THE ESKIMO ABOUT BERING STRAIT

BY

EDWARD WILLIAM NELSON

CONTENTS

ILLUSTRATIONS[1]

[1] The figures in parentheses following the titles of the illustrations refer to the numbers of the
objects in the catalog of the United States National Museum.

Page

18 ETH——2

GROUP OF KIÑUGUMUT FROM PORT CLARENCE

THE ESKIMO ABOUT BERING STRAIT

By EDWARD WILLIAM NELSON

INTRODUCTORY

The collections and observations on which the present work is based were obtained by the writer during a residence of between four and five years in northern Alaska. The fur-trading station of St Michael, situated about 65 miles north of the Yukon delta and some 200 miles southward from Bering strait, was my headquarters during the greater period of my residence in that region.

On June 17, 1877, I reached St Michael and remained there until the last of June, 1881, except during the time consumed by a number of excursions to various parts of the surrounding country. Owing to the fact that my official work was that of procuring an unbroken series of meteorological observations, whatever I did in other branches of science had to be accomplished in odd moments or during the short periods when the agents of the Alaska Commercial Company kindly relieved me of my duties by making the necessary observations.

During the first year I explored the district lying immediately about St Michael. The next year my investigations were extended over a wider field, and on the 1st of December, 1878, I left St Michael in company with Charles Petersen, a fur trader, each of us having a sledge and team of eight dogs. We traveled southward along the coast to the mouth of the Yukon, and thence up that stream to Andreivsky, which was Petersen's station and the second trading post from the sea. From this point we proceeded southwestward across the upper end of the Yukon delta, passing the eastern base of the Kusilvak mountains and reaching the seacoast just south of Cape Romanzof at a previously unknown shallow bay. From this point we proceeded southward, keeping along or near the coast until we reached Cape Vancouver, opposite Nunivak island. The second day beyond this point, Petersen, who had accompanied me thus far, said the weather was too bad to continue the journey and he therefore turned back.

From the last-mentioned point I proceeded, accompanied by an Eskimo, to the mouth of Kuskokwim river. After traveling some distance up its course we turned back toward the Yukon, which we reached at a point about a hundred miles above Andreivsky. Turning up the river the journey was continued to Paimut village, the last Eskimo settlement on the Yukon. At Paimut I turned and retraced my steps down the river and thence along the coast back to St Michael.

19

This expedition completed a very successful reconnoissance of a region previously almost completely unknown as regards its geographic and ethnologic features. A very fine series of ethnologic specimens was obtained and many interesting notes on the people were recorded; some of their curious winter festivals were witnessed, and several vocabularies were procured.

On November 9, 1880, in company with a fur trader and two Eskimo, I again left St Michael on a sledge expedition. We proceeded up the coast of Norton sound to the head of Norton bay, where we remained for some days. Thence we traveled along the coastline past Golofnin bay to Sledge island, south of Bering strait. Owing to the fact that the people of this district were on the point of starvation our farther advance was prevented and I was forced to give up my contemplated trip to Cape Prince of Wales and the islands of the strait at this time. We turned back from Sledge island and reached St Michael on April 3, after an extremely rough journey; but the series of notes and ethnologic specimens obtained on this reconnoissance are extensive and valuable.

On November 16, 1880, in company with another fur trader, I left St Michael and crossed the coast mountains to the head of Anvik river, down which we traveled to its junction with the Yukon. At this point is located the fur-trading station of Anvik, which was in charge of my companion. Bad weather delayed us at this point for some time, but we finally set out, traveling up the Yukon, crossing Shageluk island, exploring the country to the head of Innoko river, and returning thence to Anvik. From the latter place I descended the Yukon to its mouth and went back to St Michael along the coast. On the way down the river I stopped at Razbinsky and witnessed one of the great Eskimo festivals in commemoration of the dead.

As was the case in all my sledge journeys, the main object in view was to obtain as large a series of ethnologic specimens and notes on the character and customs of the people as was possible. Unfortunately my limited time on these trips prevented any extended investigation into the customs and beliefs of the people, but the series of specimens obtained is unsurpassed in richness and variety.

At the close of June, 1881, the United States revenue steamer *Corwin* called at St Michael on her way north in search of the missing steamer *Jeannette*. By the courtesy of the Secretary of the Treasury, Captain C. L. Hooper was directed to take me on board as naturalist of the expedition. During the rest of the season I was the guest of Captain Hooper and received many favors at his hands.

We left St Michael and sailed to St Lawrence island, where the Captain had been instructed to land me in order that I might investigate the villages which had been depopulated by famine and disease during the two preceding winters. The surf was too heavy on the occasion of this visit to risk landing at the desired points, so we passed on to Plover bay, on the Siberian coast. Thence we coasted the shore of Siberia to

North cape, beyond Bering strait, taking on board a sledge party which had been left there early in the season. We then returned to St Lawrence island, where a landing was effected and a fine series of valuable specimens obtained, after which we departed for St Michael where the collections were transferred to the Alaska Commercial Company's steamer for shipment to San Francisco, and the *Corwin* once more returned to the Arctic. During the remainder of the season we visited all of the Arctic coast of Alaska from Bering strait to Point Barrow, including Kotzebue sound.

The ethnologic collection obtained during my residence in the north numbers about ten thousand specimens, which are deposited in the United States National Museum, under the auspices of which my work in Alaska was done. With the exception of a comparatively small number of specimens obtained among the Athapascan tribes of the lower Yukon and among the Chukchi of eastern Siberia, the entire collection was obtained among the Eskimo.

Since my return from Alaska Mr John Murdoch has reported on the collection and observations made by the International Polar Expedition at Point Barrow.[1]

Although my collections cover many of the objects found along the northern coast, I have been more explicit in describing those from other regions visited by me rather than to duplicate the work of Mr Murdoch. The preparation of the present work has been delayed from various unavoidable causes, but despite the length of time which has elapsed since my observations were made, but little has appeared regarding the customs of the Eskimo in the region visited by me. This being the case, the data collected at a time when the life of the majority of the natives had not been so greatly modified by intercourse with white men as at present, are of particular value. Since then the introduction of missionary schools and the gold-mining excitement have resulted in greatly changing the status of many of the people, and as a natural consequence their old customs and beliefs are rapidly falling into disuse or are becoming greatly modified.

In this work I have confined myself to recording the information obtained and have made no attempt to elaborate any of the matter by generalizations. However imperfect my observations were in many cases, I trust the information gained will serve as a basis for fuller investigation of a very interesting field. I was placed under great indebtedness for favors received from the Alaska Commercial Company and its officers at St Michael during my residence at that point. Through the cordial assistance of Mr Rudolph Neumann and the late M. Lorenz, who volunteered to carry on my meteorological observations during periods of absence from St Michael, I was enabled to accomplish much work that would have been impracticable without such aid. I am also indebted to Mr Neumann for several of the tales from St Michael.

---

[1] Ninth Annual Report of the Bureau of Ethnology, 1887–88.

The fur traders, one and all, furthered my work with voluntary assistance.   To Messrs McQuesten, Petersen, Fredericks, and Williams I owe many favors.   I am particularly grateful to the late Professor Baird for the opportunity to accomplish the field work which resulted in the accumulation of the material on which the present report is based.   I have also to extend to the authorities of the National Museum my appreciation of their courtesy in placing the entire Alaskan ethnological collection at my disposal during the preparation of this report, and for other favors.   To Professor Otis T. Mason and Dr Walter Hough, of the United States National Museum, I am under special obligations for their unfailing courtesy and cordial assistance during the preparation of this work.   I wish also. to express my sense of obligation to Mr Wells M. Sawyer, illustrator of the Bureau of American Ethnology, for many suggestions and other favors while arranging the illustrations.

ALPHABET

The following alphabet is used in writing all Eskimo names of places, etc, in this memoir:

a   as *a* in father.
ă   as *a* in what.
ä   as *a* in hat.
â   as *aw* in law.
ai   as *ai* in aisle.
au   as *ow* in how.
b   as *b* in blab.
ch   as *ch* in church.
d   as *d* in dread.
dj   as *j* in judge.
e   as *e* in they.
ĕ   as *e* in then.
f   as *f* in fife.
g   as *g* in get.
g'   an aspirated *g*.
gh   a harshly aspirated *g*.
h   as *h* in ha.
h'   a soft aspiration.
hl   a sound formed by placing the tongue in the position assumed at the end of the pronunciation of *l* and then giving an aspirated continuation of the sound.
i   as *i* in pique.
ĭ   as *i* in pick.
j   as *z* in azure.
k   as *k* in kick.
k'   a soft aspiration of the *k* sound.
kh   a hard palatal prolongation or aspiration of *k*.

kn   a nasal sound formed in the roof of the mouth by the blending of the *k* into the *n*.
l   as *l* in lull.
l'   an aspirated *l*.
lh   a harsher aspirated sound than *l'*.
m   as *m* in mum.
n   as *n* in nun.
ñ   as *ng* in sing.
o   as *o* in note.
ŏ   as *o* in home, with a short pronunciation.
p   as *p* in pipe.
ph   an aspirated *p*.
r   as *r* in roaring.
s   as *s* in sauce.
sh   as *sh* in should.
t   as *t* in touch.
tl   as *tle* in little.
ts   as *ts* in tsar.
u   as *u* in rule.
ŭ   as *u* in pull.
û   as *u* in but.
v   as *v* in valor.
w   as *w* in wish.
hw   the *w* sound, beginning with an aspiration.
y   as *y* in you.
z   as *z* in zone.

The color scheme used in the drawings representing totem marks. grave boxes, masks, etc., is shown in figure 1, page 26.

EIGHTEENTH ANNUAL REPORT PL. II

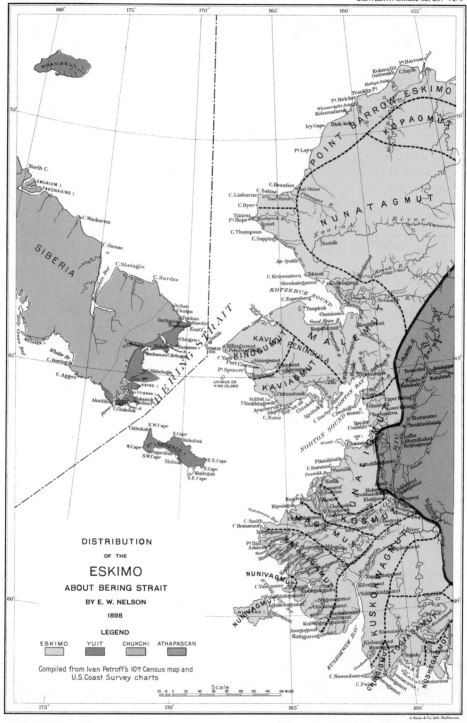

SKETCH OF THE WESTERN ESKIMO

GEOGRAPHIC FEATURES OF THEIR RANGE

That portion of the western Eskimo described in the present work is found mainly within the limits of the area which I have designated elsewhere as the Alaskan-Arctic district. This region includes the treeless coast belt, from 3 to 100 miles in width, which extends from the peninsula of Alaska northward to Point Barrow, including the adjacent islands. The Eskimo penetrate the interior of the country to the forested region along the courses of the larger streams. Their range into the interior is mainly along Kuskokwim, Yukon, Kowak, and Noatak rivers. On all of these streams they are found several hundred miles from the coast, and at their upper limits are in direct contact with the Athapascan or Tinné tribes. In addition to the Eskimo of the Alaskan mainland and adjacent islands, within the limits just mentioned, I visited also the Eskimo of the neighboring Siberian coast from East cape to Plover bay and St Lawrence island. The lives of these people adjacent to the Tinné, as well as those of the Siberian coast who are in constant contact with the Chukchi, have been somewhat modified by their surroundings, although in their language and customs they are still unmistakably Eskimo. The people of the Siberian coast and of St Lawrence island are the most aberrant group of Eskimo encountered within the area covered by my work.

The belt bordering the Alaskan coast of Bering sea belonging to this district is mainly low, and much of it consists of broad, marshy tracts which are but little above sea level. This is particularly the case in the large, roughly triangular area lying between lower Kuskokwim and Yukon rivers. To the northward of this the country is more broken or rolling in character, rising gradually in many places to low, mountainous masses, several hundred feet in height and coming down to the coast at intervals as bald headlands. The islands of Bering straits are small and rocky and rise precipitously from the water, as does much of the adjacent Siberian shore. St Lawrence island is large and has an undulating surface with rocky headlands at intervals along the coast.

North of Bering strait the country is generally rolling, with flat areas about the head of Kotzebue sound and north of Icy cape. South of the strait the coast country has a mildly arctic climate, but to the northward the results of a more rigorous environment appear in both plant and animal life. The climate of the Siberian coast is much severer than that of the adjacent Alaskan shore.

Everywhere south of Point Hope a plentiful arctic vegetation is found. Although the country is destitute of trees, along the courses of streams and in sheltered spots on the southern slopes of hills a more or less abundant growth of willows and alders is found. This is the case even at the head of Kotzebue sound, directly under the Arctic circle. Over a large portion of the low, gently rolling country are beds of sphagnum interspersed with various grasses and flowering plants. Inland, along the water courses, there occur spruce and white birch in addition to the plants which are found nearer the coast. The villages of the western Eskimo are located always near the sea or directly along the water courses, such situations being necessitated by their dependence for the greater portion of their subsistence on game and the fish obtained from the waters in their vicinity.

Driftwood is abundant along most parts of the American coast within the region discussed in this work, and the food supply also is more abundant than is found in most regions inhabited by the eastern Eskimo, so that the conditions of life with the Alaskan people are much more favorable. The shores of Bering sea north of the Kuskokwim mouth are icebound from early in November until about the end of May or early June of each year. North of Bering strait the sea ice is present for a somewhat longer period.

Although the aborigines living along the American coast from Point Barrow to Kuskokwim river are not separated by physical barriers, they are divided into groups characterized by distinct dialects.

DISTRIBUTION OF TRIBES AND DIALECTS

The Shaktolik people told me that in ancient times, before the Russians came, the Unalit occupied all the coast of Norton sound from Pastolik northward to a point a little beyond Shaktolik. At that time the southern limit of the Malemut was at the head of Norton bay. They have since advanced and occupied village after village until now the people at Shaktolik and Unalaklit are mainly Malemut or a mixture of Malemut and Unalit. They added that since the disappearance of the reindeer along the coast the Malemut have become much less numerous than formerly.

Various Russians and others, who were living in that region in 1872 and 1873, informed me that at that time there were about two hundred people living in the village of Kigiktauik, while in 1881 I found only about twelve or fourteen. At the time first named the mountains bordering the coast in that neighborhood swarmed with reindeer, and in addition to the Unalit many Malemut had congregated there to take advantage of the hunting.

During November, 1880, I found a family of Malemut living in a miserable hut on the upper part of Anvik river. As stated elsewhere, these people have become spread over a wide region. About the middle of March, 1880, between Cape Nome and Sledge island, I

MALEMUT FAMILY FROM SHAKTOLIK

found a village occupied by a mixture of people from King island in Bering strait, Sledge island, and others from different parts of Kaviak peninsula. These people had united there and were living peaceably together in order to fish for crabs and tomcods and to hunt for seals, as the supply of food had become exhausted at their homes.

There are few places among the different divisions of the people living between Yukon and Kuskokwim rivers where a sharp demarkation is found in the language as one passes from village to village. In every village in this region they have had friendly intercourse with one another for many years, and intermarriage has constantly taken place. They visit each other during their festivals, and their hunting and fishing grounds meet. All of these causes have aided, since the cessation of the ancient warfare which served to keep them separated, in increasing the intercourse between them and have had a tendency to break down the sharp distinctions that existed in their dialects. The language used in this region, south of the Yukon mouth, is closely related to that of the Unalit along the shore of Norton sound north of the Yukon.

The greatest distinctions in language appeared to be in the curious modification of the sounds of the vowels, these being lengthened or shortened in a different manner, thus causing the pronunciation to be differently intoned in the two districts. The Nunivak island people and those living at Cape Vancouver, however, appear to speak a language quite sharply divided from that of their neighbors.

As it is, one of the natives from any portion of the district south of the Yukon mouth, except on Nunivak island or Cape Vancouver, can readily make himself understood when visiting villages of the lower Yukon or among the Unalit of Norton sound. The distinction between the Unalit and Kaviagmut Eskimo, or the Unalit and the Malemut, is considerable, and people speaking these tongues do not readily communicate at once, although it takes but a short time for them to learn to talk with one another. The dialect of the people of Point Hope appears to differ but slightly from that used at the head of Kotzebue sound. There is such a general resemblance between the dialects spoken by the Eskimo of the Alaskan mainland that a person belonging to one district very quickly learns to understand and speak other dialects. My Unalit interpreter from St Michael accompanied me on the *Corwin*, and when at Plover bay, on the eastern coast of Siberia, managed to understand a considerable portion of what the people of that point said. He had great difficulty, however, in comprehending the language of the St Lawrence islanders, and in fact could understand but few words spoken by them. Both at East Cape and at Plover bay, on the Siberian coast, there were many words that I could understand from my knowledge of the Unalit tongue gained at St Michael. The people of St Lawrence island and Plover bay are closely related and the dialects spoken by them are very similar, so that they have no difficulty in communicating with each other.

The Point Barrow Eskimo occupy the coast from Cape Lisburne to Point Barrow. The Malemut inhabit the country from Point Hope around the shores of Kotzebue sound to beyond Cape Espenberg, and thence south to Uñaktolik river. From this point southward to the Yukon mouth, including St Michael island, are the Unalit or Unaligmut. The people of Cape Prince of Wales, Port Clarence, and King island are the Kiñugumut. The people occupying the coast from Port Clarence and around to Cape Nome, Golofnin bay, and Nubviukhchugaluk, including the interior of the peninsula back from the coast country as well as Sledge (Aziak) island, are Kaviagmut.

The people of the Diomede islands and of East cape, Siberia, are a group of Eskimo of whom I failed to obtain a special designation.

South of this point the Eskimo of Plover bay and the neighboring coast form another group. The people of St Lawrence island form still another group, and of these also I failed to record any special designation.

The people of the lower Yukon, from Paimut down to the vicinity of Pastolik, including the Yukon delta, are the Ikogmut. The Magemut are the people occupying the low, marshy country back from the lower Yukon, between it and the Kuskokwim, extending from a line just back of the Kuskokwim northwesterly to the coast between Cape Romanzof and the Kusilvak branch of the Yukon mouth.

The Nunivagmut are the people of Nunivak island and the mainland at Cape Vancouver.

The Kaialigamut are the people occupying the coast northward from Cape Vancouver to Kushunuk, Kaialigamut, and the adjacent villages. The Kuskokwagmut are the people occupying the villages along the lower Kuskokwim and the adjacent country to the north of that point to a line where begin the other divisions already named.

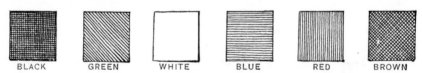

BLACK   GREEN   WHITE   BLUE   RED   BROWN

Fig. 1—Scheme of color on masks and mask-like objects, grave boxes, and totem markings.

PHYSICAL CHARACTERISTICS

The Eskimo from Bering strait to the lower Yukon are fairly well-built people, averaging among the men about 5 feet 2 or 3 inches in height. The Yukon Eskimo and those living southward from that river to the Kuskokwim are, as a rule, shorter and more squarely built. The Kuskokwim people are darker of complexion than those to the northward, and have rounder features. The men commonly have a considerable growth of hair on their faces, becoming at times a thin

KIÑUGUMIUT MAI E. SU-KILJIK. Age 25.

beard two or three inches in length, with a well-developed mustache (plates IV, V). No such development of beard was seen elsewhere in the territory visited.

The people in the coast region between the mouths of the Kuskokwim and the Yukon have peculiarly high cheek bones and sharp chins, which unite to give their faces a curiously pointed, triangular appearance. At the village of Kaialigamut I was impressed by the strong develop- ment of the superciliary ridge. From a point almost directly over the pupil of the eye, and extending thence inward to the median line of the forehead, is a strong, bony ridge, causing the brow to stand out sharply. From the outer edge of this the skull appears as though beveled away to the ears, giving the temporal area a considerable enlargement beyond that usually shown. This curious development of the skull is rendered still more striking by the fact that the bridge of the nose is low, as usual among these people, so that the shelf-like projection of the brow stands out in strong relief. It is most strongly marked among the men, and appears to be characteristic at this place. Elsewhere in this district it was noted only rarely here and there.

All of the people in the district about Capes Vancouver and Roman- zof, and thence to the Yukon mouth, are of unusually light complexion. Some of the women have a pale, slightly yellowish color, with pink cheeks, differing but little in complexion from that of a sallow woman of Caucasian blood. This light complexion is so exceptionally striking that wherever they travel these people are readily distinguished from other Eskimo; and before I visited their territory I had learned to know them by their complexion whenever they came to St Michael.

The people of the district just mentioned are all very short and squarely built. Inland from Cape Vancouver lies the flat, marshy coun- try about Big lake, which is situated between the Kuskokwim and the Yukon. It is a well-populated district, and its inhabitants differ from those near the coast at the capes referred to in being taller, more slender, and having more squarely cut features. They also differ strik- ingly from any other Eskimo with whom I came in contact, except those on Kowak river, in having the bridge of the nose well developed and at times sufficiently prominent to suggest the aquiline nose of our southern Indian tribes.

The Eskimo of the Diomede islands in Bering strait, as well as those of East cape and Mechigme and Plover bays on the Siberian coast, and of St Lawrence island, are tall, strongly built people, and are generally similar in their physical features (plates XI, XII). These are characterized by the unusual heaviness of the lower part of the face, due to the very square and massive lower jaw, which, combined with broad, high cheek bones and flattened nose, produces a wide, flat face. These features are frequently accompanied with a low, retreating forehead, producing a decidedly repulsive physiognomy. The bridge of the nose is so low and the cheek bones so heavy that a profile view will frequently show only the tip of the person's nose, the eyes and upper portion of the nose being completely hidden by the prominent outline of the cheek. Their eyes are less oblique than is common among the people living southward from the Yukon mouth. Among the people at the northwestern end of St Lawrence island there is a greater range of physiognomy than was noted at any other of the Asiatic localities.

The Point Hope people on the American coast have heavy jaws and well-developed superciliary ridges. At Point Barrow the men are remarkable for the irregularity of their features, amounting to a positive degree of ugliness, which is increased and rendered specially prominent by the expression produced by the short, tightly drawn upper lip, the projecting lower lip, and the small beady eyes. The women and children of this place are in curious contrast, having rather pleasant features of the usual type.

The Eskimo from upper Kowak and Noatak rivers, who were met at the summer camp on Hotham inlet, are notable for the fact that a considerable number of them have hook noses and nearly all have a cast of countenance very similar to that of the Yukon Tinné. They are a larger and more robustly built people than these Indians, however, and speak the Eskimo language. They wear labrets, practice the tonsure, and claim to be Eskimo. At the same time they wear bead-ornamented hunting shirts, round caps, and tanned deerskin robes, and use conical lodges like those of the adjacent Tinné tribes. Among them was seen one man having a mop of coarse curly hair, almost negroid in character. The same feature was observed in a number of men and women on the Siberian coast between East cape and Plover bay. This latter is undoubtedly the result of the Chukchi-Eskimo mixture, and in the case of the man seen at Hotham inlet the same result had been brought about by the Eskimo-Indian combination. Among the Eskimo south of Bering strait, on the American coast, not a single instance of this kind was observed. The age of the individuals having this curly hair renders it quite improbable that it came from an admixture of blood with foreign voyagers, since some of them must have been born at a time when vessels were extremely rare along these shores. As a further argument against this curly hair having come from white men, I may add that I saw no trace of it among a number of people having partly Caucasian blood. As a general thing, the Eskimo of the region described have small hands and feet and the features are oval in outline, rather flat, and with slightly oblique eyes.

Children and young girls have round faces and often are very pleasant and attractive in feature, the angular race characteristics becoming prominent after the individuals approach manhood. The women age rapidly, and only a very small proportion of the people live to an advanced age.

The Malemut and the people of Kaviak peninsula, including those of the islands in Bering strait, are tall, active, and remarkably well

BUREAU OF AMERICAN ETHNOLOGY

KĬÑUGUMUT MALE, KOMIK-SÉNER, Age 23

built. Among them it is common to see men from 5 feet 10 inches to 6 feet tall and of proportionate build. I should judge the average among them to be nearly or quite equal in height to the whites.

Among the coast Eskimo, as a rule, the legs are short and poorly developed, while the body is long, with disproportionately developed dorsal and lumbar muscles, due to so much of their life being passed in the kaiak.

The Eskimo of the Big lake district, south of the Yukon, and from the Kaviak peninsula, as well as the Malemut about the head of Kotzebue sound, are, on the contrary, very finely proportioned and athletic men, who can not be equaled among the Indians of the Yukon region. This fine physical development is attributable to the fact that these people are so located that their hunting is largely on open tundra or in the mountains, thus producing a more symmetric development than is possible among those whose lives are passed mainly in the kaiak.

There were a number of halfblood children among the Eskimo, resulting from the intercourse with people from vessels and others, who generally show their Caucasian blood by large, finely shaped, and often remarkably beautiful brown eyes. The number of these mixed bloods was not very great.

As a race the Eskimo are very hardy and insensible to cold. While the *Corwin* was at anchor in Hotham inlet during the fall of 1881, I found a Malemut woman with two little girls, one about two years and the other five years of age, lying fast asleep on the deck of the vessel clothed only in their ordinary garments. A very raw wind was blowing at the time, and it was difficult for us to keep warm even while moving about in heavy overcoats.

While I was at the head of Norton sound during February, when the temperature stood at minus 40° Fahrenheit, a boy 10 years of age, with a sled and three dogs, was sent back several miles along the previous day's trail to recover a pair of lost snowshoes. He started off alone and returned a few hours later with the snowshoes, his cheeks glowing red from the cold, but without other indication of the effect of the temperature.

The men lead a hard and perilous life in the districts bordering the sea, where much of the hunting is done in kaiaks. In spring they go long distances offshore, and are sometimes cast adrift on the moving ice, requiring the greatest effort to return to the land. In a number of instances that came to my notice men were forced to spend one or two days fighting their way back to shore in their kaiaks, after having been driven seaward by a strong wind.

In addition, the constant wetting and exposure throughout the entire year helps gradually to undermine the strength of the natives; as a result, consumption and rheumatic complaints are common, and but few live to an advanced age. Families rarely have more than two or three children, and it is not uncommon for them to have none.

CLOTHING

GARMENTS IN GENERAL

The garments of the western Eskimo are similar in general plan to those worn by their relatives farther eastward, but vary locally in pattern and style of ornamentation. The upper part of the body of both men and women is covered with a frock-like garment put on over the head, and in the greater part of the area visited these garments are provided with a hood. In addition, both men and women wear trousers. Those of the men are made to reach from the hip to the ankle, the feet being clothed with socks of deerskin or grass, over which skin boots are drawn. The lower garments of the women are combined boots and trousers reaching to the waist. Over the feet are sometimes drawn skin boots, but frequently a sole of oil-tanned sealskin is attached directly to the trousers.

On the Diomede islands, along the eastern shore of the Chukchi peninsula, and on St Lawrence island the women wear a curious garment having a loose waist, flowing sleeves, and very baggy trousers reaching to the ankles. They put this on by thrusting the head and feet into a slit-like opening in the back, which is then laced up. The feet and lower part of the legs are then encased in skin boots tied about the ankles. Usually these combined garments are loosely made, without hoods, and are opened broadly at the neck, with a narrow trimming of wolverine or other fur about the border. They are worn usually with the hair inside, and the smooth outer surface becomes greasy and begrimed so that they present a curious appearance. Small children dressed in these garments waddle about and appear to move with the greatest difficulty. Very young children on the coast named are placed in these combination garments with the ends of the sleeves and legs sewed up, so that nothing but the face of the child can be seen.

In addition the women of this region wear a frock-like outer garment reaching down to midway between the waist and knee and provided with a hood. The hood is trimmed with wolverine skin or other fur, the long hairs projecting halo-like about the face. In front is a broad bib-like flap, usually made from the short-hair skin taken from the reindeer's legs, which hangs down over the breast. Sometimes, however, these flaps are replaced by a long, narrow gore of white reindeer skin, sewed over the shoulder on each side of the neck and extending down the front. Very little effort is made to ornament the garments among any of the people save those of St Lawrence island, where they are ornamented with tassels made from strips of fur taken from the hair-seal pup and dyed a reddish brown. Rows of the crests and horny bill sheaths from the crested auklet are also sewed along the seams. Similar ornamentation was observed in lesser degree along the Siberian shore.

The illustration (plate XIV) from a photograph taken of a party of women and children from East Cape, Siberia, gives an idea of the garments described. The woman on the left wears one of the combination garments with the fur side out, the one on the right having the garment turned with fur inward, and the two central figures wear the frock in addition.

Most of the garments worn by these people are made from the skins of tame reindeer, although those of wild reindeer are used to a limited extent. The handsomely mottled coats of the tame deer serve to render some of the clothing rather ornamental in appearance. On St Lawrence island and the Diomedes the skins of waterfowl are sometimes used for making the outer frock-like garment for both men and women of the poorer class. Their boots are usually of reindeer skin, generally taken from the leg of the animal, with a sole of tanned sealskin.

Crossing Bering strait to the American shore we find the garments for men and women closely alike in general style over a wide area. They are practically identical in pattern northward to Point Barrow and southward to the Yukon mouth, including King and Sledge islands.

The garments worn by the men consist of a skin frock, which is put on over the head and has a hood variously bordered by strips of skin. These borders are made usually of an outer strip of wolfskin with the long hairs standing out like a halo, as before described. Just within this is sewed another belt or band of skin from the wolverine so that the long outer hairs lie back against the wolfskin border, producing a pleasing contrast. These halo like borders, when the hood is drawn up, surround the face and give a picturesque appearance to the wearer (plates IV, XIII*b*, XV*a*). The back of the hood is made usually of several pieces sewed in such a way as to take the form of the head. A gore usually extends from the top of the shoulders at the base of the hood down on each side of the chest, and is generally of white-hair skin from the belly of the reindeer. The sleeves and lower border of this garment are fringed with a narrow band of wolf or wolverine skin. These garments may be made of the skins of wild or tame reindeer, Parry's marmot, muskrats, mink, or waterfowl, such as cormorants, auklets, murres, eider ducks, or loons, and in the region southward of the Yukon mouth the skins of emperor and white-front geese are also used for this purpose. One such garment is made from the skins of scaup ducks, with the hood of Parry's marmot skins, and is bordered around the bottom with a narrow fringe of wolfskin. On the lower Yukon very poor people utilize even the skins of salmon for making their frocks.

The trousers of the men extend from the hips to the ankles and are rather awkwardly made. They are fastened about the waist with a drawstring in a loop of skin sewed along the border. A variety of materials are used, including wild and tame reindeer, sealskin, dogskin, and white-bear skin. The trousers made from the skins of reindeer are sometimes worn with the hair inward during cold weather or with the hair outward when it is warmer. Of late years these people during the summer wear shirts and trousers of calico and drilling obtained from the fur traders. Ordinary cotton shirts also are worn by them.

Reaching the lower Kuskokwim and adjacent country to the north, the men wear frocks similar to those hitherto described, but so long that when at full length they reach the ground about the wearer's feet. When traveling these frocks are drawn up and belted about the waist until the lower border reaches only to the knee. They are made usually from the skins of Parry's marmot or a species of whistler found in the mountains south of the lower Kuskokwim district, and are ornamented with the tails of the animals, which are set on, fringe-like, with each skin hanging all about the person. They are made generally without hoods and the neck is bordered by the skin of the Arctic hare or white fox, or more commonly by a roll-like edge of deerskin with the hair on. A gore is set in on each side of the neck over the chest, or sometimes a single broader gore extends down the middle in front. The sleeves may be bordered by the white-hair skin of the reindeer's belly, and bands of the same are sometimes set in around the body or near the lower border. In place of hoods the wearers of these frocks have fur caps with ear-laps for tying under the chin. Their trousers are similar to those already described.

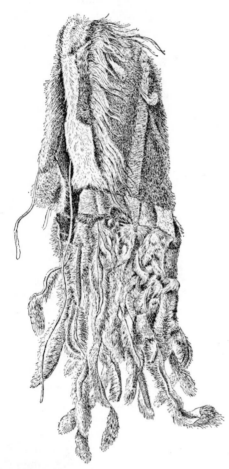

FIG. 2— Man's hood from Koñigunugumut ($\frac{3}{16}$).

On the tundra between the Kuskokwim and the lower Yukon there are worn similar, but shorter, hoodless frocks. In place of the fur caps described as worn by the Kuskokwim people these tundra men wear curious headdresses made of various skins.

One of these (figure 2), from Koñigunugumut, is a hood made of the skins of Parry's marmot with a border about the face of reindeer skin with the hair on. The hood is bordered also along its lower edge by a

KIÑUGUMUT MALE, ISER-KYNER, Age 20

strip, about two inches wide, of reindeer skin and has a narrow band extending up from this over the crown. About the lower border, on the sides and behind, extends a fringe consisting of narrow strips of reindeer skin, 12 to 15 inches in length, which hangs down the back.

Another variety of hood worn in this district is made of a band of deerskin, with the hair on, sewed to fit about the brow like a turban with the crown of skins of Parry's marmot, or of white or blue foxes. When the marmot skins are used they are usually sewed in a series so as to hang behind like an open sack. If the fox skins are used they are sewed so that the head of the fox rests on the crown of the wearer with the body and tail hanging down over the back. These caps are very picturesque and give the wearer a remarkably dignified appearance.

FIG. 3—Fox-skin cap.

In the region about Askinuk curious small fur caps or hoods are worn, fitting snugly about the head and fringed behind by a few little tags or strips of skin, but which do not hang far down the back like those last described. These hoods are made in ornamental patterns from various kinds of skin.

A hood of reindeer and marmot skin from Askinuk (figure 4) has

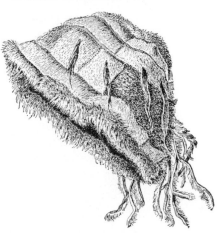

FIG. 4—Man's hood of reindeer and marmot skin and mink fur (⅛).

a circular piece of reindeer skin set in the middle of the crown; this is surrounded by two strips of white reindeer skin taken from the leg of the animal with the hair clipped. Following this is a broader strip of similar reindeer skin, alternating with a square of dark-hair reindeerskin on the top and marmot skins on each side, succeeded by another strip of reindeer skin and bordered about the face by a narrow fringe of mink fur. Similar caps were obtained at Koñigunugumut.

In summer the Eskimo of Noatak and Kowak rivers wear bead-ornamented caps similar to those of the Tinné along the upper Yukon. On the shore of the Arctic at Point Hope the specimen represented in figure 5 was obtained. This

18 ETH——3

is a handsomely made hood fashioned from the skin of a wolf's head, the nose of the animal resting directly over the brow and extending back over the head, so that the ears of the animal lie on the nape of the wearer's neck. From just back of the nose to a point nearly between the ears the skin is slit and an oval piece of skin, tanned with the hair off, is set in, and along it are sewed ten parallel, longitudinal rows of blue beads. Little strings of red, white, blue, and black beads are attached to the sides of the head from just back of the wolf's nose, down along each side, two-thirds of the way to the ears. Sewed to the front border of the hood is a strip of long-hair wolfskin, and two strings at the corners in front serve to tie it about the wearer's chin.

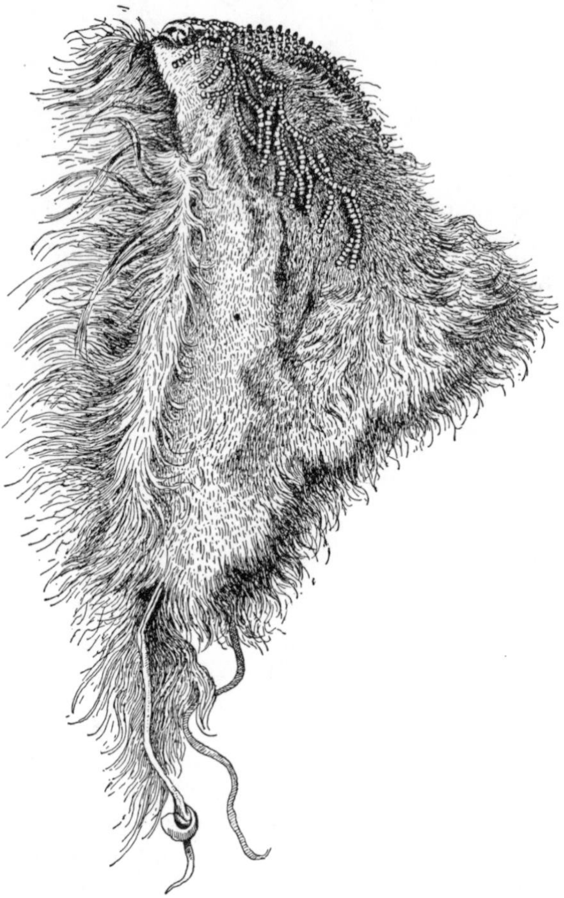

From the Yukon mouth northward to Point Barrow the frocks of the men are cut a trifle longer behind than in front. South of the Yukon these garments are cut nearly the same length all around.

Many of the Kowak and Noatak men seen at Hotham inlet wear hunting shirts of tanned moose-skin similar to those used by the Tinné of the inte-

FIG. 5—Man's wolf-head summer hood from Point Hope (½).

rior, from whom they were probably obtained. These Eskimo also wear robes made from reindeer-skin tanned with the hair on. These are made to fasten over the shoulders by two cords, and fall behind nearly to the ground like a cloak. They are usually bordered with a fringe formed by cutting the skin into little strips, and on the inside the totem signs of the owners are marked in red paint.

From one of the Diomede islands I obtained the garment illustrated in plate XVI, a frock without a hood, made from the skin of a guillemot.

KIÑUGUMUT FEMALE. KOK-SUK. Age 23.

Around the back of the neck is a border of black-bear skin with the long hair erect. The lower border of the garment is edged with a narrow strip of white-reindeer skin, succeeded by a border of red-bear skin with tufts of white-bear fur sewed on all around at short intervals.

The people on the islands of Bering strait and the adjacent shores use a kind of face protector made of a ring of white-bear skin, which is drawn on over the head and fitted round the face. These are held in place by a narrow band of the same material extending over the top of the head; another strip from each side joins the other at the back.

During summer the men usually wear a light frock made from the skins of the marmot, mink, muskrat, fawns of reindeer, or the summer reindeer with its light coat of hair. In winter two of these garments are frequently worn, and those of the winter deerskin with its heavier coat of hair are used in severe weather.

A man's frock from Cape Vancouver (plate XVII) is made of reindeer-fawn skin and has a hood which forms a part of the garment instead of being worn separately as is done farther inland. From the shoulders hanging down both in front and behind depend broad strips of reindeer skin with the fur cut short and having attached to their tips strings of white, red, and blue beads from five to six inches in length with narrow strips of wolverine fur. From the middle of the hood behind hangs a strip of reindeer skin, tipped with wolverine fur. Little tassels of red-bear skin are attached to strips of white-deer skin, set in, gore-like, over the tops of shoulders. Two sharp-pointed gores of white-deer skin are set in above the waist.

The hood has an inner border of arctic-hare skin followed by a strip of wolf skin. The lower end of the sleeves is bordered by a band of white-deer skin, edged by a narrow border of mink fur, the lower edge of the garment being bordered in the same manner. This is one of the most ornamental garments of the kind seen in that district.

The frocks worn by the women of this region are made similar to those of the men except that they are cut up a little farther on the sides so as to make a more conspicuously pendent flap before and behind.

From the Yukon mouth northward the women's frocks are much more handsomely made, the mottled white skin of the tame reindeer, obtained from the Siberian people, affording a good material for the production of ornamental patterns. Some of these garments are very richly ornamented; they are deeply cut up along each side, so that before and behind the skirt hangs in a long, broad, round flap. The hoods are bordered by wolverine and wolf skin, and the ends of the sleeves and the lower edge of the garment are trimmed with wolf or wolverine skin, usually the latter. A typical garment of this kind (number 64272), from Cape Prince of Wales, has the hood made of a central oval piece extending up from the back of the garment as a narrow strip which broadens above. The hood is bordered on each side by short-hair white-reindeer skin which extends to the shoulders and then divides and forms a long, narrow gore down the front and back of the garment. Between the white skin on the sides and the brown deerskin forming the back or central part of the hood, extends a series of five narrow strips of white deerskin with the hair shaved close and having welted into the seams narrow strips of black parchment-like skin. Two of these welted seams bordering the central one have little tufts of red wool set along at intervals of about one-fourth of an inch. Across the shoulders from front to back extend a similar series of strips of white deerskin with black welted seams, and the lower border of the garment is ornamented with a broader band of the same handsome pattern. From the top and back of the shoulders, as well as on the middle of the back, are attached tassel-like strips of wolverine skin eight to ten inches in length.

The frocks of the women of the lower Kuskokwim have the sides cut up to a lesser degree than those to the north, and are provided with a hood bordered with wolf, wolverine, or other skin with the fur on. Set across the body before and behind are bands of white-hair deerskin, having narrow welted strips of dark skin in the seams. The sleeves and lower edge of the garment are bordered with a band of white-hair reindeer skin fringed with wolverine skin. In addition, the women's frocks of this district have strung along the patterns of white deerskin in front and back little strings of beads an inch or two in length. The trousers worn by the women from the lower Kuskokwim to Point Barrow are made usually of skin taken from the legs of reindeer, and commonly by sewing in alternating strips of different colors to produce ornamental patterns. The specimen shown in plate XVIII, from the head of Norton sound, is a woman's handsomely made frock. The body of the garment is of marmot skins, while skins from the crowns of the same animal are pieced together on the crown of the hood. The skirts and ornamental pieces are of white-hair reindeer skin, and the trimming is of wolf and wolverine fur.

The example from Mission, illustrated in plate XIX, is made of salmon skins tanned and worked with a scraper until they have become pliable. Most of the seams are ornamented with bands of brownish dyed fish-skin, on the surface of which are sewed narrow strips of white parchment-like skin from the throats of seals. On each shoulder are inserted two gore-like pieces of fish-skin dyed brown and having ornamental strips of white sewed along them and following their outline.

WATERPROOF GARMENTS

In addition to the upper garments already described the Eskimo make waterproof frocks from the intestines of seals. The intestines are dried and slit open, and the long, ribbon-like strips thus formed are then sewed together horizontally to form a frock similar in shape to those of fur worn by the men, as already described. About the sleeves a braided sinew cord is inclosed in a turned-down border to form a drawstring for fastening the garment securely about the wrist, in order that the water may not enter. In addition the border of the

KIÑUGUMUT FEMALE. UNGER-KEE-KLUK. Age 22

hood about the face is provided with a similar string, the ends of which hang down under the chin so that this portion of the garment may be drawn tightly for the same purpose. These garments are worn over the others during wet weather on shore as well as at sea. Their most important use, however, is while the hunters are at sea in kaiaks. At such times, when the weather becomes rainy or rough, the hunter dons his waterproof frock and the skirt is extended over the rim of the manhole in which he sits. A cord provided for the purpose is wound around the outside, fastening the border of the skirt down into a sunken groove left for the purpose below the rim on the outside of the kaiak. When this cord is made fast and the drawstrings about the face and sleeves are tightened, the occupant of the kaiak is safe from being drenched by the dashing spray, and no water can enter his boat.

These garments are strong and will frequently withstand the pressure of the water even when the wearer is entirely submerged beneath the combing sea. Among the breakers, however, they are not to be relied on, as the writer knows from experience, the weight of the water striking heavily from above, tearing them and permitting the water to enter the boat.

The seams of these waterproofs are frequently ornamented by sewing in seals' bristles

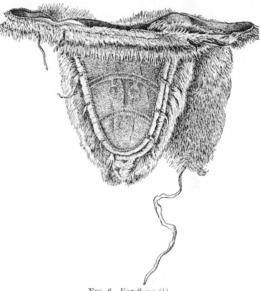

FIG. 6—Ear-flaps ($\frac{1}{3}$).

or the fine hair-like feathers of certain waterfowl. About the islands in Bering strait and on the bordering Asiatic shore the horny sheaths from the base of the mandibles of the crested auklet are sewed along the seams of some of these frocks as ornaments. Narrow strips of black, parchment-like tanned skin are frequently welted into the seams for ornamental purposes, and the lower borders are sometimes narrowly fringed with a strip of woolly fur from small hair-seals. Garments of this kind made for the use of women are cut up on each side to produce flaps similar to those of the ordinary frock.

EAR-FLAPS

About Chalitmut and the adjacent district on the tundra between the Kuskokwim and the Yukon, where men's frocks are made without the hood, ear-flaps are commonly used. These are made of oval flaps of deerskin with the hair side inward and having the base truncated and sewed to a narrow band of skin to go around the head. The flaps are then tied under the chin by means of strings. The tanned outer surface of these flaps has various ornamental patterns in white hairs from reindeer sewed on with sinew thread, the designs produced being parallel lines, either straight, curved, or in circles. Figure 6 represents a pair of these ear-flaps.

GLOVES AND MITTENS

From the Yukon northward to Kotzebue sound and thence to Point Barrow, mittens and gloves are found in common use. The gloves are made usually with places for each finger and the thumb. From the Yukon mouth to Point Barrow were obtained gloves having each of the fingers made of a separate piece sewed upon the hand, the thumb in both cases being sewed on in the same manner and having an awkward, triangular shape.

A pair from Sledge island (number 45085) are made of sealskin with the hair removed and the wrists bordered with a fringe of white-bear fur. A pair from Point Hope (plate XX, 1), of the usual pattern described, is of tanned reindeer skin with the hair side inward. The wrists are bordered with a fringe of little strips of tanned reindeer-skin, dyed reddish brown, and on the back are numerous little pendent strings of red-and-white and red-and-blue beads, with other beads strung on the fringe bordering the wrist. These gloves are joined by a double string of little copper cylinders, spaced by blue beads, reaching up to the central loop of soft, tanned skin, for going completely around the neck, thus holding the gloves without danger of their being lost if suddenly taken off.

Plate XX, 3, shows a pair of deerskin gloves of the common pattern from Kotzebue sound. The skin is tanned with the hair left on and turned in on the inside of the hand and all around on the fingers. The back of the hand and the thumb are covered with a piece of white-hair deerskin, on which hang four tassel-like strips of wolverine skin. The wrists are bordered with a series of narrow bands of reindeer skin, with the white hair clipped short, and between the strips a narrow band of parchment-like skin is welted in. Midway in this series of strips a seam is bordered by a series of small, regularly spaced tufts of red worsted. A narrow band of wolverine fur completes this ornamental border.

Other gloves from Bering strait are made of skin tanned with the hair left on and turned inward; others have the hair entirely removed.

A peculiar pattern of glove is common to the Diomede islands and the adjacent shore of Siberia. The fingers and the hand are of one piece, with three pieces of skin of a different color set in gores along the back and divided to extend down as a gore along the inside of each

KIÑUGUMUT FEMALE

finger. Plate xx, 7, illustrates an example of these gloves from King island.

Another curious pair of gloves, from Norton sound, is shown in plate xx, 5. These are made with separate divisions for the thumb and the forefinger, the other fingers being provided with a single cover. They are made like other gloves used along the American coast in that they have the parts covering the fingers in separate pieces sewed on the piece forming the hand.

The gloves illustrated in plate xx, 6, were obtained on the Diomede islands, Bering strait; they are made of tanned reindeer-skin, with the hair side inward. The front of the gloves is a dingy russet brown in color and the skin on the back is hard-tanned and colored chestnut brown. The back of the hand and the wrist have ornamental patterns in red, white, and blackish stitching, made by sewing in white reindeer hairs and red woolen yarn with sinew thread. These are made in the style peculiar to these islands and the coast of Siberia already described, the pieces of skin sewed into the gores being pale buff in color.

The glove shown in plate xx, 2, from Anderson river, British America, is similar in style to the gloves from the head of Norton sound. It is made of reindeer skin. The mittens used are of a common pattern, with a triangular thumb. They are made of the skin of seals, reindeer, dogs, wolves, white bear, cormorant, murre, and salmon, and are sometimes of woven grass.

For use while at sea long mittens reaching to the elbow or above are made of well-tanned sealskin and are provided at their upper border with a cord for drawing them tightly against the arm. These mittens are waterproof and protect the hands of the hunter from water during cold weather.

Plate xxi, 6, represents a typical pair of these mittens measuring 21 inches in length. They are well made, with a piece of tanned skin welted into the main seam. Near the upper border is a broad strip of sealskin, and a strip of the same extends down each side of the seam, running thence to the end of the thumb. Set about the lower border is a wide band of skin; near the upper edge and also along each side of the bands running to the thumb are tufts of white seal bristles with little tufts of young seal fur dyed a reddish brown.

From Sledge island I obtained a similar pair of mittens made from waterproof tanned sealskin, and which reach only a little above the wrist. One of these is shown in plate xxi, 3.

On lower Yukon and Kuskokwim rivers mittens made of salmon skin are also used. Along all of the coast region the skin of the hair seal, tanned with the hair on, is used for this purpose. All three of the latter kinds are used mainly during wet weather in summer or at sea.

Mittens of woven grass are also made on the lower Yukon and thence to the Kuskokwim. For winter use they make clumsily shaped mittens from the skins of dogs, reindeer, wolves, and cormorants.

All along the coast where seals are hunted on the ice during the spring months, huge mittens of white bearskin or white dogskin are made to reach from the hand to a little above the elbows. These are worn by the hunters, while creeping prone upon the ice, to serve as a shield, the left arm being carried bent across in front of the face and head as the hunter slowly creeps along. The bushy white hair on the mitten, being similar in color to the surface of the snow, serves as a blind to prevent the seal from observing the approach of the hunter.

FOOT-WEAR

BOOTS

Among the Eskimo boots are the most common style of foot-wear; they are made with a hard-tanned sealskin sole and a top reaching just below the knee. The tops are generally of sealskin tanned with the hair left on, or of reindeer-skin tanned in the same manner. The sealskin boots of this class may have the hair side worn either inward or outward; for this purpose the skin of the *Phoca vitulina* is most commonly used. When topped with reindeer-skin, the hair is worn usually outward. The feet and ankles of the latter variety of boots are made of reindeer-skin in the brown, short-hair summer coat; the legs are made usually in some pattern formed by combining pieces of the white-hair skin from the belly of a reindeer with strips of brown-hair skin from the legs of that animal. For this purpose skin from the white-hair tame reindeer of Siberia is highly prized. The tops of the boot-legs are surrounded usually by one or two bands of white-hair deerskin with the fur shaved close to present a velvety surface, the seams along these borders having narrow strips of black skin welted in with little tufts of red worsted strung along some of the seams. Between these bands of shaved skin and the lower portion of the legs commonly is sewed a strip of wolverine skin, with long projecting hair, and generally two or more little tassels of the same kind of skin hanging before and behind. The soles are of hard, oil-tanned sealskin bent up around the border and crimped about the heel and the toe by means of a smooth, pointed ivory crimper. The uppers are frequently sewed directly to the sealskin soles, but sometimes a narrow intervening strip of tanned sealskin is sewed in around the border. A long, narrow strip of rawhide has one end sewed to the sole on each side of the ankle to fasten the boot to the foot. These straps are raised and drawn across the rear just above the heel and then passed around in front of the ankle and back again, and may be tied either in front or on the sides. At the top the boots are fastened tightly over the trousers by means of a drawstring. This style of boot is common from the lower Yukon to the Arctic coast northward of Kotzebue sound. The specimen from Kotzebue sound shown in plate XXI, 12, is a typical example of this style of foot-wear, but the pattern of ornamentation varies according to individual fancy.

WOMAN OF MECHIGME BAY

WOMAN OF EAST CAPE

SIBERIAN ESKIMO

On the tundra south of the lower Yukon this general style of boot is made in a somewhat different fashion. The sewing is much more crudely done in that district than in the region to the northward. Plate XXI, 9, shows a pair of winter boots typical of the lower Kusko-kwim district; they are made of deerskin tanned with the hair on and the hairy side turned in, but with a long, oval flap turned down in front from the top, thus having the hairy side outward on this portion. The outer flap is bordered by one or more narrow strips of white-hair deer-skin with little tags of worsted scattered along the lower edge, and is finished by a narrow strip of mink fur.

The soles of the shoes worn in this district are of sealskin sewed on in the same manner as already described, but in a very crude fashion, owing to the unskilfulness of the needle women in this part of the country.

On the lower Kuskokwim and southward to Tikchik lake the boots worn are more like those from the region north of the Yukon, except in the example shown in plate XXI, 8, from Tikchik, which have the front and rear of the legs ornamented with little tags of red worsted and white hair, and along the sides of the seams a series of little strips of reindeer-skin two or three inches in length.

The top of the boot has two bands of white-hair reindeer-skin sewed around, each bordered above by a narrow strip of plucked beaver-skin. The lower of these white bands is bordered on its lower edge by strips of plucked beaver-skin, three or four inches in length, hung in pairs. These boots have two pairs of little leather ears—one on each side of the toes and the other on each side of the ankles. A long cord is passed across the top of the foot through the first of these, the ends of which are crossed over the foot and passed through the ears at the sides of the ankles, thence crossing behind and around forward and tied, as already described.

On King island and the Diomedes in Bering strait some of these deer-skin boots are handsomely ornamented, as shown in the accompanying illustration (plate XXI, 7) of a typical pair from the first named locality. They are made of white-hair reindeer-skin taken from the legs of the animal, and have a hard-tanned sealskin sole and a narrow strip of tanned sealskin of russet color between the sole and the uppers. The legs are handsomely ornamented with pattern work sewed on in colors— red, black, white, blue, and yellow being used. The white work is done mainly by sewing in long reindeer hairs. In addition colored threads are used for the red and blue. A fine, yellow checked pattern work is produced by drawing narrow strips of yellow-tanned seal intestine through little slits cut along the strips of russet-colored tanned sealskin which are set into the sides of the legs. Along these bands and on the borders of the pattern work are set little tufts of hair from the pup seal, dyed a deep chestnut red, alternating with little square tags of white-hair skin. As usual, around the top are several bands of white-hair skin, between the upper two of which is a strip of wolverine skin with long projecting hair. These strips of skin along the upper border have welted into the seam between them a narrow strip of hard, black-tanned skin, so as to produce a black line along each seam. These boots are fastened to the foot as in the first pair described from the American mainland. The soles are crimped in the same manner as those from the adjacent coast, and both sewing and crimping are well done, as is characteristic of all work of this kind performed by the women throughout the region.

For summer wear the common style of boot is of tanned sealskin with the hair side outward or with the hair removed. The latter kind is made waterproof, and the oil-tanned uppers are either black or dyed a deep reddish brown by the use of alder bark. The seams between the soles and the uppers, as well as those along the legs, are generally heavily welted, and commonly have the tops surrounded by a band of white parchment-like tanned sealskin, turned in to hold a drawstring for fastening the boot to the leg. The straps for fastening these boots are made usually of white-tanned sealskin attached to the seams between the soles and uppers on each side of the middle of the foot. They are then crossed over the top of the foot, and after passing through the ear or lap of sealskin which is sewed to the sole on each side of the ankle, they are again crossed above the heel and carried forward around the front, then back again to be tied as already described. Plate XXI, 10, shows one of a typical pair of these boots from St Michael.

The legs of these boots usually reach to just below the knees, but some are made to extend to the hips for wearing while hunting or fishing, and many are made that reach just above the ankle. These latter are more in the style of dress boots, being worn about the villages or while traveling in umiaks. Their uppers are made commonly of white, parchment-like tanned sealskin, but sometimes from the stomach of a large seal or walrus, which makes a beautiful white, parchment-like leather. The uppers are variously ornamented by welted seams and strips sewed in successively around the edge of the sole, as shown in plate XXI, 4, from Golofnin bay.

These short summer boots are made sometimes of tanned sealskin, with the hair left on and turned inward, so that the softened inner surface of the skin is exposed. They are surrounded at the upper border usually by a white, parchment-like band with a drawstring, and the portion of the uppers over the toes and sides of the foot in front have sewed upon them strips of russet and white-tanned skin with fine yellow and black checked patterns, produced by drawing narrow strips of white tanned parchment through little slits cut in the material. Plate XXI, 11, represents a typical example of this class of ornamentation. The women living on the islands of Bering strait are noted for doing handsome work of this kind.

ESKIMO MEN—MECHIGME BAY, SIBERIA

In addition to the boots described, socks made of deerskin or sealskin with the hair not removed, and reaching a little above the ankles, commonly are worn in winter. For wear at all seasons socks are made of woven grass, the patterns of weaving varying to a certain extent and sometimes different colored grasses being used to produce ornamental patterns, as shown in the sole of the example from the lower Kuskokwim, illustrated in plate XXI, 2.

Plate XXI, 1, shows a typical grass sock from Razbinsky, on the lower Yukon, and plate XXI, 5, also represents a common style of grass sock from that district. The bottoms of boots of all kinds are usually stuffed with a grass pad made by taking wisps of long grass stalks and binding them over one another to form a long cushion for the bottom of the foot. This gives a soft footing and absorbs the moisture that penetrates the sole, so that it requires a long time for water to reach the foot.

At night the socks and the grass pads are removed and hung to dry either over the lamp in the house or in a convenient place in the room, so as to be ready for use on the following morning.

CLOTHING BAGS

Along the lower Yukon and thence to the Kuskokwim large numbers of bags are made for various purposes from the skins of salmon. Some are used for stor-

FIG. 7—Fish-skin clothing bags ($\frac{1}{10}$).

ing clothes, and still smaller ones for various small objects, such as trinkets and small odds and ends of different kinds. Others are made very large, frequently with a capacity of a bushel or two, and are used for the storage of dry fish, which is kept in them in the storehouses until needed.

Figure 7 (2) illustrates a salmon-skin bag for storing clothing. This example, from Tikchik lake, is ornamented with bands of russet-colored fishskin and white, parchment-like skin from the throats of seals, and is neatly sewed with sinew thread. The upper border of the bag is hemmed, and a series of rawhide loops are sewed at intervals around the top, through which is run a cord of the same material for use as a drawstring in closing the bag. The bottom is oval in outline and has a piece of fishskin sewed into it, with the seam inside. These bags are in common use from the lower Yukon to the lower Kuskokwim.

Figure 7 (1) represents a handsomely ornamented bag from St Michael, made from the skins of salmon trout. The bottom of the bag is fashioned from a piece of deerskin with the hair side inward. The sides are ornamented with strips of white, parchment-like leather made from the gullets of large seals. These strips are edged with narrow bands of russet-color leather, sewed with ornamental seams of black and white. On each of four upright white bands which cross the side of the bag are sewed two circular pieces and a four-pointed piece of the shiny black skin of the sea-wolf, the round pieces being edged with strips of russet skin.

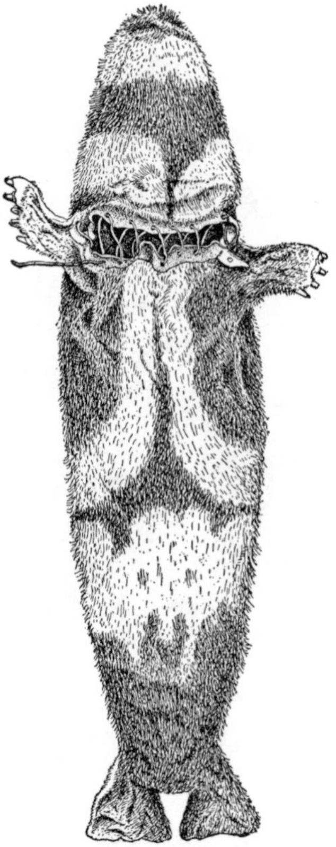

Figure 8 represents a sealskin clothing bag from Sledge island. It is made from the skin of the ribbon seal, taken off entire, including both flippers. The nose and the eyes are sewed up; the only opening is a cut extending crosswise between the fore flippers. The edges of this cut are bound with a border of stout rawhide, pierced with holes at intervals of about two inches, through which is run a strong rawhide cord for lacing the opening. This skin is tanned with the hair left on.

Bags of this character are made from skins of all of the smaller seals, and are useful for storing clothing from the fact that their shape makes them convenient for handling in umiaks or while on sledge journeys; at the same time their waterproof character serves to protect the contents from getting wet. Every family has from one to three of these bags, in which are kept their spare clothing, dressed skins, and valuable furs.

FIG. 8—Clothing bag of sealskin ($\frac{1}{6}$).

PERSONAL ADORNMENT

LABRETS

The wearing of labrets and the custom of tattooing are very general among the Eskimo of the Alaskan mainland and islands northward from Kuskokwim river. The style of the labrets, as with the extent and the pattern of tattooing, varies with the locality. The custom of

ICY CAPE

CAPE PRINCE OF WALES

CAPE PRINCE OF WALES AND ICY CAPE MEN

wearing labrets is almost lost among the Eskimo of the Asiatic coast and of St Lawrence island. One man seen at the latter point had a circle tattooed on each side of his chin to represent these ornaments (figure 15 b). Some of the natives on Mechigme bay, just south of East cape, Siberia, had labret holes in their lips. The Eskimo of the Yukon and the Kuskokwim who live nearest the Tinné have also generally abandoned the practice of wearing labrets, and the custom is becoming obsolete at other points where there is constant intercourse with the whites.

During my residence at St Michael it was rather uncommon to see very young men among the Unalit with their lips pierced, and throughout that time I do not think a single boy among them had been thus deformed. Many of the old men also have ceased to wear labrets, although the incisions made for them in youth still remain.

Among the Eskimo of Bering strait and northward, where contact with the whites has been irregular, labret wearing is still in full force. Increasing intercourse with civilized people makes it only a matter of time for this custom to become entirely obsolete. In the district southward from the Yukon mouth labrets were not universally worn among the men, as is the case in the country northward from Bering strait, and in every village some of the men and many women were found without them. The labrets of the women are of a curious sickle shape, but vary in detail of arrangement, as shown by the accompanying illustrations. Most of them are made with holes in the lower border for the attachment of short strings of beads. The women who wore labrets had the under lip pierced with one or two holes just over the middle of the chin.

The use of these labrets, in the country visited by me, seemed to be limited to the district lying between Yukon and Kuskokwim rivers and Nunivak island. Elsewhere I did not see labrets of any kind used by women. In the villages of Askinuk, Kushunuk, and other places in that region the common form was a small, flattened, sickle-shape piece of ivory, with a broad, flattened base for resting against the teeth, and the outer tip brought down to a thin, flat point. Of this style there are some variations, the most common of which is to have the two ordinary sickle-shape labrets joined by a crosspiece of ivory cut from the same piece and uniting the two sickle-shape parts just on the outer side of the lip.

Another form was to join the inner ends of the labrets so that the portion resting against the teeth united the bases of the two sickle-shape points. In a labret (plate XXII, 2) from Koñigunugumut the piece joining the two sickle-shape points is flattened vertically. In another specimen (plate XXII, 3), from Kulwoguwigumut, this crosspiece, uniting the bases of the two projections, is flattened horizontally. In another (plate XXII, 4) from the lower Kuskokwim, the two sickle-shape projections unite exteriorly to the lip so that a single orifice in the middle of the lower lip serves for the insertion of the stem.

The National Museum collection contains two specimens of women's labrets (one of which is shown in plate XXII, 10) obtained on Nunivak island by Dr W. H. Dall, which differ from most of those of the main-land in having the broadened bases for resting against the teeth made of separate pieces of ivory. These pieces are small, flattened disks with holes in the center through which fits the inner end of the labret, after piercing the lips. These differ also in external form, as shown by the figures.

Another specimen (plate XXII, 1) obtained on Nunivak island has the common sickle-shape parts joined by an external bar, and the inner end is enlarged by means of similar small perforated disks of ivory set on the rounded inner end of the labret. This specimen has attached to its outer border three short, double strings of beads, which hang down over the chin. Plate XXII, 5, showing a specimen from Askinuk; figure 7, one from Kulwoguwigumut, and figure 6, one from Kushunuk, are the ordinary forms of women's labrets of sickle shape.

The labrets worn by men in the district between the Yukon and the Kuskokwim are rather small and are commonly formed of a long, thin, curved ivory flange for resting against the teeth, with a hat-shape pro-jection for extension through the lip to the surface. The hat-shape projection is provided with a central hole, through which extends a wooden pin. This pin reaches beyond the outer border of the ivory and has fitted upon it some kind of bead, a round piece of stone, or, as in one specimen from Nunivak island, a truncated cone of lead.

Another style of labret obtained from Nunivak island by Doctor Dall is shown in plate XXII, 10. It has the usual hat-shape piece for pierc-ing the lip, with the wooden pin extending through and bearing on its outer end a white bead. Beyond this bead is attached a well-cut piece of serpentine, apparently representing the tail of a whale. This labret is two inches long and the serpentine tip is an inch and five-eighths in width by an inch and a quarter long.

From the lower Yukon was obtained a large, flat labret (plate XXII, 16) having a rectangular outline with the sides slightly rounded and on the inner surface a pin five-eighths of an inch in length which serves to pierce the lip. On this is fitted a long, oval piece of ivory an inch and a half long and five-eighths of an inch in width, made convex in front and concave behind, with a slot in the middle for fitting it on the pin. This labret is to insert in the lip and then the last described por-tion is fitted on it from the inside, thus holding it in place. The face of this labret measures an inch and seven-eighths in length by an inch in breadth and is made of fossil mammoth ivory.

Northward from the Yukon the commonest style of labret is the hat-shape form shown in plate XXI, 21, of white quartz from Sledge island. This specimen has the inner side smoothly excavated to fit upon the teeth and the outer border has a groove across its face. This labret is about half an inch across its exposed face and nine-tenths of an inch along the portion resting against the teeth.

TYPICALLY DRESSED WOMEN AND CHILDREN FROM EAST CAPE, SIBERIA

Similar labrets are shown in plate XXII, 19, 20, from Sledge island, which are from an inch to an inch and a quarter along the beveled inner flange, and five-eighths of an inch across their outer faces; these are made of hard stone, mottled black and white. Figure 9 shows a pair of lignite labrets worn by a King island man.

The specimen shown in plate XXII, 9, was obtained on King island in Bering strait. The base is the ordinary hat-shape labret of walrus ivory, having a slot cut in its outer face in which is fitted a well modeled piece of serpentine two inches in length and three-fourths of an inch in breadth, representing the tail of a right whale, and is fastened in place by means of a wooden pin which passes through a hole drilled across the top of the labret and through a corresponding hole in the

FIG. 9—King island man with labrets of lignite.

border of the piece of serpentine inserted in the slot. Its similarity of shape to the specimen (plate XXII, 10) from Nunivak island is curious, and probably represents an ancient and widely spread form that is now rare. A labret obtained on Nunivak island by Doctor Dall (plate XXII, 11) is elaborate in form, having a hat-shape ivory base with six short strings of beads forming the outer part, which are held in position by flat ivory spacers. Another style (plate XXII, 12) from the same locality has an ivory base with a lead tip in the form of a truncated cone.

In the neighborhood of Bering strait and Hotham inlet, large, flat labrets made of jadite were not uncommon. The beautiful specimen (plate XXII, 15) obtained in Hotham inlet by Mr Woolfe measures one and seven-eighth inches by an inch and a quarter on its outer surface. It has an oval button on the inside an inch and a half in width; the outline of the exposed surface is quadrangular, with the two sides rounded; the surface is plain, beveled at each end and crossed lengthwise by a groove. Other styles of labrets worn along this coast, in addition to those already described, have a large inner flange beveled to fit the teeth, and a large, rounded, knob-like head to project through the lips; these are made from various materials, usually some kind of stone.

The specimen (plate XXII, 14) from Kotzebue sound is the finest labret obtained. It is made of nephrite and measures three and a half inches long by an inch and a quarter wide on its outer surface. It is reduced in thickness uniformly, is very regular in outline, and has a well-made button-shape projection on the inner surface for fastening it in the lip.

Some large labrets made of white quartz were obtained at Point Hope; they are circular in outline on their outer faces, measure an inch and a half in diameter, and have the ordinary flanged projection inside for holding them in position. Some of these have the outer face plane and a few have half of a large blue bead fastened to the center of the outer surface. Others have the middle of the outer surface plane and thence to the border slightly beveled. The labret shown in plate XXII, 18, is a good example of the variety with the bead in relief. Plate XXII, 17, shows one with plane surface.

The collection also contains a specimen obtained by Mr Woolfe from Point Hope, which has a large blue bead fitted upon a wooden peg which pierces the hat-shape portion of the labret in a manner exactly similar to those from the island of Nunivak and adjacent mainland.

Among the males labrets are worn only after puberty, as the lips of the young boys are not pierced until that period. The hole is made just below each corner of the mouth and at first a long, thin, nail-like plug of ivory, about an inch in length, having a slight enlargement at the inner end, is thrust through the opening and left for some time. After the wearer becomes accustomed to this, a somewhat larger plug is made, like that shown in plate XXII, 22, from Sledge island, and inserted in the hole for the purpose of enlarging it. This process is repeated, a larger plug being used on each occasion until the hole is of the size desired. In many cases it is so large that the teeth are visible through the opening when the labret is not in place.

To complete the process of enlarging the hole, a man uses a series of from six to eight or ten of these little plugs, which he afterward pierces at their small ends and keeps strung upon a sinew cord, as shown in plate XXII, 25, from Koyukuk river and figure 23 of the same plate from Uñaktolik. These he may keep among his small effects or they may be hung as pendent ornaments to the end of his wife's waist belt, or to the strap of her needle case. When they are used in this way as ornaments, the men frequently etch little patterns upon them, as shown in some of the specimens (plate XXII, 23), which have about their center a double band of incised lines, making a zigzag pattern, with the raven totem mark toward the larger end. Various other figures are also drawn upon these ornaments as fancy may dictate.

KAVIAGMUT

KUSKOKWOGMUT

TYPICAL DRESS OF KAVIAGMUT AND KUSKOKWOGMUT MEN AND WOMEN

The people of Kowak and Noatak rivers, like those of Point Hope and the adjacent Arctic coast, wear large labrets, varying from half an inch to nearly two inches in diameter. The materials from which these are made varies greatly, among them being granite, syenite, jadite, quartz, slate, glass, lignite, and wood, as well as walrus and fossil mammoth ivory. The heads, as already described, may be round, squarely beveled, angular, knoblike, or of various other forms. The photographs of men taken at Point Hope and Kotzebue sound show the appearance of these objects when in place (plate XXIII and figure 10).

FIG. 10—Kotzebue sound Malemut men and women.

The specimen from Point Hope, figured in plate XXII, 24, is a knob-head labret made of a dark green stone. Another from the same locality (plate XXII, 13) has a hat-shape base of ivory with a large blue bead on a wooden pin inserted in a hole made in the basal portion of the labret.

In wearing large stone labrets, the lip is dragged down by their weight, so that the lower teeth and gums are exposed. It is the usual custom to wear but one of the larger size at a time, one of smaller dimensions being inserted on the opposite side of the mouth. While traveling with these people in winter, I found that during cold days the labrets were invariably removed in order to prevent the lip from freezing, as must have occurred had they remained in place. The labrets were removed and carried in a small bag until we approached a village at night, when they were taken out and replaced, that the

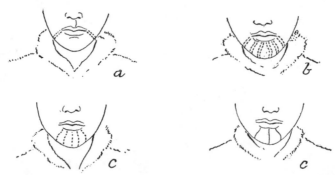

Fig. 11—Tattooing on women (*a*, South of Yukon mouth; *b*, East cape, Siberia; *c, c*, Head of Kotzebue sound).

wearer might present a proper appearance before the people. They are also sometimes removed when eating and before retiring for the night.

TATTOOING

Tattooing is universally practiced among the women of the Bering strait region, but has attained its greatest development on the Siberian coast and St Lawrence island. On the tundra south of the Yukon only part of the women are tattooed, and I was informed that the practice is comparatively recent among them. They claim to have adopted it from the women of Nunivak island, who had straight lines on their cheeks, and also from having seen tattooing on the faces of Tinné women. The common pattern used in this district is a pair of lines across the chin from each corner of the mouth, as shown in figure 11,*a*.

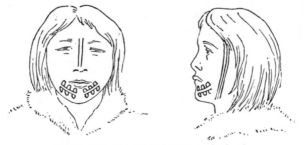

Fig. 12—Tattooing on a St Lawrence island girl.

Malemut women, as well as those from Noatak and Kowak rivers, cross the chin with series of lines of tattooing radiating from the lower lip, as shown in figure 11, *b*, *c*; they also frequently have straight lines across the back of the wrist and forearm. On St Lawrence island and

MAN'S BIRDSKIN FROCK (ABOUT ONE-SEVENTH)

the adjacent Siberian coast women have the sides of their faces (figure 12) and their arms and breasts covered with finely designed patterns of circles and scroll work, sometimes crossed by straight lines.

At East cape, the women ordinarily have six or eight pairs of lines crossing their chins, and on each side of their faces patterns of circles

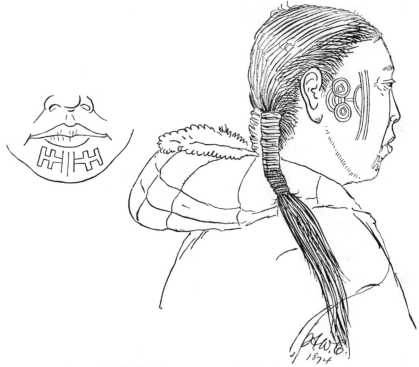

Fig. 13—Tattooing on a woman of St Lawrence island.

and spiral lines; also, two or three vertical, parallel lines crossing their temples and extending to the chin. The patterns on the cheeks usually cover a space about four inches in width extending from the ear toward the nose and from the eye to the lower jaw.

On the inside of the forearm two long parallel lines usually extend from the elbow to the border of the palm. These are crossed just below the elbow by two short lines, and the wrist is crossed by four lines which sometimes

Fig. 14—Tattooing on a woman's arm, East cape, Siberia.

completely encircle that part of the arm (figure 14). On the body the tattooing covers the breast and sometimes the shoulders and upper arms.

The pattern shown in figure 12 was seen on the face of a little girl of St Lawrence island. Figure 13, showing the tattooing on the face of a woman of this island, is from a sketch made and kindly presented to me by Mr Henry W. Elliot.

At Mechigme bay, Siberia, a man was seen who had a double circle connected by radiating lines on each cheek (figure 15, *a*). At Plover bay a boy had the raven totem over each eye, as shown in the illustrations of totem markings. On St Lawrence island a man had circles, representing labrets, near the lower corners of his mouth, and two short, parallel lines on each temple (figure 15, *b*).

BEADS AND EARRINGS

The practice of piercing the septum of little girls is still common among the Eskimo of the Alaskan mainland. While the children are small they wear one or more beads about the size of buckshot pendent from this hole so that they rest upon the upper lip. When the girl reaches maturity, the nose beads are not worn, and I never observed any use made by women of the hole in the septum except for carrying

a   *b*

FIG. 15—Circular forms of tattooing (*a*, on a Mechigme bay man; *b*, on a St Lawrence island young man).

small objects like needles, which are frequently thrust through the opening and held in place by the pressure of the wings of the nose on either side.

On the Asiatic coast large boys and young men were frequently seen wearing two or three beads strung on their hair so as to hang down over their foreheads. The hair and the clothing of little girls and young women of the district south of the lower Yukon are highly ornamented with beads. These are hung in parallel strings, held in position as flat bands by means of small, flat, ivory rods, or by strips of heavy skin pierced with holes at short intervals, through which pass the cords on which the beads are strung. Loops of these bands sometimes hang from the earrings over the shoulders to the breast; others are attached to the braids of hair above the ears. To these loops is frequently attached a heavy copper ring.

The practice among women of piercing the lobe or outer edge of the ear is common in all the territory occupied by the Eskimo visited by me. In some instances only the lobe is pierced, and in others holes

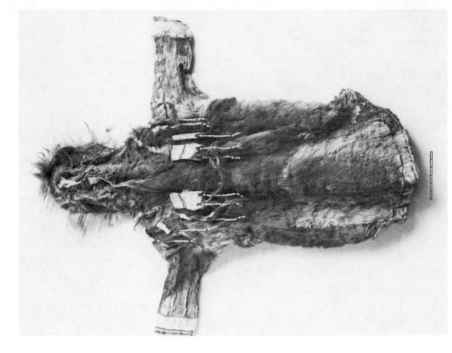

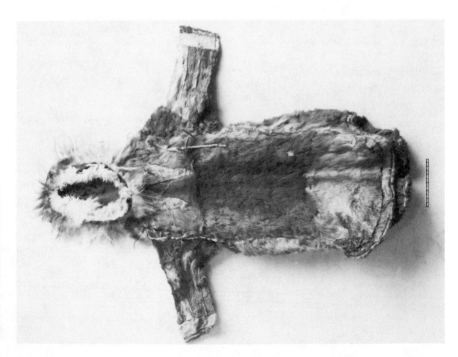

FRONT AND BACK OF MAN'S DEERSKIN FROCK (ONE-TWELFTH)

are made along the outer border above the lobe. It is also common for men to have their ears pierced, particularly in the district between the Yukon and Kuskokwim, where they wear huge earrings, from which frequently hang strings of beads, extending under the chin from ear to ear in a long loop. The variety of earrings worn by the women in the vicinity of the Yukon and the Kuskokwim is very great, as shown by the series illustrated in plates XXIV and XXV; they are made of ivory, with occasional settings of beads or other objects. Elsewhere along the coast very much less variety in the ornamentation of these objects was observed.

It is interesting to note that the greatest richness of ornamentation and variety in form of earrings is found among the people of the district south of the lower Yukon, which coincides with the elaborate style of their carvings on masks and other objects.

Earrings worn by men of the tundra between the Yukon mouth and the lower Kuskokwim are made of ivory and are very large. They are usually rectangular and measure from an inch and a quarter to two inches in length by three-quarters of an inch to an inch and a quarter in width. Frequently there are four plane sides, but some of them have the lower end rounded, while others have this portion beveled from each side to the center. They commonly taper slightly from above downward. The front is excavated, leaving a narrow rim of ivory around the border, the sides of the excavation being parallel with the outline of the tablet-like piece forming the ornament. Frequently this excavated space is crossed midway by a narrow ridge of ivory, which subdivides the central opening into upper and lower divisions of equal size. This sunken area is then filled with some kind of cement, probably made from spruce gum, in which are set various shining objects.

The following descriptions cover some of the most interesting forms of men's and women's earrings contained in the collection. The specimen from Kaialigamut shown in plate XXV, 12, measures an inch and a quarter in length by three-quarters of an inch in width and has its outer face divided by an ivory ridge. The excavated spaces are filled with a black cement, and set in each subdivision are three small, square pieces of lead, making six on each earring. The lower end is beveled to a point, and like all of these large earrings has a boss on the posterior surface near the lower border, which is pierced with a hole for fastening the ends of little pendants of beads. In addition, this specimen has a longer string of beads passing beneath the chin to the opposite side. The hook for attaching these ornaments to the ear is cut from the same piece of ivory and extends back and downward nearly to the lower point of the carving.

Another example from Kaialigamut (plate XXV, 10) is similar in shape to the one last described, with the lower end beveled to a point. It is two inches in length by an inch and one-eighth wide, and has set in the cemented outer face several fragments of bottle glass. On the back is the usual long, stout hook, and a small pierced knob or boss is provided near the lower point for the attachment of strings of beads.

The earring from Nunivak island shown in plate XXV, 13, is an inch and five-eighths long by an inch wide, with the lower end of bow shape. The excavated front surface is not subdivided by an ivory ridge, but has an insertion of some white substance crossed by regular black lines forming a diamond-shape pattern over which is neatly fitted a piece of window glass.

Another specimen (plate XXV, 11), from Big lake, is of quadrilateral outline and has an ivory septum across the center forming two subdivisions filled with cement, in which are set four rounded fragments of brass, one at each corner, with a round bead of iron in the center. A smaller specimen than this, from the same locality, has four white beads set in the cement at each corner of the subdivisions, with fragments of glass in the center. Another earring, from Koñigunugumut, has small fragments of mica imbedded in the cement.

The greatest variety of carving, however, is shown in the earrings worn by women. These are sometimes plane-face, quadrate, or oval pieces of ivory with a stout hook in the back; but, as a rule, the fronts are variously carved and ornamented.

A common style of ornamentation consists of a series of concentric rings with a round pit or dot in the center. Their faces are frequently crossed by fine, etched, ray-like lines. Another form is that of the circles and ray-like lines shown in plate XXIV, 18, from Askinuk. All these rings have a stout hook for attaching them to the ear, and a pierced boss near the lower border, on the posterior side, for the attachment of a string of beads.

From Cape Vancouver was obtained the specimen shown in plate XXIV, 5, which exhibits another form, consisting of a circle five-eighths of an inch in diameter, with a round hole in the center and a knob on each corner, and a long, narrow bar at its lower edge, all carved from a single piece of ivory. The front is surrounded by a series of seven neatly etched concentric circles.

From the same locality is a similar earring (plate XXIV, 1), having the circles spaced in pairs, between the outer and the next to the outer set of which are a series of round, sunken dots.

The example illustrated in plate XXIV, 2, from Nunivak island, is an inch and an eighth long by three-fourths of an inch wide. The upper portion is circular, with concentric rings, and the central hole is filled with a little ivory plug; the borders have on each corner a little spur, also of ivory, and below, extending downward, two oblong ivory projections with rounded ends which are pierced by a small, round hole. The front surfaces of these are convex and are covered with a series of five concentric circles; etched lines extend from the outer circle down on the front of the lower projections, and a little circle surrounds each of the holes near the lower end.

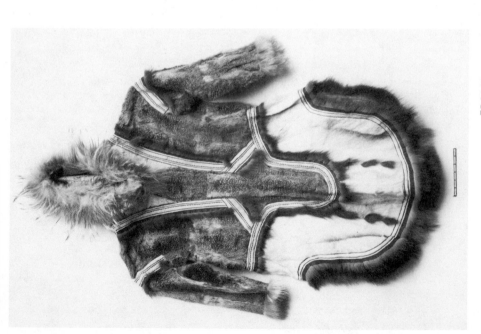

FRONT AND BACK OF WOMAN'S FROCK (ONE-TWELFTH)

The specimen from Chalitmut figured in plate XXIV, 6, is small and rounded; it is a little over half an inch in diameter, and has a rounded knob at each corner. The center has a black spot and two concentric rings with spaced dots scattered around these and a dot in the middle of each corner projection.

Another small set (plate XXIV, 8) from Chalitmut measures half an inch in diameter and is rudely oval in shape, with five small circles and dots arranged in the form of a cross on a slightly convex face.

A single earring obtained from St Michael (number 129265) exhibits two circles, joined one below the other, and each having the front covered with concentric rings with a piece of lead set in the center. There is a hole at the lower end for the attachment of a string of beads.

A pair from Nulukhtulogumut (plate XXIV, 3) measure three-quarters of an inch in width. They are of the usual rounded pattern with projecting corners, and with the center excavated and set with half of a blue bead, which is surrounded by two concentric circles, the outer one having spur-like etched lines drawn from it to the corner projections.

Another example (plate XXIV, 4) from Kaialigamut, is three-quarters of an inch in diameter, with rounded outline and convex face, in which is set half of a large, amber-colored glass bead.

In addition to the styles already described, the country between the lower Yukon and the Kuskokwim affords a considerable variety of these ornaments, upon which are carved the features of men, animals, and *tunghät*. These are usually oval in outline, measuring from half an inch to three-quarters of an inch in diameter, but some are oblong in shape. A pair from Chalitmut (plate XXIV, 15) are square, with the features raised in relief in the center.

A pair from Kushutuk (plate XXIV, 13) are each three-quarters of an inch in length and in shape represent a small seal.

The ornamentation of the specimen from Cape Vancouver illustrated in plate XXIV, 16, represents the features of a *tunghák*, and on another from the same locality (plate XXIV, 14) is shown the face of a short-ear owl.

Northward from St Michael to Bering strait the earrings used are more oblong in shape, being longer and narrower in proportion; they are also less handsomely ornamented, and the entire workmanship is more crude. These measure from half an inch to an inch and a half in length and from an eighth to half an inch in diameter.

An oblong, convex-face pair (plate XXIV, 19), from Sledge island, measure a little over an inch and a quarter in length and three eighths of an inch in breadth, and have half of a large blue bead set in the front of each. Most of the earrings from this island have the faces crossed by deeply incised lines, although there were obtained one or two pairs which are perfectly plain.

The specimen from Cape Vancouver shown in plate XXIV, 7, is a disk with a series of concentric circles on its face; another (plate XXIV, 11) from the same locality represents a grotesque human face with tufts tied on each side to represent a woman's braided hair, while another (plate XXIV, 17), obtained also at the same place, represents the features of a seal.

The only metal earrings obtained were collected on the lower Yukon. They are made of copper, of the usual round style worn by women, with concentric circles on the face and projecting knobs at the corners.

A pair of earrings (plate XXIV, 9), obtained at St Michael by Mr L. M. Turner, show smooth, disk-like faces three-eighths of an inch in diameter, back of which project for about a quarter of an inch rounded ivory pins extending downward three-quarters of an inch to roughly truncated tips pierced for the reception of the ends of a string of beads. These are the only earrings of this description that were seen.

A pair from Cape Vancouver (plate XXIV, 12) are long, narrow, and oval in shape. They are an inch long, by three-eighths of an inch wide, and taper down to a narrow, flattened point pierced as usual for attaching a string of beads. Extending lengthwise along the median line of the faces is a ridge from which the surface is beveled away on both sides. On this doubly beveled surface is represented, by means of incised lines and dots, a grotesque human face with labret holes below the corners of the mouth.

Another pair, from Nulukhtulogumut (plate XXIV, 10), are broadly oval in outline with a grotesque human face on the front; they measure seven-eighths of an inch long by nearly three-quarters of an inch wide.

Plate XXV, 9, shows a pair from Chalitmut, three quarters of an inch long by half an inch wide, having an oval outline and a slightly convex face. An incised line extends vertically through the center, with two pairs of beveled lines extending thence diagonally downward to the border on each side. In the three spaces thus made along each side of the surface are three small circles and dots. From the lower ends of these rings hang two pendants of beads two and one-half inches in length, and a string of beads twelve inches in length connects them below the chin.

A pair of rounded earrings from Sfugunugumut (plate XXV, 7) are about seven-eighths of an inch in diameter and have knob-like projections on four corners, each of the latter having an incised dot in the center. The faces are marked by two concentric circles, with a hole in the center, which is plugged with wood. A hole in the lower edge of these rings serves to attach the upper edge of a band over four inches in length, made of seven strings of beads, which are spaced near the upper end by a flattened ivory rod an inch and a half long, pierced with a hole for each string. Near the lower end they are held in place by a similar strip made from a thick piece of sealskin.

On the islands as well as on both shores of Bering strait, the women frequently wear pendent from their earrings, in place of beads, strings of the little orange-color horny sheaths from the angle of the bill of

FRONT OF MAN'S FISHSKIN FROCK (ONE-SIXTH)

the crested auklet, in a double row four or five inches in length and terminating in one or more beads.

HAIR ORNAMENTS AND COMBS

The tonsure is universally practiced by the Eskimo wherever I traveled among them, whether on the American or on the Siberian coast, with the possible exception of some of them in the upper Kusko-

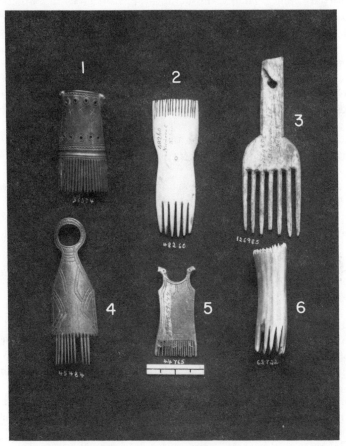

FIG. 16—Hair combs ($\frac{3}{10}$).

kwim region. The general style is to shave the top of the head, leaving a narrow fringe of hair about the border, which usually is kept trimmed evenly two or three inches in length around the head.

The women dress their hair by parting it along the median line and arranging it in a pendent braid or club-shape mass behind the ear, as shown in the accompanying illustration (plate XXVI) of some women at Cape Smith. Sometimes the ends of the braids are united at the back of the head, or they may be arranged with strips of fur or strings of beads into club-shape rolls hanging down to the shoulders or even over the breast. Very often the strips of fur worn are those of the animal representing the family totem, and when wrapped about the hair in this manner they indicate the gens to which the woman belongs.

South of the Yukon mouth the women are especially fond of ornamenting the pendent rolls or braids of hair by hanging bands and strings of beads upon them with ivory ornaments attached, some of which are figured. They usually represent the faces of animals or of grotesque semihuman creatures. The ornament from Big lake illustrated in plate XXV, 1, is of ivory and represents the face of a wolf. Another (plate XXV, 2), from Koñigunugumut, represents a grotesque, semihuman face. On one from the lower Kuskokwim (plate XXV, 3) there is a representation of a human countenance, while one from Agiukchugumut (plate XXV, 4) shows also a grotesque face. Another specimen from Big lake (plate XXV, 6) is ornamented with a conventional pattern.

Combs used by the Eskimo for the hair are made by cutting slots in the straight edge of flat or slightly curved pieces of deerhorn, walrus ivory, or bone.

A rather elaborately made deerhorn comb (figure 16, 1) is from the lower Yukon. It has a series of teeth along one edge; the handle has a bear's head in relief on each side, and a ring of the material is left on the back to strengthen the comb and to afford a better grip for the hand. The upper side of the handle is crossed by parallel grooves and a zigzag pattern formed by a series of circles pierced with central holes.

A specimen from Sledge island (figure 16, 5) is a flat tablet of deerhorn with a series of teeth in one end and two projecting animal heads carved on the upper end of the handle. Another, from St Michael (figure 16, 4), is of deerhorn, with the handle ornamented by lines and dots and terminating in a ring. In figure 16, 6, is shown a comb, from the Diomede islands, made from a hollow bone, which has a series of teeth of different sizes surrounding each end.

Figure 16, 2, shows an example from Nunivak island made from a piece of walrus ivory, and has one end provided with large teeth and the other with smaller ones. Another, from St Lawrence island (figure 16, 3), is cut from a paddle-shape piece of bone. It has large rounded teeth and a slender handle, pierced near its upper end.

BRACELETS

Bracelets of iron, brass, or copper are worn by women and girls throughout the region visited. The men also use bracelets made of a sealskin cord on which is strung one or more large beads of ivory or other substance. They are generally used while at sea for rolling under the end of the sleeves of the waterproof skin frock. In plate XXV, 5, is shown an example of these bracelets from Nunivak island.

MEN'S GLOVES

BELTS AND BELT BUTTONS

Throughout the Eskimo country from the lower Kuskokwim to the Arctic coast, a favorite waist belt worn by the women is made from the incisors of reindeer. These are obtained by cutting off the tip of the lower jaw, leaving sufficient bone to retain the teeth in their natural position. These rows of teeth are sewed along a strap of rawhide, one overlapping the next in scale-like succession, so that they form a continuous series along its entire length.

Some of these belts have a double row of such teeth, and as each set represents a reindeer, it is evident that a long period of hunting is necessary ere a sufficient number can be accumulated.

In addition to the belts made of reindeer incisors, they have others made by fastening along the surface of a strap of tanned sealskin a series of smooth brass buttons in close succession, or they ornament the entire length of the outer surface of the belt with circles and lines of beads arranged according to the fancy of the wearer.

When worn, the belts are brought loosely around the waist and held in place by a toggle or button, which is attached to the belt by a short cord tied through a hole pierced in the button for the purpose. These cords are attached to the belt about a foot or fifteen inches from the ends, so that the latter hang down in front of the hips on each side.

The belt buttons are passed through a cord loop on the opposite side of the belt and thus hold it in place. They are made of ivory, bone, or reindeer horn, and have very great variety of form. Some are merely rounded knobs, or are made from the tooth of a bear or walrus pierced in the middle, while others are in the form of hooks. Flat button-shape carvings, with squared, circular, or oval outlines are common, but most numerous of all are those made in the forms of seals, walrus, birds, and men.

A number of these objects have been illustrated (plate XXVII) in order to show their great variety and to demonstrate the skill and ingenuity in carving which these people possess.

The following notes describe the character of those figured, which are made of ivory except where other substances are indicated.

The specimen from Cape Nome, illustrated in plate XXVII, 1, is a good example of this style of fastener. A similar object, shown in figure 2 of the same plate, is from Chalitmut; this is a fragment of deerhorn, an inch and three-quarters long and three-quarters of an inch in diameter. smoothly rounded, and pierced with a central hole. Another (figure 4), from Kotzebue sound, consists of a long, quadrangular piece of walrus ivory an inch and a half long by half an inch in width, with a narrow, raised ear or projection on the middle of the inner surface, which is pierced lengthwise for the passage of a cord; the front is marked with incised lines. Figure 5 illustrates a specimen from Chalitmut, which is somewhat similar in shape to the last, except that it is round and about half an inch in diameter. It has a flattened projection on one side, which is pierced to receive the cord.

Another example from Cape Nome (plate XXVII, 6) is a narrow, oblong piece of ivory, having the front strongly convex and the back slightly concave, with a projection near the middle, through which passes a broad opening for the cord. Another, from Chalitmut (plate XXVII, 25), is a roughly oval, plummet-like piece of ivory, with a stem-like projection on one end which is pierced for the cord; the surface is crossed by incised lines extending around each face and by a similar line around its greatest diameter, between which and the stem are four sets of circles and dots.

The specimen from Anogogmut, illustrated in plate XXVII, 16, is a neatly made carving of a seal an inch and three-eighths long, with a projecting ear-like piece on its lower surface, through which a triangular hole admits a cord. Another, from Nunivak island (plate XXVII, 15), is a double oval carving, with an angular projecting ear on the lower surface for the attachment of the cord. On the front the double oval surface meets at a narrow neck, each end having etched upon it a grotesque countenance, probably representing the face of a seal.

The fastener shown in plate XXVII, 12, from Sfugunugumut, is an inch and a half long, made from walrus ivory in the shape of a white whale, and is pierced through the side. Figure 3 shows a carving from Agiukchugumut, two and a quarter inches in length, slightly resembling in outline the incisor of a bear; on the truncated end is a grotesque semihuman face, and etched upon the sides are lines, circles, and dots, including the representation of fore and hind limbs. It represents some being recognized in the mythology of the Eskimo.

Plate XXVII, 7, represents a neatly made carving, an inch and three-quarters long, in the form of a walrus, the flippers of the animal being conventionally shown in relief. It is from the lower Kuskokwim.

Plate XXVII, 11, shows a miniature carving, from Sledge island, representing a white bear; it is an inch long and is pierced through the side for the cord.

Plate XXVII, 8, illustrates a fastener, from Nunivak island, representing a walrus. It measures two and a half inches in length and is pierced vertically for the cord.

An unnumbered piece from Kushunuk is a small carving representing on its front a grotesque figure of a woman; it is pierced on the back for the passage of the cord.

Plate XXVII, 10, represents a small carving, from Nunivak island, an inch and three-eighths long, almond-shape in outline, flat on the lower edge and concave on the upper; the latter surface has marked upon it the figure of a fish, with a broad, deeply incised, crescent-shape mouth; it is pierced vertically for the cord.

Plate XXVII, 14, shows a fastener from Cape Nome; it measures an inch and a half in length and represents the heads of two polar bears

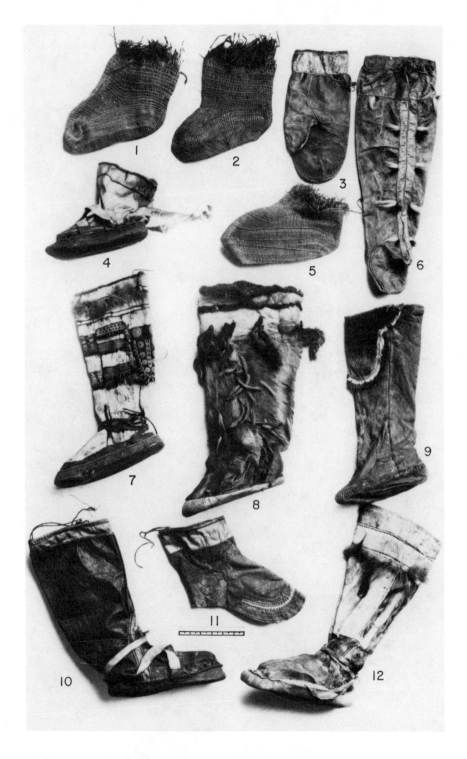

BOOTS, WATERPROOF MITTENS, AND STRAW SOCKS (ABOUT ONE-NINTH)

with open mouths and joined at the necks. A hole passes laterally through the bases of the necks for the cord; the heads are divided by a deep, broad incision, separating them from each other at their bases.

Another fastener from Cape Nome (figure 17) is a fine piece of composite carving. Held in one position it represents the head of a white bear; turned with the other surface upward it represents a seal, the ears of the bear serving in that case for the fore-flippers of the latter animal, while a ridge along both sides of the posterior portion of the seal's body marks the position of its hind flippers and serves to outline the lower jaws of the bear. This object can also be used as a cord handle.

Plate XXVII, 13, from Point Hope, is an excellent representation of the skull of a walrus an inch and a half in length. Figure 21 of the same plate represents a fastener from Askinuk, in the form of a seven-fingered human hand.

Another style of button or belt fastener is made from a rounded, oval, or quadrangular flattened piece of ivory or bone, pierced through the center with a single hole for the accommodation of the belt cord.

The following fasteners are also illustrated in plate XXVII:

Figure 19, from the lower Yukon, is a thin, square piece of ivory, pierced in the center by a hole for the cord; its border is surrounded by a series of etched lines, forming a wave pattern; extending toward the center from each corner are etched the tridentate marks representing the raven totem.

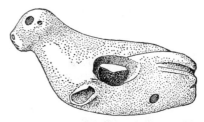

FIG. 17—Ivory belt fastener.

Figure 20 is from Cape Vancouver. It has a circular face, with four projecting knobs at the corners, and etched upon the front are seven concentric circles; the knobs at the corners are pierced and the holes are plugged with wood; two circular lines surround the holes.

Figure 22, from Cape Prince of Wales, is a round, convex-face piece of ivory, with the surface neatly carved in relief with a wave pattern alternating with rings; a large ear-like projection on the back is pierced for the cord.

Figure 18, from Anogogmut, is an inch and a quarter long, rounded above and square below, with a slightly oval front, on which, in low relief, is a grotesque human face. The usual ear-like ring on the back serves for attaching the cord.

Figure 17, from Nunivak island, is an inch and three-eighths long and an inch and a quarter wide. It is excavated at the back, and on the front has a well-made representation of human features, with the mouth and the eyes pierced, and with lines representing snow goggles across the eyes; on the back is a strong ear for attaching the cord.

Figure 24, from Cape Vancouver, represents the head of a salmon;

it is hollow and has an ivory pin passing through its base, to which a cord may be attached.

In addition to the button-like objects described, other belt fasteners are made in the form of hooks. These vary from plain hooks, as in plate XXVII, 30, to the elaborately carved forms shown in this plate.

Figure 26, from Agiukchugumut, has its surface marked by incised lines inclosing the eye at the base of the hook, passing thence to a point, where they unite. A similar but larger specimen is more elaborately ornamented on its surface.

Figure 27, from Chalitmut, represents a fish, and has an incision along the entire length, following its outline.

Figure 23, also from Chalitmut, is a square, flattened piece of ivory with a slit-like notch cut in on one side to a hole in the center, and with a beveled edge on one face. Both surfaces are marked by heavily incised lines.

Figure 28, from the mouth of the Yukon, is a rudely made hook with the head of an animal carved upon the outer end, the other end being pierced by a hole for the cord; along the back of the animal, from between the ears, extends an incised line, from which other lines extend diagonally down the sides as though outlining segments.

Figure 29, from the northern end of Norton sound, is a curiously made hook in the shape of a human figure, represented as sitting on its legs with the body bent forward and the head supported by the hands placed on either side of the face; the area inclosed between the neck and the arms serves for attaching the belt cord, and the legs extending forward and upward parallel to the body serve as a hook for insertion into the opposite loop.

Figure 9, from Kushunuk, represents a rudely outlined, grotesque human figure.

Figure 30, from Agiukchugumut, shows a plain hook with an eye for the cord and two lines etched along the surface, surrounding the eye and following the outline.

The men and boys wear belts of various kinds. Sometimes these may be simply a rawhide cord or strap of tanned skin; more commonly, however, they are made of the skin taken from the feet of a wolverine or wolf, the claws being left on. It is soft-tanned without removing the hair and the edges are sewed together to make a continuous band; on the back is sewed the skin of the animal's head, the nose being attached to the belt and the tail fastened to the lower end. These belts are highly prized, and it is very seldom that a man or a boy, unless he be very poor, does not possess his wolverine or wolf-skin belt. It is supposed to give the wearer a certain strength and prowess similar to those qualities in the animal from which the skin was taken.

Belts representing the totem animal of the owner are also worn, and sometimes the mummified bodies of the little weasel are attached to them in front, in the belief that some of the animal's prowess will be conveyed

LABRETS (NINE-SIXTEENTHS)

to the wearer. These weasel belts were most frequently seen among people from the head of Norton bay and Kaviak peninsula, where they seemed to be particularly prized. The people from that section offered as much as two dollars' worth of furs for the skin and the head of a weasel for this purpose.

UTENSILS AND IMPLEMENTS

LAMPS

Throughout western Alaska, including the islands of Bering strait, and upon the coast of Siberia, open lamps are used for burning seal oil; they are made of clay, soap-stone, or other easily worked stone, and present considerable variety of form.

At Point Barrow I saw a fine soapstone lamp (figure 18), 2 feet long and 10 inches broad, weighing about 30 pounds. The owner refused to sell it, but the accompany-

FIG. 18—Lamp from Point Barrow.

ing sketch made at the time shows the manner in which it is subdivided by ridges of stone, with sunken interspaces; it is symmetrical in form and suboval in outline, with the convexity greatest on one side.

At East cape, Siberia, I saw a stone lamp lying upon a grave, just back of the village, which is similar in outline to the Point Barrow lamp described, but it lacked the subdivisions across the interior; it is about 15 inches long and proportionately broad.

FIG. 19—Ivory carving representing a lamp and stand (full size).

The specimen illustrated in plate XXVIII, 3, was found on the eastern coast of Siberia; it is made of stone, is suboval in outline, deeply excavated at the back, and slopes upward to a broad ledge in front; this ledge is crossed by a ridge of stone cut through in the center for holding the wick.

On the Diomede islands similar lamps were found in use, but a child's toy, made from ivory in shape of a lamp, was obtained on one of these islands, which shows a different form (figure 19). It is suboval in outline and deepest in the center, with a ridge extending along each side just above the bottom, and with a groove cut through the middle of each side for the wick. This lamp is represented as standing upon a stool-like frame, which is supported by four legs, with a crosspiece on each side and two crosspieces on the ends to hold the legs in place.

An example (number 64223) from Hotham inlet is of stone, subtriangular in outline, with the convexity greatest on one side, toward which the bottom slopes; the long, nearly straight, unnotched edge forms the ledge on which the wick rests.

From St Lawrence island a number of lamps were obtained, showing considerable variety of form.

Plate XXVIII, 7, represents a lamp made of clay, 11¼ inches long, 9½ wide, and 2¾ deep; it is suboval in outline, with a tray-shape bottom; a high, thin ridge runs along each side, just above the bottom, which projects upward, and inclines a little outward; a deep notch is cut through the middle of these ridges close to the level of the bottom for receiving the wick. The form of this lamp is precisely that indicated on the toy carving from the Diomede islands above described (figure 19).

Plate XXVIII, 8, illustrates a lamp from St Lawrence island, 14½ inches long by 12¼ wide and 2¾ deep. It is like the last in general shape, but slopes gradually from the sides downward to within a short distance of the bottom, when it drops suddenly to a depressed area about an inch deep, which occupies the entire bottom of the lamp; along each side of the bottom projects a ridge, which slopes upward and a little toward the middle. These ridges are pierced by a round hole near each end, about on a line with the bottom of the lamp, through which the wicks were inserted. Both this lamp and the one last described undoubtedly stood upon framework supports, and were used probably for cooking purposes.

A tray-shape clay lamp (number 63569) from St Lawrence island is 15½ inches long by 10¾ wide; it has two projecting ridges on the inner sides, midway between the rim and the bottom, for supporting the wick. This, like the other large lamps from this island already described, was undoubtedly used for cooking.

Plate XXVIII, 4, shows a tray-shape lamp from St Lawrence island, which undoubtedly was used solely for illuminating purposes. It has the upper border flattened smoothly on three sides; along the front the slope extends gently backward toward the deepest part. Extending lengthwise, midway between the bottom and the front border or lip, is a thin projecting ridge; the front border of the lamp above this ledge shows signs of having been burnt; evidently the wicks had their bases supported against the raised ridge while their upper edges projected from the lip.

Plate XXVIII, 5, represents the support for the last-described lamp. It is made of clay, and is in the form of a pot 5 inches high and 6¾ wide. It has a flat bottom, with the sides rounded to the front, where a crescentic depression is made in the border, with a slightly raised point on the rim at each side. The lamp was placed on the mouth of the vessel, the depressed portion of which is just beneath the point where the wick rests along the outer edge of the lip, so that any drippings of oil which might run down would be caught in the vessel below.

The lamp from St Lawrence island shown in plate XXVIII, 9, is somewhat similar in shape to the preceding, but having the bottom flattened

KOTZEBUE SOUND MALEMUT MEN AND WOMEN WITH LABRETS

and on the posterior side a handle like projection which extends outward for two inches from the general outline of the lamp. Along the opposite side the bottom slopes gradually from the border to the side next to the projection just described, where its deepest point is found. Just below the border is a ridge for supporting the wick, which rests along the upper edge of the lamp in front. Plate XXVIII, 10, represents a wooden bowl-like holder or support for this lamp. It is excavated into a smoothly oval, gourd-shape depression, and has the bottom flat to insure its retaining an upright position.

All of the lamps from St Lawrence island are made with nearly flat bottoms, with the exception of that shown in plate XXVIII, 4, in which the base is rounded.

Plate XXVIII, 12, from Norton bay, is a crescentic toy lamp made of stone, with a sharp edge extending almost straight across one side, the remainder of the border approaching a semicircle.

Figure 11 of the same plate is a clay lamp from St Michael, very similar in shape to the preceding; it is the ordinary form used at that locality and in other villages of the Unalaklit.

From St Michael there is a toy lamp (number 43470) made apparently by utilizing a natural hollow in a small stone. There is also a small toy lamp of stone (number 6475), from Cape Darby, of crescentic outline, and sloping from the nearly straight border to the deepest point below the rim on the opposite side.

Figure 6 represents a stone lamp obtained by Mr L. M. Turner at St Michael; it is nearly pear-shape in outline, with a smoothly sunken depression.

Figure 2, from Big lake, shows a round, saucer-shape toy lamp of clay, with the bottom rounded and the interior regularly depressed. A series of three parallel grooves are incised around the outer edge, near the border; inside the border are seven incised parallel grooves, succeeded by two others which encircle the center of the bottom and are connected with the series on the side by four spoke-like rays, each of which is formed by a series of four incised lines with an intermediate row of dots.

Similar round, saucer-shape lamps are in common use from the Kuskokwim to the Yukon mouth and are found also along the shore of Norton sound to St Michael. One of these lamps from the lower Yukon bears Museum number 38078a. It has two grooves encircling the outside, near the border; inside are four heavy grooves, and a large cross is incised in the center of the bottom.

DIPPERS, LADLES, AND SPOONS

In the neighborhood of Norton sound and the lower Yukon the most common form of dipper is made by cutting a long, thin strip of spruce, three to six inches wide, and fashioning one end into the form of a handle; the other end is thinned down to a long, wedge-shape point,

18 ETH——5

and the wood is steamed and bent upon itself so that the thin edge rests against the strip just inside of the base of the handle. It is then held in position by means of two pairs of sticks clamped upon opposite sides and tied by a wrapping of cord or spruce rootlets. After the frame becomes dry the clamps are removed and a series of holes are punched through the overlapping wood. The bottom of the cylinder formed by the sides has a groove extending around it, in which is fitted a circular or an oval piece of wood, with the edges chamfered. When this bottom is in place the stitching of rootlets is passed through the series of holes in the overlapping ends, holding them permanently in position.

Plate XXIX, figures 6 and 7, illustrate dippers of this description from Norton sound and Sledge island, respectively. The latter is not colored; the former has on the outside of the handle a band extending around the upper and lower edges of the sides, and a strip around the sides of the bottom painted red. The red borders on the sides are outlined on their inner edges by narrow black lines in a slight groove.

Figure 8 of the same plate represents a dipper of slightly different pattern from the lower Yukon. It is obovate in horizontal section, and near the beveled edge of the end of the strips of wood which form the sides of the dipper there is a slightly raised boss extending across it as a strengthener. Exactly opposite this is a similar thickening of the side, which strengthens it and renders the curves around the ends uniform, in the same manner that a thickening in the center of a bow braces it and governs the curves. After being steamed the wood is bent until two notches cut in the upper edge come together at the points where one end of the strip should overlap the other inside of the handle. The ends are then held in place by means of four short, stout sticks, which are bound in pairs on the outer and inner sides by means of tightly wrapped spruce roots, which form a strong clamp. In this manner the wood is held firmly in place until it dries, after which the clamps are removed and a double series of holes are pierced for sewing. A groove is cut on the inner side near the lower edge, into which the chamfered edges of the bottom are sprung. Spruce rootlets are then sewed along the holes pierced in the side, and the dipper is ready for use.

Plate XXIX, 12, from Ikogmut (Mission), represents a round, bowl-shape dipper cut from a single piece of wood, with a flat handle projecting on the inner side; its capacity is about a quart.

Figure 10 of the same plate, from St Lawrence island, is a flat-bottom, bowl-shape dipper, a little smaller than the preceding, which has a round handle projecting from one side with a quadrate opening cut through it.

The dipper from Cape Nome shown in plate XXIX, 9, is made from the horn of a Dall's sheep. It has a deep spoon-shape bowl, with a long, slender handle provided with an ivory pin, held in place by two ivory pegs set in a slot cut through its outer end and projecting down-

EARRINGS

ward with a recurved hook. This is intended to prevent the hand from slipping. Dippers similar to this were obtained from Kotzebue sound.

Among the handsome dippers observed was one seen at Point Hope, made from fossil mammoth ivory. It was oblong in outline, with a deeply excavated interior and a handle projecting at one end.

Plate xxix, 3, from Cape Nome, shows an oval, spoon-shape ladle, with a rounded handle, pierced by two orifices, projecting from one side. A ladle similar to the preceding in form of handle is common along the coast of Bering strait from Cape Nome to the Diomede islands. A specimen from Sledge island, shown in figure 2 of plate xxix, is similar as to the form of the bowl, but has a handle more ornately carved.

The dipper from Chalitmut, shown in plate xxx, 24, has a handle smoothly rounded, with a long, slender, oval hole pierced through it. The inside of the bowl is surrounded by a checked pattern in black, with a curious figure representing some mythological being marked on the center in black paint. This paint is very durable, since it shows no signs of defacement, although the utensil has been used in hot water and in greasy compounds.

Plate xxx, 19, from the lower Kuskokwim, is somewhat similar in outline to the last. The handle is provided with a very small hole, and the edge of the bowl is elevated like a rim above the point of insertion of the handle. This spoon has its inner border encircled by two black lines with crosslines, and in the center is painted, in black, the form of a seal with a spear attached to its back, to which is fastened a line with a float at its outer end. Near the upper edge of the handle are black crossbars.

Plate xxx, 20, from Cape Vancouver, shows a spoon somewhat similar in shape to the preceding, but with the handle differing in outline and the inside of the bowl bordered by a black line, with a conventional drawing of some mythological animal.

Plate xxix, 5, from Chalitmut, has the outer end of the handle truncated and a long, narrow, triangular slot cut through it; the inside of the bowl is ornamented with two drawings, in black, of the killer whale, and the exterior surface is painted red; the handle is crossed by red and black bars.

Dipper numbered 38630, is similar in outline to that just described. On the inside the figure of a man, a circle, and two skins, apparently of otters, are painted in black; the border of the bowl is surrounded on the inside by a black line. The handle and the lower border are red and the former is crossed by a black band.

Plate xxx, 21, from Sfugunugumut, is similar in outline to the last mentioned. It has a seal-like animal painted on the bottom, showing details of its internal anatomy, and inclosed by two long arms with the hands extended and the palms pierced similarly to the hands. Similar figures are seen on masks from this district.

A ladle with a deep bowl, from Paimut, illustrated in plate xxx, 25, has the handle narrowed near the base, then widened and narrowed again toward the top, ending in a rounded point; a triangular slot is cut through the handle, and near the top is a circular hole; its upper surface is carved around the border, and a quadrangular area with incurved sides is sunken near the base and painted black; on the lower surface a groove extends in toward the handle on each side and surrounds the bottom. The form of a small fish is painted in black on the bottom of the bowl, which, near its border, is surrounded by two black rings connected by crossbars.

Plate XXX, 23, from Chalitmut, has the handle made in two parts, joined by a crossbar near the outer end; the lower side of the bowl and part of the handle are painted red; above this the handle is crossed by one red and two black bands. On the inside of the bowl are painted figures of the curious hybrid animal known in Eskimo mythology as the metamorphosis of the white whale into a combination of wolf and whale.

Plate XXX, 22, from Sfugunugumut, is similar in form to others described. It has the inside of the spoon outlined by a black line, and in the center a pattern like that seen on women's earrings in this district, being a circle and a dot with four projecting points which form corners on the outside of the circle.

Figure 9 of the same plate, from Koñigunugumut, is a round-handle spoon, the handle being surrounded at equal intervals with three beads cut in the wood; it is not painted.

Figure 10, from Chalitmut, is a plain-handle spoon having the form of a seal painted in black on the inner surface.

Figure 16, from the Kuskokwim, is a plain-handle spoon having a double-head bird painted in black on the inside; the inner border of the bowl is surrounded by two black lines.

Plate XXIX, 4, shows a spoon from Sabotnisky with a plain handle narrowed near the bowl, which is pear-shape in outline and has the figure of an otter painted within it. The border is surrounded near the upper edge by two black lines; the edge of the rim is red, as are also the borders of the handle on each side, which are connected by a crossbar of red in the middle; the two quadrangular areas of plain wood thus left on the upper surface of the handle are outlined in black.

Plate XXX, 17, also from Sabotnisky, is a long, oval spoon, with the bowl continued to form the handle; it has both the upper and the lower surface ornamented with figures in black.

Plate XXIX, 1, represents a rudely shaped ladle from Big lake. It has a long handle, flattened above and oval below, and is painted red except on the inner surface of the bowl. On this unpainted portion is outlined a figure of the head and fore part of the body of a mythological animal, combining features of the wolf and the killer whale. The fin of the whale is shown rising from the shoulders of the animal, while the fore feet and the head of the wolf are also represented.

Plate XXIX, 11, from St Lawrence island, is a broad, flattened scoop, with a short, projecting handle on the inner end and nearly square

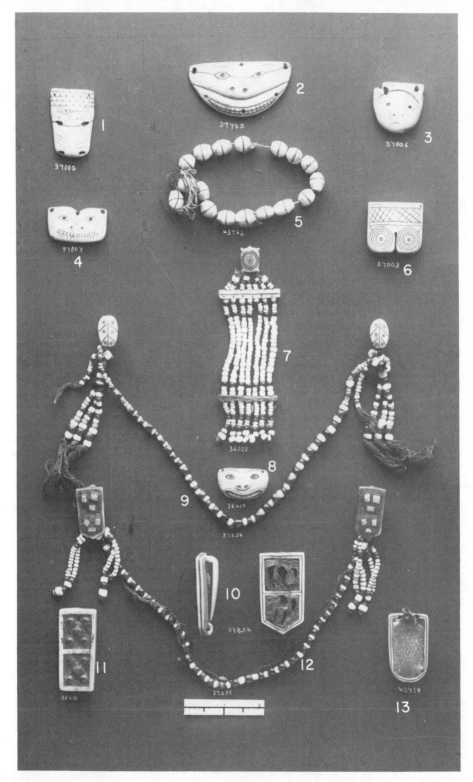

EARRINGS AND OTHER ORNAMENTS (SEVEN-SIXTEENTHS)

across its outer border. This utensil is used for skimming oil or for taking the scum from boiling meat.

Plate XXX, 15, represents a small, rudely fashioned wooden spoon from St Lawrence island, somewhat similar in outline to the scoop last described.

Plate XXX, 18, from Sledge island, is a spoon with a deep bowl and a short, neatly turned handle.

Plate XXX, 11, from Kulwoguwigumut, is a short-handle spoon having a narrow black line extending around the inner border of the bowl, in the center of which are the figures of three reindeer and a large pair of antlers in black.

Plate XXX, 14, from Kushunuk, is a short-handle spoon with a square, shovel-shape edge.

Plate XXX, 13, is similar to the last in shape, but has on the inside of its bowl the figure of a reindeer in black.

Plate XXX, 12, from Kaialigamut, is a scoop-shape spoon, with a conventional representation of a wolf-like animal on the bowl, which is also ornamented with bordering lines of black, and is dotted over with round, red spots.

Plate XXX, 7, from Point Hope, is a small ivory spoon, with a hole in the handle, to which is attached a piece of rawhide cord.

Fig. 20—Marrow spoon ($\frac{1}{2}$).

Plate XXX, 4, from Anogogmut, is a flat spoon, made from reindeer horn, having its smooth upper surface ornamented with three concentric circles and a black dot, and two parallel incised lines which extend around the surface just inside the border.

Plate XXX, 3, from Kushunuk, is a long, narrow spoon of deerhorn, with a hole in the end of the handle for attaching a cord.

Plate XXX, 5, from Kushunuk, is a deerhorn spoon, oval on the inner side and straight on the outer side, with a short handle projecting spur-like on one side.

Plate XXX, 8, from Kushunuk, is a spoon with a shovel-shape bowl and a projecting arm-like handle at one corner.

Plate XXX, 6, from Kushunuk, is a long-bowl, scoop-shape spoon without any distinct handle.

A rudely made spoon of walrus ivory, from St Lawrence island, is represented in plate XXX, 2. It has a hole at one end of the handle for attaching a cord. Spoons similar in shape were obtained also on the Diomede islands.

Plate XXX, 1, from Pastolik, is a spoon for extracting the marrow from bones. The handle is scalloped to receive the fingers; two parallel lines are etched along the borders of the scallops, which terminate below with the raven totem mark. A deerhorn marrow spoon from Kigiktauik has a rounded tip and scalloped handle, as shown in the accompanying figure 20.

WOODEN DISHES, TRAYS, AND BUCKETS

The Tinné of the lower Yukon, adjoining the territory occupied by the Eskimo, are expert in woodworking. They fashion from spruce large numbers of wooden dishes, buckets, trays, and ladles, which they ornament with red and black paint, and the maker usually places his totem mark on each utensil. They make trips down the river for the purpose of selling their products to the Eskimo, and travel as far as St Michael on the seacoast. In addition to this trade with the Eskimo, the articles manufactured by these people are distributed over a much greater extent of territory by means of intertribal trading among the Eskimo themselves.

Besides the ware of this kind obtained from the Tinné, the Eskimo make similar articles themselves, which are as a rule equally well made. Examples of this class of work are shown in the ladles, dippers, and spoons already described and illustrated. The simplest form of tray or dish made by the Eskimo is that cut from a single piece of wood, and this variety of utensil is found over a wide area.

Plate XXXI, 1, represents a rude bowl-shape wooden dish from Icy cape, slightly flattened below to enable it to stand safely.

Figure 2 of the same plate, from St Lawrence island, is a slightly pear-shape, dipper-like dish, with a flattened bottom and a short, projecting handle on one side. This is rather rudely made, as are all the articles obtained on this island.

Figure 9, from the same island, is a tray-like dish with a long, obovate outline above, and slightly flattened below, with the handle projecting upright from one end. It is rudely made and is without ornamentation.

Figure 6, from the lower Yukon, is a handsomely made, tray-like dish, cut from a single piece and bordered around the edge, outside and in, with a band of red paint, inside of which are two parallel narrow black lines connected by similar straight crosslines.

Figure 5, from Chalitmut, is a deep tray, oval in outline and having the head of an animal at one end, which serves as a handle. At the other end is a short, quadrate projection representing the animal's tail. It is bordered around by a band of red, succeeded by an uncolored area and a red line in a groove around the outside. The bottom, both within and without, is uncolored.

Figure 4, from Big lake, is a smoothly finished, deep, tray-like dish. The rim is bordered with red and the inside is painted black. At one end projects a carving representing the head and neck of a human being. The face is turned upward and a short string of beads hangs from each ear. Two white beads are inlaid to represent labrets, and a blue bead hangs from the pierced septum. A circular piece of wood was cut from the rear of the head, through which the latter was excavated, and the

WOMEN AND CHILDREN OF CAPE SMITH

mouth and the eyes were pierced into the hollow interior. This orifice is closed with a neatly fitted circular piece of wood.

Figure 8 represents a very well made tray-shape dish from Big lake; it is oval in outline and is cut from a single block. Projecting from each end are carved figures of grotesque human heads which serve as handles; the eyes are represented by white beads, and others are set around the grooved upper edge of the dish. The lower surface is not painted. A groove around the inside, below the edge, is painted black, succeeded by a red border, below which is a narrow black line. The inside bottom is ornamented with a large figure of a quadruped with a short tail and a curious bird-like head marked with a crest.

Another kind of shallow tray or dish is made from two pieces of wood, the bottom shaped like a truncated cone, the base of which is turned up and chamfered to fit in a groove on the inside of the rim.

In most specimens the narrow, ledge-like rim is made from a thick strip of wood, softened by steam, and then bent around with the beveled ends overlapping and fastened together with wooden pegs. These are in general use on the American coast and on the islands of Bering sea.

Specimens from St Lawrence island are made in the same way except that the overlapping ends are sewed together with whalebone. The ledge-like borders are beveled to a central ridge on the inside and are plane along their outer surfaces; in the middle on each side these bordering strips are thickened slightly, in order that in bending them the curves shall be thrown out regularly.

A tray of this kind from Nulukhtulogumut, represented in plate XXXII, 3, is painted red around the rim and on the inside to cover the border. Just inside this is a narrow black line, and on the bottom is painted in black a grotesque figure of some mythologic animal having upraised hands with pierced palms; along one side of this figure is a row of five walruses and on the other five seals.

Plate XXXII, 8, shows a handsomely made tray of similar character, also from Nulukhtulogumut. It is about fourteen inches in length and has inlaid around the beveled inner edge of the rim a series of eight neatly cut, almond-shape pieces of white stone. The rim, both outside and in, is painted red, as is the upper edge on the inside. Just below this, on the inside, are two parallel, narrow black lines, and painted in black on the bottom is a grotesque figure of some mythological animal, showing anatomical details.

Plate XXXII, 2, from the same locality as the last, is similar to it in form and has two mythological figures with heads like reindeer painted in black on the inside.

Specimen number 45494, from Ikogmut (Mission), is a large tray measuring about 28 inches in length and 18 inches in width. It is painted red around the border, and has two parallel black lines inside. On the bottom appears an alligator-like coiled figure, inside of which a mythologic animal is painted in black.

Plate xxxii, 7, from St Lawrence island, is another type of tray made from a broad, flat piece of spruce, which has a square groove cut across inside of each end; a strip of wood is bent upward to meet the end pieces, which are fitted into the grooves and held in place by means of thin strips of whalebone sewed through holes in both edges. This is a rude piece of work, showing none of the finish characteristic of specimens from the American coast. It is the only tray of this kind that was seen.

Another style of utensil made in a similar manner to the trays, but with the overlapping ends sewed in two parallel seams by means of spruce roots, are the large tubs used for containing water, seal oil, berries, and other food supplies.

Specimen number 45495 is a tub of this kind from Ikogmut. Its sides are 11½ inches high above the upper edge of the bottom, which is excavated and of tray shape, with chamfered edges to fit into a groove around the inner edge of the side. The outline of the utensil is an elongated oval and measures twenty-two inches in length. Some tubs are larger than this; others are smaller and serve for many uses in the domestic economy of these people. One of the smaller sizes, from St Lawrence island (plate xxxii, 1), 9 inches long, 2½ inches deep, is the ordinary style of urine tub used by the Eskimo throughout the coast and islands visited. This with others of the same form obtained on St Lawrence island, have the overlapping ends united by sewing thin strips of whalebone through slit-like holes made for the purpose. The buckets used for carrying water are similar in form, the only difference being that they are provided with a handle or bail.

A specimen from St Lawrence island (number 63237) has a bail made of a narrow, curved piece of bone cut from the jaw or rib of a whale and fastened at each end by whalebone strips passed through holes pierced in the edges of the bucket and in the ends of the handle. A small bucket from Cape Vancouver (plate xxxii, 6) has the overlapping ends of the sides fastened by means of two seams sewed with spruce roots. The bail is a thin, narrow strip of reindeer antler, with a hole pierced in each end; it is bent and sprung over the inwardly projecting ends of two short bone pegs which are inserted through the rim on each side.

Plate xxxii, 4, from Kushunuk, is very similar to the preceding, except that the curved handle has the holes in its ends fitted over a round, slender rod of wood which extends across the top of the bucket, piercing the rim on each side.

Figure 5 of the same plate, from Kaialigamut, has the handle made from spruce roots, several turns of which are passed through holes made for the purpose in the sides of the rim and then united by having the end wound around the strands crossing the top of the bucket and fastened at one side. From one side of the handle hangs a feather attached by a sinew cord.

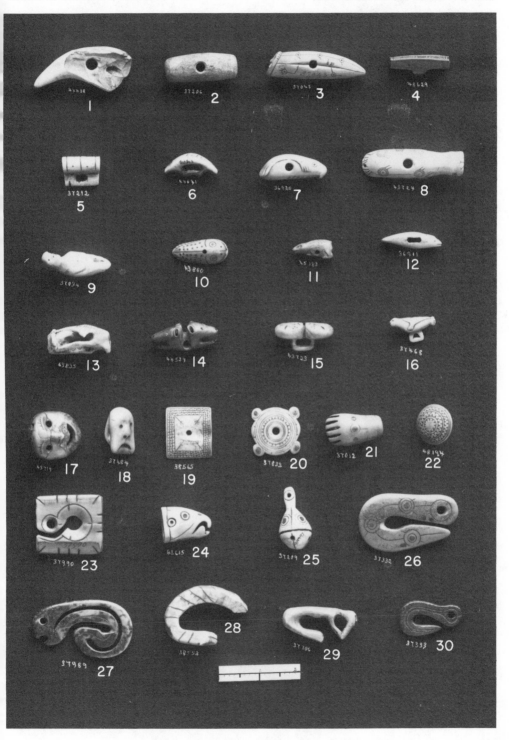

BELT FASTENERS (SEVEN-SIXTEENTHS)

PESTLES

In connection with the round-bottom trays used to contain food, broad-head wooden pestles are used for crushing berries, seal fat, or livers of birds and fish with which various pastry mixtures are made.

Plate XXXI, 3, from the lower Yukon, and plate XXXI, 7, from Ikogmut, represent typical examples of these implements. They are made of wood, with large spreading heads and slightly convex lower surfaces; they taper in somewhat conical form toward the handle, which in one consists of a large ring cut from the same piece as the head, and in the other has a flaring rim shaped like the bottom of a goblet.

BLUBBER HOOKS AND CARRIERS

Figure 8, plate XXXIII a, illustrates a hook for handling blubber, obtained on Nunivak island by Doctor Dall. It consists of a short wooden handle curved to a pistol-like grip at the upper end, and having a slot on the inside of the lower end, in which is set the butt of a sharp-pointed ivory spur, which is pierced with a large hole, through which passes a strong rawhide lashing, which also passes through the wooden handle a little above the insertion of the ivory point. The base of the ivory point is held in position in the slot by means of an ivory pin, which is inserted through a hole made in the handle and in the base of the hook.

A curious article, intended for carrying small pieces of meat or other articles when traveling (figure 9, plate XXXIII a), was obtained at Chalitmut. It consists of a wooden handle about seven inches long, slightly curved along the middle and pierced near both ends to admit the points of a crescentic rod of deerhorn, truncated at one end and pointed at the other, which is passed through one end of the wooden handle and wedged in by a wooden pin; the pointed end fits into the hole in the opposite side. Just above this the handle is pierced to receive a rawhide loop, by which it can be hung up or carried. Pieces of meat or other objects are placed upon the carrier by being slipped upon the rod, which is withdrawn for the purpose, after which it is returned and the point again inserted into the hole in which it fits.

BAGS FOR WATER AND OIL

For carrying water or seal oil while making hunting trips at sea or on land small bags made from the stomachs or the bladders of reindeer, white whale, seal, or walrus are in common use. They hold from one to four quarts, and usually are provided with ivory nozzles, which are inserted in the narrow necks of the bags, and are then firmly lashed with sinew cord above the projecting ridge at the inner ends of the nozzles. In order that they may be filled easily these nozzles are made usually with a slightly flaring mouthpiece, which sometimes is surrounded by a flaring, somewhat spoon-shape rim. The orifice is usually rather small, and is provided with a wooden plug or stopper. Occasionally a funnel is used for filling water bags or small oil bags of this character.

One specimen of this kind of nozzle from St Michael (figure 11, plate XXXIII*a*) is of wood. The top is of spoon shape, rather flat in outline, with one end in the form of a grotesque walrus head with small ivory tusks and eyes represented by inlaid ivory pegs; the other end represents the hind flippers of the walrus, and the fore flippers are painted on the inside of the top near the edge. The broad top is excavated downward to the center, where it is perforated by a round hole. The lower surface is convex, with a round, projecting, stopper-like base for inserting in the mouth of the bag.

Figure 5, plate XXXIII*a*, from St Michael, is a spoon-shape nozzle, with a projection below through which the hole passes. It is provided with a wooden stopper attached to a sealskin cord which is fastened into a hole made in a handle-like projection at one end.

Figure 6 of the same plate, from Nunvogulukhlugumut, is a somewhat similar spoon-shape nozzle, with a wooden stopper attached to a cord fastened into a hole at one end.

Figure 2, from Agiukchugumut, is a funnel-shape mouthpiece, with a wooden stopper inserted in a hole in the lower part of the wide-mouth upper end. The outside is marked with raven totem signs.

Figure 3, from Anogogmut, has a funnel-shape mouthpiece, with its outer rim marked with raven totem signs.

Figure 4, from the lower Kuskokwim, is a funnel-shape ivory nozzle, with the interior beveled. The outlines of a wolf and a white whale are incised on opposite sides of the opening in the interior. The outer border is marked with the raven totem sign.

Figure 12, from Norton sound, is a nozzle made from walrus ivory; the surface is ornamented with etched lines and patterns, and the form of a seal's head and back appear in relief on two sides.

Figure 7, from St Michael, is a conical mouthpiece without ornamentation.

Figure 10, from Sfugunugumut, is a water bag, with a funnel-like wooden nozzle provided with a wooden stopper attached by a cord.

RAKES

Plate XXXV, 2, represents a rake, from Sabotnisky, made from a piece of reindeer antler with the tips curved inward; the handle is worked down flat on the lower and flattened a little on the upper side, and has a notch for lashing it to a stout wooden haft, the lashing passing through a hole in the handle. This implement is used for taking away the refuse in the fire hole of the *kashim* or for clearing away refuse material while building a house. It is used also for cleaning

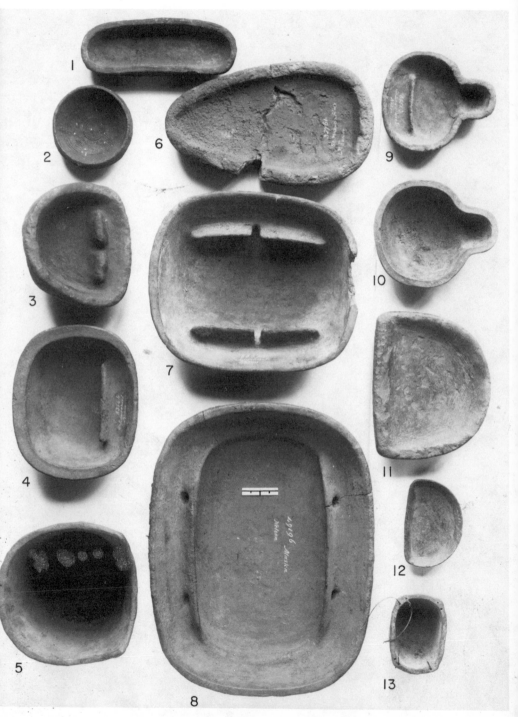

LAMPS AND POTS (ONE-FIFTH)

drift material from about the place where nets or fish traps are set in rivers or small streams.

ROOT PICKS

Small picks, made from bone or ivory, with wooden handles, are used by the women for digging the edible bulbous roots of a species of grass which grows on the plains from the Kuskokwim northward to Bering strait.

Figure 3, plate XXXIII *b*, illustrates one of three picks from Norton sound. It has a flat, wooden handle with two large scalloped incisions near the butt to aid in grasping with the hand; it is grooved and pierced by two holes. The pick is made from a long, pointed, slender rod of walrus ivory, held in position against a groove along the front of the handle by rawhide lashings which pass through the holes.

Figure 1 of the same plate shows a pick obtained on Nunivak island by Doctor Dall. It has a rounded, wooden handle, with a knob-like head, flattened in front to receive the pick and pierced by two holes for lashings. The pick is half of a walrus tusk, and its flattened side is bound against the front of the handle by rawhide lashings passing through two holes in the handle and two corresponding holes in the pick.

Figure 2, from Cape Nome, is a small ivory handle for a root pick, grooved along the front to receive the pick and pierced by two holes for binding it in position; a third hole, midway of the lower side of the handle, is intended for another lashing, to form a brace on the lower part of the pick.

BONE BREAKERS

For the purpose of breaking large bones in order to extract the marrow, stone implements are used. These in some cases are simply hammer-like stones, used without handles, but they are frequently of very hard stone, ground to a smooth polish and fastened by thongs to a short handle of wood or other material.

Plate XXXIX, 3, represents a small hammer-shape bone breaker of pectolite from Cape Nome. It is somewhat oblong in cross section, with rounded corners. The sides are smoothly polished, but the ends are battered and worn down by use.

At Point Hope there was seen a handsome stone breaker of clear white quartz. It weighed about a pound and a half and was polished to four very regular surfaces, with the corners somewhat rounded, and was secured to a wooden handle by a rawhide lashing.

FIRE-MAKING IMPLEMENTS

The method of obtaining fire, common to so many savage races, from the heat developed by the friction of a stick worked with great rapidity on a piece of soft wood by means of a cord, was found in common use among the Eskimo throughout the region visited, and the people of the lower Yukon and thence southward to the Kuskokwim were specially expert in its application.

A small notch is cut in the fire stick, in which the point of the drill is inserted, while the upper end, which usually is capped with a piece of stone or bone, is held in the mouth; the rapid revolution of the drill develops sufficient heat to set fire to the dust produced by the friction which accumulates around the pivot of the drill. This fire is then transferred to a small piece of punk or tinder and fanned into a flame.

Plate XXXIV, 3, represents a flat stick, from Norton sound, used for fire making. It is of dry spruce, having a deep groove along its upper surface, with a series of little notches opposite each other in pairs along the whole length; near one end are four small circular pits, where the drill has been used. Figure 2 of this plate shows the drill intended for use with the fire stick. It is a round, slightly tapering stick of spruce, about 19 inches in length, and has the upper end painted red; the bow also is made of spruce, and is about 16 inches long, with a rawhide sealskin cord attached to the holes in the ends. With this is used the ordinary mouthpiece cap (figure 1 of the same plate) slightly crescentic in form, with a square piece of white quartz set in its lower side.

Figures 4, 5, 7, and 8 of plate XXXIV illustrate a set of fire-making implements, from Chalitmut, consisting of a large drill, the cap of which has a piece of obsidian set in its lower surface, a double-hand drill cord with handles made from the points of small walrus tusks, and a broad fire stick with a step-like ledge on one side and several holes along the center where the drill has been used.

In plate XXXIV, 9, is shown a broad fire stick obtained at Cape Vancouver. It is made with a ledge along one side which slopes inward a trifle toward the center, where holes have been bored in making fire. The surface of this specimen is covered with deep holes, showing that it has frequently been used.

Plate XXXIV, 6, represents a tinder box from St Michael. It is 6½ inches in length, and is made from a section of reindeer horn, truncated at each end and of roughly oval shape in cross section. It has a long, oval opening on one side, through which the interior was excavated.

In addition to procuring fire by means of drills the Eskimo make common use of flint and steel. Sometimes the steel is replaced by a piece of iron pyrites, but usually a fragment of an old knife-blade or other steel object is carried. The flint is held between the thumb and forefinger of the left hand, just above a little wad of tinder which frequently consists of fur plucked from a garment. The steel is grasped in the right hand, and as the downward blow is struck the spark ignites the tinder, which is then transferred to the bowl of the pipe, or to a larger piece of tinder surrounded by fine shavings if the operator wishes to kindle a fire.

Of late years matches have been sold by the fur traders and are greatly prized by these people, who are always anxious to obtain them.

LADLES AND DIPPERS (ONE-FIFTH)

SNOW BEATERS

For beating snow from boots, clothing, and other articles made of fur, the western Eskimo use a long, flattened piece of bone, ivory, or deerhorn. Some of these are nearly straight, while others are more or less curved.

Figure 21, 1, represents a beater of this kind, from Sabotnisky, made from walrus ivory, smaller at one end, where a strip of wood is lashed on the inner side by means of rawhide cord in order to give a firmer grip. This implement is suboval in cross section and is much heavier than is usually the case.

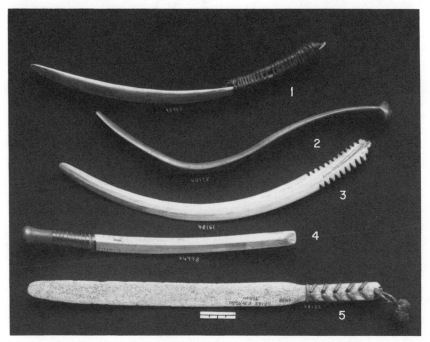

Fig. 21—Snow beaters ($\frac{3}{10}$).

A strongly curved beater from the lower Yukon (figure 21, 2) is made from split deerhorn with a knob, carved into the form of a man's head, terminating the handle. A snow beater brought from St Lawrence island is exactly like the one from the lower Yukon in shape and material, including the knob at the end of the handle, except that the latter is not carved.

The specimen from Sledge island shown in figure 21, 4, is made from walrus ivory, with a rounded wooden handle fitted upon one end; on the inside it has a central ridge and on the back is a broad, shallow groove.

A long snow beater from Cape Prince of Wales (figure 21, 5) is made of a thin piece of whalebone, narrowed a little toward the handle and pierced with a series of holes, through which cords are passed and wrapped around the handle to give a stronger grip. A double cord, about two inches in length, with a knob made from a little roll of cloth at its upper end, is attached to the handle, and serves for buttoning this implement to the belt so that it may be carried conveniently.

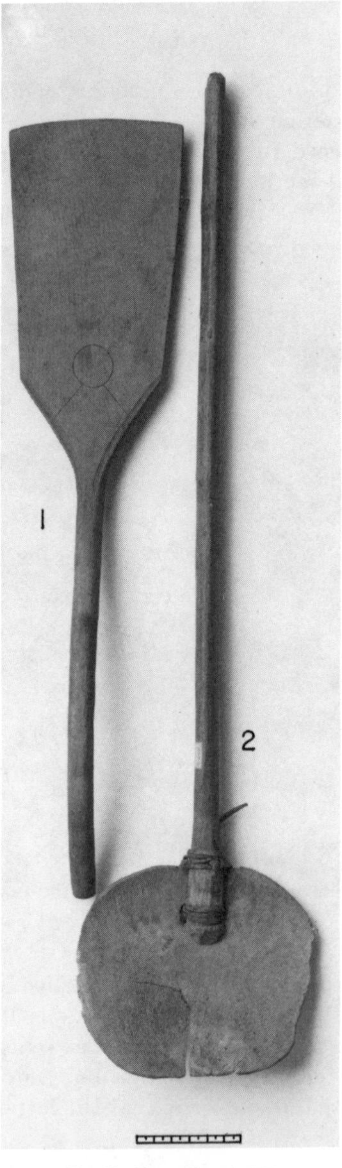

Another specimen from Cape Prince of Wales (figure 21, 3) consists of a long, tapering piece of ivory, nearly flat on one side and beveled to three surfaces on the other; the handle has a series of notches along each border.

Strongly curved beaters of deerhorn, similar to those found on St Lawrence island and the lower Yukon, were observed in use among the natives of the eastern Siberian coast.

SNOW SHOVELS AND ICE PICKS

In the region visited, the Eskimo use wooden or bone shovels for clearing away snow from around their houses or for excavating the snowdrifts.

Picks of walrus ivory or deerhorn are also used for removing frozen snow, for cutting holes in the ice for fishing, and for other purposes.

A fine wooden snow shovel from Point Barrow is represented in plate XXXV, 4. The blade is broad, nearly flat, and formed of three pieces, held together by means of lashings of whalebone passed through holes bored for that purpose; the lower edge of the wood is fitted by a tongue into a groove, in a sharp, flat piece of walrus ivory, which is fastened by a series of wooden pegs. A blue bead is inlaid on the upper part of the blade near the handle. The handle is 18 inches in length and subtriangular in cross section; the upper end is bound with braided cord of sinew, to give a firm grip for the hands, while on the lower end, near the blade, is a lashing of whalebone.

Figure 22, 2, from St Lawrence island, is a rude shovel made from a

FIG. 22—Snow shovels (1/12).

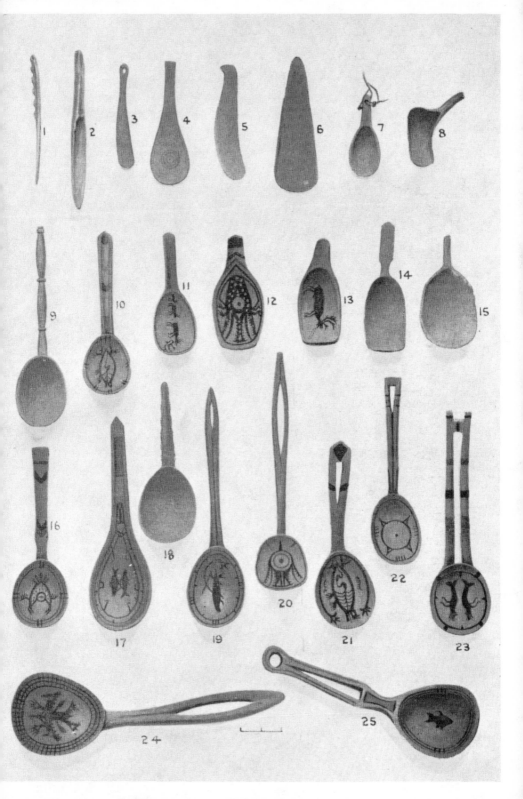

SPOONS AND LADLES (ABOUT TWO-NINTHS)

piece of the jawbone of a whale, worked down to a thin, flat blade, roughly rounded in outline. On its upper edge is a projection to which a stout wooden handle is fastened by means of a strong lashing of rawhide, which passes through two grooves and two holes in the blade.

Figure 22, 1, from Ikogmut, is a wooden shovel with a long, flat blade and curved handle carved from one piece. The back surface of the blade is slightly convex, with a medium ridge which extends upward to the handle. The back and the portion of the handle where held are painted red. On the inner surface of the blade, near the handle, is the private mark of the owner, consisting of an incised circle and two straight grooves extending obliquely outward from its upper edge to the shoulders of the blade.

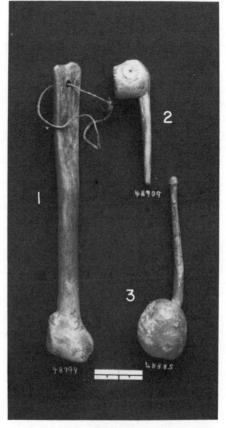

Plate xxxv, 1, represents an ice pick obtained at Point Barrow. It is made from a small walrus tusk attached to a flat wooden handle by strong rawhide lashing passed through a hole in the handle and two holes in the butt of the pick. The handle is wrapped in two places with braided sinew cord, to afford a firm grip for both hands, above which are slight projections of the wood to prevent it from slipping.

MALLETS

Mallets of wood or deerhorn are used for breaking ice from the framework of fish traps

FIG. 23—Mallets (¼).

and sledge runners, for driving small pegs, and for other similar purposes.

Figure 23, 1, from Sabotnisky, is a deerhorn mallet about 12 inches in length, with one end worked down to a flattened handle and the other having a rounded knob truncated upon one face. The handle is pierced for the reception of a rawhide cord, by means of which the mallet can be suspended from the wrist.

Figure 23, 3, from Ikogmut, is a small wooden mallet with a slender rod-like handle about 5½ inches in length; the head is made from a

rounded growth of wood which had formed an excrescence on the
branch which serves as the handle.

Figure 23, 2, from Sabotnisky, is a small deerhorn mallet with a handle 3½ inches in length, pierced at its outer end for a cord and with
the head rounded above and truncated below. In the front are carved
two large, eye-like cavities with a rudely shaped nose and a slightly
incised groove to represent the mouth, giving the front a resemblance
to a grotesque human face.

IMPLEMENTS USED IN ARTS AND MANUFACTURES

IVORY AND BONE WORKING TOOLS

In former times the tools used by the Eskimo for working ivory, bone,
and deerhorn were chipped from flint or other hard stones, and sometimes for etching or scoring deeper lines the canine teeth of small
mammals were used, mounted on a short handle. Since iron and steel
have become common among them, however, tools made from these
metals have superseded to a great extent the more primitive implements. The tools now in use are scrapers, scoring or etching implements, wedges for splitting the material, and narrow pieces of thin iron
with serrated edges for use as saws.

Figure 9, plate XXXVIa, is a small saw obtained at Port Clarence by
Dr T. H. Bean. The blade is set in a handle in a manner similar to
that of a table knife.

Figure 10 of the same plate is a saw from Cape Prince of Wales,
evidently modeled from those in use by white men. It is 11 inches
long; the blade is a long, narrow strip of iron with teeth cut in the lower
edge; it is riveted into slots in small round pieces of ivory which are
fastened into a wooden frame. A wooden rod extends across the
middle of the frame into which it is dovetailed; a double cord of rawhide is stretched across the frame, between the two strands of which
a piece of bone is inserted for twisting the cords and thereby tightening the blade of the saw in the frame.

Another style of saw is made by inserting a narrow piece of iron with
a serrated edge in a slot cut in a long piece of ivory, horn, or bone.
Sometimes these saws are mere strips of iron with teeth cut in one
edge and without either handle or frame.

Figure 6, plate XXXVIa, represents a frame for one of these saws from
Unalaklit. It is made of reindeer horn and has a projecting spur on its
upper side, the same end being bent downward to serve as a handle.

Figure 7 of this plate is a scoring or etching implement from the
Yukon district. The iron point is wedged firmly into a slit in the end
of the handle, which has a conical hole on one side, having evidently
served as a cap for a drill.

Figure 8, from Cape Darby, is a handle for one of these tools, made
from two pieces of bone with a slot for fitting in an iron point; the two
pieces are riveted together by wooden pins, and a rawhide cord is

TRAYS AND PESTLES (ONE-FIFTH)

wrapped tightly around the lower end to hold the iron point firmly in position.

Figure 3 is an iron pointed awl, from Chalitmut, used as an etching tool in ivory working as well as for a bodkin.

Figure 1, from St Lawrence island, is a similar tool of slightly different construction, being made with a slot on one side of the handle into which the end of the blade is placed; a wooden plug is then fitted over the slot, and the end wrapped around with a sinew cord to hold the blade and plug in position. From St Lawrence island another implement of this kind was obtained; it is made in the ordinary style, with the blade wedged into a hole cut in the bone handle.

From the same locality came another specimen (figure 4, plate XXXVIa) which has the blade fitted into a slot cut in the side of the wooden handle, and held in position by a wrapping of whalebone, one end of which is set in a slit in the handle. This is one of the rudest implements of the kind obtained.

Figure 5, from St Lawrence island, is an ivory working tool with a curved blade made of iron set in a notch in the end of the handle. Figure 2, from St Michael, is another style of ivory working tool. It has a curved handle with a small iron blade set in a slot near the end of the handle on the lower side.

DRILLS, DRILL-BOWS, AND CAPS

Drills are used for piercing holes in bone, ivory, reindeer antler, or wood. They consist of a wooden shaft with a point of stone or iron merely inserted in the wood or sometimes held firmly in place by wrapping with sinew or rawhide. A cap is fitted over the upper end, and the shaft is made to revolve rapidly by means of a stout rawhide cord passed twice around it and sawed backward and forward by the operator who grasps handles in the ends of the cords. The large drills, used for boring holes in wood when manufacturing the frames of umiaks, kaiaks, and sledges, or in bone for sledge runners, are worked by two men, one of whom presses down on the cap of the stem and keeps it in position while the other works the cord.

Smaller drills, with finer points, for more minute work are operated by one man, a bow being used instead of a loose cord, which enables the operator to use his left hand to hold the shaft in position by pressing on the cap. If the material be hard and difficult to drill the cap piece is grasped in the teeth and both hands used to work the bow; or sometimes, if a small object is to be drilled, it is held in the left hand, the cap is held in the teeth, and the drill bow worked by the right hand.

Plate XXXVII, 8, obtained at Point Barrow by Lieutenant Ray, is a large drill with a wooden stem, and with a well-made flint point inserted in its lower end and held fast by a wrapping of sinew cord. It is intended to be used with the double-hand cord.

Figure 7 of the same plate, also obtained by Lieutenant Ray from

18 ETH——6

the same locality, has a flint point mounted in a hollowed bone ferrule to fit on the lower end of the shaft.

Figure 10, from Norton sound, is a drill having the iron point mounted in a bone head, the base of which is divided by a wedge-shape slot in which the wooden shaft is mounted and held in place by a wrapping of rawhide.

Figure 9, from Cape Nome, is also an iron-point drill, mounted similarly to the preceding except that the wooden shaft is held in position in the bone head by rivets.

Figure 3, from St Lawrence island, is a drill with a broad, flat point of iron inserted in the wooden shaft without any wrapping or other fastening.

Figure 4, from St Lawrence island, is somewhat similarly mounted, but the point of the shaft is tapered down and wrapped with a strip of whalebone.

Figure 5, from Norton sound, has a greenstone point mounted in the end of a wooden shaft and held in place by a wrapping of sinew. Another specimen, from Hotham inlet, is provided with a finely made nephrite point.

Figure 6, from Paimut, is a similarly made greenish stone drill point.

Figure 2, from St Lawrence island, is another small drill. It has the lower end of the stock narrowed down and wrapped with sinew to hold the point in position.

The large canine teeth of bears are commonly used for the cross handles at the ends of the drill cords; they are drilled crosswise through the middle, and the cord is then passed through and fastened at each end. Figure 21, from Norton sound, is an example of these handles. Various other forms of drill handles are used; some are made from the wing-bones of waterfowl; others are carved from deer-horn or ivory to represent seals, fish, or other forms.

Figure 14, from Kotzebue sound, shows one of a pair of handles made from smooth bars of walrus ivory, slightly curved on their outer surface and having a double curve on the inside, in which the fingers rest when grasping it.

Figure 15, from St Michael, is another of these handles carved from walrus ivory to represent two heads of a white bear.

Figure 20, from Paimut, represents a pair of handles, each in the form of a fish-like creature with the tail of a white whale. Caps for drill shafts to be used with double-hand cords are made usually with the top smoothly rounded; sometimes they are large enough only for one hand, but ordinarily are made for grasping with both. Nearly all of these objects are provided with a hole in one end for attaching to the drill cord when not in use. They are generally made of wood, with a piece of stone set in the lower side, in which is a small conical depression to receive the top of the shaft.

TRAYS AND BUCKETS (ONE-FIFTH)

Figure 30, from St Lawrence island, is a piece of walrus tusk, about five inches in length, roughly oblong in shape, with a conical depression in one side for receiving the top of the shaft.

Figure 29, from the same locality, is another rough piece of walrus tusk, made with a conical depression in each side for receiving the top of the shaft. These two are the rudest implements of this description that were obtained.

Figure 27 is a cap having the wood rudely carved into the form of a seal, with a square hole through the tail, in which the drill cord can be tied when not in use. This specimen is from the Kuskokwim.

Figure 22, from Norton sound, is a cap with an oval piece of white quartz set in the lower side and the wooden portion carved in the form of a wolf fish.

Figure 28, from Cape Nome, has a square piece of grayish-white stone set in its lower surface, and the two long arms, one at each end, are carved to represent the heads of white bears. This drill cap is intended to be used either singly, with the crossbar mouthpiece, or by grasping the ends with the hands. Figure 27, from the Kuskokwim, is a similar cap, having inserted a piece of stone, mottled green, black, and white in color.

Figure 23, from Agiukchugumut, is made in the form of a seal, with a hard, milky white, flat stone set in its lower surface.

Figure 25, obtained on Nunivak island by Dr W. H. Dall, is made from an oval piece of white quartz with a conical depression in its lower surface. A groove extends around the side, in which is fastened a rawhide cord with a loop at one end to which the drill cord can be fastened.

Figure 24, from Sabotnisky, is a long, oval, green and black stone, having the usual conical pit in one side; this, like the preceding, is made for holding in one hand.

Figure 26, from Cape Nome, is a long, rather slender cap or handle of wood, having a small, square piece of stone set in its lower surface and provided with a projecting block on its upper side for grasping with the teeth; it is carved at each end to represent a wolf's head, and is intended for use with either a large or a small drill. A cap obtained at Cape Darby is also made to serve for both kinds of drills.

The caps to be used exclusively with the small drills, worked with a bow, are always provided with a projecting block on the upper surface for grasping with the teeth, and are much more elaborately made than are those used with the larger drills. They are commonly somewhat crescentic in form, and have a piece of stone or lead set in the convex lower surface; where stone is used it is cut usually into a square or rounded outline and is neatly inlaid. Two specimens, however, are of walrus ivory and are without any stone setting, the conical depression being made directly in the material of the cap. Of these, figure 16 is from Cape Nome and figure 17 from the Diomede islands.

Figure 11, from the lower Yukon, has a crescentic outline and is carved on the convex surface at one end to represent a human face and at the other the head of some animal. A round piece of stone is inserted in the center.

From Yukon river and Nunivak island were obtained rudely made specimens similar in character to those used with the double-hand cord, except that they have the back carved to permit of their being seized in the teeth.

Figure 13, from Kotzebue sound, is a crescentic piece of wood with a square stone inlaid in its lower surface; a crossbar of wood for grasping in the teeth is fastened on the upper surface by means of strong rawhide wrappings.

Figure 1, from Cape Nome, is a crescentic piece of wood pierced with a triangular hole near each end, and a round stone is set in the center.

Figure 18, from Norton sound, is a crescentic piece of wood with a square piece of iron set in the center, and a crescentic incision on each side of the thin upper border to give a hold for the teeth.

Figure 19, from Norton sound, is a long, slender cap, having a grotesque head on each end.

Figure 12, from the Diomede islands, is strongly crescentic, with a high ledge inside for grasping with the teeth, and with blue beads inlaid on each side of the stone center.

Drill bows, some of which are nearly straight while others are strongly curved, measuring from 12 to 18 inches in length, are in common use over all of the region visited. They are square, suboval, or triangular in cross section, and commonly have one or more of the surfaces covered with etchings representing various incidents in the life of the owner, such as a record of the animals killed by him on various hunts, the number of skins of certain animals he has possessed, or other personal data.

Figure 7, plate XXXVI*b*, from Sledge island, is a slender, nearly straight ivory bow, with one surface etched to represent houses, people, and umiaks.

Figure 10 of the same plate, from the same locality, is triangular in cross section, and the three sides are covered with a great number of figures and scenes.

Figure 11, from the Diomede islands, is a nearly straight ivory rod with the surfaces etched.

Figure 3, from Cape Nome, is triangular in cross section and has the three sides covered with a multitude of small etched figures.

Figure 9, from Cape Darby, is triangular in cross section and has one side etched with figures.

Figure 1, from Cape Darby, is oblong in section and strongly curved, with figures etched on two of its surfaces. Figure 2 shows a specimen from the same place that is etched on all of its sides.

Figure 5, from Norton sound, is oblong in cross section, with two of its surfaces etched.

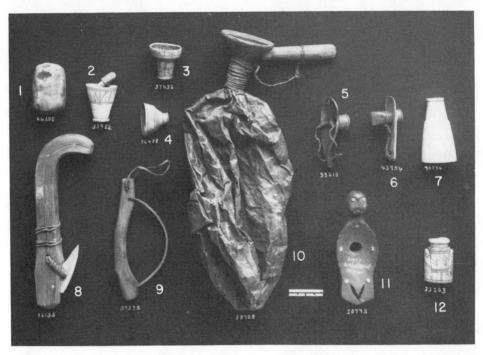

WATER BAG, MOUTHPIECES, BLUBBER HOOK, AND CARRIER (About one-sixth)

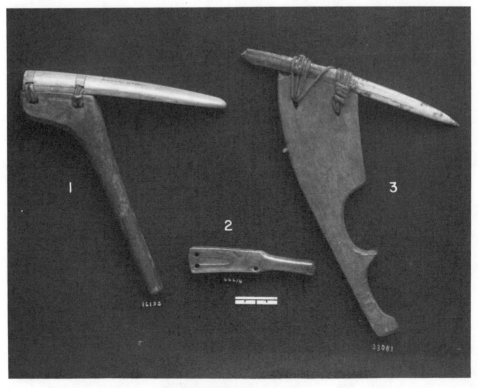

ROOT PICKS (About one-fifth)

IMPLEMENTS AND UTENSILS

Figure 6, from Norton sound, has one end terminating in a figure representing the head of some animal and with etched lines and patterns along two sides.

Figure 4, from Norton sound, is a curved piece of deer antler, quadrangular in outline and etched on three of its sides.

Figure 8, from Point Hope, is triangular in cross section, with the angles cut into scalloped outlines.

KNIVES

For whittling, carving, and finishing all kinds of woodwork the Eskimo use what is commonly called a "crooked knife," the curved blade of which varies from one to three inches in length, and is made usually from hoop iron or some similar scrap, but sometimes a portion of a steel knife blade is cut and bent for this purpose. The handle of bone, horn, or wood tapers downward to a point, and is from four to fifteen inches in length. This knife is the principal tool used in fashioning and finishing a great variety of boxes, dishes, trays, tubs, spearshafts, bows, arrows, and frames for umiaks, kaiaks, sledges, and other woodwork. The wood is first blocked out with an adze, after which it is cut into the desired shape, smoothed, and finished by patient labor with the knife. It is surprising to notice the dexterity with which this tool is used, and the excellent work produced with it.

One of these knives (plate XXXVIII, 26), from Norton sound, has the blade set in a groove in the inner edge of the handle near the end, and with no other fastening. The handle is wrapped with spruce roots just above the blade, in order to give a better grip for the hand. The under side of the handle has a conical depression, showing that it has been used as a cap for a small drillhead.

Figure 31 of the same plate, from Nunivak island, is the rudest of all the knives of this kind that were obtained. It has a short, thick piece of iron wedged into a slot in the handle, while the inner end of the blade is held in place by sinew lashing. The lower side of the handle has a small conical depression, marking its use as a cap for a drillhead.

From St Lawrence island were obtained two knives of this description, made of long, tapering pieces of iron set into wooden handles, but in a manner different from the foregoing. One of these (plate XXXVIII, 27) has the inner end of the blade set in a deep, flat hole in the end of the handle, somewhat as the blade is set in an ordinary table knife. The handle is oval in cross section, with a slightly enlarged truncated end, and is only about four inches in length. Next to the blade is a groove, which serves to receive a sinew wrapping.

Plate XXXVIII, 29, shows a knife of similar shape, but the end of the blade is fitted into a gore-shape slot sunk in the side of the handle, into which is fitted a thin strip of wood, filling it out so that the outline is continuous with the rest of the handle. Over this is wrapped a sinew cord for holding the blade in place.

Plate XXXVIII, 30, from Kulwoguwigumut, is a knife with a bone handle about four inches long, crossed with diagonal, zigzag, etched lines, and scored with a series of straight lines running its length, with a groove around it near each end.   In the end of the handle is wedged a short, straight, iron blade about two inches in length with a heavy back and a sharp edge.   At the other extremity of the handle is a rawhide loop fastened into a hole by a wedge.

Figure 25 of this plate, from Hotham inlet, has the blade fastened to the handle by two iron rivets; the upper surface of the handle is grooved for about four inches next the blade to enable a firm grasp; the under surface of the handle is excavated.   In the handle two holes are pierced for fastening the end of a cord by which a leather sheath is attached.

Figure 22, from Hotham inlet, has the blade attached in the same manner as the preceding and has a handle of similar shape.   Instead of grooves, as in the preceding specimen, this knife has a series of holes pierced along the front of the handle extending upward for about four inches, through which are passed two rawhide cords; these are wound around a narrow strip of wood, holding it in place against the front edge of the handle to give a better grip for the hand.   Attached to the handle is a leather sheath.

Figure 19, from Norton sound, has a handle of two parts; the lower piece, to which the blade is riveted, is of bone, and the upper of wood. They are neatly joined by a close wrapping of spruce root.

Figure 28, from St Michael, has the blade fitted into a groove or slit made in the inner edge of the bone handle, which is wrapped with a stout rawhide cord to hold the blade in place, and has three ships etched upon it.

CHISELS

A flat, round-pointed, chisel-like implement of bone is in common use for making incised grooves in wood preparatory to splitting it for use in the manufacture of various articles.   Specimens of these tools were obtained at different localities from the mouth of the Kuskokwim northward to Kotzebue sound.

Plate XXXVIII, 14, represents a typical implement of this kind from Kotzebue sound.   It is made of bone and has a sinew cord forming a loop for suspension passed through a hole near the head of the instrument. Another specimen, from Kushunuk (plate XXXVIII, 12), is similar in form, but slenderer.

Plate XXXVIII, 16, from Sledge island, is a small tool of this character made of reindeer horn.   It is very slender; the handle is bent at an angle with the shank and has the top neatly carved in the form of a reindeer hoof.   The thin, narrow point is used for making small incisions in the wood of arrow or spear shafts for the purpose of inserting feathers, also for making little slits in which are fastened the ends of sinew wrappings of spears, arrows, or other implements.

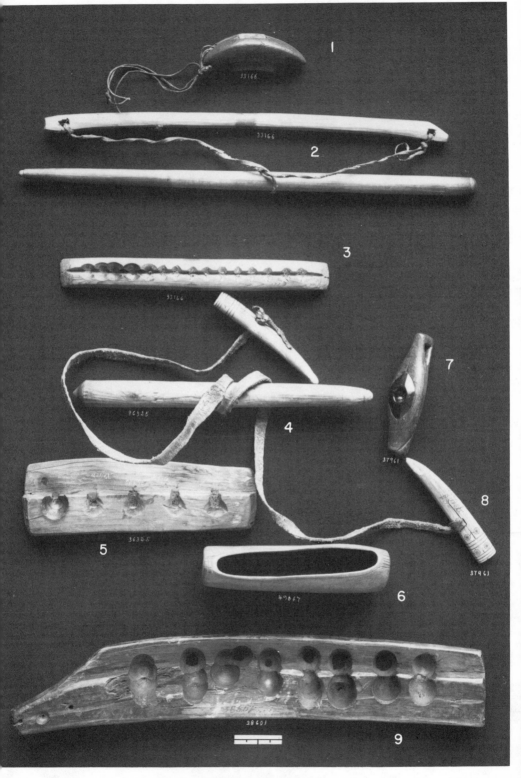

FIRE-MAKING IMPLEMENTS (ONE-FIFTH)

Plate XXXVIII, 9, from Kushunuk, is another slightly curved implement of bone, suboval in cross section and brought down to a flattened, rounded, wedge-shape point. The handle is wrapped with a fine rootlet to afford a firmer grasp for the hand, and has a round hole near the end for attaching a cord.

Plate XXXVIII, 15, from Ikogmut, is another of these wood-working chisels, made of bone, having the raven totem etched on the upper surface and a grotesque human countenance on the end of the handle; just below the head it is encircled by a series of ornamental lines and dots. Figure 13 of the same plate, from Sledge island, is a similar implement.

In the accompanying figure 24, 2, is shown a curved chisel of deerhorn for making wooden splints. It is very much discolored from age, and upon the inside of the curve are etched two raven totem signs. This chisel is from Kushunuk.

Plate XXXVIII, 18, from the lower Kuskokwim, is another of these tools. It terminates at the upper end in a carving which represents the head of a gull. Figure 24, 1, from Nunivak island, is a broad-handle chisel of bone, roughly crescentic in cross section. It has the convex upper surface covered with etchings representing a seal with anatomical details; the interspace is filled with a complicated mixture of other figures representing fishes and various animals and conventional signs.

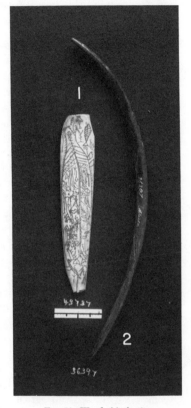

FIG. 24—Wood chisels ($\frac{1}{4}$).

POLISHING AND FINISHING TOOLS

For producing a smooth surface and for finishing woodwork of all kinds when it is desired to complete it with more than usual neatness, a variety of small implements of deer antler are used, in which are cut notches of varying form for the purpose of rubbing along the projecting angles and edges of the article in course of manufacture.

Plate XXXVIII, 7, represents an implement of this kind from Sledge island, having a broad notch in each end. Plate XXXVIII, 3, obtained at Port Clarence by Dr T. H. Bean, is somewhat similar in character to the preceding. Figure 6 of this plate, from the lower Yukon, has a single notch in one end and a long, curved handle. Figures 1, 4, and 8 are from the lower Yukon, and vary in the arrangement of the points and notches. Figure 2, also from the lower Yukon, has the end cut into two notches with two points of different shape, one on each side. Figure 5, from the lower Yukon, shows still another form.

Plate XXXVIII, 11, from the lower Yukon, is a bent piece of deerhorn having a screw-driver set in one end; the other end is fashioned into notches to form a finishing tool.

Plate XXXVIII, 10, from Kotzebue sound, is a small piece of fossil mammoth ivory, with a rounded handle and a knob-like head, the lower surface of which is convex in shape and smoothly polished. The sides and the top of the handle are provided with hollows to receive the thumb and the first two fingers.

WEDGES AND MAULS

Wedges of wood, bone, deerhorn, and ivory are used for splitting wood; they vary considerably in size, but the majority are from six to eight inches in length. Heavy wooden mauls are used for driving them.

Plate XXXIX, 5, shows a wedge, from the Diomede islands, made from the butt of an old walrus tusk, beveled from both sides. Around the lower end is a broad, sunken groove for the attachment of a handle, thus permitting the use of the implement as an ax.

Plate XXXIX, 6, represents a small wooden wedge used in making splints for fish traps. It has a short groove, painted red, on each side, which is said to represent the track of a land otter in the snow and to be the private mark of the maker. Two more of these wedges were obtained from the same man, one of them being about five inches and the other eleven inches in length.

Plate XXXIX, 4, represents a deerhorn wedge from the lower Yukon. From Point Hope was obtained a rude wedge, made from a piece of the jawbone of a whale and beveled on one of its two sides.

Plate XXXIX, 2, from Nunivak island, obtained by Dr W. H. Dall, is a curiously shaped wedge of reindeer horn, having a projecting prong on one side. In the middle is fastened a little tuft of reindeer hair by means of a peg inserted in a hole made for the purpose.

Plate XXXIX, 7, from St Lawrence island, is a wedge of walrus ivory.

Plate XXXV, 3, from Hotham inlet, is a heavy maul or beetle made from a section of fossil mammoth tusk about 18 inches in length.

ARROWSHAFT STRAIGHTENERS

Straighteners for arrowshafts are in common use throughout western Alaska, and the collection contains a large series of implements of this kind. Deerhorn and walrus ivory are the materials commonly employed in their manufacture, and considerable ingenuity is shown in shaping them.

Plate XL, 9, from the lower Yukon, is a small, roughly made shaft straightener of deerhorn, as is figure 6 of the same plate, from the same

SNOW SHOVEL, PICK, RAKE, AND MAUL (ONE-FIFTH)

locality. A specimen (figure 11) from Golofnin bay, made from deer-horn, has one end shaped to represent the head of a deer. Figure 4, from Cape Nome, has a well-carved head of a reindeer on the larger end, with the eyes formed by inlaid beads; the other end terminates in a representation of a hoof.

Plate XL, 3, from Cape Nome, has the larger end terminating in the form of the head and forelegs of a white bear, the eyes being represented by blue beads.

Plate XL, 12, from Sledge island, is of deerhorn, and has the head of a deer carved upon its larger end with blue beads for eyes. Another specimen from Sledge island is of ivory and shows signs of great age. It is the only one of these objects showing much effort at ornamentation by etched figures; scattered over the surface a number of reindeer are represented. Plate XL, 2, from the Diomede islands, is of ivory and has two bears' heads rudely carved on the larger end. Figure 7, rom Hotham inlet, is a beautiful specimen representing a reindeer in a recumbent position, with the legs folded beneath the body. Figure 8, from Kotzebue sound, is another fine carving, representing a reindeer lying down with the legs folded beneath the body; the horns are represented by two spikes of iron set in the head; the eyes were represented by beads, which have been lost. Figure 10, from Point Hope, has the larger end rounded into a knob-like termination which is crossed along its upper edge by a series of incised grooves. Specimens similar in form to that shown in figure 6 were found over a wide area and seem to be the most general type of these implements.

Plate XL, 1, from Norton sound, made from deerhorn, and figure 5, of wood, from the same locality, are somewhat similar in form to straighteners for arrowshafts, but are used for straightening and setting arrowpoints.

BEAVER-TOOTH TOOLS

A tool made from the chisel-shape tooth of the beaver is used as a gouge for making the hollows for the fingers in throwing-sticks, for cutting grooves, and for excavating hollows in fashioning boxes, masks, spoons, and wooden dishes. The smooth back of the tooth is used also as a polishing instrument for finishing woodwork, and the carved outer edge serves for sharpening knives by rubbing it sharply along the blades. These tools are still in use, but to some extent they have been superseded by implements of steel and iron, since these metals have become more easily obtainable. Plate XXXVIII, 21, from Chalitmut, is a typical example of these implements, having a beaver tooth set in a wooden handle and held firmly in place by a wrapping of rootlets.

Figure 25, 3, from Port Clarence, is a beaver tooth for sharpening steel or iron knives, set in a short wooden haft with a wrapping about the end. Figure 25, 2, from Norton sound, is a beaver-tooth knife sharpener, with a strip of tanned skin, about seven inches in length, fastened about the center for attaching it to the belt. Figure 25, 1, from Norton sound, is a similar implement, with a strip of skin lashed to the butt with a sinew cord for attaching it to a belt.

Plate XXXVIII, 23, from the lower Yukon, is a double-end tool of this kind, having a tooth set in each extremity of the handle.

BIRCH-BARK TOOLS

Implements for stripping bark from birch trees are used in Alaska wherever those trees are found.

Plate XXXVIII, 20, represents two of these tools from the lower

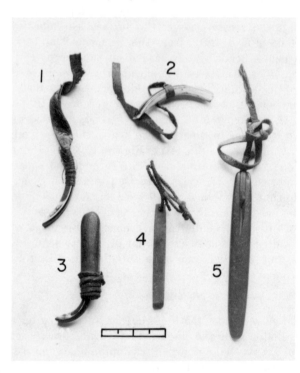

FIG. 25—Knife sharpeners (₁/₁₀).

Yukon; they are intended to be used together and are coupled by a rawhide cord. One of them has a short, knife-like blade, which projects a little more than half an inch from the handle and has two sharp points which are used to mark the outlines of the sheets of bark to be stripped from the tree; the handle consists of two pieces of spruce, between which the blade is inserted and is kept in place by strong wrappings of raw hide cord. The other implement is a long, knife-like piece of bone, on which the raven totem is rudely cut. After the birch-bark has been scored by the first-described implement, the point of the other is inserted between the bark and the wood and forced around the trunk of the tree to separate and remove the bark.

Plate XXXVIII, 17, from the head of Norton sound, is a long bone knife for removing birch-bark from the tree. It is sharpened at the point and on one edge; the butt is heavily etched with zigzag patterns and with the raven totem mark.

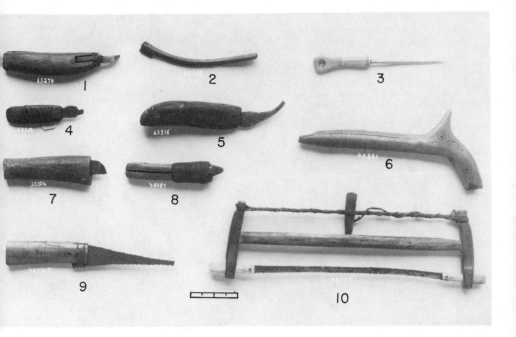

(ONE-FOURTH NATURAL SIZE)

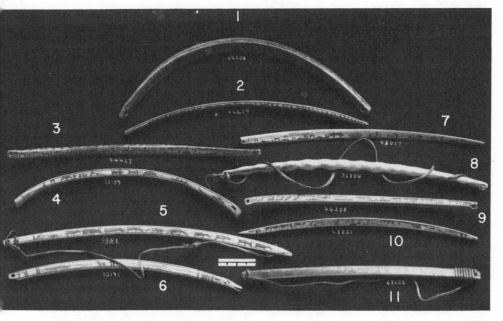

(ONE-FIFTH NATURAL SIZE)

IVORY-WORKING TOOLS AND DRILL BOWS

STONE IMPLEMENTS

Celts and axes of nephrite or other hard stone are fashioned by grinding into shape and sometimes by pecking, and are finished by grinding or friction with other stones. Knife blades, lance points, and whetstones are also made from these substances in a similar manner. The stone celts, axes, and wedges are mounted on handles of wood and deerhorn and are very skilfully used by the Eskimo for hewing and surfacing logs and planks, although at the present time they are being displaced by iron and steel tools obtained from white traders. In a *kashim* on the lower Yukon a plank was seen that was made many years ago by use of a stone adz. It was 25 feet long and four or five inches thick. The surface bore so many marks made by the hacking of

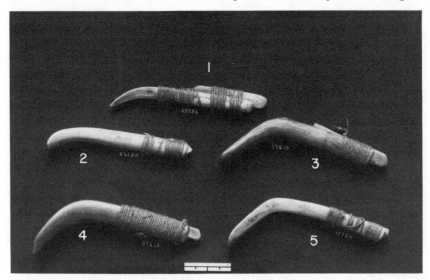

FIG. 26—Flint flakers (¼).

stone adzes that it looked as if it might have been cut by beavers. Flint knives, spearheads, and arrowpoints are made by flaking. The flakers are made of small, rod-like pieces of deerhorn, wood, or ivory, fastened into a slot at the end of a handle, usually of ivory or deer-horn, with wrappings of sinew or rawhide cord.

Figure 26, 3, represents one of these flaking implements from Kotze-bue sound. Figure 26, 4, is another flaker from the same locality, with a handle made from fossil mammoth ivory. Figure 26 2, from Hotham inlet, and figure 26, 1, from Point Hope, represent flakers with similar handles. Figure 26, 5, from Kotzebue sound, has a handle of deerhorn.

Formerly small fragments of flint were used for scraping down the surfaces of bone, ivory, or deerhorn articles in the course of manufacture, but for this purpose steel or iron implements are now in common use, and naturally produce much more satisfactory results.

Plate xxxix, 14, from Norton sound, is a wooden-handle adz, with a deerhorn head in which is fitted a point of hard, greenish-colored stone, ground to a sharp edge. Plate xxxix, 10, also from Norton sound, is another wooden-handle adz, with a deerhorn head in which is fitted a small, greenstone point, with a smoothly ground edge. These two specimens are hafted in the style commonly employed before iron was brought to the country by the Russians.

A considerable variety of stone blades or celts for use as adzes was obtained from points between the lower Kuskokwim and Kotzebue sound.

Plate xxxix, 12, from Sledge island, is a fine large celt of nephrite, measuring 9 inches in length, 3 inches in width, and an inch and a quarter in thickness; it is roughly quadrate in cross section, and the point is smoothly beveled on both sides to a chisel-shape edge. Plate xxxix, 8, from Cape Prince of Wales, is a small adz blade of nephrite intended for setting into the bone or deerhorn head of the implement. Plate xxxix, 3, from Cape Nome, is a pale, olive-greenish colored stone adz, having two grooves around its upper end to admit rawhide lashings, by means of which it can be attached directly to a haft.

Plate xxxix, 11, from the lower Kuskokwim, is a curiously shaped celt, partly ground and partly pecked into shape; the point is roughly flattened on one side and oval on the other. A groove is pecked around the upper part of the head, by means of which, with the shoulder lower down on the same face, the head is attached directly to the handle and secured by rawhide lashings.

Plate xxxix, 13, represents a celt from the lower Yukon, somewhat similar in style to the last specimen. Plate xxxix, 9, from the lower Yukon, is an adz head made from slate.

Figure 1 of the same plate is an adz handle from the lower Yukon, made from reindeer antler. It has been sawed from the lower end nearly to the head, and a piece of wood inserted for the purpose of enlarging the shaft and affording a better grip for the hand. Another piece of horn, having a slot in the lower end for the reception of a stone blade, is bound firmly to it by rawhide cords.

On one of the Diomede islands a piece of nephrite was obtained from which ax heads had been cut. It was said to have been brought from the Kaviak peninsula. It measures $9\frac{1}{4}$ inches broad and $2\frac{1}{2}$ inches in thickness. The longest edge is smoothly polished and has a coarse groove down the center, showing where a roughed-out celt has been detached.

Nephrite is used largely for making whetstones; slate is also in common use for this purpose, and other hard stones are occasionally employed. A nephrite whetstone from Kotzebue sound (plate LXV, 1) has a deep longitudinal groove on each side, terminating in a hole through which is passed a loop of sealskin for attaching the implement to the waist belt.

Figure 25, 5, shows a smaller stone of similar character from Unalaklit. The specimen shown in figure 25, 4, was obtained on St Lawrence

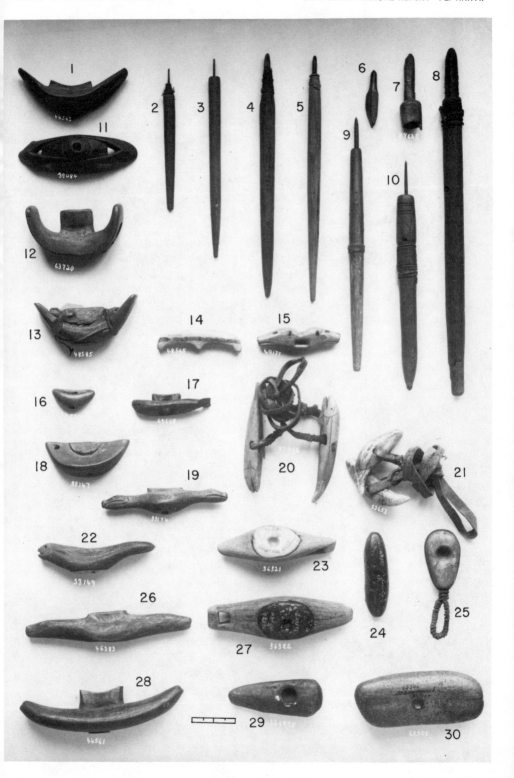

DRILLS, DRILL CAPS, AND CORDS (ONE-FOURTH)

island; it is made of slate, and is pierced at one end for the reception of a sinew cord.

TOOL BAGS AND HANDLES

Large oblong bags or satchels made of skin are in common use among the Eskimo for holding tools and implements of all kinds, including arrow and spear points, and other odds and ends which may have been accumulated. They have slightly arched handles of ivory or bone stretched lengthwise across the open mouth. Peculiarly shaped, long, narrow wooden boxes are also used for the same purpose; these are often carved into a variety of forms with great ingenuity.

One of these tool bags from Cape Darby is illustrated in plate XLI, 7. It is made from the skin of four wolverine heads, with a bottom of tanned sealskin with the hair side turned inward. The walrus ivory handle, 17 inches in length, has etched along its lower surface representations of thirty-four wolverine skins, and the ends are carved to form heads of animals; the upper surface is plain, with the exception of a groove in one side.

Plate XLI, 2, is an ivory bag handle from Sledge island, which has etched on it the representation of eight tails of whales and numerous wolverine, fox, and wolf skins.

Figure 4 of the same plate, also of ivory, from Kotzebue sound, has scalloped edges, and etched upon the convex surface are the outlines of whales and skins of wolverines and otters. On the convex side is represented a man pointing a gun at a bear, seven other bears, a man in a kaiak pursuing a whale, and another shooting waterfowl with a bow and arrow.

Figure 6 of this plate, from Kotzebue sound, has both surfaces covered with etchings of the skins of various fur-bearing animals.

Figure 5, from Point Hope, is a slender handle of deerhorn, having a series of etched figures of deer and men along one side and terminating in the head of a deer at one end and in a sharp point to represent the tail at the other.

Figure 1 shows an ivory handle from Hotham inlet, with the convex surface marked at one end with a representation of wolf skins, and along the entire length beyond these are a number of waterfowl in the act of swimming.

Figure 3, from Cape Nome, is another ivory bag handle, both surfaces of which are filled with etchings representing occurrences in the life of the Eskimo, including dragging home a seal, the pursuit of a whale, traveling with dog sledges, launching of umiaks, walrus hunting, and other similar occupations.

TOOL BOXES

A tool box obtained at Cape Nome (number 45385) is 14 inches long, 4½ high, and 5 wide. The ends are dovetailed into the sides, and the bottom is fastened on with wooden pegs. The lid, in which half a blue bead is inlaid, is attached by rawhide hinges and has a loop of rawhide and a double-end cord for tying it down. A split in the cover has been neatly mended by means of thin strips of whalebone passed through holes pierced on opposite sides. A small scalloped rod of ivory forms a handle to the cover, held in place by a loop of rawhide passed through two holes at each end into corresponding holes in the cover and the ends knotted inside.

Plate XLII, 10, represents a box from Sfugunugumut, oval in shape, rather truncated at the smaller end and beveled toward the center. One end is carried upward in the form of a neck, terminating in a grotesque human head, having a prominent nose and an incised crescent-shape mouth with two pieces of white crockery inlaid at the corners to represent labrets; the other end has a pair of seal's flippers, the entire design being intended to represent a mythical being, with the body of a seal and a human head. It is painted in a bluish tint, except the head, which is black, and the incised lines that outline the flippers, which are red. The cover is slightly convex above and concave below, with a broad groove cut in its upper surface; it is hinged by two rawhide cords, and a double-end cord is fastened in two places on the side and passed twice around the box and tied to hold the cover in place and to fasten it.

Another box (number 36242) from Sfugunugumut is similar in outline to the latter, except that it lacks the head, and, like the preceding, the body of the box is fashioned from a single piece of wood. The exterior is painted a dull red and has three grooves extending around it, which are colored black, and set in them at regular intervals are broad-head pegs of ivory, which are ornamented with a circle and dot. The interior of the box is divided into two compartments, unequal in size; the smaller, conical in shape, has been used for storing fragments of red ocher and other substances used as paints. The cover is hinged with rawhide and is fastened by a loop of rawhide which passes over a peg in front of the box. On the top of the cover is painted in black the figure of a curious mythical creature, so conventionalized in outline that it is difficult to identify it. From marks on the inside of the cover it has evidently been used in cutting tobacco.

Plate XLII, 4, from Askinuk, is a box, suboval in shape, flattened above and below and truncated at each end, cut from a single piece of wood. The interior is neatly excavated to about an inch in depth, leaving a ledge crossing from side to side about an inch inward from each end. The sides of the box are painted black while the top and the bottom are of a bluish tint. On each of the four surfaces a shallow groove extends from end to end; on the sides they are of equal width, but on the top and the bottom they are narrow in the middle, broadening gradually toward each end. These grooves are painted red. The cover is slightly convex without and concave within. On its inner surface are painted in red and black a number of rude figures representing two sledges, men, and various beasts, among the most conspicuous of which are wolves and reindeer.

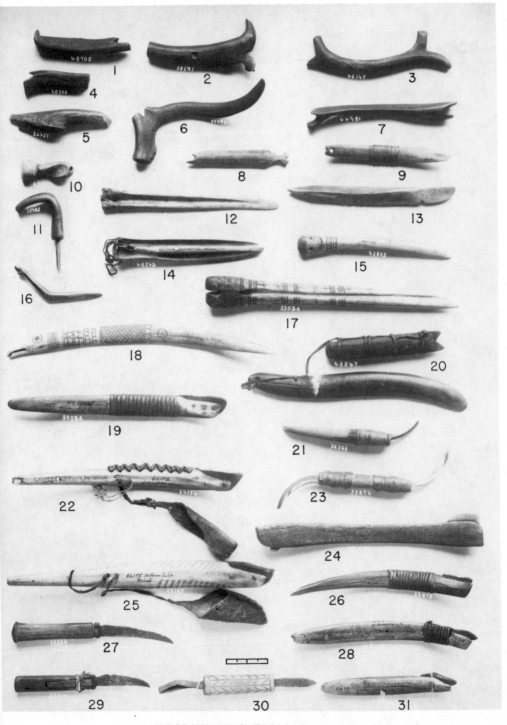

WOOD-WORKING TOOLS (ONE-FOURTH)

A box from Cape Vancouver (number 37357) is flattened oval in out-line, with a seal's head carved upon it, the eyes of which are represented by a piece of marble on one side and a fragment of porcelain on the other; ivory pegs form the nostrils, and at the corners of the mouth are ivory pegs with beads set in the center to represent labrets. On the top and on each side of the head small blue beads are inserted. A groove painted black extends around the sides of the box, in which seven ivory pegs are inserted. The cover is attached as usual by hinges of rawhide. The box is cracked, and has been mended by raw-hide cords laced through holes on each side of the fissure. A rawhide loop passing over a peg set in the front of the box serves as a fastening.

A box from Pastolik (plate XLII, 11) is made in three pieces, the bottom being fastened on with wooden pegs; it is rather flattened oval in outline, and represents the body of a seal. The head is represented with the mouth open and with wooden pegs for teeth; the nostrils are marked by ivory pegs, and for the eyes are inlaid small oval pieces of ivory with a hole in the center to represent the pupil; the flippers are carved in relief on the sides and at the rear; the tail is represented on the upper surface of the box and forms a thumb-piece for raising the cover. The cover is slightly convex without and con-cave within, with a groove extending its entire length; a groove is also cut around the body of the seal, and another below it extends the whole length of the box. The surface is painted black, except the grooves and the interior of the mouth of the seal, which are red.

The inside of the cover is decorated with figures in red and black, representing human beings and animals. On one side the thunderbird is represented grasping a deer with one claw and a man in a kaiak with the other; on the opposite side the thunderbird is seizing a whale with one claw and a seal with the other. One curious figure represents a double-head wolf with four legs and connected by a black line with the hand of a man.

Another box from Pastolik (number 38739) is made from separate pieces, the ends being mortised into the sides; wooden wedges are driven into the tenons to fasten them more firmly in the slots; the bottom is attached by wooden pegs. On the inner surface of the lid are painted in red a number of figures of men and animals, many of which are obscene. The outer surface is not colored, but is covered with neatly made parallel grooves extending lengthwise and following the outlines of the box.

A box from Kaialigamut (number 37562) is made of wood, and is oval at one end and truncated at the other; about an inch from the truncated end a crosspiece is inserted in slots on each side, which are cut narrow at the edges and flaring toward the inside, so that the edges of the crosspiece, which are cut in corresponding shape, hold the ends of the box firmly in position. The sides are formed by one piece, which is bent to form the oval figure; the bottom is attached by wooden pegs, and the cover is hinged with rawhide. For fastening, a loop passes down over a projecting peg on the bottom of the box. Following the outline of the box around the bottom, about one-third of an inch from the edge is cut a bead in strong relief, and around the sides extends a groove. The cover is carved to represent the flattened form of a seal with a large, broad head; the hind flippers are cut in relief; the eyes are represented by two small white buttons, and the nostrils by two white beads inlaid in the wood. The box is painted red, with the exception of the groove around the sides and the incisions outlining the flippers and the sides of the seal, which are black. The inside of the cover has a curious conventional design painted in black, intended as a private mark of the owner.

Plate XLII, 6, is a long oval box from Anogogmut, cut from a single piece of wood and divided into two compartments of unequal size by leaving a partition at the smaller end when the interior was excavated. The cover is neatly fitted and is hinged by two rawhide cords, and the

FIG. 27—Wooden trinket box (⅓).

fastening consists of a loop of rawhide tipped with a small ivory button, in which is a hole which fits over a bone peg. A groove is cut around the top and the bottom of the box about half an inch from the edge, and another passes around the center. The surface is painted red, with the exception of the grooves, which are black. In the center of the cover is set a round piece of white porcelain, and six smaller pieces are inlaid in one of the grooves.

Figure 27 is a box from Anogogmut made from a single piece of wood, flattened oval in outline, slightly convex above and very strongly so on its lower surface. It is deeply excavated and has a neatly fitted cover held in position by two rawhide hinges and fastened by a loop of cord passed over a wooden peg on the lower edge of the box. On the upper surface of the cover the figure of a seal is carved in relief, having in the center of the back a grotesque semihuman face, also in relief, probably intended to represent the shade of the seal. The bottom of the box is carved in the form of a larger seal with the flippers in relief and a

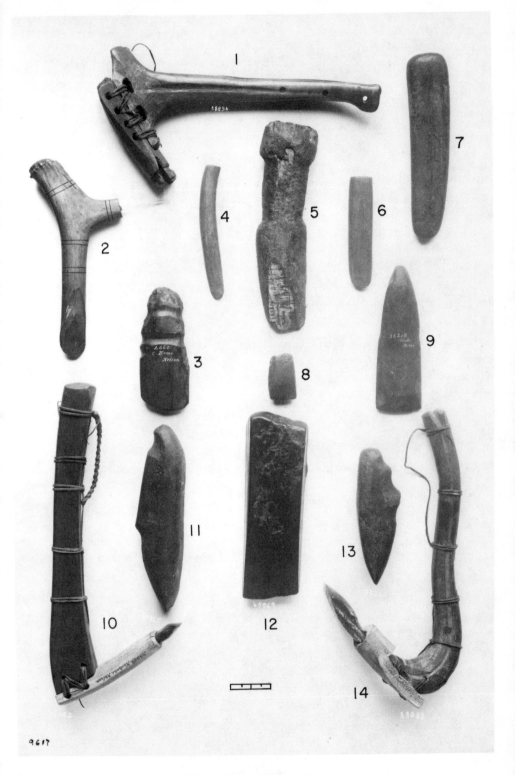

WEDGES AND ADZES (ONE-FIFTH)

deeply incised, crescentic mouth. The eyes and the nostrils of the larger seal and the eyes of the smaller seal are formed by the insertion of ivory pegs. Ivory pegs are also set around the edges of the body of the seal on the cover. This is a very old box, and if it was ever painted the coloring has long since disappeared.

Another old box (number 37553), from Askinuk, is oval in outline and has one end carved to represent the head of an animal. The nostrils are formed by blue beads, between which projects an ivory peg. Oval pieces of bone serve for the eyes, with a slit in the center for the pupil. The cover is an oblong strip of wood truncated at one end and the other tapering to a projecting point, which serves as a thumb-piece by which it can be raised. It is held in position by pegs at each end and by a thin strip of spruce rootlet passed through a hole on each side of the box.

Plate XLII, 7, is a box from Sfugunugumut, composed of three pieces of wood. The sides were formed by a strip bent and joined on beveled edges at the ends. The bottom is slightly convex and is attached by wooden pegs. The cover is similar in outline, but one end extends upward and forms the head of a seal, the eyes of which are of ivory, with small blue beads for the pupils. Ivory pegs form the nostrils, and others are set at the corners of the mouth to represent labrets. Fore-flippers are cut in relief on each side of the cover, the intention having been to represent a seal lying on its back. A groove extends around the side, in which are set small ivory pegs, with a round hole in the center of each. Similar pegs ornament the surface of the cover, which has the usual rawhide hinges and loop passing over a peg in the front of the box for a fastening.

From Kaialigamut is a box (number 37863), cut from a single piece of wood, the interior excavated and the cover neatly fitted. It is in the form of a seal, the tail forming a thumb-piece by which the cover can be raised. The mouth is incised, the nostrils are flattened spots on the muzzle, and both are painted red. The eyes are represented by small ivory pegs. Extending along each side and the top of the cover is a long groove, broad in the center and narrowing at each end, on which are depicted various figures of men and animals in black on the background of red with which these grooves are painted. The body of the seal is colored a dull blue. Three black stripes extend from the crown along the sides. The center of the back and the outlines of the flippers are also black.

Figure 28 is an oblong box from the lower Yukon. It is made from thin boards fastened together with wooden pins. On all the surfaces except the bottom, rows of ivory pegs are inserted. On the upper surface are two small rectangular doors extending across the box from side to side and opening into little shallow box-like compartments. They are hinged with strips of sealskin neatly sewed in place by chain stitches of spruce root, and fastened to them are pieces of rawhide, by

18 ETH——7

which they can be raised. In the center, extending lengthwise, are
two other doors, and on each side, just below the upper edge, is another
little door. A loop of cord extending over and tied across the middle
of the box keeps all these doors shut.

WOMEN'S WORKBOXES

Small wooden boxes are used by the women for the safekeeping of
their needle cases, sinew and fiber thread, scraps of skein, earrings,
pieces of coloring matter. and various other small articles used by them
in their work.

Figure 3, plate XLII, represents one of these workboxes from Sfugunugumut. It is oval in outline, and the top and bottom are in the shape
of flattened, truncated cones, their thin bases resting on the sides of the
box. On the front and back. crossing the sides vertically, are inlaid flat

Fig. 28—Trinket box (about ⅓).

strips of ivory, with a series of three circles and dots engraved upon
them; extending around the sides are a series of round, button-like pieces
of ivory, their surfaces covered by a number of concentric circles with
black centers. A hook-shape knob of ivory projects from the front,
over which a rawhide loop fastened to the cover is passed to keep the
lid closed. A slender ivory rod, four inches in length, having its upper
surface etched with circle and dot patterns, forms a handle and is
attached to the top of the cover by a rawhide cord at each end.

Figure 5 of the same plate shows a box, from Ikogmut, made from a
single piece of wood in the shape of a seal lying on its back with the
head and hind flippers turned upward; the fore-flippers are also carved
in relief on the surface. On the cover a flattened ivory rod is fastened
with pegs to the main part of the box. On the upper surface of the
cover, in the center of a broad circular groove in which ivory pegs are

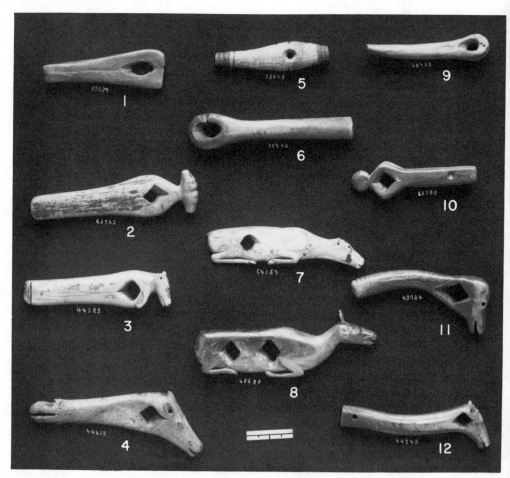

ARROWSHAFT STRAIGHTENERS AND POINT SETTERS (ONE-FOURTH)

set, is a semihuman face carved in relief; it has ivory labrets at each corner of the mouth, and inlaid pieces of ivory represent the eyes.

Figure 9 of the plate shows a box, from Sabotnisky, cut from a single piece of wood, flattened and slightly oval in outline, with truncated ends. The form of a salmon is carved in relief on both the top and the bottom, and a groove extends along the sides. The cover is attached in the usual manner by rawhide hinges, and a cord is provided for fastening it in front.

Another box from Sfugunugumut (number 36245) is made from a single piece of wood, oval in outline, truncated at one end, with a sunken ledge around the upper edge to receive the cover, which is slightly convex and projects upward at one end to form a thumb-piece for raising it. This projection is carved in the form of a cormorant's head, the eyes being represented by incised circles.

Figure 8, plate XLII, from Koñigunugumut, is a long, quadrate, wooden box, the top, bottom, and sides of which are made from separate pieces, the edges of the cover and the bottom being beveled. It is fastened together with wooden pegs, and the cover is attached as usual by rawhide hinges and fastened by a loop passing down over a projecting peg in front. The bottom of the box is painted black around the edges and crossed by black bars; the ends of the top and sides are painted red, and a broad, black band extends around the middle.

Figure 2, plate XLII, from St Lawrence island, is a workbox, circular in form, made by bending a thin piece of spruce, three inches wide, so that the ends overlap, and are sewed together with strips of whalebone passed through slits pierced in both thicknesses of the beveled ends. The top and the bottom are truncated cones in shape, chamfered and fitted into grooves cut around the inner edges of the sides. A round hole in the top serves for putting in and taking out small objects.

Figure 1, plate XLII, from Sledge island, is a box 4 inches high and 4¼ inches square, made of thin pieces of spruce smoothly finished. The bottom is attached by wooden pegs; the sides are neatly mortised together. The cover is hinged by two pieces of rawhide and is fastened in front by a double-end string passing through a rawhide loop pendent from the cover. The handle on the cover consists of two pieces of rawhide cord tied together in the middle, the ends passed through holes and knotted inside, forming a loop about an inch and a half in length. The box is grooved around the top and the sides in parallel lines; the outer grooves, painted black, are broad and shallow, while those on the inside are narrower and red in color both on the cover and sides. On the center of the cover is a pointed oval groove, black in color. The bottom of the box and a broad band around the sides are not painted.

A circular box, from Sledge island (number 45093), is seven inches high and over nine inches in diameter, made from a strip of spruce bent until the beveled edges overlap, and sewed together with a double

row of stitching with spruce rootlet. The bottom is chamfered and
fitted into a groove like the head of a barrel; the cover is slightly convex above and concave within; three parallel grooves cross the top at
equal intervals, and two others, about an inch apart, extend around
the edge. The body of the box has also a broad and a narrow groove
near each edge. The cover is painted red and a band of this color
extends around each edge of the box; the grooves are all colored
black. A cord loop, two inches in length, forms a handle for the cover,
which is hinged with sinew cord and is fastened by two ends of a rawhide cord which project through a hole in front of the box and pass
through a loop pendent from the lid.

Another box (number 176081), from Sledge island, is oval in outline,
but is contracted in the middle by means of a stout, sinew cord passed
through holes on each side, forming a stout cross-stay. The sides are
made of two pieces with the ends lapping, sewed together in the same
manner as in the preceding specimen, and the bottom is similarly fitted
into a groove by a chamfered edge. The cover is also hinged in the
same manner and is provided with a similar fastening. A looped rawhide handle, each end of which is divided into two parts, is passed
through four holes and knotted on the underside.

HANDLES FOR WORKBOXES AND WATER BUCKETS

Handles for women's workboxes and for water buckets are frequently
made of ivory or of bone. They present a considerable variety of
form and many of them are handsomely carved. A large number
were obtained, of which the following specimens, illustrated in plate
XLIII, present the principal variations:

Figure 16, from Norton sound, is a plain rod of ivory, nearly square
in cross section.

Figure 5, from Unalaklit, is a rod of ivory, suboval in cross section,
with the upper surface etched in parallel lines extending obliquely
from the middle of the top to the edge.

Figure 11, from Sledge island, is a small, flat rod, broadened vertically at each end to be pierced for a cord. The upper surface is marked
with raven totem signs and a simple etched pattern.

Figure 24, from Shaktolik, has the lower side scalloped and the upper
side etched coarsely with lines and points.

Figure 10, from Norton sound, is slightly curved and has the upper
portion covered with zigzag patterns.

Figure 26, from Cape Darby, is suboval in cross section and has
across its upper surface the figures of ten whales carved in relief.

Figure 17, from Unalaklit, is a flattened ivory rod, carved at one end
to represent the head of a seal, and with the figures of several whales
etched upon its upper surface.

Figure 13, from Norton sound, is nearly square in cross section,

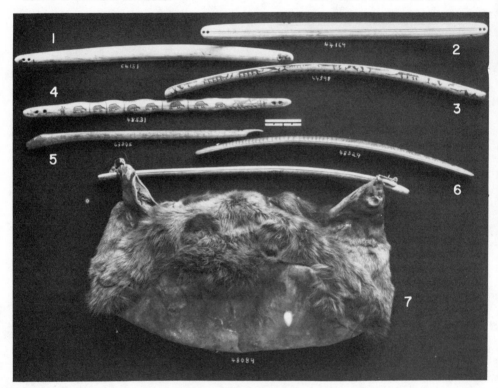

TOOL BAG AND HANDLES (ONE-FIFTH)

scalloped along each side, and grooved along the middle of the upper surface; the ends terminate in the head of an animal which has been much worn by long use; the details are consequently obliterated.

Figure 9, is a handle obtained by Mr L. M. Turner from Norton sound. It is suboval in cross section, and has in relief along its upper surface the figures of thirty seal heads; on each side of the two holes in which the cord is fastened to attach it to the box or bucket is also carved in relief the figure of a right whale.

Figure 14, from Cape Darby, is an ivory rod, suboval in cross section, with the figures of seven right-whale tails projecting from one side. Specimen 45157, from Sledge island, is a small rod, evidently used for a box cover, having along its upper edge, in an upright position, the figures of twelve whale-tails joined by their tips.

Figure 12, from Point Hope, is an ivory rod, oblong in cross section. Carved on one side of the middle is the projecting figure of the tail of a right whale, and on the upper surface are etched the figures of two right whales and the tails of four others.

Figure 6, from Kigiktauik, is a bucket handle of ivory, strongly curved and having in relief along its upper surface the figures of nine seal heads, several etched figures of seals with spears in their backs, rude figures representing otters, and a framework for storing objects above ground.

Figure 8, from Point Hope, is a slender ivory rod, triangular in cross section, doubly scalloped along both sides, and having a slight bordering pattern of etched lines.

Figure 1, from Sledge island, is a bucket handle consisting of a flat, ivory rod about four inches in length, with a neatly carved, five-link chain of ivory depending from a loop in each end. These chains terminate below with a carving, representing the head of a small seal. Through the flat surface near each end of the handle is a large, round hole in which fits, swivel-like, a small, round rod of ivory, terminating above in the figure of a seal's head, the eyes and ears of which are represented by a black substance inlaid in the ivory, while the mouth and the nostrils are etched. The lower ends of these handle rods are pierced with holes for receiving the cords connecting them with the bucket.

Figure 22, from Sledge island, is a heavy rod of ivory, suboval in cross section, terminating in a ring in which hangs by another ring the image of a right whale's tail about two inches in length. Upon the middle of the upper surface are etched figures of two right whales, and across the rod, near each end, are carved in strong relief two other figures of right whales. This carving is remarkably well done and is a very artistic piece of work.

Figure 7, from Kigiktauik, is a plain, slightly curved handle of reindeer horn, suboval in cross section.

Figure 2, from St Michael, is a handle of deerhorn, round in cross section, and bent at an obtuse angle in the center. It has a shallow groove along its convex upper surface, in which are a number of small, round points.

Figure 4, from Nunivak island, is a thin, curved piece of deerhorn with the ends rounded, and having a rounded protuberance in the sides at about one-third of the distance from each end. The upper surface has two parallel incised lines extending nearly its entire length, which are intersected at the widened points by a series of concentric circles with holes through the center.

Figure 23, from Cape Prince of Wales, is a large, strong handle of walrus ivory, with a doubly serrated edge on one side but smooth on the other. Two parallel grooves extend along the upper surface; the lower surface is convex.

Figure 20, from the Diomede islands, is a bar of walrus ivory. The ends are flattened, but the center is curved upward. Carved at each end is the figure of a polar bear in a standing position, looking outward.

Figure 21, obtained at St Michael by Mr. L. M. Turner, is a rounded bar of ivory, flattened on its lower surface and convex above, with a well-carved head of a polar bear, facing outward, on each end. A large hole is pierced lengthwise through this handle to admit the passage of a cord for attaching it to a water bucket.

Figure 18, from Unalaklit, is a flattened bar of ivory with the figure of a right whale, facing inward toward the center, carved in relief upon its upper surface at each end. In the back of each whale, near the tail, are two large, vertical holes for attaching the cord.

Figure 15, from Cape Prince of Wales, is a bar of walrus ivory, flat on the lower surface. On the upper side two right whales, facing outward, are carved in relief on one end, and on the other end is the figure of a wolf.

Figure 3, from Point Hope, is a small carving intended for a work-box handle, with a pair of seals' heads, facing outward, in high relief on each end of the upper surface. Between these heads are deeply incised lines forming a simple pattern.

Figure 19, from St Michael, is a rod of ivory carved in the form of a wolf, the legs being represented by the downward-projecting knobs, which are pierced for the attachment of cords.

Figure 25, from the Diomede islands, is an ivory handle for a water bucket. It is a flat bar, $8\frac{1}{2}$ inches long and $1\frac{1}{2}$ broad, having each end rounded and pierced with a hole three-quarters of an inch in diameter. In the center is another smaller round hole. In the holes at the ends are round pins, in which are holes with grooves below them at each side to admit the cords for attaching the handle to the bucket. The heads of the pins are carved to represent the heads, shoulders, and forelegs of white bears in an upright position, facing inward toward the center. Inside the bears' heads, on the upper surface, near the hole in the center,

TOOL AND TRINKET BOXES (ONE-FIFTH)

are carved in relief two figures of seals with their heads facing inward. The whole group represents two seals lying on the ice near their hole and two polar bears rising from the water at the edge of the ice, close to the seals.

NEEDLE-CASES

The women have a great variety of cases for holding their needles, differing widely in form and made from a diversity of materials, showing the remarkable ingenuity of these people in their adaptation of ornamental designs to practical purposes.

In the country about the lower Yukon and southward to the Kuskokwim a favorite form of needle-case is made from a section of the hollow wing-bone of a goose or other large waterfowl, plugged at each end with wooden-stoppers, one representing the head and the other the tail of a fish. The surfaces of these cases are covered with a variety of incised patterns, as will be seen by the following figures comprising plate XLIV:

Figure 35, from Kushunuk, is one of these needle-cases, representing a fish. Figure 33, from Cape Vancouver, and figure 34, from Sabotnisky, also represent fishes and have tufts of seal hair inserted around the wooden head and tail.

Figure 36, from Kushunuk, has the stopper carved in the shape of the head of a young white whale. Figure 30, also from Kushunuk, has a flat stopper in one end and a round knob on the other.

Figure 38, from Norton sound, is an ivory tube in the form of a woman's leg, with etched lines to represent the seams of the trousers.

Figure 37, from Koñigunugumut, is made of wood, over which are placed five empty cartridge shells. The stopper is in the shape of a cormorant's head.

Figure 46, from Unalaklit, is an octagonal tube of ivory.

Figure 30, from Hotham inlet, is a round, ivory tube with a figure of an Arctic hare in strong relief on two opposite sides, near one end.

Figure 32, from St Michael, is an ivory tube, round at one end and broadened by a ridge on each side near the other. It has the raven totem etched upon it.

Figure 48, from Unalaklit, is a short, ivory tube plugged at one end and with blue beads inlaid around it. The surface is surrounded by zigzag etchings and raven totem marks.

Figure 29, from Sledge island, has in relief on two sides the figures of two white whales.

Figure 45, from the lower Yukon, is a tube in the form of a woman standing with her arms held against her sides.

Figure 40, from King island, is a round tube carved with two human figures, facing inward from each end, in a sitting position, with the elbows resting upon the knees and the hands folded under the chin. This is a fine piece of carving, and from the fact that it has been much worn by handling it is doubtless of great age.

Figure 31, from the lower Yukon, is a tube with the head of a walrus in relief on each of two sides near one end and the head of a seal on the other end.

Figure 28, from Kotzebue sound, is of ivory in the shape of a small flask closed by a wooden stopper. The wooden bottom is held in place with wooden pegs. In relief on one side of the neck is the figure of a right whale, and on opposite sides are two bears.

Needle-cases are sometimes used without stoppers, in which case a large cord of sealskin is passed through the center, which terminates in a hook of bone or ivory for holding thimbles, or hung to it by small cords are various little pendent ornaments, which consist sometimes of the canine teeth of various animals, but are often small carvings representing arrowheads, human faces, miniature belt fasteners, and various animal forms. When this style of needle-case is used the needles are thrust into the sealskin cord and are drawn into the case by pulling on the other end of the cord, and when needed can be withdrawn by a reverse movement.

Figure 25, obtained on Norton sound by Mr L. M. Turner, is a good example of this style of needle-case with sealskin needle holder.

Figure 26, from St Michael, is a small, neatly carved needle-case pendant representing a reindeer's foot.

Figures 22, 23, and 27 represent a number of these small pendants, all of which were obtained at Kushunuk. The last mentioned is in the form of a frog with a large head but without the fore-limbs.

WOMEN'S "HOUSEWIVES"

The little cases or bags for materials used in sewing and for other articles for women's work, commonly called "housewives," are in general use among the western Eskimo. They are made from skins of various kinds and embellished with needlework in ornamental patterns. The lower end terminates usually in a bag and the upper end is rounded; to the latter a rawhide cord is attached, having at its end a slender cross-piece of bone, ivory, or deerhorn from three to eight inches in length, which is generally carved into various designs with the ingenuity characteristic of these people. When not in use the "housewife" is rolled up, the cord is wound several times around it and fastened by thrusting one end of the cross-piece under the cord.

A specimen of these housewives from Kaialigamut (number 37918) is made from the skin of reindeer ears and pieces of skin from other parts of the same animal. The upper end is rounded and trimmed with stripes of white, black, and russet leather parallel to the curved edge, the seams being sewed in black and white. The lower end terminates in a bag, the inner surface of which is divided into square sections by double rows of stitching, along which are painted bordering red lines. Along the outer edges is a narrow strip of white reindeer fur succeeded by a little strip of plucked beaver, outside of which is a coarse fringe made from little strips from the edge of the skin of reindeer ears.

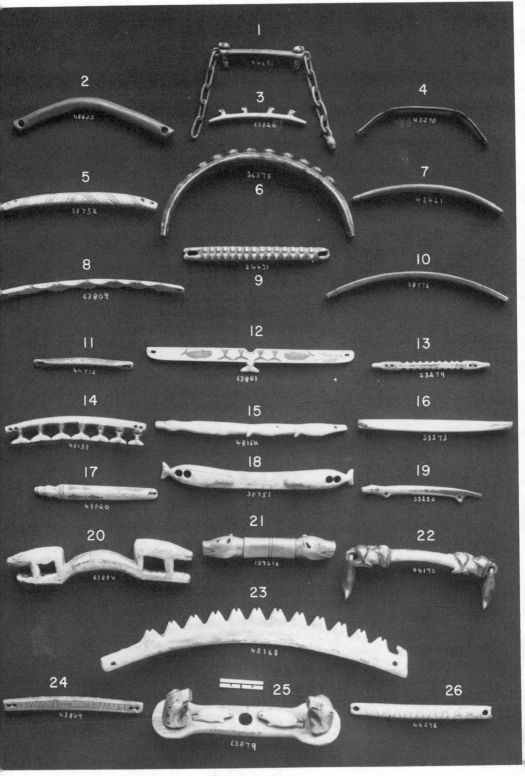

BUCKET AND BOX HANDLES (ABOUT ONE-FOURTH)

Plate XLV, 14, from the lower Yukon, is a small housewife covered on the inside with ornamental patterns of red, white, and black. It contains three pockets, and is bordered with a narrow strip of muskrat skin; the back is made of fishskin.

Plate XLV, 32, from the lower Yukon, is a piece of fishskin intended to form the outer ends of a large housewife. It is sewed with ornamental patterns, oval in outline on three sides and straight across the other, and bordered by a narrow fringe of sealskin.

Plate XLV, 31, obtained on Nunivak island by Dr W. H. Dall, is a good example of a housewife made from the skin of reindeer ears, bordered by a fringe of small strips of the same material. The sides have a border of white reindeer skin, surrounded by a narrow strip of sealskin and mink fur around its upper edge. The interior is divided into quadrate spaces by parallel seams of black and white and rows of small beads. At intervals around the outer edges are little tags of red worsted. The string for fastening is covered with beads.

Plate XLV, 15, shows a specimen from Big lake, with a central band of deerskin about an inch and a half wide by ten inches long, bordered along each side with skins from six reindeer ears sewed together along the sides. On one end is a semilunar piece of skin, having its front covered with rows of beads and an ornamental pattern of white and reddish sealskin, sewed with sinew thread and strips of white quills. The inside is crossed by parallel rows of stitching with red-painted border lines; the inclosed areas are not colored, but are adorned with small clusters of beads in their centers.

A large number of the fastening rods were obtained. The following, figured in plate XLV, illustrate a few of the variations in form and outline:

Figure 29, from Nunivak island, and figure 30, from Big lake, show two fastening rods in the shape of salmon.

Figure 27, from Koñigunugumut, and figure 28, from Agiukchugumut, are also fish-like in form.

Figure 24, from Ukagamut, is a neatly carved rod in two sections, united by a cross bar. On one side is represented a white whale, and on the other a seal, the figures being very much elongated and slit through the backs.

Figure 26, from Nulukhtulogumut, is a round fastening rod, representing a seal; it has an eye at the lower end for attaching the cord.

Figure 25 shows a rod from Big lake which terminates in the head and tail of a wolf, the legs of the animal being represented by etched lines on the surface.

Figure 17, from the lower Yukon, is a small, rod-like piece of ivory with a grotesque head at each end, one side apparently representing that of a bird and the other that of some other creature.

Figure 13, from Chalitmut, is a handsome, flat, ivory rod, having on one side at each end the figure of a seal carved in relief, and in the center the head of a man surrounded by a raised border with ray-like, etched lines extending out from it, evidently intended to represent a hood with a fur border. On the other side is the face of a woman with tattooed lines on the chin and a similar indication of a fur hood, and also two seals in relief.

Figure 21, from Big lake, is a round, slender rod terminating in the head of an unknown animal.

Figure 12, from the lower Yukon, is a slender rod having an eye at the lower end for the attachment of a cord, and is composed of a series of oval sections divided by grooves and raised beadings.

Figure 18, from the lower Yukon, is another round rod surrounded by grooves and beadings.

Figure 10, from Cape Nome, has an eye on one end for attaching the cord, and is sharpened at the other to serve as a bodkin. It is etched near its base with the raven totem.

Figure 16, from Nubviukhchugaluk, is triangular in cross section and notched along two of the corners; on one side is etched the raven totem. This piece also terminates in a point for use as a bodkin.

Figures 3 and 11 are both from Cape Vancouver, and have their ends flattened to serve as sole-creasers in making boots.

Figure 8, from the lower Yukon; figure 4, from Big lake; figure 7, from Chalitmut; figure 6, from Kushunuk, and figure 5, from Koñigunugumut, are all double rods, divided along the middle but joined near the outer ends.

Figure 9, from Chalitmut, has two detached rods united by four round iron pegs or rivets, the two rods not touching anywhere along their length.

Figure 20, from the Yukon; figure 1, from Sabotnisky; figure 19, from Koñigunugumut, and figure 2, from Chalitmut, are variously ornamented with lines and circles etched upon the surfaces.

Figure 23, from Sfugunugumut, is a round ivory rod, with a seal carved in relief on the upper side.

Figure 22, from the lower Kuskokwim, is a flattened image of a seal carved in ivory.

NEEDLES AND BODKINS

Formerly bone needles were used exclusively by the Eskimo, the holes for the stitches being pierced with a fine-pointed bodkin or awl of bone, ivory, or deerhorn; but since intercourse with white men has become more frequent they have obtained steel needles and pieces of iron, from which needles are made by themselves. Although many bodkins are now pointed with iron, a great majority of those in use are still made from bone, ivory, or horn.

Figures 1 and 2, plate XLVIII a, from St Michael, are ivory needles used for sewing coarse seams in making boat covers or for similar heavy work.

In the collection there is a small, flat, wooden tablet (number 44264),

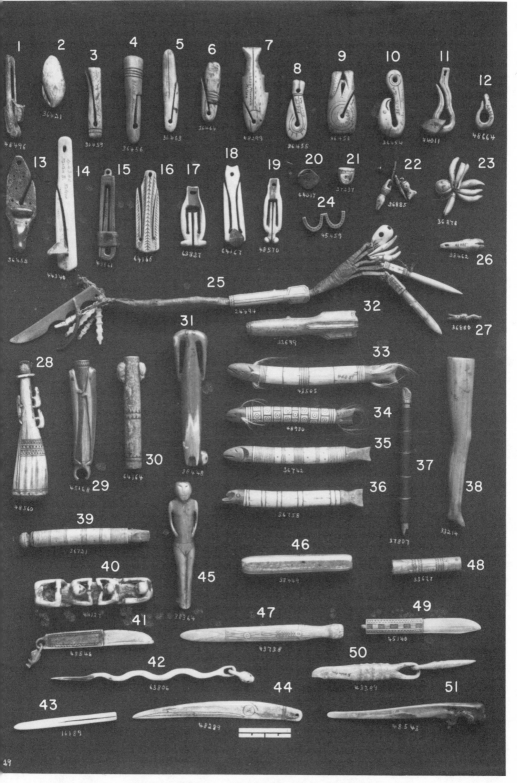

THIMBLE GUARDS, NEEDLE-CASES, AND BOOT-SOLE CREASERS (ABOUT ONE-THIRD)

from Cape Darby, four and one-half inches long by three-quarters of an inch wide and an eighth of an inch thick, used for supporting a bone or an ivory needle while the eye is being pierced. The following specimens are shown in plate XLVI:

Figure 15, from Sabotnisky, is a sharp-pointed bodkin, made from the wing-bone of a large bird.

Figure 13, from Kushunuk, is another bodkin, made from the hollow wing-bone of a bird. It has a neatly made wooden head, inserted like a plug in its upper end.

Figure 1, from St Michael, is of deerhorn, the upper end in the form of a human figure, with a face represented on both sides. A stick passing through a hole in the body and projecting on either side forms the arms. The lower end is rounded and grooved, with a hollow at the tip, in which is fitted a slender, tapering point of deerhorn that can be removed and replaced at will. This is the only implement of its kind that was seen. It is fashioned after iron-pointed tools used for a similar purpose.

Figure 14, from Razbinsky, is a slender, tapering bodkin of ivory, having its upper end cut into the form of a fish-head.

Figure 9, from Cape Prince of Wales, terminates in a link, by which is attached a loose piece cut in the form of a bird-head. Little tufts of seal hair are inserted in holes around the upper end of the handle and in the bird-head, held in place by means of wooden pegs.

Figure 8, from Big lake, is made of ivory; it has two links in its upper end, and the top is carved to represent a fish-head.

Figure 11, from Cape Vancouver, is triangular in cross section and has little strings of beads attached to the handle, the top of which is surmounted by a knob.

Figure 10, from Askinuk, is terminated by a link with a pendant in which blue beads are set.

Figure 12, from Cape Prince of Wales, is triangular in cross section, with the upper end neatly cut into the form of a reindeer head.

Figure 7, from the Kuskokwim, is a handsome ivory bodkin terminating in three links, with the hind flippers of a seal pendent from the top.

Figure 4, from Chalitmut, has an iron point and a handle of walrus ivory terminating in two links, the top one in the form of a fish-tail.

Figure 2, from Cape Vancouver, is a long iron point with a handle of walrus ivory in the form of a salmon, along the body of which are set little tufts of seal hair.

Figure 6, from the lower Yukon, is an iron-pointed bodkin with a wooden handle and a little wooden sheath for slipping over the point.

Figure 16, also from the lower Yukon, is a specimen of the larger bodkins or awls used for piercing heavy skins employed in making kaiaks and for other similar work.

Figure 3, from Nulukhtulogumut, is a strong iron implement with an ivory handle fashioned in the shape of a seal.

Figure 5, from Chalitmut, has an ivory handle terminating in two knobs, one above the other, and separated by a projecting beading.

BOOT-SOLE CREASERS

For crimping or creasing the sealskin soles of boots around the toe and heel, small, sharp-edged, flat-pointed pieces of ivory or bone are used. Sometimes these are knife-like in shape, as in figure 49, plate XLIV, from Sledge island, or are smooth, plain pieces like the specimen shown in figure 43 of the same plate, which was obtained by Doctor Dall from Nunivak island.

Figure 47 of the plate referred to represents a creaser in the form of a walrus; the head and tusks are carved, and the flippers and certain other anatomical details are etched on the back of the implement. This specimen is also from Nunivak island.

Plate XLIV, 42, from Point Hope, is an elaborate boot creaser of this kind, to the upper end of which, attached by a link, is a carving representing the head of a white bear. The body of the implement is sinuous nearly to the end where it is flattened to a wedge shape.

FIG. 29—Boot-sole creaser (full size).

Plate XLIV, 41, from Kotzebue sound, is a creaser made from ivory in the form of a knife, with a pendant attached by a link to the butt.

Plate XLIV, 50, from Cape Prince of Wales, is a creaser with a link at one end, to which is attached a short bodkin.

Plate XLIV, 51, from Kotzebue sound, is a creaser made by shaping down the small end of a piece of bone.

The accompanying figure 29 is an ivory boot-sole creaser from Nushagak; it is triangular in cross-section, with pictures etched on the three sides. The side represented shows a house with smoke issuing from the smoke hole, an elevated storehouse to the left, and some people approaching with a loaded sledge from the right.

Plate XLIV, 44, from Nunivak island, is a creaser in the form of a murre's head.

WOMEN'S KNIVES

The knives used by Eskimo women for skinning and cutting up game and fish vary considerably in form. Some consist simply of a broad piece of slate, roughly crescentic in shape, with the curved side ground to a thin edge.

Figure 8, plate XLVII, from Razbinsky, represents one of these rough slate knives.

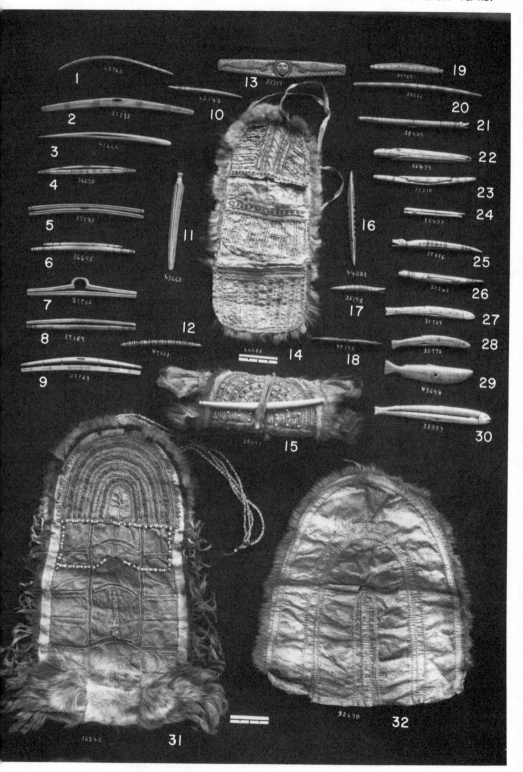

"HOUSEWIVES" AND FASTENINGS (ONE-FIFTH)

Figure 6, plate XLVII, from Kushunuk, is a small knife made of slate set in a slot in the end of an oval wooden handle.

Figure 7, plate XLVII, from the lower Yukon, is made of a fine-grain stone very similar in appearance to slate, set into a wooden handle. This specimen is more neatly made than is usually the case with these implements.

Figure 5, plate XLVII, from the lower Yukon, is a rough piece of slate set in a rudely made wooden handle.

Figure 9, plate XLVII, from the lower Yukon, is a slate knife attached to a wooden handle by means of a rawhide cord passed through a hole in the back. It has a sheath made from two pieces of wood fastened together with a rawhide cord.

Figure 10, plate XLVII, from St Michael, is a long slate blade fitted into a slot in the end of a wooden handle and bound in place with a lashing of untanned sealskin.

Figure 4, plate XLVII, from Koñigunugumut, is a specimen of the iron-blade knives which, since the introduction of iron into Alaska, are gradually displacing the old stone and slate implements. It is set in a neatly made wooden handle.

Figure 1, plate XLVII, from Sfugunugumut, is another iron-blade knife with a solid ivory handle.

Specimens of wooden-handle knives, similar in character to those from the American coast, were obtained on St Lawrence island, but they show the customary rude workmanship of that district.

THIMBLES AND THIMBLE HOLDERS

Thimbles for women are made usually from small, oval pieces of tough sealskin, having a slit extending across one edge, forming a loop-like strap, through which the forefinger is thrust, so that the strap rests across the nail and the pad of skin in the inner side of the finger (see figure 20, plate XLIV, from Nubviukhchugaluk). Some of the women use metal thimbles obtained from the traders, which are also imitated in ivory by themselves, but most of the women prefer the old-fashioned sealskin thimbles.

Figure 21, plate XLIV, from Chalitmut, is one of these ivory thimbles made to rest like a cap over the end of the finger; the back is cut away except for a strap or band across the inner border. In form this is a combination of the metal thimble of the white people and the old style made from a piece of sealskin.

Sealskin thimbles are carried usually on a holder or guard attached to the end of a cord, which is either fastened to the workbag or forms a pendant to the strap of the needle-case. These holders vary greatly in form, but are most frequently of hook shape.

Figure 1, plate XLIV, from St Michael, is a thimble holder made from a plain piece of bone from the leg of a bird; it is the rudest and simplest form of this article.

Figure 24, plate XLIV, also from St Michael, is in the form of a double crescent, with a hole in the middle over which the thimble is slipped and retained in place by the crescent-shape bar.

Figure 14, plate XLIV, from Norton bay, is a plain, hook-like holder.

Figure 19, plate XLIV, from Kotzebue sound; figure 18, from Hotham inlet, and figure 17, from Point Hope, are all made from ivory and represent different forms of this little implement.

Figure 2, plate XLIV, from St Lawrence island, is a rude hook made from a walrus tooth. Figure 4, from Kushunuk, is a rather rudely made hook of deerhorn. Figure 3 is another deerhorn hook from the same locality as the last. Figure 7, from Nunivak island, is a hook made from walrus ivory in the form of a salmon.

Figures 5, 8, 9, 10, and 13, of plate XLIV, represent various forms of this implement made from ivory. All are from Kushunuk.

Figure 11, plate XLIV, from Nubviukhchugaluk, and figure 12, of the same plate, are ivory hook-shape holders from Kotzebue sound.

Figure 15, plate XLIV, from Unalaklit, is a hook-shape holder having a leather band which slips down over the hook, holding it closed and preventing the thimble from dropping off.

Figure 6, plate XLIV, from Kushunuk, is a specimen which has a wrapping of spruce rootlets around the shank and inside the slot which forms the hook to keep the thimble in place.

Figure 16, plate XLIV, is a double thimble guard of ivory from Point Hope.

IMPLEMENTS FOR MAKING THREAD AND CORD

Thread for sewing clothing or other small articles is made of sinew from the legs of reindeer, dried and beaten with a maul to loosen the fibers, which are then divided and cleaned. From the Kuskokwim northward to Kotzebue sound and the islands of Bering strait, small comb-like implements with from two to four teeth are in use for this purpose. On the lower Yukon a species of tough grass is obtained and utilized for making thread and for other purposes. After being dried and beaten it is hatcheled with the combs which are used for making thread from sinew. Cords are made in different ways and of various materials. according to the uses for which they are intended. The kind most commonly in use is made from tanned sealskin, which is trimmed to an oval shape, from which a continuous strip is cut. Sometimes an entire skin is made into an unbroken cord. For heavier cords the skin of the walrus is utilized. Tanned reindeer skins are also cut into thongs, and sinews of reindeer and seals are twisted into cords of various sizes. On the lower Yukon and in the interior territory occupied by the Eskimo, cord is made from the inner bark of the willow. Strips of whalebone are also frequently employed for lashings on sledges, boats, and various implements.

Figure 5, plate XLVIIIa, from Norton sound, represents one of the combs used in making thread from sinew.

Figure 6, plate XLVIIIa, from the Diomede islands, is a comb or sinew

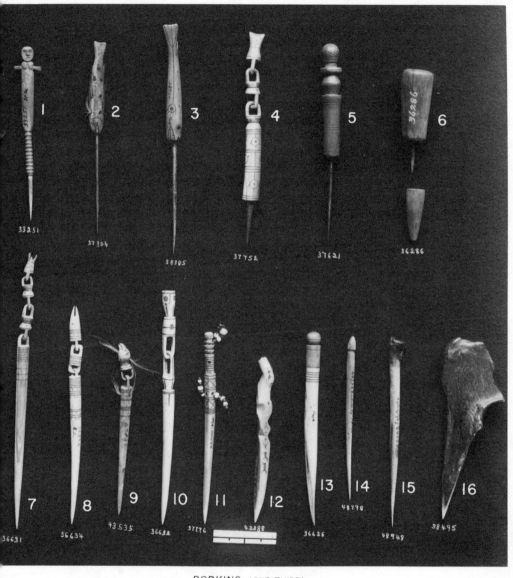

BODKINS (ONE-THIRD)

shredder of walrus ivory, with four large, coarse teeth and a narrow handle.

Figure 1, plate XLVIII a, from Sledge island, is a three-toothed sinew shredder with a flattened knob-like blade at the end of the handle.

Figure 3, plate XLVIII a, from Cape Nome, is a small, flat piece of deerhorn with three flat teeth on one end, and figure 2, plate XLVIII a, from Sledge island, is a similar implement made of ivory.

Figure 4, plate XLVIII a, from Cape Darby, is a toothed ivory implement of this kind, one tooth being attached to the side of the main piece by means of a strong wrapping of willow root.

Figures 7 and 9, plate XLVIII a, from the lower Yukon; figure 8, from Mission, and figure 10, from Sabotnisky, are specimens of combs which have been used in making grass thread.

The accompanying figure 30, from Sledge island, represents some of the implements used for twisting sinew cords. A full set consists of two flattened ivory rods with a small knob or head at each end, and four bodkin-like ivory rods each with the figure of a deer-head at the upper end. These implements are all pierced with holes and strung

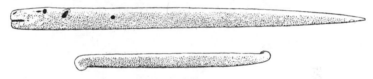

Fig. 30—Sinew twisters (½).

on a rawhide cord in order that they may conveniently be carried and not readily mislaid.

Figure 8, plate XLVIII b, from Cape Vancouver, and figure 5 of the same plate, from Nunivak island, represent reels on which thread is wound. They are sometimes used also as shuttles in making small meshed nets.

Figures 4 and 6, plate XLVIII b, from Nunivak island, are specimens of thread reels carved to represent mythical beings, half woman and half seal, with the hands held against the sides of the faces.

Figures 3 and 7, plate XLVIII b, from the same island, are ivory reels carved to represent seals.

Figure 31 represents a sinew cord spinner from St Lawrence island. This object is made of ivory and consists of three parts; these are a quadrate base for holding in the hand, and pierced in the middle of the outer surface for the insertion of one end of a slender rod having a knob at its other end. A flattened rod is pierced near one end and slipped upon the first-named rod, upon which it revolves. The sinew to be spun is attached to the flattened rod at the shoulder, just below the hole, and by a rapid circular motion of the hand the flattened rod is caused to revolve rapidly, giving the desired twisting to the cord.

No implements of this kind were seen among the Eskimo elsewhere in the region visited, and it is quite possible that the St Lawrence islanders obtained the idea from some of the whaling ships which stop so frequently along their shore.

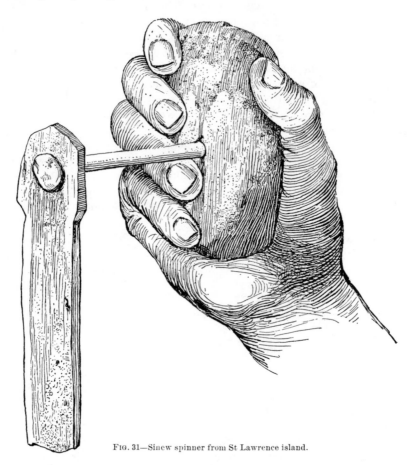

FIG. 31—Sinew spinner from St Lawrence island.

SKIN-DRESSING TOOLS

For dressing and tanning skins several different implements are used, the most important of which are scrapers for cleaning the fat and water from the surface, and polishers for the purpose of softening the hide. From the lower Kuskokwim to the northern part of Norton sound and the coast of Bering strait, stone-blade scrapers with long handles are the prevailing style, although on the coast and islands of Bering strait a short-handle scraper is frequently seen, while from Kotzebue sound northward they are all of the latter type, with the handle made to fit the hand and elaborately carved.

Plate XLIX, 17, from Big lake, represents one of these scrapers of

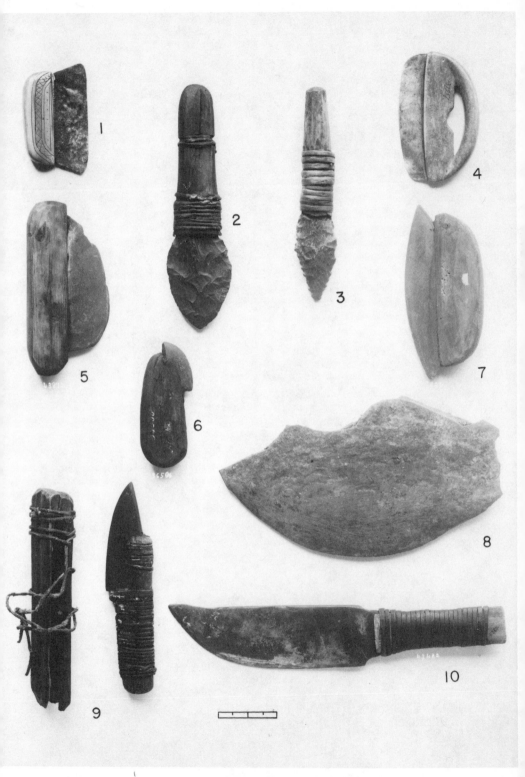

FISH AND SKINNING KNIVES (ONE-THIRD)

hard, green schistose ground to a crescentic edge, fitted to a wooden handle eleven inches in length, which extends downward, overlapping about one-half the length of the blade, and held in place by a rawhide lashing which is prevented from slipping by a ridge along the lower edge of the wood. The upper part of the handle is bent downward for convenience in grasping.

Plate XLIX, 19, from the lower Yukon, is a slate scraper similar in design to the last, with a wooden handle attached by a lashing of spruce root, the upper part bent downward nearly to a right angle.

Plate XLIX, 20, from Nubviukhchugaluk, is a scraper consisting of a chisel-shape blade inserted in a broad wooden handle which overlaps the upper part and is held in position by a lashing of spruce root. On the upper surface of the handle is a groove to receive the forefinger, on the inner side is another groove to receive the thumb, and two grooves on the under surface of the downward-turned end of the handle admit the remaining three fingers.

Plate XLIX, 15, from the lower Yukon, is a short scraper with a wooden handle curved downward to a pistol-like grip, and a heavy blade of black chert ground to a chisel-shape edge, fitted to the handle with an intervening pad of grass. The blade is held in position by means of a strong lashing of spruce root.

Plate XLIX, 12, from the lower Yukon, has a broad, flattened blade of slate, chisel-shape at the edge, with an overlapping wooden handle held in place by a spruce-root lashing. The handle is bent downward to form the grip.

Plate XLIX, 18, from Norton sound, has a large, slate blade with a rounded, chisel-shape edge. It is fitted into a groove in the wooden handle, which is held securely in place by a rawhide lashing. The handle is broad near the blade and narrows gradually to a rounded grip, which is bent abruptly downward; a groove extends along the upper surface, and others, on two sides, below the grip, form a rest for the forefinger and the thumb.

Plate XLIX, 10, from Sledge island, has a flat blade of slate with a rounded edge fitted against a shoulder on the lower surface of the overlapping wooden handle, which has a projecting spur just above the grip, intended to rest between the thumb and the forefinger when the implement is in use.

Plate XLIX, 13, from Cape Prince of Wales, is a small scraper with a flat, chisel-like blade of black slate, held in position against the short oval wooden handle by a rawhide cord. Another scraper from Cape Prince of Wales (number 43405) consists of a rudely chipped flint blade, fitted into a mortise in the rough wooden handle and secured by a lashing of sinew. The upper end of the handle is bent downward and has two grooves on the lower surface to receive the second and third fingers.

Plate XLIX, 11, from Sledge island, has a thin, chisel-shape blade of

18 ETH——8

black slate wedged into a slot in the wooden handle, which is broad near the socket and tapers gradually to the grip, where it is enlarged to form a broad oval to rest in the palm of the hand. A broad groove runs down the front of the handle, and the sides are flattened to form rests for the thumb and the forefinger.

Plate XLIX, 7, from Kotzebue sound, is a short handle for a scraper, made of fossil mammoth ivory, with a slit in its lower end for the insertion of a flint blade. It is hollowed on the lower side of the bent upper portion to receive the thumb. On the outer surface are two grooves for the second and third fingers. The first finger is intended to rest at the base of the blade.

Plate XLIX, 8, from Kowak river, has a chisel-point, chipped flint blade, inserted in a plain handle of fossil mammoth ivory. Another specimen (number 48627), from Kotzebue sound, has a chipped flint blade inserted into a slot in the mammoth ivory handle, which has a groove on the inside for a thumb rest and two on the upper surface for the first and second fingers. A deep slot on the under surface is intended to receive the third and fourth fingers.

Plate XLIX, 14, from Hotham inlet, is a wooden handle larger than that last described, but grooved in the same manner to receive the fingers.

Plate XLIX, 3, also from Hotham inlet, is a short handle of mammoth ivory, with a slot for the insertion of a flint blade. The back of the handle forms a flaring edge intended, when in use, to rest on the under surface of the hand near the base of the thumb, while the first and second fingers are placed in a deep groove in front and the third and fourth fingers lie in a deep excavation on the under surface.

Plate XLIX, 2, from Point Hope, is a handle made from fossil mammoth ivory, with a deep groove on the inside for receiving the thumb, two grooves on the upper surface for the first and second fingers, and an excavation on the lower surface for the third and fourth fingers.

Plate XLIX, 4, from Point Hope, is a scraper consisting of a small flint blade fitted into a handle of mammoth ivory. On the inside is a shallow depression for the reception of the thumb, and another above for the first and second fingers; a deep slot across the lower surface is for the third and fourth fingers.

Plate XLIX, 9, from Point Hope, has a blade of brown flint in a wooden handle, which has a deep slot for the thumb on the inner side, two grooves for the first and second fingers on the upper surface, and a deep excavation below for the third and fourth fingers.

Plate XLIX, 6, from Point Hope, is a very curious specimen, roughly triangular in shape; the chipped flint blade is fitted into a groove in a wooden handle, which has a large blue bead inlaid on the upper part; on the inside is a deep slot for the reception of the point of the thumb; along the front of the top is a deep excavation bordered above by three grooves for the ends of three fingers, and on the outside a hollow for the little finger.

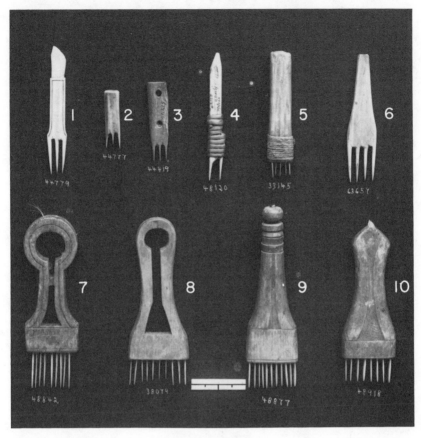

GRASS COMBS

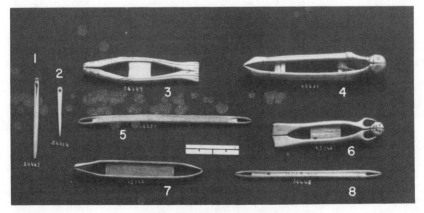

THREAD SHUTTLES AND NEEDLES

THREAD AND CORD MAKING IMPLEMENTS (THREE-TENTHS)

Another form of scraper, used specially for cleaning the skins of birds and small mammals, is somewhat knife-like in shape. Plate L, 5, is a specimen of this type of implement from Nunivak island. It is made of deerhorn with a slightly spoon-shape blade, and has incised parallel lines across the upper side of the handle.

Plate L, 6, from Big lake, is also of deerhorn, and is somewhat similar in shape to the preceding.

Plate L, 3, from Ikogmut, is of ivory. The edge is sharp and across the butt of the handle is a series of notches forming short teeth, which are used in cleaning fat, blood, and other matter from among the feathers or hair of the skins and for softening hard spots. On the lower side of the handle are four round projections, each pierced with a large hole, and on the back etched lines form a conventional pattern.

Plate L, 2, from Norton sound, is another of these ivory knife-like scrapers with a notched butt.

Plate L, 15, from Norton sound, is an ivory scraper generally similar in form to the preceding, but lacking the toothed butt.

Plate L, 1, from St Michael, is of ivory and has a number of small knobs on the handle and a coarsely-toothed butt.

Plate L, 4, from Cape Prince of Wales, also of ivory, has a long, tapering blade and a toothed butt. It has four grooves on the lower side of the handle to form a grip for the fingers.

Plate L, 9, from St Michael, is a ruder implement of this kind, semilunar in shape and with a flat back.

Plate L, 11, from Point Hope, is a tray-shape implement about 4 inches long and 2½ inches wide, deeply excavated inside and with a sharp edge all around the exterior rim. It is used by placing the thumb inside with the fingers grasping the back and pressing either side or end against the skin.

Plate L, 12, is a rudely made scraper from the Diomede islands.

Plate L, 8, from Point Hope, is a scoop-shape scraper made from fossil mammoth ivory; the inside is slightly excavated and the lower edge is sharpened. It is used by placing it in the palm of the hand with the grooved end resting against the inside of the fingers, the convex under surface against the palm, and pushing it from the operator. This is the only implement of this kind that was seen, all the other scoop-shape scrapers being used by drawing toward the person.

Plate L, 7, from Sledge island, is a flat rod of deerhorn beveled to an edge on one side; each end is pierced with two holes in which a strong rawhide cord is fastened, by which the ends are drawn toward each other until they form a horseshoe-shape curve; it is used by grasping the cross cord and drawing the edge of the scraper along the skin toward the operator.

Plate L, 18, from Kotzebue sound, is a scraper made from the shoulderblade of some animal; the butt is sawed down and shaped to serve as a handle; the outer end is also cut off and the thin lower portion cut to a straight edge.

Plate L, 13, from Chalitmut, is a deerhorn scraper with a well shaped upcurved handle, a blade formed like an obliquely truncated half of a spoon, and a sharpened edge.

Plate L, 16, from Sledge island, and figure 17, of the same plate, from the lower Yukon, are sections of deerhorn with one surface flattened and cut to a sharp edge.

Plate L, 14, obtained on St Lawrence island by Captain C. L. Hooper, is a crescent-shape piece of reindeer horn with a sharp edge, flat upon one side and beveled to three surfaces on the other, with a groove running down the center of each.

Plate L, 10, from St Lawrence island, is of ivory, dish-shaped, somewhat oval in outline and nearly straight on the upper or thicker side; the other side is curved and thinned down to a sharp edge. It is used by resting the thumb on the interior and grasping the back with the first and second fingers.

Plate XLIX, 1, obtained by Mr L. M. Turner at St Michael, is a rounded

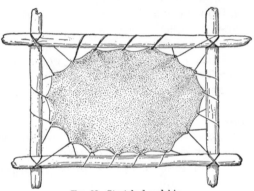

FIG. 32—Stretched sealskin.

bowlder-like piece of granite about 5 inches in its longest diameter for rubbing and softening skins; the lower surface is smoothed and polished by use.

SKIN DRESSING

Among the Eskimo it is customary for the men to dress the skins of large animals such as reindeer, wolves, wolverines, bears, seals, and walrus, while the women prepare the skins of smaller creatures such as fawns, hares, muskrats, marmots, and waterfowl, and sometimes assist the men in the preparation of the larger skins.

In dressing sealskins and walrus hides they are first scraped to free them from the adherent particles of flesh and fat, then rolled into a bundle with the hair side inward and kept in the house or the kashim until they become sour and the hair loosens; small sealskins are sometimes dipped in hot water to hasten the loosening of the hair; the hair is then scraped off and the skin is stretched on a wooden frame, made from sticks of driftwood (figure 32), by stout cords passed through slits around the edges and over the side bars of the frame, when they are again scraped and placed outside the house to dry. When dry they are removed from the frames and folded compactly into flat, oblong packages (figure 33), for convenience in carrying or storing. If the skin is to be tanned with the hair on, for use in making boots or

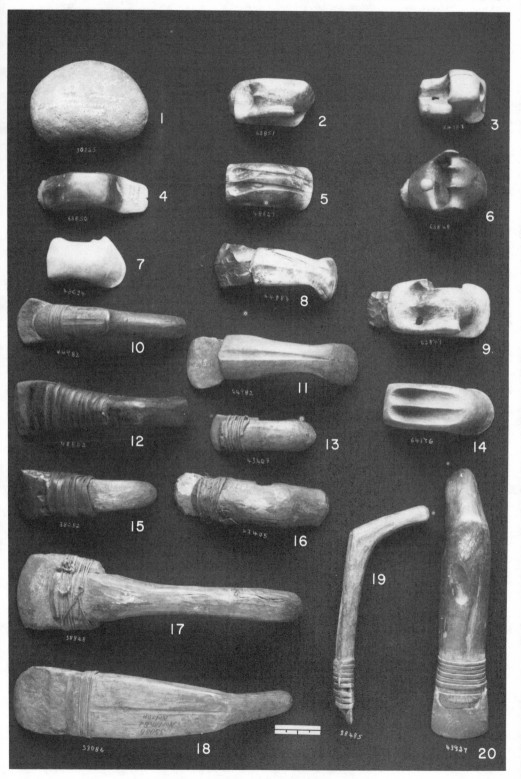

SKIN SCRAPERS (ONE-FOURTH)

clothing, it is soaked thoroughly in urine to remove the fat, then stretched, scraped, and dried in the manner described.

The beautifully white, parchment-like leather used for boots and ornamental work is made from small sealskins from which the hair has been removed. The skin is then soaked in urine to free it from the oil, stretched upon the drying frame and exposed in the open air during the coldest months of winter; the intense cold and the beating of the dry snow upon the surface of the skin bleaches it to a satiny whiteness. A finer quality of white leather is obtained from the gullets of large seals and walrus treated in the same manner. The russet-colored seal-skin, used for ornamental work, is made by washing the surface of this white, parchment-like leather with dye obtained from alder bark.

The skin of the wolf-fish (*Annarrichas lupus*), called *kä-chú-hlúk* by the Eskimo, when stretched and dried makes a thin, blackish, parchment-like material, which is cut into narrow strips and frequently welted into the seams of boots and other articles of clothing, or used for other ornamental purposes. The white woolly skin of the new-born fur seal, after being tanned, is dyed a rich brown by an infusion of alder bark and cut into narrow strips for borders to garments or for making tassels for boots and frocks.

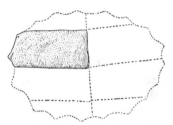

FIG. 33—Method of folding sealskin.

To tan reindeer skin with the hair on, the fleshy side of the skin is wetted with urine; it is then rolled into a compact bundle, with the hair side outward, and permitted to remain a few hours in the warm kashim, after which it is unrolled and any remaining fragments of sinew or flesh are removed with a scraper. It is then dried and again thoroughly scraped and hung up open in the kashim while a fire is burning, and dried until it becomes hard and almost as brittle as pasteboard, when it is taken down and scraped carefully and lightly on the inner side. This breaks the grain of the leather and covers the epidermis at the roots of the hair with numberless little cracks, rendering the skin very pliable. After this treatment the skin is scraped again more thoroughly, and boiled fish eggs, while still warm, are rubbed on the inner surface. It is then rolled up and permitted to lie for a few hours, after which it is unrolled and worked and rubbed between the hands until it becomes dry and soft; a final scraping then removes any remaining roughness or adherent matter and completes the process of tanning. Reindeer skins tanned in this manner are beautifully white on the inside and the leather is as soft and pliable as chamois skin.

Small skins are soaked in urine to remove the fat, after which they are stretched and worked with the hands and finally rubbed with pieces of pumice until dry. Urine is so much used in tanning and for other purposes that every house is provided with one or more tubs in which a constantly renewed supply is kept.

Marmot skins and the skins of muskrats and birds are rubbed and worked in the hands, after which the women use their teeth to chew the harder parts to render them soft; they are then stretched and dried and a slight wash of oil is applied to render them more pliable.

The skins of salmon and losh are dressed and used for making bags, boots, mittens, and waterproof garments by the Eskimo of the lower Yukon. The intestines of seals, cleaned and inflated, are dried, and form a kind of translucent parchment, which is cut into strips and sewed to form the waterproof frocks worn by the men when at sea in the kaiaks or when out on land in rainy weather. These garments will shed water for several hours. Coverings for the smoke holes in roofs of houses and kashims are made of this material, which is used also for covering bedding during transportation or in open camps.

The Eskimo who live away from the coast, lacking the sea animals, use the intestines of deer and bears for similar purposes.

HUNTING AND HUNTING IMPLEMENTS

ANIMAL TRAPS AND SNARES

Owing to the rapid extermination of reindeer in the neighborhood of the coast of Norton sound, the natives depend on hunting the various kinds of seals and on fishing for their main supply of food. For over a hundred miles along that coast, during my residence at St Michael, not a dozen reindeer were killed each year. Twenty years earlier reindeer were extremely numerous throughout the same district, but the introduction of firearms, after the Americans took possession of the country, resulted in a wasteful slaughter by the natives, who soon succeeded in virtually exterminating these animals in the larger portion of the coast region.

Before the introduction of firearms the Eskimo had various ingenious modes of capturing and killing deer. They were stalked in the usual manner by hunters, armed with bows and arrows, who approached the herds by creeping from one shelter to another until within bow shot. At other times two hunters went together, and when a herd of reindeer was seen one of the hunters walked immediately behind the other, so that their two bodies were in contact. Then, while keeping step as one man, they walked directly toward the herd. The deer would permit them to come within a certain distance and then make a wide circuit for the purpose of passing behind the advancing hunters; the man in the rear then took advantage of the first hollow or other shelter to throw himself on the ground and lie hidden while his companion continued onward, apparently without paying the slightest attention to the game; as a result the deer would circle in behind him, and while watching him were almost certain to run within bow shot of the con-

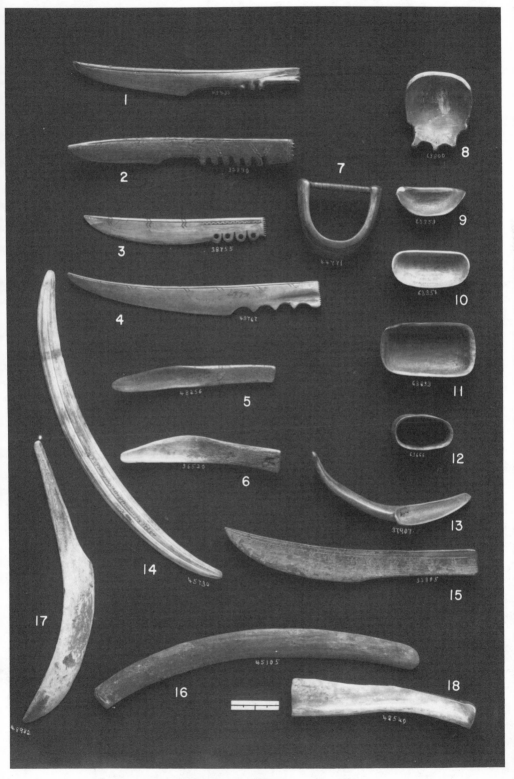

SKIN-CLEANING TOOLS (ONE-FOURTH)

cealed hunter; when they were near enough he would spring up and discharge his arrows; this would distract their attention from the first man, who in the meantime had also concealed himself. In running to escape from the hunter who had just discharged his arrows, the game would frequently circle within shot of the other man and become so confused as to run wildly back and forth, approaching each man in turn several times before the survivors regained their wits sufficiently to make their escape.

Another method was to close the lower end of a rocky pass through which the deer were accustomed to travel, and then make a drive from the open valley and inclose an entire herd at once, when they were killed with lances and arrows. The people said that in cases of this kind they were accustomed to kill every deer thus inclosed, without regard to number, and that frequently such large numbers were killed that they were unable to utilize them, and they were left where they fell.

Deer were also snared with strong nooses of rawhide, which were tied to stout bushes and held open by light strings of grass or sinew connecting them with other bushes, or with small stakes planted in the ground. In feeding, the deer would entangle their antlers or thrust in their heads, so that they were held or strangled by the nooses closing around their necks.

Another method practiced by the young men in early summer, when the fawns were born, was to look for them, and when a fawn only a few days old was found they would run it down. The hunters considered this sport to be a great test of agility and endurance, for instead of shooting the fawn with arrows, as might readily

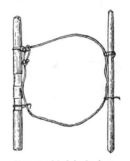

Fig. 34—Model of a deer snare.

have been done, it was a matter of pride to pursue the animal until it became so tired and its feet so tender that it stopped and permitted itself to be captured.

At the time of my visit to Point Barrow in 1881, reindeer were still common in the low mountains to the south and southeast of that place, but it had become very easy to obtain breech loading guns and ammunition from the whalers, and the people were destroying the deer very rapidly. One old man and his son, it was claimed, had nearly five hundred skins in storage, and others had an abundance of them.

Dall's sheep were also killed in large numbers by these people and by the Eskimo of Kowak river, judging from the number of skins seen among them.

Figure 34 shows a model of a deer snare from the lower Yukon; it consists of two straight sticks, to the larger of which the end of the snare is firmly attached, while the outer side of the loop is lightly held by a smaller stick which serves to keep the snare in place.

This method of snaring deer is illustrated in figure 35, which represents a boot-sole creaser from Nushagak. It is etched on three sides, and on the side shown are two reindeer caught in rawhide snares, with another snare still set between them.

The white bear is found only at very rare intervals on the mainland south of Bering strait. A single young white bear was killed a few miles south of St Michael during my residence there, and was said to have been the first one seen in many years. On St Lawrence island they are frequently seen on the ice during winter and spring. The hunters there kill them by concealing themselves among the ice hummocks in the course the bear is pursuing, and as he passes shoot him in the head between the eye and the ear. This spot is chosen on account of the thinness of the skull, as the .44-caliber breech-loading guns which they use have not power enough to kill the bear if shot in any other part. I saw a great many skulls of these animals on the island named, and all of them had bullet holes in the same place.

From Point Hope to Point Barrow bears are not uncommon, and a number of Eskimo living along the coast from Bering strait northward have been frightfully disfigured by encounters with them. A man from Point Hope told me of an encounter with one of these animals

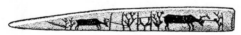

FIG. 35—Etching on ivory, showing deer snares (⅔).

that took place near his village in the winter of 1880. Two men left the village and went out on the sea ice during the night to set their nets for seals; while they were setting the nets, at some distance from each other, one of them heard the snow cracking under the feet of a white bear which was approaching. The hunter was without weapons of any kind, and as it was too dark to see the animal he quietly lay down flat upon his back on the ice, hoping to escape notice. The bear came directly up to him, and stopping, began smelling along his body, until finally he pressed his cold muzzle against the hunter's nose and mouth and sniffed vigorously several times. As he did this the hunter held his breath until his head swam. Suddenly the bear heard the other hunter moving about and raised his head to listen; then he sniffed at the hunter's face again and started off on a trot toward the other man. When the bear had been gone a few moments the prostrate hunter sprang to his feet and fled for his life toward the shore, hearing the death cry of his comrade as he ran. About noon the next day, when the sun came to the horizon, the villagers armed themselves and went out on the ice, accompanied by the wife of the missing hunter. They reached the place at dawn and found the bear still feasting on the hunter's remains. The wife fired the first shot at him, followed by the others, and the bear fell; then the woman drew a hunting knife and rushing at the bear slashed its sides until the skin hung in shreds, when she stopped from exhaustion.

Another man in that region has the scalp and flesh from one side of his head, including one eye, torn away by a stroke from the paw of one of these animals.

Formerly, after bears had been brought to bay by dogs they were killed with stone or iron-pointed lances, and, indeed, the people of the Siberian shore still kill many in this old fashion.

Wolves are killed with guns or arrows or are taken with various kinds of traps; steel traps have been introduced by the traders, but the ancient devices are still sometimes used for both wolves and foxes.

One of the common methods of killing wolves in ancient times, which is still practiced to a slight extent, was by the use of spits made of whalebone. A slender piece of bone, 8 or 9 inches in length and a third of an inch wide is pointed at each end, and, after being softened, is bent upon itself in folds 1½ or 2 inches in length. It is then bound in position by a strip of cord and laid aside until it becomes dry, when it retains the form in which it has been bent. The cord is then taken off and the whalebone is soaked in oil for a short time, then wrapped in tallow, blubber, or sometimes a piece of fish-skin, after which it is placed in a locality frequented by wolves and foxes.

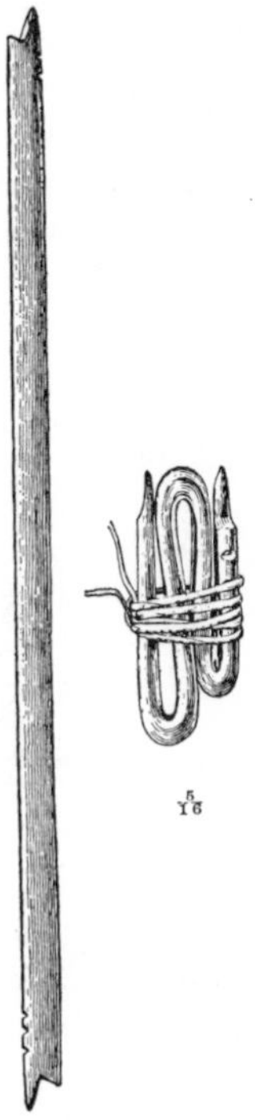

Discovering this morsel the animal begins to devour it, but finding that it is not easily masticated, swallows it entire, doubtless mistaking it for a piece of gristle. When the whalebone becomes warm and is moistened in the stomach, it straightens out and the pointed ends pierce the beast to death or cause such pain that it is soon found and dispatched by the hunter who has followed its trail.

Figure 36 shows examples of this implement both in the folded and extended form; they were obtained at St Michael. Dead falls, used as traps for minks, foxes, and sometimes for larger animals, are made by build-ing a small inclosure of sticks driven into the ground, over the entrance to which a heavy log is supported by an ordinary 4-shape device.

FIG. 36—Game spits.

Plate LI, 6, illustrates a bait spit for use in one of these "4-traps," which was obtained at Port Clarence by Doctor Dall. It consists of a double-pointed bone spit about seven inches in length, with a notch an inch from one point, against which is fastened the end of another bone spit resting against the notch, and projecting at the other end opposite the point of the first named.

Near Andreivsky I saw snares for catching lynxes made by building a dome-shape pile of brush, with one or more narrow openings leading to the bait, which was placed on the ground under the center. At the mouth of each of these openings a rawhide loop was so arranged that the lynx could not reach the bait without getting its head or legs entangled, and as the animal drew back the snare would close and hold it fast.

Another common style of snare was made by setting a noose over a path used by animals and digging a deep hole in the ground below it. To the lower end of the snare a heavy stone was attached, hanging in the mouth of the pit; the upper part of the snare was held open by attaching it by strings to surrounding objects, and a trigger was so arranged that at a touch from a passing animal the stone would be freed and drop into the hole, causing the snare to close and draw the animal's neck down to the ground and hold it fast.

Sometimes a noose was set at the entrance to a tunnel made in the frozen snow, with a bait of meat at the rear end, and in endeavoring to reach this the animals were snared. I was informed that animals as large as reindeer, and even bears, were formerly caught by means of snares, and that they were in general use for taking red and white foxes.

Fig. 37—Fox or wolf trap with sinew spring.

South of the mouth of the Yukon the Eskimo formerly made pits for catching wolves by digging in summer square holes down to the permanently frozen earth, and then making a wall about the sides and grading the earth in a gentle slope up to the outside edge, thus making a pit so deep that no animal could jump out; it was then covered with a frail roof concealed by straw and weeds, with the bait laid on the center. In winter the roof was covered with snow. According to the old men this was the commonest style of trap used in ancient times, and with it many animals were caught.

One of the most ingenious traps found among the Eskimo was one by means of which the tension of a set of strong, twisted sinew cords was used to throw a lever and brain the animal that sprung it. These traps were known to the people from the northern shore of Norton sound to Kotzebue sound; they are not now used on the American coast, as they have been superseded by steel traps, but I was informed that formerly they were in common use.

On St Lawrence island were found many pieces of such traps that were large enough to kill foxes, and from this I conclude that they are still in use in that district. The accompanying sketch (figure 37) from

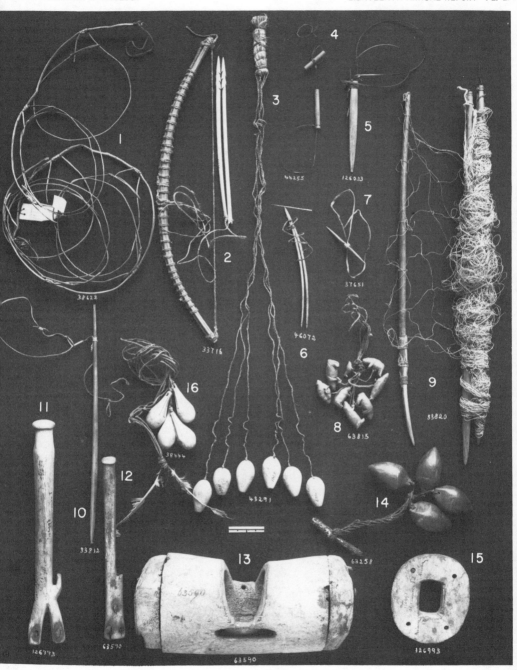

NETS, SNARES, AND TRAPS (THREE-SIXTEENTHS)

a model made by an Eskimo living at the head of Norton sound, shows the parts and illustrates the working of this ingenious contrivance:

1—1 is a cylinder of wood, that material or bone ordinarily being used for these traps; 2—2 are crosspieces of wood or bone, bound together by strong sinew cords; 3 is an ivory or bone block; 4 is an ivory or bone pin, fitting into 3, and is attached to a cord passing through a hole in the cylinder to the bait at 10; 5 is a slot cut through the side of the cylinder; 6 is a stout lever of bone with a knob at its inner end, which is inserted through the cords connecting 2—2; 8 is a pointed spike of bone or ivory (a nail is sometimes used on St Lawrence island); 7 is a peg projecting from the side of the lever. 2—2 are twisted in opposite directions until the twisting of the connecting cords, which pass around them and through the cylinder, causes a strong tension, thus holding the crosspieces so firmly against the ends of the cylinders that they can not slip back. This also draws the cord so taut in the cylinder that when the lever, 6, is drawn back to lie parallel with 9, a great resistance is encountered, acting like a spring to throw it back to its first position. The lever, 6, is held in position next to 9 by passing 4 over 7 and into 3. The bait is tied to the end of a cord attached to 4 at 10, so that it lies just within 8. The trap is then fastened firmly to the ground and concealed with earth, but care is taken to insure the free working of the lever. The bait is then exposed in line with the lever and when a slight pull is given, the pin, 4, is freed and the lever springs sharply over, burying the spike set in its end in the skull of the animal.

These traps work very nicely and strike a heavy blow. They are ordinarily made for killing foxes and wolves, but I was told that formerly they were sometimes used for bears.

Figure 13, plate LI, illustrates a cylinder for one of these traps from St Lawrence island. It is 12 inches long and 5 inches in diameter, and is made from a piece of the jawbone of a whale. It is capped at each end by a ring of bone held in position by four iron nails. A deep notch is cut in the middle of one side of the cylinder, at one end of which is a slot and at the other a round hole through the side.

Figure 11, plate LI, from the same island, is a lever made of bone, forked, and armed at the outer end with iron spikes. The inner end terminates in a rim of bone. This is the striking arm of one of these traps. It has a notch on one side for receiving the trigger. With this arm is a bone ring (plate LI, 15), pierced with four holes, intended for a cap, at one end of the cylinder.

Figure 12, plate LI, from the same island, represents another striking arm for a trap, with three iron spikes set in it.

For trapping beavers in their houses square nets, 4 or 5 feet across, with meshes large enough for the beaver's head to pass through, are fastened over the entrance to the animal's house below the surface of the water, so that in going out or in the animal will become entangled and drown. These nets are sometimes used in the same way for otters.

Hares are snared and netted in spring by setting the nets or snares among the bushes which they frequent, so that they become entangled while moving about, or by setting fine sinew nets in open spaces among the bushes and then making a drive and frightening the animals into them. This method is practiced for taking both the large Arctic hare and the white rabbit.

Parry's marmot is a common animal in many parts of Alaska, particularly about the head of Norton sound and along the shore of Kaviak peninsula. Their skins are highly prized for making light frocks for summer use and form a prominent article of trade among these people. They are best when taken early in spring, soon after the marmots have come out of their holes and while they are still in the soft, grayish winter fur. They are taken in several ways. One method consists of a noose fastened to the end of a willow or alder stick 4 or 5 feet long, with the large end planted firmly in the snow or ground. The small end, having the noose attached to it, is bent down so that the noose hangs just over the marmot's runway in the snow or on the ground, and is held in place by a small cross stick above it, which is hooked under a stick bent across the runway with its ends thrust into the ground. It is fastened so lightly that as the animal passes a touch releases the trigger and the bent stick springs up and catches it.

Figure 4, plate LI, is an example of this style of snare from Cape Darby. The noose is made of whalebone, and is passed through a small wooden cylinder, which causes it to run freely and at the same time helps to hold it in position.

Similar nooses were obtained from the head of Kotzebue sound with the cylinders made from the hollow wing-bones of birds. In these latter a hole is made in one side of the bone at the lower end, in which is tied the end of a fine rawhide line. This line passes up through the cylinder, and has a small, round block of wood tied crosswise at the other end of the cylinder.

Figure 38 is another style of marmot trap, from the head of Norton sound, made from a cylinder of wood a little over eight inches in length. The cylinder is made in two parts, fastened together by means of a willow-bark lashing through holes made along the line of junction on both sides. A slot is cut through the upper side and a deep groove runs around the inside from it, and there are two holes near the other end. A strong running noose, made from feather vane or whalebone, is inserted through the upper slot and lies concealed within the groove on the inside. At the upper end of the noose is a sinew cord, which is attached to a bent stick having one end planted firmly in the ground and held in position by a strand of willow bark tied to it, passed down through the two holes in the cylinder, and knotted on the under side. As the animal comes out of a hole or along a runway, where the trap is set, it enters the cylinder, and finding the passage barred by the strand of willow bark across the end, bites it off. This releases the bent stick, which flies up and draws the concealed noose taut about the animal's body and holds it against the upper side of the cylinder until it is strangled or the trapper comes to remove it.

Among the people living to the south of the Yukon mouth thousands of muskrats and minks are caught every fall and winter in small wicker fish traps, such as are used for taking the blackfish (*Dallia*). These traps are set in creeks and small rivers, beneath the ice, with a close wicker or brush fence extending as wings from either side and completely shutting off the stream except at the opening occupied by the funnel-shape mouth of the trap. In this way from ten to twenty mink have been known to be taken in a single day. The traps are completely submerged, and, of course, when the animals swim into them they are unable to rise to the surface, and quickly drown. At

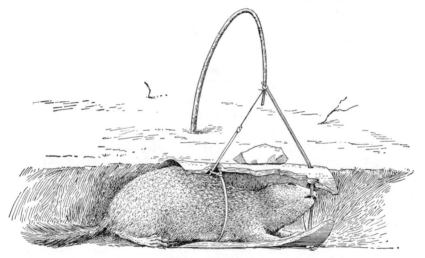

Fig. 38—Marmot trap.

times animals even as large as the land otter enter these traps and are taken.

The skins of minks, muskrats, and marmots are taken off, by a slit between the hind legs, and dried on stretchers, with the flesh side outward. The stretchers are made by fastening together two long, slender sticks by means of crossbars, which permit them to be brought together by a hinge-like motion and pushed into the inside of the skin; they are then spread, thus stretching the skin and holding it until it is dry. This contrivance and the "figure-4" dead-fall were probably introduced by white men.

Land otters and beavers are taken at their holes by means of steel traps.

The hunting of fur-bearing animals of all descriptions commences with the first heavy frost of autumn and continues until the short cold days of midwinter. Then a period of cessation ensues until February, when the hunting and trapping are resumed and continued until the sun in April renders the fur too harsh and brittle to be of value.

The hunting of seals, whales, and walrus is conducted in a variety of ways, according to the season.

Each year about the first of September the hunters on the coast of Norton sound begin to overhaul their seal nets, repair broken or weak places, and rig them with sinkers and floats. The nets used are from 10 to 15 fathoms in length and from 1½ to 2 fathoms in depth, made from rawhide, with a mesh large enough to admit easily the head of a seal; they are buoyed with wooden floats, or sometimes with inflated bladders; the floats are frequently made in the form of sea fowls or the heads of seals. The lower side of the net is strung with sinkers of stone, bone, or ivory, and is anchored at each end by a large stone tied with a heavy rawhide cord. These nets work precisely like the gill nets used for salmon fishing, and are very effective.

By the middle of September fur seals of two or three species begin to come in shore and pass about the rocky points or around reefs which guard the entrances to the bays and coves which they are in the habit of entering. The nets are watched by the owners, and when a seal is caught the hunter goes out in his kaiak and brains it with a club or stone, fashioned for the purpose; then if the net has been damaged it is repaired and reset.

During the dark nights of midwinter seals are netted beneath the ice. The blowholes of the seals are located during the day; at night the hunters go out and make four holes in the ice, in the form of a square, at equal distances from the seal hole; a square net is then placed under the ice by means of a long pole and a cord, so arranged as to cover the access to the hole from below, and held in place by cords passing up through the holes in the ice. When the seal rises to breathe it becomes entangled in the net and is captured. This method of netting is common from Bering strait to Point Barrow.

Another method of netting seals through the ice was observed on the shore between Bering strait and St Michael. In swimming along the shore the seals are obliged to pass near the rocky points and headlands. Taking advantage of this, the hunters make a series of holes through the ice at intervals of from 10 to 15 feet, and then, by use of a pole a little longer than the distance between the holes, a stout sealskin line is passed along from hole to hole until the cord is run out to the distance desired, and is used to drag the long net below the ice. Sinkers are fastened to the lower edge of the net, and it is held in position at each end by a stout cord tied to a crossbar at the hole or to a stake set in the ice. While swimming beneath the ice during the night the seals become entangled in the net and drown.

For light sinkers on these nets, long, pointed, ivory weights are used by the people from the northern end of Norton sound to the coast of Bering strait.

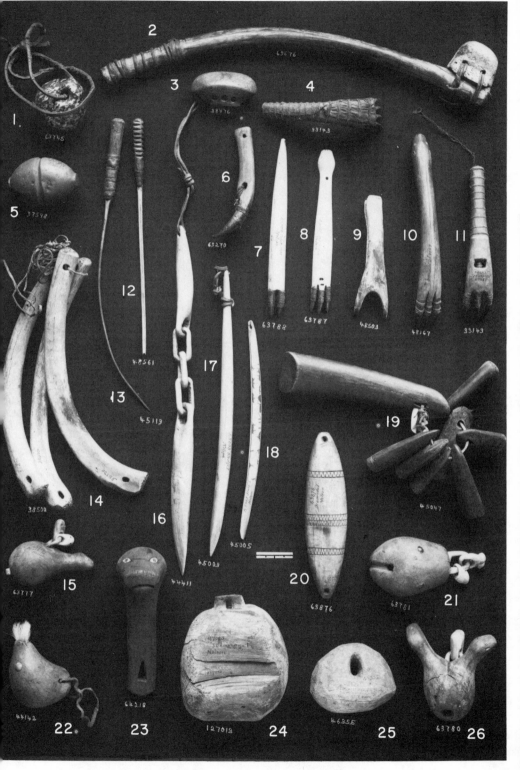

BRAINING CLUBS AND SEAL-CAPTURING IMPLEMENTS (ONE-FIFTH)

Figure 17, plate LII, is an example of one of the ivory sinkers from Sledge island; it is long, rounded, and tapers from the middle toward each end.

Figure 16, plate LII, from Cape Nome, is another sinker of this description, made from a walrus tusk, with three links in the middle.

Figure 18, plate LII, is a light ivory sinker, from Sledge island, with etchings on its surface representing boats and houses.

Figure 2, plate LII, from Cape Espenberg, is a club used for killing seals; it has a rounded, curving, wooden handle, with a rawhide cord wound around it to afford a good grip. A rounded knob of bone, grooved to fit against the side of the handle, is fastened to the head by a lashing passing through two holes and around a groove at the back.

Figure 5, plate LII, from the head of Norton sound, is an oval braining stone, having a groove around the middle and the ends brought down to a truncated point. This stone is used on the end of a stout cord, which is fastened firmly about the groove.

Figure 1, plate LII, from Point Hope, is a braining stone of mottled black and white color, roughly oval in outline, with a hole pierced through one end, in which is fastened a stout rawhide loop, by means of which the hunter swings the stone and brings it down upon the head of the animal.

Figure 3, plate LII, from Kigiktauik, is an oval bone head for a braining club, with a prominent ridge along the face and truncated on the back; it is provided with three holes, by means of which it is lashed to the handle.

Figure 23, plate LII, from the Diomede islands, is a float for a seal net, with a long, flattened handle, oval in cross section and pierced at the lower end for attachment to the net cord.

Figure 22, plate LII, from Cape Nome, is a float in the shape of a seal head, with blue beads inlaid for eyes and tufts of hair inserted on each side of the nose to represent bristles. A hole is pierced through the neck, through which the cord is passed for fastening it to the net.

Figure 15, plate LII, from Point Hope, is a curiously made float representing a seal, with a rounded body, terminating at the rear in an ivory ring for attachment of a cord; on the back a larger ivory ring is inserted and held in place by a wooden pin. In this ring are linked two ivory pendants, having upon their outer surfaces incisions representing the eyes, nostrils, and mouth of an animal, probably a seal. The eyes of the seal in the head of the float are represented by inlaid white beads.

Figure 21, plate LII, represents the head of a seal, with the eyes formed by inlaid blue beads. A large bone ring is inserted in the mouth, from which hang two ivory pendants.

Figure 26, plate LII, represents a double-head seal, with a hole made through the wood on the back end for the attachment of the cord, and an ivory pin, with a single link pendant, inserted in the breast.

Figure 25, plate LII, is a rudely oval, wooden net float, pierced on one side. It is from Icy cape.

Figure 24, plate LII, from St Lawrence island, is a wooden net float, somewhat rounded in outline, with an ear on one side, which is pierced with a hole for the attachment of the line.

Figure 14, plate LII, from St Michael, are specimens, made from walrus ribs, of a class of implements which serve a double purpose; they are used as sinkers and as handles for hauling in the seal or beluga nets.

Figure 20, plate LII, from one of the Diomede islands, is an elongated oval sinker for a seal net, made of walrus ivory; it is surrounded with etched bands of zigzag pattern.

About the end of February the Eskimo from Bering strait southward begin to hunt seals at the outer edge of the shore ice, where the leads are open at that season. On the 28th of February, 1880, I met a party of people on their way from the head of Norton bay to Cape Darby, where they were going to hunt seals on the ice until spring opened.

At midnight on March 28, the same season, I reached a village on the northern shore of Norton sound as a party of seal hunters came in from the outer edge of the ice, bringing several fine, large hair seals. The entire village was up awaiting their return, and we were cordially welcomed to the ensuing feast, which lasted until well into the morning. The entrails and other parts of the viscera were cooked and passed around as special delicacies, while the people of the village who had come to share in the feast assisted in dressing the animals.

At this season, also, the people about St Michael begin their usual spring hunting upon the ice. They leave their village, hauling their kaiaks, spears, guns, and other implements on small, light sledges made specially for the purpose. Whenever open water is to be crossed the kaiak is launched, the sled placed upon it, and the hunter paddles to the opposite side, where he resumes his journey upon the ice. The method of obtaining seals at this time is by the hunter concealing himself on the ice close to the water, and from this point of vantage shooting or spearing them as they swim along the edge. Sometimes a seal is shot or speared while lying asleep on the ice.

When the ice breaks up, so that there is much open water, with scattered floes and cakes of varying size, the hunters make long hunts in their kaiaks, searching for places where the seals have hauled up onto the ice.

On the 10th of May, one season, I met a party of Eskimo between Pastolik, near the Yukon mouth, and St Michael. They had umiaks of ordinary size on sleds, drawn by dogs, and were going with their families to the outer edge of St Michael island to hunt seals, planning to return to the Yukon mouth in the umiaks when the ice had left the coast.

During the early spring months the small hair seals come up through holes in the ice to be delivered of their young. These holes are sometimes covered by the hunter with an arch of snow, and the seals are surprised and speared as they come up. When stalking these seals as they lie sleeping or sunning themselves on the ice, the hunter wears a pair of knee protectors made of white bear or white dog skin, which reach from just above the knee to the ankle, and have the long shaggy fur outward. They are secured upon the leg by strings along their edges, like a legging, but they do not inclose the leg in the rear. A huge mitten of the same skin, reaching from the hand to a little above the elbow, is also worn on the left arm. Armed with a spear, which has a long line fastened to a detachable point, the hunter approaches erect as near to the seal as is prudent, then lies flat upon the ice and places his bent left arm before him so that the huge fur mitten forms a shield between him and the seal. The fur hood is raised over his head, so that the long border of gray or whitish fur blends with the mitten. The color of the fur harmonizes so well with that of the snow that the hunter can creep to within the desired distance of the seal without being detected. He is always careful to keep his body flat and in a direct line behind the mitten, and trails his gun or spear behind him with his right hand until near enough to make sure of his aim. When stalking a seal in this manner the hunter carries a small wooden scratcher, consisting of a neatly carved handle, tipped with seal claws. If the seal becomes uneasy or suspicious, the hunter pauses, and with this implement scratches the snow or ice in the same manner and with the same force as a seal while digging a hole in the ice. Hearing this the seal seems satisfied and drops asleep again. This is repeated, if necessary, until the hunter is within reach of the animal, when he drives his spear into it, braces himself, and holds fast to the line. If close to a hole, the seal struggles into it. By holding the line the hunter prevents its escape, and the animal soon drowns and is hauled out. Of late years guns are commonly used for this class of hunting, and the seal is shot through the head, so that it remains on the ice.

On the Diomede islands I obtained a typical pair of white bear skin knee protectors, having a triangular piece of sealskin sewed on their upper edge to extend above the knee, along the leg, and provided with a cord which extends thence up to the waist belt of the hunter.

Figure 7, plate LII, from Point Hope, is an ivory-handle scratcher with a ring in the upper end; the handle is crescentic in cross section. The lower end is divided into two parts, on which two claws are held firmly in position by a sinew lashing.

Figure 8, plate LII, from Point Hope, is a similar scratcher with an ivory handle, and with three claws fitted on the lower end in the same manner as in the preceding specimen. The upper end of the handle is carved to represent the head of a seal.

Figure 9, plate LII, from St Michael, is a very ancient scratcher obtained in the ruins of an old village. It is made of reindeer horn and has two points forming a Y-shape end, on which the seal claws

18 ETH——9

were fitted. The handle has a groove around it for the sinew cord that served to hold the claws in place.

Figure 6, plate LII, from St Lawrence island, is a small scratcher with a wooden handle, and with three large claws upon the tip, which are held in position in the usual manner by sinew cords.

Figure 11, plate LII, from Norton sound, is a wooden-handle scratcher with three claws fastened in position by fine sinew cords passed through a hole in the handle. The upper end of the handle is bound with sinew cords to afford a firm grip, and a loop of similar cord is fastened to the butt for suspending the implement from the wrist.

Figure 10, plate LII, from Cape Prince of Wales, is a handsomely made scratcher with a long wooden handle, having three claws on the lower end, attached in the usual manner. The handle is carved on both sides, above and below, and terminates in the image of a white bear's head, having blue beads inlaid for eyes.

Figure 4, plate LII, from St Michael, is a rather rudely made scratcher, with a wooden handle having four claws at the tip, held in position by a strip of rawhide pierced with four holes and drawn over the claws, with a flap extending back on the handle and bound by a cord lashing.

Another method of approaching seals on the ice is by the hunter covering a light framework with white sheeting and placing it upon a kaiak sled in such a way as to conceal himself and the sled, which he pushes cautiously before him until he is within range and shoots the seal with a rifle. Should he not be provided with a rifle, he uses a spear, but approaches near enough to be sure of the cast and then fixes the barb firmly in the animal's body.

After having killed a seal at sea the hunter is sometimes able, if the seal be small, to drag it upon the kaiak and thrust it inside; but if it be large this is impossible, and he is compelled to tow it to the shore or to the nearest ice, where it can be cut up and stowed in the interior of the kaiak. The towline is made fast to the animal by cutting slits in the skin through which cords are passed, or the flippers are tied together by cords and drawn against the body and a cord passed through a slit in the upper lip and the head drawn down on the breast. In order to pass the cord between the slits in the skin without difficulty, small, slender bone or ivory probes are sometimes used, having a notch at the upper end and a groove along both sides. The cord is looped and placed over the notched end; the hunter holds the two ends in his hands and passes the doubled cord through from one slit in the skin to another.

Figure 12, plate LII, represents an implement of this kind obtained on Kotzebue sound. It is of deerhorn, with a wooden handle fastened on by sinew cords and heavily grooved on four sides to enable the holder to secure a firm grip.

During the winter and late in the fall seals are usually fat enough to float when killed in the water, but in spring, and sometimes at other seasons, they are so thin that they sink and the hunter loses them.   To insure their floating while being towed, it is a common practice to make slits in the skin at various points and, with a long pointed instrument of deerhorn, to loosen the blubber from the muscle for a space of a foot or more in diameter.   Then, by use of a hollow tube, made from the wing-bone of a bird or from other material, air is blown in and the place inflated; wooden plugs are then inserted in the slits and driven in tightly to prevent the air from escaping.   By the aid of several such inflated spots the seal is floated and the danger of losing it is avoided.

Figure 13, plate LII, from Sledge island, is one of the probes used for loosening the blubber in the manner described.   It consists of a long, curved rod of deerhorn, round in cross section and pointed at the top. It is set in a slit made in the round wooden handle and held in position by means of a lashing of spruce root.   A similar instrument was obtained at Cape Nome.

Figure 19, plate LII, from Sledge island, shows a set of eight of the described wooden plugs, flattened oval in cross section.   They are fashioned to a thin, rounded point at one end and are broad and truncated at the other, giving them a wedge shape.

During the latter part of August and early part of September nets are set near rocky islets or reefs to catch white whales.   These nets are similar to those intended for seals, except that they have larger meshes and are longer and wider.   Whales enter them and are entangled exactly as fish are caught in gill nets, and, being held under water by the weight of heavy anchor stones, are drowned and remain until the hunter makes his visit to the net.   As these nets are set so far from shore that it is impossible to observe them from the land, a daily visit is made in a kaiak to inspect them.   Sometimes white whales are captured in seal nets near the shore, but this occurs only once or twice in a season.   Occasionally a school of these whales, while swimming in company, encounter one of these nets set for them and by their united strength tear it to pieces and escape.

BIRD SNARES AND NETS

The Eskimo have various ingenious methods of taking ptarmigan and water fowl.   During the winter small sinew snares are set among the bushes where the ptarmigan resort to feed or to rest.   Sometimes little brush fences are built, with openings at intervals in which the snares are set so that the birds may be taken when trying to pass through.   Figure 10, plate LI, illustrates one of these snares, from Norton sound.   It consists of a stake nearly 14 inches in length, having a rawhide running noose attached to its upper end by a sinew lashing; a twisted sinew cord about a foot in length serves to attach the snare and stake to the trunk or branch of an adjacent bush.

As spring opens the male birds commence to molt and the brown summer plumage appears about their necks. At this time they become extremely pugnacious and utter loud notes of challenge, which so excite other males within hearing that desperate battles ensue. The birds occupy small knolls or banks of snow, which give them a vantage point from which to look over the adjacent plain. If, when on his knoll, the male ptarmigan hears another uttering his call within the area he considers his own he flies to the intruder and fiercely attacks him. This habit is taken advantage of by the Eskimo, who stuff the skin of one of these birds rudely and mount it upon a stick which holds the head outstretched. This decoy is taken to the vicinity of one of the calling males, and it is planted on a knoll or snowdrift so that it forms a conspicuous object. The hunter then surrounds it with a finely made net of sinew cord supported by slender sticks. Both netting and sticks are pale yellow in color, and are scarcely discernible at a short distance. The hunter then conceals himself close by and imitates the challenge note; the bird hears it and flies straight to the spot. As he flies swiftly along within a few feet of the ground he sees his supposed rival, dashes at him, and is entangled in the net. The hunter secures him, after which he carries the decoy and the net to the vicinity of another bird.

Figure 9, plate LI, illustrates one of these fine-meshed ptarmigan nets, from St Michael. It is made of sinew cord, and is about 16 feet in length. At each end it has a wooden spreader, in the form of a round stake, about 18 inches in length, tapering at the lower end, to which a deerhorn point is securely lashed. In the middle of the net is a similar wooden spreader.

In the collection from Cape Prince of Wales is a similar but stronger sinew net (number 43354) having the two end spreaders and three wooden sticks for use along the middle of the net for holding it in position.

Once when hunting near the Yukon mouth in the month of May, while patches of snow still covered the ground in places, I saw my Eskimo companion decoy ptarmigan by molding some soft snow into the form of a bird; around the part representing the neck he placed a bunch of brown moss to imitate the brown plumage. This image was placed on a small knoll; from a short distance the imitation of a ptarmigan was excellent and the hunter succeeded in calling up several birds that were in the vicinity. He told me that hunters used to call the birds in this manner to shoot them with arrows when they were hunting on the tundra and had no food.

After the first snow of winter great flocks of ptarmigan migrate southward across the Kaviak peninsula and resort to the valleys of Yukon and Kuskokwim rivers for the winter. They fly mainly at night, and usually begin to move just as it is becoming dusk, when it is still possible to distinguish objects at a distance of 75 or 100 yards. A favorite direction for these flights is down the valleys of the rivers flowing southward into Norton bay.

When the migrating season commences the people take advantage of it to capture the birds with salmon nets. Each net is from 50 to 100 feet in length and is spread open by wooden rods; a man or a woman at each end and another in the middle holds the net flat on the ground; when a flock of ptarmigan come skimming along within two or three feet of the ground, the net is suddenly raised and thrown against and over the birds, so as to cover as many as possible. The persons at the ends hold the net down, while the one in the middle proceeds to wring the necks of the captured birds. After throwing them to one side the net is again placed in position. In this manner a hundred birds or more are sometimes captured in a few minutes.

Gulls are taken about the northern shore of Norton sound and the coast of Bering strait by means of bone or deerhorn barbs, pointed at both ends and having a sinew or rawhide cord tied in a groove around the middle, the other end of the cord being fastened to any suitable object that will serve as an anchor; or a long line is anchored at both ends and floated on the surface of the water with barbs attached to it at intervals. Each barb is slipped lengthwise down the throat of a small fish which serves as bait. As the gulls in their flight see the dead fish floating on the water they seize and swallow them; when they attempt to fly away the barbs turn in their throats and hold them fast.

Figure 7, plate LI, represents one of these barbs made of deerhorn; it was obtained from Norton sound.

Along the northern coast of Norton sound the people gather the eggs of sea fowl from the cliffs by means of seal nets, which they roll into a cable and lash in that shape with cords; the nets are then lowered over the cliffs and the upper ends firmly fastened to rocks or stakes. The egg gatherer fastens a sash about his waist, removes his boots, and goes down the net, hand over hand, to the ledges below, the meshes of the net forming excellent holding places for the fingers and toes; the hunter then fills the inside of his frock above the sash with the eggs and climbs to the top of the cliff.

In a camp at Cape Thompson, on the Arctic coast, I saw many dead murres which had been caught by letting a man down by a long line from the top of the cliff to the ledges where the birds were breeding; there he used a scoop net and caught as many birds as he wished by putting it over them while they sat stupidly on their eggs.

On the islands of Bering strait the people catch great numbers of auklets with scoop nets, and also by placing the rudely stuffed skin of one of the birds on a rocky ledge and a fine-mesh net or snare about it. These birds swarm around the rocky cliffs like bees and continually alight near each other, so that the hunter has only to place the snares in position and come out of concealment to take the birds as they are caught.

Figure 5, plate LI, illustrates one of these snares from St Lawrence island. It consists of a wooden stake, about five inches in length, having about its upper end a wrapping of whalebone which secures the middle of another strip of whalebone extending outward about a foot in each direction, each end of which is made into a running noose.

Figure 1, plate LI, represents a set of snares, from Big lake, used for catching ducks or other wild fowl about the borders of grassy lakes. It consists of a strong spruce root, three or four feet in length, with a rawhide cord fastened to each end, by which it is firmly attached to stakes. Spaced at regular intervals along this root are eight running nooses, also made of spruce root, spliced by one end to the main root, leaving a point projecting outward about two inches, which serves to hold the noose open. The snares are set just above the surface of the water across the small openings in the floating grass and weeds, and as the birds attempt to pass through they are caught. Similar snares of whalebone were obtained along the shore of Norton sound, and thence northward to Kowak river and Kotzebue sound.

An ordinary sling, consisting of a strip of leather in the middle and two long strings at each end, for casting a stone, is used among the Eskimo from the mouth of the Yukon to Kotzebue sound for killing birds. A compound sling or bolas is used for catching birds by the people of the coast from Unalaklit to Kotzebue sound, the islands of Bering strait, St Lawrence island, and the adjacent Siberian coast. It is used but little by the people around the northern end of Norton sound, but in the other districts mentioned it is in common use. These implements have from four to eight braided sinew or rawhide cords, varying from 24 to 30 inches in length, united at one end, where they are usually bound together with a tassel of grass or fine wood shavings; at the free end of each cord is a weight of bone, wood, or ivory, usually in the form of an oval ball, but occasionally it is carved into the form of an animal, as in the specimen from Point Hope, illustrated in figure 8, plate LI, which has ivory weights representing five white bears, a bird, and a seal. Another example, from Nulukhtulogumut, shown in figure 16, plate LI, has four pear-shape ivory balls, with raven totem marks etched upon their surfaces at the lower ends of the rawhide cords; to the united upper ends are attached two white gull feathers to guide the implement in its flight. The specimen represented in figure 14, plate LI, which was obtained at St Lawrence island, has four oval wooden balls united by a braided sinew cord; another from Port Clarence, shown in figure 3 of the same plate, has six oval balls of bone attached to sinew cords.

When in search of game the bolas is worn wound around the hunter's head like a fillet, with the balls resting on the brow. When a flock of ducks, geese, or other wild fowl pass overhead, at an altitude not exceeding 40 or 50 yards, the hunter by a quick motion untwists the sling. Holding the united ends of the cords in his right hand, he seizes the balls with the left and draws the cords so tight that they lie parallel to each other; then, as the birds come within throwing

ST MICHAEL HUNTER CASTING A SEAL SPEAR

distance, he swings the balls around his head once or twice and casts them, aiming a little in front of the flock. When the balls leave the hand they are close together, the cords trail behind, and they travel so swiftly that it is difficult to follow their flight with the eye. As they begin to lose their impetus they acquire a gyrating motion, and spread apart until at their highest point they stand out to the full extent of the cords in a circle four or five feet in diameter; they seem to hang thus for a moment, then, if nothing has been encountered, turn and drop to the earth. While in the air the cords do not appear to interfere with each other, but when the sling reaches the ground the cords will be found to be interwoven in a perfect network of entanglement; if a bird is struck it is enwrapped by the cords and its wings so hampered that it falls helpless.

It is curious to note the quickness with which this implement changes its course if one of the balls encounters any obstruction. At Cape Wankarem I saw the Chukchi capture many eider ducks by its aid, and frequently saw one of the extended balls or its cord touch a duck, when the other balls appeared as if endowed with intelligence; their course was rapidly changed, and the bird enwrapped as completely as if it had been struck squarely by the sling. Owing to the space covered by these implements they are very effective when cast among a flock of birds. They are used mostly on low points over which waterfowl fly at certain hours of the day.

The Eskimo of the Yukon delta and the low country to the southward make drives of waterfowl on the marshes during August, when the old birds have molted their wing-feathers and the young are still unable to fly. Salmon nets are arranged by means of stout braces and stakes to form a pound with wings on one side; the people form a long line across the marsh and, by shouting and striking the ground with sticks as they advance, drive the birds before them toward the pound. As they approach it, the line of people converge until they reach the wings, and the birds, thus inclosed, are driven in and killed with sticks. Thousands of downy young are thus slaughtered and thrown away, while umiaks are filled with the larger or adult birds. One of the fur traders told me that he witnessed a drive of this kind where about a ton of young birds were killed and thrown aside, while several umiaks were loaded with the larger birds, among which were many varieties of ducks and geese. These drives and the constant egg gathering that is practiced every spring are having their effect in rapidly diminishing the number of waterfowl in this district.

SEAL SPEARS

The ordinary types of weapons used for spearing seals from a kaiak vary from 4 to 4½ feet in length. They have a light wooden shaft, rounded or slightly oval in cross section, of about the same size from butt to point, with a long, rounded head of bone or ivory having a hole in the tip in which is fitted a wooden socket with an oval slot, to receive the wedge-shape base of a detachable barbed point of bone or deerhorn. The heads of some of these spears are shaped into rounded, tapering points, which are inserted in the ends of the wooden shafts; in others the heads have deep, wedge-shape slots in which the beveled ends of the shafts are fitted, and have a small shoulder at their upper ends to prevent the lashings from slipping. In all instances the heads are held firmly in position by strong lashings of braided sinew cord, which sometimes extends up the shaft in a long spiral, with from one to three bands of wrapping at the upper end, inclosing the quills of feathers placed near the butt, the other ends of the feathers being inserted in deep slits in the shaft, as are also the ends of the sinew cord, to hold the wrappings in position. The ivory points for these spears are from an inch to three inches in length, and have two or three barbs along each side, with the points and edges formed by four beveled faces, and are pierced near the base to receive a sealskin cord which connects them with the hafts. When the spear is thrown, the barbed point, when imbedded in the animal, is immediately detached from the head of the shaft, to which it remains attached only by the sealskin cord which has been wrapped around the shaft; as it unwinds the shaft of the spear is drawn crosswise after the retreating animal, and serves as a drag to exhaust its strength and render it more easily overtaken by the hunter. The method most frequently used, however, is to attach to the barbed point a line about 3½ feet in length, which is divided at about two-thirds of its length into two ends, which are attached to the shaft about two feet apart, a little nearer to the head than to the butt, and are then wound tightly about the shaft. Plate LIII, drawn from a photograph, illustrates the attitude of a St Michael man casting a seal spear from a kaiak.

Figure 2, plate LIV, from Unalaklit, is made with the head, point, and lashings placed upon the hafts in the usual manner, but the butt is without feathering.

Figure 4, plate LIV, a typical spear of this class, from Norton sound, has on the butt three feathers from a cormorant's tail, but is otherwise very similar in its finish to the one just described.

Figure 3, plate LIV, from St Michael, is a spear having an ivory head fitted upon the shaft by means of a slot. The barbed point is attached to the shaft by a line about 16 inches long, fastened just above the lashing which binds the head to the shaft.

Figure 5, plate LIV, from Big lake, has an ivory head, roughly triangular in cross section, with angles rounded and the butt cut down to a smaller size and inserted in a slot on the end of the wooden shaft, which is attached to the head by a rawhide lashing passed through a hole in the shaft and in the adjoining part of the head. Outside of this the usual sinew lashing holds the shaft firmly over the end of the head.

Figure 6, plate LIV, from Cape Vancouver, is another spear, with a double-feathered butt and an ivory head carved at the end to represent

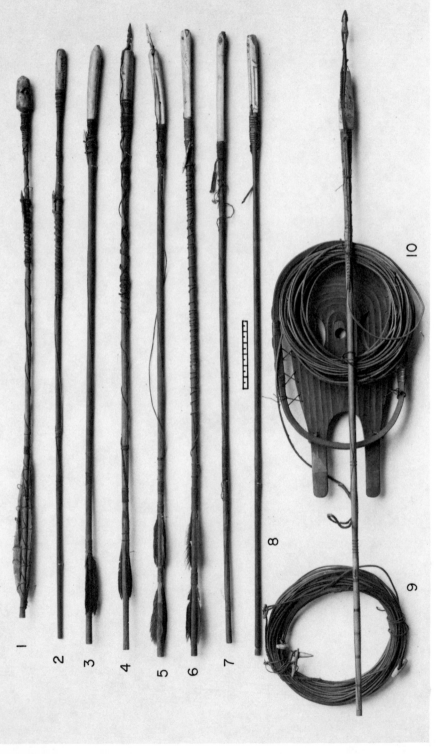

SMALL SEAL SPEARS AND LINES (ABOUT ONE-EIGHTH)

the head of an otter. The inner end of the head has a wedge-shape slot, in which the beveled point of the shaft is fitted; in the base of the head is a hole through which a rawhide lashing is passed and wound tightly around the projecting sides of the slot, holding the head firmly against the shaft. A braided sinew cord is also wound about the shaft from the head to the butt, where the featherings are held in place by a tight wrapping.

All the small spears with featherless shafts which were collected came from the shores of Norton sound; those with single feathering were obtained between Bering strait and the Kuskokwim, and those with the double feathering from Nunivak island and the adjacent mainland at Cape Vancouver, Chalitmut, and other villages of that district.

These spears are the lightest weapons of this character used by the Alaskan Eskimo, and serve mainly for the capture of the smaller seals. Throwing-sticks are in general use for casting them.

Figure 1, plate LIV, from Nunivak island, is an example of another style of seal spear intended to be used with a throwing-stick; the head is short and thick and the feathered butt of the shaft has attached to it a bladder float, over which is a light netting of twisted sinew cord.

WALRUS AND WHALE SPEARS

For taking the larger and more vigorous seals, walrus, and white whales, a spear of about the same size and length is used in connection with a float and float-board. The dragging of the shaft against the water, in the kind of spears just described, is sufficient for retarding the flight of the smaller seals after they are struck, but for the larger animals the greater resistance of a large float on a long line is required. This latter style of implement is in use from Kotzebue sound to Bristol bay. The haft is not feathered, and the head is rather longer and slightly heavier than that on ordinary spears of the class just described. The heads are of ivory or bone, and, in the region about Nunivak island and the adjacent mainland, are commonly carved into the conventional forms of wolves or land otters.

Figure 7, plate LIV, from Nunivak island, is such a spear, with the end of the head carved to represent the head of a land otter, with blue beads inlaid for eyes.

Figure 8, plate LIV, from the lower Kuskokwim, is a spear with the shaft carved to represent the conventionalized form of a wolf. The ivory head has a wedge shape point by which it is fitted to the shaft, and is bound firmly in place by a spruce-root lashing in place of the usual sinew or sealskin cord.

Figure 10, plate LIV, from the Yukon mouth, is a spear with the float line and board attached. The barbed ivory point has a triangular iron tip inserted in a slot, and is united to the head by a rod of deer-horn inserted in a hole in its lower end. The point is pierced through the middle for the insertion of a strong rawhide line, which passes back and is looped to the lower end of a strong sealskin line six to eight fathoms long, connecting the spearhead with the float, which consists of the entire skin of a seal with all of the openings closed and having a nozzle by means of which it is inflated. A cord loop in the front end serves to attach it to the end of the float line, which also has a permanent loop for this purpose.

The float-board consists of a strong, oval hoop of spruce made in two U-shape pieces, with the ends brought together and beveled to form a neatly fitting joint, which is wrapped firmly with a lashing of spruce root; the sides have holes by which a thin board is fastened to the under side, the ends of which are notched in front to form a coarsely serrated pattern with five points that are inserted in slots cut in the front of the hoop. The front of the board is oval, and the sides taper gradually to the points of two projecting arms, which extend four or five inches behind the bow; between these arms a deep slot is cut, with the inner border rounded. The board has a round hole in the center and a crescentic hole on each side (plate LIV, 10).

On the kaiak the float-board is placed in front of the hunter, with the arm-like points thrust beneath the cross lashing to hold it in position, and upon it lies the coil of float line with the spear attached and resting on the spear guards on the right rail of the boat; the end of the line is passed back under the hunter's right arm to the float which, fully inflated, rests on the deck just back of the manhole.

When the spear is thrown the coil runs off rapidly and the float is thrown overboard. In some cases, when the prey is vigorous and leads a long pursuit, another line, like that shown in figure 9, plate LIV, is made fast through the semilunar orifices in the center of the float-board, which latter, when drawn through the water by means of this cord, assumes a position nearly at a right angle to the course of the animal and forms a heavy drag to impede its progress.

When hunting on the ice the float-board, with the line coiled upon it, is carried in the left hand of the hunter and the spear in the right hand while he watches along the borders of the leads or holes for the appearance of the seal. When he succeeds in striking it, he holds firmly to the line until the animal is exhausted, or if necessary the float-board attached to the line is cast into the water, while the hunter hurries to his kaiak and embarks in pursuit.

In addition to the smaller spears used in connection with the throwing stick and float-board, larger spears are used to cast directly from the hand. These spears have a stout wooden shaft from four to seven feet long, with a finger-rest of bone or ivory lashed on at about one-third of its length from the butt. The head is of bone or ivory, rounded and fitted to the wooden shaft by lashings in a manner similar to that of the smaller spears. It is pierced near the base for the reception of the line by which it is attached to the shaft. Several feet of this line are wound about the shaft, so that when the point is detached the cord will unwind and the shaft will form a drag to impede the animal in its efforts

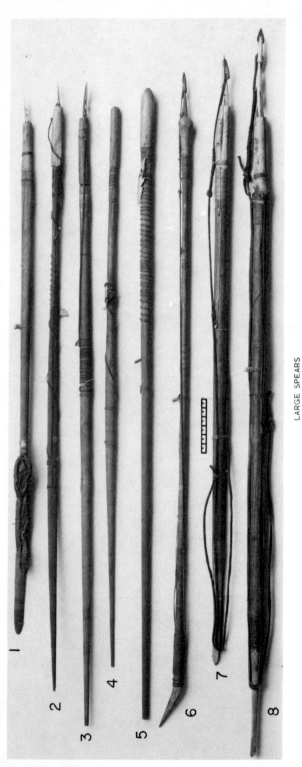

LARGE SPEARS

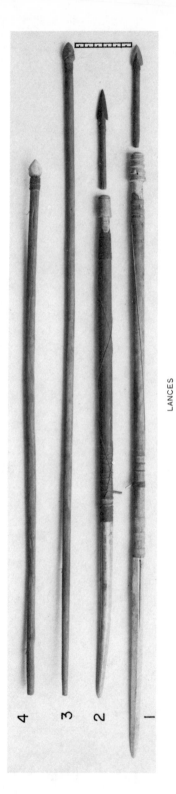

LANCES

SPEARS AND LANCES (ONE-TENTH)

to escape. Figure 2, plate LVa, is a typical spear of this kind from St Michael.

Figure 3, plate LVa, illustrates a typical example of this kind of spear which was obtained at Sledge island. The shaft is a little over six feet long, tapering from the middle toward both ends, the upper end being the smaller. The private mark of the owner is marked on the shaft in red and black paint. The head is held in place by a combination of sinew and rawhide lashings. Spears very similar to this are in common use on the shores of Norton sound and Bering strait.

Figure 1, plate LVa, from Norton sound, is an example of the large spear used in that locality.

Figure 8, plate LVa, is another spear of this kind, about seven feet in length, from Port Clarence. The shaft is strongly lashed with rawhide in several places, the lashings being held in place by small bone pins, and a strong finger-rest in the form of a seal-head is attached to one side for use in casting; the butt has a tapering, rounded point of bone, fastened by a rawhide lashing which passes through an orifice in the bone. The bone head is inserted in a groove in the wooden shaft, against which it is held firmly by a rawhide lashing; an ivory rod about seven inches in length is inserted in the top and on it is fitted the detachable harpoon point, the tip of which is slit and a triangular piece of brass inserted to form a sharp point. The detachable point has a hole through which is passed the cord which attaches it to the shaft.

Figure 7, plate LVa, from Sledge island, is a similar but shorter walrus and whale spear, having the bone head worked into an image of a white bear's head, with pieces of blue beads inlaid for eyes. Spears of this character were found also in use along the coast of Kotzebue sound and northward to Point Barrow.

From St Lawrence island a similar but ruder spear of this kind was obtained. It has a long, rounded shaft, with a small ivory head and a finger-rest at the middle; the short bone tip at the butt is sharpened to a wedge-shape point. This specimen, which measures nearly eight feet, is the longest of any of the spears that were seen.

Figure 6, plate LVa, from Norton sound, is a spear used for walrus and whales, somewhat similar in general character to those already described, but the long, slender shaft has a spur-shape point of bone inserted in its upper end and fastened by a rawhide cord. This projects obliquely from the shaft instead of being in line with it, as in the other specimens described. The usual lashings of rawhide are around the shaft, but the bone head is smaller and terminates in a knob, in which is inserted the bone peg on which is fitted the detachable point. This point has a flat, triangular, iron tip and a hole through the base for the attachment of a stout rawhide cord that passes backward through two grooves in the bone head and thence along the shaft to the butt, where it is coiled and attached to a float.

Figure 5, plate LVa, from Chichiñagamut, is the style of large hand spear used on Nunivak island and the adjacent mainland, between the Yukon and the Kuskokwim. A deerhorn peg is inserted in the side of the shaft to serve as a finger-rest for casting. The shaft is largest near the head, round in cross section, and tapers gradually back to the truncated tip. A modification of this style is seen in figure 4, plate LVa, from Pastolik, which has the finger-rest formed of a small bone pin inserted in the side of the shaft, but with the latter oval in cross section and tapering each way, like the Norton sound spears of this kind.

FLOATS

The sealskins used as floats in connection with spears in capturing large seals, walrus, and white whales, are taken from the seals entire and are tanned usually with the hair removed. To stop the holes made in them by spears or in other ways, and to prevent their fastenings from becoming loose and the consequent loss of the float and the game, plugs of wood, bone, ivory, or deerhorn are used, which are stud-like in form, with spreading heads and a deep groove around the side. The hole in the skin is first sewed up or patched, if necessary, leaving a very small orifice, through which the stopper is pressed until it projects far enough on the inside for the workman to wrap a stout lashing of thin rawhide or sinew cord around the groove and make it fast. This work is done through a hole left open at the muzzle of the skin, after which the nozzle through which it is inflated is inserted and fastened by rawhide lashings. Some of these stoppers are plain, but most of them have the upper surface carved in a great variety of ornamental designs.

Figure 5, plate LVI a, illustrates a specimen of one of these stoppers obtained at Koñigunugumut, having the top in the form of a cone.

Figure 7, plate LVI a, from Nubviukhchugaluk, has a conical head with half of a blue bead set in the top.

Figure 1, plate LVI a, from Koñigunugumut, has an oval head.

Figure 4, plate LVI a, from the same locality, has an oval head with the raven totem sign etched upon its surface.

Figure 6, plate LVI a, also from the same locality, has a round, flat top, with two concentric circles surrounding a wooden plug set in the center.

Figure 3, plate LVI a, from Cape Nome, has the top surrounded by a circle with an inlaid bead in the center and a conical base.

Figure 10, plate LVI a, from Cape Nome, has the top in the form of a seal's head, with the eyes, nostrils, and ears indicated by round wooden pegs inlaid in the ivory.

Figure 14, plate LVI a, from Sledge island, is a large, round, wooden plug, on the surface of which are three concentric incised circles.

Figure 13, plate LVI a, from Cape Vancouver, has the upper surface very slightly rounded and bearing the features of a woman in low relief. The eyes, nostrils, and mouth are incised; there are two labret holes on each side of the lower lip, and radiating lines from the middle of the mouth indicate tattooing.

Figure 15, plate LVI *a*, from Agiukchugumut, is of ivory and has a human face carved on the surface of the head.

Figure 9, plate LVI *a*, from Cape Vancouver, is an ivory plug, oval in outline, with the face of a short-ear owl on its upper surface.

Figure 2, plate LVI *a*, from Chalitmut, is a small stopper with the face of a seal in relief on its surface.

Figure 8, plate LVI *a*, from Cape Darby, is a stopper with a stem in the form of a link, with its base projecting and pierced with a hole, through which a crosspiece of ivory is inserted to hold the lashing in position. In the link, and carved from the same piece of ivory, is a seal-head with bristles set in by plugs of wood to indicate the whiskers; the eyes, nostrils, and ears are represented by wooden plugs.

Figure 12, plate LVI *a*, from Cape Darby, is another link plug, having carved on it a seal-head, the nostrils and eyes formed by inlaid beads. The base has the usual constricted neck, but is conical instead of flattened.

Figure 11, plate LVI *a*, from Sledge island, is made like the preceding, with

FIG. 39—Sealskin float (about 1/10).

a conical base attached to the open link by a narrow neck. In this link is another one, the outer end of which is carved to represent the end of an inflated float.

Figure 16, plate LVI *a*, from Kushunuk, is a long, slender float with an ivory nozzle. It is made from the intestines of a seal, and is intended to be attached to the shaft of a hand spear. Some of these floats are made from the bladders or stomachs of seals and walrus, and are usually oval in shape.

Figure 39, from Nunivak island, is a sealskin float, tanned with most of the hair removed. It has an ivory nozzle fitted in the place of one of the fore-flippers. The front of the skin is bent downward and wrapped with rawhide cord, with an ivory peg stuck through to pre-vent the cord from slipping. The cord has a loose end about three feet in length with a loop for attaching it to the float line.

The nozzles for the smaller floats, which are attached to the shafts of spears, are made usually of ivory; they are round and have a projec-tion at one end which is pierced for the attachment of a line to bind the nozzle to the shaft of the spear; an enlarged rim prevents the lashing from slipping off. In some specimens the base is not pierced, but a projecting piece is left which is concave on the lower surface and convex on the upper and serves to retain the lashing.

Figure 29, plate LVI a, represents a nozzle or mouthpiece obtained at Cape Vancouver. It is intended for a small float.

Figure 24, plate LVI a, is a nozzle from Cape Darby. The projection on the side has a single hole for the passage of the cord and a shoulder on the projecting end which is grooved for the lashing.

Figure 27, plate LVI a, from Unalaklit, is another mouthpiece with a single flattened hole through its projecting lower side.

Figure 17, plate LVI a, from Kushunuk, is a large mouthpiece having a raven totem mark on one side of the base, which is pierced with three holes for the lashings.

Figure 20, plate LVI a, from St Michael, has two holes through the base for the attachment of the cord.

Figure 18, plate LVI a, from St Lawrence island, is another nozzle, as is also figure 19 of the same plate, from Cape Darby. Both of these are of ivory, and the latter has etched upon its surface several raven totem signs.

Figure 21, plate LVI a, from the Yukon mouth, is made of deerhorn, and has three holes along the base for the attachment of cords.

Figure 28, plate LVI a, from Cape Nome, has four holes along the base for the attachment of cords.

Figure 25, plate LVI a, from Koñigunugumut, is carved in the form of a walrus head, the projecting tusks below forming one side of the opening at the base for the attachment of the cords.

For the purpose of attaching one float line to another when greater length is needed, or for joining lines along the shafts of spears, small ivory blocks are used, which are made in great variety of form, and considerable ingenuity is displayed in carving their surfaces into vari-ous figures and patterns. One form consists of a small block with a round hole across its length, near the underside. Another larger hole runs from below and extends obliquely upward, continuing on the upper surface as a groove around the base of an enlarged head on the upper side of the block, in which a permanent loop is inserted. When the hunter wishes to attach another cord to lengthen his line he passes the looped end through the hole on the underside to the upper surface and

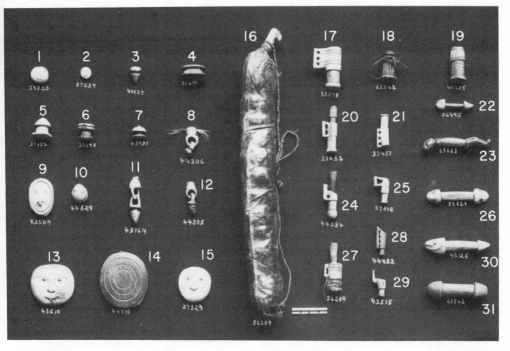

FLOAT, FLOAT PLUGS, AND MOUTH PIECES

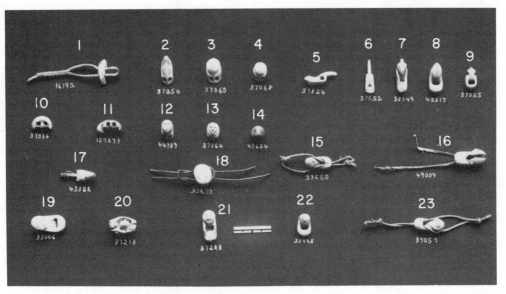

CORD ATTACHERS

HUNTING AND FISHING APPARATUS (THREE-SIXTEENTHS)

slips it over the head, where it falls into the slot or neck and forms a firm attachment.

Figure 20, plate LVI *b*, represents one of these blocks, obtained at Paimut. It is carved on the underside to represent a bear, with the fore-paws extended around in front. When this figure is turned over, the hind-legs and the tail, which appear on the opposite side, are seen to form the fore-legs of another bear, while the fore-legs of the first form the hind-limbs of the latter. In the space inclosed by the legs of the last-named bear is the figure of a seal-head in strong relief, which forms the head over which is passed the loop of the cord to be attached.

Figure 19, plate LVI *b*, from Chalitmut, is a block having the head carved to represent a grotesque face.

Figure 21, plate LVI *b*, shows a specimen from Kaialigamut, the head of which is carved to form a human face and on the opposite end is etched the head of a seal.

Figure 16, plate LVI *b*, from Sabotnisky, is a plain block with a deep groove cut in the head for the permanent loop, instead of a hole sidewise through it.

Figure 15, plate LVI *b*, from St Michael, is one of these blocks with a grotesque face on the head. Two rawhide loops are placed in it in position to show the manner of making the attachment of lines.

Figure 7, plate LVI *b*, from Nulukhtulogumut, has a diamond-shape head projecting forward to a point.

Figure 8, plate LVI *b*, from Nunivak island, has an almond-shape head, crossed lengthwise by an incised line.

Figure 22, plate LVI *b*, from St Michael, has the head decorated with incised concentric circles arranged in two pairs.

Figure 9, plate LVI *b*, from Kushunuk, has the head cut into an oval form, with a strong ridge along its top, which turns abruptly downward in front.

Figure 6, plate LVI *b*, from the lower Kuskokwim, has a long, beak-like projection for the head, as does figure 5 of the same plate, from Koñigunugumut.

Figure 23, plate LVI *b*, from Askinuk, represents a grotesque countenance. In it are inserted two loops to show the method of attachment.

Another style of cord attacher, commonly used to fasten the end of the float line to the short loop on a detachable spearhead, consists of a bar-like piece of ivory, pierced with two holes through which is passed the end of a rawhide loop, forming the permanent attachment, which projects beyond the side of the bar far enough to permit another loop to be run through it, passed over the bar, and drawn back; the bar lies across the end of the second loop and prevents slipping. Attachers of this kind are commonly made in the form of a double crescent joined along one side, having two parallel holes for the permanent loop; the upper sides are convex and the lower ones slightly concave.

Figure 1, plate LVI *b*, represents one of these cord attachers, in the form of a white whale, with the loop in position to show the method of attachment. It is from the coast between Yukon and Kuskokwim rivers. Figure 11 of the same plate, obtained at St Michael by Mr L. M. Turner, is in the form of a seal, and figure 10 shows a specimen from the Yukon mouth, also fashioned in the form of a white whale.

Still another form of these cord attachers consists of a rounded, upright block, pierced with two parallel holes for the attachment of the permanent loop, just above which is a deeply grooved constriction or neck to receive the temporary loop.

Figure 13, plate LVI b, shows a specimen of this form of the implement, obtained at Askinuk; on it is a human face, with labret holes at the corners of the mouth, and a raised rim around the face representing a fur hood. The raven totem mark is incised on the sides.

Figure 12, plate LVI b, from Sledge island, is similar in form, and has a woman's countenance upon the upper surface, with two labret holes in the middle of the lower lip.

Figure 4, plate LVI b, from Kushunuk, has a grotesque face upon its upper surface.

FIG. 40—Cord attacher (about ⅔).

Figure 14, plate LVI b, from Cape Vancouver, has the face of an owl upon the upper surface.

Figure 2, plate LVI b, from Kushunuk, has a wolf-head upon the upper surface.

The accompanying figure, 40, from Unalaklit, is very well carved to represent a hair seal; blue beads are inlaid for eyes.

Figure 41 a shows a well carved attacher from Golofnin bay; at one end the nostrils of a seal are indicated by round holes, with the cord hole for a mouth; in the top is a deep excavation, in the middle of which stands a projecting knob carved to represent a seal-head, over which the loop of the temporary attachment is passed; on the lower side (figure 41 b) is the figure of a whale in relief.

Figure 3, plate LVI b, from Kulwoguwigumut, has the upper surface plain, except for a median ridge running lengthwise across it.

Figure 18, plate LVI b, from Norton sound, is a long, flat-head specimen, with a cord inserted to show the manner of attaching the loops.

Figure 17, plate LVI b, from Cape Prince of Wales, is a handsomely made ivory swivel for attachment to a float line to prevent it from becoming twisted by the movement of the float; the block, or main portion, is handsomely carved in the form of a white bear's head, in which fragments of blue beads are set for eyes. The swivel is formed by an ivory rod, about an inch in length, with the head carved in the

shape of a closed human fist; it is placed in a hole in the lower side of
the bear head and projects to the rear.

The front ends of large floats are commonly provided with a cross bar
of ivory, which serves as a handle for raising them, and at the same
time is convenient for looping the lines.

Figure 26, plate LVI a, from Unalaklit, is such a handle bar with the
head of a seal carved at each end.

Figure 23, plate LVI a, from the Diomede islands, is another such bar carved
in the form of a woman.

Figure 22, plate LVI a, from the lower
Kuskokwim, has one end cut into the
form of a grotesque head, and figure 30
of the same plate, from Sledge island,
has upon one end the head of a salmon
and at the other a seal's hind flippers.

Figure 31, plate LVI a, from St Lawrence island, is a wooden bar, rounded
in cross section, with a rounded knob
at each end.

LANCES

In addition to the spears for killing
whales and walrus, two distinct kinds
of lances are used by the Eskimo. The
ordinary form is found generally on the
Asiatic and American coasts of Bering
straits and thence northward along the
Arctic coast. It consists of a slender
wooden shaft, from six to seven feet in
length, with a rounded point of flint,
nephrite, or other hard stone, held in
position by rawhide or willow-root iash-
ings. In recent years some of these
lances have been tipped with iron, but
the use of stone for this purpose is connected with the superstition that exists
among these people which prohibits the
use of iron in cutting up these animals.

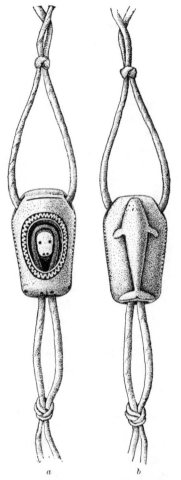

Fig. 41—Cord attacher, obverse and
reverse (about ⅜).

Figure 3, plate LV b, from Cape Nome, is a typical example of this
style of lance. It has a shaft about 5½ feet in length, oval in cross section, with a rounded point of chipped flint set in the slot at the end and
bound firmly in position with a sinew lashing.

Figure 4, plate LV b, from St Michael, is a shorter shafted lance, with
the point made from marble ground down to the leaf-shape outline

18 ETH——10

common to the stone points of these weapons.   Usually the shafts of these lances are plain, but a specimen (number 33891) from Norton sound, has a finger-rest of bone bound midway on the shaft.

The other form of lance is a peculiar one used along the coast of Norton sound, about Nunivak island, and in the region lying between the mouths of Yukon and Kuskokwim rivers.   It is from 4 to 4½ feet in length and has a walrus ivory butt from 20 to 24 inches in length fastened to the end of the wooden shaft.   The end of the butt has two holes, through which a sinew cord is passed and wound tightly around the junction of the two parts of the shaft.   The head has a round hole for the reception of the point, which is held in position by a stout lashing of sinew cord.

Figure 2, plate LV *b*, represents a specimen of this kind of lance obtained on Nunivak island.   It has a butt made from a walrus tusk, along each side of which is etched a long, slender figure of an animal, having a blue bead inlaid for the eye; the tip of the butt is shaped to a tapering point.   In the wooden shaft, just above the ivory butt, a deerhorn peg is inserted for a finger-rest.

Another example (number 168579) from Nunivak island has the ivory butt etched with the outline of a long arm, with a hand at the lower end and the palm pierced.

Figure 1, plate LV *b*, from Nunivak island, has a round bone head with three deep grooves extending around it, leaving four ridges terminating in a shoulder next to the shaft, bound in position by a cotton cord, evidently obtained from some trader.   A long, tapering ivory butt, triangular in cross section, is fastened to the wooden shaft, and about the junction is a strong binding of cord similar to that used on the head.

All the points used on these lances are detachable, and every hunter carries a small bag made from sealskin or other hide, containing eight or ten additional points.

Figure 17, plate LVII *a*, from the lower Yukon, is a fish-skin bag for holding a set of spearpoints.   These points vary somewhat in character, but are from 8 to 10 inches in length, with thin, triangular tips of stone, glass, iron, or other material.   Sometimes the points are made of ivory or bone, but this is not common.   Slate is perhaps most frequently used, and occasionally flint or iron points are seen.

Figure 5, plate LV *b*, from Chalitmut, is a lance with a wooden shaft on which a raven totem mark is incised.   The point to this is of slate, beveled on both sides to a sharp edge, and set in a wooden foreshaft; with it is a wooden sheath, to slip over the point and protect it when not in use (figure 25, plate LVII *a*).   Figure 27, plate LVII *a*, represents another form of these wooden sheaths for lance points.

Figure 19, plate LVII *a*, shows a lance from Port Clarence, Bering strait.   It has a wooden shaft, with a chipped flint point inserted in a slot in the end and held in position by a wrapping of whalebone.   The upper end of the shaft is wrapped with whalebone to prevent splitting, and a small tuft of seal hair is inserted in a narrow slot on the side.

Figure 22, plate LVII *a*, from Cape Nome, and figure 21 of the same plate, from Norton sound, are lances of this kind, with the points bound to the wooden shafts by wrappings of whalebone.

Figure 18, plate LVII *a*, from Unalaklit, has a wooden shaft, with a long, slender point of flint, shaped like the flint arrow-tips used in that region for hunting deer.

Figure 24, plate LVII *a*, from Cape Vancouver, has a long, gracefully shaped head of slate, set in a wooden shaft.

Some of these lances, instead of a plain wooden shaft or a wooden shaft with an ivory butt, have the upper part or foreshaft made of bone or ivory.

Figure 23, plate LVII *a*, from the lower Kuskokwim, has a bone foreshaft set in a slot in the wooden shaft and held in place by a sinew lashing. It has a triangular slate point, between which and the foreshaft is a deep notch forming a barb.

Figure 26, plate LVII *a*, from Anogogmut, has a bone foreshaft with a triangular slate tip. The foreshaft is excavated at its posterior end for the reception of the end of the wooden part, which is thrust into this hole without other fastening.

Figure 16, plate LVII *a*, from Chalitmut, has an ivory foreshaft with a triangular iron point set in a slot in its end. On the side of the foreshaft a sharp-pointed ivory spur is set, pointed backward, and made to serve as a barb to fix the point in the body of the animal. With this specimen is a neat sheath, made from two pieces of wood carefully excavated to the form of the head and bound together by a spruce-root lashing.

Figure 20, plate LVII *a*, obtained on Nunivak island by Doctor Dall, has the head made from a piece of iron riveted to a wooden shaft, which is pierced with a hole in which a strong rawhide loop is fastened, evidently for attaching the head to the line, so that the weapon could be withdrawn and used repeatedly on the same animal. A long sheath of wood, wrapped with spruce roots, serves to protect this point when not in use.

These lances are used when the seal or walrus has been disabled, so that it can not keep out of reach of its pursuers, when the hunter paddles up close alongside and strikes the animal, driving the detachable head in its entire length. The head remains in the animal, and the hunter immediately fits another point into the shaft and repeats the blow, thus inserting as many of the barbed heads as possible, until the animal is killed or the supply of points exhausted. Every hunter has his private mark cut on these points, so that, when the animal is secured, each is enabled to reclaim his own.

SPEAR AND LANCE HEADS

Figure 34, plate LVII *b*, illustrates a round ivory head for one of the smaller seal spears used with a throwing stick, obtained at Big lake.

Figure 18, plate LVII *b*, represents one of the barbed deerhorn points used in the small spears. They are from St Michael. Figure 17 of the same plate shows a seal spearpoint notched along one side. It also came from St Michael.

Figure 20, plate LVII *b*, from Norton bay; figure 16, plate LVII *b*, from Cape Nome, and figure 19, plate LVII *b*, from Nunivak island, are examples of the points used in the large hand spears thrown by means of a finger rest on the side of the shaft.

Figure 33, plate LVII *b*, from Anogogmut, is a head for a light spear cast with a throwing stick and used in connection with the detachable harpoon head and sealskin float.

Figure 12, plate LVII *b*, from Kigiktauik, is the point for one of these spears made entirely of deerhorn. Ordinarily these points are tipped with iron, copper, or stone set in a slot in the end of the point. When not in use these points, which have a permanent loop fastened to them, are kept in a wooden sheath to prevent the thin metal or stone tip from being broken.

Figure 14, plate LVII *b*, from Kushunuk, is one of these points having a triangular copper tip. On both the front and the back of the point raven totem signs are etched.

Figure 15, plate LVII *b*, from Kaialigamut, shows another of these points with the sheath in position over the tip.

Figure 5, plate LVII *b*, from Chalitmut, is an iron point for a walrus spear, fastened to the bone rod which connects it with the spearhead. The rod is lashed to a wooden butt which fits into the spearhead.

Figure 6, plate LVII *b*, from Sledge island, is a detached point for one of these spears with a triangular tip of thin iron. It terminates at the inner end in a single beveled point.

Figure 8, plate LVII *b*, from Sledge island, is a point for one of these spears made entirely from iron worked down to a shape similar to that of the others.

Figure 13, plate LVII *b*, from St Lawrence island, is a curiously shaped point for one of these spears made from bone with a thin iron tip inserted in a slot.

Figure 11, plate LVII *b*, from Unalaklit, is a bone point for a large hand spear, the inner end terminating in two sharp points.

Figure 4, plate LVII *b*, obtained on Nunivak island by Doctor Dall, is a good example of a head for a large spear, with a sheath made of wood and wrapped with spruce root.

Figure 7, plate LVII *b*, from Sledge island, is a specimen of the ivory rods used to connect the detachable spearpoint with the head of the spear shaft.

Figure 1, plate LVII *b*, from Cape Nome, is a walrus ivory spur, such as is used at the butt of the large hand spears for walrus and whales. This specimen is very old, and has etched along its surface upon one side scenes of whale and walrus hunting in umiaks, and wolves and the killer whale upon the other.

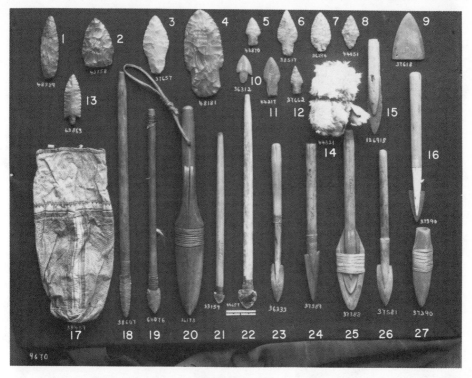

LANCE POINTS, ETC.

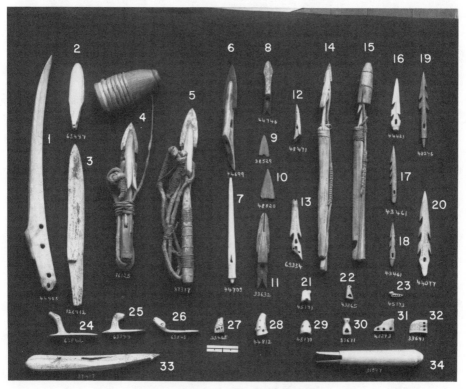

SPEAR HEADS, POINTS, FINGER-RESTS, ETC.

OBJECTS USED IN HUNTING

Figure 3, plate LVII *b*, from St Lawrence island, is a bone spur such as is used on the ends of walrus spears on that island.

Figure 2, plate LVII *b*, from St Lawrence island, is another spur for a walrus spear shaft.

Figure 9, plate LVII *b*, from the lower Yukon, and figure 10 of the same plate, from Razbinsky, represent triangular slate tips for use on detachable points of walrus and seal spears.

Figure 6, plate LVII *a*, from Kigiktauik, is a handsome flint lance-point of bluish stone, very regular in form.

Figure 9, plate LVII *a*, from Norton bay, is a triangular slate lance-point with the border beveled down on both sides to form the edge.

Figure 4, plate LVII *a*, from Cape Prince of Wales, is a large, round-pointed, flint lancehead.

Figure 1, plate LVII *a*, is an old flint lancehead obtained from an ancient village site at St Michael.

Figure 10, plate LVII *a*, from Kushunuk, is a curiously formed slate lancepoint.

Figure 11, plate LVII *a*, from Cape Darby, is a leaf-shape slate point.

Figure 2, plate LVII *a*, from King island, is a handsomely made flint point, subtriangular in outline.

Figure 8, plate LVII *a*, from Nubviukhchugaluk, is a diamond-shape, flint lancepoint.

Figure 5, plate LVII *a*, from Unalaklit, is made of quartz crystal.

Figure 7, plate LVII *a*, from Big lake, is a handsomely made, oval lance-point of bluish flint.

Figure 13, plate LVII *a*, from Point Hope, and figure 12 of the same plate, from Kotzebue sound, are well-chipped flint points.

Figure 3, plate LVII *a*, from Kotzebue sound, is a handsomely made flint point of dull greenish color.

Figure 15, plate LVII *a*, from St Lawrence island, is a lancehead of bone, tipped with a thin, oval iron point which is riveted in place by an iron pin; it has a deep slot at the upper end in which the wooden shaft is fitted, and has a hole just below the slot through which passes the rawhide cord which binds it to the shaft.

Figure 42 (2), from Kotzebue sound, is one of the points used on the three-point bird spears. Figure 42 (8), obtained on St Lawrence island by Captain C. L. Hooper, is a rudely made prong for a bird spear-point. Figure 42 (7), from Cape Nome, is a bone point such as is used on the shafts of bird spears. Figure 42 (3), from Cape Nome, and figure 42 (4), from Cape Prince of Wales, represent points for bird spears. Figure 42 (6), from St Lawrence island, is a prong or spur for attachment to the side of the shaft of a bird spear. Figure 42 (5), from St Lawrence island, shows the bone points for a small, three-point bird and fish spear.

In places where there is considerable whale and walrus hunting, each hunter has several lancepoints, which are kept wrapped in some kind of skin to protect them from injury.

Figure 14, plate LVIIa, from Cape Darby, illustrates a wrapper of this kind for lancepoints, made from the skin of a swan's neck, with the feathers left on, and having a rawhide cord attached to one end as a fastening. The lanceheads are so wrapped that each has a fold of the skin between it and the next.

On the shafts of the large hand spears various kinds of finger-rests are used. Sometimes a small pin of ivory, deerhorn, or bone is driven into the shaft and left projecting from half an inch to an inch, sloping slightly backward to afford a firm rest for the finger.

From Point Hope three finger-rests of deerhorn were obtained. Figures 25 and 26, plate LVIIb, illustrate these specimens, each of which has the head of a deer carved on the outer end. Figure 24 of the same

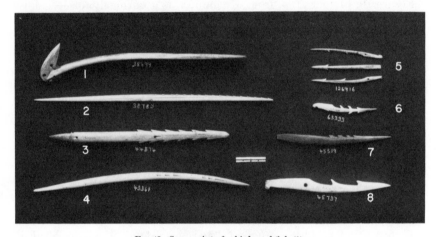

FIG. 42—Spearpoints for birds and fish (⅙).

plate shows the other example, which is carved to represent the head of an unknown animal, the eyes being formed by inlaid blue beads. The base of each of these finger-rests is in the form of a long, thin strip for lashing along the shaft of the spear.

Figure 28, plate LVIIb, from Sledge island, is a handsomely carved finger-rest, with the head of a white bear on the outer end and the base made concave to fit the spear shaft. There is a hole through the base to receive the cord which fastens it in place.

Figure 29, plate LVIIb, from the same locality as the specimen last described, represents the head of a seal.

Figure 27, plate LVIIb, from St Michael, represents the head and shoulders of a seal. The base has three holes to receive the cord.

Figure 22, plate LVIIb, from Unalaklit, has a triangular hole in the base for the cord.

ST MICHAEL MAN CASTING A BIRD SPEAR

Figure 21, plate LVII *b*, from Sledge island, is carved to represent the head of a seal.

Figure 30, plate LVII *b*, from Koñigunugumut, is a round piece of ivory, with the interior excavated and crossed by a triangular hole for the passage of a cord.

Figure 32, plate LVII *b*, from the lower Yukon, and figure 31 of the same plate, from Nunivak island, are roughly triangular finger rests of a very common style. They have three holes along the base for the cord.

Figure 23, plate LVII *b*, from Sledge island, is a small, curved object, with a seal-head on the top and pierced with five small holes along the base for the attachment of cords by which it is lashed to the shaft of the spear. This device serves to hold a cord at a point where it is desired to pass it along the shaft in a different direction without forming a knot. Ordinarily small pegs are inserted in the shafts of these spears for this purpose, but in some instances objects of this kind are used.

In addition to the use of spears for killing seals, walrus, and white whales, the Eskimo have several forms of spears for capturing birds, which vary considerably in length and in other details. The commonest form consists of a round wooden shaft, varying from 3 feet 9 inches to 4 feet 3 inches in length, with three long, rounded, tapering points, barbed along the inner side with a series of serrations curved slightly outward and set in the form of a triangle in grooves around the lower end of the shaft. A strong sinew lashing, about one-third of the distance from their lower end, secures them to a small central knot on the end of the shaft, thence to their lower ends they are wrapped about with a braided sinew cord, which afterward passes spirally about the handle to the butt, where it is fastened. Plate LVIII, after a photograph, illustrates the method of casting bird spears at St Michael.

Figure 5, plate LIX, from Anogogmut, is a typical example of these spears. The shaft is not feathered.

Figure 6 of the same plate, from Cape Nome, has a shorter shaft, near the butt of which are inserted three feathers from the tail of a cormorant. Figure 2, from Norton sound, is a bird spear with three rudely made points of deerhorn, the serrations on which are made to turn to the sides instead of toward the center as is the usual custom. Figure 3, from St Michael, has three deerhorn points, with serrations on their outer sides. Figure 4, from Nunivak island, has three bone points, triangular in cross section, with serrations in pairs facing inward.

From Nunivak island and the adjacent mainland some spears were obtained similar to the preceding, except that they were not feathered and have four points. Figure 1, plate LIX, from Nulukhtulogumut, is a typical specimen of these four-point bird spears. It has serrations on the inner faces of the points.

The most curious bird spears are those with a long point of bone, ivory, or deerhorn, serrated on one or both sides, inserted in the end of the wooden shaft. Set in the shaft, at about one-third of the distance from the butt, are three points of bone, ivory, or deerhorn, which are lashed in position with their sharp points extending obliquely outward, forming a triangle. These spears are from 4 to 6 feet in length and frequently have handsomely made points.

Figure 8, plate LIX, from Nunivak island, is one of these spears with a bone point triangular in cross section and 22 inches in length. It is grooved along all the angles, which have serrations along them in pairs, at intervals of an inch or more, with a series of coarsely made serrations near the butt. The points on the shaft are triangular in cross section and are barbed along their inner edges. This specimen is without feathering at the base of the shaft.

Figure 9, plate LIX, represents a spear obtained by Mr L. M. Turner at St Michael. It has three cormorant feathers on the shaft and three barbs, on two of which the serrations face outward and on the other they are inward. The point is of ivory, hexagonal in cross section, and barbed on two sides.

Figure 7, plate LIX, from St Michael, has an ivory point, roughly oval in cross section, with two sets of barbs on the edges; three barbs on the shaft are of deerhorn serrated along their inner edges.

Figure 11, plate LIX, from Razbinsky, is a large and heavily made bird spear, with a strong point of deerhorn and three heavy points on the shaft.

Figure 10, plate LIX, from St Michael, is another spear of this description, having the point set in a slit at the upper end of the wooden shaft and secured by a rawhide lashing. Three bone points are lashed to the shaft near the butt.

Bird spears are used for capturing waterfowl, particularly during the late summer and fall, when the geese and ducks have molted their wing-feathers and are unable to fly; also for catching the young of various water birds. The object of the three prongs on the shaft is to catch the bird by the neck or the wing when the point may have missed it. In using the spear but little attempt is made to strike the bird with the point, but it is thrown in such a manner that it will diverge slightly to one side as it approaches the quarry, so that the shaft will slide along the back or the neck and one or more of the points will catch the neck or the wing.

THROWING STICKS

The Eskimo are very expert in casting spears with the throwing stick. The small, light spears used in hunting seals are cast from 30 to 50 yards with considerable accuracy and force. I have seen them practice by the hour throwing their spears at young waterfowl, and their accuracy is remarkable. The birds sometimes would see the spear coming and dive just before it reached them, but almost invariably the

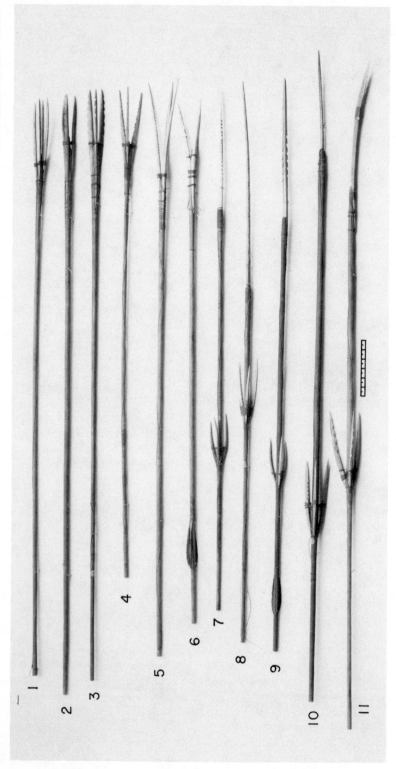

BIRD SPEARS (ONE-TENTH)

weapon struck in the middle of the circle on the water where the bird had gone down. Bird spears are generally cast overhand, so as to strike from above, but if the birds are shy and dive quickly, the spears are cast with an underhand throw so that they skim along the surface of the water. I have seen a hunter throwing a spear at waterfowl on the surface of a stream when small waves were running; the spear would tip the crests of the waves, sending up little jets of spray, and yet continue its course for 20 or 25 yards. This method is very confusing to the birds, as they are frequently struck by the spear before they seem to be aware of its approach. When throwing spears into flocks of partly fledged ducks or geese that are bunched together, two or even three are sometimes impaled at once upon the triple points.

Hunters in kaiaks are able to follow a seal or a diving waterfowl in calm weather by the lines of bubbles which rise from the swimming animal and mark its course beneath the surface. On one occasion I amused myself for nearly half a day with two Eskimo companions in kaiaks by pursuing half-fledged eider ducks in the sea off the end of Stuart island. After a little instruction from my companions I was surprised to see how readily the birds could be followed, for when they came to the surface they were always within easy range of a cast of the spear.

In using the throwing stick for casting the spear in a curve through the air by an overhand motion, the throwing stick is held pointing backward; the end of the spear shaft is laid in the groove on its upper surface, resting against the ivory pin or other crosspiece at the outer end; the shaft of the spear crosses the fingers and is held in position by grasping with the thumb and forefinger around the throwing stick. The under side of the spear rests upon the extended end of the third finger, which lies along a groove in the throwing stick. This gives the outer end of the spear an upward cant, so that when it is cast it takes a slightly upward course. If the cast is to be made directly forward with a vertical motion of the hand, the spear is held with the groove upward; but in throwing the spear along the surface of the water the throwing stick is so held that the groove faces outwardly. In using throwing sticks that have pins set along the side for finger-rests, the spear is held in position by the thumb and second finger instead of with the thumb and first finger, as is usual with other throwing sticks. In the case of the three-peg throwing sticks the spear rests upon the turned-in ends of the first and third fingers, while the thumb and second finger hold it in position from above.

The throwing sticks used by the Unalit Eskimo are made of a length proportioned to the size of the person who is to use them; this is determined by the measurement of the forearm from the point of the right elbow to the tip of the outstretched forefinger. Throwing sticks used with the spears for hunting white whales are made longer by the width of the forefinger than those used for seal and bird spears.

The ordinary length of the seal spears used with throwing sticks by the Unalit is calculated as three times the distance from the point of the maker's elbow to the tip of the outstretched forefinger, with the added width of the left thumb for each of the first two cubits and the width of the left hand added to the last. Seal hunters are not so careful about the precise length of their throwing sticks as the white whale hunters, who are extremely exact in their measurements.

Figure 43 (6) represents a throwing stick, from Sledge island, with the tapering point deeply grooved and provided with an ivory pin against which the slightly excavated tip of the spear is intended to rest. The handle is rounded near the end and notched on the sides to receive the thumb and the little finger. Small, rudely made depressions in the upper surface serve for the ends of the second and third fingers, and a

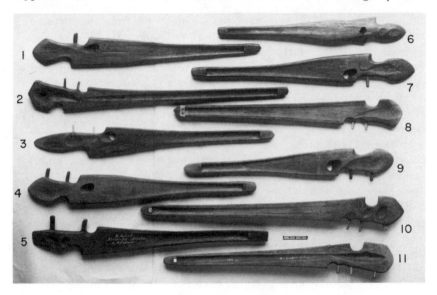

Fig. 43—Throwing sticks (⅛).

hole running obliquely through is intended for the insertion of the forefinger.

Figure 43 (1) shows a throwing stick, from Sabotnisky, with a peg of ivory in the groove on its upper surface to receive the butt of the spear. The handle has a hole on the underside to receive the forefinger, a wooden pin on the inside as a rest for the second finger, with a deep notch opposite for the thumb, and the upper surface of the slightly expanded butt has a flat depression to receive the ends of the last two fingers.

Figure 43 (7), also from Sabotnisky, is similar in form to the last, with a wooden peg at the end of the groove to receive the butt of the spear. Another wooden pin on the inside of the handle serves as a rest for the forefinger, while an excavation on the upper surface for the tips of the last three fingers is oval in form, with incisions representing a crane with long bill and legs, which is a totemic sign.

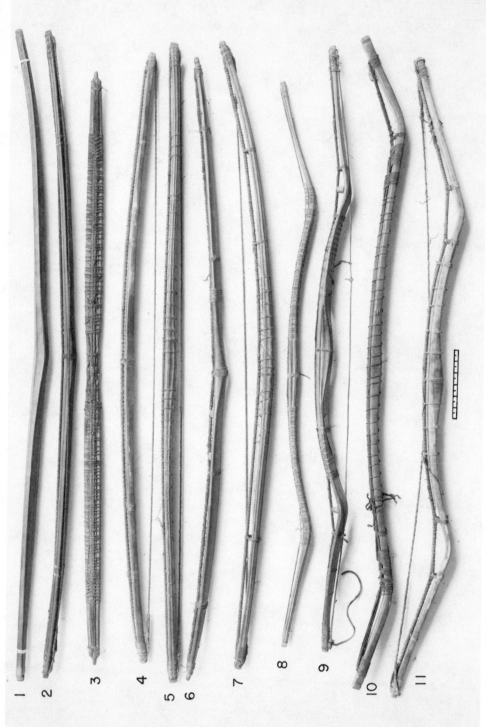

BOWS (ONE-EIGHTH)

Figure 43 (4), likewise from Sabotnisky, has two pins on the handle, against which rest the second and little fingers. The usual slot for the thumb and an aperture for the admission of the first finger are provided.

Figure 43 (5), from St Michael, has two pins, one of wood and the other of deerhorn, on the side of the handle as rests for the first and last fingers. Three hollows on the upper surface serve for the tips of the last three fingers. An upright wooden pin at the end of the groove in the handle is intended to retain the butt of the spear.

Figure 43 (3), from Norton sound, has a hole on the underside for the forefinger, a shallow depression on the upper surface for receiving the tips of the fingers, and two bone pins on the side, against which the third and last fingers may rest.

Figure 43 (9), from St Michael, has two wooden pins on the side and a depression on the upper surface as rests for the fingers, and a hole through the lower part for the forefinger, in front of which is cut the raven totem sign.

Figure 43 (2), from Cape Vancouver, is a long, slender stick, with a narrow groove on one side of the handle for the thumb, two pins on the opposite side as rests for the first and second fingers, and a deep depression on the top for the ends of the last two fingers.

Figure 43 (8), from Nunivak island, has two pins on one side of the handle as rests for the first and second fingers, a groove for the thumb, and a crossbar of ivory at the end of the groove in the upper surface, with a small spur at its side to retain the butt of the spear.

Figure 43 (11), from Kushunuk, has three pegs along one side of the handle, and a groove on the upper surface as a rest for the fingers, while a rounded slot on the opposite side is intended for the thumb.

Figure 43 (10), from Nunivak island, was obtained by Doctor Dall. It has three pegs on one side of the handle and three depressions on the upper surface as finger-rests and a deep slot to receive the thumb.

Among the throwing sticks obtained by Doctor Dall on Nunivak island is one having two bone pegs on one side and made to use in the left hand. This is the only example of the kind in the collection.

BOWS

Bows and arrows were still in common use for shooting birds and fish in some districts of northwestern Alaska during my residence there. The Eskimo hunter's rule for making his bow was that it should be the length of his outstretched arms, measuring from the finger tips. The length of the ordinary hunting or war arrow was the distance from the tip of the extended left thumb to the inner end of the right collar bone, but if the man happened to be short armed he usually measured from the tip of the left forefinger instead of from the thumb.

Among the Eskimo the making of sinew-backed bows attained a high degree of excellence, particularly in the district between lower Yukon and Kuskokwim rivers, where bows are still used more than elsewhere in Alaska. These bows are of the kind generally in use, but some are made without backing. At St Michael, and thence to the northward, bows without sinew backing were common, but the majority of all bows in this region have a backing of some kind.

A large number of bows were collected which vary considerably in form and style of backing.

Figure 1, plate LX, illustrates a bow from Askinuk, narrowed and thickened in the middle, where it is grasped by the hand; thence it broadens in each direction for a short distance and then narrows toward the tips, where it is notched for the reception of the string.

Figure 4, plate LX, from Nunivak island, is a bow with a heavy sinew cable along the back, with three sets of cross-lashings to hold it in position; the string is of twisted sinew.

Figure 2, plate LX, from the lower Yukon, is backed with a single heavy cable of sinew, with two cross-lashings near the ends and one in the middle.

Figure 6, plate LX, is a bow from Askinuk, made with a single cable as backing, which is held in position by fine cross lashings; to force up and tighten this backing two small wooden blocks, each notched on its upper side, are inserted on one side of the middle.

Figure 5, plate LX, is a broad, heavy bow from Tununuk, with a single cable along the back and a continuous lashing to hold it in position along the inner two-thirds of its length. The string is of sinew, with a wrapping of spruce root on the middle to afford a good hold for the fingers.

Figure 7, plate LX, from Nunivak island, has a single cable along the back, which is held in position by a continuous cross-lashing along the middle third and one near each end; inserted under the cable in the center of the bow is a' long strip of ivory, flattened below and grooved above, to receive the cable, which is intended as a strengthener and to give elasticity.

Figure 3, plate LX, from Unalaklit, has two flattened cables of sinew along the back, with a thin layer of skin beneath them. They are held in position by a continuous cross-lashing of sinew, which extends along the entire length from within about six inches of the ends.

Figure 8, plate LX, from Pastolik, has a single light cable along the back, with a cross-lashing extending about one-third of the length each way from the middle. This bow has a double curve about one-fourth of the length inward from each end; along the back, in this curve, is laid a piece of deerhorn, which is flat on the lower side for resting upon the bow and grooved above to receive the cable.

Figure 10, plate LX, represents a heavy bow obtained by Captain Hooper on St Lawrence island. It has a double curve about eight inches from each end and is backed with a series of braided sinew cords, the ends of which are wound around the bow and form cross-lashings for about eight inches from each end.

Figure 11, plate LX, is a bow from Cape Vancouver, with a double curve about fifteen inches from each end. It has a single cable of sinew as a backing, held in position by numerous cross-lashings, and a long strip of ivory along the middle, under the backing, to give additional strength.

Figure 9, plate LX, is a broad, thin bow from Razbinsky, with a rawhide string and a sinew cable as backing, fastened by numerous cross-lashings; there is a double curve about a quarter of the distance from each end, in which is set a short, triangular wooden pin, having a broad base, and notched above to receive the backing. A strip of wood is inserted under the backing as a strengthener.

Figure 26, plate LXI b, from the lower Yukon, represents a strip of bone, flat on one side and grooved on the other. It is intended for use as a strengthener to be inserted under the sinew backing of a bow.

Figure 2, plate LI, is a small bow from St Michael, with a sinew backing, fastened by a number of cross lashings at short intervals. Attached to the bow by means of long sinew cords are two slender bone arrows about nine inches long, with barbed points. This implement is used for killing muskrats. The hunter, having found a hole of these animals in the ground, or at the entrance of their house, sits quietly down in front of it, with one of these arrows fitted on the string ready to shoot. The moment the head of the muskrat is seen at the mouth of the hole the arrow is loosed and the barb point entering the animal prevents its escape, while the cord that attaches the arrow to the bow enables the hunter to drag it out of its burrow.

ARROWS

ARROWS FOR LARGE GAME

Several forms of arrows are used in different parts of the Alaskan mainland and on the adjacent islands. Among those collected the most important were the arrows used for hunting large game and in war. These consist of a straight wooden shaft, sometimes terminating in a foreshaft of bone or of ivory, with a stone or metal point set in a slot in the end. Others have a long point of bone or ivory with a sharp edge, either notched or smooth.

Figure 5, plate LXI a, represents an arrow from Cape Darby, having a straight bone tip, suboval in cross section, with three notches on one side, and shaped to a sharp point. The shaft has a notch for the bowstring, but it is not feathered.

Figure 9, plate LXI a, shows a deer arrow from Big lake, having a long bone point with four notches along each side, and a narrow, flattened base inserted in the split end of the shaft and firmly lashed to it by a sinew cord. At the butt of the arrow are three feathers with one side of the plume removed, the tips being inserted in little slits near the end of the shaft, and the butts, which point forward, being held in position by a sinew lashing. This is the method commonly adopted on the Alaskan mainland for attaching feathers to arrows.

Figure 1, plate LXI *a*, shows one of two arrows from St Lawrence island, both of which have long, pointed, triangular heads of ivory, the butts of which are set in slots in the wooden shafts and fastened by sinew lashings. The shafts have their fore ends triangular in continuation of the shape of the points, but toward the butt they become round, and are flattened as they approach the end. One of these shafts is broadly flattened as an aid to the feathering in guiding its flight; the other was feathered upon both sides of the flattened butt, but the feathering has been lost.

Figures 4 and 6, plate LXI *a*, are ivory-pointed arrows from St Lawrence island.

Figure 2, plate LXI *a*, represents an arrow from St Lawrence island, having a long, triangular point of ivory with four notches on one side of the point without barbing, except on the hindmost, where the point is cut to a wedge-shape for insertion in a slot in the wooden shaft. This shaft has two feathers from a cormorant tail, fastened in the usual manner.

Figure 8, plate LXI *a*, shows an arrow obtained on Nunivak island by Doctor Dall. It has a long bone point with three notches on the side and a groove running along their bases, thus marking the arrow as belonging to a man of the wolf totem. The point is inserted in a hole in the shaft, which is wound with sinew lashing; it has three feathers near the butt, held in position by a sinew cord.

Figure 3, plate LXI *a*, shows an arrow from St Lawrence island, with a long, flattened bone point with a strong barb on one surface and grooved along the other. There are two tail-feathers of a cormorant on the flattened sides of the shaft near the butt.

Figure 7, plate LXI *a*, shows an arrow obtained at St Michael by Mr L. M. Turner. The point is of bone, triangular in cross-section, but becoming round near the butt, where it is inserted in the shaft and held in place by a sinew lashing. The butt of the shaft is not feathered.

Figure 10, plate LXI *a*, represents an arrow obtained by Doctor Dall from Nunivak island; it has a foreshaft of bone, is suboval in cross-section, with a single strong notch and barb on one side and a thin, triangular tip of iron inserted in a notch at the top. It has three halves of feathers at equal intervals around the butt, fastened in the usual manner.

Figure 11, plate LXI *a*, from St Lawrence island, has a bone fore-shaft in which a triangular point is inserted, and two cormorant feathers near the butt of the shaft.

Figure 12, plate LXI *a*, from St Lawrence island, has a bone fore-shaft set on the shaft in an unusual manner. The foreshaft has a wedge-shape slot in which the wooden shaft is inserted, and an iron point is fixed in a slot in the other end of the foreshaft. Both point and foreshaft are held in position by wooden rivets, and a sinew lashing is wound around the junction of the foreshaft and shaft to bind them securely in place.

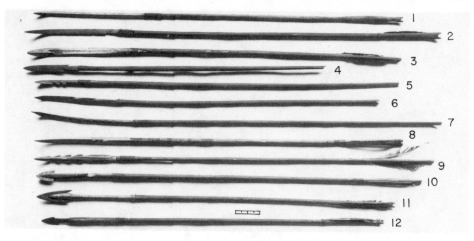

a—ARROWS FOR LARGE GAME AND FOR WAR (Three-twentieths)

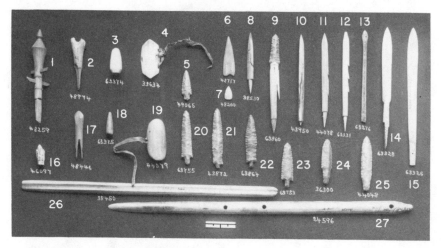

b—ARROW POINTS, WRIST GUARDS, AND STRENGTHENERS FOR BOWS AND QUIVERS (About one-sixth)

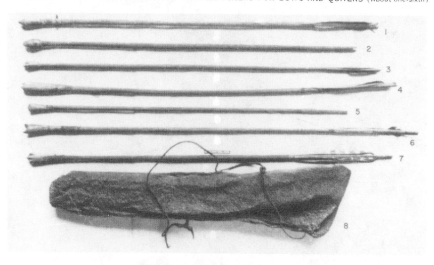

c—BIRD ARROWS AND QUIVER (Three-twentieths)

HUNTING AND WAR IMPLEMENTS

Among the arrowpoints without shafts, obtained on St Lawrence island, are several of peculiar form. Among these the specimens shown in figures 12, 14, and 15, plate LXI*b*, differ most from those already described. They are all made from bone.

Figure 11, plate LXI*b*, from Kowak river, is a double-notch arrowpoint of deerhorn, and figure 10 of the same plate is a single-notch ivory point from Nubviukhchugaluk.

Figure 8, plate LXI*b*, from the lower Yukon, is a bone foreshaft with a single notch on one side and with a small slate point.

Figure 9, plate LXI*b*, from Point Hope, is a bone foreshaft with a single deep notch and a well-made tip of chipped flint.

Figure 6, plate LXI*b*, from Razbinsky, is a triangular slate point.

Figure 7, plate LXI*b*, from Cape Prince of Wales, is a triangular point of hard, green stone.

Figure 22, plate LXI*b*, is a beautifully chipped flint arrowhead from Point Hope.

Figure 21, plate LXI*b*, is a flint point from Unalaklit.

Figures 20, 23, plate LXI*b*, are flint points from Hotham inlet.

Figure 24, plate LXI*b*, from Shaktolik; figure 25 of the same plate, from Nubviukhchugaluk, and figure 5 of the plate, from St Michael, illustrate well made flint points.

Figure 13, plate LXI*b*, is an iron point, from St Lawrence island, resembling some of the bone points in form.

BIRD ARROWS

Arrows with blunt heads of various patterns are used for killing birds.

Figure 2, plate LXI*c*, is a featherless arrow from St Lawrence island, with a rounded, conical head of ivory that has a hole in the base for the insertion of the shaft.

Figure 3, plate LXI*c*, is an arrow from Cape Darby, with a bone head that terminates in a knob-shape enlargement with a series of notches around the edge, forming a crenelated pattern.

Figure 4, plate LXI*c*, is an arrow from Pastolik, with a long bone head, which is excavated and crossed by two slots which form four points ranged in a circle around the edge. The butt has two feathers.

Figure 1, plate LXI*c*, is an arrow from Cape Vancouver, with a round head of ivory terminating in a conical point. Just back of the head the shaft is crossed by two bone pins which are passed through it at right angles, with the points projecting. The butt has three feathers which are bound on with a strip of whalebone.

Figure 5, plate LXI*c*, is a boy's bird arrow from Kigiktauik, with a knob-like head of bone which has four points around its surface. The tapering end of the shaft is inserted in a hole at the base of the head. On the butt are two feathers.

Figure 6, plate LXI*c*, shows an arrow, from Kigiktauik, with a double-pointed bone head on which the raven totem sign is engraved.

Figure 7, plate LXI c, illustrates an arrow from the lower Yukon, with a knoblike bone head notched around its edge and terminating in a small point in the center. At the base of the shaft are three feathers of the gerfalcon, fastened by sinew wrappings.

FISH ARROWS

In addition to the arrows used for killing birds and mammals, the Eskimo have others for shooting fish, which vary considerably in the shape of the heads.

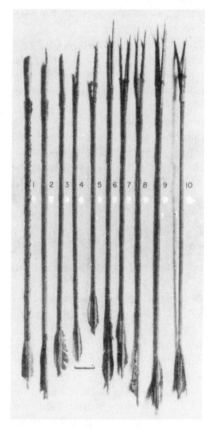

FIG. 44—Fish arrows ($\frac{1}{10}$).

Figure 44 (3) represents one of these fish arrows from Razbinsky. It has a wooden shaft, with three feather vanes at the butt and a single barbed point of bone inserted in the split end of the shaft and held in position by sinew lashing.

Figure 44 (4, 5) are fish arrows from Nunivak island, each having a single, long point with a series of barbs along the inside and a short supplementary barb on the opposite side of the shaft. The base is set in a slot in the shaft and held in place by sinew lashings. At the butt are two feathers.

Figure 44 (6) shows a fish arrow, from the lower Yukon, with two barbs of unequal length, notched along their outer edges, set into the head of the shaft with their backs nearly touching, and held in position by a strong lashing. At the butt of the shaft are three feathers, the ends of which are inserted and fastened by sinew lashings.

Figure 44 (7) shows a fish arrow, from Nunivak island, somewhat similar to the preceding specimen, having two points of bone, barbed along their outer surfaces and held in position by sinew lashings. The butt has three feather vanes.

Figure 44 (8) illustrates another double-pointed fish arrow, from Razbinsky, with barbs along the inner faces of the points.

Figure 44 (9) shows a fish arrow, from Norton sound, which has three bone points with a series of barbs along the inner face of each; the long, pointed lower ends are inserted in deep grooves in the sides of the shaft, where they are fastened by sinew lashings. At the base are three feathers.

Figure 44 (10) represents a handsomely made triple point fish arrow from Cape Vancouver, with the points serrated as in the preceding specimen and held in position by an ivory ferule slipped over them. At the base of the shaft are three tail-feathers of a cormorant. They are notched along their inner vanes and bound in place by a sinew cord at their tips and a strip of whalebone about the lower ends.

Figure 44 (2) shows a fish arrow from Cape Vancouver; it has a bone head, provided with a detachable barbed point fastened to the shaft by a cord.

Figure 44 (1) shows a fish arrow from the Yukon mouth, having a detachable point, with a long sinew cord, which is divided on its inner half and attached at two widely separated points to the shaft. When a fish is struck and the point freed, the shaft floats and forms a drag to impede its escape.

ARROWPOINTS

Figure 2, plate LXI*b*, is a bone arrowhead from Sabotnisky, the tip of which is notched to form four points. The base forms a wedge-shape point for insertion in the shaft.

Figure 17, plate LXI*b*, from Kigiktauik, is a bone point beveled down to form five faces.

Figure 1, plate LXI*b*, from Nunivak island, is a conical point of wood having two short, iron crossbars inserted at right angles through the head. The inner end is cut down to a wedge-shape point for insertion in the shaft.

Figures 3 and 18, plate LXI*b*, show conical points of ivory from St Lawrence island. Their bases are excavated, with a round hole for receiving the points of the shafts.

Figure 16, plate LXI*b*, from Nunivak island, is of ivory, with the base excavated to receive the shaft. The conical point is surrounded by rounded auxiliary points, formed by incisions along the sides, making a crenelated pattern.

QUIVERS

Figure 8, plate LXI*c*, represents a fish-skin quiver from the lower Yukon. It has a cord attached at the upper edge and at another point about midway on one side.

Figure 27, plate LXI*b*, shows a long ivory rod which was obtained at St Michael by Mr Turner; it is intended for insertion along the side of a quiver to stiffen it. It is crescentic in cross section and large at one end, which terminates in the figure of a wolf's head. The back of the rod has three holes for the passage of a lashing.

WRIST-GUARDS

Figure 4, plate LXI*b*, shows a bone wrist-guard from St Michael, made to wear upon the left wrist to prevent the bowstring from striking it.

18 ETH——11

It is bound on by a strip of rawhide, which is passed through two holes on one side and one upon the other.

Figure 19, plate LXIb, illustrates a bone wrist-guard from Kowak river, with a single hole on one side for the attachment of a cord. Wrist-guards are all made crescentic in cross section, in order to fit the curve of the wrist.

BOXES FOR ARROW- AND SPEAR POINTS

The Eskimo store and carry the thin, flat points for arrows, spears, and lances in small wooden boxes, in the manufacture of which they display considerable ingenuity.

A box of this kind (number 36248), from Kushunuk, is flattened and square in outline and made from a single piece of wood; the excavated interior is shallow; it is grooved just below the upper edge to receive the sliding cover, which has a notch on the top near one end for a thumb-rest in drawing it out. On two corners of the box a rawhide loop is fastened for hanging it to the belt or for attaching it to any other object.

Figure 10, plate LXII, is a long, flattened box from Cape Nome. It is less than an inch in height, is 7½ inches long, and has a sliding cover. The sides and top are ornamented with a variety of incised cross-line patterns.

Figure 5, plate LXII, is a long, thin box from Nunivak island, slightly convex above and below, pointed oval at one end and truncated at the other. It has a long, narrow cover, fitting like a stopper and resting at each end on a sunken ledge, and a thumb-piece for raising it projects at the rear. On the upper side of the front end of the box are incised the outlines of the mouth, nostrils, and eyes of some animal.

Figure 1, plate LXII, from Pikmiktalik, is a rudely oval box, grooved around the sides and along the bottom, but otherwise is not ornamented.

Figure 4, plate LXII, represents a box, from Cape Nome, fashioned in the form of a fish known as the losh. The eyes are formed by small ivory pegs with the centers excavated for the pupils; the gill openings are marked by incised crescentic lines; the mouth is incised, and the tail is represented as doubled and lying forward midway along the body. It has a long, oval, stopper-like cover resting on a sunken ledge at each end.

Figure 6, plate LXII, shows a box, from Askinuk, in the shape of a seal. The eyes and the mouth are incised and the front flippers are in relief; the cover is a long-pointed oval in outline and fits into the side, thus differing from the ordinary method of fitting it either in the upper or the under surface.

Figure 3, plate LXII, illustrates a box, from Norton sound, representing a seal in flattened outline. The head is well made, the eyes and nostrils being formed by inlaid pieces of ivory. The cover represents another seal, the projecting head and neck forming the thumb-piece for raising it. The eyes and the nostrils are marked by ivory pegs.

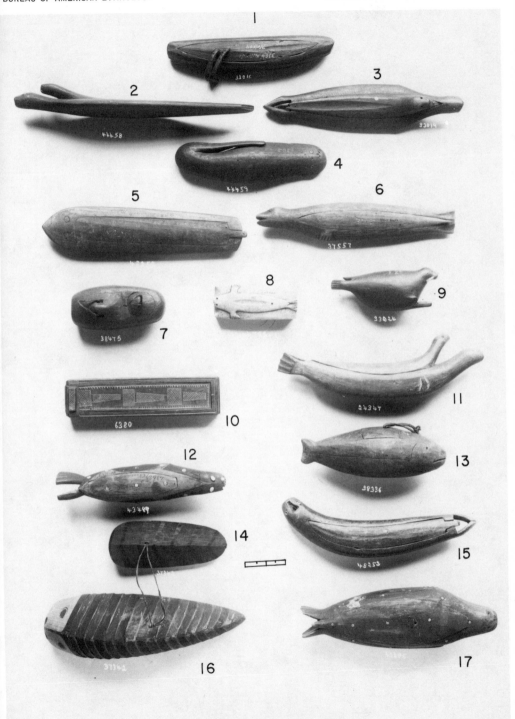

BOXES FOR ARROWPOINTS AND PAINTS (ONE-FIFTH)

A box (number 64220) from the Diomede islands represents a rude, heavily-made figure of a right whale cut from a piece of wood; the mouth and blowholes are incised; the lower surface of the body is excavated, forming a somewhat rounded, conical orifice on which fits a stopper-like cover in the shape of a seal; this is held in place by means of a rawhide cord passing through a hole in the under surface of the whale, thence through two holes in the shoulders of the seal, and is fastened on the under surface. Toward the rear of the seal's back a loop of cord is attached, the end of which passes through a hole in the tail of the whale and through which the cord is passed for fastening. This box is a kind of fetich in which are kept the small spear- and lance-points used in killing whales.

A box (number 63268) exactly like the preceding was obtained on St Lawrence island.

Figure 2, plate LXII, shows a flattened oval box, from Cape Nome, representing a seal with a smaller one on its back; the latter forms a long, pointed, oval cover; the eyes of the larger seal are indicated by blue beads. The top of the box is crossed by a series of parallel lines extending from the middle diagonally backward toward the border.

FIREARMS

Although primitive forms of weapons are still largely used, guns are common everywhere among the Eskimo. The guns obtained by them during the early period of their contact with the Russians were extremely clumsy, and the Russians brought with them the forked supports for these weapons which they were accustomed to use in Siberia. In some of the more retired parts of the country between the lower Yukon and the Kuskokwim these supports still exist, as the poor quality of the guns and the scarcity of ammunition render its aid necessary in hunting to secure a fair degree of accuracy and success.

Figure 31, plate LXIII, illustrates one of these forked supports, from Chalitmut, having two legs tipped with ivory points and a crossbar of ivory to hold them in position. Along each of the three outer faces of these legs is a groove in which small, round, ivory pegs are set at intervals; at the upper end the support has a rounded head in which is a deep slot; through the sides is a hole in which fits an ivory pin, fastened by a rawhide cord. A deerhorn disk is fitted into the slot and is held in place by a pin; it has a long, flattened projection on one side which is grooved to receive the gun barrel and has three holes for the lashings by which it was secured; as this disk moved freely on the pin the support folded down parallel to the gunstock when being carried, and could be readily set in position when needed.

Figure 24, plate LXIII, from Kigiktauik; figure 25 of the same plate, from Chalitmut; and figure 26, from Kushunuk, illustrate examples of the pieces of deerhorn intended for securing the lower side of the gun barrel to connect the forked rest with the gun.

Figure 8, plate LXIII, represents a pair of bullet molds, from Chalit-mut, made from two small blocks of slate neatly hollowed out and set in wooden blocks, united by pins and corresponding holes so that the faces of the molds are brought squarely together; there is a conical hole at the top by means of which lead can be poured into the mold.

Figure 16, plate LXIII, represents a bullet starter, from Cape Van-couver, for use in muzzle-loading guns; it is made of wood and has a bone handle. Figure 15, plate LXIII, shows another bullet starter made entirely of bone, which was obtained at Anogogmut.

Nearly all the guns in use at present among the Eskimo are muzzle-loaders, and the ingenuity of the natives is displayed in the many forms of cap boxes, powder chargers, and flasks made by them.

A common style of cap box is made of wood, flattened and rectangu-lar in shape, with a sliding cover. Some of these are plain, others have their surfaces cut into a variety of patterns. Figure 28, plate LXIII, from Pastolik; figure 30 of the same plate, from Cape Nome; and figure 29, from Sledge island, are examples of this style of box.

Other small wooden cap boxes are rounded in cross section, broadest at the base, and tapering toward the top, where they are truncated and fitted with a wooden stopper. Figure 17, plate LXIII, illustrates one of these boxes, obtained at Cape Vancouver. It has a series of grooves around the sides.

Figure 27, plate LXIII, from Kushunuk, is a round-sided box, shaped like a truncated cone, with a separate piece fitted in the bottom. Fig-ure 6 of the same plate, from Kowak river, is another tapering box of this kind, with the top turned out to form a lip, under which is fas-tened a rawhide cord for attaching the box to the hunting bag.

Another curious style of box, made to contain a few caps in each end, illustrated in figure 1, plate LXIII, was obtained at St Michael. It is a long, cylindrical box, largest in the middle and tapering toward both ends, which are truncated. It consists of two pieces, excavated, neatly fitted together, and fastened by sinew cords. Extending cross-wise through the middle is a wooden pin for the attachment of the cord which fastens the box to the hunting bag. A little wooden stopper is inserted in each end.

Other cap boxes are made of ivory, cut into various forms, with a stopper in one end and the other closed by a piece of wood which is held in position by rivets. Figure 4, plate LXIII, from Cape Nome; figure 5 of the same plate, from Norton sound; figure 7, from Nubviuk-chugaluk; and figure 2, from Kaviak peninsula, illustrate specimens of these boxes.

Powder chargers are even more varied in form, and show more inge-nuity in design than the cap boxes.

Figure 3, plate LXIII, is a small charger, made of bone, with a long, round, wooden cap box attached to it by a sinew cord. It was obtained at Norton bay.

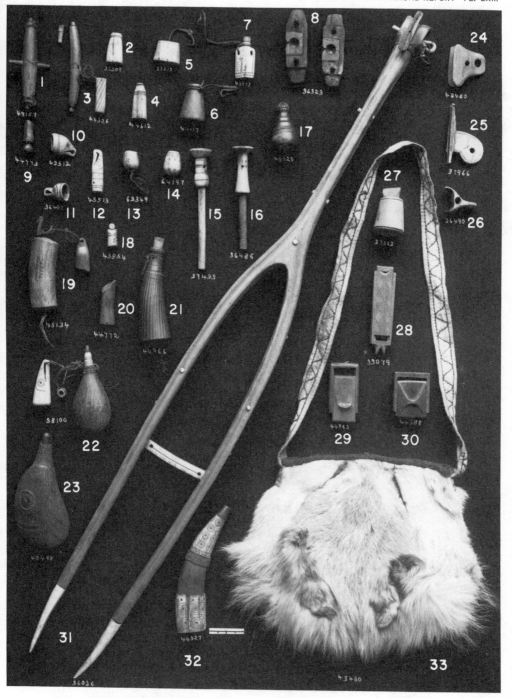

OBJECTS USED WITH GUNS AND IN HUNTING (ONE-FIFTH)

Figure 14, plate LXIII, represents a rounded bone charger from Hotham inlet. It has an ornamental device of circles and dots and the raven totem etched upon its surface.

Figure 18, plate LXIII, from Unalaklit, has its lower end carved into the form of a human head.

Figure 12, plate LXIII, from Cape Vancouver, represents a cormorant's head.

Figure 11, plate LXIII, from Cape Vancouver, represents the head of a skua-gull.

Figure 9, plate LXIII, from Sledge island, is a cylindrical ivory charger with a knob on the lower end.

Figure 13, plate LXIII, from St Lawrence island, is rounded with a small, spout-like projection on the rim.

Figure 10, plate LXIII, from Cape Vancouver, represents a falcon's head.

Figure 20, plate LXIII, from Sledge island, is a rounded bone charger with a wooden stopper; it is intended for carrying a charge of powder ready for putting in the gun when needed.

Figure 19, plate LXIII, represents a powder flask obtained at Kotzebue sound; it is made from a section of deerhorn, excavated and fitted with a wooden stopper at each end; one of these is perforated and a small plug of wood inserted, by removing which an inlet is formed for the powder. A charger of deerhorn is attached to the flask by a sinew cord.

Figure 23, plate LXIII, from Cape Vancouver, is a wooden powder flask in the form of a sea parrot's head. The small end at the neck is bound together with sinew lashings, and a rounded stopper is fitted in the hole.

Figure 22, plate LXIII, from Nulukhtulogumut, shows a small, leather-covered flask with an ivory mouthpiece in which a wooden stopper is fitted; to this is attached an ivory charger in the shape of a cormorant's head. With this charger is a small ivory disk, having a conical perforation in the center, which is intended to be placed over the nipple of the gun for priming it.

The form of both of the preceding flasks is an imitation of those sold by the fur traders.

Figure 21, plate LXIII, from Sledge island, is a wooden powder flask with the sides carved in a twining pattern.

Figure 32, plate LXIII, from Norton bay, is a wooden flask fitted at each end with an ivory cover and having an iron tip at the nozzle.

The Eskimo of Plover bay on the Siberian shore and on St Lawrence island, as well as those along the shores of Bering strait and thence up the Alaskan coast to Point Barrow, are successful hunters of the right whale; for this purpose the old-fashioned barbed spear is the weapon ordinarily used, but it is being superceded by firearms wherever the people have been able to obtain them. At Plover bay the natives had a bomb gun which they had obtained from some whaler. While on a summer cruise on a whaling ship some of the men had learned the use of this gun and they took the earliest opportunity to obtain one; in the fall it was planted on the ice near the entrance to the bay, and as the whales swam slowly along the narrow lead that remained open in midchannel the bomb lances were fired into them without any lines attached. This was always done while the whales were heading up the bay, so that they might swim as far as possible toward the head of the bay and die under the ice; a few days later the gases would inflate their bodies to such an extent that the carcasses would burst through the ice and indicate their position to the people, who would at once cut them up, using the blubber for food and keeping the whalebone to be traded to the whalers in the spring. The people at Point Barrow have also used a whaling gun for some time.

The walrus is found on many parts of the coast, but is rarely seen near St Michael; about Nunivak island and the coast of the adjacent mainland it is caught during fall and spring. Near the mouth of the Kuskokwim the hunters endeavor to surprise herds of walrus in the shallow bays along the coast. When they succeed, they form a line of kaiaks between the animals and the sea, and by shouting and striking the sides of the kaiaks with their paddles, so alarm them that they are driven ashore, where they are easily killed. In the fall of 1879 thirty of these animals were captured by a drive of this kind just south of Cape Vancouver. This method, however, can be employed only where the water is very shallow, so that the walrus can not escape by diving and passing beneath the kaiaks.

Although spears and lances are still used in walrus hunting, as firearms become more plentiful among the natives many of these animals are shot with rifles, which are used in addition to the old-style weapons for killing the beluga or white whale. This animal is sometimes stranded at low water and is then easily killed. These whales are treated with great respect by the Eskimo, and when one is taken certain ceremonies must be observed to avoid offending it. At St Michael I saw the hunters haul a recently killed beluga ashore, and before it was completely dragged out of the water one of them poured some urine in its mouth and then addressed several sentences to its shade in propitiation for having killed it. At Point Hope one was killed during the visit of the revenue cutter *Corwin* to that place in the summer of 1881, and while it was being drawn ashore the people gathered on the beach and sang a song of welcome such as is used in the kashim during certain dances.

HUNTING BAGS AND HELMETS

Hunting bags are made in various forms and are worn by a strap over the shoulders; in them the hunters carry their powder, bullets, cap boxes, and other small articles needed in the chase. Bags of this kind made from the skins of wolves' heads are highly prized.

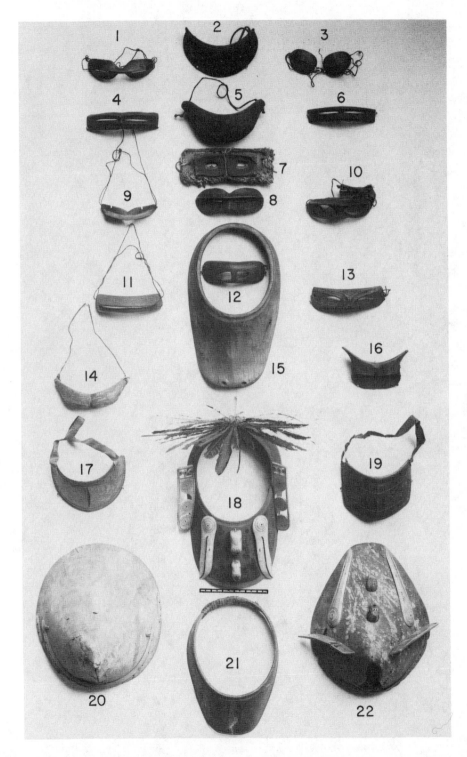

HUNTING HELMETS, VISORS, AND SNOW GOGGLES

Figure 33, plate LXIII, from St Michael, is such a bag made from the skins of two wolves' heads, bound around the edge with red flannel and lined with white cotton. A shoulder strap made of white cotton and ornamented with stitching of red worsted is attached to it.

At St Michael I obtained a long, slender hunting bag (number 38458) made of alternating strips of white and brown deerskin, with a fringe of the same cut in little strips around the lower end. It is bordered above by a trimming of skin from a loon's throat, which is succeeded by ornamental bands of deerskin and a strip of wolverine fur.

The people of the seacoast between Yukon and Kuskokwim rivers use conical wooden helmets to protect their eyes from the glare of the sun when hunting at sea; these are ornamented with carved ivory images or are painted with various devices.

At Kushunuk were seen many of these hats which were painted white, on which were various phallic pictures in red; these pictures had a certain significance connected with the religious beliefs of the people, which I failed to ascertain. The same idea was shown in a phallic picture on a pair of paddles obtained at this village, each of the two having one-half of the picture upon it, so that it was completed by joining them at their edges.

From the mouth of the Yukon northward, wooden visors are used to shade the eyes; these are somewhat similar in shape to the helmets but they lack the conical top; the forepieces of the visors are often ornamented with ivory carvings and have at the back a plume of feathers from the tails of old squaw ducks.

Figure 22, plate LXIV, represents one of these conical helmets from Kushunuk. It has a strip of deerhorn lashed around the base at the rear to hold the bent ends in position. On both sides are fastened, by sinew cord passed through holes, wing-like pieces of ivory, carved with open-work pattern and ornamented with groups of concentric circles, with a central hole in each. On the middle of the front are two carved walrus heads of ivory, and on each side of these are two ivory strips representing heads of gulls. The outer surface of this helmet is painted slate color splashed with white.

Another helmet, from Kaialigamut (figure 20, plate LXIV), is without ivory ornaments on the front. It is held together at the back by a strip of deerhorn pierced with holes, through which pass lashings of cord; the edges, where they are held together in the rear, are fastened together with spruce-root lashings. The outer surface is painted white and decorated with red figures; bordering grooves on the top and bottom are also red.

The visors worn by the people of Norton sound and the lower Yukon are usually plain, but sometimes are made to represent the head of some animal. They consist of a fillet of wood passing around the back of the head, with the front carried out to form a long, rounded forepiece.

Figure 21, plate LXIV, illustrates one of these unornamented visors, which was obtained at Razbinsky. It has a groove around the edge and a deep, broad groove down the front; at the rear the overlapping ends are lashed together with willow bark. The specimen from St Michael, shown in plate LXIV, 15, is more heavily made. On the middle of the front is a groove. The front is carried out to represent the head of a pike, with a mouth formed by a deeply incised groove, in which are set numerous small reindeer teeth; two deep holes represent the nostrils, and two amber-colored beads are inlaid for eyes. One side of the visor is black, the other side is not colored. Visors from the shore of Norton sound are sometimes ornamented with ivory figures lashed to their sides and front, like the helmets from south of the Yukon mouth.

Figure 18, plate LXIV, illustrates a visor of this kind, which has a wing-like piece on each side and the head of a gull in front; the median ridge is ornamented with the ivory images of two walrus heads. The back of the visor has an oval ring of shavings projecting upward and stuck full of feathers from the tails of cormorants and old wife ducks.

Figure 2, plate LXIV, from Chalitmut; figure 19 of the same plate, from Norton bay; and figure 17, from Sledge island, represent visors made from pieces of wood, with a rawhide strip or cord attached on each side for passing over the back of the head. The first specimen mentioned is painted black on both sides and has a series of ivory pegs and white beads inlaid in two rows on the upper surface. The visor shown in plate LXIV, 19, has a shallow groove, painted red, around the upper edge; inside of this is a deep, narrow groove, which, with the remainder of the visor, is uncolored. The third specimen (plate LXIV, 17) has the lower part of the visor, a band around the edge, and a long, oval groove down the front, painted black. A shallow groove, extending around the borders above and below inside the black line, is colored red.

The ornamentation of helmets with ivory carvings varies but little in the several localities. Usually there is a long, flat, wing-shape piece on each side and the head of a bird in front; the middle is occupied by carvings of walrus heads or figures of other animals.

The following specimens, shown in figure 45, illustrate some of the ornaments:

Number 8 represents one of the wing-shape pieces from Shaktolik, with open-work pattern and a series of circles and dots. Number 7 shows one of the ivory strips obtained at Kushunuk; it is carved to represent the head of a cormorant. Another, from Askinuk (number 6), represents the head of a gull. A specimen from St Michael (number 5) is an ivory walrus head for the front of a helmet. Another, from Kushunuk (number 3), represents a land otter, the eyes of which are represented by inlaid blue beads, and similar beads are inlaid in the centers of circles etched along the back. A thin band of deerhorn from the lower Yukon (number 2) is flattened on one side and beveled to three faces on the other; it is pierced with holes, in pairs, to receive the lashings, with which it is bound on the back of a helmet to hold the bent ends of the wood in position. A walrus head, cut from ivory, from Kushunuk (Museum number 38719), is for ornamenting the front of a hunting helmet. A similar ornament from Anogogmut (number 1) represents the flattened image of a seal, with eyes formed by inlaid blue beads. Another of these ornaments (number 4), from the lower Yukon, is a flattened, conventionalized image of a wolf. Along the

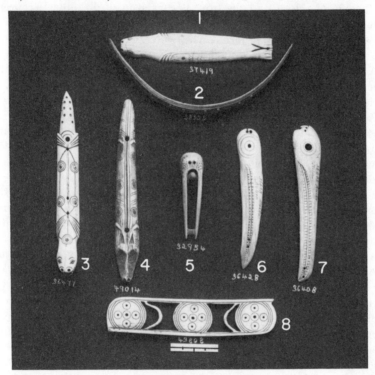

Fig. 45—Ivory ornaments for hunting helmets (¼).

back and the sides it is ornamented with etched lines and a series of three pairs of concentric circles, each having a wooden peg inserted in a central hole.

SNOW GOGGLES

To preserve the eyes from the glare of the sun on the snow in the spring and thus prevent snow blindness, goggles are in general use among the Eskimo. They vary considerably, according to locality, but the specimens illustrated give the principal variations in form among those collected.

Figure 5, plate LXIV, represents a flattened, funnel shape specimen of these goggles, obtained from the lower Yukon. The projecting front extends out both above and below in a gradual slope to the edges of a single broad slit, the upper border slightly overhanging the lower. They have a rounded notch for fitting over the nose, and are held in position by a cord which passes over the back of the head. A specimen from Point Hope, shown in plate LXIV, 11, is somewhat similar to the preceding, except that the slit is smaller and the upper front border projects farther beyond the lower.

Another pair from the Lower Yukon (plate LXIV, 4) have two narrow slits divided in the middle by a septum. A notch is cut on the inner surface for the nose, and the front is carved in slight relief to represent a human face, with the nose between the eye slits. The forehead projects at the eyebrows to form a visor-like edge. The inside and top of the goggles are painted black and the front red.

A pair from Norton sound (figure 6, plate LXIV) have two slits, a notch for the nose resting against a strong septum in the middle, and a visor-like projection along the top in front. The goggles from Sabotnisky (figure 13, plate LXIV) have a notch for the nose and two flattened eye slits divided by a rudely made septum. The top is grooved to represent hair, and a nose is shown between the slits, giving them a mask-like appearance. They are painted red in front, but are not colored behind.

Figure 8, plate LXIV, represents spectacle-shape goggles from Cape Darby, with two narrow eye slits and a visor-like projection in front. There is a deep groove for the nose and the outline is narrowed in the middle, so that the eyepieces are suboval in shape.

Another pair (figure 1, plate LXIV), from Norton bay, are still more like spectacles than the preceding, being greatly narrowed in the middle between the two slits for the eyes. The front slopes gently to the borders of the slits and there is no visor. Another example of neatly made goggles (figure 9, plate LXIV), also obtained at Norton bay, are narrowed in the middle with two narrow slits and a visor in front. The upper borders of the eyepieces are deeply notched to permit the circulation of air about the eyes. The pair shown in figure 3, plate LXIV, are also from Norton bay. They consist of two suboval eyepieces, held together by two sinew cords which are strung with beads. Each of these eyepieces has a long, narrow eye slit.

Figure 14, plate LXIV, represents spectacle-shape goggles from Kushunuk; they are fashioned to extend forward, surrounding the large, oval eyeholes in a flattened, tubular form; the insides of the eyeholes are painted black, as is the upper portion of the outside, with the exception of the borders of the eyeholes which are red.

A specimen from St Lawrence island, figure 12, plate LXIV, consists of a trough-shape piece of wood, concave within and convex on the outside; it is somewhat crescentic in form, with a notch on the lower side for the nose; the eyeholes are straight within against the wooden crossbar or septum which divides them, and their outer edges are oval; they are large, and without any arrangement for shading them.

KNIFE SHARPENER AND DAGGER OF NEPHRITE, WITH SHEATH (ONE-HALF)

A pair of goggles (figure 10, plate LXIV) obtained at Port Clarence by Doctor T. H. Bean, are made from three pieces of wood; both the upper and lower pieces are grooved to admit the insertion of a fragment of common window glass in each oval eyehole; they are lashed together with whalebone cord passed through holes; a projecting visor over-hangs the front; inside a bar of wood is lashed, which is notched on each side over the eye to permit circulation of air.

A clumsily made pair from the Diomede islands (figure 7, plate LXIV) consist of two pieces of canvas sewed together; eyeholes are cut in the middle of each, in which are inserted pieces of window glass; the can-vas is backed by a rudely formed wooden framework, rather quadrate in outline. These are the only goggles of this kind that were seen.

Figure 16, plate LXIV, represents a pair of wooden goggles from Nor-ton sound; they are notched for the nose, and project at the sides as long, oval ends reaching to the temples; the tubular front has two large, oval holes, and a strip of rawhide, rounded in front, is pegged to the upper surface to form a visor.

HUNTING AND SKINNING KNIVES

The stone knives formerly in universal use among the Eskimo have been almost entirely displaced by the ordinary butcher knives sold by the traders. Some of these old-fashioned flint knives were procured at Hotham inlet, and were in actual use when obtained; they are illus-trated in plate XLVII, figures 2, 3. They consist of leaf-shape, chipped flint blades, set in short wooden handles split at the lower end to receive the blade which is held in place by a wrapping of rawhide or sinew cord, or (as in figure 3) by a lashing of willow root.

From the northern end of Norton sound a beautiful knife (plate LXV, 3) was obtained. The narrow, leaf-shape blade of nephrite is $8\frac{1}{4}$ inches in length and $2\frac{1}{4}$ inches wide at its broadest part, and is slightly convex on one side; the other side is slightly grooved near each edge and has a broad, slightly elevated, flat ridge running down the center to near the point; it is double-edged and brought to a slightly rounded point. The handle is of ivory, oval in cross section, $3\frac{1}{4}$ inches in length; the blade is set in a slot, the sides of which overlap about 2 inches, through which ivory pegs are inserted to hold it in place. In the handle are seven holes, through which a rawhide cord is wound and crossed to afford a firm grip for the hand. The wooden sheath (plate LXV, 2) follows the outline of the knife and extends halfway up the handle; it is in two parts, which are fastened together by thin strips of whalebone passed through holes in the edges. Across one side of the sheath, near the butt, are two small, parallel grooves which form the private mark of the owner. This specimen, from its large size and the beauty and regu-larity of its finish, is probably unique. It was purchased at Nubviukh-chugaluk from a Kaviak Eskimo who said that it had been an heirloom in his family for many generations; although now of no practical utility he prized it very much from its association, and it was only after two years of careful effort that I succeeded in obtaining it by paying what he considered a large price. Other jade knives, somewhat similar to this but much smaller and with less perfect blades, were also seen.

Knives are usually worn by the Eskimo in a sheath strapped to the outside of the right thigh, just below the hip, so that the handle may readily be grasped; some of the men, however, have the sheath suspended from the waist belt.

DRAG HANDLES

Drag handles, attached to a stout permanent loop of sealskin cord, are used for hauling dead seals or other heavy weights over the snow or ice. They are made of wood, bone, ivory, or deerhorn, carved in a variety of forms, considerable ingenuity being exercised in adapting the designs to the shape of the handle and to the purpose for which it is to be used.

Plate LXVI, 16, from Kushunuk, is a cylindrical wooden handle, grooved around the middle for receiving the loop.

Plate LXVI, 4, from St Michael, is an ivory handle, in the form of a crossbar, with the head of a white bear carved on each end and a square slot crosswise through the middle for receiving the cord.

Plate LXVI, 18, from Cape Darby, represents two white whales lashed together on their ventral surfaces and pierced through the middle for receiving the ends of the cords, which project

FIG. 46—Cord handle of ivory (½).

through their mouths and form a loop on that end. The other ends of the whales terminate in a ring from which are suspended six links of ivory; to the last link of one of these chains is suspended a small carving in the form of a whale's tail.

Plate LXVI, 14, shows a handle, from Sledge island, in the form of a white bear. A cord passes through the lower surface.

A rounded block, carved in the form of two seals lying face to face, with their fore-flippers along their muzzles, is illustrated in plate LXVI, 1. It has two holes pierced in one end which join and issue as a single hole at the other end. It was obtained at Unalaklit.

Plate LXVI, 15, represents a handle, from Sledge island, in the shape of a white whale, which is pierced transversely for the cord.

Figure 46 shows an ivory cord handle from Sledge island. It is an extremely artistic carving, representing the head of a white bear with a small seal in its mouth. On the lower surface of the head is a figure, in relief, of another seal.

Plate LXVI, 19, shows another elaborate drag handle from Cape Darby. The central portion consists of a piece of ivory, pierced by two round holes, and a third one forming a slot through which is passed the cord for the loop. From one of these rings is hung, as a link, the tail of a whale, and from the other two chains, each consisting of eight links,

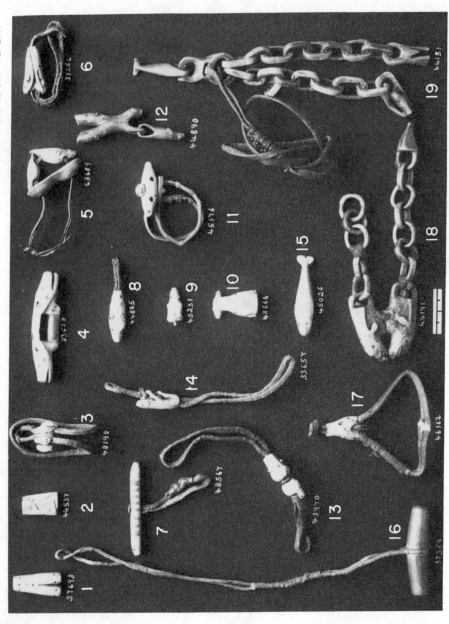

CORD OR DRAG HANDLES (ABOUT ONE-FOURTH)

one of which terminates in the head and fore-legs of a white bear and the other in the tail and hind-flippers of a seal.

Plate LXVI, 12, from Sledge island, is a four-prong ivory rod, with white-bears' heads carved upon two of the points and a seal's head on another; the fourth point terminates in a ring in which is linked a pendant representing the head and shoulders of a seal.

Plate LXVI, 2, from Cape Nome, is a small ivory handle, pierced with a hole at one end, which forks and terminates in two holes on the other end. On one side is carved in relief the form of a seal, and on the other the form of a white bear.

Plate LXVI, 17, is a handle, fashioned in the form of a white-bear's head, with blue beads inlaid for eyes. The two cords form one loop, projecting from the bear's mouth, and on the other side they project from separate holes at the rear.

Plate LXVI, 11, from Sledge island, is an ivory image of a seal, with a hole through the back, in which is fitted an ivory pin, terminating above in the figure of a seal's head. To the lower end is attached the cord forming the loop.

Plate LXVI, 5, from the Diomede islands, is a handle made of a bar of ivory, an elongated oval in outline, with a convexity near each end on the lower side and slightly excavated within. In the middle of this excavation is a hole, through which passes the cord forming a loop. On the upper side the cords pass through holes in two figurines of seals, which rest with their heads down against the outer borders of the bar.

Plate LXVI, 8, from Sledge island, has carved on one end the head of a seal and on the other that of a white bear.

Plate LXVI, 10, from Kotzebue sound, is in the shape of the head of a white bear, represented as holding a seal crosswise in its mouth; it is pierced lengthwise on the under side for the passage of a cord.

Plate LXVI, 7, from Kotzebue sound, is an elongated bar, with a seal's head on each end. The handle is surrounded by eight series of etched parallel lines.

Plate LXVI, 3, from Cape Prince of Wales, has four images of seals carved in high relief on the small ivory center through which the cord passes.

Plate LXVI, 13, from Nubviukhchugaluk, is a handle in the form of a white-bear's head, represented as holding a stick crosswise in its mouth, and just back of this, carved from a separate piece, the head of a seal.

FISHING AND FISHING IMPLEMENTS

METHODS OF FISHING

Fishing forms one of the main sources of food supply among the western Eskimo, and in its pursuit a variety of methods and implements are employed. The fishing season along the coast of Norton sound opens about the end of March or early in April of each year; at this time the spring tides begin to show along the shore, where the water forces its way up through the cracks in the ice. During the cold weather of winter the tomcod and the sculpin remain in deep water, but as spring approaches they begin to return to the vicinity of the shore, and holes in the ice are made through which they are caught by means of hook and line. During May, as the weather grows warmer, the tomcod become extremely numerous, and at this time the old men and women may be seen scattered about on the ice, a few hundred yards from the shore, where they fish during many hours of the day. Figure 47, from a photograph taken at St Michael, shows a man at one of the fishing holes.

Fig. 47—Tomcod fishing through sea ice at St Michael.

For fishing through the ice a hole from six to eight inches in diameter is made. The ice pick employed for this purpose consists of a stout wooden staff, usually provided with a point made from the end of an old chisel or a flat piece of iron; but formerly, and indeed frequently during my residence in Alaska, picks pointed with reindeer horn or ivory were in use.

Figure 10, plate LXVII, illustrates one of these picks from Norton sound; it consists of a wooden staff, nearly four feet long, terminating in a deerhorn point, which is lashed firmly to the staff with cords of sealskin.

As the ice is generally several feet in thickness, the hole becomes filled with small fragments as the work of digging progresses. To

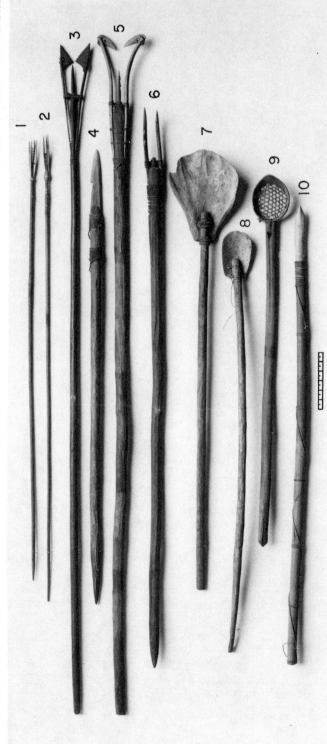

ICE PICK, SCOOPS, AND FISH SPEARS (ONE-TENTH)

remove these, as well as to skim out the film of ice that constantly forms on cold days, a small scoop with a netted bottom is used by the natives of the coast from the mouth of the Kuskokwim to Kotzebue sound. A typical specimen of an ice scoop, from St Michael, is illustrated in figure 9, plate LXVII. The rim consists of a band of deerhorn bent into a circle, the overlapping ends being pierced and lashed together with rawhide cord. The upper edge has a long, rounded point in front; the lower edge has holes in pairs, through which is passed the rawhide cord, which is netted across the bottom in a hexagonal pattern. This scoop is fastened to the handle with a lashing of sinew cord, which passes through a hole in the handle and over the rim. The wooden handle is oval in cross section, and is about 34 inches in length.

In the vicinity of Bering strait the net of some of these implements is formed of a cord made of twisted filaments of whalebone.

Another variety of this implement, from St Lawrence island, is illustrated in figure 8, plate LXVII; it consists of a slightly grooved wooden handle, to which is attached a scoop-shape piece of bone. Still another, from the same locality, is shown in figure 7, plate LXVII; it is made from the shoulder-blade of some animal, pierced near its small end with two holes, through which a lashing is passed, which fastens it firmly to a wooden handle four feet in length.

The implements used in fishing for tomcod consist of a short pole, from 25 to 36 inches in length, and a long line made from whalebone, sinew, rawhide, or the feather quills of gulls or other large waterfowl. These are split and worked a little to render them more pliable, and knotted together while moist, forming a tough and durable line. On the lower end of the line, six to ten inches from the bottom, a sinker of stone, bone, or ivory is attached, pierced at each end for attachment to the line. The hooks usually have a straight ivory or bone shank, with a hole at the upper end for the line, and two holes near the lower end, at right angles with each other, through which are thrust small, double-pointed iron skewers, with their ends bent upward, forming a hook with four points. The rods are usually provided near the top with an ivory or bone guide, perforated near the tip for the passage of the line, and fastened to the rod by sinew cord. The base of the rod is notched, so that the line may be wound on it when not in use. In connection with these rods a slender stick of about the same length is used. It is held in the left hand, and so manipulated as to enable the fisherman to bring the hook to the surface without rising from his seat on a mat spread on the ice. As the fish comes to the surface it is thrown to one side on the ice and disengages itself, as the hook is not barbed. The fisherman then gives it a rap with the stick to prevent it from struggling back to the hole, and returns his hook to the water. No bait is used, as the fish nibble at the white ivory shank, and are caught by a continued up-and-down movement of the hook.

In autumn the tomcod are extremely abundant near St Michael. At this season cold north winds generally blow and render it very uncomfortable to remain for hours in one position on the ice. To remedy this, small shelters are arranged, consisting of grass mats, held on a framework of sticks, to the windward of the hole. In November, soon after the ice is formed, a fisherman frequently catches 200 pounds of tomcod in a day, but from 10 to 40 pounds is the average result of a day's fishing.

Figure 24, plate LXVIII, represents an outfit for tomcod fishing, from Cape Nome, consisting of the two rods, a whalebone line, stone sinker, and hook as described. The line is guided through the notch in the end of the rod, which is cut in at each end so that it forms a shuttle-like stick, upon which the line is wound when not in use. In some instances the four hooks are arranged around the sinker and held in place by means of short, elastic leaders of whalebone or quill.

Among the fishermen of Norton sound and along the American shore of Bering strait the lines on which these hooks are held usually pass through holes in the sinker and are wedged in place. On St Lawrence island, sinkers are made with a hole at the bottom for suspending a hook, and four other holes for a similar purpose at each of the rounded corners. Figure 5, plate LXVIII, represents one of the sinkers from this island; the hooks are made of iron and have from three to four points on the end of a straight shank, which is lashed to a whalebone leader by a sinew cord; the upper end of the leader is passed through the holes in the sinker and knotted. Accompanying this specimen is the stick for manipulating the line when landing the fish (figure 32, plate LXVIII). Figure 31, plate LXVIII, illustrates another tomcod fishing outfit, from Norton sound, consisting of a shuttle-like rod notched at each end and a thin rawhide line with an ivory sinker, which is in two parts, excavated in the middle and filled with lead; the two halves are held together by a lashing of whalebone; a whalebone loop extends from the bottom of the sinker and to it is attached a small hook made by lashing a small iron point across the lower end of a whalebone shank; just above the sinker a leader of whalebone is attached to a line with a similar hook.

Figure 28, plate LXIX, represents a large sinker, from St Lawrence island, made from a piece of the jawbone of a whale. On two of the sides, a little below the middle, are holes through which pass whalebone leaders about nine inches long, on which are hooks with bone shanks having conical knobs on the lower ends; there are three slits on one shank and two on the other, in which upstanding points of bone are inserted and fastened in position with fine cord made from whalebone.

From Cape Nome was obtained an obovate ivory sinker, shown in figure 4, plate LXIX. It has three holes in the sides, in which are inserted three upstanding points of ivory over an inch in length, held in position by a wrapping of fine whalebone; lower, through one side of the

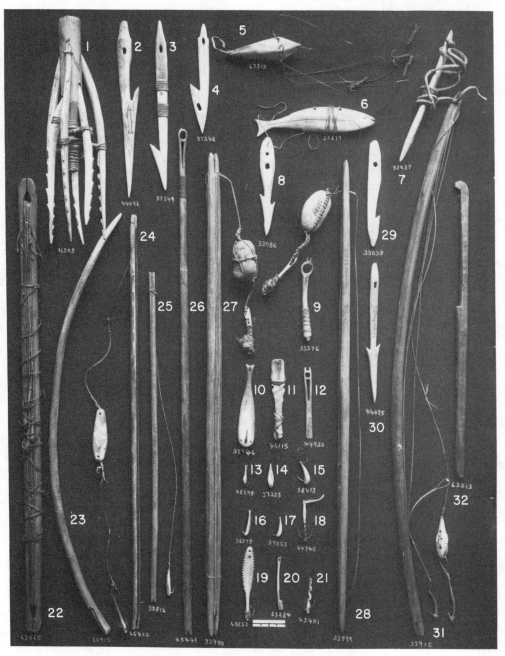

FISHING IMPLEMENTS (ONE-FIFTH)

sinker, passes a whalebone leader with a small hook at each end; these hooks have an ivory shank through which is passed a pointed iron spike bent upward at the point. Hanging from the lower end of the sinker is another leader of about the same length as the others with a straight shanked hook of the ordinary style, with four points.

The style of tomcod hook used from the Yukon mouth to the Kuskokwim is illustrated in figure 3, plate LXIX. This specimen, obtained at Askinuk, has a long, round shank of deerhorn, with a knob at the upper end for attachment of the line, and the lower end is enlarged to a doubly conical base, which has three slits at equal intervals, narrowed on the outside and widening within. Above these, on the upper cone, are three similar slits alternating around the surface with the first-named. Into these slits are fitted long, slender, sharp-pointed spines of deerhorn, $3\frac{1}{2}$ to 4 inches in length, projecting upward and slightly outward. This hook is moved slowly up and down in the water, and catches the fish by piercing them from below while they are gathered about the ivory sinker.

Figure 21, plate LXVIII, from Cape Prince of Wales, is a common style of ivory-shanked tomcod hook, with four projecting iron points. It varies from the ordinary style in having the shank made in a series of curves instead of being straight.

A peculiar style of tomcod hook and sinker, from Cape Nome, is shown in figure 10, plate LXIX. The sinker is made from an old, stained piece of ivory, fashioned into the shape of a fish. Two blue beads are inserted in rings of ivory near the lower end to represent eyes, and another is inlaid on the lower surface. The tail is formed of a piece of white ivory attached to a truncated end of the dark material by a lashing of fine cord; the mouth is represented by a hole, in which is a leader, attached to which, below the sinker, are three orange-yellow pieces from the bill of the crested auklet, which are strung on a fine sinew cord with two blue beads, serving to attract the fish. At the lower end of the leader is a hook, with the upper part of the shank of ivory and the lower of deerhorn. These are fastened together with small bone pegs and a lashing of fine cord around the joint. At the base were four iron points, one of which has been broken off.

Figure 26, plate LXVIII, from Cape Nome, is a rod used for fishing for tomcod, with an ivory line guide in the end. Figure 20, plate LXVIII, from St Lawrence island, are bone shanks for tomcod hooks, made with two slits on the sides at the lower end, in which may be inserted upright bone barbs; the upper end is broadened and flattened a little and pierced for the attachment of a line. Figure 22 of the same plate, from St Lawrence island, is a rather flat, shuttle-shape rod, notched at each end and having wound upon it a long line made from whalebone, with a set of four tomcod hooks at the ends of leaders, which are of the ordinary straight-shank pattern with four barbed points of copper. Figure 9, plate LXVIII, from St Michael, is a deer-

18 ETH——12

horn guide from a tomcod rod.   Figure 12, plate LXVIII, shows another tip for a tomcod rod, from Sledge island.

Another set of hooks and sinker from Hotham inlet are shown in figure 5, plate LXIX.   The sinker is of greenish slate, with a rounded ivory tip at the upper end, excavated to admit the pointed end of the stone, which is riveted in place.   There are two holes in the middle of the stone, at right angles to each other, for the passage of the leaders. Only a single pair of leaders are in place, the other set having been lost.   Figures 14 and 16, plate LXVIII, illustrate forms of tomcod hooks, obtained at Sfugunugumut, which are used also for catching smelts. When tomcod are abundant along the coast in autumn and spring, smelts also are plentiful, and often are caught on the same hooks; but in some localities special hooks are made for taking smelts, one of which, from Nunivak island, is illustrated in figure 13, plate LXVIII. This has a straight ivory shank, largest near its lower end, in which a recurved copper hook is set and held in place by a wooden plug.

While fishing for tomcod, sculpin of several species are frequently caught in shallow water.   A number of hooks made especially for taking these fish were obtained at Cape Nome.   Sculpin hooks from the northern shore of Norton sound and from Bering strait are made from pieces of stone and ivory, fitted together to form an oval shank (figure 21, plate LXIX).   The surface of the stone is grooved to receive the ivory, which forms the lower end, and is fastened by a lashing.   The hook, either of iron or copper, passes through the shank and the point is upturned in front.   The shank is ornamented with little tags of sinew cord at the lower corners, to which are attached blue beads and the sheaths from the bills of auklets.   The stone chosen for these hooks varies considerably, but is usually of some bright color.   Sometimes the lower end is made also of stone of another color instead of ivory, as in the specimen from Cape Nome, illustrated in figure 12, plate LXIX, which is used also as a grayling hook.

A sculpin hook and sinker of dark-colored stone is represented in figure 14, plate LXIX.   It was obtained at Cape Nome.   The sinker is pierced at the upper end for the attachment of the rawhide line; to this upper end is fastened a finely braided sinew cord, having an orange-yellow piece from an auklet's bill at its lower end.   The other end of the sinker has a white ivory cap fitted over it and held in place by a wooden peg; in the lower end is a hole in which is a small sealskin band, to which are attached some pieces of skin from the legs of birds, and below this extends a leader, terminating in a flat-shank hook.   The leader is also ornamented with a blue bead and a piece from the bill of an auklet.   The shank of the hook is composed of three pieces, the upper and lower of ivory, and the middle one of stone, neatly fitted in grooves in the ivory and fastened by a lashing; a single-point copper barb is inserted through the shank and bent upward in front.   In the truncated base of the ivory of the shank are two holes below the place where the hook is inserted, to which are hung

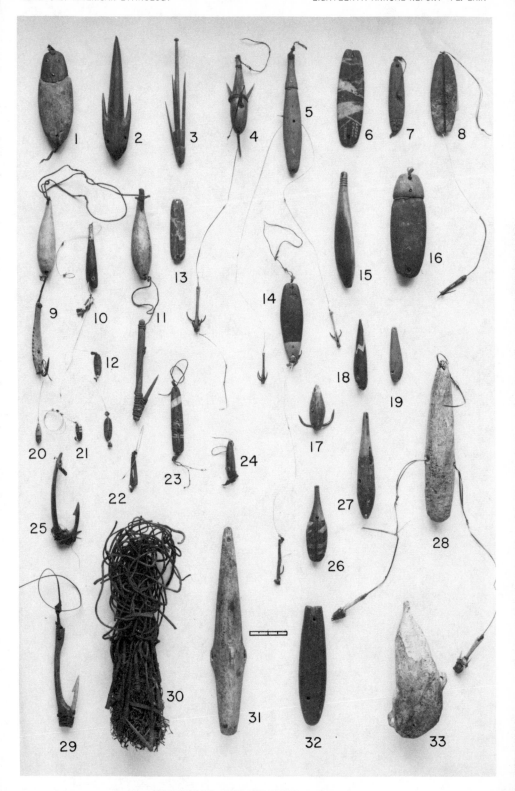

FISHHOOKS AND SINKERS (ONE-FIFTH)

two short sinew cords, on each of which is strung a blue bead and an orange-colored piece from the bill of an auklet. These various ornaments are intended as lures for the fish. Another of these sculpin hooks from Cape Nome is shown in figure 22, plate LXIX. It is attached by a leader to a small ivory sinker, which is yellow on one side and blackened on the other; on the dark side are inserted two white ivory eyes with a dark-colored wooden plug in the center of each to represent the pupil. On the other side is a hole for attaching the leader; small bits of red flannel are fastened to this end for lures. The other end terminates in a flattened point, in which is a hole for the line. Strung on the leader is a blue bead and an orange-yellow piece from the bill of an auklet. The shank, which has near the end two holes for the line, is made from deerhorn and flattened,' becoming larger toward the lower end, where an oblong piece of ivory is inserted just back of the point of the hook, which is a single, sharp-pointed iron barb inserted through the lower end of the shank and bent upward in front. At each of the lower corners of the shank is a short sinew cord, on which are strung a blue and a white bead and an orange sheath from the bill of an auklet.

Another sculpin hook from the same locality is represented in figure 8, plate LXIX. It is made from a stout piece of iron, the ends bent together and the points sharpened and upturned. It is attached to a sinker of gneiss, which is elongated-oval in shape and fastened to the line by a lashing of whalebone, which passes around it from end to end. A small hook from Sledge island (figure 20, plate LXIX) is made from two pieces of ivory joined by a small connecting rod, on which is strung a flat blue bead. It is shaped to represent a fish. At the lower end are two small, dark-colored wooden pegs set in to represent eyes. A short copper hook projects on the inside. Another sculpin hook, from Cape Nome (number 45281), is made in three pieces. The lower part is of dark chocolate-colored stone, the middle of reddish granite, and the upper part of ivory. They are lashed together in the usual manner.

For catching salmon trout and the large-fin grayling, small, ornamented hooks are made of stone and ivory. These hooks are similar in character to those used for catching smelts and sculpin along the shore of Norton sound and the coast of Bering strait. One of these grayling hooks from Cape Nome is shown in figure 12, plate LXIX. It is made from two pieces of stone, the upper of which is chocolate-color and the lower reddish white. They are neatly joined together and held in position by a sinew lashing, which passes through a hole in one piece and around a groove along the middle line of the other. A small iron pin is passed through the lower part of the shank and curves upward in front to form the hook. Attached to the upper and lower ends of the shank are orange-yellow sheaths from the beak of an auklet, the lower end having also a blue bead.

Figure 21, plate LXIX, represents two hooks from the Diomede

islands. One is similar in form and ornamentation to the last preceding specimen, but the lower portion is of yellowish bone and the
upper part of greenish-gray stone. The other is similar in shape, but
the upper half of the shank is of white ivory, with two encircling
grooves in which narrow strips of skin from the legs of an auklet are
bound, and the lower half of the shank is of dark-colored ivory. A
grayling hook from Unalaklit (figure 48) has a leader of whalebone.
The white ivory shank has a dull green spiral band, produced by stain-
ing the ivory in some unknown manner.

Figure 30, plate LXIX, represents a set of hooks from the Lower Yukon,
which are intended for catching losh. They have tapering wooden
shanks, split at the lower end to receive the butts of long wooden or
deerhorn points, which are lashed in position with spruce
root. Most of these hooks are provided with rawhide
leaders, but one leader is made from a strip of whalebone.
They are held together by thrusting the points into a
rounded mass of fine shavings bound together with a
strip of spruce root.

A hook from the Lower Yukon (figure 15, plate LXVIII)
has an obovate shank of deerhorn, with a spur-like barb of
iron thrust through the lower end. The upper end is tapering, flattened, and pierced with a hole for the reception of a
line. Hooks of this kind are used for small whitefish and
losh in the streams back from the coast. A losh hook from
the head of Norton bay (figure 17, plate LXIX) has an obovate shank of ivory, bored across through the shank and
filled with lead to give additional weight. The lower end
has a hole through which is thrust a small, double-point
rod of iron, bent upward at the ends to form two barbs.
A hook used for catching large whitefish or nelma (figure 10, plate LXVIII) was obtained at Paimut. It has a
curved deerhorn shank, broadening toward the lower
end, in which are incisions representing the mouth and
eyes of a fish. Between the eyes is inserted a strong

FIG. 48—Grayling
hook (½).

iron barb, bent upward at the point. The upper end of the shank is
forked like the tail of a fish, and has a hole for the line. A hook for
catching pickerel and whitefish, illustrated in figure 19, plate LXVIII,
is from Unalaklit. The shank is broad and flattened toward the upper
end, where it has two holes for attachment of the line. The edges are
serrated. Near the lower end it is slender and has an upcurled barb
of iron fastened with a lashing of sinew cord. Another hook, obtained
at Sledge island, is somewhat similar to the preceding, but the barb,
instead of being fastened by a lashing, is inserted through a hole in
the shank, the upper portion of which is broad and has only two
notches on the sides (figure 11, plate LXVIII). Two hooks, from St.
Michael, used for catching wolf fish, illustrated in figures 9 and 11

plate LXIX, are attached to rounded, tapering sinkers of ivory. One of them has a deerhorn shank, serrated on the edges, with a stout iron barb inserted through the lower end. The other hook has a rude, straight shank, made from a stick about four inches in length, with a notch at the upper end for attaching the line, which passes downward to the lower end, where a pointed spine of deerhorn is lashed obliquely across it. Another variety of hook is a rudely made specimen from St Lawrence island (figure 25, plate LXIX). It is cut from a piece of walrus ivory and is provided with a long barbed point. It was used for catching wolf fish, but probably both this and the two preceding examples were also used for cod-fishing.

A similar hook from the same locality is shown in figure 29, plate LXIX. In this case, however, the shank is of wood with a barbed point of bone fitted in a slot at the base. The upper end of the shank has a hole for attaching the whalebone line. This hook was used probably for catching codfish. An outfit for catching wolf fish, illustrated in figure 27, plate LXVIII, was obtained at the head of Norton sound. It consists of a shuttle-like rod, 28 inches in length, on which is wound a rawhide line, near the end of which a rounded piece of lava, reddish in color, is fastened with a basket lashing. The hook has a straight deerhorn shank, to the lower end of which is lashed crosswise an iron nail with the projecting end pointed. In the fork between the hook and the shank a kind of bait composed of sinew-like material is secured by a lashing. Figure 28, plate LXVIII, shows a similar outfit from Norton sound, with the sinker made of a rounded granite pebble grooved at each end for the attachment of the rawhide lashing Another outfit (figure 25, plate LXVIII), from Norton sound, for catching blackfish (*Dallia*) is a long, slender, shuttle-like rod 20 inches in length, on which is wound a short line of sinew with a small hook at one end. This hook has a straight, rounded ivory shank and is provided with a pointed iron pin through the lower end, with the tip upcurved.

Along the shore of Bering sea and the adjacent Arctic coast considerable ingenuity is displayed by the people in manufacturing sinkers for fishing lines, and a great variety are made. For several species of fish the sinker is intended to attract the fish, as well as to serve as a weight for the line, and is made of a variegated white and dark colored stone. Other sinkers, of ivory, have a portion of the surface blackened, and some of the stone sinkers have an ivory cap. A large collection of these objects was obtained, from which typical examples have been selected for illustration.

A specimen from the Diomede islands (figure 32, plate LXIX) is a piece of bone, discolored to a chocolate-brown, pierced with a hole and grooved near the upper end to receive the line. The lower end has a hole for fastening the leader for the hook. The lower end represents the head of a fish, with an incision for the mouth; a blue bead represents one eye and a piece of lead the other. Another example from the same locality (figure 16, plate LXIX) is a long, oval stone with a rounded ivory cap, held in position by a deerhorn pin passed through both substances. A hole for the line is in the upper end of the ivory cap and another in the lower end of the stone portion. A similar sinker (figure 1, plate LXIX) was obtained at Port Clarence by Dr Dall. It is made from a piece of granite and has a cap of chocolate-color ivory, held in position by an iron rivet through the two pieces; the ivory portion has a flattened point, and on the sides a pair of eyes are represented by two inlaid rings of ivory, in which blue beads are set. A similar sinker, from Cape Nome (figure 7, plate LXIX) is made of stone, with a small ivory cap fastened by a rivet. The long, round stone sinker shown in figure 27, plate LXIX, was obtained on Sledge island. It tapers below to a blunt point, where it is pierced for a leader. The upper end is truncated, and has fitted on it a long, round tail-like piece of ivory, lashed in position with a strand of whalebone passed through holes in the two parts. In the stone is a hole to receive a long leader for two hooks. Another sinker, of variegated black and white stone, from the same locality (figure 26, plate LXIX), has an ivory cap fastened with a lashing passed through a hole in the lower end of the ivory and around a groove in the stone. A black and white stone sinker from Cape Nome (figure 23, plate LXIX) has been broken in the middle and neatly mended with a strong lashing of whalebone passed through two holes and around a deep groove in the sides. A small sinker of greenish stone from Sledge island (figure 19, plate LXIX) is rudely shaped to represent a fish, having ivory pegs with black centers inlaid for eyes. It has a small hole at each end for attaching the lines. Another specimen from the same locality (figure 13, plate LXIX) is a handsome sinker of variegated white and brown stone, with a deep groove on each side near the ends, in which holes are bored for attaching the lines. The black and white ivory sinker shown in figure 18, plate LXIX, was obtained on Nunivak island. Eyes, also black and white in color, are inlaid in the black upper surface.

The black and white, flattened stone sinker shown in figure 6, plate LXIX, is from Cape Nome. A long ivory sinker from Hotham inlet (figure 15, plate LXIX) has a hole at each end; the upper end is surrounded by four grooves and raven totem marks. On one side is a rude etching representing a framework for drying fish. The bone sinker from St Lawrence island, shown in figure 31, plate LXIX, is triangular in cross section and pierced at the upper end for the line; on the lower half, at each of the angles, is an ear containing a hole for attaching a leader. Another example from the same place (figure 33, plate LXIX) is a rude bone sinker, roughly obovate in shape, with a hole at the upper end for a line and two ear-like projections near the lower end for attaching leaders. A heavy ivory sinker (figure 2, plate LXIX) was obtained at Plover bay by Mr W. M. Noyes. It has holes around the sides and the bottom for attaching leaders. The upper end is oval in cross section and tapers to a thin, flat point, pierced for the line. About the base are three upright spines, projecting slightly outward, carved from the same piece, which serve as additional hooks for capturing fish that may gather around, attracted by the white ivory. This sinker has been used in fishing for tomcod and other small fish. In the deep water off the headlands, from Golofnin bay to Cape Nome, large crabs are very abundant; sometimes specimens are seen measuring three feet from tip to tip of their outstretched claws. They are caught during March and April by the use of a bait of dead fish tied to the end of a line and sunk to the bottom through a hole in the ice. In March, 1880, near Cape Darby, I saw large numbers of people fishing for crabs by this method, and on the 10th of March, west of Cape Darby, I found a party of about twenty-five people, from Sledge island, who had been starved out at home and were camping there, living on the tomcod and crabs, which were abundant. Their crab lines were fastened to small sticks set in the snow beside the holes in the ice, thus enabling one person to watch several holes. When the crab seized the bait the stick was moved sufficiently to attract the attention of the watcher, who at once drew in his line. Small snow shelters were built beside the holes to protect the fishermen from the wind; they were open on one side and had a crescentic base with the convexity toward the direction of the wind, while some of them were partially arched over. The crabs were so plentiful that one day, soon after my arrival, a man and a woman came in bringing about two hundred pounds, which they had taken during the day.

As soon as the ice leaves the coast of Norton sound, in June, herrings arrive and spawn on the seaweed about the rocky points and shores of the small bays. At this time many of them are caught by means of small seines made from rawhide or sinew cord; but about the latter part of June commences what to these people is the most important of all fishing seasons. This is the time for the arrival of the salmon. The king salmon enter the rivers first, and are followed during the season by two or three smaller species of inferior quality. Along the entire coast, from the Kuskokwim to Point Barrow and up Kuskokwim and Yukon rivers, the Eskimo are very busy during July and August catching and curing these fish. The cleaning is done by the women. The fish are split from the head to the base of the tail, the entrails removed, and the fish thrown over a raised framework and left hanging until dry, when they are stored away in bales or bunches. The large king salmon (*chow-chee*), after being split, are slashed crosswise at short intervals to open the flesh and thus facilitate drying; the backbone is also generally removed and dried separately. When dry, the smaller species, called dog salmon, are always tied in bunches of twenty, and are stored or sold in this shape.

FISH TRAPS

Along the entire seacoast salmon are caught in gill nets, which are placed at intervals along the shore. On lower Yukon and Kuskokwim rivers wicker fish traps are set, with a brush and wicker-work fence connecting them with the shore. These fish traps form an elongated cone, with a funnel-shape entrance in the larger end. Each has two long poles at the sides of the mouth or broad end and another at the small end, by means of which it is raised or lowered. It is set at the outer end of the wicker-work fence with the mouth facing downstream, and held in place by poles driven in the river bottom with their ends projecting above the water.

A model of a trap from the lower Yukon, used for catching salmon, is illustrated in figure 14, plate LXX. The funnel-shape mouth is fastened to a square framework, with handle-like extensions along the upper and lower sides, by means of which poles are fastened for guiding the trap in setting, and which rest against the poles driven into the river bottom to keep the trap in position.

The Eskimo living near the base of the Kuslevak mountains go to the Yukon delta to fish for salmon. Norton bay and the shores around the head of Norton sound are occupied by people from the surrounding districts, who gather there during the fishing season. Nearly all of the Sledge islanders resort to the adjacent mainland at this time.

Throughout the region the people go out from their villages to summer camps at places where the run of fish is known to be greatest, and all enjoy a season of plenty, always anticipated with pleasure by the entire community.

At times fish are so plentiful on the lower Yukon in July, while the dog salmon are running, that the wicker fish traps, which measure 4 to 5 feet in diameter and about 10 feet in length, have to be emptied several times a day to prevent their breaking. The gill nets are also watched constantly by the owner, who goes out in his kaiak whenever the motion of the floats shows there are fish in them, and, drawing up the net so that the heads of the fish are above water, he stuns them by a blow from a short club and removes them from the net.

Figure 2, plate LXX, represents one of these clubs for killing fish, which was obtained at Sabotnisky. It is made of spruce and is reduced in size downward to form a slender handle, suboval in cross section, grooved on each side, and wrapped with spruce root at the grip. Toward the end it becomes larger and is rounded, and then tapers again to a truncated point. Another club of this character, from Sledge island, is shown in figure 1 of the same plate. It is 30 inches long, and is oval in cross section.

The blackfish (*Dallia pectoralis*) is common wherever sluggish streams and lakelets occur from Kotzebue sound to Kuskokwim river. Throughout this region they are taken by means of small wicker traps, about 18 inches in diameter and 5 feet long, which are set in small streams, with a wicker fence leading from the mouths of the traps to the shore.

A model of one of these traps, from St Michael, is illustrated in

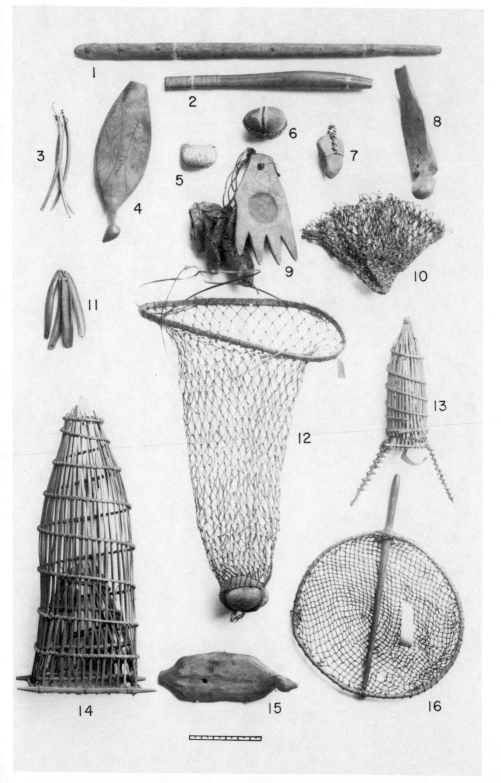

OBJECTS USED IN FISHING (ONE-EIGHTH)

figure 13, plate LXX, showing the method of construction. Splints of spruce are fastened together in a bunch to form the small end of the trap, and are held in position by a rawhide or spruce-root lashing; thence toward the mouth they are held in place by a wrapping of spruce root, which is wound spirally several times around the circumference to the mouth, forming a cone-shape basket; the splints are fastened to the wrapping by a lashing of spruce root or rawhide, which is wound around the crossings of the framework; in the mouth of the trap is a conical mouthpiece attached to a square framework of four sticks and inserted in the larger end of the trap, where it is fastened by lashings on each side.

By means of traps of this character vast quantities of blackfish are taken in the waters of the low country between Yukon and Kuskokwim rivers, where they are very abundant, and form one of the principal sources of food supply for the people during several months of the year.

After the salmon season, the main trapping for fish is done along the lower Yukon and in the adjacent region in autumn, just before and after the streams become frozen; at this time the salmon traps are set again and vast quantities of whitefish, losh, pickerel, and blackfish are secured and preserved by freezing for use later in the season. The traps are kept out until midwinter, but the main catch is while the fish are crowding in from the small streams. Plate LXXI, from a photograph, shows the method of setting these traps through the ice on the Yukon, near Ikogmut (Mission).

On Norton sound, when high gales blow from the north during September and October, very low tides ensue, and the women go out among the exposed rocks to gather mussels, ascidians, and several kinds of fish which are found concealed beneath the large stones off the rocky points.

NETS

Gill nets for salmon are set usually on a line leading from the shore. The inner end of the line is made fast to a stone or a stake, and the owner carries the other end out to the proper distance and anchors it with a stone. At the outer end of the net is fastened a wooden marker-float, commonly made in the form of a bird. Rounded wooden floats, varying considerably in form, are also strung at intervals along the upper edge of the net. A specimen of these net floats, from Ikogmut, is illustrated in figure 4, plate LXX. It is fashioned in the shape of a loon, with a long, projecting neck, and is made from a single piece of wood. A hole runs through it for attaching the cord; two incised grooves outline the wings, and a wide, shallow groove extends around the edge. All of these grooves are painted red; the center of the back has a greenish tint, but the wings are not colored.

At Cape Blossom, on the Arctic coast, the people were seen using gill nets about 25 feet in length, strung with floats and sinkers in the usual

manner. A stout cord held one end fast to a stake on the shore, while
the owner, by means of several slender poles lashed together, pushed
the anchor stone on the outer end out to its place, thus setting the net.
When the floats gave indication that fish had been caught, the net was
pulled in hand over hand, the fish removed, and the net reset. This
plan appeared to work very successfully, as evidenced by the large
number of fish on the drying frames close by.

On Kotzebue sound, in the month of September, I saw a party of
Malemut catching whitefish with a seine. The net was fitted with
wooden floats and stone sinkers in the usual manner, and was about
60 feet long, the ends being spread by stout stakes secured by lashings
of cord. The shore end of the net was held by two men standing at
the water's edge; the other end was pushed out from the shore to its
full extent by the aid of several long poles. A long, rawhide line was
made fast to the outer end of the net and another to the middle of the
string of poles, by which it was pulled along. One man carried the inner

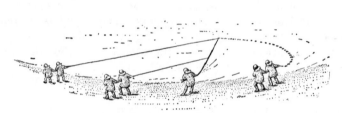

FIG. 49—Seining on Kotzebue sound.

end of the pole along the beach between the two rear line men and the
men holding the net. In this way the net was drawn along the beach
for 100 or 200 yards, and when the fish were running large hauls were
made. The accompanying figure 49, showing this method, is from a
sketch made at the time.

Between Cape Romanzof and the mouth of Kuskokwim river the
greater part of the fishing is done by means of dip-nets, but great
quantities of stickleback and other small fish are taken in small nets
or seines of fine rawhide cord. Large dip-nets for whitefish are made
of the same material, and among the people south of Cape Vancouver
this style of net is used more than the gill net. A dip-net obtained by
Lieutenant Stoney at the head of Kotzebue sound is about three feet
long, and is made of twisted sinew cord. The upper third of the net has
meshes about an inch in diameter; this is joined to the finer-mesh
lower portion by a rawhide cord, which is knotted into the adjoining
meshes of the two parts. The meshes of the lower portion are less
than half the size of those of the upper part. On the lower point
of the net is a rawhide loop, by means of which it can be raised and
the contents discharged. A small dip-net obtained at Ikogmut is

SETTING FISH TRAP THROUGH THE ICE ON THE YUKON, NEAR IKOGMUT

shown in figure 16, plate LXX. The hoop at the top is a round willow stick, with the beveled ends overlapping and bound together. The handle extends across the hoop and projects four and one-half inches on one side. The net is shallow, made of twisted sinew cord, and is joined to the hoop by a spiral wrapping of spruce root, which passes around the frame and through the bordering meshes.

The accompanying figure 50 shows the mesh of a larger dip-net from Sabotnisky. This net is about thirty inches in diameter, is made of twisted sinew cord, and is used for catching various kinds of small fish. A small, strongly made dip-net of willow bark, obtained by Lieutenant Stoney from the region back of Kotzebue sound, is shown in figure 10,

FIG. 50—Mesh of dip-net made of sinew (about ⅔).

plate LXX. It is only about fifteen inches in diameter; the meshes are of diamond shape around the border and quadrate on the bottom. The mesh of a large dip-net used for catching salmon and whitefish (figure 51) was obtained from Sabotnisky. It is about six feet in length and the same in diameter, and is made of willow bark. The

hoop is of spruce wood, with a long, slender handle of the same material, which crosses the hoop. Figure 12, plate LXX, represents a dip-net from Plover bay, Siberia, made of whalebone, which is used for catching small fish in the lakes and streams of that vicinity. The mouth of the net is held open by a stout rim of whalebone. Four strands of the same material are attached at intervals around the rim and fastened together about sixteen inches above it. A heavy granite bowlder, grooved to receive the lashing, is fastened to a whalebone ring in the bottom of the net, which is used by being thrown out into the water and then hauled to the shore by a cord.

FIG. 51—Mesh of dip-net made of willow bark (⅔).

A herring seine of sinew cord, from St Michael (figure 52), has a number of rounded, subtriangular wooden floats pierced at their small end for attachment to a sealskin cord which runs along the upper edge of the net; to a cord stretched along the lower border are lashed pieces of deerhorn four to five inches in length, which serve as weights and also as handles by which the net can be hauled to the shore. A seine of twisted sinew cord similar to the preceding, obtained at Hotham inlet (number 63612), is about thirty inches in width, with a stretcher of wood at each end. It has oval wooden floats and deerhorn and stone sinkers.

A small-mesh seine of sinew cord, used for herring and whitefish, obtained at Cape Prince of Wales, is shown in figure 53. It is nearly thirty inches wide, and has wooden stretchers at each end, a series of rounded, tapering floats along the upper edge, and handle-like sinkers of ivory along the lower border. Another small-mesh herring seine, about five feet wide, obtained at St Michael (figure 54), is made from fine sealskin cord. Along the bottom is strung a series of small oval stone sinkers, notched above and below to secure the lashings.

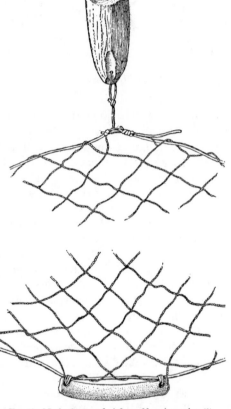

FIG. 52—Mesh, float, and sinker of herring seine (¼).

Floats for nets are sometimes carved in the shape of birds and in other forms. Figure 15, plate LXX, represents a float rudely fashioned in the form of a grebe; another, from the lower Yukon (plate LXX, 8), represents the head of a man and the flattened tail of a bird. A float from St Lawrence island (figure 55) is round in cross section, large in the middle, and tapers gradually to both ends, where there are slight shoulders to retain the cords by which it is made fast. Others are merely rounded blocks of wood, pierced for attachment to the net.

In addition to the wooden floats, others are made from the inflated bladders or stomachs of various animals. Figure 9, plate LXX, illustrates a set of three such floats and a wooden marker-float for use on one end of the net. The latter is a thin, curved piece of wood in the form of a thumbless hand, with a round, excavated depression in the center, which, with the inside of the finger tips, is painted black. This hand is similar to that represented so frequently in this region on masks and in paintings of mythological beings. Figure 7, plate LXX, illustrates a stone sinker for a net, obtained at Point Hope, consisting of a roughly triangular pebble with a lashing of rawhide terminating in a loop for attaching it to the net. It is not grooved, advantage being taken of the natural shape to secure the lashings. Another example (figure 6, plate LXX), from the Diomede islands, is a rounded bowlder, with two pecked grooves extending around it in opposite directions, around which is a stout sealskin cord. The lashings on both this and the preceding sinker are permanent, and the attachment to the net is made by a separate cord.

Ivory or bone weights frequently alternate with stone sinkers on the nets, and serve both as sinkers and handles. They vary from five to six or seven inches in length, are more or less curved, and have a hole at each end for fastening them

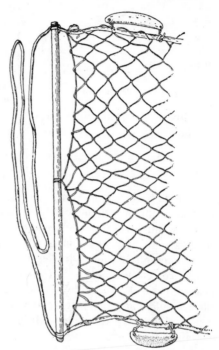

FIG. 53—Herring seine, with stretcher at one end and with float and sinker (⅓).

to the net. A small bone handle of this kind (number 36395), with the raven totem mark on its inner surface, was obtained at Kushunuk. A set of four such handles from the lower Yukon are shown in figure 11,

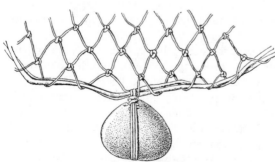

FIG. 54—Sealskin-cord herring seine with stone sinker (⅔).

plate LXX. Another set of four handles, from Cape Vancouver, illustrated in figure 3, plate LXX, are slender, curved, bone rods, with a hole at each end. The suboval weight of walrus ivory shown in figure 5, plate LXX, was obtained on St Lawrence island.

Directly after the freezing of the Yukon in the fall there is an annual run of lamprey, which pass up the river, just below the ice, in great numbers. Holes are kept open in the ice by the people who watch for the first appearance of these fish. As soon as the first one is seen everybody seizes a dip-net or a stout stick with a short cross-piece at

FIG. 55—Wooden net float (⅜).

the lower end and throws out as many as possible. When the main body of the fish have passed, the people run up the river for some distance, cut other holes, and repeat the catch. This is continued until the people are exhausted by the violent exertion or a neighboring village is reached, when they are compelled to stop and give way to those living in that locality.

NET-MAKING IMPLEMENTS

GAUGES

Various tools are used by the Eskimo in the manufacture of nets, several forms of which were seen in different districts. From St Lawrence island several curiously shaped whalebone gauges for the meshes of nets were obtained. One of these (number 127020) is a trifle over six and one-half inches in length, and is a flat, oblong tablet, with a small projection at each end on one side. From the holes through it near one end it had evidently been used previously as part of a sledge runner. The specimen illustrated in figure 4, plate LXXII, is similar in form and material to the preceding, but is smaller. Similar but shorter examples are shown in figures 2 and 3, plate LXXII. Each of these has a long, curved handle projecting from one corner and a short spur from the other.

A whalebone gauge from Kotzebue sound (figure 7, plate LXXII) is notched along each side to receive a sinew cord to secure it to the wooden handle in which it is inserted. The specimen from Sledge island (figure 13, plate LXXII) is a long-blade gauge of ivory, with a heavy back. The handle is grooved to receive the fingers, and terminates in an image of a seal's head, with eyes, ears, and nose represented by inlaid, blackened wooden pegs.

The long-blade ivory gauge with heavy back, from Cape Darby (figure 12, plate LXXII), has a long, tapering deerhorn handle riveted and lashed to its upper side. The example from the Diomede islands (figure 14, plate LXXII) is a large, heavy, ivory gauge with a plain handle, which has a rude projection at the inner end to prevent it from slipping. The deerhorn gauge from Cape Nome (figure 8, plate LXXII) is fastened in the split end of a wooden handle by a lashing of spruce root. A gauge similar to this was obtained on Nunivak island. A small, double-end gauge from Sabotnisky (figure 10, plate LXXII) is slightly different in size at each end. The handle is enlarged in the middle and has a stick lashed to it by spruce roots to make it large enough to afford a convenient grip for the hand. The single-blade

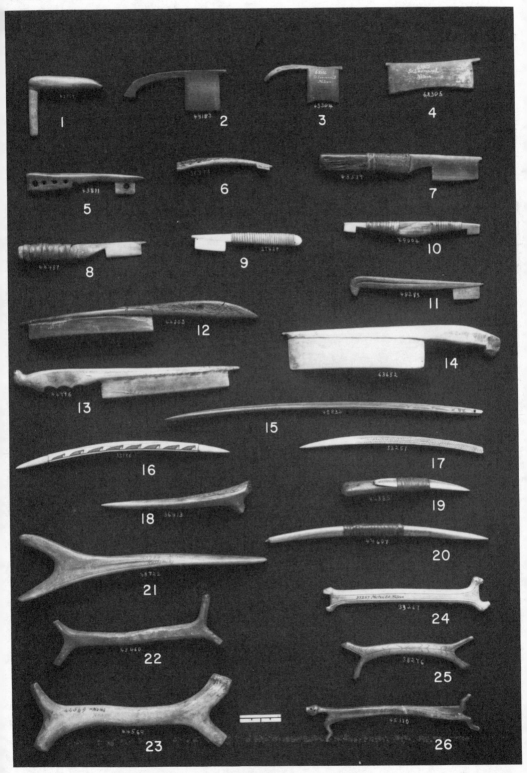

NET-MAKING IMPLEMENTS (NEARLY ONE-FOURTH)

deerhorn gauge from Shaktolik (figure 5, plate LXXII) is similar in form to the preceding; it has a circular hole through the middle, surrounded by an incised circle; the handle is pierced with four holes, three of equal size and one larger. Figure 9, plate LXXII, shows a handsomely made ivory gauge from Cape Vancouver, with a handle wrapped by spruce roots, and figure 6, plate LXXII, illustrates a small gauge from Kushunuk, made of deerhorn, with a handle enlarged toward the butt. The deerhorn gauge from Nunivak island shown in figure 11, plate LXXII, is grooved along the upper edge and has a handle terminating in a hook curved downward.

The specimen from Nubviukhchugaluk (figure 1, plate LXXII) is a small gauge entirely different in form from the others. It is of deerhorn, with a handle oval in cross section, from which it projects at a right angle a little over two inches.

SHUTTLES AND NEEDLES

The shuttles used in making nets also vary considerably in size and form, according to locality and to the purpose for which the nets are to be used.

Figure 14, plate LXXIII, illustrates a small wooden shuttle from Sledge island, used for making fine-mesh nets. The long, slender, ivory shuttle, shown in figure 26, plate LXIII, is also from Sledge island.

The long, slender shuttle from Cape Nome, shown in figure 25, plate LXXIII, has the central portion of wood and the two ends made of bone, with a wedge-shape notch on the inner side, into which the tapering ends of the wooden portion are fitted and held in position by means of a series of cross rivets.

The shuttle from the lower Yukon (figure 28, plate LXXIII) is made of deerhorn and has conventional figures and patterns etched on one surface. Another deerhorn shuttle from Cape Nome (figure 18, plate LXXIII) has four reindeer etched on one side. The specimen from Kotzebue sound (figure 27, plate LXXIII) is a long, plain, deerhorn shuttle.

The deerhorn shuttle from Nunivak island (figure 19, plate LXXIII) has the end openings deeper than usual and the borders along the sides are raised above the plane of the flat, central portion. One of the arms is made from a separate piece and is attached by means of sinew cords passed through three holes in the main part of the shuttle.

The specimen from Cape Nome shown in figure 24, plate LXXIII, is a long wooden shuttle. At the bottom of the notch in each end it is crossed by a sinew lashing, to prevent it from splitting, the lashing passing through two holes on each side of the edge. A deep groove runs along the sides between the notches in the ends. The long wooden shuttle from Sledge island represented in figure 23, plate LXXIII, has a deep groove along the sides between the notches.

Figure 20, plate LXXIII, shows a large, heavy, wooden shuttle, such as is used in making nets for catching white whales or large seals. It was obtained on one of the Diomede islands. The large wooden shuttle from Cape Vancouver (figure 8, plate LXXIII) has two sides made of separate pieces, which are held together by crossbars which pierce the sides at the bottom of each notch. The inside is excavated to form two long, triangular borders.

Figure 21, plate LXXIII, represents a large, rather broad, wooden shuttle from Nunivak island. It has a flat groove extending between the notches.

The wooden shuttle shown in figure 10, plate LXXIII, is from Paimut, as is also that shown in figure 9 of the same plate, which is made of one piece with two long openings in the middle.

The specimen from Norton sound (figure 22, plate LXXIII) is a large wooden shuttle used in making nets for capturing seals and white whales.

The deerhorn shuttle from Nulukhtulogumut (figure 16, plate LXXIII) contains some fine, twisted sinew cord.

A long, narrow, wooden shuttle from Sabotnisky (figure 15, plate LXXIII) has the two ends lashed with sinew cord to prevent the wood from splitting; wound upon it is some fine cord made from the twisted inner bark of the willow. The large wooden shuttle from the lower Yukon (figure 17, plate LXXIII) is also filled with cord made from material similar to that in the preceding specimen.

The shuttle from St Lawrence island (figure 12, plate LXXIII) is made of whalebone in the shape of an arrowpoint, with the center excavated, leaving a long, tongue-like point projecting from the base toward the tip. Another shuttle (figure 11, plate LXXIII) from the same locality is filled with well-made, twisted sinew cord.

Figure 13, plate LXXIII, represents a shuttle, obtained on the coast of Japan by General Capron, which is similar in pattern to the preceding. The Eskimo of eastern Siberia and of St Lawrence island must have derived the pattern of their shuttles from farther south, and the imported design thus replaced the ordinary kind in use among their relatives of the islands of Bering strait and the American shore.

Figure 7, plate LXXIII, represents a long, wooden, netting needle, tapering toward both ends, with a large hole in the middle; it is used for mending the broken meshes of nets. The double-point ivory netting needle from Askinuk (figure 4, plate LXXIII) is similar in shape to the preceding.

The ivory netting needle, pierced at one end, shown in figure 6, plate LXXIII, was obtained at Cape Nome. The large, curved needle of deerhorn represented in figure 5, plate LXXIII, is from the lower Yukon.

Figure 3, plate LXXIII, from Ukagamut, and figure 1 of the same plate, from Kushunuk, represent small needles used in mending the meshes of small nets. A needle from St Michael (figure 2, plate LXXIII) is somewhat similar to the preceding, but has a hole near the center instead of near one end.

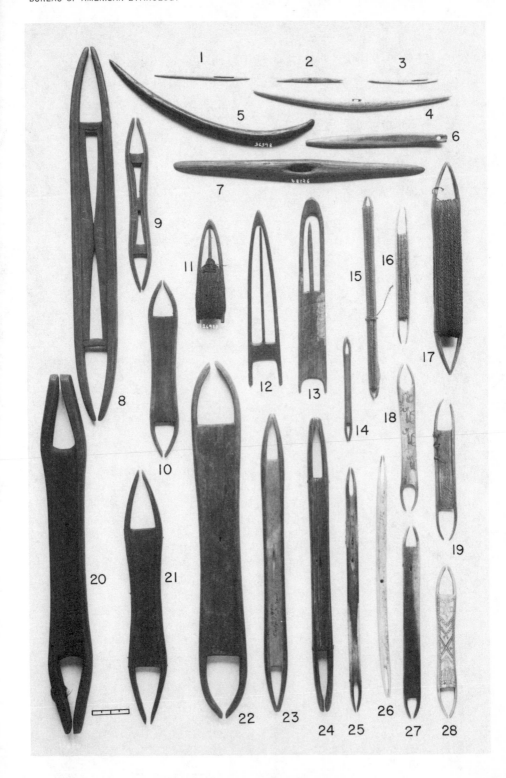

NET-MAKING IMPLEMENTS (ONE-FIFTH)

MARLINSPIKES

Marlinspikes are used for tying and slipping meshes while making nets; they also serve for slipping meshes to enlarge or to reduce their size when it is desired to change the uses of nets.

Figure 21, plate LXXII, illustrates a large marlinspike, from Razbinsky. It is made from reindeer horn, tapers to a blunt end, and has the upper end forked.

Figure 18, plate LXXII, shows an implement, from the lower Kuskokwim, similar to the last mentioned but smaller in size. A curved marlinspike from Pastolik (figure 17, plate LXXII) is made of ivory and is oblong in cross section. Another example, from Cape Nome (figure 19, plate LXXII), has an ivory

FIG. 56—Ivory marlinspike (¼).

point fitted into a slot in a wooden handle and held in place by a rawhide lashing.

Figure 16, plate LXXII, represents a marlinspike from Norton sound; it is made of ivory and is double pointed; it is nearly plain on two sides and convex on the other. A line of walrus is etched upon one side, houses on another, and a conventional pattern ornaments the third.

Figure 56 shows a marlinspike used for slipping knots in large nets. It is from Nunivak island and is round in shape, the handle terminating in a figure of the head of a murre, with the mouth, nostrils, and eyes marked by incised lines. A marlinspike from Norton sound (figure 57) has a bone point set in a slot in the wooden handle and held in position by lashings of spruce root. The example from Cape Nome

FIG. 57—Marlinspike with bone point (¼).

(figure 20, plate LXXII) has a large, blunt point at one end and at the other a small, spur-like point which serves for loosening knots.

Figure 15, plate LXXII, represents a marlinspike from Kotzebue sound; it is a long, slender rod of ivory, triangular in cross section, having all its surfaces ornamented with etched figures of whales, walrus, and hunting scenes. A specimen from the lower Yukon has a round ivory point set in a wooden handle and held in place by a lashing of sinew cord.

REELS

Several forms of reels are employed for holding the small cord used in making nets.

Figure 24, plate LXXII, represents one of these reels from Norton sound. It is neatly grooved; at the tips of the arms of the fork at one end are two seal-heads, and the hind-flippers are at the other end; a grooved pattern extends down their backs and the fore-flippers are indicated by etched lines.

A grotesquely made reel of deerhorn, from Sledge island, is shown in figure 26, plate LXXII. One end is ornamented with the head of a wolf; the opposite side is forked to represent the legs of the animal, and two forked arms at the other end represent the hind-limbs.

A reel of deerhorn from Sabotnisky (figure 25, plate LXXII) has the tops of the arms at one end, as well as one of the arms at the other end, carved in the shape of animal heads. On the sides are etched patterns.

Figure 23, plate LXXII, from Cape Nome, and figure 22 of the same plate, from Kigiktauik, represent deerhorn reels without ornament.

FISH SPEARS

In the fall season holes are made in the ice at places where the water is sufficiently clear to render objects visible several feet below the surface. Through these holes fish are speared, and large quantities of whitefish and pickerel are obtained by this method.

Figure 3, plate LXVII, shows a typical example of these fish spears from St Michael. It consists of a wooden shaft about six feet in length, with a sharp, deerhorn point, surrounded by narrow pieces of deerhorn with triangular points which are secured by a lashing to a shoulder on the shaft. At the base of these points a wooden crossbar, fastened by a strong leather cord, holds the points in their relative position. When a fish is struck with the central point, the triangular sidepieces spread a little, grasp the fish firmly with their inner edges, and hold it until it can be drawn out of the water. A somewhat similar fish spear from Razbinsky (figure 5, plate LXVII) has the central point barbed, instead of smooth as in the preceding specimen; the sidepieces are fastened against a shoulder on the shaft by rawhide cords, and the points are lashed across the ends in a similar manner. Figure 42, 1, represents a deerhorn prong for one of these fish spears from the lower Yukon. Another fish spear, from Razbinsky (plate LXVII, 6), has two points of reindeer horn with two notches on one side of each. A short-handle fish spear from the lower Yukon (plate LXVII, 4) has only one large, single barb point lashed against the side of the shaft. The head of a fish spear from Nunivak island, (plate LXVIII, 1) has the central point surrounded by six others, inserted in slits in the end of the shaft and held in place by a lashing of spruce root. All of these points are barbed for about four inches along one edge.

A small fish spear from Nunivak island (figure 2, plate LXVII) has a central point, surrounded by three other points, forming a triangle; these points are inserted in the shaft and held in position by a rounded ivory ferule. The shaft is very slender, round in cross section, and

about four feet in length; it is in two sections with overlapping ends
beveled and held together by a lashing of twisted sinew cord.

Another spear from the same locality (figure 1, plate LXVII) is similar to the preceding except that it has four points instead of three
surrounding the central point, which are also held in position by an
ivory ring. The inner sides of all the points on both of these spears
are notched to form barbs.

From the lower Kuskokwim northward to Kotzebue sound spears
used for taking salmon and whitefish have large points of bone, deerhorn, or ivory, with from one to three barbs. They are pierced near the
butt for the attachment of a cord, and at this end are of a rounded
wedge shape for insertion into a slot in the end of a long wooden shaft;
a stout sealskin line is made fast to the point, drawn up along the
shaft, and terminated in a coil, which is held in the hand of the fisherman. When a fish is struck the shaft becomes detached, leaving the
barbed point in the fish, which is hauled ashore by aid of the line.

The points of these spears vary considerably in character, as is shown
in the examples described; they are intended for capturing large fish in
the streams flowing into the sea, or in the tributaries of the larger
rivers in the interior; but they are also sometimes used for spearing
white whales.

Figure 7, plate LXVIII, illustrates one of these points from Norton
sound; it is made of bone and has four barbs, two on each side; to
the hole in the butt is attached a piece of stout rawhide line. A slender point of deerhorn, from Kowak river (figure 30, plate LXVIII), has a
barb on each side. Another from the same locality (figure 2, plate
LXVIII) is a flat, slender point of bone with a single barb. A bone
point from Chalitmut (figure 3, plate LXVIII) has a single barb and is
made in two pieces; the overlapping ends are riveted together and
wrapped with two rawhide lashings. A short, rudely made bone point
from Norton sound (figure 8, plate LXVIII) has two barbs, one on each
side, and two holes near the base. Figure 4, plate LXVIII, from Agiukchugumut, and figure 29 of the same plate, from Norton sound, represent bone points with one barb.

To attract pickerel and large whitefish within reach of their spears
while fishing through holes in the ice, the Eskimo of the lower Yukon
make use of the figure of a fish about six or seven inches long. They
have two holes pierced through the back for sinew cords, which are tied
together a few inches above and continue thence upward as a single
string. These images are well fashioned, with the eyes, gill openings,
scales, and lateral line indicated by etched lines. The fisherman stands
directly over the hole and dangles the image a few feet below the surface of the water, holding the spear in his hand ready to thrust on the
approach of the fish, which rush at the lure and are readily speared.
Figure 6, plate LXVIII, represents one of these lures, which was obtained
at Razbinsky.

ARTS AND MANUFACTURES

BONE AND IVORY CARVING

The Alaskan Eskimo are remarkable for their dexterity in working wood, bone, ivory, and reindeer horn. This is particularly noticeable among the people on the islands of Bering strait and the mainland coast from Point Hope southward to the mouth of Kuskokwim river. Within this area the implements used in hunting and for household purposes are handsomely made and often are elaborately ornamented; special skill is shown in adapting the forms of mammals, birds, and fish, with which they are familiar, to the ornamentation of useful articles. In addition to utilizing animal forms for this purpose, they display considerable imaginative faculty in the conception of designs for fanciful carvings, as well as in ornamental patterns, which are frequently etched on the surface of various objects. Many of their carvings are really artistic, and the skill with which animal forms are carved in relief is admirable. The beauty of their work is the more surprising when we consider the rude tools with which it is accomplished. Of the articles obtained many are very ancient, and, the old men told me, had been made by the use of flint tools. The execution of these carvings is equal to that of the specimens produced by the use of iron and steel tools at the present time.

While a considerable degree of artistic taste and skill is quite general, there are some districts in which the people seem to have a greater amount of ability in this direction than the average. The most notable instance of this is among the people living between the Yukon delta and the lower Kuskokwim, which is amply illustrated in the collection, obtained in that locality, of elaborate masks, handsomely ornamented wooden boxes and trays, and a great variety of beautifully executed ivory work. The villages of Askinuk, Kushunuk, Agiukchugumut, and others in this vicinity, supplied a fine series of ivory carvings, well-made wooden dishes, and numerous implements of wood and ivory, all marked by excellence of workmanship. The people of Ukagamut were living in the greatest squalor, even for Eskimo, yet among them were found beautiful specimens of ivory carving.

Before working bone, deerhorn, or ivory, it is the custom to soak the material thoroughly in urine in order to soften it, and indeed it is frequently wetted with the same liquid as the work progresses. For rendering the etched lines on the surface of carvings more distinct, a black paint is made from a mixture of gunpowder and blood, which is rubbed into the freshly cut incisions, making a permanent stain.

In places where ivory is plentiful the men appeared to delight in occupying their leisure time in making carvings from that material or from bone, sometimes for use, but frequently merely for pastime, and many little images are made as toys for children. The articles thus produced are not regarded by them as having any particular value, and I was often amused at the delight with which they sold specimens of their work for one or two needles, a brass button, or some similar trifle.

The women of the district between the Yukon delta and Kuskokwim river are not very proficient in needlework or in ornamenting their garments, the artistic skill appearing to be confined to the men; but on the islands and the adjacent American shore of Bering strait, while the men make very handsome ivory work, the women are equally skilful in beautiful ornamental needlework on articles of clothing. This is notably the case with the finely decorated sealskin boots for which the natives of Diomede and King islands are noted.

The men at Point Hope, on the Arctic coast, are also, skilful in ivory work. About the shores of Kotzebue sound and Bering strait various articles and implements, such as celts, knives, knife sharpeners, and labrets, are made from nephrite.

On the Asiatic shore the Eskimo appear to have lost much of their skill in carving and other ornamental work; consequently their clothing and implements, both on the mainland coast and on St Lawrence island, are rudely made.

In ascending Yukon and Kuskokwim rivers, as the coast districts are left behind skill in carving becomes less and less marked among the Eskimo, until those living as neighbors to the Tinné appear to have but little ability in that art. Paimut, the last Eskimo village on the Yukon, was notable for the fact that the tools and other implements in use were as rude as those of the adjacent Tinné.

In addition to their skill in carving, the Eskimo of the coast display great ability in etching upon tools and implements, notably on ivory drill-bows, scenes from their daily life, records of hunts, or other events. They also produce a great variety of ornamental designs, composed of straight or curved lines, dots, circles, and human or grotesque faces. Upon the surfaces of their wooden dishes they frequently paint a ground color of red, upon which, as well as upon those that are not colored, are drawn in black various well made patterns and figures representing totem animals, personal markings, or mythological creatures.

DRAWING

The Eskimo also possess considerable skill in map making. While traveling between the Yukon delta and the Kuskokwim, several men drew for me excellent maps of the districts with which they were familiar, although probably they had never seen a map of any kind made by a white man. At other points to the northward of St Michael considerable skill was manifested by several persons in sketching outlines of the coast, with its indentations and projections.

During one winter at St Michael a young Eskimo, about 23 or 24 years of age, came from the country of the Kaviak peninsula and remained about the station. While there he took great pleasure in looking at the numerous illustrated papers we had, and would come day after day and borrow them; finally he came and asked me for a pencil and some paper, which I supplied him. Some days later I chanced to go to his tent, and found him lying prone upon the ground, with an old magazine before him, engaged in copying one of the pictures on the piece of paper which I had given him.

When he saw me he seemed to be very much abashed and tried to conceal the drawing, but I took it up and was surprised at the ability he had shown. He had done so well that I asked him if he could draw me some pictures of Eskimo villages and scenes. He agreed to try to do so. He was furnished with a supply of pencils and paper, and the result was a series of a dozen or more pictures which were remarkable, considering that they were made by a savage whose ideas were similar to those of his people, except what he had learned by looking over the papers I had loaned him a short time before.

WRITTEN RECORDS

The Eskimo also have an idea of keeping records or tallies of events, as was illustrated in a trading record kept by a Malemut during a winter trading trip which he made from St Michael to Kotzebue sound. It was kept for his own reference and without any suggestion from another. It was drawn on small fragments of brown paper and was a good example of picture writing; small, partly conventional outlines were made to represent the various articles of trading goods, which were drawn beside a representation of the skins for which he had exchanged them. On the same paper he drew a route map of his journey, marking the villages at which he had stopped.

PAINTS AND COLORS

A picture, image, paint, or color is called *ä'-lhĭñ-ûk* by the Unalit. Fine shades of color are not differentiated by these people, but they have names for most of the primary colors.

Black is called *tûñ-u'-lĭ;* white, *kä-tûgh-û-lĭ;* red, *kau-ĭg'-û-lĭ;* brown or russet, *kau-ĭg'-û-lĭkh-lu'-g'ûk;* green, *chuñ-ûkh'-luk* or *chuñ-ûg'-û-lĭ.* Various other shades are distinguished as being colored like natural objects; gray or clay color is called *kĭ-gu'-yû-gnäl'-ĭñ-uk* (from *kĭ-gu'-yûk,* clay, and *ä'-lhĭñ-ûk,* color); purple is *kĭ-uñ' ä'-lhĭñ-ûk;* blue is *ku-logh'-ûn ä'-lhĭñ-ûk.*

Coloring matter is obtained from various sources. The dark reddish shade which is given to tanned sealskin is obtained by soaking the inner bark of the alder in urine for a day and washing the skin with the infusion. White is made from a white clayey earth; yellow and red from ocherous earths; red is also obtained from oxide of iron; black is made from plumbago, charcoal, or gunpowder, the two latter being mixed with blood; green is obtained from oxide of copper.

For the purpose of storing their fragments of paint the Eskimo use boxes somewhat similar in general character to those used for tools, save that they are very much smaller. These boxes also serve for keeping other small articles, such as fishhooks, spear- or arrow-points, etc.

Figure 8, plate LXII, illustrates a small ivory paint box obtained from Norton sound by Mr L. M. Turner. It is about four inches long by an inch and a half wide, and with the exception of the cover is made from one piece. It is oblong, and has a sunken ledge at each end to receive the cover. On one end a human face is carved in relief, on the other end the mouth and nostrils of an animal, and on the bottom the figure of a seal. A small wooden box from St Michael (number 33021) is oval in outline and represents the body of a seal. The cover is in the form of a smaller seal, of which the projecting head and neck serve as a handle for raising it. Another paint box, from the lower Yukon (figure 13, plate LXII), is cut from a single piece of wood and represents a salmon, the eyes, nostrils, mouth, gill openings, and lateral line being indicated by incised lines. A square cover fits like a stopper in the top and has a rawhide loop on its center for raising it. A box from Norton sound (figure 11, plate LXII) represents two seals, one on the back of the other, with their heads turned to the left, the upper seal forming the cover. The eyes of both are represented by inlaid beads, the nostrils and mouths are indicated by incised lines, and the fore-flippers of the larger seal are carved in relief on its sides. A somewhat similar box (figure 15, plate LXII) was obtained on Nunivak island, but it represents the figure of only a single seal.

A curious colored box (figure 12, plate LXII) was obtained at Cape Vancouver. It represents a seal with the mouth open and with the teeth in relief; the fore-flippers are carved in relief on the sides, the eyes and nostrils are indicated by ivory pegs, and various other pegs are inserted on the surface of the body. The back- and fore-flippers are painted a dull bluish color; the sides are red, and the same color extends forward over the top of the head to the muzzle; the chin, throat, lower surface of the body, and outline of the flippers, with triangular spots to mark the ears, are black; the teeth are outlined in red. A similar box from the same locality (figure 17, plate LXII) represents a banded seal. The lower surface of the body and a large, triangular space from the crown to the shoulders are colored black; the remainder of the upper surface is alternately banded with red and black lines.

A paint box from Norton sound (figure 9, plate LXII) is made from a single piece, and represents a seal. The fore-flippers are in relief, the tail and hind-flippers are carved free, and the whiskers are represented by little tufts of seal hair set in on each side of the muzzle. The cover, which is of spoon shape, fits like a stopper and is provided with a projecting rod which serves as a thumb-piece for raising it.

A curiously shaped box from Big lake (figure 16, plate LXII) is intended to represent the larva of some insect. It is cut from a single piece and has an oval, stopper-like cover, with a cord loop in the center for raising it. A series of alternately red and black grooves encircle the sides of the body; the crescentic mouth is incised, two beads represent the nostrils, and two incised rings outline the eyes. The mouth, nostrils, and eyes are painted red, the rest of the face showing the natural color of the wood.

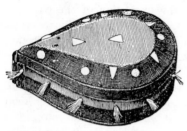

FIG. 58—Wooden paint box (about ⅔).

A box from the lower Yukon (figure 58) is flattened above and below, and is pear-shape around the sides, which are formed by bending a thin strip of wood, the ends being sewed together with spruce root; the bottom is fastened on with wooden pegs, and a stopper-like cover, with a flaring rim, fits into the top, on which a series of small triangular and circular pieces of ivory are inlaid. The colors which originally ornamented this box have disappeared through long use. A box from Pastolik (number 33014) is somewhat similar to the preceding, but the cover is held in place by a long cord which is wound several times around the box and fastened over a peg which projects in front.

A rudely oval box from the lower Yukon (figure 7, plate LXII) is cut from a single piece of wood, and has two compartments to each of which is fitted a stopper-like cover, one rounded in outline and the other with one end truncated; they are provided with small cord loops for lifting them. The body of the box has a groove extending entirely around the sides; another starting from it passes under the bottom to the opposite side.

A handsome wooden box from Big lake (figure 59) is carved from a single piece, and has a stopper-like cover. The body of the box represents a seal with the front flippers in relief and the eyes formed by white beads; the wrists of

FIG. 59—Wooden paint box (about ⅔).

the flippers are crossed by a small inlaid bar of ivory. At one end of the cover is a human face carved in relief, the mouth and eyes being represented by pieces of ivory neatly inlaid. This face and a circle about the eyes of the seal, as well as a long ridge connected with the flippers and the bottom of the box, are colored red. The rear end of the cover is blue, and the remainder of the box is black.

An oval box from St Lawrence island (number 65267) represents the rude outline of a seal with a smaller one on its back, which forms the cover, fitting like a stopper. On the back of the cover are inlaid six halves of blue beads. A sinew cord projecting several inches through the cover serves for raising it. The eyes of the larger seal are formed by round pieces of ivory, with some black substance filling a hole in the center of each to indicate the pupil.

An oblong wooden box from Nunivak island (number 43878) is made of two pieces, the lower two-thirds forming the main part and the other the cover, which is held in place by two bone pegs inserted in the lower edge, at each end, and fitting into corresponding holes in the ends of the lower portion of the box. On the sides and ends of the box are inlaid square strips of ivory, about half an inch from the edge, and a number of small ivory pegs are set in the space between the inlaid strips.

POTTERY

The manufacture of pottery from clay is widely spread among the Eskimo with whom I came in contact, but the women are the only potters. The process of making vessels from clay, as witnessed at St Michael, is as follows:

A quantity of tough, blue clay is moistened and kneaded thoroughly with the hands until it assumes plasticity; then short, tough blades of a species of marsh grass and a small quantity of fine, black, volcanic sand from the beach are mixed with it. A round, flat layer of the prepared clay is worked out to form the bottom of the vessel, and about the edge of this a wall is built up with a thin band of clay, carried around a number of times until the desired height is reached. The top is then smoothed, and is either left plain or slightly scalloped with the fingers. The sides of the vessels are usually left plain, but sometimes they are ornamented with a series of simple, incised lines made with a stick. Several vessels obtained at St Michael have the sides curving slightly until near the top, where they are somewhat constricted and the rim is made slightly flaring.

After the shaping and the ornamentation of the vessel are completed, it is placed near the fire until it becomes dry; then a fire is built both on the inside and the outside, and it is baked for an hour or two with as great a heat as can be obtained.

In a summer camp at Hotham inlet a number of pots were seen, varying in capacity from two to three gallons. Several of the larger ones had the tops scalloped and were slightly constricted in outline below the rim. On the sides they were ornamented with short, parallel, horizontal lines, beginning near the rim and forming a band extending to the bottom, as shown in figure 60, from a sketch made at the time.

Despite the ability shown by the Eskimo of this region in carving bone and ivory, I saw only two efforts made at modeling in clay beyond the manufacture of pots and lamps. These were both rude clay dolls, obtained at a village on the lower Yukon.

A specimen of earthenware from St Michael (number 43068) is 9 inches high by 10¼ wide. Around the inside, near the top, occurs a series of small incised dots; on the inside of the rim are five parallel incised grooves, just below a broader groove which borders the edge; the upper surface of the edge is marked also with a shallow groove. Another vessel from the same locality has three lines of dots around its outer border, near the rim, with two sets of double parallel grooves, and just inside the slightly flaring rim are four roughly made grooves.

From St Lawrence island were obtained some small clay vessels which were used for suspending over ignited lamps. One of these (figure 13, plate XXVIII) is 4½ inches long, 3¼ wide, and 1½ in depth. It is quadrate in outline, with rounded corners, each of which is provided with two holes through which are passed strips of whalebone by which it was suspended. A similar vessel from the same locality (number 63546) measures 6 inches in length, 4¾ in width, and 2 inches in depth; it has a small lug at each corner, near the upper edge, pierced for the reception of the cord by which it was suspended over the lamp. Another of these small pots from the same place (figure 1, plate XXVIII) is oval at the ends, with the sides nearly parallel. It measures 8½ inches in length by 3 broad, and a little over an inch in depth.

FIG. 60—Clay pot from Hotham inlet.

Another specimen from the same island (number 62547) is fashioned like the preceding three vessels, all of which are too small for use in cooking food, and probably served for the purpose of trying out seal oil for use in the lamps.

MATS, BASKETS, AND BAGS

From the shore of Norton sound to the Kuskokwim the women are expert in weaving grass mats, baskets, and bags. Grass mats are used on the sleeping benches and for wrapping around bedding. They are used also as sails for kaiaks, and formerly were utilized as sails for umiaks. They now frequently serve as curtains to partition off the corners of a room or a sleeping platform. Small mats are placed also in the manholes of kaiaks to serve as seats. The bags are used for storing fish, berries, and other food supplies, or for clothing. Smaller bags and baskets are made for containing small articles used in the house.

At Chukwuk, on the lower Yukon, I saw a woman making one of

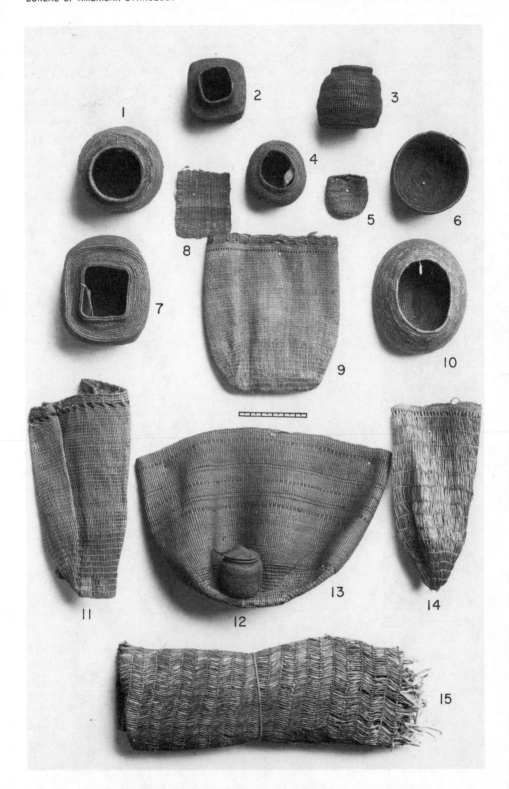

OBJECTS OF GRASS AND SPRUCE ROOT (ONE-EIGHTH)

these mats and watched the process she employed. A set of three or four straws were twisted and the ends turned in, forming a strand, a number of which were arranged side by side with their ends fastened along a stick, forming one end of the mat and hanging down for the warp. Another strand was then used as a woof. By a deft twist of the fingers it was carried from one side to the other, passing above and below the strands of the warp; then the woof strand was passed around the outer strand of the warp and turned to repeat the operation. The strands were made continuous by adding straws as necessary, and with each motion the strands were twisted a little so as to keep them firmly together. By this simple method a variety of patterns are produced.

Figure 15, plate LXXIV, illustrates a common sleeping mat of the kind used by the Eskimo from Kotzebue sound to the Kuskokwim. It was obtained on Norton sound. The size of these mats varies; the example shown is 4 feet long by 3¾ wide, but they are sometimes made twice this size.

A toy grass mat, made for use with a doll (figure 8, plate LXXIV), is also from Norton sound. It is woven in the same way as the larger mats, except that the warp is twisted at intervals and the strands are crossed, thus producing small quadrate openings in the pattern.

In making grass bags, they are started from a point at the bottom, where the strands of the warp, consisting of two or more grass stems, are fastened together and extend vertically downward. The woof is formed by a double strand of grass which is twisted about itself with the strands of the warp inclosed in the turns; both are continually twisted as the weaving progresses. In coarsely made bags, the strands of the woof are spaced from an inch to two inches apart, and those of the warp at intervals of from a quarter to half an inch. These bags have a conical bottom, which slopes from the center to the sides. At the mouth the ends of the warp are braided to form a continuous edge.

Figure 14, plate LXXIV, represents one of these loosely woven bags from Norton sound. These bags, when used for storing fish, sometimes contain from 50 to 100 pounds, which is frozen into a solid mass and packed away in storehouses for use during the months when fresh food can not be obtained. The contents become so thoroughly frozen by the intense cold of winter that when required for use the mass has to be separated by use of wedges and mauls.

Another bag from Norton sound (figure 11, plate LXXIV) is similar to the preceding, except that the bottom has a long, narrow base instead of ending in a point. Along the mouth the strands of the warp are brought together in little braids about an inch and a half in length, spaced at intervals of about half an inch and merged into a thick, braided border, which forms the rim. The weaving is done as in the specimen last described, except that the warp consists of two grass stems, extending down the sides to the bottom, without being twisted.

The woof is twisted, but the strands are spaced only a little over a quarter of an inch apart.

A bag obtained at St Michael by Mr L. M. Turner (figure 9, plate LXXIV) is somewhat similar to the preceding specimens, but the warp is divided alternately by the twisted strands of the woof, forming a slightly zigzag pattern from near the mouth to the edge of the bottom, where the warp extends again in parallel lines.

A closely woven bag, intended to hold clothing (figure 13, plate LXXIV), is from the lower Kuskokwim. It is made like the example from St Michael, except that the solid weaving of the sides extends to the braid at the mouth. The warp extends up and down the sides, as usual, and the strands of the woof are woven close together, forming a compact, thick texture. Several black lines of varying width extend around the bag, and are made by interweaving strands of blackened sinew cord. This pattern and another of ornamental black bands are made in the country between Yukon and Kuskokwim rivers and thence southward to Bristol bay. One specimen from the latter locality, in addition to the black lines, has three broken bands of russet brown, made by drawing small strips of brown leather through the warp. From the lower Kuskokwim was obtained also a grass bag, 11 inches in height and 13 inches across the bottom, woven in the same manner as the last specimen. It is circular in shape around the sides and widest near the bottom, narrowing gradually to near the top, which is suddenly constricted to an opening five inches in diameter.

The people of the lower Yukon and thence northward to Kotzebue sound make various sizes of grass baskets of a coil pattern. A strand of grass is laid in a coil forming the warp, the woof is then woven in by interlacing grass stems, and the coil is continued until the flat bottom is completed. The coils are then superimposed one upon the other until the basket is built up to the top, where it is narrowed in to form a circular, oval, or square opening. Frequently the coil is commenced on the bottom around a vacant space, from an inch to three inches in diameter, into which is sewed a piece of rawhide. The rim at the top has the grass brought over and neatly turned in on the under side, forming a smoothly finished edge.

One of these baskets (number 48139), used for storing clothing and various small articles, which was obtained from the mouth of the Yukon, measures $10\frac{1}{2}$ inches in height by 13 inches in width, with an opening at the top 10 inches in diameter. A basket of this description from Kushunuk (figure 7, plate LXXIV) is roughly quadrate in outline, with rounded corners; it has the bottom woven in the same manner as those of the bags which have been described. Another basket, obtained on Putnam river by Lieutenant Stoney (figure 10, plate LXXIV), has a flat bottom, with a long, oval piece of rawhide in the center; the sides round gradually upward to an oval opening.

A basket from St Michael (figure 1, plate LXXIV) has a flat bottom,

MALEMUT FAMILY WITH DOG SLED

with a center made from a piece of rawhide; the sides, built up of coils, narrow inward to the top, where they are suddenly constricted to a rolled rim surrounding the circular opening. The basket from the lower Yukon shown in figure 4, plate LXXIV, has a flat bottom with a circular piece of rawhide in the center. A double strand of grass is twisted into the woof between each of the coils on the sides, producing a doubly ridged surface. The top has a slight rim around the central opening.

A toy basket from the lower Yukon (figure 5, plate LXXIV) has the warp varied at intervals with grass cords passed around the surface, about a third of an inch apart, in three parallel rows. These cords consist of three strands, only one of which is woven into the warp, leaving the remainder in relief on the surface.

Figure 6, plate LXXIV, shows a basket from St Michael. In this specimen the coil starts from the center of the flat bottom; the sides slope slightly outward and end at the upper edge without being constricted, forming a dish shape. Another basket from the coast of Norton sound has the usual flat bottom; the sides slope slightly outward, swell around the middle, and then are drawn in again toward the top to form a rim around the opening.

On the lower Yukon coiled baskets are made of spruce roots, which form very strong, rigid walls. They vary in form, but all have flat bottoms. A basket of this kind, from that locality (figure 2, plate LXXIV), is roughly quadrate in form, with rounded corners. The sides are nearly straight, but are constricted abruptly above, forming a neck-like rim about an inch high, which surrounds the square opening in the top. Another specimen, from Sledge island (figure 3, plate LXXIV), is round in shape, with the sides slightly curved and constricted above to a slightly flaring tip around the opening.

The most elaborately finished specimen procured is shown in figure 12, plate LXXIV. This was obtained from the lower Yukon district. It is round in shape, with slightly curving sides, which are constricted abruptly to the neck of a slightly flaring rim. It has a flattened conical top, which has two small sinew hinges, and is fastened in front with sinew cords; a loop of the same material on the top forms the handle.

A "housewife" of woven grass, obtained on the lower Yukon, is woven with open-work similar to the bags which have been described.

TRAVEL AND TRANSPORTATION

SLEDS

The Alaskan Eskimo of the mainland and on all the islands about Bering strait, including St Lawrence island, use dogs and sleds for winter traveling. Plate LXXV, from a photograph taken at St Michael, represents a Malemut family ready to start on a journey. On the

American coast and adjacent islands sleds from 9 to 10 feet in length are built strongly of driftwood. Their runners are from 2 to 3 inches broad and from 6 to 7 inches high. They are straight nearly to the front, where they curve up regularly to the level of the bed. Along the sides four or five stanchions are mortised into the upper edge of the runners and project upward about 2½ to 3 feet; the ends of bow-shape pieces of wood are also mortised in the top of the runners, and both these and the stanchions are fastened with wooden pins. These bow-shape pieces curve upward and inward about five inches above the tops of the runners, forming the supports on which rests the bed of the sled, which is from 16 to 24 inches in width, and is formed of a kind of latticework. A crescentic or bow-shape piece of wood is fastened across the front, from which two long, thin, wooden slats run length-wise to the rear, where they rest on the upcurved bows, to which they are lashed. Across these pieces a series of thin wooden slats are lashed by rawhide cords passed through holes and corresponding holes in the longitudinal slats, which extend out to the rear line of the runners and have a long strip of wood lashed along each side. A long wooden rod is fastened firmly to the upturned point of the runner on each side and extends to the rear of the sled, resting on the tops of the stanchions, forming a rail. A stout rawhide cord is passed through holes in the top of the stanchions and wound around the rail, holding it firmly in position. The rail usually projects a few inches beyond the last stan-chion on each side, forming handles for guiding the sled. Some sleds also have a crosspiece resting on the last stanchions at the rear. On the sides a stout rawhide cord is fastened at the end of the rail and is passed down around the side bar of the bed and back to the rail again in a diagonal or zigzag pattern along the entire length, thus forming a netting, which prevents articles from falling from the sled. Inside of this netting it is customary to place a large sheet of canvas or of skins sewed together to form a covering for the load. The flaps are folded over the top, and a rawhide lashing from rail to rail holds the load firmly in place. From five to nine dogs are attached to large sleds of this character, and a considerable load can be hauled on them. With seven dogs it is customary, on trips along the coast of Norton sound, to haul a load weighing 300 or 400 pounds.

Smaller sleds, from 5 to 6 feet in length, are used about the villages or for short journeys.

Figure 16, plate LXXVI, represents a model of one of these sleds, which was obtained at the head of Norton sound. A simpler form of sled also is used by the people along the coast from Kotzebue sound to the Yukon mouth. The runners are of the same fashion as those last described, to which a stout crosspiece is fastened on the inside of the upturned ends, and two or three short stanchions, 6 to 8 inches in height, are mortised into their upper edge. A rail on each side is lashed against the crosspiece and extends backward, resting upon and lashed to the tops of the stanchions to form rails. Crosspieces connect the sides of the sled between the stanchions.

These sleds are very light, weighing only from 15 to 20 pounds. They are used for short hunting or fishing trips, and are hauled usually by the hunter himself. In the spring they are used by hunters to haul their kaiaks on the sea ice to open water, or to the cracks that are opening. When such a break is reached, the hunter places the sled on the top of the kaiak, back of the manhole, and paddles across to the other side, where he disembarks, places the kaiak on the sled, and resumes his journey. In this manner these people make long trips over the sea ice in search of seals and walrus.

Fig. 61—Kaviak hunter with hand sled.

When a hunter wishes to make a trip to the mountains in winter in search of reindeer and does not care to take dogs with him, he frequently loads his provisions, bedding, and gun on one of these light sleds and drags it to the camping place.

The accompanying illustration (figure 61), from a photograph, represents a deer hunter leaving St Michael with one of these sleds for a winter hunt in the mountains backward from the coast.

Both of the styles of sleds described are in common use over nearly the entire coast district visited.

The runners of the larger sleds are commonly shod with thin, flat strips of bone—sawed from the jawbone of a whale—of the same width as the runner, and fastened on with wooden pegs; the smaller sleds commonly have the runners unshod, although sometimes strips of bone are used for that purpose.

Figure 62 illustrates a sled from Plover bay, Siberia, which is the style used on St Lawrence island and the adjacent Siberian coast. It is modeled after those used by the Chukchi of eastern Siberia. The runners are made from pieces of driftwood; they are suboval in cross section, about 2 inches wide by 1¼ thick, and taper toward the front. To the front ends of the runners is lashed an overlapping piece of wood of the same width and about half an inch thick, which extends down the under side of the runner and is curved up over the back, reaching midway to the rear of the sled, where it is lashed to the end of a flat piece of wood which serves as the rail. Bowed pieces of reindeer horn are fixed in the tops of the runners, to which they are fastened by whalebone or rawhide lashings. Two flattened sticks extend from the top of the first bow to a little beyond the last one, to form a resting place for the bed of the sled and to which it is lashed. Crosspieces are then lashed to these sticks. On each side a brace is formed by a rod of wood, which is lashed against the side of the stringer and to the

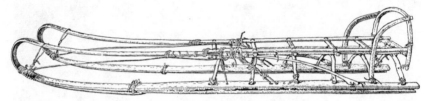

Fig. 62—Sled used on the Siberian shore of Bering strait.

runner 15 inches in front of the rear end and extending obliquely forward under the bed. At the rear end a bow of wood is lashed to the last deerhorn bow under the bottom, forming a curve about 10 inches high above the bed; from each side of this, near the top, another bow extends forward and downward to the base of the second deerhorn bow, where it is firmly lashed. To serve as a shoe, a thin, flat piece of wood is fastened to the lower side of each runner by rawhide lashings passed through the runner and through holes in the shoe, which are countersunk, so that the friction against the surface of the snow or rocks shall not cut the cord. The load is fastened on these sleds with rawhide cords, and the attachment for hauling is made to the forward part of the runners and the first crosspiece.

This form of sled is used with dogs by the Eskimo and sedentary Chukchi of the Asiatic coast, and with reindeer by the reindeer-using Chukchi of that region.

Figure 1, plate LXXVI, represents another style of sled, from St Lawrence island, used for transporting to the village the meat and blubber from the place where the game is killed. It is about 15 inches in length and the same in width, and has two stout, walrus-tusk runners about 15 inches long, an inch and a half deep, and two-thirds of an

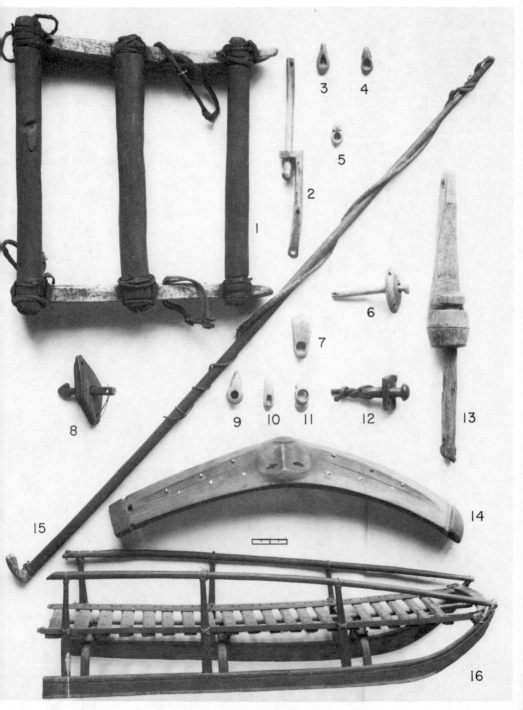

ODEL OF SLED FRAME, WITH OTHER OBJECTS USED IN TRANSPORTATION (THREE-SIXTEENTHS)

inch wide; they have a flange-like projecting edge along the outside of the upper border, and are held together by three rounded wooden crossbars 14 inches long, with two grooves in their ends, held in position by strong rawhide lashings that pass through two holes in the upper edges of the runners. The front ends of the runners are curved upward and have a large slot in them for attaching the cord by which the sled is hauled. In the rear end of each runner are two holes, in which are inserted stout rawhide loops, and a hole just in front of the second crossbar serves for another rawhide loop; these loops receive the lashings with which the load is held in place.

DOG HARNESS AND ACCOUTERMENTS

The ordinary style of harness used for dogs is made of rawhide straps. It consists of a collar with a strap extending down from the back of the neck to the middle of the back, where it meets a strap which passes from the lower part of the collar between the fore-legs and up on each side over the ribs, to be attached to the back strap; at this point is made fast the leading line, which is from three to five feet long, and is attached either directly to the front of the sled or to a single straight leading line fastened to the sled and extending forward to a distance sufficient for the attachment of all the dogs belonging to the team. When the team consists of more than three dogs, they are attached to the main leading line in pairs, with the most intelligent dog in front as a leader.

When the load is very heavy, or the dogs are too numerous to work well in a single team, they may be attached to the forward stanchions, sometimes one or even two on each side, in addition to the team in front.

On the islands of Bering strait and along the Asiatic coast, long-handle whips are used for driving dogs; specimens of these were obtained on Sledge, King, and St Lawrence islands. The handles of the whips from King and St Lawrence islands are round rods of spruce, a little over forty inches in length, and have rawhide lashes fastened to them with sinew cord.

One of these whips from St Lawrence island (figure 15, plate LXXVI) has a lash made from a piece of sealskin, with the edges sewed together, forming a round cord, with a slender strip of sealskin at the tip for a cracker. On the handle is a ferule of walrus ivory, rudely representing the head of a white bear; the end of the handle is wedged into the ferule, which projects spur-like on one side.

A King island whip (number 45407) has a stout lash made of a piece of walrus hide, with a small rawhide cracker at the tip. At the butt of the handle is a round ivory ferule, sloping to a flaring rim, which extends around it. The use of these whips also extends to the mainland of the American coast at Cape Prince of Wales, and thence northward to Point Hope on the Arctic coast.

18 ETH——14

The Eskimo to the southward of Bering strait use short-handle whips with a long lash, generally of braided rawhide, largest just in front of its attachment to the handle and tapering to a point at the end, which is provided with a sealskin cracker.

The ferules used on the handles of these whips vary considerably in form, as is shown in the specimens illustrated. One example, from St Lawrence island (figure 7, plate LXXVI), is slightly spoon-shape in outline, projecting spur-like on one side. A round ferule from the Diomede islands (figure 11, plate LXXVI) is of walrus ivory and has a lobe-like projection on each side. Figure 9, plate LXXVI, shows a round ivory ferule from Sledge island, with a carving representing the head of a white bear projecting on one side. Another, from Point Hope (figure 10, plate LXXVI), is a small ivory specimen with a flattened spur on one side.

In many localities I found in use swivels made of bone, deerhorn, ivory, or wood, which were fastened to the cords by which dogs were attached to stakes or other objects, to prevent the cords from becoming twisted by the movement of the animals.

Figure 13, plate LXXVI, represents a large wooden swivel of this kind from Razbinsky, on the lower Yukon. It consists of a round wooden rod, deeply notched on one side, with a hole pierced through the head formed by the notch, through which is inserted a stout wooden rod with a large head. In the opposite ends of the two rods are holes in which cords are fastened.

Swivels exactly similar in design, but made of deerhorn or ivory, were obtained on the Diomede islands, St Lawrence island, on Kowak river at the head of Kotzebue sound, and at Point Belcher on the Arctic coast. Figure 2, plate LXXVI, represents one of these ivory swivels from the Diomede islands.

Another style of swivel used similarly to the preceding, as well as on dog harness to prevent the lines from becoming twisted, is made by inserting a large-head rod of deerhorn or ivory in a hole in the center of a square or oval block of the same material, around the borders of which are four holes, to which are attached cords with their ends fastened together a few inches beyond their starting points. Figure 12, plate LXXVI, shows such a swivel from Unalaklit, made of deer-horn, with a square block on the head. Another swivel of this character, with an oval head (figure 6, plate LXXVI), is from Cape Nome. A similar specimen was obtained on Kowak river.

A deerhorn swivel from the lower Yukon (figure 8, plate LXXVI) has a head roughly triangular in shape, with two holes for the lines; through another hole in the center is a deerhorn rod with a large head and with a hole at the small end for the attachment of a cord.

In addition to swivels, small, double-eye blocks are also commonly used on dog harness; these are cut from bone, deerhorn, or ivory, and have holes passing through them in two directions. Blocks of this character were obtained from various localities between Norton sound and Point Hope, on the Arctic coast, and thence across Bering strait to the coast of Siberia, and on St Lawrence island.

Figure 4, plate LXXVI, illustrates a small ivory block of this character, from St Lawrence island. It is somewhat pear-shape, with a hole through one end, surrounded by a lip or bead-like elevation; this hole and a groove on each side are intended to receive a permanent cord. In a direction transverse to this hole is a larger one, through which the cord is passed in making a temporary attachment. Another of these blocks from St Lawrence island (figure 5, plate LXXVI) has an incised groove, forming a neck, between the two holes.

Some of these blocks are very rudely shaped, as is shown in figure 3, plate LXXVI, from St Lawrence island. This example is cut without any attempt to round off the corners. Another very plainly made specimen was obtained at Unalaklit.

In addition to the use of dogs for hauling sleds, it is a common practice among the Eskimo when traveling in summer to put their dogs on shore and harness them to a long line attached to the bow of the boat, one of the party remaining on shore to drive the dogs, which travel along the beach and pull the boat. By the employment of this means much labor is saved.

BREAST YOKES

From Nunivak island southward beyond the mouth of Kuskokwim river the people are in the habit of using breast yokes when carrying heavy burdens on their backs; they are made of flattened pieces of wood, crescentic in form, with a hole at one end through which a cord is fastened; at the other end is a knob-like enlargement, with a notch on its outer side, over which a loop on the end of the cord can be slipped.

Figure 14, plate LXXVI, illustrates one of these breast yokes, which was obtained on Nunivak island by Doctor W. H. Dall. It consists of a flattened board, slightly crescentic in shape, about three inches wide and half an inch in thickness. On the curved front is carved in relief a human face, the eyes, mouth, and nostrils being incised, as are also four parallel lines extending downward from near the corners of the mouth, to represent tattooing; across the front each way from the face is a broad groove which narrows to a point at the outer end, along each edge of which are set six small reindeer teeth. The face, grooves, and tips of the yoke are painted red; the remainder of the front and upper border is black. Doctor Dall obtained another yoke of this kind on Nunivak island; it has a beveled front and a slight ridge along the center, which is narrow in the middle but broader toward the ends.

A yoke from Chalitmut (number 36023) is constricted in the middle and expanded into a wing-like form toward each end.

SNOWSHOES

Among the western Eskimo snowshoes are in common use. They are of the greatest service for traveling, both over the sea ice and on land, and are used by both men and women, but more largely of course by men, as their more active life necessitates almost constant travel while hunting, visiting netting places on the ice, or traps on the shore. For traveling on land, where the snow is softer and deeper than on the sea ice, snowshoes with larger and finer netting are used. Figure 63 represents snowshoes, used for land travel, which were obtained near the head of Norton bay. They are made of two pieces of wood, spliced in front where they curve upward at the toe, held together by means of

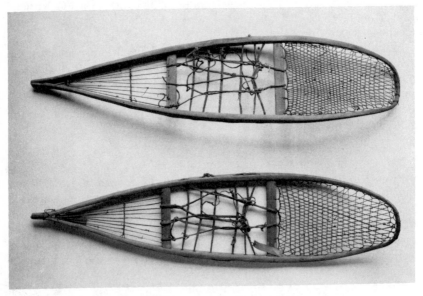

FIG. 63—Snowshoes from Norton bay.

two crossbars in the middle, before and behind the foot-rest. The netting in front of the first crossbar is hexagonal in shape, and in the rear consists of ten cords passing through holes in the hindmost crossbar and converging to the thong that binds the frame together at the heel. The foot-rest is on a stout netting made of widely spaced crosscords attached to the framework on the sides as well as to the crossbars.

This is the general style of snowshoe worn about the shores of Norton sound and thence southward to the Kuskokwim, and up lower Yukon and Kuskokwim rivers. Various forms of coarsely netted snowshoes are used on the sea ice at different points along the coast.

Figure 64 shows the style of snowshoe used at Cape Darby. The frame is in two pieces, rounded in cross section and tapering in front, where they are curved strongly upward at the ends which overlap and are lashed together. At the heel the rim tapers backward to a point and is held together by a rawhide lashing; the toe netting is replaced by a cord passing from side to side and two other crosscords which pass diagonally from near the point of the upturned toe to holes in the front of the crossbar. The foot-rest is made of a strong cord of rawhide passed through holes in the side of the frame and over the

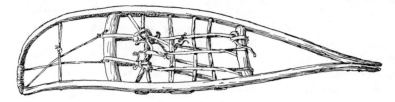

FIG. 64—Snowshoe from Cape Darby.

front and rear of the crossbars, forming a pattern somewhat similar to that in the shoes used on land.

A roughly oval shoe from Icy cape (figure 65) is rudely made and pointed at the heel. The spaces in front and behind the crossbars are filled with fine netting of babiche, which is fastened through holes in the rim. The foot-rest is made by rectangular netting fastened through holes in the sides of the framework and over the front and rear crossbars. These shoes are intermediate in character between those used on land and the ones intended for service on sea ice.

A short, stoutly made shoe from St Lawrence island (figure 66) has the framework oblong in cross section, with the corners slightly rounded and turned upward abruptly at the toe, the curve commenc-

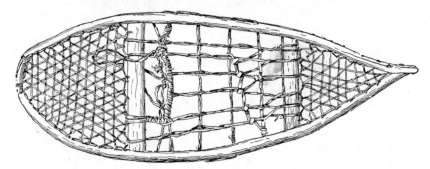

FIG. 65—Snowshoe from Icy cape.

ing immediately in front of the first crossbar. The ends of the side-pieces meet at the toe and are held firmly together by a lashing of whalebone passed through holes. The rear crossbar is close to the heel, which is held in position by the end of the cord used for the foot-rest, which passes through a hole on one side, and, crossing the triangular space behind the last crossbar, is tied through a hole in the opposite side. The space between the front and rear crossbars occupies almost the entire area of the shoe and is crossed by a stout netting of rectangular pattern, with some of the strands passing diagonally, producing a combination of patterns. These coarsely netted shoes are intended for use upon frozen snow or on the rough surface of the sea ice, for which purposes they are very serviceable, as the masses of broken ice have many small openings large enough for the foot to pass through, which render traveling very difficult without such assistance. By aid of these shoes hunters are enabled to travel safely and frequently to pass over weak places where newly made ice would not otherwise support them. On the Asiatic coast the Eskimo use snowshoes similar to those from St Lawrence island that have been described, and others rather more elongated but similar in general pattern.

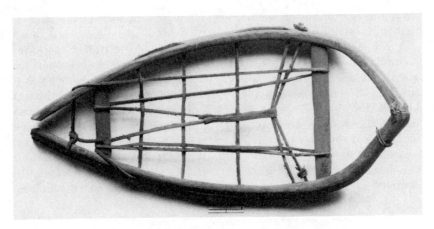

Fig. 66—Snowshoe from St Lawrence island.

ICE STAFFS

When traveling or hunting on the sea ice there is great risk of breaking through thin places which have been concealed by drifted snow. To guard against this danger the people are in the habit, at certain seasons, of carrying a stout wooden staff with a strong ivory or bone point, two or three inches long, inserted in the lower end and fastened by a strong wrapping of sinew. Around the base of this point is fastened a hoop of bone or deerhorn, hung to the staff by a cord passed through a hole above the point. A ring of bone or horn surrounds the base of the point, and between it and the outer hoop strong cross-lashings of rawhide form a sort of netting.

In walking over suspicious places in the ice the traveler plants the staff solidly before him previous to taking a step; if the ice be thin the point of the staff goes through, but the hoop comes in contact with a broader surface and prevents the staff from sinking farther. In this way the weight of the man is distributed over three points, and thus he is often enabled to pass over places which otherwise would not support him.

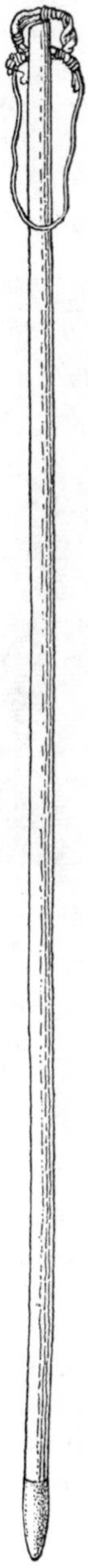

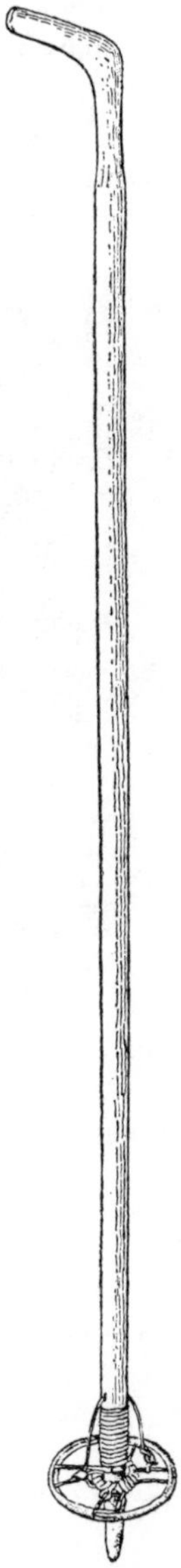

These staffs are also used in summer travel. During this season the tundras are covered with tussocks and soft beds of sphagnum, which render walking excessively laborious and difficult. By use of the staff the traveler is enabled to walk more safely, and by lessening the weight on his feet, does not sink so deeply in spongy patches of moss or in semi-marshy ground.

Figure 67 illustrates one of these ice staffs from Cape Nome.

An ice staff from Point Barrow (figure 68) consists of a round wooden staff nearly five feet in length, the lower end being tipped with a cap of ivory, held in place by a pin through its base. Through the upper end is a hole, in which is a sealskin loop for hanging the staff on the wrist.

ICE CREEPERS

Ice creepers are used to prevent the feet from slipping while traveling over the sea ice or frozen snow in spring. In some of them the central groove is deepened to form an oblong slot, piercing through, and on others the points are formed in groups near each end.

Figure 69 (3) represents a pair of ice creepers from Cape Darby, consisting of small, flat, oblong ivory rods 3½ inches in length, with the upper surface slightly rounded and the lower side having a deep, flat groove extending lengthwise along the middle, leaving two high ridges that are crossed by deep grooves, producing a row of pyramidal points along each edge. The ends are provided with two holes, in which are fastened the rawhide cords by which the creepers are attached to the sole of the boot.

FIG. 67—Ice staff (⅛).

FIG. 68—Ice staff (⅛).

A pair of ice creepers from St Lawrence island (figure 69, 5) are in the form of flat, ivory bars, about 4 inches long and an inch wide. Eight small holes are drilled into the lower surface, in which are inserted small, round-pointed iron spikes; there are

two holes through each end for the cords by which they are fastened
to the foot. Figure 69 (1 and 1a) show the upper and lower surfaces
of a broader and heavier pair of ice creepers from the Diomede islands.
They are turned up at the ends to retain them in place on the foot, and
have four rows of pyramidal points along the lower surface.

Figure 69 (2 and 4), from St Michael and St Lawrence island, respectively, represent ivory creepers with a row of pyramidal points along
each side. Through the middle, between the rows of points, is cut a

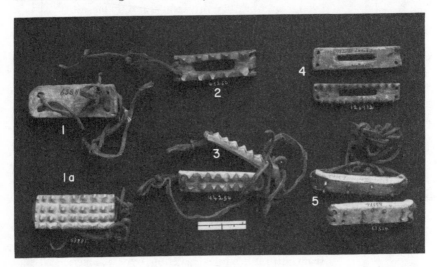

Fig. 69—Ice creepers (⅓).

long, rectangular slot, and in the ends of each are holes for the cords
by which they are fastened on.

Other creepers of similar style were obtained from Plover bay on
the Siberian shore.

BOATS

The Eskimo of the Alaskan coast, the islands of Bering strait, and
the coast of Siberia use large open boats, varying in length from fifteen
to forty feet, and made by covering a wooden framework with sealskin or walrus-hide. These are the umiaks so well known from their
use by Greenlanders. Among the people from the head of Norton
sound and northward to Point Barrow, these boats are known as
u'-mĭ'-ăk; among the Unalit of the eastern shore of Norton sound and
southward they are called añ'-i-juk. They vary in size according to
locality or to the purpose for which they are made, and their pattern
also varies slightly with the locality. Originally they were propelled
by paddles, after which slender-blade oars were adopted in some localities, and these are still used.

Although oars are in common use, yet it is not rare to see umiaks
propelled wholly by paddles, as was done in ancient times. Paddles

MODEL OF UMIAK WITH MATTING SAIL

were seen in use at Cape Prince of Wales on Bering strait, and at points northward and southward from that locality.

The oars are held in place usually by means of a rawhide lashing made fast, on the inside of the boat, to the framework. The steering is always done with a large, broad-blade paddle.

In ancient times sails sometimes were improvised by sewing together grass mats and putting them up between two long sticks, which were fastened to the framework of the umiak and stayed by means of cords so as to extend upward and outward in V-shape form, one from each side of the boat. Later, after the arrival of white men, a single upright mast with stays and with blocks made from bone or ivory, were adopted in imitation of the rigging used on the ships of the strangers.

Sails were next made from the skins of reindeer or other animals, sewed to a proper size and shape and fastened to a yard, which was raised or lowered by tackle made of walrus-hide cord passed through an ivory or bone block or through a hole in the upper end of the mast. Some sails are still made of old deerskins or light sealskins sewed together, but many are seen of light canvas or drilling obtained from vessels or through fur traders.

The framework of these boats is formed of neatly-shaped pieces cut from driftwood and lashed together with rawhide cords, which are passed through holes drilled in the wood, as shown in the model, from St Michael, illustrated in plate LXXVII, 38. The covering is of heavy sealskin or walrus-hide, tanned to remove the hair, sewed into proper shape, and drawn over the framework. In the edges many little slits are cut, through which is passed the cord which lashes it to the framework on the inside under the rail. After it is in place the lashings are drawn tightly and permitted to dry; as it contracts the cover becomes as tight as a drumhead, after which several coats of seal oil are applied to the outside and allowed to become thoroughly dry, when the cover becomes impervious to water for a week or ten days, at the expiration of which time it becomes water-soaked and it is then necessary to haul up the boat on the shore and, after allowing it to dry, to give it another coating of oil, otherwise the skins would rot. Traveling is done by day, and at night the boats are hauled up on the beach and turned bottom up or upon one edge, so that they may dry during the night. When treated carefully in the manner described, the cover of an umiak will last for several years.

In comparison with the Norton sound umiaks, I noticed that the boats used by the people of Bering strait have somewhat less sheer to the sides and are provided with flaps of sealskin about two feet wide, which are attached along the rail and folded down inside the boat in fair weather; in rough weather these flaps are raised and held in place by stout sticks lashed to the framework around the sides and their ends thrust into a series of holes or slots along the upper edge of the flap. In addition to these, the people of Bering strait carry sealskin floats, which are inflated and lashed under the rail on the outside, to prevent the boat from swamping.

Sometimes umiaks are driven out to sea by storms and their occupants are unable to regain the shore, when the dashing spray and the waves soak the cover and the rawhide lashings of the frame until they relax and the boat collapses, drowning all on board.

From Kotzebue sound northward the umiaks are very similar to those of Norton sound, but are slightly narrower. At the former place, during the summer of 1881, I saw a number of umiaks, each of which had a figure of a man painted roughly in black close to the bow. The umiaks of the Yukon and adjacent country, and thence southward, are commonly ornamented, on the middle of each side, with the figure of a mythic, alligator-like animal called *päl-rai'-yûk*; the head, with open mouth and projecting tongue, is close to the bow, while the tail reaches the stern (figure 156).

The umiaks seen among the Eskimo south of East cape, Siberia, at Mechigme bay, St Lawrence island, and Plover bay, were all very much narrower than those of Norton sound, and with very little sheer to their sides; some of them seemed to have almost perpendicular sides. All of the umiaks used in the latter region are provided with a set of sealskin floats to fasten along the outside below the rail in rough weather, which render the boats very buoyant, and but little water can be shipped even in very stormy weather. With their boats fitted in this manner with inflated floats, these people sail fearlessly along their stormy coasts and cross back and forth between the mainland and St Lawrence island.

The oars used in the umiaks of the American mainland are kept in position by means of rawhide stays, which are attached firmly to a notch in the part of the oar which rests on the rail; the stays extend fore-and-aft a short distance and are fastened to the side pieces on the inside below the rail. The steering is performed with a broad-blade paddle. On St Lawrence island oarlocks have been copied from those seen on whaling vessels. An example of these (figure 34, plate LXXVIII), made of oak, is provided with a pin to fit in a hole in the rail of the boat, and its upper portion is pierced to receive the oar.

Figure 19, plate LXXVIII, represents an ivory block, from Sledge island, used for the rigging of an umiak. Another form of these blocks, from the same place, is shown in figure 20 of the same plate. A handsomely made little block from Cape Nome (figure 21, plate LXXVIII), has the head of a seal carved in relief on the lower side.

A smaller boat or canoe, called *kai'ak*, is also used along the American coast and the adjacent islands; but I have never seen one among the people of the Siberian coast nor among the St Lawrence islanders. It is decked over, except a hole amidships, where the navigator sits. They vary somewhat in size and shape in different localities, but the general plan of construction is the same.

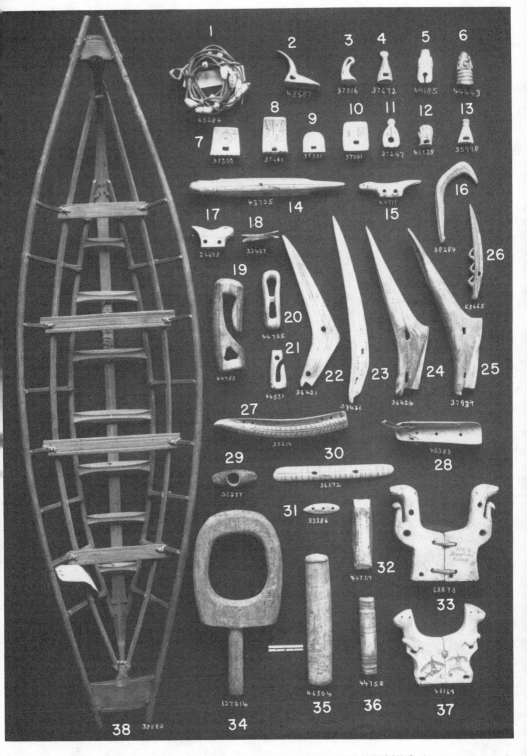

MODEL OF UMIAK FRAME AND APPURTENANCES OF UMIAK AND KAIAK RIGGING (THREE-SIXTEENTHS)

The frame consists of small strips of wood running lengthwise and brought together at the bow and stern; they are connected by curved ribs, placed at short intervals and fastened by rawhide cords; the bow has a stem piece of wood, roughly triangular in form; another piece at the stern is flattened, but varies in form according to the style of the kaiak in which it is placed. The rail is formed of a strong piece of wood, into which the upper ends of the ribs are mortised, holding the rail in place and forming a support for the deck of the boat, in the middle of which is a circular opening, forming the manhole, surrounded by a wooden hoop, which is fastened to two pieces extending to the bow and stern, and resting on the cross-pieces which support the deck. On each side of the manhole is a short stanchion mortised into the rail and the lower side of the rim of the manhole. The entire surface is covered with sealskins, tanned with the hair taken off, and sewed together with sinew cord. The seams are oiled or coated with reindeer tallow, and the entire surface of the boat is thoroughly covered with oil, which is permitted to dry before the boat is placed in the water.

In front of the manhole the deck is crossed from side to side by two stout rawhide cords, three or four feet apart, and one or two similar cords are placed at the back of the manhole; slipped on these cords at the rail, on each side, are spur-like pieces of deerhorn, ivory, or bone, which project upward and form a rest on which may be placed the paddle or the hunting spears.

Commencing with the kaiaks in use at Nunivak island, the following descriptions show the different forms used successively along the coast nearly to Point Barrow:

Figure 2, plate LXXIX, illustrates a kaiak from Nunivak island, 15 feet 1 inch long, 14 inches deep, with 29 inches beam. Another kaiak, from the same island (figure 1, plate LXXIX), is 15 feet 1 inch long, 14 inches deep, and has 29 inches beam. These kaiaks are heavily made, the framework being strong and stoutly built, in order to withstand the stormy seas which they have to encounter about this island. A similar form is in use on the coast of the adjacent mainland.

The manhole is placed a trifle back from the center; the rim is lashed to the rail by rawhide cords; the cross-pieces which support the deck are upcurved toward the middle, forming a ridge, on the top of which is lashed a stout stick extending each way from the manhole to the bow and to the stern, where it projects as a short, handle-like, quadrate spur; below this the stern slopes downward, with a slight slant toward the front. The wooden parts on top of the bow are cut out, forming a large, round opening just above the rail, around which the skin covering is cut away. On some of the kaiaks this opening is made to represent the eye of some mythological animal, the mouth of which is painted in black on the outside of the covering. In front of the stern are two loops of cord, which are attached to the central ridge, and hang on each side, so that the shafts of the spears, which lie on the ivory rests, may be thrust into them and their points placed under the crosscord to hold them firmly in place. The cross section of these kaiaks is slightly rounded along the keel, with a stronger broken curve along each side to the rail.

Figure 3, plate LXXIX, shows a kaiak from St Michael. It is 16 feet 8½ inches long and 12 inches deep, with 27½ inches beam.

The kaiaks of Norton sound are made lighter and narrower than those from Nunivak island. They are essentially the same in the plan of framework except that the projecting stern extends out even with the spur-like point of the top-piece, which reaches back from the manhole. In the bow this top-piece extends forward to the upturned point of the stem, leaving a broad, slot-like interspace. When these kaiaks are covered, the covering follows the point of the stem and of this central piece so as to leave an open space. The same is done at the stern, so that there is a slot-like opening there. This projecting point at the stern serves as a handle for lifting the kaiak, as does the projecting point of the centerpiece at the bow. The central ridge, produced by the stick fastened along the top of the upturned crosspieces of the deck, is similar to that in the kaiaks from Nunivak island.

Figure 4, plate LXXIX, represents a kaiak from King island. It is 15 feet 3 inches long, 13½ inches deep, and has 28½ inches beam. These kaiaks are comparatively short and broad, with an upcurved bow very similar in form to that of the Nunivak island type, and with the same kind of circular opening through the bow piece. The stern is quite different, however, as it extends back from the manhole nearly straight for a short distance and then curves regularly down to the level of the keel point. These kaiaks are strongly made; they are used in the stormy waters of the strait, and sometimes are taken even to the Siberian coast of the strait and to St Lawrence island.

The kaiaks of Nunivak island and of Bering strait are curiously alike in general form, corresponding in a broad bottom and in the strength of their framework. The Nunivak island kaiaks, however, are sometimes twice the size of those used in Bering strait, and at times the bow is very strongly upcurved and the projecting end piece on the top of the stern extends out, or out and down, so that the point reaches halfway to the level of the keel.

At Kushunuk and Askinuk, as well as along the southern border of the Yukon mouth, the Nunivak island style of kaiak is in use, but to the northward it gives way to the type used in Norton sound. Southward from Nunivak island there is a decrease in the size and height until they reach their minimum in the Aleutian islands.

The kaiaks in use on the shores of Kotzebue sound are much smaller and slenderer than those found elsewhere along the Alaskan mainland, and are built on a somewhat different model. This style of kaiak is found from Kotzebue sound northward to Point Barrow, but at the latter place they are made about one-fourth longer than in Kotzebue sound, and as their width is but little greater, they are proportionately slenderer.

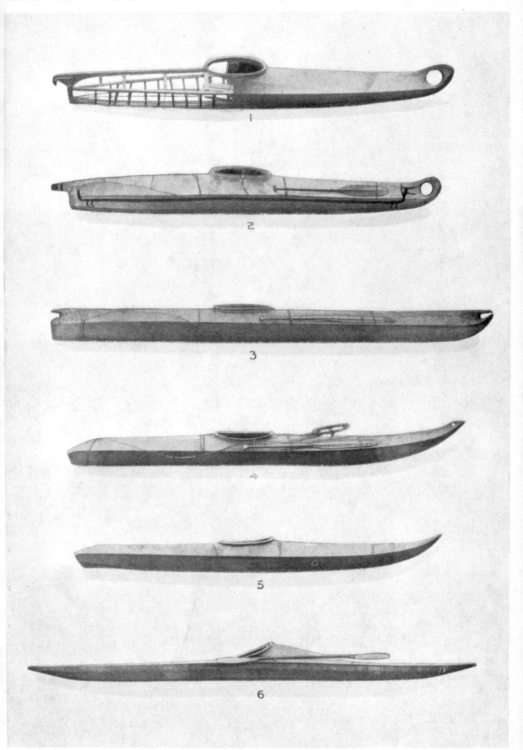

KAIAKS (ABOUT ONE-FORTIETH)

A kaiak from Cape Krusenstern (figure 6, plate LXXIX) is 17 feet 3 inches in length, 8 inches in depth back of the manhole, and has 18 inches beam. Another, from Cape Espenberg (figure 5, plate LXXIX), is 14 feet 4 inches long, 13 inches deep, and has 24 inches beam. These are examples of the Kotzebue sound kaiaks. They are long, slender, and sharp-pointed at both ends; the manhole is placed somewhat backward of the center, and the deck is flat from the rear of the manhole to the stern. Just in front of the manhole the deck is sprung upward by means of the upcurved cross-pieces so as to form a rising slope, which extends back to the rim of the manhole.

This curving surface is brought to a central ridge by means of a strip of wood bound along the tops of the upcurving cross-pieces. The manhole is fitted into position along the rear of this raised portion, with its borders sloping down and backward to the lower flat deck behind. These kaiaks lie very low in the water, and the upsprung curve of the deck just in front of the manhole serves to throw off the water and prevent the full force of the waves from striking against the occupant.

Kaiaks with two or three manholes are now used to a limited extent along the Alaskan coast. These have been introduced by the Russian traders from the Aleutian islands, but they are rarely used by the natives. They are ordinarily made for the convenience of white men, who can thus utilize native labor to propel them.

In journeying on rivers or along the coast, the Eskimo frequently fasten two kaiaks side by side by lashing cross-sticks against the front and rear of the manholes with rawhide cord. A kind of platform of sticks is also made across the deck, on which small loads of goods are placed. These are fixed usually behind the manhole, although at times a load is carried both before and behind the occupant.

On one occasion, near St Michael, I saw two kaiaks lashed together in this way, with a man in each, and just behind them was placed a small pile of household goods, consisting mainly of bedding, upon which sat a woman. In front a small mast, held in position by guys, had been raised on a crosspiece lashed on the decks near the front crosscords, and a small sail, made from parchment-like gut skin, was raised. This odd-looking vessel was making very good time on a small stream before the wind. In rough weather at sea hunters frequently lash their kaiaks together in pairs in order to rest or to prevent accident.

When the *Corwin* reached King island, in Bering strait, one stormy day in the summer of 1881, the islanders lashed their kaiaks in pairs, and came off with piles of furs and other articles of trade heaped up on the decks behind the manholes.

The rim of the manhole is made slightly flaring or with the cover constricted just beneath it next to the deck. Around this constriction a cord is passed, which fastens down the borders of the waterproof frock worn by the occupant in rough or wet weather. With this garment lashed down it is impossible for any water to reach the interior.

When occupied by skilful paddle-men these boats are very difficult to upset and will ride through extremely rough weather in safety. I was told that some of the most skilful among the coast people could upset their kaiaks and right them again by the use of the paddle, but the old men said this feat was now becoming rare as the young hunters were degenerating and were not as good kaiak men as formerly.

BOAT HOOKS

Boat hooks are used by the men on umiaks and kaiaks all along the coast and on the islands, the principal difference in them being in the larger size of those used on the umiaks. These boat hooks are of great service, particularly to men on kaiaks when landing on rocky shores or upon the ice, and those having pointed spurs at the butt are used for fending off ice when paddling about at sea during spring and autumn.

Figure 1, plate LXXX, illustrates a stout boat hook, 6 feet in length, for use in a umiak, which was obtained on Norton sound. The end of the shaft has a strong bone point lashed against a shoulder with rawhide cords; a foot inward from the lower end a strong spur of deerhorn is lashed against the side, from which it projects at a right angle. This is the style of boat hook commonly used on umiaks, the shafts varying from 6 to 8 feet in length.

A boat hook intended for use on a kaiak, obtained at Golofnin bay, is shown in figure 3, plate LXXX. It is 4 feet 9 inches in length; the shaft is rounded and tapering, with a long, spur-like hook of walrus ivory set in a notch near its end and held in place by lashing with strips of whalebone passed through holes in the spur and shaft. This hook is flattened triangular in cross section; the inner edge is thin, but it broadens toward the back; it projects backward toward the end of the shaft and ends in a tapering point.

Boat hooks of this kind are common from the mouth of the Kusko-kwim to Kotzebue sound, and vary but little in shape and in the form of the spur or hook. The backs of these ivory hooks are covered with conventional patterns of diagonally etched lines, crossed by long, horizontal grooves. This pattern is common on these implements over a wide extent of territory. A specimen in the National Museum (numbered 73797) was brought from Taku harbor, in southeastern Alaska. It is made of walrus ivory and is marked with the pattern described.

Figure 15, plate LXXVIII, shows an ivory hook from Sledge island, which has two points at one end and the other fashioned into the form of a seal-head. Another small ivory hook of this kind (figure 26, plate LXXVIII) has three walrus-heads along the back. A long ivory hook from Unalaklit (figure 23, plate LXXVIII) has etched upon it a conventional pattern of straight lines and the raven totem sign.

A deerhorn hook from Askinuk (figure 25, plate LXXVIII) has the back carved to represent the head of a walrus, the outlines of the flippers

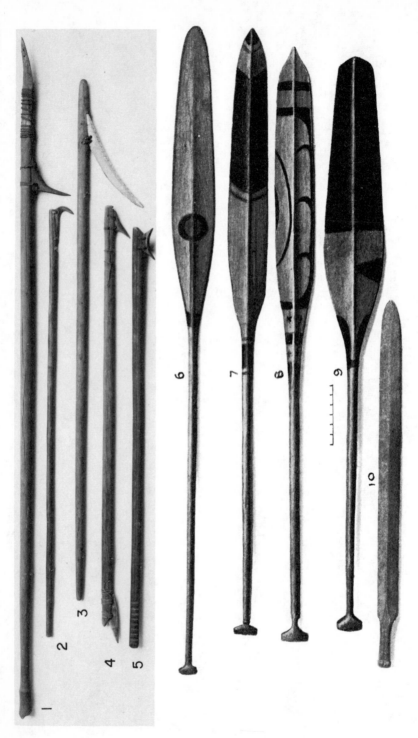

PADDLES AND BOAT HOOKS (ONE-TENTH)

being etched on the sides of the hook. A hook from Big lake (figure 22, plate LXXVIII) has two raised heads extending along each side near the middle. Another, from the same place (figure 24, plate LXXVIII), has the back carved into the form of the head and body of a wolf, with etched lines below on the sides to represent the legs. A boat hook from Sledge island (figure 5, plate LXXX) has a strong wooden shaft, 3 feet 9 inches long, grooved along both sides. It has a double-point hook of deerhorn bound to one side by a rawhide lashing, which passes through two holes in the shaft and through corresponding holes in the hook. The other end of the shaft is heavily grooved crosswise to afford a firmer grasp.

These double-point hooks are frequently notched at the ends, so that the points become double, as shown in the specimen from St Michael, illustrated in figure 18, plate LXXVIII. Boat hooks of this style are commonly used for drawing out articles from the interior of kaiaks which can not be reached with the hand.

An ivory hook (figure 17, plate LXXVIII) obtained on Norton sound by Mr L. M. Turner, has a forked point at one end and the head of a seal carved on the other.

A boat hook from the lower Yukon (figure 2, plate LXXX) has a round handle, three feet in length, with a deerhorn hook lashed with spruce roots to one side of the end; the lashing passes through two holes in the handle, then through a corresponding hole near the outer end of the hook, and around a notch at the base. The holes in the handle, through which the loops pass, are plugged with wooden pins to bind the lashings. A detached hook for a similar implement from the lower Yukon, shown in figure 16, plate LXXVIII, has its surface covered with a heavily etched pattern.

A short boat hook from the lower Kuskokwim (figure 4, plate LXXX) has a backward-pointed spur of deerhorn near one end, which is held in place by rawhide lashings through holes in the hook and in the shaft. A pointed spur of deerhorn at the butt is set in a groove in the same side as the hook at the other end, and is fastened by strong rawhide cords passed through holes in the spur and thence around the notched shaft. The ends of the lashings at each end of the hook are inserted in slits made in the shaft with a flat-point chisel of bone or ivory.

PADDLES

In Kotzebue sound the blades of the paddles used on umiaks are made rounded and very short. North of this district, at Point Hope, the paddle blades are lanceolate in shape, broadest near the handle, and taper downward to a long, sharp point.

The paddles used on kaiaks are made in two forms, one having a blade at each end and the other being provided with a single blade. The forms of the blades vary according to locality. The single-blade paddles have the handles terminating in a crossbar, which is sometimes

cut from the same piece of wood, and at other times is formed from a
separate piece pierced with a hole, by which it is fitted on the end of
the handle.

Figure 29, plate LXXVIII, shows one of these crosspieces for a paddle
handle from the lower Yukon. It is made of bone, is oval in outline,
and is provided with a projecting lip on the lower side, through which
is a round hole for putting on the end of the handle.

Figure 70 a represents an umiak paddle used in Kotzebue sound, and
figure 70 b shows a form of umiak paddle seen at Point Hope.

The kaiak paddles used by the people of Nunivak island and the
adjacent mainland are neatly made and frequently ornamented, in red
and black paint, with figures forming the private marks or totem
signs of the owner.

The Bering strait islanders decorate their kaiak paddles in patterns
of red and black, which probably form totem and ownership marks.

Figure 71 b represents a double-blade paddle from King island. It
is about 8 feet long and the handle is suboval in cross section. The
blades are long, narrow, and flat on the surface which is to be used

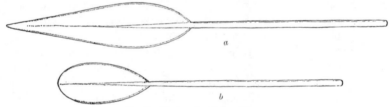

FIG. 70—Forms of umiak paddles.

against the water, and are strengthened along the backs by a ridge
down the middle. One of the blades is painted black and the other
red, and the handle is surrounded by red and black bands. Another
double-blade paddle, obtained at Point Barrow by Lieutenant Ray
(figure 71 a), is 7 feet in length, with the blades nearly flat on both sides
and much broader and more rounded than those of the preceding specimen. The backs of the blades have a very slight ridge running down
the center. A single-blade paddle from King island (figure 9, plate
LXXX) has a large, broad blade, with a central ridge on the outside.
The lower two-thirds of the blade is painted black, and a triangular
spot of black is marked on each side; the edge of the blade, where it
joins the handle at the upper end, is also black, with a ring extending
around the handle. All of these black markings are bordered by a
narrow line of red and constitute the private marks of the owner.

Another single-blade kaiak paddle, from Kushunuk (figure 7, plate
LXXX), has a crosspiece fitted on the top of the handle by means of a
square hole. The blade is long and slender and is tipped with black for
a short distance; this is succeeded by several bands, varying in width,
alternately of red, black, and uncolored wood. The handle near the

blade is surrounded by a broad, black band, with a red band above and another below it.

Figure 8, plate LXXX, represents one of a pair of single-blade kaiak paddles from Kushunuk. It has a long, narrow blade, and the crossbar at the end of the handle is cut from the same piece. The paddle is marked with black lines and bars representing a female phallic emblem, one-half of the figure being on each of the two paddles forming the set. On each side of the crossbar are incised lines representing the mouth, nostrils, and eyes of a semi-human face. On one side the mouth is curved downward, and on the other it is upcurved. The two paddles are exact duplicates as to their markings.

A single-blade paddle from Big lake (figure 6, plate LXXX) is somewhat similar in form to the preceding. On the middle of the blade on each side is painted a red disk, surrounded by a black circle, from which a black band extends up the median ridge of the blade to its upper edge, where a black ring surrounds the handle; from this point to the tip the edge of the blade is painted black.

In the vicinity of the lower Kuskokwim the paddle blades are somewhat similar in shape, but vary in the character of the figures painted on them, which indicate the totems or the ownership marks of their makers.

Figure 10, plate LXXX, illustrates a thin, sword-shape implement of wood, which was obtained at Cape Denbeigh. It is flat on one surface, down the middle of which extends a small groove, while the other surface is so ridged that the cross section forms a flattened triangle. It is employed by seal and walrus hunters for a double purpose—as a paddle for propelling the kaiak slowly and cautiously toward sleeping seals, and for striking the water with the flat side to frighten a wounded animal and cause it to dive again before it can take breath, and thus become exhausted more quickly. From the Chukchi of the Asiatic coast, northwest of Bering strait, I obtained a similar implement made from a long, flat piece of whalebone fitted to a wooden handle.

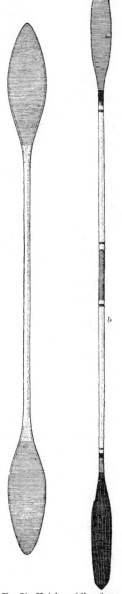

FIG. 71—Kaiak paddles from Point Barrow and King island ($\frac{1}{16}$).

Strips of bone cut from the jaw or rib of a whale are sometimes

18 ETH——15

lashed to the rails of umiaks at the point where the oars pass over them to preserve the cover from wear by friction.

One of these strips, obtained at Port Clarence by Dr Dall, is shown in figure 35, plate LXXVIII. It is flattened below, with one edge turned down, forming a slight lip; the upper portion is rounded, and has a projecting shoulder to retain the lashing which binds it to the rail of the boat.

SPEAR AND PADDLE GUARDS

In Bering strait, where considerable whale fishing is done, small ivory or bone forks are lashed to the bows of umiaks, just inside and between the front ends of the rails; in these the ends of the lances and spears rest, and through them the lines run out. The projecting sides of these forks are usually carved in the form of the heads and shoulders of white bears. They are made in two pieces and are united in the middle by an ivory or bone block mortised in and fastened by wooden or ivory pegs. In some instances the two halves are lashed together by rawhide cords passed through holes; on the outer edges are holes through which pass the lashings which attach them to the bow.

Figure 33, plate LXXVIII, shows an example of these lance guards from the Diomede islands; another (figure 37, plate LXXVIII) from Cape Prince of Wales, has been illustrated among the mythological figures to show the "thunderbird" which is etched on its surface (see plate CVIIa).

To prevent the spears and paddles from falling off the sloping deck of the kaiak, when not in use, there are used guards consisting of upstanding, spur-like pieces of bone, ivory, or deerhorn, which rest on the gunwale on each side, and are fastened to the crossline of the kaiak, which passes through a hole in the base. This base of the guard is flattened and sometimes heavily scored with grooves to give it a firmer hold against the surface of the skin covering. The guards are made in a variety of forms, the simplest of which is a subtriangular piece with the broad base downward.

Figure 4, plate LXXVIII, represents one of these guards, which was obtained at Koñigunugumut; it is rounded in outline and narrow above, where it ends in the form of a tail of a white whale. Another, from Chalitmut (figure 3, plate LXXVIII), is curved over at the end and pierced with a narrow, pear-shape hole through the tip.

Another simple form is a flattened, shell-like piece of ivory, having the bottom curved or flat for resting on the surface of the cover, with a thin, flattened or oval upturned point, the outer side of which is generally covered with etched patterns. Sometimes the inner surface is also ornamented in the same manner. Figure 8, plate LXXVIII, from Anogogmut; figure 10, plate LXXVIII, from Kushunuk, and figures 7 and 9, plate LXXVIII, from Sfugunugumut, represent examples of this kind of guard.

In many cases these spear guards are made in the form of various animal figures.

Figures 72 and 73 represent a pair of beautifully made ivory guards from Kaialigamut. One of them (figure 72) has the broad outer surface carved to represent grotesque semihuman features, and the upper end represents the face of a seal, while on the two sides are the figures of white whales. On the other (figure 73), on both sides, are carved semihuman faces, and on each side is the figure of a seal in relief, and terminating in the head of a seal. These are all beautifully executed carvings.

FIG. 72—Ivory spear guard for kaiak (⅔).

A guard from Cape Vancouver (figure 12, plate LXXVIII) is in the form of a hand, with the palm pierced and a tuft of seal hair set in the back and held in place by a wooden plug. Another, from Cape Nome (figure 5, plate LXXVIII), is carved in the shape of the head of a white bear. A rounded guard with truncated end (figure 13, plate LXXVIII) is from Sfugunugumut. A specimen from Agiukchugumut (figure 11, plate LXXVIII) is in the form of the head and shoulders of a human being, with the hands represented by a flipper etched on each shoulder. Another example from Cape Nome (figure 6, plate LXXVIII) is in the shape of the head of a white bear, with fragments of blue beads representing the eyes and another bead inlaid on the top of the head.

On Nunivak island a somewhat different form of guard is made. 'It is carved in the shape of a seal or other animal, with the body some six

FIG. 73—Ivory spear guard for kaiak (⅔).

or seven inches in length, and has a hole passing diagonally through the side, through which are passed the cross-cords. These figures then lie diagonally along the cover near the rail with the heads pointing upward.

Figure 14, plate LXXVIII, represents one of these guards, which is in the form of a land otter.

Figure 2, plate LXXVIII, shows an ivory guard, obtained at Kotzebue sound, of a pattern different from those generally used. The portion which rests on the cover of the kaiak is rounded above and tapers downward to a wedge-shape point; the upright part forms an obtuse point, which curves forward from the base. A similar guard, made from deerhorn, was obtained on Sledge island.

For repairing broken ribs or for strengthening weak places in the frames of umiaks and kaiaks, strips of ivory or deerhorn are used as splices; holes are pierced through the ends, or a shoulder is left across the upper side to retain the lashings by which they are fastened. Figures 32 and 36, plate LXXVIII, show examples of splices for use on umiaks, collected on Sledge island.

A small deerhorn splice, from St Michael, intended for use on a kaiak, is shown in figure 31, plate LXXVIII. It is pointed oval in outline, and has holes along the middle to receive the lashing.

A longer splice, from Chalitmut (figure 30, plate LXXVIII), is slightly hollowed below and convex on the outer side; it has two holes along the central line, which is grooved on the convex surface; the latter is crossed by numerous incised lines to prevent the lashings from slipping.

When paddling about among the broken ice in spring and autumn there is danger of the skin covering of the kaiak being cut at the bow by floating pieces of ice; to lessen this risk protectors are made from deerhorn and bound on the bow at the water line.

Figure 27, plate LXXVIII, represents one of these protectors from Pikmiktalik; it is $7\frac{1}{2}$ inches long, and is excavated within so as to form a hollow shoulder. One end terminates in a hollow, spoon-shape point, which rests against the bow above the water line. The lower end has a bar of the material left across it, which rests against the bow below the water line, thus permitting the curve to enter the hollow but not to rest against the interior of the protector. Holes along the sides and three notches across the outer surface serve for the lashing by which it is attached to the bow of the boat. The sides are ornamented with a conventional pattern of etched lines.

A similar bow protector from Cape Nome (figure 28, plate LXXVIII) is made of deerhorn; it has holes along the sides for attaching it to the boat. This protector is not ornamented.

The cross-cords for kaiaks are generally plain rawhide lines, but sometimes they are ornamented with beads carved from walrus ivory and strung on them. The commonest form of these represents an inflated sealskin float, generally alternated with round or elongated beads of ivory, and ornamented with etched patterns or having the surfaces of the beads pierced with round holes, in which are inserted small, black wooden pegs.

Figure 1, plate LXXVIII, represents one of these cords from King island. The ornaments strung along it are held in place by wooden wedges, inserted in the holes through which the cord passes. Examples of similar cords were collected at points from Bristol bay to beyond Kotzebue sound.

TRADE AND TRADING VOYAGES

According to traditions of the Unalit, the people on the coast of Bering strait, in ancient times, made regular summer trading voyages back and forth across the strait. Old men told me of having seen small pieces of cloth which had been brought by the people of East cape,

Siberia, and sold as curiosities to the American Eskimo, before the Russians took possession of the country. They also informed me that the use of tobacco was introduced among them, before they were brought into direct contact with white men, by means of trade with their Asiatic neighbors, who brought across Bering strait small bundles, called "hands," of Circassian leaf tobacco.

In ancient times intertribal communication along the coast was irregular and uncertain, owing to the hostile attitude of the people toward one another. For this reason trading was then confined to those villages which happened to be on friendly terms. Now the old barriers have been broken down, and active barter between the different communities has become a marked feature of their life. This is particularly the case among the people living between the Kuskokwim and Kotzebue sound. The numerous fur-trading stations which have been established among them, and the visits of trading vessels and whaling ships to the coast of Bering strait, have served to quicken and encourage among them the spirit of trade. In summer the people of Bering strait make visits to the head of Kotzebue sound and to the mouth of the Yukon, carrying the skins of tame reindeer purchased from the people of the Asiatic coast, for which they receive in barter skins of various fur-bearing animals that are used in turn for trading with vessels in Bering strait or with their Asiatic neighbors. For the latter purpose beaver and land-otter skins are the most highly prized, as the Chukchi of Siberia will always offer two full-size deerskins for one of either of the skins named. They cut them into strips for trimming the collars of their deerskin coats, and use them also for trading with the Russians.

Parties of traders from East cape, Siberia, and the Diomede islands also make yearly voyages to Kotzebue sound, where the Eskimo of Kowak and Noatak rivers hold a sort of summer fair. After the sea freezes in winter, the Eskimo, who have thus obtained a stock of reindeer skins, start out with dogs and sledges to travel along the coast and barter for furs. In the winter of 1880 I met, on Norton sound, a sledge party of Eskimo, who were making a trading trip from Sledge island to Kotzebue sound.

The Malemut along Kotzebue sound make trading trips southward to the Yukon, and even to their enemies, the Tinné, of Koyukuk river. The Malemut are the most energetic and enterprising of all the people of this region. They are great traders, and are more courageous and domineering than most of the natives with whom they deal, and are in consequence much disliked by the people with whom they come in contact.

When, in 1873–'74, the reindeer suddenly left the shores of Norton sound, these people pushed on in family parties from point to point until, in 1877–'78, they had reached Kuskokwim river, Nunivak island, and Bristol bay.

During trading voyages there are carried from one part of the country to another beads and other articles of use or ornament, as well as pieces of jadeite, which material, according to some of the Eskimo, is found in the mountains inland from Kotzebue sound and also on Kaviak peninsula. Small articles, such as green and red paint and wooden dishes, were sent out from the lower Yukon; and the people of other localities who have a surplus of seal oil, dried fish, and skins of various animals, take them to points where they can be exchanged for other desirable commodities.

During one winter at St Michael the skin of a Siberian squirrel was brought to me by an Eskimo living on Norton sound, he having obtained it on Bering strait. The skin must have come from the interior of Siberia.

In the month of August, 1879, we were visited at St Michael by an umiak from Cape Prince of Wales, and another from King island. In July, 1881, a number of umiaks arrived from the former place. These all brought deerskins and tanned hides of seal and walrus for trade. The umiaks in full sail, crowded with fur-clad people, dogs, and their various possessions, made a very picturesque sight. Among the men were some Chukchi from the northern coast of Siberia. These were recognized by our officers, who had spent a couple of weeks with them earlier in the season. The Chukchi generally start out on their trading voyages in May, traveling along the shore with dog sleds, hauling on them their umiaks, which are folded, until they reach open water, when the sleds are left at some point and the umiaks set up; then, taking the dogs and goods on board, they coast along the shore of Bering sound and over to the American side. Some of them even visit the Russian fair at Ghigiga, near Anadyr river, during the winter to dispose of the furs they have gathered on their summer trading voyages.

During one season an umiak came to St Michael from King island, but the people were poorly supplied with goods for trading, having only dried salmon and seal oil. As usual, they were very difficult to trade with on account of their slowness in closing a bargain. A man would bring in a bunch of dried fish, throw it on the floor, and then stand about as if he had no interest in anything going on, until asked what he wished; when the regular price was offered he would almost invariably refuse, and then a long talk would ensue, which ended either by his accepting what was offered or by taking away the fish. This slowness is common with these people.

I was at a trading station on the head of Norton bay one winter when a Malemut chief wished to exchange some reindeer skins for various articles. It was in the evening, and after prolonged haggling, and changing one article for another, which lasted until 3 oclock next morning, half a dozen skins were finally bought from him. We retired and were hardly in bed before the man came back to exchange for other things some of the goods which he had taken. Finally the trader put him off until next day, when he again occupied a couple of hours before he was satisfied. This may be an extreme case, but it illustrates their general methods of trading.

In July, 1881, we found at Hotham inlet a row of over 150 conical lodges set up for over a mile along the beach, which were occupied by Malemut from Selawik lake and natives from Kowak and Noatak rivers. In 1880 Captain Hooper found about twelve hundred of these people encamped at Cape Blossom, but in 1881 the main camp had been located at Hotham inlet. When we arrived there we saw a small trading schooner lying off the village, surrounded by umiaks three or four deep and the deck crowded by a dense mass of the Eskimo. Tobacco, drilling, knives, ammunition, and other small articles were used to buy from them the skins of reindeer, wolves, black bear, arctic hare, red, white, and cross foxes, etc. As we proceeded up the coast a number of umiaks were seen on their way to the camp at Hotham inlet, and at many points we saw umiaks on trading trips up the coast, and some of the people told us that they had bought rifles and cartridges from the men of Cape Prince of Wales.

At many places from Point Hope to Point Barrow we were offered whalebone, ivory, the skins of reindeer, mountain sheep, Parry's marmot, whistlers, and many white and red fox skins. Whisky and cartridges seemed to be about the only articles desired by these people in exchange. This was unfortunate, considering the fact that the object of our visit to the coast was to prevent the sale of these very articles to the natives.

Near Cape Lisburne we met nine umiaks containing about one hundred people from Point Hope, who were on their way to the vicinity of Point Barrow to trade. Their dogs were running along the shore, keeping abreast of the boats but stopping occasionally to howl dolefully. We obtained two photographs of their camp near our anchorage.

While we were anchored in Kotzebue sound in September, several umiaks passed on their way back to Cape Prince of Wales from a trading voyage up the coast. One came alongside the *Corwin* that had a huge sail made by sewing numberless pieces of deerskin into a strange patchwork.

To show the difficulty attending the navigation of these frail boats in Bering strait I will state that, although we made six passages through the strait during the summer of 1881, only once was it clear enough from fog to permit the high land of both shores to be seen. Among the islanders of Bering strait the main articles they had for barter were coils of rawhide line, tanned sealskins, and handsomely made, waterproof sealskin boots. At East cape and along the Siberian coast, including St Lawrence island, the articles of trade among the Eskimo were walrus ivory, whalebone, and the skins of white foxes and reindeer. The St Lawrence islanders make frequent trading voyages to the Siberian coast, where they obtain reindeer skins for clothing. Formerly these people went along the American coast as far as Cape

Nome, but this has not occurred recently. On a clear day the headland on the Siberian shore is visible from St Lawrence island, some 40 or 50 miles away.

During the summer of 1879 the Tinné from Anvik, on the lower Yukon, descended the river in several umiaks and visited St Michael to exchange their wooden tubs and dishes for seal oil and other products of the coast district.

UNITS OF VALUE AND MEASUREMENT—NUMERATION

UNITS OF VALUE

The skins of mammals, being the most valuable portable property among the Alaskan Eskimo, give the most convenient standard of value. In very early days, before the advent of the Russians about the Yukon district, the skin of the full-grown land otter was considered the unit of value. Equaling it was the skin of the large hair seal.

Of late years the skin of the beaver has replaced the otter skin as the unit of trade value. All other skins, furs, and articles of trade generally are sold as "a skin" and multiples or fractions of "a skin," as it is termed. In addition to this, certain small, untanned skins, used for making fur coats or blouses, are tied in lots sufficient to make a coat, and are sold in this way. It requires four skins of reindeer fawns, or forty skins of Parry's marmot or of the muskrat, for a coat, and these sets are known by terms designating these bunches. Thus:

Four fawn skins   = *no-ûkh'-kĭt.*
Forty Parry's marmot skins = *chi-gĭkh'-kût.*
Forty muskrat skins   = *i-lĭg'-ĭ-wûkh'-kût.*

The pelt of a wolf or a wolverine is worth several "skins" in trade, while a number of pelts of muskrats or Parry's marmot are required to make the value of "a skin."

The foregoing terms are of the Unalit, but similar ones are in use among all the Eskimo of this region.

UNITS OF MEASUREMENT

All units of linear measurement among these people are based on body measurements—mainly of the hand and the arm, which form the readiest standards. Such units of measurement are used also by them for gauging the size and length of all of their tools, implements, and, in fact, of nearly everything made by them.

As the length of a man's hands and arms are usually in proportion to the length of his body, it is evident that bows, arrows, spears, boat frames, etc, when made by him according to a fixed number of spans or cubits, will be in direct proportion to himself, and thus especially suitable to his use, whether he be large or small.

The following terms are from the Unalit, and cover the units of measurement commonly in use, although others probably exist:

Large, *ăñ-to'-ûk.*

Small, *mĭk'-ĭ-lĭñ'-u-ûk.*

Nĭ-g'ĭn' [1] is the measurement of the length of the mesh in the largest seal nets used for the large hair seal or *mûk-lûk.* It is found by measuring a line from the tip of the extended thumb of the right hand across the palm of the hand, the fingers being closed.

Nû-kĭ-shun' nĭ-g'ĭn' is the mesh of the small salmon (*nû-ka'*) net. This is the distance from the wrinkle or line dividing the first and second joints of the right forefinger to the line midway between the base of the thumb and the forefinger.

Tu-bukh-chun' nĭ-g'ĭn' is the size of the mesh used for nets for the large sea whitefish (*tu-buk'*). It is found by taking the width of the extended first three fingers on the palmar surface at the first joint.

Tûg-ĭ-jûk'-whûkh-chun' nĭ-g'ĭn' is the size of the mesh for the large salmon (*tûg-ĭ-shûk'-whûk*), and is measured from the base of the extended thumb along the inner surface of the hand to the tip of the extended first finger.

Ĭ-ka'-thlu-ûkh'-pûkh-chun nĭ-g'ĭn' is the mesh for the herring seine (herring = *ĭ-ka'-thlu-ûkh'-pûk*). The width of the inner surface of the two extended first fingers at the first joint.

Stokh-chun' nĭ-g'ĭn' is the mesh used in nets for the white whale (*s'to'-ûk*). The tips of the extended thumbs are placed together and the measurement taken on the palmar surface across both extended hands along the line of the thumbs.

Tun-tu-shun' nĭ-ghûk'. The length of the rawhide line used for a reindeer snare is obtained by passing the cord twice around the sole of the left foot and drawing the double loop up to the groin while sitting on the floor with feet extended.

Kai-okh'-hlĭkh-chun' nĭ-g'ĭn' is the mesh used in nets for the Arctic hare (*kai-okh'-hlĭk*). It is determined by the width of the palm at the base of the fingers.

Ă-kûj'-û-gĭkh-chun' nĭ-ghûk'. The length of the cord used for snaring ptarmigan (*ă-kûj'-ĭ-gĭk*). The distance from the tip of the outstretched forefinger along the palm and the inner side of the forearm to the point of the elbow.

Pä-lok'-tûkh-chun' kû'-bvĭ-shă, the mesh used in nets for beaver (*pä-lok'-tûk*). The distance around the head on a line with the middle of the forehead.

U-nûg'-û-mun is the distance from the tip of the extended left thumb, with fingers closed, along the inside of the extended arm to the armpit.

K'okh-kog'-û-nûk, the distance measured from the end of the left thumb across the palm of the closed hand, thence along the upper side of the outstretched arm and across the chest to the inner end of the right collar bone.

Tuj'-ĭ-mun', same as the last, but extended to the point of the right shoulder.

I-ku'-yĭg-ĭ-nûg'-û-mûk, same as the last, but extended to the point of the right elbow, the right arm being extended and flexed at the elbow.

I-gu'-yĭ-gûg'-ĭ-nûk. This is the measurement used for making the stem, or bow-piece, of a kaiak. It is found by measuring from the tip of the extended forefinger, through the palm of the hand and along the inner side of the arm, to the point of the elbow, with the added width of the left forefinger, which is placed crosswise on the angle of the elbow.

Ai'-hûg'-û-nûk is a measurement used for making boot soles, the height of kaiak frames, etc. It is a span, or the distance between the outstretched tips of the thumb and the second finger of the right hand.

Kĭñ-û' is the height of a man's knees from the ground; used in making dog-sleds.

Yäg'-û-nûk. The distance from the tip of the extended left thumb, along the arm, across the chest, and to the tip of the extended right thumb. This is the most com-

---

[1] *Nĭ-g'ĭn'* is the name given to the gauge used in measuring meshes of nets of any kind.

mon unit of measure used among these people. It is the regular measurement used for all objects having considerable length, such as rawhide lines, nets, cloth, etc. It is adopted by the fur traders, and is called a 'fathom.' By it cloth and other trading goods of that character are sold, the end of the article to be measured being taken in the left hand, with the extreme end opposite the tip of the left thumb, then the edge of the cloth is slid through the right hand and raised until it is drawn across the chest, under the chin, by the outstretched right hand; then the left hand drops its end and takes a new hold at the point of the right thumb, and so the operation is repeated until the desired length is obtained.

CHRONOMETRY

The Eskimo divide their time by moons, each moon being designated by the title of the most characteristic local phenomenon which accompanies it. The following lists of months from various localities agree in this. By the "moons" all time is reckoned during the year, and dates are set in advance for certain festivals and rites. In addition to the moons, the year is frequently divided into four seasons according to the regular occupations that occur in each—but this is indefinite and irregular as compared with the other method.

In counting years they are referred to as winters—the winter being the most impressive part of each year in this high latitude.

The following are Unalit terms:

A year, *äthl-hän'-ĭ.*
A moon, *ĭ-gha'-luk.*
Spring, *u'-pĭ-nŭkh'-kûk.*
Summer, *ki-âk'.*
Autumn, *uk-shu'-ûk.*
Winter, *uk-shuk'.*
Long ago, *â-ka'.*
Very long ago, *û-ka'-mĭ.*

Thirteen moons are counted to a year, but I failed, unfortunately, to obtain the complete series. In the following lists the moons are arranged as they correspond with our months; as a matter of course, this correspondence is not perfect, but is very close.

January, *Wĭ'-wĭk.* "To turn about," from an ancient game played with a top.

February, *Nai-ĭkh'-chĭk.* Time first seals (*nai'-yĭk'*) are born.

March, *Tĭ-gĭg'ĭ-lukh'-chĭk.* The time of creeping on game. From the custom of hunting seals on the ice by stalking.

April, *Kĭp-nŭkh'-chĭk.* The time of cutting off. From the appearance of sharp lines where the white of the ptarmigans' bodies is contrasted with the brown of the new summer neck feathers which begin to appear at this time.

May, *Kai'-äkh-tûg'-o-wĭk.* Time for going in kaiaks. The ice opens at this time so that the hunters go out to sea in kaiaks.

June, *No-âkh'-chûg'-û-wĭk.* Time of fawn hunting.

July, *Koñ-ĭn'-nĭ-g'e'-nât ĭñ-ĭj'-û-vĭ-ât.* The time of geese getting new wing feathers (molting).

August, *Kuj'-u-gut ĭñ-ĭj'-û-rĭ-ât.* Time for brooding geese to molt.

September, *Äm-i-ghai'-ghû-wĭk.* The time for velvet shedding (from horns of reindeer).

October, *Ku'-bvĭ-jâkh-pûg'-û-wĭk.* Time for setting seal nets.

November, *Ûk'-whû-tûg'-û-wĭk.* Time for bringing in winter stores.

December, *Chau'-i-ûg'-û-wĭk.* Time of the drum—the month when the winter festivals begin.

Very often several different names may be used to designate the same moon if it should chance to be at a season when different occupations or notable occurrences in nature are observed, and I have used the most common terms.

On the lower Yukon, near Mission, the following terms are used for the moons:

January, *U-i'-wûk*. The season for top-spinning and for running around the kashim.

January (last part, and first part of February), *A-ki-luh' st-a'-gu-wĭk*. Time of offal eating (from *a-ki-lŭkh-stakh-tŏk*, "he boils offal"). This name comes from the scarcity of food likely to occur at this time and the necessity that arises during such periods to eat scraps of every description. Another name used for this moon is *I-ga-luh'-lŭkh*, the cold moon.

February–March, *Kup-nŭkh-chŭk*. The time of opening the upper passageways into the houses. This term was said to come from the time long ago when they claim it was much warmer than now and when the sun began to melt the snow a month earlier than at present.

March–April, *Tĭñ'-û-mĭ-ăkh'-lhu-ŭg'-û-wĭk*. Birds come.

April–May, *Tĭñ'-û-mi-ag'-û-wĭk*. Geese come (*tĭñ-û-mi-ŭk*, goose).

May–June, *Măn-it' ăn-u'-tit*. Time of eggs (*măn' ĭk*).

June–July, *Nŭk'-săg'-o-wĭk*. Time of salmon (*nŭk'-sŭk*).

July–August, *U-ko'-go-lĭ-sŏg'-û-wĭk*. Time for red salmon (*u-kog'-o-lĭk*). Also, *Tĭñ'-û-mi-at' ĭñ-u'-tit*, Waterfowl molt.

August–September, *Tĭñ'-û-mi-ăt tĭñ-u'-ri-ăt*. Time for young geese to fly.

September–October, *Ăm-ĭ-gai'-gu-wĭk*. Time for shedding velvet (*ă-mi'-rik*) from reindeer horns.

October–November, *Chup'-whĭk*. Mush ice forms.

November–December, *Ka'-gi-tăgh'-û-wĭk*. Time of muskrats (*ka-gi'-tak*).

December–January, *Chai-ûgh'-û-wĭk*. Time of the feast (*chai'ŭk*).

Among the Eskimo just south of the Yukon delta the following moons are recognized:

January, *Wĭ'-wĭk*. From the game with a top; also the time of a certain festival in which the dancers wear straw fillets stuck full of feathers.

February, *Á-găh-lŭkh'-lŭk*. The time of much moon (long nights).

March, *Ũ-ŏgh-o-wĭk*. Time of taking hares in nets.

April, *Kup-nŭkh'-chŭk*. Time of opening summer doors.

May, *Tĭñ-mi-ăgh'-û-wĭk*. Arrival of geese.

June, *Chi-sŭgh'-û-wĭk*. Time of whitefish.

July, *Tŭg-i-yŭk'-pŭk ka-gu'-ti*. The time of braining salmon. (The fish are struck on the head when lifted from the water.)

August, *Tĭñ-û-mi-ăt ĭñ-u'-ti*. Geese molt.

September, *Ku'-gĭ-yut' ĭñ-u'-ti*. Swans molt.

October, *Tĭñ-u'-tit*. The flying away (migration of birds).

November, *Am'-ĭ-gha'-ghŭn*. Time of velvet shedding (from reindeer horns).

The name for December was not obtained.

NUMERATION

The following notes and numerals are from the Unalit Eskimo, but are typical of the system in use among all the Eskimo with whom I came in contact, except those of the Aleutian islands:

Kĭt-stchĭ', count.

Kĭt-stchi'-nŭk, counting.

Kĭt'-stchi-ok, he counts.

The intertribal communication between the mainland Alaskan Eskimo and the constant trade carried on among them have developed considerable quickness in the use of numbers up to two or three hundred; this is quite general with both old and young. Going beyond the numbers ordinarily used in trade, however, the most intelligent among them become quickly confused.

In order for them to count correctly it is necessary to have the objects lying before them, and these are placed in groups of twenties as they are counted. If required to count abstractly they soon become confused after reaching one or two score; in this, however, there is great individual variation. About the Bering strait region most boys of 10 or 12 years of age count objects very readily up to one hundred and over, and some men can reach four hundred, but it is only among the most intelligent natives of this section that four hundred can be counted, and it is rare that attempt is made to exceed that number.

The Eskimo system of counting is based on a series of fives, rising in this way to twenties. The fingers and toes furnish the counters for computing numbers, as is explained below. Among the Unalit Eskimo, as elsewhere among these people, there is great variability in individual power. The most intelligent men and boys can count very readily up to two hundred or more, while others seem incapable of counting to twenty without blundering and repeated mistakes, like a stupid, slow-witted child. At every mistake made by such persons they are compelled to return and commence at one again, being unable to hold the numbers clearly enough in mind to take them up at intermediate points. Not even the most intelligent among them seem capable of counting readily beyond the number of his fingers and toes without the aid of objects directly before him. For this purpose I usually provided gun caps or matches, which served very conveniently as markers.

In counting such small objects they commonly placed them in groups of five, and as four of these were completed they were swept into a single large group of twenty; in this way successive twenties were completed and kept separately.

When making twenty the person would sometimes count the fives, commencing each time at one, but the most intelligent usually counted on to twenty, using the numerals of the regular series as given in the list. When an Eskimo was asked to count up to twenty without using fingers or toes, his eyes would seek, involuntarily, for something with which to tally, and even when asked to count five his eyes would turn at once to one of his hands, though he might make no visible use of his fingers.

In using the fingers and toes for counting, the closed hands are held in front of the waist, palms down, and thumbs near together. Commencing with the little finger of the right hand, as one, they pass to the left, opening or extending each finger in succession as its number is called until the right thumb, or number five, is reached. Passing thence to the little finger of the left hand for six, the fingers of this hand are opened successively until the left thumb and ten are reached. As ten is said the two hands, thumbs near together and fingers all outstretched, palms down, are extended a little from the body. Then the right foot is advanced a little and the right forefinger points at the little toe of that foot as the counter says *ät-khakh'-tŏk*. This word ordinarily means "it goes down," and is used here both to indicate the descent in counting from hands to feet as well as having, at times, an acquired meaning in this connection of eleven. The toes are counted from right to left until the right great toe is reached, when both hands with open fingers, palms down, are extended toward the right foot, which is advanced a little more as the counter announces fifteen. The counter then lets the left hand fall by the side and points at the left great toe, saying, *gŭkh'-tŏk*, meaning "it goes over," and sometimes conveying in this connection the acquired meaning of sixteen, as well as the going "over" of the count from one side of the body to the other. The other toes of the left foot are then enumerated from right to left, and as the small toe is reached, if the person be sitting, he extends both feet in front of him, doing the same with his hands, palms down, and says twenty; if he be standing, then the open hands are extended downward with a slight motion and the number is spoken.

The use of *ät-khakh'-tŏk* and *gŭkh'-tŏk* for numerals, as given above, is not uncommon among the intelligent people who are able to count readily up to twenty in a single series of numerals. Among the ignorant and slow-witted twenty is reached by making up four series of numbers running from one to five. In cases of this kind these two words are used between ten and eleven and fifteen and sixteen, simply to convey their regular meaning. They are most commonly used in counting the fingers and toes, when their application is quite natural; but often they are used in counting various other objects, and seem to be in a transitional state toward becoming the regularly recognized numerals. When used as numerals, as noted above, their meaning in that sense seems to be recognized by everyone.

Two is usually *mäl'-û-ghûk*, but it is often replaced by *ai'-pă*, which means second, or a pair. This latter word is used commonly to designate one of a pair, such, for instance, as in speaking of the close friend of another person, who is referred to as his *ai'-pă*. The name for the right arm and hand taken together is *tä-hlĭk'-pĭk*.

The term for five is *tä-hli'-mĭk*. The right hand alone is called *tä-hlĭk'-pĭm ai'-hĭ* (*ai'-hĭk* = hand, either right or left).

Nine is *ko'-lĭñ-o-gho-tai'-lĭñ-un*, from *ko-lĭn'*, ten, and *tai'-tŭk*, not, or lacking; i. e., ten lacking one.

Ko-lĭn', ten, is from *ko-hli'*, the upper half or the upper part of the body, or the count of the fingers. The word half is *ko'-kän*.

Twenty is *yu-i'-nûk*, from *yuk*, man, and means "a man completed."

When the person reaches twenty he will very often say *yu-i-nakh'-tŏk*, meaning "the man is finished." If he is asked how many fingers and toes he has counted he will reply "*yu-i'-nûk*."

When forty is reached a singular change takes place in the naming of the twenties. For instance, forty is *mäl'-û-ghu-i'-pĭ-äk*, from *mäl'-û-ghŭk*, two, and *i'-pĭ-äk*, a set of animal's legs and paws, with the toes, this last coming from *i'-pĭk*, the name given to the combined leg, foot, and toes of any mammal. Thus forty becomes "two sets of animal's paws." In this way each succeeding twenty is designated by combining one of the cardinal numbers with *i'-pĭ-äk* up to four hundred. At this point a change occurs, and the idea of a man is combined with that of the animal, as follows: Four hundred is *yu-i'-näm yum i-pi'*. This may be analyzed as follows: *yu-i'-näm*, twenty; *yum*, of a man's; *i-pi'*, sets of paws; or, "twenty sets of man's paws," this meaning twenty times twenty.

The following tables of Unalit numerals, with explanatory notes and the facts already given, will render plain their system of counting.

The first column in the first table gives the numerals as commonly used when counting the fingers and toes; the second column gives the forms used in counting exterior objects or to express a complete number. These two sets of numbers are sometimes interchangeably used, so that no invariable custom defines their usage.

1. *ă-tau'-tsĭk* .... *ă-tau'-tsĭk.*
2. *mäl'-û-ghŭk*, or *ai'-pä* .... *mäl-û-ghŭk*, or *ai'-pä.*
3. *pĭñ-a'-shu-ûk* .... *pĭñ-ai'-yun.*
4. *sta'-mĭk* .... *sta'-mûn.*
5. *tä-hli'-mĭk* .... *tä-hli'-mûn.*
6. *a-ghu-bĭn'-ghŭk* .... *a-ghu-bĭn'-lign.*
7. *mäl-û-ghun'-lĭgn* .... *mäl-û-ghun'-lĭgn.*
8. *pĭñ-ai-yun'-lĭgn* .... *pĭñ-ai-yun'-lĭgn.*
9. *ko'-lĭñ-o-gho-tai'-lĭñ-ŭn* .... *ko'lĭñ-o-gho-tai'-lĭñ-ŭn.*
10. *ko-lĭn'* .... *ko-lĭn'.*
11. *ät-khakh'-tŏk*, or *ă-tau'-tsĭk* .... *ko-lä' ă-tau'-tsĭ-muk chĭ'-pĭ-tŏk.*
12. *ai'-pa*, or *mäl'-û-ghŭk* .... *ko-lä' mäl-u-gu'-nĭk chĭ'-pĭ-tŏk.*
13. *pĭñ-a'-shu-ûk* .... *ko-lä' pĭñ-ai'-yun-ĭk chĭ'-pĭ-tŏk.*
14. *sta'-mĭk* .... *ko-lä' sta'-mĭn-ĭk chĭ-pĭ-tŏk.*
15. *ä-ki'-mĭ-äk*, or *tä-hli'-mĭk* .... *ko-lä' tä-hli-mûn-ĭk chĭ-pĭ-tŏk.*
16. *gûkh'-tŏk* .... *ko-lä' a-ghu-bĭn'-lĭgn-ĭk chĭ-pĭ-tŏk.*
17. *ai'-pä*, or *mäl'-û-ghŭk* .... *ko-lä' mäl-û-ghun' lĭgn-ĭk chĭ-pĭ-tŏk.*
18. *pĭñ-a'shu-ûk* .... *ko-lä' pĭñ-ai'-yun-lĭgn-ĭk chĭ-pĭ-tŏk.*
19. *sta'-mĭk* .... *ko-lä' ko-lĭñ'-o-gho-tai'-lĭñ-ŏg'-a-g'ŭk.*
20. *yu-i'-nûk*, or *tä-hli'-mĭk* .... *yu-i'-nûk.*
21. *ă-tau'-tsĭk* .... *yu-i'-nûk ă-tau'-tsi-mûk chĭp'-hlu-ku.*
22. *ai'-pä*, or *mäl'-û-ghŭk* .... *yu-i'-nûk mäl-û-ghun'-ĭk chĭp'-hlu-ku.*
23. *pĭñ-a'-shu-ûk* .... *yu-i'-nûk pĭñ-ai'-yun-ĭk chĭp'-hlu-ku.*
24. *sta'-mĭk* .... *yu-i'-nûk sta'-mĭn-ĭk chĭp'-hlu-ku.*
25. *tä-hli'mĭk* .... *yu-i'-nûk tä-hli'-mĭn-ĭk chĭp'-hlu-ku.*
26. *a-ghu-bĭn-ghŭk* .... *yu-i'-nûk a-ghu-bĭn'-lĭgn-ĭk chĭp'-hlu ku.*
27. *mäl'-û-ghun'-lĭgn* .... *yu-i'-nûk mäl-û-ghun'-lĭgn-ĭk chip'-hlu-ku.*
28. *pĭñ-ai-yun'-lĭgn* .... *yu-i'-nûk pĭñ-ai-yun'-lĭgn-ĭk chĭp'-hlu-ku.*

29. *ko'-lĭñ-o-gho-tai'-lĭñ-ŭn* .... *yu-i'-nŭk ko-lĭñ-o-gho-tai'-lĭñ-og'-ŭ-g'ŭk chĭp'-hlu-ku.*

30. *ko-lĭn'* .... *yu-i'-nŭk ko-lĭn'-ĭk chĭp-hlu-ku.*

40. *mäl'-ŭ-ghu-i'-pĭ-äk.*

50. *mäl'-ŭ-ghu-i'-pĭ-äk ko-lĭn'-ĭk chĭp'-ĭ-hlu'-ku.*

60. *pĭñ-ai'-yun i'-pĭ-äk.*

70. *pĭñ-ai'-yun i'-pĭ-äk ko-lĭn'-ĭk chĭp'-ĭ-hlu'-ku.*

80. *sta'-mun i'-pĭ-äk.*

90. *sta'-mun i'-pĭ-äk ko-lĭn'-ĭk chĭp'-ĭ-hlu'-ku.*

100. *tä-hlĭ'-mun i'-pĭ-äk.*

400. *yu-i'-näm yum i-pi'.*

It will be noted that numerals above ten in the second column have the verb *chĭ'-pĭ-tŏk,* signifying "it is added," or "additional." Thus *ko-lă' ă-tau'-tsĭ-mŭk chĭ'-pĭ-tŏk* means, literally, "to ten one is added." Above twenty the verb *chĭp'-hlu-ku,* or *chĭp'-ĭ-hlu-ku,* is used, meaning "is added of the next." Thus *yu-i' nŭk ă-tau'-tsi-mŭk chĭp'-hlu-ku* means, literally, "twenty, and one is added of the next."

The ordinal numbers are as follows:

First .... *chi-ŏk'-hlĭk.*
Second .... *kiñ-ŏk'-hlĭk.*
Third..................... *pĭñ-a'-shu-ût.*
Fourth .... *sta'-mit.*
Fifth .... *tä-hlĭ'-mit.*
Sixth .... *ă-ghu-bĭn'-ghŭt.*
Seventh .... *mäl'-ŭ-ghun'-lĭ-ghŭt.*
Eighth .... *pĭñ-ai-yun'-lĭ-ghŭt.*
Ninth.................. *ko'-lĭñ-o-gho-tai'-lĭñ-o-ŭt.*
Tenth .... *ko'-lĭñ-o-ŭt'.*
Eleventh .... *ko-lĭm' chĭp'-nŭ-gha.*
Twelfth .... *ko'-lĭn mäl-ŭ-ghu'-gŭ-nĭk chĭp'-nĭñ-ut.*
Thirteenth .... *ko'-lĭn pĭñ-ai'-yu-nĭk chĭp'-nĭñ-ut.*
Fourteenth .... *ko'-lĭn sta'-män-ĭk chĭp'-nĭñ-ut.*
Fifteenth .... *ă-kĭ'-mĭ-a'-ghŭt.*
Sixteenth............. *ă-kĭ'-mĭ-agm' chĭp'-nŭ-gha.*
Seventeenth .... *ă-kĭ'-mĭ-äk mäl-ŭ-ghu'-gŭ-nĭk chĭp'-nĭñ-ut.*
Eighteenth .... *ă-kĭ'-mĭ-äk pĭñ-ai'-yu-nĭk chĭp'-nĭñ-ut.*
Nineteenth .... *ă-kĭ'-mĭ-äk sta'-män-ĭk chĭp'-nĭñ-ut.*
Twentieth .... *ă-kĭ'-mĭ-äk tä-hlĭ'-män-ĭk chĭp'-nĭñ-ut,* or *yu-i'-nät.*
Thirtieth .... *yu-i'-nŭk ko'-lĭn-ĭk chĭp'-nĭñ-ŭk.*
Fortieth .... *mäl-ŭ-ghuk' i'-pĭ-a'-ghut.*
Fiftieth............... *mäl-ŭ-ghuk' i'pĭ-äk ko'-lĭ-mŭk chĭp'-nĭñ-ŭk.*

The numerals of repetition are:

Once .... *ă-tau'-tsĭkh ku'-mŭk.*
Twice .... *mäl'-ŭ-ghŭkh ku'-gŭ-nĭk.*
Three times............... *pĭñ-ai'-yăkh ku'-nĭk.*
Four times................ *sta'-mŭkh ku'-nĭk.*
Five times .... *tä-hlĭ'-mŭkh ku'-nĭk.*
Six times .... *ă-ghu-bĭn'-lăkh ku'-nĭk.*
Seven times.............. *mäl-ŭ-ghun'-lăkh ku'-nĭk.*
Eight times .... *pĭñ-ai-yun'-lăkh ku'-nĭk.*
Nine times............... *ko'-lĭñ-o-gho-tai'-lĭñ-okh ku'-nĭk.*
Ten times................ *ko'-lĭñ-okh ku'-nĭk.*

Eleven times..............*ko'-lă ă tau'-tsĭkh ku'-nĭk.*
Twelve times ....*ko'-lă măl'-û-ghûkh ku'-nĭk.*
Thirteen times............*ko'-lă pĭn-ai'-yûkh ku'-nĭk.*
Fourteen times............*ko'-lă sta'-mûkh ku'-nĭk.*
Fifteen times ....*ko'-lă tä-hli'-mûkh ku'-nĭk.*
Sixteen times ....*ko'-lă ă-ghû-bĭn-lûkh ku'-nĭk.*
Seventeen times............*ko'-lă măl-û-ghun'-lûkh ku'-nĭk.*
Eighteen times............*ko'-lă pĭn-ai-yun'-lûkh ku'-nĭk.*
Nineteen times.. ....*ko'-lă ko-lĭñ-o-gho-tai'-lĭñ-okh ku'-nĭk.*
Twenty times ....*yu-i'-nûkh ku'-mûk.*
Thirty times..............*yu-i'-nûk ko'-lĭn-ûkh ku'-nĭk.*
Forty times...............*măl-û-ghûk i'-pĭ-ûkh kû'-mûk.*
Fifty times ....*măl'-û-ghûk i'-pĭ-ûkh ko-lĭñ-okh kû'-nik.*
Sixty times ....*pĭn-a'-yun i'-pĭ-ăkh ku'-nĭk.*

The distributive numerals are:

One to each ....*ä-tau'tsĭ-ŏ kă-ghakh'-lu-ku.*
Two to each ....*măl'-û-ghu kă-ghakh'-lu-ku.*
Three to each ....*pĭn-a'-shu-ŏ kă-ghakh'-lu-ku.*
Four to each..............*sta-män ka'-ghakh'-lu-ku.*
Five to each ....*tä-hli'-män ka'-ghakh'-lu-ku.*
Six to each ....*ă-ghu-bĭn'-lĭkh-kok ka'-ghakh'-lu-ku.*
Seven to each.............*măl-û-ghun' lĭkh-kok ka'-ghakh'-lu-ku.*
Eight to each.............*pĭn-ai'-yun-lĭkh-kok ka'-ghakh'-lu-ku.*
Nine to each ....*ko'-lĭñ-o-gho-tai'-lĭñ-okh'-kok ka'-ghakh'-lu-ku.*
Ten to each ....*ko-lĭñ-okh-kok ka'-ghakh'-lu-ku.*
Eleven to each.............*ko-lă ă-tau'-tsĭ-mûk chĭp'-nĭñkh kă-ghakh'-lu-ku.*
Twelve to each ....*ko-lă măl-û-ghun'-ĭk chĭp'-nĭñkh kă-ghakh'-lu-ku.*
Thirteen to each ....*ko-lă pĭn-ai'-yun-ĭk chĭp'-nĭñkh kă-ghakh'-lu-ku.*
Fourteen to each...........*ko-lă sta-män'-ĭk chĭp-nĭñkh kă-ghakh'-lu-ku.*
Fifteen to each ....*ko-lă tä-hli'-män-ĭk or, ă-ki'-mĭ-ăkh' ka-ghakh'-lu-ku.*
Sixteen to each ....*ă-ki'-mĭ-ăk ä-tau'-tsĭ-mûk chĭp'-nĭñkh kă-ghakh'-lu-ku.*
Seventeen to each..........*ă-ki'-mĭ-ăk măl-û-ghun'-ĭkh chĭp'-nĭñkh kă-ghakh'-lu-ku.*
Eighteen to each...........*ă-ki'-rĭ-ăk pĭn-ai'-yun-ĭk chĭp'-nĭñkh kă-ghakh -lu-ku.*
Nineteen to each ....*ă-ki'-mĭ-ăk sta'-män-ĭk chĭp'-nĭñkh kă-ghakh'-lu-ku.*
Twenty to each ....*ă-ki'-mĭ-ăk tä-hli'-mĭn-ĭk chĭp'-nĭñkh kă-ghakh'-lu-ku,* or
                          yu-i'-nam kă-ghakh'-lu-ku.
Thirty to each ....*yu-i'-nûk ko'-lĭñ-ĭk kă-ghakh'-lu-ku.*
Forty to each..............*măl'-û-ghu-i'-pĭ-a'-ghû kă-ghakh'-lu-ku.*
Fifty to each..... ....*măl'-û-ghu-i'-pĭ-äk ko'-lĭn-ĭk kă-ghakh'-lu-ku.*
Four hundred to each......*yu-i-núm i'-pĭ-ám kă-ghakh'-lu-ku.*

Following are a number of miscellaneous terms bearing on numeration:

How many?..............*käf'-chĭ-u'-ât?*
Several ....*käf'-chĭ-khän.*
One only................*ä-tau'-tsĭ-khûk.*
Two only ....*măl-û-ghu'-khûk.*
Three only...............*pĭn-ai'-yu-khän.*
Four only................*sta'-mă-khän.*
Five only ....*tä-hli'-mă-khän.*
Six only ....*ä-gho-bĭn'-lĭ-khän.*
Seven only. ....*măl-û-ghun'-lĭ-khän.*
Eight only...............*pĭn-ai-yun'-lĭ-khän.*
Nine only................*ko-lĭñ'-o-gho-tai'-lĭñ-o-khän.*
Ten only.................*ko-lá'-khän.*

Fifteen only..................................... *ä-ki'-mĭ-a'-khän.*
Twenty only .... *yu-i'nă-khän.*
Forty only .... *mäl'-û-ghuk i'-pĭ-a'-khän.*
One-half (in length)........................... *ko-kän'-tă-kĭn'-û-gha.*
One-half (in quantity)........................ *au-ĭlh'-hă,* or *au-ĭlh'-û-hûk.*
A part or portion, in length or quantity.......... *au-ukh'-ûk.*
All.. *tä män'.*
None.. *pi'-tûk.*

For purposes of barter four skins of the reindeer fawn—just enough to make a fur coat or parkie—are tied in a bunch and called a "parkie of fawn skins." The following set of numerals is used in counting these sets of fawn skins or parkies:

One parkie of fawn skins.............. *ä-tau'-tsĭ-kût.*
Two parkies of fawn skins .... *mäl'-û-ghu'-i-kût.*
Three parkies of fawn skins.......... *pĭñ-a-shu'-i-kût.*
Four parkies of fawn skins........... *sta-mai'-kût.*
Five parkies of fawn skins........... *tä-hli'-mai-kût.*
Six parkies of fawn skins .... *a-ghu-bĭn'-lĭkh-kût.*
Seven parkies of fawn skins.......... *mäl-û-ghun'-lĭkh-kût.*
Eight parkies of fawn skins.......... *pĭñ-ai-yun'-lĭkh-kût.*
Nine parkies of fawn skins.......... *ko'-lĭñ-o-gho-tai'-lĭñ-okh'-kût.*
Ten parkies of fawn skins............ *ko'-lĭ-kût.*
Eleven parkies of fawn skins......... *ko'-lĭ-kût ä-tau'-tsi-nĭk chĭp'-ĭ-tut.*
Twelve parkies of fawn skins .... *ko'-lĭ-kût mäl-û-ghu'-i-nĭk chĭp'-i-tut.*
Thirteen parkies of fawn skins....... *ko'-lĭ-kût pĭñ-a-shu'-i-nĭk chĭp'-i-tut.*
Fourteen parkies of fawn skins ...... *ko'-lĭ-kût sta-mai'-nĭk chĭp'-i-tut.*
Fifteen parkies of fawn skins .... *ko'-lĭ-kût tä'-hli-mai'-nĭk chĭp'-i-tut,* or *ä-ki'-mĭ-äkh'-kût.*
Sixteen parkies of fawn skins........ *ä-ki'-mĭ-äkh-kût ä-tau-tsi'-nĭk chĭp'-ĭ-tut.*
Seventeen parkies of fawn skins...... *ä-ki'-mĭ-äkh-kût mäl-û-ghu'-i-nĭk chĭp'-ĭ-tut.*
Eighteen parkies of fawn skins ...... *ä-ki'-mĭ-äkh-kût pĭñ-a-shu'-i-nĭk chĭp'ĭ-tut.*
Nineteen parkies of fawn skins....... *ä-ki'-mĭ-äkh-kût sta-mai'-nĭk chĭp'-ĭ-tut.*
Twenty parkies of fawn skins........ *ä-ki'-mĭ-äkh-kût tä'-hli-mai'-nĭk chĭp'-ĭ-tut,* or *yu-i'-nakh-kûk.*
Forty parkies of fawn skins.......... *mäl'-û-ghu-i'-pĭ-akh'-kûk.*
Sixty parkies of fawn skins .... *pĭñ-ai'-yun i'-pĭ-akh'-kûk.*

VILLAGES AND HOUSES

The Eskimo villages of western Alaska are located with reference to proximity to hunting and fishing grounds and to the most favorable landing place for their kaiaks and umiaks that may be found. The sites vary greatly, from the head of some beautifully sheltered cove to the precipitous face of a rocky slope, as on Sledge and King islands. Formerly, the constant danger from hostile raids caused the people to choose locations for their dwellings which were easy of defense. This is demonstrated by the sites of ruins on the coast of Bering sea and the ruins of former Eskimo villages on the Arctic coast of Siberia, north-westward of Bering strait.

These ancient villages were built usually on the highest points of islands, near the shore, or on high capes or peninsulas commanding a wide view over both sea and land. Formerly, as at present, the village was usually an irregular group of semi-subterranean houses built about a large central building, called by the Unalit, *käj'-ĭ-gĭ*. This term corresponds to the name *kashim*[1] of the fur traders, which has been used throughout this paper to designate structures of this kind.

These buildings are on the same general plan as the dwelling houses, but are much larger and are used as the central point of the village social life. They are ordinarily made large enough to contain all the villagers, besides guests that may come during festivals. In some of the villages, however, where the number of inhabitants is considerable, two or more of these buildings are constructed. Their size is necessarily limited by the material available, which is mainly drift logs cast up along the shore. The people of the lower Yukon have a tradition that there formerly existed below Ikogmut a village that contained thirty-five kashims; at present there are many villages in which there are two of these buildings.

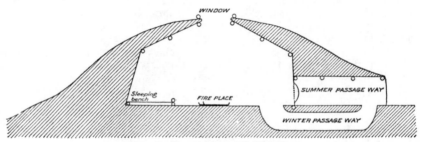

FIG. 74—Plan of house at St Michael.

Snow houses, so common among the Eskimo of Greenland and other eastern regions, are known in Alaska only as temporary shelters erected by hunters when out on short excursions from their village during winter; they are termed *ăn-ĭ-gu-yŭk'*, and their use is familiar to all of the Eskimo, although they are so rarely constructed.

On Kowak river there are villages in which the Eskimo have adopted from their Tinné neighbors the use of conical lodges for summer use, and it is worthy of note that the former appear to have adopted other customs from the same source. On Yukon and Kuskokwim rivers the contrary is the case; there the Tinné have adopted many of the Eskimo customs and usages, while the Eskimo appear to have derived very little from their Tinné neighbors.

The Eskimo of the Kuskokwim and northward to the vicinity of Bering strait have summer villages, built in a more or less permanent manner, to which they resort during the fishing season. From Kotzebue sound northward the people use tents or skin lodges while at their fishing stations in summer.

---

[1] This term is derived from the word *kaj'-ĭ-gĭm* = "my *kaj'-ĭ-gĭ*."

A typical dwelling house used by the people of St Michael is constructed by building a rectangular framework of logs, 8 or 9 feet high in the middle and 5 feet at the sides; this is covered with smaller logs or rude slabs, over which earth is thrown to a thickness of 3 or 4 feet. Raised platforms occupy three sides of the single room and are used for sleeping places, commonly by a family on each side. The front of the room has a low, arched doorway leading in from the outer covered entry, which is used only in summer, when a bearskin hangs over

FIG. 75—Storehouse at St Michael.

the doorway as a curtain; in winter this entrance is closed and an underground passage or tunnel leads from the outer end of the covered entry way to a point below the floor just inside the summer door. The place on each side of the door, or an unoccupied platform on one side of the room, is used for the storage of bags of seal oil, wooden dishes, tubs, or other domestic utensils, and of articles of food. Figure 74 is a section plan of one of these houses. Each family has a small saucer-shape clay lamp burning near its platform. On the earthen floor directly under the smoke hole is a fireplace, where cooking is done; this usually has a flat slab of stone set edgewise in the floor on the side toward the doorway to serve as a wind-break for preventing drafts from striking directly on the fire.

Many of the houses are built with a long, low, covered passageway, used both in winter and in summer, and the underground entrance is omitted; some houses are very narrow and have only one wide sleeping bench at the rear end, where one or two families are accommodated.

In some cases the entrance passage above ground is large enough to serve as a storeroom, but usually every household is the owner of a storehouse. Where timber is scarce, as in the country between Cape Vancouver and the mouth of the Kuskokwim, these are built of turf. At Point Barrow underground storerooms, with a trap in the roof, were seen. At St Michael storehouses are erected on four stout posts, made from drift logs, set firmly in the ground and projecting 10 or 12 feet, forming an equal-sided quadrangle. About 5 feet from the ground the hewed ends of timbers are inserted to form parallel stringers, on which are laid roughly hewed sticks for a floor, the ends projecting 2 or 3 feet on either side. To form the walls rough planks are fitted, with their ends locked by means of notches. The top is covered with sticks similar to the flooring, on which is placed a grass thatch or sometimes a covering of earth. The doorway in front, 2½ to 3 feet square, is framed beside one of the corner posts by a roughly hewed cap and jamb; the door is of rough plank, on rawhide hinges, fastened by a stout cord.

Outside on the projecting ends of the floor are laid the sledge, kaiak, and other objects belonging to the owner, while the inside serves as a receptacle for food supplies and other perishable articles.

The accompanying illustration (figure 75) gives a good idea of a typical storehouse of this character.

Where timber is abundant, as on the lower Yukon, these storehouses are more elaborately constructed, being raised from 6 to 8 feet above the ground, with the posts arranged and held in place in the same manner as in those at St Michael. The front and rear walls are made of well-hewed planks, set upright, with an oval door in the center of the front, access to which is gained by a notched log. The ends of the floor logs project in front far enough to support separate cross sticks, forming a narrow outside platform. On the sides, the planks forming the walls are placed horizontally. The roof has a double pitch, and is usually made of bark held in place by cross sticks or other weights. The upright planks that form the front and rear of these structures are held in position by crosspieces extending between the corner posts, as shown in plate LXXXI.

In addition to the storehouses, every village has elevated frames upon which sledges and kaiaks may be placed; this is necessary, owing to the number of dogs in every village and the danger of their eating

STOREHOUSES AT IKOGMUT (MISSION)

the rawhide covers of the kaiaks and the lashings of the sledges. These frames are formed usually of two horizontal, parallel poles, or small logs, raised on posts with forked ends or mortised into the timber, their size and strength depending on the abundance of neces-sary material.

Kashims are common everywhere among the Eskimo and have been adopted by the adjacent Tinné of lower Yukon and Kuskokwim rivers. They vary in size according to the number of inhabitants in the village. The material used for these structures is driftwood, consisting of logs and poles which float down the rivers in spring and are strewn along their banks or carried to sea and scattered along the coast during the following summer. Spruce is the most common variety. The logs are usually deprived of their bark by friction and are seasoned by exposure. Logs 15 or 20 inches in diameter are not uncommon, and some are found reaching 30 feet in length; as a rule, however, the timbers are much smaller.

In constructing a kashim the logs are laid in the form of a square to the height of 7 or 8 feet; from thence they are drawn in on every side, in alternate courses, until the last are short, and surround a square opening in the roof, directly over the middle of the room, and from 9 to 12 feet above the floor, forming a frame for the smoke hole, which is about 2 or $2\frac{1}{2}$ feet in width. If the building is small, it is covered with a heavy layer of earth, but if large, a crib-work is built around it, held together by a frame, so as to inclose the building and form a double wall, inside of which is thrown a heavy layer of earth.

The floor is usually of hewed planks laid close together, and occupies about one-third of the area of the room, in the shape of a square in the center; it is laid on sills at the end so that the planks can readily be taken up; below these there is a pit from 3 to 4 feet deep, in which the fire is built to heat the room for sweat baths, or at rare intervals in winter; but usually the heat from the bodies of the occupants keeps the temperature so high that they remain nude, or partly so, much of the time, even in winter. Other planks usually cover the ground back to the walls, although in many places, especially where wood is scarce, the floor of this portion of the room consists merely of the earth, beaten hard. The entrance consists of a long, roofed passage, built of logs and covered with earth; the outer end of this is faced with planks, over which is a square, round, or arched doorway leading into the room in summer, when it is closed only by a bearskin curtain. In winter this entrance, which is above the ground, is closed tightly, and a round hole in the floor near the outer end of the upper passage leads through a low tunnel, along which the people pass on their hands and knees to the fire pit, and thence through a circular or oval hole to the middle of the room.

These rooms are from 12 to 25 feet square. Around the inside, about 4 feet from the floor, extends a bench, hewed from a single log, 15 to 18 inches wide and usually from 4 to 6 inches in thickness, or left half rounded below; this heavy bench is supported by stout sticks placed diagonally across the corners of the room, and is used as a sleeping place, also as a seat during festivals and at other times.

At the back of the room, supported on an upright post from 2 to 3 feet high, a lamp is kept burning, by public contribution, at all times when the kashim is gloomy. A gut-skin cover is used over the smoke hole at all times, except when the fire is burning in the pit, or when the heat becomes too oppressive.

The accompanying illustration (figure 76) shows the outside of the kashim at St Michael, with the long passageway of logs. A sectional plan of one of these buildings is given in figure 77.

FIG. 76—Kashim at St Michael.

Pikmiktalik was a very populous place in the days when reindeer were plentiful along this coast, some ten or fifteen years previously to my residence in this region; but in 1878 only two or three families remained, and the kashim and other houses were falling to pieces.

Pastolik, near the Yukon mouth, is the southernmost settlement of the Unalit, and its buildings are typical. Ascending the Yukon and passing several unimportant little villages, the first characteristic settlement of the Yukon Eskimo is reached above Andreivsky. From that point up the river the towns are similar to one another, consisting of winter houses and kashims built on the ordinary plan, and of large, loosely built summer houses of hewed planks on an inner framework, with sloping roofs.

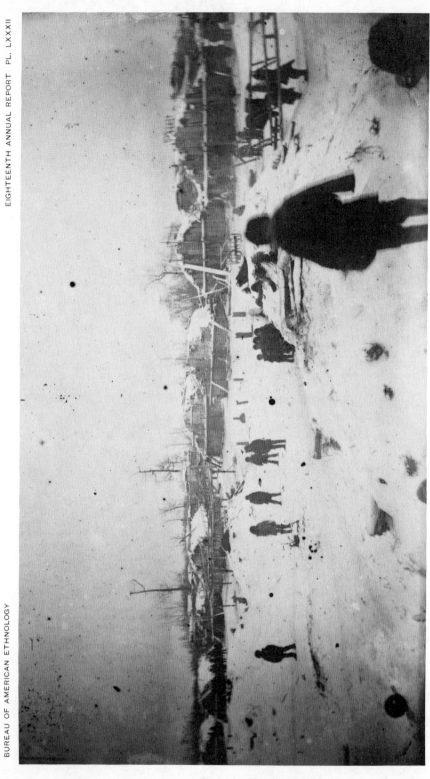

WINTER VIEW OF RAZBINSKY

The village of Starikwikhpak above Andreivsky, is built on a high bank of the Yukon in the midst of a thick growth of tall alders and cottonwoods, and contains about forty people.

Next above is Razbinsky, containing some twenty-five houses and two kashims. It is the largest existing village of the Yukon Eskimo, and the only one seen that was arranged with any degree of regularity. There the winter and summer houses are built together, and the rude alignment of the summer houses is evidenced in the illustration (plate LXXXII). The summer houses front a small creek which flows into the Yukon at that point. Back of them, in a more regular arrangement, are most of the winter houses. Near one end of this row are two kashims, and immediately back of them is the graveyard, the latter forming a part of the village and becoming so offensive in summer that it is impossible at times for the fur traders to camp in the vicinity.

The summer houses at this place and all along the Yukon up to

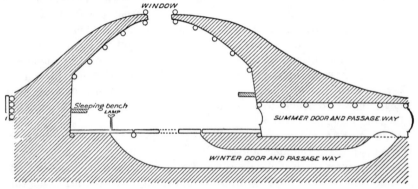

FIG. 77—Section of kashim at St Michael.

Paimut, the upper Eskimo village on the river, are alike built of heavy slabs and planks split and hewed from drift logs.

Plate LXXXII, from a photograph, is a view taken at Razbinsky in winter, showing the tops of some winter houses in the foreground and a row of plank summer houses in the background.

The summer houses throughout this part of Alaska vary so slightly in the details of their construction that a description of those seen at Razbinsky will serve as typical of all in that region. The front and rear ends are constructed of roughly hewed planks set upright; the sides are of horizontal timbers hewed and loosely fitted. About five feet from the ground a log extends from side to side of the structure, resting upon two posts in the middle, with braces at either end, having their ends set in the ground, and connected by similar logs which extend from front to rear along the eaves.

In some houses the braces at the front and rear are replaced by two tall poles set in the ground midway between the corners, two or three yards apart and projecting several feet above the top of the roof. Lengthwise over the top of the house extend hewed sticks which hold in position the upright posts and the logs that bind the upright planks.

The use of crosspieces fastened at each end to the top of upright timbers is a common method adopted by the Eskimo of Norton sound and the lower Yukon for binding the framework of their structures. Braces, which fit into a notch in an upright post with the other end planted in the ground, are also commonly used. Sometimes the walls of summer houses are built with upright sticks all around, as can be seen at Ikogmut, but more commonly the ends are formed of upright pieces and the sides of timbers laid horizontally. The inner framework is bound together by withes or wooden pins and held in place at the eaves by joists, across which are thrown poles or planks, forming an open attic or platform for the storage of dried fish and other articles of food, nets, and various implements. The roof is double-pitched and covered with slabs or planks over which pieces of bark are laid. Along the sides of the room, at from one to three feet above the floor, are broad sleeping platforms, which accommodate from one to three families. In the front, a foot or two above the ground, a semilunar piece is cut from each of two adjoining planks, forming an oval doorway about three feet high. Small square or round windows, a few inches in diameter, are sometimes cut in the walls near the sleeping platforms. There is also plenty of ventilation from other directions, as very little effort is made to prevent the wind from circulating freely through the numerous cracks.

Plate LXXXI, which represents the storehouses at Ikogmut, shows also one of these summer houses in the background.

In the winter of 1880 the people at Paimut were found living in their summer houses on a high bank overlooking the Yukon, and I was told that their winter village on the island in the river had been swept away by high water the season before.

At Chukwhûk, just above Ikogmut, the winter houses, as is usual in this district, were arranged with the sleeping platforms raised about three feet from the ground, leaving space below for storing supplies. The house at which I stopped was supplied with three of these platforms, each having its oil lamp on an upright post. Near one lamp a woman was making a pair of ornamented gloves, and by another lamp a woman was braiding a straw mat.

At a village in the Big-lake district, lying in the strip of country between the two nearest points of lower Yukon and Kuskokwim rivers, the houses were of the ordinary kind, except that they were rather smaller than on the Yukon and had extraordinarily long entrance passages.

At the base of Kuslevak mountains the houses were made of smaller timbers, brought a long distance from the coast in boats, or of a light framework of short, crooked alder trunks covered with brush from the banks of the streams in the neighborhood. These houses were very small and depended for their strength partly upon the hard, frozen covering of earth. Igiogagamut, a village lying between Kuslevak mountains and Cape Romanzof, consisted of several small hovels of this kind. Their interior plan was as near the usual type as the material would allow, as the rooms were only 4½ feet high to the small, square smoke holes, which were covered with sheets of clear ice about 4 inches thick instead of with the usual gut skin. From the smoke holes the walls sloped to the ground, making inclosures from 12 to 15 feet in diameter. These places were crowded with people. On the earthen floors were layers of soft, decaying garbage of every description, from which the heat arising from the crowded human bodies evolved a sickening odor.

Near Cape Romanof was a summer fishing village of four houses, which looked like so many mounds, about 6 feet high. We found them to be built entirely above ground and of split drift logs, held up in the usual manner and covered with earth. A square opening 3 feet high in one wall served as a door, entering directly into the room, and the square smoke hole in the roof formed the only other aperture. Sleeping platforms were rudely made on the earthen floor.

Askinuk, south of Cape Romanzof, is built on the top of an earthen mound which rises about 15 feet above the level of the surrounding country. The present village covers nearly the entire top of this mound. The inhabitants say that this elevation has accumulated from the long occupancy of the spot by their people, and its present appearance would seem to justify the assertion.

The houses are clustered together in the most irregular manner, and the entrances to the passageways leading to the interiors open out in the most unexpected places. Sometimes one of these passages opens on the top of another house built lower down on the side of the mound, or, it may be, between two houses, or almost against the side of an adjoining one. Near by is a very extensive graveyard, which has some interesting burial places, but my visit was too brief to enable me to examine it carefully.

The Askinuk kashim is like those at the next village to the south, called Kushunuk. At this place there are two kashims, the smaller one being about 30 by 30 feet on the floor and 20 feet high at the smoke hole. The walls are of split logs placed vertically, with their plane faces inward and resting at their upper ends against the logs which form the framework of the roof; the floor is of heavy hewed planks. Extending around the room on the floor, and about 3½ feet from the walls, are small logs, serving to mark off the sleeping places of the men and at the same time as head rests, the sleepers lying with their heads toward the middle of the room. Three feet above and 6 inches nearer the walls other logs extend around the room, with planks between them and the sides, affording a broad sleeping bench, supported in the middle by upright posts and at each end inserted in the wall of the structure. The roof is made by the usual arrangement of logs forming a rectangular pyramid with a flat top, in the middle of which is the smoke hole. The entrance passage is unusually high and roomy, opening directly into the kashim above ground by means of a round hole in the front of the wall.

In winter the entrance is through a hole in the floor of the entrance passage, thence through the underground tunnel as usual to an exit hole, which has on each side a walrus tusk with the point and base sunk into the plank and the curve upward, affording convenient hand-rests when going in and out and preventing the necessity of placing the hands on the wet planks at the side of the hole. The plan of this kashim is shown in figure 78.

In addition to the kashims, the village contained about twenty houses, accommodating about one hundred and twenty-five people. It

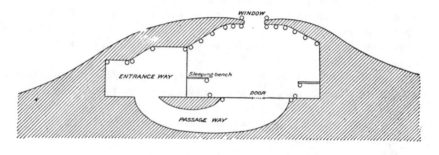

FIG. 78—Section of kashim at Kushunuk.

is built in a straggling manner on a slightly rising piece of ground, with elevated storehouses and raised frameworks for the boats and sledges. The entire area covered is about a quarter of a mile in length. Nearer the sea is the site of an ancient village that was occupied by the ancestors of these people.

To the southward of this place the next village was Kaialigamut, which contained about one hundred people and two kashims. The houses and kashims were like those of the last two villages described, except that the kashims were smaller and were provided with a second and narrower shelf above the first sleeping benches, on which the men placed their clothing and other belongings.

The early Russian traders who visited this district say that the people in these large villages had underground passageways leading from the kashim to adjacent houses, for use in case of sudden attack by an enemy. A Russian told me that he once discovered a passage of this kind from the kashim to an ancient house and from there to another house. It was further stated that in those days the people made their houses larger, so that they could use their bows in them for repelling an attack by the enemy.

The village of Ukagamut, near Mount Robert Lincoln, contained about twenty people. The huts were extremely small, owing to the scarcity of wood. The interiors were excessively filthy and permeated with the stench of decaying animal matter. The smoke holes were covered with slabs of ice, and the floors were several inches deep with an oozy mass of refuse. The dried fish stored in the houses and used for food was covered with blue and green mold, and the entire place was the most miserable that I saw in that region. The inhabitants were suffering from skin diseases and from the attacks of an ailment resembling epilepsy.

Tununuk was a summer village on Cape Vancouver at the time of my visit in December, 1879. A few people were found wintering there. Wood was scarce and the houses were small and filthy.

South of this point wood was so scarce that in several villages there was none for making elevated storehouses, and for that purpose small huts were built of turf cut into slabs and laid up in walls, which were frozen solid and covered with flat roofs of the same material. The doors, which were the only openings, consisted of slabs of frozen turf about 2½ by 3 feet and 4 inches thick. At one village I saw about twenty of these huts, all of which were 4 or 5 feet high and from 6 to 8 feet in diameter.

In the second village south of Cape Vancouver the houses were made of turf slabs laid up about the frail framework of small sticks and brush and covered with earth. This had been wet and frozen so that the walls were very firm, but the people stated that they would leave them early in the spring, for as soon as warm weather began the walls would melt and fall in.

The smoke holes of the houses in all this district were covered with slabs of ice, from which the heat inside continually caused water to drop down the walls, rendering the floor a soft and sticky mass except in the coldest weather.

From Cape Vancouver to the Kuskokwim the land is very low, and whenever the wind blows a gale in shore the coast villages are in danger of being flooded. The day before my arrival at Chalitmut the sea flowed inland and rose to a depth of three feet over the floor of the kashim; the people who were caught inside made a hole in the roof, to which they crept and stayed for hours, until the water had subsided. Every few years the ice sweeps away one or more villages in this district, causing loss of life.

At Chichiñagamut, in this district, a heavy rain fell during my stay, and the water came into the kashim from the surrounding drainage so that it was 18 inches deep in the tunnel-like entrance passage and had to be baled out twice a day. The kashim was very small and low, with no floor except the beaten earth; the fire pit in the middle of the room was in the depression which began at the walls and sloped gradually toward the center. This central depression was full of water, and the entire floor was covered except for a narrow border about four feet wide around the sides. In this kashim two lamps were burning upon supports, one on each side of the room. These supports were rudely carved in the form of a human face, representing quite a different type from the countenances of the people, and constituted the only attempt at such work that I saw among the Eskimo (figure 79). When the Kuskokwim was reached the abundance of driftwood was shown by the larger size of the houses and kashims, and by the presence of elevated storehouses and frames for sleds and boats.

From St Michael northward along the coast of the mainland there

existed a much greater variety of houses than had been noted to the southward of that place. From St Michael to Uñaktolik, including Kigiktauik, Unalaklit, and Shaktolik, with a few smaller places, the houses are of the type general among the Unalit, as the people belong mainly to that group.

Tup-hanikwa, north of Unalaklit, had in February, 1880, a single house, which was occupied by three families. The single room was 10 by 12 feet in dimension and about $5\frac{1}{2}$ feet high. On the night of my visit sixteen adults slept on the earthen floor of this small room.

At the villages of Atnuk and Nubviukh-chugaluk the houses were large, well made, and provided with a floor of hewed planks; the sleeping platforms were raised about 18 inches above the floor.

FIG. 79—Carved lamp support.

In March, 1880, the village of Ignituk, near Cape Darby, contained about one hundred and fifty people. It was built at the mouth of a small canyon leading down to the sea, and the lower houses were on the upper edge of an abrupt slope 40 or 50 feet above the beach, where were arranged on sleds the kaiaks of the villagers ready for seal hunting on the sea ice. The houses had plank floors and broad sleeping benches. They were built with a small, square anteroom, which was used as a storeroom for provisions, and from it a passage about 3 feet high and 10 to 20 feet in length led to the round hole giving access to the living room. This hole was either in the end of the passage opening through the wall of the room just above the floor, or through the floor inside the front wall. In the middle of the floor the planks were laid so that they could be taken up, as is done in the kashims. Close to the fire-

place, between it and the door, was a large flat slab of stone placed on
edge to protect the fire from the draft. Some of the houses had two
sleeping platforms, one above the other, the lower one raised very little
above the floor and the other about three feet above it. Plans of two
of these houses are shown in figures 80 and 81.

On the long strip of low, sandy coast, between Ignituk and Cape
Nome, were located a number of small houses, which were used by the
people while snaring marmots (*Spermophilus parryi*) in spring, or
when salmon fishing in summer. These summer houses, or shelters,
were conical lodges, made by standing up sticks of driftwood in a

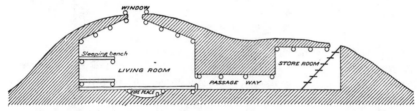

FIG. 80—Section of house at Ignituk.

close circle, with their tops leaning together, forming a structure like
an Indian tipi; they were built by first lashing together three pieces
of wood and setting them up like a tripod, the others being leaned
against them to complete the rude structure. On the inside a rough
sleeping platform was supported on four corner stakes at the back of
the room. A narrow vacant space between two of the logs, forming
the wall, served as a doorway.

In the village on the north side of Cape Nome the houses were built
very much like those of Ignituk, but varied in some particulars.

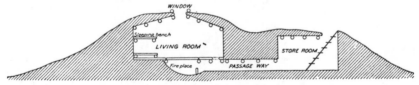

FIG. 81—Section of house at Ignituk.

They were constructed of driftwood, with an outer storeroom, which
was entered through a hole in the roof, access to which was gained by
means of a notched ladder. From this storeroom was a passage about
three feet high, which ended in a hole leading through the wall directly
onto the plank floor of the living room, which had a sleeping bench
about four feet from the floor, and below this the floor was usually occupied for the same purpose. Leading from the entrance storeroom
were one or two other passages communicating with other living rooms,
and on one side a short passage opened into a room about 8 by 10 feet
in dimension and 6 or 7 feet in height, which served as a cooking room

for the group of families living in the structure. No fires were ever lit in the living rooms. The sectional plan of one of these houses is shown in figure 82, and a ground plan in figure 83.

On Sledge island the winter village was perched on a steep slope, facing the sea, and well above the water. The houses were set one

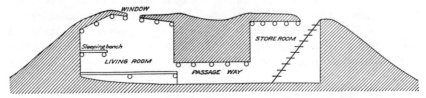

FIG. 82—Section of house at Cape Nome.

back of the other on the slope of the rocky talus that extends up to the top of the high bluff; they were built on the plan of those at Cape Nome, above described, except that the storeroom usually opened on a level with the ground in front, instead of through the roof. In July, 1881, this village was almost deserted, as the people were on the adjacent mainland engaged in salmon fishing.

In all the last-named villages elevated frameworks for boats and sledges were numerous; in those where the floors were made of hewed

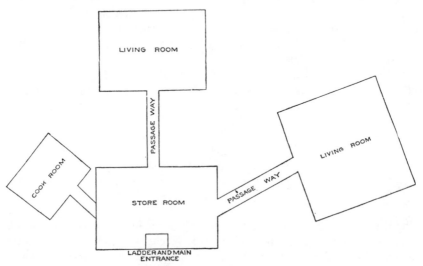

FIG. 83—Ground plan of house at Cape Nome.

planks, long use had worn them smooth and the inmates were careful to keep them clean, sweeping them as often as necessary with a little wisp of twigs.

King island, in Bering strait, is a rugged mass of granite rising sheer from the water for hundreds of feet on three sides, and on the fourth side, where the village is located, it is very difficult to make a landing. In July, 1881, the *Corwin* anchored a few hundred yards off the shore; the rugged granite walls rose in sharp, serrated, angular slopes almost perpendicularly from the edge of the water to the village and thence upward to the high crest. Along the edge of the water great granite bowlders added to the difficulty of landing, thence up to the village a broken path zigzagged sharply up the jagged slope. From the vessel the village presented the appearance of a cluster of cliff-swallows' nests on the face of the island, the entrances to the houses looking like rounded black holes among the granite bowlders used for their walls. As the anchor chain went rattling out, the people, who had been watching us from the houses, gave a loud shout and ran down to the water, leaping from rock to rock and looking like pigmies, so dwarfed were they by the gigantic background.

The winter houses at this place were made by excavating the loose rocks, thus forming a deep niche in the steep slope, and by walling up the front and sides with stones placed over a driftwood framework. Access to these houses was gained by a long, arched stone passageway, which sloped from the outer entrance in and up to a hole in the plank floor. The inside of the living rooms were arranged with plank floor and benches, just as on Sledge island, but there were no outer storerooms or cooking rooms in the passageway. Driftwood was abundant there, but the principal material used for covering the houses was broken granite.

The summer houses were remarkable structures; they were square inclosures, made wholly of tanned walrus hide, with a slightly arched roof of walrus skins drawn snugly over the wooden framework and lashed firmly in place. The houses were elevated and held in place by a framework which consisted of two main poles standing upright with their bases fastened among the rocks and connected by a wooden crossbar lashed to them 10 or 20 feet from the ground. From this crossbar other bars extended on a level back to the slope of the hill, where they were made fast. The floor was of roughly hewed planks, and at the back rested against the face of the hill. From the hillside a plank extended to one of the corners of the house, and a little plank walk passed thence around the side of the house to the front, being railed by a pole lashed, at about the height of a man's hand, to uprights set in the rocks. On the seaward side was a circular opening, which served as a combined door and window. Figure 84 represents one of these summer houses.

In some of these houses one corner was walled off from the room with walrus hide as a square inclosure to serve as a sleeping room. In one of the houses the entire rear half was walled across and again subdivided by a walrus-skin partition, forming two sleeping rooms, entrance to which was given by a round hole cut in the skin. Each of these inner rooms served for a family, and contained their bedding and various small possessions, the longer outer room being a general sitting and work room and a receptacle for dried fish and other stores. The translucent walrus hides rendered these houses very light, and they were kept quite clean. In summer fresh meat and fish were kept in a great cleft in the cliff close to the landing place, and accessible only from the water. There were various elevated frameworks here for storing the boats.

On the larger Diomede island, in the middle of Bering strait, the villages differed in several respects from those of the King islanders.

FIG. 84—Walrus skin summer house on King island.

The summer houses were built among the winter dwellings, and were above ground, with stone walls and gravel-covered roofs. An arched stone passage, similar to those of the winter houses, but shorter, led to the living room. With the exception of being less carefully built to exclude water, these summer houses were very similar to those used in winter. Raised on four posts over or very near the entrance to each summer house was a storehouse, the supporting posts and framework of which were made from driftwood, and the sides and roofs of walrus hide, like the elevated houses on King island.

At Cape Prince of Wales, on the American shore of Bering strait, there were two villages. One near the hill at the southern side of the cape was called the "hill village," and the other, located on the flat, was called the "spit village." They were separated by a space of about 75 yards. The houses were built of driftwood covered with earth, and were very similar to those of the Diomede islands. The people of these two villages had a standing feud that occasionally broke into open quarrels. Those of the "spit village" were the most aggressive, and were hated and feared by the others.

Crossing the strait a large Eskimo village was found on the point of East cape, Siberia. This was built on a steep slope fronting the sea, and its dome-shape houses with small outer openings gave it the same appearance of being a cluster of cliff swallows' nests that we had

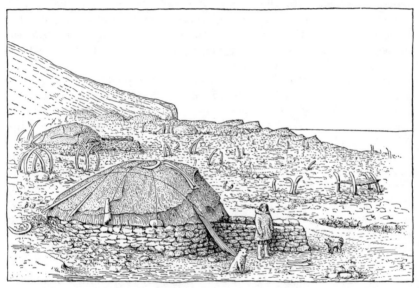

Fig. 85—Eskimo village at East cape, Siberia.

noticed on our approach to King island. From the anchorage fifty-four occupied houses were counted; these must have contained over two hundred and fifty people.

Just around the cape, to the north, was a village of equal size, which was not visited. The village on the point was built on a slope of loose granite fragments inclined at such an angle that there was space for only a narrow trail in front of most of the houses, and then a sharp descent of some yards. The houses consisted of a stone wall laid up two or three feet from the ground, in oval form, and continued in the shape of an arched or open-top entrance passage three or four yards long, as shown in figure 85.

Upon this stone wall was a framework of whale-ribs arched to a common point over one side of the entrance, where they were met by the jawbone of a whale, the upper end of which was slightly curved inward to meet the ribs crossed on the top. The jawbone, held in place by lashings and heavy stones, was thus made to sustain the weight of the structure. Over this framework tanned walrus hides were laid and secured by lashings and heavy stones or whale vertebræ attached to the ends of cords. The front part of the room was used for storing various articles of food and property, and the rear part was supplied with pologs, or small rooms, made by sewing reindeer skins into the form of a covered square or rectangular box without a bottom, about 7 or 8 by 10 or 12 feet square and about 4 feet high, which were held in place by rawhide ropes extending from each upper corner and the middle of the sides to the framework of the roof. In this way very close, warm rooms were made inside the house, in which, on a small raised platform of planks or beaten earth, the beds were placed. Each family had its own polog. Wood seemed to be very scarce among these people. The illustration shows the situation of the village and the position of the houses. The elevated platform on the right, for sleds and boats, is made of whales' jawbones (figure 85).

Scattered along the hillside among the occupied houses were the remains of many ruined houses, which were similar in character to the dwellings seen on the Diomede islands—partly underground, with external stone walls—and a very large number of pits showed the sites of still older houses. It was evident that in earlier times these people had used underground houses exclusively, but more recently had abandoned them and built their dwellings in the manner described.

At Plover bay, on the same coast, the village consisted mainly of walrus-hide huts similar to those at East cape, except that they had no stone walls about the bases, and the frames were composed of driftwood instead of whale ribs; but the interior arrangement of deerskin pologs was the same. The illustration (plate LXXXIII a), from a photograph, will give an idea of the exterior of these houses.

A few small, half underground houses of driftwood and whalebones covered with earth in the regular Eskimo style, were found here. On the northern side of the mouth of the bay a zigzag path leads high up on the bluffs to a rock-walled shelter used as a lookout to watch for whales or for vessels at sea.

This village is not very populous, and through the introduction of whisky and of various diseases by the whalers, who call here every season, the Eskimo at this point are in a fair way to become extinct. The accompanying illustration (plate LXXXIV) represents two women from this locality.

St Lawrence island had several large and populous villages previous to the year 1879. During the winter of 1879-'80 a famine, accompanied by disease, caused the death of at least two-thirds of the entire population of the island, and several villages were completely depopulated.

During the summer of 1881 I visited these villages on the revenue

b—NOATAK SUMMER LODGE

a—HOUSE AT PLOVER BAY

ESKIMO DWELLINGS

cutter *Corwin*, and found the tundra surrounding the village sites covered with corpses of the inhabitants; and dozens of them were still lying where they had died in the houses.

In two villages at the southwestern end of the island were several summer houses of walrus skin, like those used at Plover bay, and various winter houses. These latter were framed with the jawbones and ribs of whales, which were planted in the ground, arching in at the top, forming an oval framework supporting the roof. The latter was made of similar bones with a little driftwood added, and the entire structure was covered with earth. Owing to the scarcity of material these houses were small and rude, but were very similar to buildings on the northern shore of Norton sound.

Close by the winter houses were elevated storehouses, upheld on four jawbones of whales planted upright in the ground. Most of the summer houses were framed of long strips of bone sawed lengthwise from whales' jaws, with one end planted in the ground and the other bent over toward a stout jawbone of a whale standing upright in the ground, on one side of the oval area inclosed by the bone strips. Alternating with these strips were whale ribs, which also curved over toward the upright post. The frame pieces were planted very shallowly in the ground and were held steady by a rock weighing over 100 pounds, which was hung from the post-like jawbone which formed the main strength of the structure. An idea of these frames is given by the accompanying sketch (figure 86).

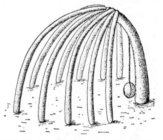

FIG. 86—House frame of whale ribs and jawbone.

The interior of these summer houses measured about 20 feet in diameter, and were supplied with pologs made of reindeer skins sewed together and suspended from the roof, as is done on the Siberian coast. Exteriorly they were covered with walrus skins, which were lashed on and held in place by heavy weights of stone, driftwood, and bones, to prevent their being toppled over by the frequent gales.

In a large village on the northern shore of the island, where all the inhabitants had perished, I found many similar summer houses, also some partly subterranean winter houses, differing from any others seen in this region. They were roofed with whalebones and driftwood, over which was the usual layer of earth. Over the outer end of the passageway was a roofed, stockaded shelter made of driftwood, with one side or a part of one side left open, facing away from the direction of the prevailing wind. These shelters were from 5 to 8 feet across and about 5 or 6 feet high. In the floor opened a square hole, giving access to the passageway, which was 2 or 3 feet high and from 50 to 75 feet in length and built wholly underground. In several instances they were curved laterally or turned at an angle, as if to cut off a draft; but it is possible this may have been caused by starting at both ends of the tunnel when excavating it and failing to meet in a direct line. The houses had two sets of broad sleeping benches on the right and left sides of the room. Over the center of the floor was a square hole in the roof; just back of

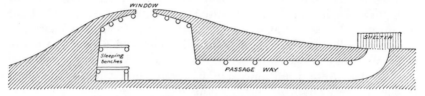

FIG. 87—Section of house on St Lawrence island.

this a round opening had been made, in which was fitted a large vertebra of a whale hollowed out to form a short cylinder, serving as a smoke hole or ventilator, which could be left open during stormy weather when the larger opening was covered. The accompanying section of one of these houses (figure 87) explains the method of their construction.

FIG. 88—Summer camp at Hotham inlet.

At Cape Espenberg, on Kotzebue sound, in July, 1881, we found a camp of traveling Malemut. They had several low, round-top tents, 3½ to 4 feet high and 6 to 7 feet wide, made of drilling drawn over slender poles crossed and bent, with their ends thrust into the ground. One conical lodge, also covered with drilling, was about 10 feet high and 8 feet in diameter on the ground.

WOMEN OF PLOVER BAY, SIBERIA

At Hotham inlet, near the head of Kotzebue sound, on the 15th of July of the same year, a large gathering of Eskimo from Kowak and Noatak rivers was seen.   They were living in a row of conical lodges extending in a line for more than a mile along a low, sandy spit parallel to the shore of the sound.   Figure 88, from a photograph, illustrates this camp for the season of 1881.   This camp was arranged with almost military precision; along the beach, above high-water mark, with their sterns to the sea, were ranged between sixty and seventy umiaks, turned with the bottom upward and toward the prevailing wind, tilted on one rail, the other being supported on two sticks 3½ to 4 feet fong.   Seventy-five yards back from the umiaks, in a line parallel to the beach, were ranged over two hundred kaiaks, supported about three feet from the ground on low trestles made of branching stakes. Below each kaiak, supported on a rest 3 or 4 inches above the ground, was the set of spears, paddles, etc, belonging to the boat.   The kaiaks were all of the long, slender pattern common at Kotzebue sound, and were ranged parallel to each other, pointing toward the sea, in a line with the umiaks.   Fifty yards back from the kaiaks, and ranged in a line parallel with them, were the conical lodges occupied by the people; they were framed by slender poles standing in a circle, with the upper ends meeting and held in place by a strong wooden hoop lashed to the poles with

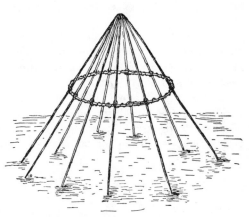

FIG. 89—Frame for summer lodge, Hotham inlet.

rawhide cord midway between the ground and the top.   The accompanying sketch (figure 89) shows the manner of arranging the framework.

The frames were about 10 feet high and from 12 to 15 feet in diameter at the base; they were covered with untanned winter deerskins sewed into squares containing about six deerskins, which were thrown over the framework with the hair outward.   Several of these squares were necessary for each lodge.   In some cases the deerskins were covered with a large sheet of drilling or calico, as shown in plate LXXXIII *b*. Behind the lodges were stakes to which each family had tied its dogs, fastened so as to be just out of reach of each other.

This was a summer trading camp of these people, and contained from six to eight hundred persons.   Figure 90 shows the plan of the encampment.

In size and methodical arrangement this camp presented a very striking appearance and was the only one I ever saw in which the

Eskimo had followed a deliberate plan. The large number of boats, and the necessity for having clear space to enable each crew to launch without interfering with its neighbors, must have brought about this plan, which could not have been improved, as the entire camp could embark and paddle to a trading vessel in less than five minutes.

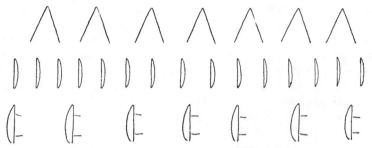

FIG. 90—Arrangement of summer camp at Hotham inlet.

This was a temporary camp which is located here for a few weeks each summer for the purpose of trading with vessels which cruise in these waters, as well as for meeting and trading with the people from both shores of Bering strait.

At Point Hope, just north of Kotzebue sound, was found a large Eskimo village, containing between three hundred and four hundred people, living in conical summer lodges. The winter village of semi-subterranean houses was on the outer edge of the cape, the summer village being nearer the mainland.

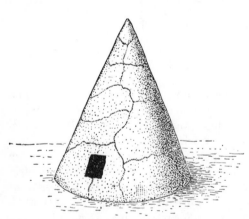

FIG. 91—Summer lodge at Cape Thompson.

Near Cape Thompson was found a small party of people, from Point Hope, who were on their way up the coast and were waiting here for better weather. They were living in conical lodges covered with a patchwork of sealskins sewed together. The entrance to each lodge was through a square hole in one side, about two feet from the ground, as shown in the accompanying illustration (figure 91).

At Cape Lisburne was found another camp of Point Hope people on their way northward Two photographs of this camp were obtained, from one of which plate LXXXV was drawn. This camp had the usual conical lodges, some of them being round-topped like those seen at Cape Espenberg.

SUMMER CAMP AT CAPE LISBURNE

Just north of Cape Lisburne three or four winter houses were seen, but it could not be determined whether they were occupied.

Near Icy cape were several summer camps of Point Barrow people. They were living in conical lodges, many of which were covered with canvas taken from wrecked whaling vessels. In front of each camp was erected a stout post from 12 to 20 feet high, notched on the sides for convenience in climbing. Near the top was a crossbar, used as a seat or perch. The coast in this part of the district is very flat and low, and these posts are used as lookout points whence the people are able to see the " blowing " of whales or the approach of ships. As we passed by the shore each post was usually occupied by a man who waved his shirt to induce us to stop.

From here to Point Barrow were several similar summer camps of from two to ten lodges each. At Point Barrow the winter houses were of the ordinary half-underground type with a long, tunnel-like entrance way; scarcity of driftwood had necessitated the use of whale ribs and jawbones in framing these houses. At this point the storehouses for meat were built very nearly in the style of the winter houses, except that the only entrance was by a trapdoor in the roof, so that they were really half-underground cellars.

Near the winter houses were platforms 6 to 8 feet above the ground, on which were stored spears, nets, and various hunting and household paraphernalia. At the time of our visit in August the inhabitants were living in conical lodges.

RUINS

Ruins of ancient Eskimo villages are common on the lower Yukon and thence along the coast line to Point Barrow. On the Siberian shore they were seen from East cape along the Arctic coast to Cape Wanka-rem. Various circumstances prevented the recording of more than a few superficial notes in regard to them, which are here inserted for the purpose of bringing them to the attention of future workers in that region. On the shore of the bay on the southern side of St Michael island I dug into an old village site where saucer-shape pits indicated the places formerly occupied by houses. The village had been burned, as was evident from the numerous fragments of charred timbers mixed with the soil. In the few cubic feet of earth turned up at this place were found a slate fish knife, an ivory spearhead, a doll, and a toy dish, the latter two cut from bark. The men I had with me from the village at St Michael became so alarmed by their superstitious feelings that I was obliged to give up the idea of getting further aid from them in this place. I learned afterward that this village had been built by people from Pastolik, at the mouth of the Yukon, who went there to fish and to hunt seals before the Russians came to the country.

On the highest point of Whale island, which is a steep islet just off-shore near the present village of St Michael, were the ruins of a kashim and of several houses. The St Michael people told me that this place was destroyed, long before the Russians came, by a war party from below the Yukon mouth. The sea has encroached upon the islet until a portion of the land formerly occupied by the village has been washed away. The permanently frozen soil at this place stopped us at the depth of about two feet. Here, and at another ancient Unalit village site which was examined superficially, we found specimens of bone and ivory carvings which were very ancient, as many of them crumbled to pieces on being exposed.

Along the lower Yukon are many indications of villages destroyed by war parties. According to the old men these parties came from Askinuk and Kushunuk, near the Kuskokwim, as there was almost constant warfare between the people of these two sections before the advent of the Russians.

Both the fur traders and the Eskimo claim that there are a large number of house sites on the left bank of the Yukon, a few miles below Ikogmut. This is the village that the Yukon Eskimo say had 35 kashims, and there are many tales relating to the period when it was occupied. At the time of my Yukon trips this site was heavily covered with snow, and I could not see it; but it would undoubtedly well repay thorough excavation during the summer months. One of the traditions is that this village was built by people from Bristol bay, joined by others from Nunivak island and Kushunuk. One informant said that a portion of this village was occupied up to 1848, when the last inhabitants died of smallpox, but whether or not this is true I was unable to learn.

Another informant told me that near the entrance of Goodnews bay, near the mouth of the Kuskokwim, there is a circular pit about 75 feet in diameter, marking the former site of a very large kashim. A few miles south of Shaktolik, near the head of Norton sound, I learned of the existence of a large village site. Both the Eskimo and the fur traders who told me of this said that the houses had been those of Shaktolik people, and that some of them must have been connected by underground passageways, judging from the ditch-like depressions from one to the other along the surface of the ground. The Shaktolik men who told me this said that there were many other old village sites about there and that they were once inhabited by a race of very small people who have all disappeared.

From the Malemut of Kotzebue sound and adjacent region I learned that there are many old village sites in that district. Many of these places were destroyed by war parties of Tinné from the interior, according to the traditions of the present inhabitants.

On Elephant point, at the head of Kotzebue sound, I saw the site of an old village, with about fifteen pits marking the locations of the houses. The pits sloped toward the center and showed by their outlines that the houses had been small and roughly circular, with a short passageway leading into them, the entire structure having been partly underground.

The Eskimo of East cape, Siberia, said that there were many old village sites along the coast in that vicinity. These houses had stone foundations, many of which are still in place. There is a large ruined village of this kind near the one still occupied on the cape.

On the extreme point of Cape Wankarem, and at its greatest elevation, just above the present camp of the reindeer Chukchi, a series of three sites of old Eskimo villages were found. The accompanying sketch map of the cape shows the relative sites of these villages, and also indicates another fact which may give a slight clew to the age of one of them.

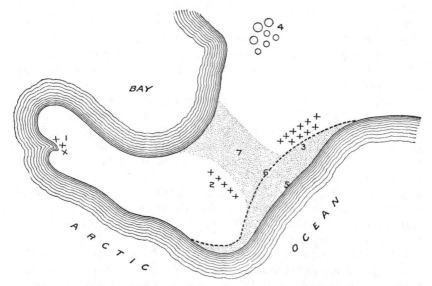

Fɪɢ. 92—Sites of ancient villages at Cape Wankarem, Siberia.

Number 1 is the site of a village which at present contains the ruins of three houses; other houses have evidently been washed away by the encroachment of the sea. These three houses are of mound shape, with a pit or depression in the middle, and a trench-like depression leading out from each of them toward the sea shows the position of the entrance passage. Numerous ribs and jawbones of whales lie scattered about, and the decaying end of a whale's jawbone, projecting through the top of one of the mounds, shows the material used in framing them.

Number 2 represents a series of five similar house sites, facing the dotted area on the sketch map; and at number 3 is indicated still another series of ten house sites like the preceding, all unquestionably of Eskimo origin.

Number 4 is the site of the present Chukchi camp, consisting of skin lodges, as we found it at the time of our visit. No recent whale bones were seen about the Chukchi camp, but there were many vertebræ and other bones gathered from the ruins of the Eskimo houses. A man was seen digging up a whale's jawbone from one of the old house sites, and there were evidences that many others had been removed in the same manner by the present inhabitants.

During repeated visits made to these ruins I was impressed by several circumstances which may serve to shed light on their age, as shown by the following observations:

Villages 1 and 2 are on a high knoll which rises like an island from the low, flat shore, the sides sloping down to the narrow, pebble-covered neck of land (at 7) which separates a lagoon on one side from the open sea on the other. Number 4 is on higher ground than the neck at number 7, and is made up of sand and gravel. Number 5 is the present seashore or water line. Number 6 is a well-marked ancient water line, close to the edge of which was built the village marked 3. There is a gravelly beach between the present and former water lines. Number 7 is a pebble-covered beach, probably two feet above extreme high water line at present.

It will be noticed that number 2 fronts directly upon 7 and is located exactly as an Eskimo village would be placed if 7 were an open channel. The western Eskimo have an almost invariable custom of building their villages facing the water and parallel with the shore line. I think it may safely be stated that none of these people ever placed a village site in the relation to the sea that the site of number 2 now bears, and it consequently follows, almost as a demonstrated fact, that village number 2 was built and occupied when 7 was an open waterway, separating the high knoll of Cape Wankarem from the mainland and thus forming it into an island.

I think number 2 marks the most ancient of the villages, for number 3 is so placed in regard to the ancient beach (6) that it could not have been safely inhabited until the sea came to occupy nearly its present water line. I should conclude that the land had been raised about three feet from its ancient level at the time the water line stood at 6, when village number 3 was occupied. The gradual upraising of the coast must have made village number 2 untenable and caused the people to change to number 3, that and number 1 probably being the last villages occupied by the Eskimo, who had disappeared from this part of the coast before the historical period.

The severity of the Arctic climate on this bleak coast renders it very difficult, if not impossible, to make an estimate of any value (basing calculations upon the decay of perishable articles) as to the length of time that has elapsed since an ancient site was occupied. If data were at hand to estimate the rate of the rise of the land on the northwestern Alaska and Siberian coasts, we would have a key to the approximate age of villages 2 and 3 at Cape Wankarem, and probably to the age of numerous other settlements along the same shore.

FOOD

Being a race of hunters and fishermen the food supply of the Eskimo is essentially composed of game and fish, which are prepared in a variety of ways. But little attention is paid to cleanliness in the preparation of food among these people. The flesh of reindeer, mountain sheep, bears, seals, walrus and other large game are commonly boiled in sea water to give it a salty flavor.

Meat is frequently kept for a considerable length of time and sometimes until it becomes semiputrid. At Point Barrow, in the middle of August, 1881, the people still had the carcasses of deer which had been killed the preceding winter and spring. This meat was kept in small underground pits, which the frozen subsoil rendered cold, but not cold enough to prevent a bluish fungus growth which completely covered the carcasses of the animals and the walls of the storerooms.

Meat killed in summer is often dried, as are also the various kinds of salmon, which are split down to the base of the tail and hung on wooden frames until dry. The smaller species of salmon, known as dog salmon, are tied in bunches of twenty when dry and placed in storehouses for future use.

The large flakes of dried king salmon are usually packed away in bales or bundles. Tomcod, sculpin, and whitefish also are dried, the smaller species, such as tomcod and sculpin, being hung upon strings. The roe of herring is gathered on the seaweed during spawning time and some of this is dried and preserved for winter use, when it is boiled and eaten with great relish.

On the lower Kuskokwim and thence to the Yukon the people try out the oil from a species of whitefish found there and store in bags for winter use the clear white fat thus obtained.

Fish are boiled and sometimes are roasted over an open fire as is frequently done with meat, but boiling is the usual method of preparing both fish and meat. Fish taken in winter are usually placed in grass bags and kept frozen until required, when they are eaten raw, while still frozen, or are boiled. Crabs, mussels, and ascidians are boiled.

In the district between the Yukon and the Kuskokwim, the heads of king salmon, taken in summer, are placed in small pits in the ground surrounded by straw and covered with turf. They are kept there during summer and in the autumn have decayed until even the bones have become of the same consistency as the general mass. They are then taken out and kneaded in a wooden tray until they form a pasty compound and are eaten as a favorite dish by some of the people. The odor of this mess is almost unendurable to one not accustomed to it, and is even too strong for the stomachs of many of the Eskimo.

The back fat of the reindeer is cut into small pieces and chewed by the women until it becomes a pasty mass, which is put into a wooden dish. When enough of this has been prepared, a quantity of snow and

some salmon or cranberries are mixed with it and the who_e is kneaded
until it becomes a homogeneous mass. This compound is regarded as
the greatest delicacy that can be served to guests and at feasts.

The blubber of seals, walrus, or whales is stored and often eaten in
its natural form; or the oil may be tried out and stored in bags and
used for food as well as for burning in lamps. When used as food it
is placed in a small wooden tray or dish and the people dip their dried
fish or other meat into it. The oil is never drunk by them except when
desiring to take it as a purgative; at such times a large draft of seal
oil is usually effective.

The oil obtained from whitefish is regarded as a great delicacy when
eaten with dried salmon. Walrus flippers and the skin of the white
whale are also among the choice bits of the Eskimo larder. The blood
of seals or other large game is made into a stew called kai-u'-shăk. The
soup of boiled meat is called mĭ-chu'-ă and is greatly relished.

On the mainland it is customary for the women to go out every spring
and search the marshes for the eggs of wild fowl which breed there.
Upon the islands waterfowl are caught and their eggs taken from the
cliffs facing the sea, and many geese and ducks are speared or netted
while molting at the end of the breeding season.

In autumn the women gather a large supply of blueberries, heath
berries, salmon berries, and cranberries, which they store for winter
use. At this season is also gathered a kind of wild sorrel, which is
boiled and crushed with a pestle and then put into a wooden tub or
barrel and covered with water, where it is left to ferment in the sun.
This makes a very pleasant acid relish, which is added to various dishes
in the winter and is called ko-pa'-tŭk. Young willow leaves are also
boiled and eaten.

The women also gather the bulbous roots of a species of grass, which
are either boiled or eaten raw; they have a sweetish, nutty flavor. They
also search for the little stores of these roots which have been gathered
by field mice. They feel around among the grass-covered knolls with
a long-handle staff until a soft spot is found, showing the location of
the hidden store, which they quickly transfer to their baskets.

All the Eskimo are forced by the harsh nature of their climatic surroundings to provide a supply of food for winter, but they are careless
and improvident in many ways. They frequently consume nearly all of
their stores during midwinter festivals and live in semi-starvation
throughout the early spring.

The seal nets set out in the fall are of the utmost importance to the
natives, as they depend upon the catch of seals at this time for food
and for a supply of oil for their lamps and other purposes, as well as
the skins for buying necessary articles from the traders.

Just before the netting season, one of my paddle men, an unusually
industrious hunter, found that there was some whisky in a village
where we stopped. Before I knew it he had traded off his only seal
net for enough whisky to make himself intoxicated, in which condition

he immediately proceeded to place himself. The result was that he and his family were very short of food during the following winter.

The terrible famine and accompanying disease which caused the death of over a thousand people on St Lawrence island during the winter of 1879 and 1880 was said to have been caused by the use of whisky. The people of that island usually obtained their supply of food for the winter by killing walrus from the great herds of these animals that go through Bering strait on the first ice in the fall. The walrus remain about the island only a few days and then go south, when the ice closes about and shuts the island in till spring.

Just before the time for the walrus to reach the island that season, the Eskimo obtained a supply of whisky from some vessels and began a prolonged debauch, which ended only when the supply was exhausted. When this occurred the annual migration of the walrus had passed, and the people were shut in for the winter by the ice. The result was that over two-thirds of the population died before spring. The following spring, when the *Corwin* visited the islands, some of the survivors came on board bringing a few articles for trade. They wished only to purchase rifle cartridges and more whisky.

During July, 1881, the *Corwin* made a visit to this famine stricken district, where the miserable survivors were seen. Only a single dog was left among them, the others having been eaten by the starving people. Two of the largest villages were entirely depopulated.

In July I landed at a place on the northern shore where two houses were standing, in which, wrapped in their fur blankets on the sleeping platforms, lay about 25 dead bodies of adults, and upon the ground and outside were a few others. Some miles to the eastward, along the coast, was another village, where there were 200 dead people. In a large house were found about 15 bodies placed one upon another like cordwood at one end of the room, while as many others lay dead in their blankets on the platforms.

In the houses all the wooden and clay food vessels were found turned bottom upward and put away in one corner—mute evidences of the famine. Scattered about the houses on the outside were various tools and implements, clay pots, wooden dishes, trays, guns, knives, axes, ammunition, and empty bottles; among these articles were the skulls of walrus and of many dogs. The bodies of the people were found everywhere in the village as well as scattered along in a line toward the graveyard for half a mile inland.

The first to die had been taken farthest away, and usually placed at full length beside the sled that had carried the bodies. Scattered about such bodies lay the tools and implements belonging to the dead. In one instance a body lay outstretched upon a sled, while behind it, prone upon his face, with arms outstretched and almost touching the sled runners, lay the body of a man who had died while pushing the sled bearing the body of his friend or relative.

Others were found lying in the underground passageways to the houses, and one body was found halfway out of the entrance. Most of the bodies lying about the villages had evidently been dragged there and left wherever it was most convenient by the living during the later period of the famine. The total absence of the bodies of children in these villages gave rise to the suspicion that they had been eaten by the adults; but possibly this may not have been the case. The strongest evidence in this regard, however, was in one village where there were over two hundred dead adults, and although I looked carefully for the bodies of children, none could be found; yet there was no positive evidence that cannibalism had been practiced by the natives. That this custom sometimes prevailed, however, in ancient times, during famines, I learned from the Unalit; nevertheless they openly expressed their abhorrence of the practice.

On the bluff at the northwest point of this island we found a couple of surviving families living in round-top, walrus-hide summer houses. At the foot of the hill not far from their present camping place was a winter village, where about 100 people lay dead; the bodies were scattered about outside or were lying in their blankets in the houses, as we had seen them in other places.

The two families living there consisted of about a dozen people; the adults seemed very much depressed and had little animation. Among them were two bright little girls, who had the usual childish carelessness, and kept near us while we were on shore. When I shot a snow bunting near the village they called to me and ran to show me its nest on the hillside.

When I asked one of the inhabitants what had become of the people who formerly lived on that part of the island, he waved his hand toward the winter village, saying, "All *mucky mucky*," being the jargon term for "dead."

I tried to obtain a photograph of the women and little girls, and for that purpose placed them in position and focused the camera. While I was waiting for a lull in the wind to take the picture, the husband of one of the women came up and asked in a listless, matter-of-fact tone, "All *mucky* now?" meaning, "Will they all die now?" He evidently took it for granted that my camera was a conjuring box, which would complete the work of the famine, yet he seemed perfectly indifferent to the consequences.

A curious trait noticed among these survivors was their apparent loss of the customary fear which the natives usually show when near a spot where many persons have died. The death of all their friends and relatives seemed to have rendered them apathetic and beyond the influence of ordinary fear of that kind. The two families mentioned were camped on the hill just above the village full of dead bodies, and whenever they went down to the shore to launch their umiak they were forced to pass close to the dead, yet they seemed oblivious to their gruesome surroundings.

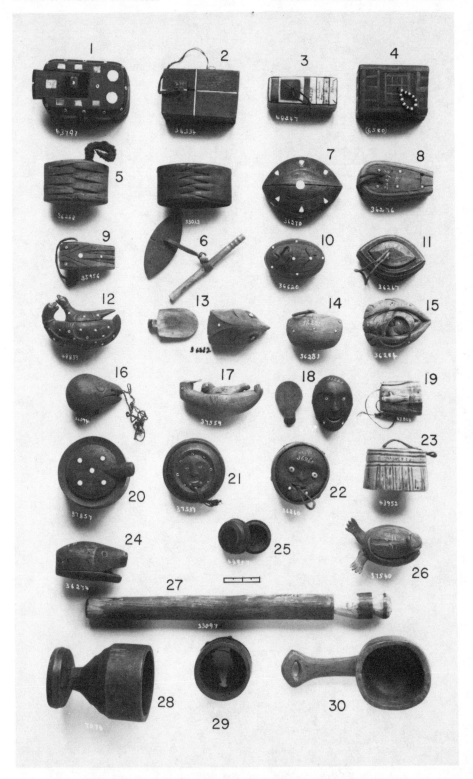

TOBACCO AND SNUFF BOXES AND SNUFF-MAKING IMPLEMENTS (ONE-FIFTH)

TOBACCO AND SMOKING

METHODS OF USING TOBACCO

Tobacco was first introduced among the Alaskan Eskimo from Asia, by way of Bering strait, by their Siberian neighbors, and by the same route came the pipes with cylindrical bowls and wide rims, similar to those used in eastern Asia.

Tobacco is used in different forms by both sexes; the women usually chew it or take it in the form of snuff, but rarely smoke it; the men use it in all these ways. The tobacco now used by these people is obtained from the traders, and is usually in the form of the natural leaf, tied in small bunches called "hands."

For chewing, the tobacco is cut into shreds on small boards which are usually merely plain tablets from a few inches to a foot or more in diameter, but they are sometimes ornamented with an incised pattern. When the tobacco has been cut sufficiently fine it is mixed with ashes obtained from tree fungus and kneaded and rolled into rounded pellets or quids, often being chewed a little by the women in order to incorporate the ashes more thoroughly. The tree fungus from which the ashes

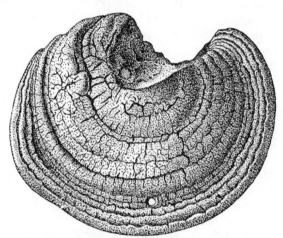

FIG. 93—Fungus used for making ashes to mix with tobacco.

are made forms a regular article of trade with the Tinné of the interior, who bring it to the coast every summer and sell it to the Eskimo. Figure 93 represents a specimen of this tree fungus, which was obtained at St Michael from a trading party of the Yukon Tinné. Figure 118 illustrates one of the tobacco boards.

It is common when traveling among these people to see the women engaged in cutting up tobacco, kneading it with ashes, or chewing it into quids in order to supply their husbands or other male relatives with a stock for use on the ensuing day. From four to eight of the pellets are prepared at one time; these are packed in little boxes ready for use.

The men do not usually chew the quids, but hold them in the cheek, and rarely expectorate the juice. After holding a quid in his mouth for some time, if the chewer wishes to rest, eat, or drink, he takes it out, and after rolling it into a little ball, places it behind his right ear, where it remains until again needed.

In addition to the usual tobacco mixed with fungus ashes these people are also fond of using the nicotine that accumulates in their pipestems. At intervals every smoker opens his pipestem and carefully removes the oily mass of tobacco extract, which he places with his chewing tobacco; a portion of this is combined with the quid and adds greatly to his enjoyment, owing to its strong narcotic influence. I have frequently seen them place this material in their mouths almost undiluted and in quantity that appeared sufficient to cause the individual's death, yet apparently without producing the least nausea or other ill effect.

Some of the writers on the Eskimo have claimed that they eat this concentrated tobacco, but I think this a mistake, as I frequently saw them placing it in their mouths and holding it there in the same manner that they did ordinary quids.

For smoking the tobacco is cut very fine, then a little tuft of fur is plucked from the clothing and wadded at the bottom of the narrow, cylindrical bowl of the pipe, and the tobacco is placed on top of this until the bowl is full. A small fragment of tinder is then lighted with flint and steel and placed on the tobacco. The smoker gives two or three short, sharp draws, which thoroughly ignite the tinder and tobacco, and then draws the smoke into his lungs by a long, deep inhalation, which consumes all the tobacco contained in the pipe. After retaining the smoke as long as possible it is exhaled, and the smoker puts away the pipe.

For making snuff the tobacco is finely shredded, and is then thoroughly dried, after which it is pounded in a small wooden mortar with a wooden pestle until reduced to powder. These mortars are generally more or less goblet-shape, although I obtained one specimen from the lower Yukon, shown in plate LXXXVI, 30, which is like a small wooden dipper, with a hole near the end of the handle for suspending it. Another typical example of these mortars (plate LXXXV, 28) was obtained at Razbinsky. The pestles usually consist of sticks from an inch to an inch and a half in diameter, rounded at the lower end, and from 10 to 15 inches in length. A good specimen of these implements, from Kigiktauik, is shown in figure 27.

After the tobacco has been reduced to powder it is sifted, to remove the coarser particles, until it is finally of the fineness required. For this purpose there are used small sieves, similar to the specimen from Razbinsky (figure 29), which are made by cutting out a cylinder of wood about two inches long, and fastening over one end a cover of parchment made from some thin skin or from the intestine of some animal, which is punctured with numerous small holes, and the edges bound to the cylinder by a sinew cord wrapped around a groove in the border. The sieve frames are sometimes made from bark, and one such specimen collected on the lower Yukon has the sieve made from a piece of coarse sacking.

FUNGUS ASH BOXES AND TOBACCO BAGS (ONE-FOURTH)

TOBACCO IMPLEMENTS

SNUFF-BOXES

The snuff is kept in neatly made boxes, and is used by placing one end of a tube (made from the wing-bone of a goose or other water fowl) successively in each of the nostrils and inhaling vigorously from the snuff-box in which the other end of the tube is placed.

The boxes used for containing snuff vary greatly in form, many of them showing remarkable skill in carving and ingenuity in conception of the designs.

A snuff-box from Kigiktauik (number 33074) is formed of a band of bone bent into a circle and riveted at the ends by pieces of iron; this serves as a foundation on which is fitted a top and a bottom in the form of truncated cones, the top having a round hole in the center, capped with a wooden cover. The band of bone has a few circles and dots etched on its surface.

A circular wooden snuff-box from Kaialigamut (figure 20, plate LXXXVI) is slightly narrower at the top and is beveled inward from the rim both above and below to the convex top and bottom; the cover has a projecting arm, extending slightly beyond the edge of the box, by which it can be raised. In both top and bottom are set five small ivory pegs with broad heads. The box is painted black, except the beveled edge of the rim above and below and the lever-like handle on the cover, which are red. Another specimen, brought from Norton sound, is shaped similarly to the preceding, but has four grooves around the outside, forming bead-like ridges, the upper and lower ones being the largest.

The snuff-box from Anogogmut (figure 21, plate LXXXVI) is somewhat similar to the above-described specimen from Kigiktauik, but the top and the bottom are carved in relief to represent a human face surrounded by a beveled ridge; two beads are inlaid to represent labrets, and the mouth and the eyes are indicated by inlaid pieces of ivory. A series of beads is set in a groove around the middle of the box, which is painted red.

An oval wooden box from Kushunuk (figure 11, plate LXXXVI) forms a sharp angle at each end; the top and bottom are slightly convex. The sides are painted with alternate stripes of black and red; on the top the red is replaced by dull blue, the bottom also being of that color. A loop of sealskin cord three and a half inches long forms a handle on the cover.

Another oval box, obtained at St Michael (figure 6, plate LXXXVI) has the sides made of leather covered with black whalebone, the ends of which are notched and interlocked. The top and bottom are of wood neatly fitted. To the center of the top is fastened a stout rawhide cord about three inches long, which has attached to its end a small tube for inhaling snuff.

18 ETH——18

A curious box from Chalitmut (figure 15, plate LXXXVI) is oval in shape and is cut from a single piece of wood. The oval cover is set in one side and has a rawhide handle. On the sides, carved in strong relief, are two grotesque, seal-like animals facing each other. The bodies are painted red and the intervening area black. The entire surface of the box is marked with crescent-shape incisions and studded with white beads of different sizes.

A box from the lower Yukon (figure 12, plate LXXXVI) represents a large seal upon its back with the head and the tail upraised and a smaller seal lying upon it, this latter forming the cover. This is a well-made carving in strong relief, with numerous small ivory pegs and white beads set about the surface. Around the neck of each seal is fastened a flattened piece of bird quill. The seals are represented with open mouths and beads form the eyes.

The small square box from Nunivak island (figure 3, plate LXXXVI) is made of ivory, with the top and bottom of separate pieces fastened by pegs. Across the top three strips of brass are inlaid, and the small wooden lid has a loop of rawhide for a handle. The sides of the box are etched with two parallel lines connecting a series of circles and dots.

A square wooden box from Nulukhtulogumut (figure 2, plate LXXXVI) has the bottom neatly fitted and a small, square lid near one end with a loop of sinew for a handle; around the sides and the top, passing over the middle in both directions, narrow strips of ivory are inlaid. The bottom of the box, the sides of the top, and the end farthest from the lid are painted red; the remainder is black.

A round-cornered box from King island (figure 1, plate LXXXVI) has square pieces of lead and bone inlaid around the sides and the top. In the top are two circular pieces of white bone, and white beads are inserted over the surface, except on the bottom. The lid is a thin piece of wood which slides in a groove and has a projecting thumb-piece at one end. A box very similar to this was obtained on Nunivak island; its surface is inlaid with strips and squares of brass and numerous white beads.

Another box from Nunivak island (figure 4, plate LXXXVI) is of wood heavily inlaid with cross-bands of brass. The lid, which is inlaid in the same manner, consists of a small, square, wooden cap fitted into the beveled edges of a small hole in the center of the top.

An oval box from Kushunuk (figure 5, plate LXXXVI) is made of birch-bark which is bent and the overlapping ends cut and interlaced. The top and the bottom are fitted with wooden stoppers, the upper one having a strip of beaver skin for a handle. Another box from Kushunuk (figure 7, plate LXXXVI) is of wood, oval in outline. The bottom and the cover are pointed oval in form, and the latter has a projecting thumb-piece at one end. It is painted black and pieces of white crockery are inlaid in regular series over the surface.

A large ivory snuff-box from Nubviukhchugaluk (figure 23, plate LXXXVI) is neatly made from a hollowed-out cross section of a walrus tusk. The top and the bottom are of wood and the surface is grooved horizontally and vertically.

SNUFF-TUBES

For taking snuff from the boxes, tubes made from the hollow wing-bones of geese and other water fowl are used; they are truncated at both ends, and vary in length from $3\frac{1}{4}$ to $5\frac{1}{2}$ inches. Frequently they are attached to the cover of the snuff-box by a rawhide cord, but sometimes they are carried separately. They are in general use from the Kuskokwim northward to Kotzebue sound, and the method of using them is the same as previously described.

The surface of these implements is sometimes plain, as in the specimen shown in plate XC, 1, from Cape Nome, which has merely a rude groove around the middle for the attachment of a cord.

Another tube (figure 2, plate XC) from Kushunuk, is also plain, and has wound around it, near one end, several turns of a smooth rootlet, the ends being tucked under to hold it in place. The specimen from Anogogmut (figure 4, plate XC) is likewise plain, but its ends are slightly reduced in size, and near the shoulder, around the tube, are three parallel incised lines.

A tube from the lower Yukon (figure 3, plate XC) has the ends slightly reduced and the sides beveled to form eight faces. Another, from Razbinsky (plate XC, 13), is encircled with smooth, parallel grooves extending in a regular series from end to end, producing a scalloped surface, the intervening ridges being neatly rounded. The specimen from Cape Vancouver (plate XC, 14) is similar to this, but has an incised groove around the top of each ridge.

Another tube (figure 5, plate XC) from Askinuk, has two broad grooves near each end, with three incised lines around the bordering ridges. Another specimen from the same place (figure 15, plate XC) is handsomely etched with lines, circles, dots, and cross patterns, and has numerous tridentate marks representing the raven totem.

The specimens illustrated in figures 6 and 12, plate XC, are from Chalitmut.

Tubes variously ornamented with etched lines are shown in figure 11, from the lower Yukon; figure 9, from Koñigunugumut; figure 10, from Askinuk; figure 7, from the lower Yukon, and figure 8, from Cape Vancouver.

BOXES FOR FUNGUS ASHES

For storing the wood fungus ashes, which are used with chewing tobacco, small boxes are made; these are usually rather tubular in shape and are made from a considerable variety of materials. Among the large series obtained are specimens made from sections of reindeer antler hollowed out and fitted with a cap of wood or antler at each end. Some are made from the butts of walrus tusks hollowed out and fitted with covers, and others are of wood or bone.

One of these boxes, from Hotham inlet (figure 7, plate LXXXVII), is made from a piece of walrus ivory and shaped something like the hoof of a reindeer. About its upper end is sewed a piece of cloth provided with a puckering string for closing it. The surface is plain, except for a series of circles and dots which extend around its upper border.

A box from Golofnin bay (figure 5, plate LXXXVII) is made from the butt of a large walrus tusk, and has a wooden bottom held in place by wooden pins set through holes drilled in the ivory. The sides of this box, which have been split, are repaired with small copper clamps and a sinew cord wound around the middle. The top is neatly made of walrus ivory, oval in outline, with a sunken shoulder to fit in the opening of the box. In the back are two holes through which a rawhide cord is passed and tied; the cord then runs up through a hole in the edge of the cover and along a slot on the top, then down again near the front edge and through a hole just below the top of the box, from which hangs its free end. By the use of this simple contrivance the cover can be raised or closed without danger of dropping it. This device for the covers of these boxes is in common use along the coast from the Yukon mouth to Kotzebue sound.

A specimen from Hotham inlet (plate LXXXVII, 4) is made from a piece of reindeer antler and has a wooden bottom held in place by snugly fitting the outline of the box. The top is a simple wooden piece with a short rawhide cord, with a knot in its end, projecting from the middle of the upper surface, by which it can be lifted out. The box is oval in shape, and has incised lines in pairs around the outside, dividing it into four nearly equal sections, in which are etched a variety of figures, including birds, mammals, boats, sledges, trees, waterfowl, and people. The etching is deep and is rendered very distinct by having dark-reddish coloring matter rubbed into the incised lines. On one side is etched the raven totem, with a circle and dot just in front, similar to the mark described as existing on a kashim cover at Kigiktauik, and undoubtedly intended to represent the same idea of the raven's tracks in the snow, with the mark left where it had eaten meat (see figure 116, page 325).

Number 64184 is a tall box of walrus ivory, flattened-oval in shape, also from Hotham inlet. Around the base on one side are etched the figures of six reindeer; on the other side is represented a house with an elevated cache and a man shooting at the hindmost of the deer. Around the upper border is carved a zigzag pattern, pendent from which is a series of raven totem marks. On another specimen of similar shape, from Razbinsky, on the lower Yukon, each of the borders is ornamented with a zigzag pattern and with raven totem marks extending thence toward the middle of the box.

Another box from Hotham inlet (figure 8, plate LXXXVII) is made from a piece of reindeer antler, with a knob on the side, and a wooden lid which is held in position by a cord fastened on one side and strung through holes in the cover, as in the specimen shown in figure 5 of the same plate. The surface of the box is covered with circles and dots, and has etched around the middle a series of conical summer lodges.

A long, cylindrical specimen from Sledge island (figure 9, plate LXXXVII) has the surface carved in a series of scallops and ridges extending around it. The bottom is fastened with four wooden pins. The box is provided with a wooden lid.

A box from Nunivak island (figure 3, plate LXXXVII) is of reindeer antler, with a wooden top and bottom. In slight relief upon its sides are represented the fore and hind flippers of a seal, with circle-and-dot patterns elsewhere along the sides.

Figure 12, plate LXXXVII, represents a box, from Kotzebue sound, made from a piece of whalebone. The bottom is formed of a rounded piece of the same material. On the surface are etched the arms and the breast of a woman with a curious fish-like head; on the back a small, square piece of iron is inlaid. A specimen from Norton sound (number 33199) has a zigzag border pattern on both ends and raven totem marks extending toward the middle.

A vase-shape wooden box from Kaialigamut (figure 14, plate LXXXVII) is four inches in height and is very regular in outline. It has a flaring rim and a wooden cover; the sides are set with small, round, ivory pegs symmetrically arranged, and around the rim are inserted four white beads. Another round wooden box (figure 11, plate LXXXVII) has a beveled edge, like the chime of a barrel, and the bottom is neatly inserted. In the center of the lid is set a piece of wood, convex in outline, on which is carved in relief a grotesque face intended to represent some mythological being. The eyes are formed by ivory pegs with large heads, and the sides of the box are ornamented with similar pegs, as well as with long, triangular pieces of ivory neatly inlaid near the upper edge, with the smaller ends pointing downward. The box is painted black around the sides, with a red border, and a black circle surrounds the cover. The face on the cover has a red forehead, a broad black band across the eyes, a red band across the mouth and cheeks, and a black chin. From each corner of the mouth extends a stout rawhide cord about four inches in length, which serves as a handle for raising the cover.

An oval wooden box, from the country south of the Yukon mouth, has a groove incised around its border in two directions. The top and the bottom are made of thin pieces of wood set into holes cut parallel to the sides of the box. The surface is inlaid in symmetrical patterns with small square, triangular, and round pieces of white crockery.

A square wooden box from Kushunuk (figure 13. plate LXXXVII) has the corners beveled and scored with a deep, vertical groove; another groove encircles the bottom of the box, which also has a circular groove on the center. The neatly fitted cover is a thin piece of wood, with an incised circle about the middle and a projecting thumb-piece which fits upon beveled shoulders on the rim at one side.

A round wooden box from the lower Yukon (figure 6, plate LXXXVII) is a little less than 5 inches in height and 2 inches in diameter. It has a deep incision around the base, with a flaring, rim-like bottom. The cover is fitted, like a stopper, into the top, and is incised to form a flaring rim; it has a knob on the top.

Another round box from the Yukon (figure 10, plate LXXXVII) has the middle part formed by a narrow band of bone bent and fastened with bone rivets and pegs. The excavated top and bottom are made of wood in the form of truncated cones with slightly projecting rims; they fit stopper-like into the bone circle. On the bone part are etched circles and dots with a continuous zigzag border. On the top of the box a round section of walrus tooth is inlaid in the center, and five smaller pieces are set at regular intervals around the beveled edge. On both the upper and the lower edge of the border are inserted small tufts of seal hair fastened with pegs.

QUID BOXES

Figure 16, plate LXXXVI, represents a small quid box, obtained on Nunivak island by Dr W. H. Dall. It is shaped in the form of a murre's head, the lower mandible forming a thumb-piece for raising the lid. The cover is formed by the jaw and throat; the eyes are outlined by incised circles; the nostrils consist of a hole pierced through the mandible in front of the eyes, in which is a sinew cord for attaching the box to the belt or for hanging it around the neck of the owner.

A quid box from Chalitmut (figure 8, plate LXXXVI) is flattened above and below, and is oval in outline, with one end truncated. It is cut from a single piece, with the exception of the cover, which fits into the top flush with its edges, on which a rawhide loop serves as a handle. Around the sides, near the upper edge, is a deep groove, in which nine ivory pegs are set at regular intervals. Six ivory pegs are inserted in the top and seven on the bottom along an incised line following the border. In the truncated end are five others, one at each corner and one in the middle.

A specimen from Kushunuk (figure 14, plate LXXXVI) is an oval box large enough to hold only one or two quids of tobacco. The top is rather more flattened than that of the preceding box, and has a stopper-like cover. Each end is carved to represent the features of some animal, incised lines marking the mouth, nostrils, and eyebrows. On its surface are several inlaid white beads, and similar beads represent the eyes and nostrils.

A quid box from Askinuk (figure 17, plate LXXXVI) represents a walrus, with projecting tusks, lying on its back. On its abdominal surface is the figure of a young walrus, which forms the lid and fits stopper-like into an oval opening in the larger animal. The flippers are carved in relief, and the eyes are represented by inlaid beads, those of the larger walrus being red, those of the young one white. One of the tusks of the larger animal is made of wood and the other of bone. Those of the smaller walrus are both of bone. Another specimen from Askinuk (figure 26, plate LXXXVI) is a curiously grotesque box, rather oval in shape, with two long, flipper-like projections on one end. The cover rudely represents a seal-head turned up to form the thumb-piece, while the neck and shoulders slope downward and have a stopper-shape base which fits into an oval hole in the top of the box.

A box from Anogogmut (figure 9, plate LXXXVI) is egg-shape in outline and flattened above and below. It is carved from a single piece of wood, except the stopper, which fits neatly into the top. Around the sides are inlaid beads and circular bits of crockery, and a gored pattern is cut in relief on the surface of the sides. This box, which is apparently made of birch, is a very neat piece of workmanship.

The handsomely carved box from Kulwoguwigumut (figure 13, plate LXXXVI) is rather flat on its upper surface and oval on the other sides; the cover, more or less square in shape, fits like a stopper into the upper surface and has a projecting thumb-piece about half an inch long. Holding this box with the cover downward it represents a grotesque figure of a porcupine; the mouth is deeply incised; the eyes, formed by ivory pegs, are in saucer-shape depressions with incised crescentic lines back of the eyes; the nostrils are indicated by small pieces of ivory. On the rear side of the figure are three round-head ivory pegs set in a triangle.

A circular box from Kushunuk (figure 22, plate LXXXVI) is formed of a band of spruce, with the overlapping ends beveled and fastened by some kind of gum or cement; the bottom is fitted into a groove in the rim and the top is also neatly fitted. The cap of the box fits stopper-like into the top and is slightly convex in outline, having the face of a man carved in low relief on its upper surface. The eyes and labrets are represented by round-head ivory pegs, and the mouth is a crescentic incision with a hole in the center, through which is fastened a rawhide loop, serving to lift the cover.

A round wooden box from Sledge island (figure 25, plate LXXXVI) is made in two nearly equal parts which fit together by an inner border on the under half. It is cracked on one side and bound together by a sinew cord.

A small wooden box from Chalitmut (figure 18, plate LXXXVI) has the form of a human head; the face is carved in relief, the eyes and labrets are represented by inlaid white beads; the mouth is deeply incised and crescentic in form. In a groove which extends around the face are set a series of round-head ivory pegs; the back of the head has a hole in which fits a cover with a projecting thumb-piece crossing a notch on the edge of the box. The face is painted red, the back of the head black, and the cover bluish.

Another box from Chalitmut (figure 24, plate LXXXVI) is carved in shape of a bear's head; it is painted black, with the open mouth and nostrils in red; one eye is formed by an incised circle with a black center, the other is an oval incision with a small fragment of glass set in the center to represent the pupil. The cover is ingeniously made so that the lower jaw of the open mouth serves as a thumb-piece by which it can be raised. There is a circular orifice in the head into which the cover fits, with a flaring rim, forming a continuous outline with the body of the box.

An oval wooden quid box from Kushunuk (figure 10, plate LXXXVI) has the top and the bottom neatly fitted; a groove is incised around the side and three grooves in the cover, which has a rawhide loop. Round ivory pegs are inlaid on all the surfaces; it is painted bluish and the grooves are red.

An ivory quid box from Unalaklit (figure 19, plate LXXXVI) has carved on the surface, in relief, the figures of four seals. A braided grass cord is attached for a handle, and the bottom is closed by a wooden stopper. The cover has been lost.

PIPES

The tobacco pipes used by the Eskimo on the mainland and adjacent islands of northern Alaska vary considerably in different localities, as shown in the series illustrated, but in general their remarkable likeness to pipes used in China and Japan is noteworthy, and suggests the source whence the patterns were derived. All of them have a small, cylindrical bowl, with a flaring top of greater or less breadth. The bowls are ordinarily made of stone, lead, or copper. They are set on the end of the stem and held in place by rawhide or sinew cord passed around the stem or through holes pierced in it.

Exceptions to this style are found in some pipes from Kotzebue sound, Cape Prince of Wales, Cape Nome, and St Lawrence island, which are made with the bowl and the stem in one piece; but in general character they are similar to the others.

Pipe stems are usually of wood, with a mouthpiece of bone or ivory, although sometimes the wood itself is rounded to serve this purpose, or it may be tipped with an empty brass or copper cartridge shell, with a hole bored in the head. On Norton sound and in the Yukon district the stems are made usually of two pieces of wood, hollowed out and lashed together with a rawhide cord, so that they can be separated to obtain the nicotine, which is removed occasionally and mixed with the chewing tobacco.

On the coast of Bering strait and at Cape Nome, Port Clarence, Cape Prince of Wales, Sledge island, and Kotzebue sound, the pipes, which are made in one piece, have small, door-like pieces fitted neatly

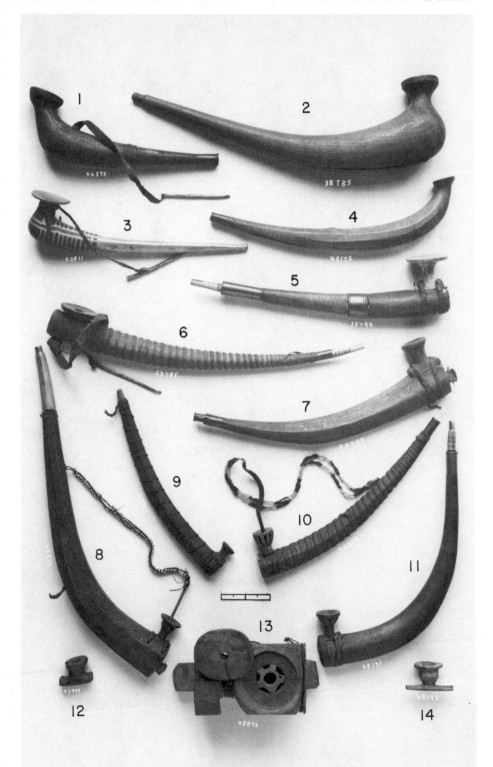

PIPES AND PIPE MOLD (ONE-FOURTH)

in the lower part of the stem, which can be removed at will to enable the owner to clean out the accumulated nicotine. Each pipe is usually provided with a small metal implement, which is used for cleaning the bowl and for tamping the tobacco; it is attached to the stem by a string or band of beads, or sometimes by a strip of tanned rawhide.

In addition to those described, there are handsomely ornamented pipes made of ivory, with metal bowls. These are not very numerous, but were seen at widely separated localities from the Yukon mouth northward through Bering strait to Kotzebue sound. They are of the ordinary type, but have a narrow stem, beveled on four sides, and are handsomely ornamented with etched scenes, illustrating native customs and life, similar in general style to the etchings on drill bows.

Figure 13, plate LXXXVIII, represents a wooden mold used by the Eskimo for casting the wide-mouth leaden bowls for their pipes. It was obtained at St Michael. It consists of five pieces; the two side pieces in which the shape of the pipe is excavated are held together by sinew cords in notches at each end; below a square stick forms the base, on which stands a small, upright. round stick to form the hole in

FIG. 94—Pipe from Kotzebue sound (about ¼).

the bottom of the bowl, on the inside of which is a ring of wood with five spoke-like projections reaching to the edge of the mold, which serves to produce the pattern that is seen on the bowls of many of the pipes. A round wooden cover fits snugly over the top of the mold, which has a round hole in the center through which the molten lead is poured.

From among the large number of pipes obtained from widely separated localities, the following specimens have been selected for illustration as representing the principal varieties found among them:

A pipe from Kotzebue sound (figure 94) is a huge affair, very heavy and clumsy. The wooden stem, 18 inches in length and 3 inches in diameter near the bowl, is beveled to form eight sides, and has two neatly fitted square tablets, about 4½ inches long, fitted into its lower side; these have a projection on one end to enable them to be lifted out for the purpose of extracting the accumulated nicotine. The bowl of the pipe is of lead, and several roughly oval pieces of the same metal are inlaid on the stem near the bowl; the mouthpiece is a tapering tube of lead about 2½ inches in length.

A wooden pipe from Cape Prince of Wales (figure 4, plate LXXXVIII) is cut from a single piece, the slightly flaring bowl being lined with tin, and an empty cartridge shell is fitted on the end of the stem for a mouthpiece. The lower end of the stem has three long pieces of wood fitted into openings to permit the removal of the nicotine from the interior. Fragments of a large blue bead are inlaid on the stem.

The pipe from Cape Nome (figure 1, plate LXXXVIII) is somewhat similar to the preceding, but the end of the stem is made in a separate piece, fitted into the larger part by a tapering joint, and wrapped with rawhide cord; a copper cartridge shell forms the mouthpiece. The underside of the pipe has a long oval piece of wood set in an opening, the rear end of which is guarded by a strip of tin, having its two ends inserted in the wood and fitted against the curve of the surface. An iron picker about three inches in length is fastened to the stem by a strip of rawhide. This picker is neatly made, with one end bent over against a notch in the stem, forming an eye for the strap; the lower end is octagonal and has a chisel-shape tip.

A pipe from Sledge island (figure 2, plate LXXXVIII) is very similar to the preceding. The bowl forms a part of the stem and is lined with lead; on the underside of the stem, near the bowl, is inserted a long, narrow piece of wood, to cover a hole made for removing the nicotine, and a similar hole appears near the mouthpiece, on the upper part of the stem. The mouthpiece is made by shaping the tip of the stem to a rounded point, leaving a shoulder about one-third of an inch from the end.

The pipe from St Lawrence island (figure 3, LXXXVIII) is similar in shape to the preceding, but both the stem and the bowl are of lead. On the lower portion of the stem, next to the bowl, is an open pattern, in which are inlaid small pieces of wood; the bowl is fitted on the top of the stem, and held in place by a rawhide cord which passes around the enlarged end of the stem, the lower surface of which has the usual long, narrow tablet for covering an orifice.

A pipe from Unalaklit (figure 5, plate LXXXVIII) has a wooden stem made in two pieces, the rear section jointed to the forward by a shoulder and a long, cone-shape, beveled point, which is inserted in the other section and fastened by a ring of brass, the ends of which are united by copper rivets. The mouthpiece is a smoothly tapering piece of ivory fitted into the stem, the joint being surrounded by a broad copper ring. A plug of wood fits into the front end of the stem to permit the removal of the nicotine, for which purpose the joint in the stem is also contrived. The small cylindrical bowl is of lead with a broad flaring rim; on its base are two shoulders for securing the bowl to the stem by a rawhide cord, which is wound several times around the shoulders and the end of the stem and tucked under itself at each side.

The pipe shown in figure 11, plate LXXXVIII, is more strongly curved

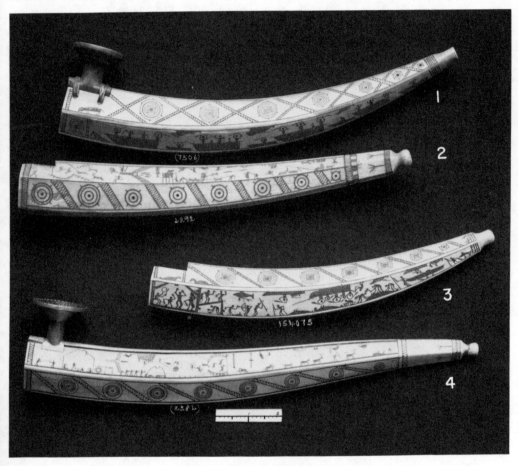

IVORY PIPESTEMS (ONE-THIRD)

than the preceding, with a tapering wooden stem on which is mounted a neatly made copper bowl, with openwork patterns on the flaring rim, and with shoulders for the cord by which it is attached to the stem. Two narrow tablets are inserted on the lower side of the stem, and the front end is excavated and the hole closed by a wooden plug; the mouthpiece is of ivory, neatly made and fitted into the wood, the joint being covered with a ferrule made from a brass cartridge shell.

The pipe from Cape Nome (figure 8, plate LXXXVIII) is somewhat similar in shape to the preceding and has a well-made copper bowl and a wooden stem, in which are two holes; through them a cord is passed and wrapped around shoulders on the bowl, making two or three turns on each side, the ends being fastened by tucking them under. In the front of the stem is a small wooden plug with a projecting end to enable the owner to remove it with his teeth; a small tablet is also fitted into a hole in the stem and provided with a tag of sealskin to facilitate its removal. The well-made mouthpiece of ivory is fitted into the wood and the joint is wrapped with sinew cord. A small iron picker is attached to the upper part of the stem by a string of beads about seven inches in length.

A pipe from Port Clarence (figure 7, plate LXXXVIII) is very similar in shape to the preceding, but its bowl is made from soft stone lashed on with sinew cord passed around the end of the stem. The mouthpiece consists of a small cartridge shell fitted into the wood, and over the joint is a copper thimble.

Figure 10, plate LXXXVIII, represents a pipe of the style generally in use about Norton sound and southward to the lower Kuskokwim. The wooden stem is split lengthwise and the two parts are held together by a continuous wrapping of sealskin cord, which serves also to hold the leaden bowl in position on the stem. The bowl is neatly made, with openwork around the flaring rim. The mouthpiece is a copper cartridge shell fitted over the end of the stem. An iron picker is attached to the stem by a band of beads made of six strings, separated by leather spacers and fastened by the lashing on the stem.

A pipe with a stem similar to the preceding (figure 6, plate LXXXVIII) is from Point Hope. A mouthpiece of walrus ivory is fitted to the stem by a copper cartridge shell. The flaring rim of the bowl is made from bituminous coal lined with a thin sheet of iron, and is set directly on the stem without the usual neck-piece between. An iron picker is attached to the stem by a rawhide strap fastened with a sinew cord.

At present pipe bowls generally are made of metal, copper and lead being most in use, but formerly stone bowls, similar in shape, were common, and a few specimens of these were obtained, principally from the vicinity of Bering strait.

Figure 12, plate LXXXVIII, represents one of these bowls, made of hard, olive-gray stone. It was obtained at Nubviukhchugaluk.

A bowl made of walrus ivory (figure 14, LXXXVIII) was dug from the site of an old village near St Michael. It is slightly different in pattern from either the stone or the metal bowls. It is very old, antedating the arrival of the Russians on the shore of Norton sound.

A wooden-stem pipe from Cape Prince of Wales (figure 95) has a small brass bowl. Pipes of this shape are occasionally seen between Norton sound and Kotzebue sound.

Figure 1, plate LXXXIX, represents an ivory-stem pipe with a stone bowl which was obtained at St Michael. The stem is diamond-shape in cross section, and has its surface elaborately etched. On one side a series of umiaks and kaiaks are pursuing a walrus; on the other side are reindeer that have just crossed a river, and a man in a kaiak has thrown a spear into the back of the last one as it emerges from the water, while at the farther end a man is shooting another with an arrow. On the remainder of the surface is a series of conventional designs.

Another handsomely etched ivory pipestem (figure 3, plate LXXXIX) was obtained at Norton sound. On the side shown in the illustration are various hunting scenes in which are whales, walrus, and seals, and

FIG. 95—Pipe from Cape Prince of Wales (½).

a man is shooting with a bow and arrow just in front of a kashim in which people are dancing to the music of a drum.

The handsomely etched pipestem shown in plate LXXXIX, 2, was obtained in Kotzebue sound by Lieutenant Stoney. It has the raven totem marks near the mouthpiece, and a variety of hunting and other scenes of Eskimo life, besides various conventional designs, over its surface. Another handsome pipe (figure 4, plate LXXXIX) was also obtained at the same place by Lieutenant Stoney. The leaden bowl has an old clock-wheel inlaid in the top of the flaring rim. Like the preceding, the stem has the raven totem mark near the mouthpiece, and is elaborately etched with scenes from the life of the people, among which are the hunting and trapping of game and fish, dancing in the kashim, and playing football.

TOBACCO BAGS

With the pipes are carried small, round-bottom tobacco bags, made from various kinds of ornamental fur or skin, the borders often having handsome patterns formed by different colored skins, fur, or beadwork tassels. The top is generally bordered by strips of fur of the wolverine, mink, or other animal, or sometimes by a band of ornamental needlework.

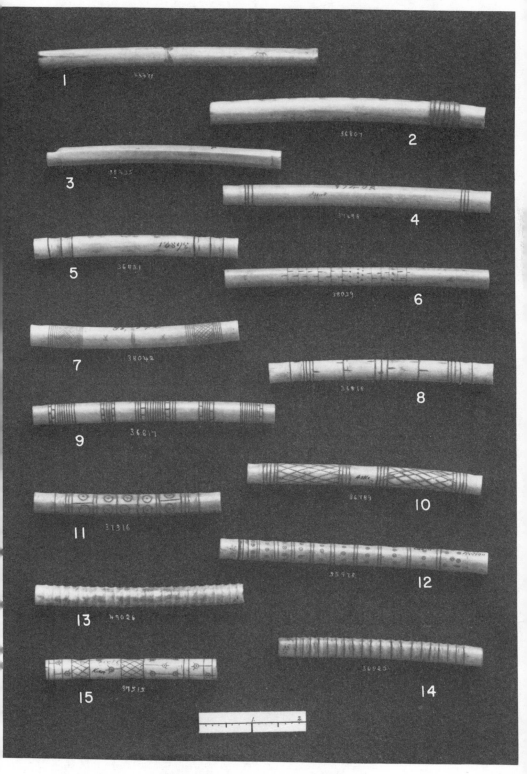

SNUFF TUBES (ABOUT NINE-SIXTEENTHS)

Figure 2, plate LXXXVII, represents one of these bags, which was obtained at Paimut, on the lower Yukon. It is about 10 inches deep, and is intended for carrying the pipe, tobacco, flint, steel, and tinder. The back is of winter reindeer skin, with the hair cut close; the front is of the skin of Parry's marmot; around the lower edge and near the upper border are sewed strips of wolverine skin. The lower two-thirds of the bag is ornamented by a pattern of white-hair deerskin with two narrow strips of black skin welted in the seams, and a row of small tufts of red worsted spaced around at regular intervals. The mouth of the bag is surrounded by pattern work of white and dark threads on narrow strips of yellow and black skin, the extreme edge being bound with calico.

A similar bag, of nearly the same size and shape (number 48136), was obtained at Cape Darby. As is usual in all these bags, the bottom is rounded and the top straight. The lower two-thirds is fringed with a narrow strip of mink skin, inside which is a pattern made with strips of white reindeer skin, with narrow strips of black skin welted into the seams, and two series of small red worsted tags spaced all around. The border of the bag is of white, parchment-like sealskin, and the string for closing it is of the same material.

Figure 1, plate LXXXVII, represents a smaller bag of the same shape, but with less ornamentation. It is 5½ inches deep, and is made of deer-skin, which is worn nearly bare of hair by use. A band of skin is sewed around the mouth and little strings of red and white beads, about an inch in length, hang in pairs around the lower border and sides, each string having pendent from it a small tuft of mink fur.

HOUSE-LIFE AND SOCIAL CUSTOMS

THE KASHIM

Among the Eskimo in every village of the Alaskan mainland and the islands of Bering strait the *kashim* is the center of social and religious life. In it every man has a recognized place according to his standing in the community, and it is also the common sleeping place for the men. The women and the children live in houses apart and the men sleep with their families only occasionally.

When a new kashim is to be built the villagers of Norton sound make a song of invitation to people of the same tribe living in neighboring places, which is learned by one of the young men, who is then sent to invite the guests. The messenger goes to the designated village, where he enters the kashim and during a dance sings his song of invitation to both men and women. When an invitation of this kind is given all respond and join in building the new kashim. This is said to produce friendly feeling between the neighboring places, which will render them successful in their hunting.

The men are nearly always to be found in the kashim when in the village, this being their general gathering place, where they work on tools or implements of the chase, or in preparing skins.

Dances and festivals of all kinds are held in this building, and there the shamans perform some of their most important ceremonies. The old men gather there and repeat the traditions of their fathers. The younger ones are thus instructed and become familiar with the tales and wisdom of the elders.

It is the usual place for the reception of guests; and there is scarcely an occurrence of note in the life of an Eskimo man which he can not connect with rites in which the kashim plays an important part. This is essentially the house of the men; at certain times, and during the performance of certain rites, the women are rigidly excluded, and the men sleep there at all times when their observances require them to keep apart from their wives.

Games are played there in winter by men and boys, and twice or three times a day food is brought by the women from the surrounding houses. Unmarried men sleep there at all times, as they have no recognized place elsewhere, except as the providers of food for their parents or other relatives dependent on their exertions. The sleeping place, near the oil lamp which burns at the back of the room opposite the summer entrance, is the place of honor, where the wise old men sit with the shamans and best hunters. The place near the entrance on the front side of the room is allotted to the worthless men who are poor and contribute nothing to the general welfare of the community, also to orphan boys and friendless persons.

The first time a child is taken into a kashim in the village of its parents, the latter present a gift to each person present at the time as a propitiatory offering and to secure the good will of their neighbors. A similar custom is observed by all strangers arriving at the village; they are required to dance and sing a little and, if on an ordinary journey, are supposed to make presents according to their means.

All messengers who reach villages for the purpose of announcing a festival or an invitation to other observances in their own town, deliver their message in the form of a song while dancing in the kashim.

In the summer of 1879 a party of Eskimo from East cape, Siberia, and the Diomede islands in Bering strait, came to St Michael. On their arrival they sang and danced in the kashim, making offerings to the people. The songs and dances were very similar to those I had seen performed on Sledge island in honor of the fur trader and myself during our winter visit to that place.

At the time of this visit we entered the kashim and gave the headman some tobacco to distribute among the men present and some needles for the women. These he divided among them, and afterward the men who took part in the dance as representatives of the community gave us each a small present, which was considered as establishing friendly feeling between us, extending the privilege of the kashim, and as a testimony of the good will of the inhabitants.

South of the Yukon the fur traders make a practice of complying with this custom of giving presents whenever they visit a village for the first time, and at St Michael we did the same whenever we were invited to attend the first autumnal festival; but the Eskimo do not expect the white men to dance and sing, as would be obligatory with their own people.

The presents are always handed to the headmen of the village, who divide and distribute them among their fellow townsmen. All guests whom it is desired to honor are given seats on the side of the kashim where the old men of the village sit. If that side of the kashim chances to be fully occupied, some of the men make room for their guests. At a village near the head of Norton sound I was given the usual place of honor in the kashim, and when the women brought in food a dish of boiled seal intestines was presented to me as a special delicacy.

The observance of giving presents and of placing the old men and the guests at the head of the kashim is customary also among the Tinné of the Yukon, who have adopted these customs from the Eskimo.

The men usually wear no clothing while in the kashim, but this being the custom it does not excite the slightest notice. The women frequently sit upon the floor by their relatives until the latter have finished their repast, or sometimes leave after delivering the food and return later to remove the empty dishes. During festivals, dances, and other ceremonies the women gather in the kashim as spectators and sometimes take part in the performances.

SWEAT BATHS

In these buildings sweat baths are taken by men and boys at intervals of a week or ten days during the winter. Every man has a small urine tub near his place, where this liquid is saved for use in bathing. A portion of the floor in the center of the room is made of planks so arranged that it can be taken up, exposing a pit beneath, in which a fire of drift logs is built. When the smoke has passed off and the wood is reduced to a bed of coals, a cover is put over the smoke hole in the roof and the men sit naked about the room until they are in profuse perspiration; they then bathe in the urine, which combines with the oil on their bodies, and thus takes the place of soap, after which they go outside and pour water over their bodies until they become cool. While bathing they remain in the kashim with the temperature so high that their skin becomes shining red and appears to be almost at the point of blistering; then going outside they squat about in the snow perfectly nude, and seem to enjoy the contrasting temperature. On several occasions I saw them go from the sweat bath to holes in the ice on neighboring streams and, squatting there, pour ice water over their backs and shoulders with a wooden dipper, apparently experiencing the greatest pleasure from the operation.

Throughout the region visited the men, while taking their sweat baths, are accustomed to use a cap made of the skin of some water fowl, usually the red- or black-throat loon. The skin is cut open along the belly and removed entire, minus the neck, wings and legs; it is then dried and softened so as to be pliable and is fastened together at the neck in such a way that it can be worn on the head. Owing to the intense heat generated in the fire pit, the bathers, who are always males, are obliged to use respirators to protect their lungs. These are made of fine shavings of willow or spruce bound into the form of an oblong pad formed to cover the mouth, the chin, and a portion of the cheeks. These pads are convex externally and concave within; crossing the concave side is a small wooden rod, either round or square, so that the wearer can grasp it in his teeth and thus hold the respirator in position.

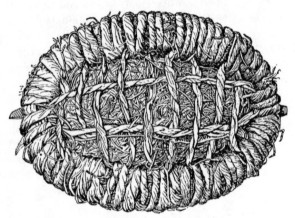

FIG. 96—Respirator, front view (½).

Some of the respirators are made of shavings bound together at each end by a few strands of the same material and furnished with a wooden holder. Others are more elaborately made, as in the example from Shaktolik shown in figure 96. This is a little over 5 inches in length and 4 inches broad, and is made of fine wood shavings; it is smoothly oval in outline, with the border rounded by means of a rope-like band of shavings tightly wound with a cord made of the same material. Inclosed within this oval ring is a soft mass of shavings held in position by a loosely twisted cord made of the same. On the inner side the shavings are packed loosely and held in position by the rod or mouthpiece which crosses the pad horizontally.

DWELLING HOUSES

The dwelling houses are the domain of the women. From one to three families may occupy the platforms in the single room which the house contains, but each is quite separate and independent in all of its domestic arrangements. Each woman who is the head of a family has an oil lamp beside her sleeping bench where she sews or carries on her household work. Her own cooking utensils and wooden dishes for food, together with the stock of seal oil, dried salmon, and other articles of domestic economy, are kept at one side of the platform or in a corner of the room devoted to this purpose.

When the time approaches for the preparation of a meal, a fire is built in the middle of the room and the food made ready, after which each woman places a quantity in one or more wooden dishes, takes it to the kashim, and sets it beside her husband, father, or whoever she has provided for.

CHILDBIRTH

During childbirth old women who are reputed to have skill in such matters act as midwives. Formerly, among the Unalit, when a woman was confined with her first child she was considered unclean and put out in a tent or other shelter by herself for a certain period. This custom is now becoming obsolete, but it is still observed by the Eskimo of Kaviak peninsula, by the Malemut, and by other remote tribes. In one case that came to my knowledge a young Malemut woman was confined with her first child at a village on the lower Yukon. It was midwinter, but she was put outside in a small brush hut covered with snow and her food handed her by her husband through a small opening. Despite the intensely cold weather, she was kept there for about two months.

When a child is born it is given the name of the last person who died in the village, or the name of a deceased relative who may have lived in another place. The child thus becomes the namesake and representative of the dead person at the feast to the dead, as described under the heading of that festival. In case the child is born away from the village, at a camp or on the tundra, it is commonly given the name of the first object that catches its mother's eyes, such as a bush or other plant, a mountain, lake, or other natural object.

The name thus given is sometimes changed. When a person becomes old he takes a new name, hoping thereby to obtain an extension of life. The new name given is usually indicative of some personal peculiarity, and, after a person makes a change of this kind, it is considered improper to mention the former one. Some of the Malemut dislike very much to pronounce their own names, and if a man be asked his name he will appear confused and will generally turn to a bystander, asking him to give the desired information.

Formerly it was a common custom to kill female children at birth if they were not wanted, and girls were often killed when from 4 to 6 years of age. Children of this sex are looked upon as a burden, since they are not capable of contributing to the food supply of the family, while they add to the number of persons to be maintained. When infants are killed they are taken out naked to the graveyard and there exposed to the cold, their mouths being filled with snow, so that they will freeze to death quickly.

Near St Michael I saw a young Malemut girl of 10 or 12 years,

who, soon after birth, had been exposed in this manner with her mouth
filled with snow. Fortunately for the child, this occurred close to a
trading station. By accident the trader found her a few moments
later, and by threats succeeded in making the mother take her back.
The child was afterward reared without further attempt on the part of
the parents to take its life.

One of the Eskimo told me that if a man had a girl not more than 5
or 6 years old who cried much, or if he disliked it for any reason, or
found it difficult to obtain food for the family, he would take it far out
on the ice at sea or on the tundra during a severe snow storm, and
there abandon it to perish by exposure.

A man at St Michael was in my house one day and told me in a
casual way that his wife had given birth to another girl, and added,
"At first I was going to throw it away on the tundra, and then I could
not, for it was too dear to me." This man was one of the most intelligent Eskimo I knew. He had been associated with the Russians and
other white men since early boyhood, and was one of the so-called con-
verts of the Russian church; yet the idea that a man was not perfectly
justified in disposing of a girl child as he saw fit never for a moment
occurred to him.

On the other hand, a pair of childless Eskimo frequently adopt a
child, either a girl or a boy, preferably the latter. This is done so that
when they die there will be some one left whose duty it will be to make
the customary feast and offerings to their shades at the festival of the
dead. All of the Eskimo appear to have great dread of dying without
being assured that their shades will be remembered during the festivals, fearing if neglected that they would thereby suffer destitution
in the future life.

In March, 1880, while on a journey to Sledge island, just south of
Bering strait, we were accompanied for the last 75 miles by the wife of
our Eskimo interpreter, who was a fine looking woman of about 30
years and was heavy with child. She went with us in order that her
confinement might take place among her own people, who lived on the
island. Notwithstanding her condition, she tramped steadily through
the snow with the rest of us day after day, and on the morning of our
arrival at the island she was in the room with us talking and laughing
when she became suddenly ill, went to her mother's house, and was
delivered of a fine boy in less than half an hour. Directly after the
birth a shaman came in and borrowed from me a drum and a small
ivory carving of a white whale, which I had purchased on the road.
The father explained that the image of the whale was borrowed to put
in the child's mouth so as to feed him upon something that would make
him grow up a fine hunter. The shaman beat the drum and sang for
half an hour over the boy to make him stout-hearted and manly. The
woman remained at this village a few days and then walked back the
75 miles to her home, carrying the child on her back.

PUBERTY

Among the Malemut, and southward from the lower Yukon and adjacent districts, when a girl reaches the age of puberty she is considered unclean for forty days; she must therefore live by herself in a corner of the house with her face to the wall, and always keep her hood over her head, with her hair hanging disheveled over her eyes. During this time she must not go out by day and but once each night when every one is asleep, but if it is summer the girl commonly lives in a rough shelter outside the house. At the end of the period she bathes and is clothed in new garments, after which she may be taken in marriage. The same custom formerly prevailed among the Unalit, but at present the girl is secluded behind a grass mat in one corner of the room for the period of only four days, during which time she is said to be ă′-gû-lĭn-g′a′-gŭk, meaning she becomes a woman, and is considered unclean. A peculiar atmosphere is supposed to surround her at this time, and if a young man should come near enough for it to touch him it would render him visible to every animal he might hunt, so that his success as a hunter would be gone. Should a considerable time pass after a girl reaches puberty and no suitor appear, the father accumulates a large amount of food and makes a festival for the purpose of announcing that his daughter is ready for marriage.

MARRIAGE

Among the Unalit when a young man sees a girl he wishes to marry he tells his parents and one of them goes to the girl's parents to ask their consent. Having obtained this, the suitor dresses in his finest clothing and goes to the bride's house with a new suit of garments, which he puts upon her and she becomes his wife. If the parents of either party have no children at home, the newly married couple go to live with them; otherwise they set up an establishment of their own, either building a new house or sharing one with some one else.

The Unalit frequently marry first cousins or remote blood relatives with the idea that in such a case a wife is nearer to her husband. One man said that in case of famine, if a man's wife was from another family she would steal food from him to save her own life, while the husband would die of starvation; but should a woman be of his own blood she would share fairly with him. The wife is considered to become more a part of the husband's family than he of hers. However, brothers and sisters, and step-brothers and step-sisters, do not intermarry.

From the lower Yukon to the Kuskokwim child betrothals are common and may occur in two ways. The parents of a very small girl who have no son may agree with the parents of several sons that one of the boys shall live with them and become the girl's husband. Again, a young boy may sometimes choose a family, containing a girl, in which he would like to live. In such case he takes with him his clothing and implements, besides a fine suit of clothes for his future bride, and leaving his own parents, goes to the people whom he has adopted, and transfers filial duty of every kind to his adopted father to the exclusion of his own parents. In such cases the girl is frequently not over 4 or 5 years of age. Sometimes such arrangements are made by a couple to take effect when the first girl is born.

In these child marriages when the girl reaches puberty both she and her husband are considered unclean, and neither of them is permitted to take part in any work for a month, at the end of which period the young husband takes presents to the kashim and distributes them. After this he enjoys the rights of other heads of families.

Men who are able to provide for them frequently take two or even more wives. In such cases the first wife is regarded as the head of the family and has charge of the food, but either may carry food to the kashim for the husband. A man may discard a wife who is a scold, or unfaithful to him, or who is niggardly with food, keeping the best for herself. On the other hand, a woman may leave a man who is cruel to her or who fails to provide the necessary subsistence. When a husband finds that his wife is unfaithful he may beat her, but he rarely avenges himself on the man concerned, although at times this may form an excuse for an affray where enmity had previously existed between the parties. An old man told me that in ancient times when the husband and a lover quarreled about a woman they were disarmed by the neighbors and then settled the trouble with their fists or by wrestling, the victor in the struggle taking the woman. It is a common custom for two men living in different villages to agree to become bond fellows, or brothers by adoption. Having made this arrangement, whenever one of the men goes to the other's village he is received as the bond brother's guest and is given the use of his host's bed with his wife during his stay. When the visit is returned the same favor is extended to the other, consequently neither family knows who is the father of the children. Men who have made this arrangement term one another *kin'-ĭ-g'un'*; each terms the other one's wife *nu-lĭ-u'-yŭk*, and the children of the two families call each other *kät-knun'*. Among people south of the Yukon the last term is sometimes used between children of two families where the man has married the discarded wife of another.

It is frequently the case that a man enjoys the rights of a husband before living regularly with the woman he takes for a wife, and nothing wrong is thought of it, unmarried females being considered free to suit themselves in this regard.

MORAL CHARACTERISTICS

Blood revenge is considered a sacred duty among all the Eskimo, and it is a common thing to find men who dare not visit certain villages because of a blood feud existing, owing to their having killed some one whose near relatives live in the place. On different occasions I had men go with me where they dared not go without the protection afforded by a white man's presence. In one place a man kept by me like a shadow for two days and slept touching me at night. The man who held the feud against him would come into the house where we stopped and sit for hours watching the one with me like a beast of prey, and the mere fact that my Eskimo companion was with a white man was all that saved him.

In another case a boy of 14 years shot and killed a man who had murdered his father when the boy was an infant. The duty of blood revenge belongs to the nearest male relative, so that if the son is an infant, and too young to avenge his father at the time, it rests with him to seek revenge as soon as he attains puberty. If a man has no son, then his brother, father, uncle, or whosoever is nearest of kin must avenge him.

In the case of the boy mentioned, the man who had killed his father lived in the same village with him until he became grown. One morning, as the man was preparing to hitch up his dogs and start on a trip, the boy's uncle handed him a loaded rifle and told him that it was time to avenge his father's death; the boy at once went outside and, taking deliberate aim, shot the man dead. Fortunately the dead man had no relatives, or it would have devolved upon them to retaliate by killing the boy.

Owing to this custom, a man who has killed another watches incessantly, and in the end his eyes acquire a peculiar restless expression which the Eskimo have learned to recognize at once. Several of them told me that they could always recognize a man who had killed another by the expression of his eyes, and from cases observed by myself I think that this is undoubtedly true.

The desultory feud existing between the Kotzebue sound Malemut and the Tinné of the interior partakes of the character of blood revenge, except that each side seeks to avenge the death of relatives or fellow tribesmen upon any of the opposing tribe.

Stealing from people of the same village or tribe is regarded as wrong. The thief is made ashamed by being talked to in the kashim when all the people are present, and in this way is frequently forced to restore the articles he has taken. An old man at St Michael told me that once a number of men took an incorrigible thief and while some held him others beat him on the back of his hand until he roared with pain, but that the fellow stole just the same afterward, and nothing further was done except to talk to him in the kashim. To steal from a stranger or from people of another tribe is not considered wrong so long as it does not bring trouble on the community.

The Eskimo living about the trading stations have adopted some ideas in regard to this matter from the whites. As a result of this, coupled with the memory of some wholesome chastisements that have followed theft at various times, the property of white men is tolerably safe in most places.

The only feeling of conscience or moral duty that I noted among the Eskimo seemed to be an instinctive desire to do that which was most conducive to the general good of the community, as looked at from their point of view. Whatever experience has taught them to be best is done, guided by superstitious usages and customs. If asked why they do certain things, they would almost invariably reply, "We have always done so." But in most cases an underlying reason could be obtained if they were questioned further, and if they had sufficient confidence in the questioner to express themselves to him freely regarding their deepest beliefs.

A curious innate distrust of strangers, or of people apart from themselves, was shown by the common demand for pay in advance when they were asked to do anything for white men. This was seen repeatedly among the Unalit, yet I do not suppose that in all their dealings with white men during recent years they had known of an instance in which one was employed without being paid in full.

In the same way they would hesitate and even refuse to give white men any articles of value to be paid for at another time. On the other hand, it was a constant practice among them to obtain credit at the trading stations, to be paid when they should have procured the necessary skins. In this, however, they were very honest, paying all debts contracted in this manner.

During my residence at St Michael I saw men trusted for goods who came from distant villages and were scarcely known by sight to the traders. This would often happen when the man lived in a village 100 or 200 miles away.

On one occasion an Eskimo came to St Michael in midwinter from near Kotzebue sound, bringing a mink skin to settle a debt which he had contracted with the trader the previous year. If this man had desired to do so, he need not have come and the trader would have had no means of obtaining his pay. This was but one of many such cases that came to my notice.

A curious part of this custom was that very often the same Eskimo who would be perfectly honest and go to great trouble and exertion to settle a debt would not hesitate to steal from the same trader. Among themselves this feeling is not generally so strong, and if a man borrows from another and fails to return the article he is not held to account for it. This is done under the general feeling that if a person has enough property to enable him to lend some of it, he has more than he needs. The one who makes the loan under these circumstances does not even feel justified in asking a return of the article, and waits for it to be given back voluntarily.

My interpreter, a full-blood Eskimo, once told me that he had loaned an old pistol the season before and the borrower had never returned it. I asked him why he did not ask for it, as they lived near each other in the same village. To this he replied that he could not, and must wait for the man to bring the pistol back of his own accord.

Begging is common only among those Eskimo who have had considerable intercourse with white men. This custom has evidently come about through indiscriminate giving of presents. From St Michael southward to the Yukon mouth, and thence up the river to Chukwhûk, the people have had more dealings with white men than elsewhere in the region covered by my travels. They were also the most persistent beggars that I met, and in some villages were so importunate that they fairly drove me away

The people not accustomed to meeting white men were little addicted to begging, and their manners were usually much more frank and attractive.

Hospitality is regarded as a duty among the Eskimo, so far as concerns their own friends in the surrounding villages, and to strangers in certain cases, as well as to all guests visiting the villages during festivals. By the exercise of hospitality to their friends and the people of neighboring villages their good will is retained and they are saved from any evil influence to which they might otherwise be subjected. Strangers are usually regarded with more or less suspicion, and in ancient times were commonly put to death.

During my sledge journeys among them I experienced a hospitable reception at most of the places, but on a few occasions the people were sullen and disobliging, apparently resenting my presence. At Cape Nome and on Sledge island during a winter visit I found the people extremely kind and hospitable.

At the time of our arrival at Sledge island the inhabitants were so destitute that their dogs had all died of starvation, and some of the people were living upon scraps. Owing to the lack of food for our dogs the trader and myself decided to return at once to the mainland, but the headman and several of the other villagers surrounded us, urging us to stay over two nights, in order that they might show their appreciation of our visit, and assuring us at the same time that they would find something for our dogs.

True to his promise, the headman went out among the villagers and the women soon came to us, bringing little fragments of seal meat, blubber, and fish, so that we finally gathered enough food for our dogs. We were shown to the best house in the place, and in the evening, when we had unrolled our blankets, the headman asked if we wished to sleep. When we replied that we did, he at once sent out all of the people who had congregated there with the exception of the owners of the house.

Stopping on Sledge island at this time we found a number of King islanders from farther north in Bering strait. They had come down the coast, visiting at various villages in order to live upon the people, as the food supply at their own home had been exhausted. They were a strong, energetic set of men, and, being bold and dishonest, did not hesitate to bully and otherwise terrify the more peaceable villagers into supplying them with food.

In the morning after my arrival at Sledge island a knife was stolen from my box of trading goods, and on making this known to the headman he sent out a small boy, who returned in a few moments with the knife, everyone apparently knowing who had committed the theft.

A little later one of the King island men, who was sitting close by me, and who had traveled down the coast with the trader and myself the previous day, tried to steal a small article from me but was detected in the act, and I at once ordered him to leave the house. To this he paid no attention. I then seized him by the right arm, and when he saw that I was in earnest his face grew dark with passion, but he did not hesitate to take up his mittens and leave the room. He did not return during the day, but that evening when the people had left the room and the trader and myself were preparing for bed, we noticed that the headman of the village was still seated by the entrance way on the other side of the room, although everyone else had left and the family occupying the house were asleep. Making down our beds upon the floor, we wrapped ourselves in the blankets. We had a suspicion that the cause of the headman's presence was due to the trouble that I had had with the King islander during the day, and I awoke several times during the night and found him sitting wakeful by the entrance hole. About 3 oclock the next morning I was awakened by a slight noise, and, raising my head cautiously, heard someone creeping in through the passageway. A moment later the head of the thief whom I had sent out and shamed before his companions the day before was thrust into the room. In an instant the watchful headman had taken him by the shoulder and spoke rapidly to him in an undertone. In a few minutes the King islander drew back and went away. The headman remained in his place until we arose in the morning. During the day we left the island and at a hut on the mainland encountered the same King islander, he having left the village immediately after going out of the house.

I have always considered that the watch kept by the headman during that night was all that prevented an attempt by the King islander to obtain revenge for my having offended him.

When we came to the first hut on the mainland, upon our return from the island, the Eskimo living there urged us to remain all night, and when we refused to do this he insisted on our going in to eat some crabs and dried fish with him before resuming our journey.

Near Cape Darby we were welcomed in a cordial way and made to join in a feast of freshly killed seal, and in villages on the lower Yukon I met the same hospitable treatment.

At some other places our reception was the reverse of this. In the large village of Koñigunugumut, near the mouth of the Kuskokwim, I was given a very surly reception, and it was almost necessary for me to use force before I could get anyone to guide me to the next village. On the contrary, at Askinuk and Kaialigamut, in the same district, the people ran out at our approach, unharnessed our dogs, put our sledges on the framework, and carried our bedding into the kashim with the greatest good will.

At King island, in Bering strait, the same spirit was shown by the people during the visit of the *Corwin*, when they insisted on having us enter their houses. Their attention sometimes became embarrassing, as in one instance when I was stopping in a house on the outer side of St Michael island. An old man came home from fishing in the afternoon and was given a small tray containing tomcod livers and berries, kneaded by his wife into a kind of paste. From his trinket box he took an old spoon fastened to a short wooden handle and began eating the mixture with great pleasure, until he suddenly remembered that there was a guest present. At this he stopped eating and, wiping the bowl of the spoon on the toe of his sealskin boot, gravely handed it and the dish to me, whereupon I declined them with equal gravity.

That morning I had fallen into the water while hunting, and as a consequence remained in the house all day to dry my clothes. At one time or another during the day nearly everyone in the village came to see me, and in every instance my hostess placed a few tomcods before the callers.

This practice of offering a small quantity of food to guests is considered to be proper among the Eskimo. Wherever I visited them, and any people of the same village came in in a social way, they were given food, unless everyone was on the verge of famine.

On October 3, 1878, I arrived at Kigiktauik in a large kaiak with two paddle men. As we drew near the village one of the men welcomed us by firing his gun in the air, and then ran down to help us land, after which he led the way to his house. The room was partly filled with bags of seal oil and other food supplies, and the remaining space was soon occupied by a dozen or more villagers, who came to see us and were regaled with the tea that was left after I had finished my supper, and soon after my blankets were taken to the kashim, where I retired.

A small knot of Eskimo were gathered in the middle of the room around a blanket spread on the floor, and were deeply interested in a game of poker, the stakes being musket caps, which were used for chips. Scattered about on the floor and sleeping benches were a number of men and boys in varying stages of nudity, which was entirely justified by the oppressive heat arising from the bodies of the people congregated in the tightly closed room. Two small seal-oil lamps, consisting of saucer-shape clay dishes of oil with moss wicks, threw a dim light on the smoke-blackened interior. In a short time the planks were taken up from over the fire pit, and a roaring fire was built for a sweat bath. The men and boys brought in their urine tubs, and wore loon-skin caps on their heads. Each one had a respirator made of fine wood shavings woven into a pad to hold in the teeth to cover the lips and nostrils, without which it would not have been possible for them to breathe in the stifling heat. When the wood had burned down to a bed of coals the cover was replaced over the smoke hole in the roof, and when the men had perspired enough they bathed and then went out to take a cold-water douche.

In the winter of 1880 I traveled around the northern coast of Norton sound and found many of the villages on the verge of famine. This was due mainly to the fact that they had eaten most of their supplies early in the season, trusting to the weather being such that they could take sufficient fish for their needs later on. As the winter turned out to be excessively severe, nearly all of the dogs along this coast were starved and the people were on very short allowance for a long time. Just north of Unalaklit I camped in a small hut 10 by 12 feet in area and 5½ feet high in the middle. Three families were living in this house, and including my party numbered sixteen adults who occupied the room that night. The air was so foul that when a candle was lighted it went out, and a match would flare up and immediately become extinguished as though dipped in water. After making a hole in one corner of the cover of the smoke hole the air became sufficiently pure for us to pass the night without ill effect.

At the village of Uñaktolik, just beyond the last place mentioned, I found a room 15 by 20 feet in area and 6 feet high, where we numbered twenty-five people during the night of our stay.

Wherever we found the people with a small food supply they were usually quiet and depressed; but at a village on the northern shore of Norton sound, where food was plentiful, everyone appeared to be in the greatest good humor.

During the summer food is more abundant than in winter, and the people are more cheerful at that season and inclined to give a heartier welcome to a stranger. The winter season being one of possible famine, there is generally a slight feeling of uncertainty regarding the future.

When we landed from the *Corwin* at a summer trading village on the shore of Hotham inlet, in Kotzebue sound, we were surrounded at once by two or three hundred people, all shouting and smiling good naturedly. They crowded about us with the greatest curiosity, and several at once volunteered to carry my camera and box of trading goods to one of the lodges. We walked along in the midst of a rabble of fur-clad figures and a great variety of strong odors which they exhaled. The dirty brown faces, ornamented with the huge stone labrets of the men and the tattooed chin lines of the women, were alive with animation; their mouths were wide open and their eyes glistened with curiosity and excitement. Before us moved a crowd of fat children, who tried to run ahead and look back at the same time, so that they were constantly falling over one another. Entering one of the lodges where the owner had carried my stock of trading goods, I proceeded to purchase such ethnological material as was brought me by the people.

The eagerness to see the strangers was so great that a dense crowd outside pressed against the frail walls of the lodge until the framework was broken in several places. At this the owner became offended and insisted on my giving him a present to pay for the damage thus done by his fellow-villagers.

At Cape Espenberg we landed at another summer village of five lodges, where some thirty people were stopping. Several upturned sleds and umiaks, and supplies of dried seal and walrus meat lay scattered about, and a freshly killed seal was lying under an old piece of sealskin.

Fastened to stakes in a circle about the camp were over twenty dogs, which set up a howl of welcome as we landed, their cries being joined by the voices of the children. The women and children ran down to the shore to meet us, and the whole party was very friendly.

At Cape Lisburne we found a camp of people from Point Hope. Nine umiaks were drawn up on the shore and braced up on one edge by sticks and paddles. Scattered about on the ground were sealskin bags of oil and large pieces of walrus and whale meat. Just back of the umiaks were the conical and round-top lodges, where the men and the women of the camp were walking about or sitting in the sun, engaged in sewing or in other work. These people were dressed in fur clothing, which was very ragged and daubed with dirt and grease, presenting an extremely filthy appearance. In one of the lodges an old woman, stripped to the waist, was rolling up a bed. Children played about the lodges with small, fat puppies, and numerous well-fed dogs prowled listlessly through the camp.

Between the lodges ran a clear, sparkling brook, entering the sea over the pebbly beach, and just back of the camp rose high cliffs, fronting the shore.

Before we left they broke camp. The umiaks were launched, oil bags, tents, clothing, meat, and supplies were bundled into them, and several dogs being harnessed to the towline from each umiak, they started up the coast, a single person from each umiak remaining on shore to drive the dogs.

The people of the islands and shore of Bering strait and Kotzebue sound are notorious among the trading vessels for pilfering. On several occasions the villagers of Cape Prince of Wales fairly took possession of vessels with small crews, and carried off whatever they wished.

While in the village at East cape, Siberia, the children were constantly trying to steal small objects from me and repeatedly attempted to take my handkerchief from my pocket. At Point Hope, while I was buying ethnological specimens in the village, one of the men suddenly began talking and demanded some tobacco, saying that he had not been paid enough for something which he had sold me. He assumed an air of anger and in a loud voice and with many gestures tried to bully me into giving him something additional; while he was motioning with his hands to emphasize his demands I noticed that he had concealed in his palm a small comb, which I at once recognized as having been stolen from my box of trading goods. I immediately grasped his wrist and wrested the comb from his hand, calling him a thief. His companions, who had undoubtedly seen him take the article, laughed at him in ridicule at his being caught, whereupon he slunk away without further word.

As with all savages, the Eskimo are extremely sensitive to ridicule and are very quick to take offense at real or seeming slights.

When among their own tribesmen in large villages they frequently become obtrusive, and the energetic, athletic people about the shores of Bering strait and northward are inclined to become overbearing and domineering when in sufficient numbers to warrant it. On the other hand, when traveling away from their native places in small numbers, among strangers, they become very quiet and mild-mannered. When we landed at Point Hope a great crowd of people came running down to the beach, crying, "ă-sĭn', ă-sĭn'," meaning "a present, a present," and caught hold of us on either side. They hung to our arms and clothing, continually asking for presents. Two men ran along on each side of the captain of the *Corwin*, begging for the gloves he wore, while others kept trying to steal some tobacco leaves which I was carrying under my arm.

The whalers give the people of this locality a bad reputation, as they do likewise those of Point Barrow. During the summer of our visit a whaling vessel was crushed by the ice pack just off Point Barrow, and the crew threw upon the ice a large quantity of provisions, clothing, and other articles before the vessel sank. The Eskimo at the point had seen the accident and with their dog sleds hurried out to the wreck where they at once set to work to loot everything they could get hold of. They ran aloft like monkeys and cut away the sails, which, with the sails of the small boats, they carried ashore.

They stole the clothes chests of the officers, the chronometers, charts, and the ship's books; the latter they tore up, and the next day, when the officers tried to recover some of their clothes, they refused to deliver them, and wore them about before the eyes of the owners. The wrecked crew went ashore and camped near the place occupied by the Eskimo, who were living upon canned meats and crackers from the ship's stores, and refused to permit any of the whalers to take any unless it was paid for with some of the small supply of tobacco which had been saved. As a consequence, the wrecked crew were forced to give up what few things they had been able to save and were forced to live for some time upon seal and walrus meat, while their Eskimo neighbors were feasting upon the provisions from the wreck.

Owing to the constant danger of being wrecked at this point and cast ashore among these people, the whalers fear to offend them and constantly make them presents. The Eskimo recognize this as being a sort of peace offering resulting from a feeling of fear, and they are therefore insolent and overbearing. When they came on board the *Corwin* they were sulky, and any slight contradiction seemed to render them very angry.

The Malemut at the head of Kotzebue sound are another vigorous, overbearing tribe. As among the Eskimo of Bering strait, they are quarrelsome and have frequent bloody affrays among themselves. The Unalit and Yukon people regard them with the greatest fear and hatred and say that they are like dogs—always showing their teeth and ready to fight. The Malemut are the only Eskimo who still keep up the old feud against the Tinné, and are a brave, hardy set of men. They are extremely reckless of human life, and a shaman was killed by them during my residence at St Michael, because, they said, "he told too many lies."

They buy whisky from trading vessels and have drunken orgies, during which several persons are usually hurt or killed. In 1879 a fatal quarrel of this kind took place on Kotzebue sound; the people said it was the fault of the Americans for selling them whisky, and the relatives of the dead men threatened to kill with impunity the first white man they could in order to have blood revenge.

They also had the reputation of being extremely treacherous among themselves, not hesitating to kill one another, even of their own tribe, when opportunity offered while hunting in the mountains—a gun or a few skins being sufficient incentive. As a consequence, hunters among this tribe would not go into the mountains with each other, unless they chanced to be relatives or had become companions by a sort of formal adoption.

One intelligent Malemut, who was a fine hunter, told me it was very hard work to hunt reindeer in the mountains, as a man could only sleep a little, having to watch that other men did not surprise and kill him.

One winter, while preparing for a sledge journey into the Malemut country, my Unalit interpreter begged me not to go, saying that the Malemut were very bad people. He was soon followed by the headman of the Unalit at St Michael, who repeated the injunction, assuring me that the "dogs of Malemut" would surely kill me if I went.

On the other hand, the Malemut despise the Unalit, saying that they are cowards and like children. When the *Corwin* anchored off Cape Prince of Wales in Bering strait, the people came off to us in a number of umiaks. They halted at some distance from the vessel and shouted, "*nú-kú-rúk, nú-kú-rúk,*" meaning "good, good," in order to assure us of their friendly disposition. When they were motioned to come along-side, they approached hesitatingly until some of them recognized me, having seen me during a visit they had made to St Michael the previous year. At this they began to shout vociferously to attract my attention, and immediately came on board. This lack of confidence was caused by the fact that these people had looted a small trading vessel the year before, and later in the same season, when they boarded a larger ship, they had been very roughly handled.

When the trading umiaks from the shores of Bering strait made their summer visits to St Michael, the people were always remarkably civil and quiet, in marked contrast to their manner when seen about their native place. At Cape Prince of Wales I went ashore in a small boat with a couple of men. On our way we met an umiak with twelve or fifteen paddlers; as they came near they turned and paddled straight at our little dingy, whooping and shouting at the top of their voices and coming so directly at us that I feared they would run us down. When within a boat's length the paddle men on one side suddenly backed water while those of the other side made a heavy stroke, causing the big umiak to turn as on a pivot and shoot astern of us. As we landed several hundred people ran down to meet us and as many as could get hold of our boat seized it along the sides and dragged it some 25 or 30 yards up the beach with us still seated in it; afterward, when I wished to go on board, it was only with the greatest difficulty that I could get one of them to help launch the boat.

As already noted, the people at Point Hope were boisterous and confident when we saw them at home, but later in the season when we met several umiaks with people from that place near Cape Lisburne, they came within about 150 yards of the *Corwin* and then all raised their empty hands over their heads, shouting "*nû-kú-rúk, nû-kú-rúk,*" until the officer of the deck called to them, after which they came on board, but were very quiet.

The Malemut extend their wanderings from Kotzebue sound even to Kuskokwim river and Bristol bay, but hardy as they are they have the same prudence in avoiding trouble while away from home. One case illustrating this came to my knowledge in connection with a party of them who were camping beside a village of Kuskokwim Eskimo. One of the Malemut became enraged at a Kuskokwim man, and hastened into his tent to obtain a weapon. Two of his companions went after him and tried to persuade him to give up his idea of revenge for the slight affront, but he refused to listen to them and went out. His two fellow tribesmen then took him, one by each arm, and walked along, still trying to dissuade him from his project. When he again refused to listen to them, the man on his right suddenly drew his long sheath knife and slashed him in the abdomen, completely disemboweling him, so that he sank down and died in a few moments. In speaking of it afterward, the man who had done the killing said that if they had been among their own people he would not have interfered, but added: "We were only a few among the Kuskokwim men, and if our companion had killed one of their men they would have killed all of us, and it was better that he should die."

It was not uncommon among the Eskimo, particularly about the shores of Bering strait and northward, for some man of great courage and superior ability to gather about him a certain following and then rule the people through fear; such men usually confirmed their power by killing any one who opposed them. In order to keep their followers in a friendly mood, they made particular effort to supply them with an abundance of food in times of scarcity, or to give them presents of clothing at festivals; they also try to secure the good will of white men whenever they think it to their interest to do so.

At Point Hope we saw such a chief, who had killed four men and had the entire village terrorized. The people were overawed by his courage and cunning, and hated him so much that a number of them went quietly to the captain of the *Corwin* and begged him to carry the man away.

During our stay at Point Hope this fellow was never seen without a rifle in his hand, and the people said he always carried it. During the trading on the *Corwin*, whenever one of the villagers was offered a fair price for one of his articles and began to haggle for a greater one, this man would quietly take the goods offered and give them to the other, who would then accept them without another word. I tried to procure his photograph, but he became very nervous and could not be made to stand quiet, until he was told that it would be very bad for him if he did not. As soon as I had taken his photograph he insisted on having me stand in the same position that he had taken while being photographed. Then he looked under the cloth covering the camera, and when he saw my image on the ground glass he appeared to be greatly pleased, seeming to think that he had thus counteracted any ill effect that might follow in his own case.

While stopping at a village near the head of Norton sound I was shown a man who was badly crippled, and my informant gave me the history of the manner in which he received his injury. He went out with three companions hunting reindeer in the mountains, back of the head of Norton sound. At night they made camp, and placing a spruce log under a light shelter, all lay down, side by side, using the log for a pillow. A man who entertained enmity against one of the party had followed them from their own village; in the night, while they were asleep, he crept up and fired his rifle into the head of the man upon one side in such a manner that it was in line with the heads of the others, and the ball passed through the heads of three of the men, killing them instantly. The other one sprang to his feet, but before he could collect his wits he was struck down by the clubbed gun in the hands of the murderer, and beaten until he appeared to be dead. The murderer then calmly returned to the village as though nothing had happened. In the course of the next twenty-four hours the man who had been beaten managed to crawl back to the village, where, after a long illness, he finally recovered, but was badly crippled for life. The one who had done the killing made no further effort to molest him, and no one attempted to avenge him for the murder of the other three men. The murderer and the survivor continued to live in the same village for years.

The Alaskan Eskimo, so far as I observed, have no recognized chiefs except such as gain a certain influence over their fellow-villagers through superior shrewdness, wisdom, age, wealth, or shamanism. The old men are listened to with respect, and there are usually one or more in each village who by their extended acquaintance with the traditions, customs, and rites connected with the festivals, as well as being possessed of an unusual degree of common sense, are deferred to and act as chief advisers of the community.

On the lower Yukon and beyond to Kuskokwim river such leaders are termed näs-kuk, meaning literally "the head." Among the Unalit Eskimo they are called äñ-ai-yu-kŏk, "the one to whom all listen."

These terms are also applied to men who gain a leadership by means of their greater shrewdness, whereby they become possessed of more property than their fellows, and by a judicious distribution of food and their superior force of character obtain a higher standing and a certain following among the people.

The man who has accumulated much property, but is without ability to guide his fellows, is referred to merely as a rich man or tú-gu.

All Eskimo villages have a headman, whose influence is obtained through the general belief of his fellow villagers in his superior ability and good judgment. These men possess no fixed authority, but are respected, and their directions as to the movements and occupations of the villagers are generally heeded.

In some cases a headman may be succeeded by his son when the latter has the necessary qualities. An example of this was the Eskimo named Täl-yá-lûk, the headman at Unalaklit, whose father had been one of the best headmen in that region.

In some villages, where trading stations are established, the traders are accustomed to make a sort of chief by choosing men who are friendly to the whites, and who at the same time have a certain amount of influence among their people. In order to have any standing in a position of this kind a man must be endowed with a greater amount of good sense and ability than the majority of his fellows. Usually these headmen have greater force of character than their associates and are either feared or liked by them; in either case their position is assured. If at any time another man shows superior ability or skill in promoting the welfare of the village, the older leader may be replaced by common consent.

Among the Malemut, as also among the Eskimo of Bering strait and the adjacent Arctic coast, an active trade is carried on. In this region it is common for the shrewdest man in each village to accumulate several hundreds of dollars' worth of property and become a recognized leader among his fellows.

The Eskimo are very jealous of anyone who accumulates much property, and in consequence these rich men, in order to retain the public good will, are forced to be very open-handed with the community and thus create a body of dependents. They make little festivals at which are distributed food and other presents, so that the people appreciate the fact that it is to their interest to encourage the man in his efforts toward leadership, in order that they may be benefited thereby.

In every trading expedition these men are usually the owners of the umiaks, and control the others, even to the extent of doing their trading for them, but the authority of such a leader lasts only so long as he is looked upon as a public benefactor. Such men make a point of gathering an abundant supply of food every summer in order that they may feed the needy and give numerous festivals during the winter. Sometimes they obtain a stronger influence over the people by combining the offices of shaman with those of headman.

Whenever a successful trader among them accumulates property and food, and is known to work solely for his own welfare, and is careless of his fellow villagers, he becomes an object of envy and hatred which ends in one of two ways—the villagers may compel him to make a feast and distribute his goods, or they may kill him and divide his property among themselves. When the first choice is given him he must give away all he possesses at the enforced festival and must then abandon the idea of accumulating more, under fear of being killed. If he is killed his property is distributed among the people, entirely regardless of the claims of his family, which is left destitute and dependent on the charity of others. This was done at the time of the killing of Ă-gûn-ă-pai'-äk, at Unalaklit. This man was a native of the Kaviak peninsula, on the coast of Bering strait, and had been forced to leave there after having killed a man, for fear of the dead man's relatives taking blood revenge. He had located at Unalaklit, and by his domineering character and ability as a trader became one of the most prominent leaders among the people of that region. He plotted to capture and rob the trading station at St Michael, and was prevented from carrying out the plan only by the timidity these people manifest when dealing with white men.

He constantly made trading voyages by umiak to Bering strait in summer, and in winter made long sledge journeys. Wherever he went he was accompanied by various hangers-on and was feared by the people he visited. During my residence I knew of several murders he had committed, some of which were very atrocious. In one instance he

18 ETH——20

wished to go to St Michael in his umiak during the summer, and being short of an oarsman he seized a woman living in Unalaklit and thrust her aboard the boat. The woman's husband was crippled so that he needed her services, and to prevent his wife from going he hurried down to the shore and tried to detain her. This enraged the headman, who drew his knife and killed the húsband on the spot, and, leaving him where he lay, pushed off and made the trip, the wife serving at the oar during the entire time. The following winter this man became extremely overbearing and very free with his threats toward various people, and at last threatened the life of his brother-in-law for having refused to join in the murder of some people in order to get their furs. The brother-in-law received information of this, and entering the man's house one night while he was sleeping, struck him on the head with an ax, killing him instantly. The man's son, a grown youth, was sleeping in the room and sprang up at the sound of the blow and was struck down by his uncle, who had just slain the father. After this occurrence the people of the surrounding villages felt greatly relieved. Yet, from that time forth, the man who had done the killing was constantly under the influence of fear from the expectation that blood revenge might be taken by relatives of the dead man.

The nephew of this man killed a fur trader on Kuskokwim river in a very brutal manner and was arrested by the fur traders at St Michael in the spring of 1877. His younger brother had been implicated in the murder, and as soon as Kûn'-û-gän was arrested he turned to the men who took him, saying, "Kill me, but do not hurt my brother." He kept repeating this, evidently thinking that the men would execute vengeance on him at once. He was placed on board a vessel and sent to San Francisco, where he was condemned to five years' imprisonment. There he was reported to have become an industrious workman and a favorite with the prison officials.

The men who aspire to be leaders make it a special point to put themselves as nearly as possible on an equal footing with white men, and become very sullen and angry if they are not treated with greater consideration than their fellows.

From Bering strait northward the rich man becomes known as *u'-mĭ-a'-lĭk*, or the umiak owner. During the time that war was carried on between the tribes the best warrior planned the attack, and was known among the Unalit as *mû-gokh'-ch-tă*. He, however, had no fixed authority, as each one fought independently of the others, but all combined in the general onslaught. An enemy was termed *um'-i-kĭs'-tû-gă*, or "one who is angry with me."

One born in another village is termed *a-um'-tă*. A stranger is *tûñ-ĭn'-û-hâkh'*, or "seen the first time." This term is also applied to strange objects of any kind. A person belonging to the same clan is recognized as a relative, *u-jo'-hŭk'*.

The Eskimo of Norton sound speak of themselves as *Yu'-pĭk*, meaning fine or complete people. An Indian, or Tinné, is termed *Ĭñ-kĭ'-lĭk*, from *ĭñ'-kik*, "a louse egg;" this is a term of derision, referring to the fact that the long hair of the Tinné is commonly filled with the eggs of these parasites. The Eskimo practice the tonsure, so that their hair is not so conspicuous as that of the Tinné. The Russians are termed *Käs-äk*, from Cossack; all other whites are known as *A-g'ĭl'-ûk.*

Among the Unalit, with the exceptions mentioned below, whatever a man makes, or obtains by hunting, is his own.

When a man dies some of his implements and other articles are placed by his grave and the remainder are divided among his children and other relatives, the former usually receiving the larger share. The wife generally makes the distribution soon after her husband's death, often on the day of the funeral. In some cases, however, if a man's blood relatives are greedy, they make the division among themselves, leaving very little for the family.

To the sons usually pass the hunting implements, while the ornaments and household articles go to the wife and daughters. If there are several sons the eldest get the least, the most valuable things being given to the youngest. Articles of particular value, such as heirlooms (*pai·tûk*), go to the youngest son, as does also the father's rifle, which, however, is used by the eldest brother until the younger one is old enough to use it.

When a man dies his sons, if old enough, support the family; otherwise they are cared for by relatives.

The most productive places for setting seal and salmon nets are certain rocky points which guard the entrances to bays. The right to use them is regarded as personal property, and is handed down from father to son. After the death of the father the sons use these places in common until all of the brothers, save one, get new places at unoccupied points. If anyone else puts a net in one of these places the original owner is permitted to take it out and put down his own. These net places are sometimes rented or given out on shares, when the man who allows another to use his place is entitled to half the catch.

The first deer, seal, white whale, or other kind of large game killed by a young man is brought to the village, and there one of the old men cuts it up and divides it among the villagers, without leaving a particle for the young hunter; this is done, they say, that the young man may be successful afterward in hunting. If a net is set for any particular game and something else is caught, the latter also is divided among the villagers in the same way, it being said that if this is done other animals of the same kind will come to the net. This is the practice when a white whale is caught in a seal net or a seal in a salmon net.

Seals killed with gun or spear may be taken at once to the village, but all seals taken in nets in the fall must be stored in a cache built of stones and covered with logs and stones. These storage places are built on the shore near the places where the nets are set. The cache

is called *kñ-û-nûk'*. If a seal carcass is taken from the netting place
or from the cache and carried to the village before the netting season
is over, it is claimed that all the other seals will know it and become
angry, so that no more will be taken during that season.

If meat is needed a piece of flesh may be cut from the seals and
carried overland to the village, but a person must be very cautious
and keep away from the shore. At the close of the netting season the
seal bodies may be taken from the cache and carried to the village by
water.

The idea that unexpected game is a kind of treasure trove is firmly
fixed in the minds of these people. On occasions when I sent men out
to shoot waterfowl and they chanced to kill a seal they always considered the latter their own property, although they were hired to hunt
and were paid for their time. In such instances if I obtained the seal
it was by paying for it in addition to the regular wages. Their invariable reply when asked about this would be: "You said nothing about
killing a seal, so it is mine."

On one occasion, while stopping for a short time in a small village
just west of Cape Darby, on the shore of Norton sound, I refused to
buy the ivory carvings and other ethnological specimens offered, telling
the villagers that I would return in a few days and buy the things they
had to sell. On my return I found the entire village was offended at
my having refused to buy their articles on the former visit, and not one
of them would trade with me.

As a rule the Eskimo sold their implements and ivory carvings at
prices fixed by myself and seemed to regard it as a great piece of sport
that anyone would be simple enough to purchase such objects. At
Sabotnisky, on the Yukon, the people took whatever I offered, and
laughed over obtaining such prizes as needles, buttons, tobacco, etc,
in exchange for such objects, saying that I was giving away my goods.

In large villages the people would frequently struggle to get within
reach of me, each striving to be first, saying that my goods would be
gone before they could get any of them. At a village on the lower
Yukon it was amusing to witness the absurd delight some of the natives
exhibited when I bought their carvings and other small objects.

About St Michael the children were always pleased to be employed
on little errands or jobs of light work, and they were eager to trap and
bring me mice and shrews for specimens. They were given in return
gun caps, matches, or ship's bread, and the deliberate gravity with
which some of them would decide what they would have for a mouse
was very amusing. They are very mischievous in a quiet way, delight-
ing in petty practical jokes on one another. One day I surprised a boy
10 years of age who was following close behind me mimicking my
motions, while his comrades stood at a safe distance greatly entertained by the performance.

The young men are cheerful, light-hearted, and fond of jokes and amusement. During my hunting excursions, whenever I had several young men along they were continually telling stories, joking, singing, etc. When in camp and during all-night festivals in winter I frequently heard them laugh at one another for being sleepy. At one of the bladder feasts a young fellow who could scarcely keep his eyes open replied to the sallies made at his expense by saying that he saw three of everything he looked at and accused his comrade sitting next to him of being unable to find his mouth with the food before him.

Among the furs offered us at Point Hope was the skin of an Arctic hare with the tail of a fox sewed upon it as a practical joke. After they had sold all of their valuable articles, they were persistent in offering worthless things, and would laugh heartily when these were rejected. The same men would return again and again, repeatedly offering something which had been refused, and seemed to be greatly amused each time.

They are quick to express their ideas by signs when dealing with people who do not understand their language. At Point Hope the men kept holding up their hands together in a cup-shape position, locking the palms and wagging their heads from side to side in a droll way to indicate that they wished to get some whisky with which to become drunk.

On the lower Yukon and southward there is a trading custom known as *pă-tukh'-tŭk*. When a person wishes to start one of these he takes some article into the kashim and gives it to the man with whom he wishes to trade, saying at the same time, "It is a *pă-tukh'-tŭk*." The other is bound to receive it, and give in return some article of about equal value; the first man then brings something else, and so they alternate until, sometimes, two men will exchange nearly everything they originally possessed; the man who received the first present being bound to continue until the originator wishes to stop.

The fur traders sometimes take advantage of this custom to force an Eskimo to trade his furs when they can get them in no other way. A fur trader told me of securing in this way from one man the skins of 30 mink, 8 land otters, 4 seals, and 2 cups and saucers; finally the Eskimo wished to give his rifle, but at that the trader stopped the transaction.

TREATMENT OF DISEASE

In treating diseases the most common method is for the shamans to perform certain incantations. There are cases, however, in which more direct methods are pursued; blood letting is commonly practiced to relieve inflamed or aching portions of the body. For this purpose small lancets of stone or iron are used. In one instance I saw a man lancing the scalp of his little girl's head, the long, thin, iron point of the instrument being thrust twelve or fifteen times between the scalp and the skull.

One of these lancets (figure 97) was obtained on the northern shore of Norton sound. It is a small, thin, double-edge blade, of hard, pale-greenish stone, an inch and an eighth in length, broadened at the butt,

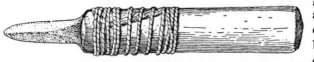

FIG. 97—Lancet pointed with nephrite (⅔).

which is inserted in the split end of a short wooden handle and wrapped tightly with a strong sinew cord. I saw other old instruments of this kind made of slate, but at present most of the lancets are similar in shape but are made of iron.

An aching tooth is extracted by placing the square point of a piece of deerhorn against it and striking the other end a sharp blow with an object used as a mallet.

On the islands in Bering strait I saw men using long-handle scratchers to relieve irritation caused by eruptions on the skin or by parasites. Figure 98 illustrates one of these implements which was obtained on Sledge island. It consists of a wooden rod about 17 inches in length, having a thin-edge ivory disk an inch in diameter fitted on one end. In the collection obtained in Labrador by Mr L. M. Turner, there is a specimen of a similar instrument.

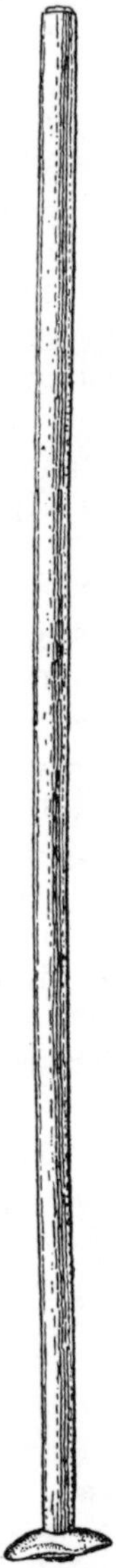

MORTUARY CUSTOMS

The burial customs of the Eskimo with whom I came in contact vary so greatly that I have given in detail an account of the observances noted in different localities, beginning with the Unalit at St Michael.

The following are Unalit terms used by the St Michael people:

Corpse .... *tŭ'-ko-mäl'-ŭ-g'ĭ-a* (dead one).
Spirit or shade.............. *tä-g'un'-ŭ-ghăk.*
Ghost, or visible shade...... *a-lhi-ukh'-tok.*
Grave .... *kuñ-u'.*

When a person dies during the day his relatives, amid loud wailing, proceed at once to dress him in the best clothing they possess, using, if possible, garments that have never been worn. Should the death take place at night, the body is not dressed until just at sunrise the following morning. Some of the male relatives or friends go out and make a rude box of drift logs in the usual burial place, which is a short distance back of the village. During this time the body lies in its place on the sleeping platform, with the oil lamp burning day and night close by, until the burial, while the relatives and friends sit about on other sleeping benches. When the box

FIG. 98—Back scratcher (⅛).

is completed, either on the same day or the next, the body is placed
in a sitting posture with the heels drawn back against the hips and
the knees resting against the chest; the elbows are drawn down
against the sides, and the forearms and hands are bent so as to clasp
the abdomen, the right hand and arm being placed above the left.
Figure 99 shows the position of the body ready for burial. It is then
wrapped in grass mats or deerskins and bound tightly with rawhide
cords. By means of cords the body is usually raised through the smoke
hole in the roof, but is never taken out by the doorway. Should the
smoke hole be too small, an opening is made in the rear side of the house
and then closed again. The body is taken to the grave and placed
upon one side in the box, below it being placed the deerskin bed of
the deceased, and over it his blankets. If the deceased be a man, his
pipe, flint and steel, tinder, and pouch of tobacco are placed in the box,
and, if a snuff taker, his snuff-box and tube. Then the cover of rough
planks or logs is put on and fastened down
with logs or stones. In case of a man, his paddle is planted blade upward in the ground near
by, or is lashed to a corner post of the box itself,
so that the relatives and friends may see the
ä'-hliñ-ŭk or totem mark, and thus know whose
remains lie there.

Fig. 99—Position of burial of
the dead at St Michael.

If the grave box is made of planks the totem
picture is usually drawn upon its front in red or
black, or sometimes the front bears the picture
of some animal which the father of the dead
man excelled in hunting. If the father took
part in a war party against the common enemy
of his tribe, then the figure of a bow is painted
on the box. Should this receptacle be of such
a nature as not to permit the making of pic-
tures upon its surface, they are drawn on a small piece of board made
for the purpose and fastened to the end of a stick five or six feet long,
and the latter is planted at the side or at one end of the box. In a conspicuous place on a corner post of the grave, or on posts set up for
the purpose, are placed the dead man's snowshoes, spears, bow and
arrows, or gun; upon the ground by the grave is laid his open work
bag, with all the small tools in place, and his kaiak frame is set
close by.

Should the deceased be a woman, her workbag, needles, thread, and
fish knife are placed beside her in the box. Her wooden dishes, pots,
and other belongings are placed by the grave, and to the corner post
are hung her metal bracelets, deer tooth belt, and favorite wooden dish,
and sometimes a fish knife. The markings upon the grave box, or on
the small board made for the purpose, are those of her family totem,
or illustrate the exploits of her father, as is done in the case of a man.

These customs, with certain variations, are still observed. At St Michael I saw a father's grave marked with his totem picture, while on the grave box of his son close by was the picture of the animal which the father had excelled in hunting.

When the grave with its various belongings is arranged, the relatives make small offerings of food of different kinds, and pour water on the ground beside it, after which all go home.

During the day on which a person dies in the village no one is permitted to work, and the relatives must perform no labor during the three following days. It is especially forbidden during this period to cut with any edged instrument, such as a knife or an ax; and the use of pointed instruments, like needles or bodkins, is also forbidden. This is said to be done to avoid cutting or injuring the shade, which may be present at any time during this period, and, if accidentally injured by any of these things, it would become very angry and bring sickness or death to the people. The relatives must also be very careful at this time not to make any loud or harsh noises that may startle or anger the shade.

In ancient times the Unalit of this vicinity exposed their dead on the open tundra back of the village, throwing their weapons and tools beside them. It was the custom to lay the body at full length on its back and plant two sticks about three feet long, one on each side of the head, so that they would cross over the face. The old man who told me this said that everyone used to be thrown on the ground in this manner, but he thought that it was from seeing the grave boxes made for the dead in other places that the Unalit had been led to adopt the present custom. The use of grave boxes undoubtedly came from the south, as it was observed that their greatest elaboration was found south of the territory occupied by the Unalit, while to the northward the Malemut still throw out many of their dead. My informant added that it was better to keep the dead in grave boxes, for it kept their shades from wandering about as they used to do; besides, it was bad to have the dogs eat the bodies.

If the deceased was a hunter, the totem of his father was usually painted on his grave box at the time of the burial, but if he was not a hunter this totem picture was not made on the box until the stake of invitation to the feast of the dead was planted by the grave the following winter. (See account of festivals to the dead.) If the person was disliked, or was without relatives to make a feast, no totem markings were put on the box. If he was a very bad man he was buried in a box, while food and water were offered to the shade; but no weapons or other marks of respect were placed beside the grave, no feast was made to his memory, and he was forgotten.

About eight miles from the village of Kigiktauik I saw the remains of a body with a sled. My Eskimo companions told me it was the body of a man who had died in the village from a loathsome disease, and the people had brought it out there and abandoned it without any attendant observances.

Among the Unalit the graveyard is usually quite close to one side of the village, generally behind it or on a small adjacent knoll. The illustration (figure 100) from a photograph taken near St Michael, will show the method of disposing of the dead in that vicinity.

During my residence at St Michael a shaman died, and the following notes were made on the observances that followed:

FIG. 100—Method of disposing of the dead at St Michael.

In consideration of the fact that the deceased had been a shaman, no one did any work in the village for three days following his death. The body, however, had been prepared and placed in the grave box on the morning that he died. The night following, when the people prepared to retire, each man in the village took his urine tub and poured a little of its contents upon the ground before the door, saying, "This is our water; drink"—believing that should the shade return during the night and try to enter, it would taste this water and, finding it bad, would go away.

During the first day after the death everyone near the village was said to be soft and nerveless, with very slight power of resistance, so that any evil influence could injure him easily; but the next day the people said they were a little harder than before, and on the third day the body was becoming frozen, so that they were approaching hardiness again.

On the evening of the second day the men in every house in the village took their urine buckets and, turning them bottom upward, went about the house, thrusting the bottom of the vessel into every corner and into the smokehole and the doorway. This, it was said, was done to drive out the shade if it should be in the house, and from this custom the second day of mourning is called *ă-hluñ'-ĭg-ut*, or "the bottom day." After this was done and the people were ready to retire for the night every man took a long grass stem and, bending it, stuck both ends into the ground in a conspicuous place in the middle of the doorway. They said this would frighten the spirit off, for should it come about and

FIG. 101—Position of burial of the dead on the lower Yukon.

try to enter the house it would see this bent grass, and, believing it to be a snare, would go away, fearing to be caught. On the third morning, before eating, every man, woman, and child in the village bathed in urine, which cleansed them of any evil that might have gathered about their persons, and also rendered their flesh firm, so that they were hardy and able to withstand the ordinary influence of the shade.

On the lower Yukon, below Ikogmut, the following customs were observed:

These people are very averse to having a dead body in the house, and the corpse is placed in the grave box at the earliest possible moment. This is so marked that the relatives frequently dress the person in the new burial clothing while he is dying in order that he may be removed immediately after death. After death the body is placed in a sitting posture on the floor; the knees are drawn up and the feet back, so that the knees rest against the chest and the heels against the hips; then the head is forced down between the knees until the back of the neck is on a line with the tops of the knees; the arms are drawn around encircling the legs above the ankles and just under the forehead. It is then tied with strong cords to hold it in this position and drawn up through the smoke hole in the roof and carried to the graveyard, where it is placed upon the top of an old grave box while one is being made for it. Figure 101 illustrates the position of the body ready for burial. When the box is ready, usually the next day, the body is placed in it upon a deerskin bed, while other deerskins or cloth covers are thrown over it. All of the small tools of the deceased are placed in the box and a cover of rough planks is fastened down over the top with wooden pegs. Just before the body is placed in the box the cords that bind it are cut, in order, they say, that the shade may return and occupy the body and move about if necessary.

The grave boxes in this vicinity are made of hewn slabs or planks, squared at the ends, and supported by a stout central piece from below, and frequently with four corner posts, which extend some distance above the box. None of the relatives touch the body, this work being done by others. The housemates of the deceased must remain in their accustomed places in the house during the four days following the death, while the shade is believed to be still about. During this time all of them must keep fur hoods drawn over their heads to prevent the influence of the shade from entering their heads and killing them. At once, after the body is taken out of the house, his sleeping place must be swept clean and piled full of bags and other things, so as not to leave any room for the shade to return and reoccupy it. At the same time the two persons who slept with him upon each side must not, upon any account, leave their places. If they were to do so the shade might return and, by occupying a vacant place, bring sickness or death to its original owner or to the inmates of the house. For this reason none of the dead person's housemates are permitted to go outside during the four days following the death. The deceased person's nearest relatives cut their hair short along the forehead in sign of mourning.

FIG. 102—Grave boxes, Yukon delta.

During the four days that the shade is thought to remain with the body none of the relatives are permitted to use any sharp edge or pointed instrument for fear of injuring the shade and causing it to become angry and to bring misfortune upon them. One old man said that should the relatives cut anything with a sharp instrument during this time, it would be as though he had cut his own shade and would die.

Near the upper end of the Yukon delta is a small graveyard in which was seen a newly made box placed over an old one made for a member of the same family. This new box was made of heavy hewn planks, painted red, and supported about a foot above the old one by the same set of corner posts, as shown in figure 102.

To the pole erected before this grave were attached a cup, a spoon and a kaiak paddle, and a pair of umiak oars were placed against the box, which contained the body of a boy, the son of an old man in the village, who, it was said, was prohibited from doing any work for three moons following the death of his son.

At each end of the boxes at this place was erected a post, to the top of which was fastened a cross-board bearing some articles of ornament or of value belonging to the deceased. The boxes were all supported two feet or more above the ground by corner posts, which extended several feet above their tops.

At Razbinsky the graveyard is placed immediately behind the kashim in the winter village, so near that the odor arising from the bodies becomes almost unbearable in the warm weather when spring opens. These grave boxes are well made and are ranged roughly in rows, forming an irregular square. At the time of my visit there were about thirty of them, some of which are shown in plate XCI.

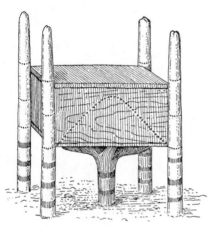

FIG 103—Burial box at Razbinsky.

They were made of hewn planks about $3\frac{1}{2}$ by 3 feet in horizontal measurement and 2 feet deep, and were raised about two feet from the ground on corner posts, with a fifth support formed by the butts of small trees so planted that the spreading roots upturned supported the bottoms of the boxes, which were all painted red, and the posts were banded with the same color. The fronts of the boxes were ornamented with rows of bone pegs, as shown in the illustration (figure 103), and the corner posts were also ornamented in the same manner.

On some of the boxes were rude figures in black of a man shooting with bow and arrow at a deer or bear. The number and arrangement of the bone pegs varied, but the general plan was the same.

At Razbinsky most of the utensils of the deceased were placed in the boxes with the bodies. A few old reindeer horns and some posts bearing invitation effigies for the feast to the dead were the main objects to be seen about these boxes. Beside some of them, however, were hewn boards five or six feet long, supported six or seven feet from the ground on two posts, and bearing the figures of skins of animals and other objects on their fronts.

At the village of Starikwikhpak, just below Razbinsky, were two grave boxes almost exactly like those just described. On the front of one of them was a large figure in black, representing a man shooting with bow and arrow at a reindeer.

GRAVEYARD AT RAZBINSKY

At Kushunuk, near Cape Vancouver, the dead are placed with the knees drawn up against the chest, and the wrists are crossed and tied to the ankles in front. They are then buried in rude boxes, made of small drift logs, which are built on the ground near the village. About and upon the boxes are placed the tools and weapons of the deceased.

Tununuk village, at Cape Vancouver, faces the sea; on a small flat and about 20 yards in front of the entrance to the kashim, between it and the sea, were three large wooden posts, representing human figures, and several subordinate posts. They were of drift logs, 6 or 7 feet high by 12 to 15 inches in diameter, without bark, and not carved except on the top. These were ranged in a row parallel to the beach and across the front of the kashim. The top of each post was carved to represent a human head and neck. Commencing on the left, as I faced them, the following account describes them in succession:

The first post had its head covered with the remains of a fur hood, such as is worn by the people of this vicinity. The mouth and eyes

FIG. 104—Memorial images at Cape Vancouver.

were made of ivory, inlaid in the wood; from each shoulder of the figure a walrus tusk curved outward and upward to represent arms. These tusks were notched above to form places for hanging objects; that on the right side bore suspended from it an ivory-handle fish knife, and near the body were several iron bracelets. From the tip of the left arm hung a small wooden dish, and nearer the body were more iron bracelets. About where the hips should be was another pair of walrus tusks inserted parallel to the upper ones, representing legs. The post was painted in broad, alternating bands of colors, commencing at the head and going down in the following order, namely, red, white, black, white, red. To the left of this was a plain, upright post, to which hung an iron bucket, and on the ground near its base was a wooden box containing a woman's workbag and outfit of clothing.

The next large post represented a man, whose mouth and eyes were of inlaid ivory, and with tusks for arms and legs, as in the post first described. Two large bead labrets were at the corners of the mouth.

At the base of this post a bow and quiver of arrows were fastened. Just behind it was a box full of man's clothing and small tools.

On a small post to the right there was a wooden model of an umiak, and on another post to the left were five wooden models of kaiaks. Close to these last was another post, bearing on the board across its top nine images of the large hair seal. A fourth post bore a model of a kaiak, in which was a man holding a spear poised ready to cast. These symbols were explained to me as follows: The umiak and kaiak models showed that the person represented had made and owned these boats. The nine hair seals were the result of his greatest day's hunting, and the kaiak with the man seated in it showed that he had been a hunter at sea.

The third large post was very old and dilapidated from long exposure. Its mouth, eyes, and arms, like the others, were of ivory, but it was not provided with legs. On two posts close by were models of a large hair seal and a reindeer, with a third post to the right bearing the figure of a man in a kaiak with poised spear. This man was said to have been a good hunter both on land and at sea, especially at sea.

These posts (figure 104) were said to represent people who had been lost and their bodies never recovered. The first post was for a woman who had been buried by a landslide in the mountains, while the men were drowned at sea. I was told that among the people of this and neighboring villages, as well as of the villages about Big lake, in the interior from this point, it is the custom to erect memorial posts for all people who die in such a manner that their bodies are not recovered.

Each year for five years succeeding the death a new fur coat or cloth shirt is put on the figure at the time of invitation to the festival for the dead, and offerings are made to it as though the body of the deceased were in its grave box there. When the shade comes about the village to attend the festival to the dead, or at other times, these posts are supposed to afford it a resting place, and it sees that it has not been forgotten or left unhonored by its relatives.

At several villages between Cape Vancouver and the mouth of Kuskokwim river were found grave boxes rudely made of driftwood, and about them were placed the usual display of guns, bows and arrows, paddles, and similar objects.

At the next village to the south, beyond Cape Vancouver, the graves were located on a high knoll overlooking the village, and were unusually conspicuous on account of the long poles of driftwood which were erected near each, and to the tops of which an ax or a gun was usually fastened crosswise.

At Big lake village, on the tundra, midway between Yukon and Kuskokwim rivers, are a number of small wooden figures similar in character to those above described, and, like them, raised in honor of people whose bodies were lost. In front of many of the graves at this place were large headboards, made of hewn planks about four feet long, placed across the top of two upright posts. To the middle of these were pinned from two to three wooden maskoids, representing human faces with inlaid ivory eyes and mouths; from holes or pegs at the ears hung small strings of beads, such as the villagers wear, and below the masks were bead necklaces, some of the latter being very valuable from the Eskimo point of view. The accompanying illustration (figure 105), from a sketch made on the spot, shows two of these maskoids. The graveyard at this place was very curious, having a large number of maskoids and images with curious ornamentation, but I was unable to remain long enough to give it a thorough examination.

I was informed that the graveyards of the villages on the Kuskokwim, below Kolmakof Redoubt, are full of remarkable images of carved wood. One was described to me as being roofed with wooden slabs, and consisted of a life-size figure, with round face, narrow slits for eyes, and four hands like a Hindoo idol. Two of the hands held a tin plate each for votive offerings, and the body was dressed in a new white shirt and bore elaborate bead ornaments. The abundance of carved figures in the graveyards of this district, as was noted also among those of the adjacent Tinné of the lower Yukon, is very remarkable, and their use does

FIG. 105—Monument board at a Big-lake grave.

not extend northward of the Yukon in a single instance, so far as could be learned.

On lower Kuskokwim river the Eskimo believe that the shade of a male stays with the body until the fifth day after his death; the shade of a female remains with the body for four days. On the Yukon and among the Eskimo to the north the shades of men and women alike are believed to remain with the body four days after death. Throughout this region the villagers abstain from all work on the day of the death, and in many places the day following is similarly observed. None of the relatives of the deceased must do any work during the entire time in which the shade is believed to remain with the body.

Along the coast north of St Michael there is much less elaboration in the mode of burial. On the beach near Cape Nome, on the northern shore of Norton sound, several summer fishing camps were located, and among these were a few rude graves made by building up slight inclosures of drift logs and covering them with similar material. At one place in this vicinity was a cone-shape inclosure made by standing drift logs on end in a circle eight or nine feet in diameter, with their upper ends meeting. From the top of this projected a long pole, and inside was a wooden box containing the remains of a shaman, swung by cords midway between the ground and the top of the structure. This man, I was told, had caused himself to be burned alive two years before the time of my visit, in the expectation of returning to life with much stronger powers than he had previously possessed; but the hope of the shaman failed to become realized at the appointed time, so his body was inclosed in a box and the cone of driftwood was erected over it.

Near the village at Cape Nome was a large burial box (figure 106) supported about five feet above the ground on four posts. This box was made of rude, hewn planks cut from drift logs, and was said to be the grave of a noted shaman who could breathe fire from his mouth. The other graves about the village at this cape were roughly made of drift logs, with the remains of totem marks, stones, and imple-

FIG. 106—Grave box at Cape Nome.

ments about them, very much like the drift-log burial places near St Michael, previously described.

On Sledge island, in Bering strait, I examined several graves on a sharp rocky slope of the island just above the village. These consisted of shallow pits among the rocks, surrounded by rude lines of stones, forming rims, over which were laid drift logs held in place by heavy stones. No implements or other marks of distinction were observed about these graves, possibly on account of their age.

In July, 1881, I climbed the rocky hill above the Eskimo village at East cape, Siberia, and found the graves located just above and back of the houses among the rocks covering a long ridge. They were very rude, consisting of a shallow pit formed by taking out the stones and laying them to form a rectangular inclosure 6 or 8 feet long and 2 or 3 feet wide. In these places the bodies were laid at full length upon their backs, with deerskin beds below, and over the top was a covering of rude planks or drift logs, or sometimes a small cairn. Upon and about the graves lay various implements of the deceased.

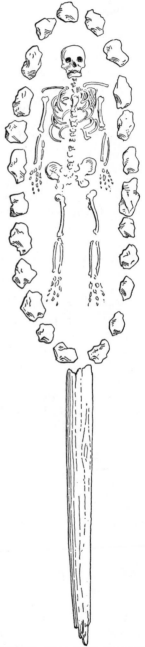

Graves of men in this spot were marked with spearheads; those of the women with potsherds and stone lamps; at one of these graves was the skull of a polar bear, and at another a few reindeer horns. The inclosures were so roughly and lightly made that the village dogs had robbed many of them of their contents. The graveyard extended along the hillside for nearly a mile just above and in sight of the village, and as I reached one of the graves quite near the houses I found a dog devouring the remains of a boy 10 or 12 years of age. Some village children who had followed me did not pay the slightest attention to this, although but a few days before the dead boy must have been their playmate.

On the southern point of St Lawrence island I found the graveyard located about a mile back of the village. Some bodies had been placed under a cairn and others were laid at full length on the ground, with a ring of stones ranged around them and a stick of driftwood six or eight feet long either on the ground at the foot of the grave or planted so as to project at an angle like the bowsprit of a ship (figure 107). No implements were seen here. From the lack of graves near other villages visited on this island, it is probable that the villagers place their dead at a distance from their houses, as is the custom at Plover bay, Siberia. This may possibly account for the absence of children's bodies among the scores of victims of famine and disease which were found in two or three villages visited on this island. At Plover bay, Siberia, the burial place was located at the base of the low spot on which the village stands, and about a mile from the houses. Some graves were on the flat at the foot of a rocky slope, and others on the rocky bench, about a hundred feet above. Many of the bodies were laid at full

FIG. 107—Grave on St Lawrence island.

18 ETH——21

length in shallow pits made by removing the rocks, and were covered with stones. Along the edges of the graves lines of small stones were arranged in a rude oval. Over the heads of some of them were piled four or five pairs of reindeer antlers.

A musket and numerous spears, with other implements, all broken so as to render them useless, were scattered about. Many of the bodies had been laid upon the ground and surrounded by an oval of stones, with a stick of driftwood at the foot, exactly as in graves seen on St Lawrence island. At none of those made in this manner were there any implements or other things deposited, and they may have been the burial places of people from St Lawrence island.

At Point Hope, just beyond Kotzebue sound, was a large graveyard, in which the bodies were placed in rude boxes built of driftwood, above the ground, and surrounded by implements. Still north of this, at Cape Lisburne, I found a solitary grave on the side of a ravine by the shore. It was an irregularly walled inclosure in rectangular shape, about 3 feet high, 3 feet wide, and 6 feet long, built of fragments of slate rock, and covered with drift logs. This grave was very old, as the skeleton was nearly destroyed by weathering, and no implements whatever were found.

TOTEMS AND FAMILY MARKS

From Kuskokwim river northward to the shores of Bering strait and Kotzebue sound the Eskimo have a regular system of totem marks and the accompanying subdivision of the people into gentes. It was extremely difficult to obtain information on this point, but the following notes are sufficiently definite to settle the fact of the existence among them of gentes and totemic signs:

Pictures, carvings, or devices of any kind, totemic or otherwise, are called ä'-lhĭñ-ûk by the Unalit. People belonging to the same gens are considered to be relatives, termed u-jo'-hŭk' by the Unalit.

FIG. 108—Arrowpoint showing wolf totem signs (½).

The gray wolf is called kĭg'-û-lun'-ûk; the wolf totem or mark, kĭg-û-lun'-û-go'-ûk; the wolf gens, kĭg'-û-lun'-û-go-älh'-ĭ-gĭt.

Arrows or other weapons marked with the sign of the wolf or other animal totem mark are believed to become invested with some of the qualities of the animal represented and to be endowed with special fatality.

Among other totem marks that of the wolf is well represented on some arrows with deerhorn points, used for large game by a party of Malemut who were hunting reindeer on Nunivak island. These arrows have two isolated barbs with a line along their base to repre-sent a wolf's back with upstanding ears, which are indicated by the two barbs. The same idea is expressed on the base of the arrowpoint, where an incised line about an inch in length is drawn along the surface of the bone with the two short, parallel, incised lines projecting from it. The arrowpoint illustrated to show this (figure 108) was

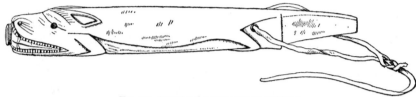

FIG. 109—Spearhead representing a wolf ($\frac{7}{16}$).

obtained on Nunivak island, but was made and used by a Malemut from the vicinity of Kotzebue sound.

The wolf totem is exhibited on numerous spearheads of walrus ivory obtained at various places from the shore of Norton sound south-

FIG. 110—Spearhead representing a wolf (about $\frac{3}{8}$).

ward to Kuskokwim river. These spearheads are usually well made, showing the mouth of the wolf open, with the line of teeth in relief around the open jaws, in the front of which is a hole lined with a wooden socket, in which the conical butt of the spearpoint is placed.

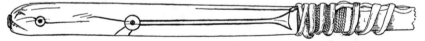

FIG. 111—Spearhead representing an otter ($\frac{1}{3}$).

The nostrils and the eyes of the wolf are often represented by blackened incised lines; or they may be circular pits in which wooden pegs are set, or filled with a black substance, so as to show prominently. The wolf's ears are usually carved in relief, or are made of sharp-pointed pegs of

FIG. 112—Spearhead representing an ermine ($\frac{3}{8}$).

ivory set in the sides of the head. In the latter case the eyes also are made of round pegs of ivory, and the holes for the nostrils are plugged with wooden pins. Others have the eyes represented by blue or black beads inlaid in the ivory. The accompanying illustrations of two of these give an idea of their general character. Figure 109 is from lower Kuskokwim river and figure 110 from Nunivak island.

Nearly all the wolf spearheads have represented upon the surface the form of the wolf's body in low relief, with the legs and feet extending around the under side.

The representation of the wolf or of some other animal totem seems to be common on this class of weapons, which are used principally for killing white whales or walrus.

Figure 111 illustrates a similar spearhead obtained on Nunivak island. It is of ivory and represents the land-otter totem. The muzzle is rounded, with a circular perforation for the eye. The mouth, nostrils, and muzzle are outlined by incised lines, but no teeth are shown. Along the sides are other incised figures, as shown in the illustration.

A spearhead from Chalitmut (figure 112) is carved to represent an ermine, indicating the totem mark of the owner.

Women belonging to the wolf gens braid strips of wolfskin in their hair, and young men and boys wear a wolf tail hung behind on the belt. It is said to have been the ancient custom for all to wear some mark about the dress by which the gens of each person might be distinguished.

Another gens among the Unalit is that of the gerfalcon (*Falcorusticolus gyrfalco*). The name for gerfalcon is *chĭ-kŭbv′-ĭ-ŭk;* the gerfalcon totem, *chĭ-kŭbv′-ĭ-a-go′-ŭk;* the gerfalcon gens, *chĭ-kŭbv′-ĭ-a′-go-ŭhl′-ĭ-gĭt.* On spears and arrows this totem mark is made by bars of red paint, which are said to represent the bars on the gerfalcon's tail. These bars are shown on the arrow illustrated in the accompanying figure 113. On the bow represented in the same figure this totem is indicated by a red and black line along a shallow groove in the middle of the inside of the bow.

The raven totem or mark is represented by an etched outline of the bird's foot and leg, forming a tridentate

FIG. 114—Simple forms of the raven totem.

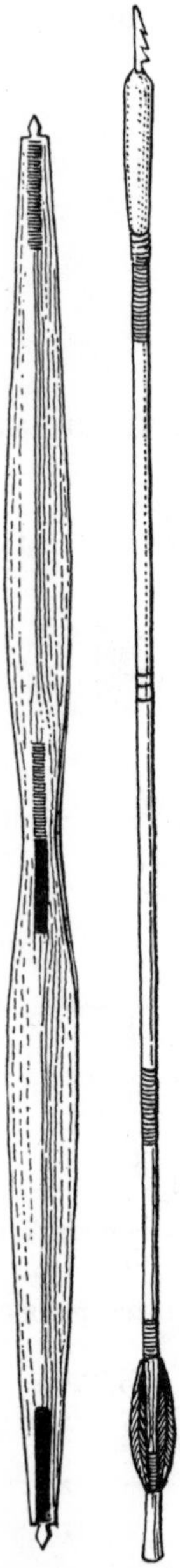

FIG. 113—Gerfalcon totems on bow and seal spear.

mark, or sometimes merely by an outline of the foot. Forms of this totem are shown in figure 114.

At East cape, Siberia, I saw numerous arrow- and spear-heads of bone or ivory bearing the raven mark, and the same mark was seen tattooed on the forehead of a boy at Plover bay (figure 115).

These marks are frequently seen on carvings, weapons, and implements of almost every description. On clothing or wooden utensils it may be marked with paint. On the gut-skin smoke-hole cover of the kashim at Kigiktauik two raven signs were drawn close together, with a red spot in front of them, as shown in figure 116.

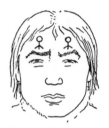

FIG. 115—Raven totem tattooing on a Plover bay boy.

On inquiry I was told that the man who presented the kashim with this cover had marked upon it his totem sign, and that the red spot in front was intended to represent the bloody mark in the snow where the raven had eaten meat. My informant added that sometimes a ring was drawn before the raven tracks on the cover to represent a seal hole in the ice.

If a man who presented a cover to the kashim belonged to another gens, or if his ancestors excelled in hunting a special kind of large game,

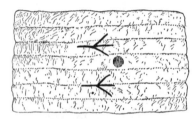

FIG. 116—Raven totems on smoke-hole cover.

the figure of that animal was drawn on the cover. One man, whose ancestors were noted for being successful hunters of sea animals, drew three <-shape marks on the cover which he presented to the kashim, as follows: < < <. These marks were said to represent the rippling wake of an animal swimming in the water.

It is customary for hunters to carry about with them an object representing their totem. A man belonging to the raven gens carries in his quiver a pair of raven feet and a quill feather from the same bird. The gerfalcon man carries in his quiver a quill feather of that totem bird.

There are other marks which are somewhat different in significance from the totem mark, but which may be adopted for various reasons. At St Michael a man told me of three hunters who went out one winter during a famine, and after hunting for a long time could find no game. Finally one of them went back to their sledge and took from it the

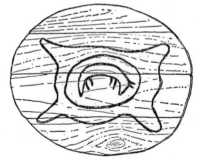

FIG. 117—Wolf totem signs on a storehouse door.

ham of a dog which he had brought with him. After eating some of this he started off again, carrying the bone with him. He had gone only a short distance when he encountered a seal and killed it. This, it was said, was due to the dog's ham-bone which he had with him, and thereafter he carried this bone and adopted a mark to represent it in place of his totem sign, as did his son after him.

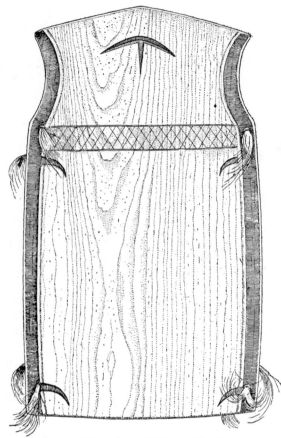

At Sabotnisky, on the lower Yukon, I saw an oval door of hewn boards in a storehouse, on which was marked, with red ocher, the outline of an extended wolfskin with the rude figure of a wolf outlined on the skin and surrounded by a circle (figure 117). In reply to a question, one of the villagers told me that it was the family mark of one of the villagers. "All of our people," he added, "have marks which have been handed down by our fathers from very long ago, and we put them on all of our things."

Another man at this village said that his ancient namesake

FIG. 118—Tobacco board with bear and loach signs.

had been a famous bowman, and once while hunting, having nothing but blunt-head arrows, such as are used for killing rabbits and other small game, came across a large red bear, which he immediately began to shoot; finally he broke all of the bear's bones and killed it. After this he adopted the red bear as his sign and his descendants still use this mark.

Figure 118 represents a thin board, on which tobacco is cut, which was obtained at Sabotnisky. There is a broad, shallow groove along each side,

FIG. 119—Figures on a grave box.

succeeded by a small groove along its inner edge. The broad groove has two incised curved marks representing bear claws. On each side and near the end on each side is an incised crescentic mark with a pointed groove below, said to represent the mouth and barbel of a loach. At the base of each bear claw is inserted a tuft of white seal bristles, with another tuft on the edge close by and one on the tip of the barbel of the loach. About one-third of the distance from the front are crosslines representing a fish net stretched across the board. The edge of the board, including the broad groove, bear-claw incisions, and loach mouth, is painted red; the net is of dull bluish color. All of these marks have totemic meanings which I did not have an opportunity to determine.

Figure 119 illustrates the figures painted on a grave box at Stari-kwikhpak, which indicates that the father of the deceased was a noted reindeer hunter.

WARS

Previous to the arrival of the Russians on the Alaskan shore of Bering sea the Eskimo waged an almost constant intertribal warfare; at the same time, along the line of contact with the Tinné tribes of the interior, a bitter feud was always in existence. The people of the coast from the Yukon mouth to Kotzebue sound have many tales of villages destroyed by war parties of Tinné. Back from the head of Norton bay and Kotzebue sound, during the time of my residence in that region, several Tinné were killed by Malemut while hunting reindeer on the strip of uninhabited tundra lying between the districts occupied by the two peoples. During the summer of 1879 a party of three Malemut from the head of Kotzebue sound ambushed and killed seven Tinné who were found hunting reindeer in the interior.

As related by various Eskimo questioned by me, it appeared that a favorite mode of carrying on their ancient warfare was to lie in ambush near a village until night and then to creep up and close the passageway to the kashim, thus confining the men within, and afterward shooting them with arrows through the smoke hole in the roof. Sometimes the women were put to death, at other times they were taken home by the victors; but the men and the boys were always killed.

In those days villages were built on high points, where defense was more easily made against an attacking party and from which a lookout was kept almost constantly. When the warriors of one of the Unalit villages wished to make up a party to attack an enemy, a song of invitation was made and a messenger sent to sing it in the kashims at other friendly villages; meanwhile the men of the village originating the plot set to work in the kashim and made supplies of new bows and arrows and prepared other weapons while waiting for their friends. The people invited would join the men from the first village and all would set out stealthily to surprise the enemy during the night. If they failed in this an open battle ensued, unless the attacking party became discouraged and returned home. Near St Michael there were shown me some of the old lookout places where the watchmen were stationed to guard against the approach of the Magemut, who lived just south of the Yukon mouth and were the chief enemies of the Unalit.

Near St Michael, on the top of an elevated islet close to the coast, is the site of an ancient village which had been surprised and destroyed by this last-named people long before the arrival of the Russians in that region. Digging in some of the pits marking the places once occupied by houses, I found charred fragments of wood and various small articles belonging to the former occupants.

The following account of the ancient warfare of the Eskimo on the lower Yukon and adjacent region southward was given me in January, 1881, by an old man living near Andreivsky:

The people of the lower Yukon and Pastolik fought against those living on the southern part of the Yukon delta and the country south-ward, including the villages at Big lake and in the Kuslevak mountains and the Magemut of the coast just south of the Yukon mouth. The old man said that the main war between these people started in a great village located near Ikogmut. Two boys were playing with a bone-tip dart, and one of them accidentally pierced his companion's eye; this so enraged the father of the injured boy that he caught the other and destroyed both his eyes. The fathers of the two boys then fought, one armed with a beaver-tooth knife and the other with a bone bodkin, the fight resulting in the death of both men. The quarrel was taken up by relatives and friends on both sides, the village became divided, and the weaker party was forced to leave the Yukon and go southward, where they settled. From that time continual warfare was carried on between them.

Battles took place usually in summer, and the victors killed all they could of the males of the opposing side, even including infants, to prevent them from growing up as enemies. The dead were thrown in heaps and left. The females were commonly spared from death, but were taken as slaves.

When young men fought in their first battle each was given to drink some of the blood and made to eat a small piece of the heart of the first enemy killed by them, in order to render them brave. An Unalit at St Michael told me that in former days each of their young warriors always ate a small piece of the heart of the first enemy killed by him on a hostile raid.

During the battles on the Yukon the best fighters used to throw themselves on their backs and kick their heels in the air in derision of the enemy when they approached one another. When any of the men exhausted their supply of arrows they would stand in front of their comrades and break those of the enemy with their spear shafts by striking them as they flew past. No shields were used. They said that if an arrow was coming straight at a man he could not see it, so it was very hard to avoid being hit, but that a man could readily see one flying toward another. Some of the warriors are said to have been very expert bowmen. My old informant told me that his namesake was a famous bowman. On one occasion he was said to have pinned an enemy to a wall of a house with an arrow so that he could not release himself.

If a fight lasted a long time, so that both parties became tired and hungry or sleepy, a fur coat would be waved on a stick by one side as a sign of truce, during which both parties would rest, eat, or sleep, and then renew the conflict. During the truce both sides stationed guards who watched against surprise. Sometimes, the old man said, a man would be shot so full of arrows that his body would bristle with them, and, falling, be held almost free from the ground by their number.

At times volleys of arrows were fired in order to render it more difficult for the enemy to escape being hit. When one of the warriors had shot away all his arrows and chanced to be surrounded by the enemy, he could sometimes escape death for a long time by dodging and leaping from side to side, but finally would be killed by some of them striking him upon the head with a warclub having a sharp spur of bone or ivory on one side. The defeated party was always pursued and, if possible, exterminated.

The Magemut are said to have been stronger in battle than the Yukon men, and a larger number of the latter were always killed in a conflict between these two people. Neither side had any recognized chief, but each fought as he pleased, with the exception that some of the older men had general supervision and control of the expedition.

When a man on either side had relatives in the opposing party, and for this reason did not wish to take part in the battle, he would blacken his face with charcoal and remain a noncombatant, both sides respecting his neutrality. In this event, a man with his face blackened had the privilege of going without danger among the people of either side during a truce.

The Magemut always carried off the women after a successful raid, but my Yukon informant told me this was not done by his people, which statement was probably made merely from a desire on his part to give his own people the advantage in my eyes. He admitted, however, the superior fighting qualities of his enemies, the Magemut.

When possible night raids were made by the villagers on both sides, and the people were usually clubbed or speared to death. The conquered village was always pillaged, and if a warrior saw any personal ornament on a slain enemy which pleased him, he seized it and wore it himself, even placing in his lips the labrets taken from the face of a dead foe. If one of the conquerors chanced to see a woman wearing handsome beads or other ornaments, he would brain her and strip them off.

The old man told me that in battles between the people of lower Kuskoquim river and those of Bristol bay the victors made a practice of cutting off the heads of their slain enemies and placing them on the top of sharp stakes set in the ground, with arrows thrust crosswise through their noses.

The last battle fought between the Yukon people and the Magemut was about the time the Russians first established themselves at St Michael. This fight took place on a flat piece of ground at the head of the northern branch of the Yukon mouth. Several low mounds visible on this little flat are said to mark the places where the dead were left in a heap after the battle.

In ancient times the Eskimo of Bering strait were constantly at war with one another, the people of the Diomede islands being leagued with the Eskimo of the Siberian shore against the combined forces of those on King island and the American shore from near the head of Kotzebue sound to Cape Prince of Wales and Port Clarence. An old man from Sledge island told me that formerly it was customary among the people of the Siberian coast to kill at sight any Eskimo from the American shore who might have been driven by storm across the strait, either in umiaks or on the ice.

I was also informed that at one time the inhabitants of the lesser Diomede island became angry with those of the greater Diomede island and united with the people of Cape Prince of Wales against them, but were defeated. The last war party in this district came in a fleet of umiaks from East cape, Siberia, and the Diomede islands, and sailed up Port Clarence, but meeting a large force of the American Eskimo, both sides agreed upon a peace, which has not since been broken.

During the wars formerly waged among the people living on the coasts and islands of Bering strait, there was in common use a kind of armor made of imbricated plates of walrus ivory fastened together with sealskin cords. Plate XCII illustrates a nearly complete set of this body armor, which was obtained on the Diomede islands.

Plates of ivory for armor of this kind were seen on St Lawrence island, and on the Siberian shore at Cape Wankarem.

The people about the shores of Norton and Kotzebue sounds were also familiar with the use of armor in ancient times. During my residence at St Michael two or three of the natives who lived turbulent lives were reputed to have worn light iron armor under their fur frocks, which it was claimed had been purchased from vessels, and from the description must have been shirts of chain mail.

GAMES AND TOYS

The Eskimo of the lower Yukon, the Alaskan coast district of Bering sea, and the Arctic ocean have a considerable variety of games, both for outdoor and indoor amusement, and most of them have a wide range. The following detailed descriptions of some of them, although taken mainly from the Unalit of Norton sound, represent games found among other tribes. The greater portion of them are played while the men are confined to the villages during the short, cold days of winter.

In the vicinity of St Michael and some other trading stations the Eskimo have learned to play cards, usually poker, and are passionately

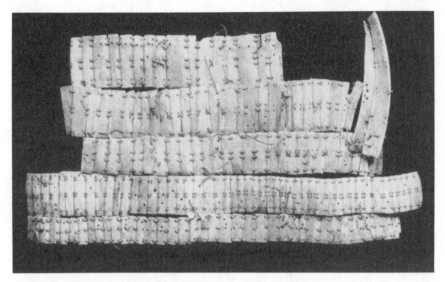

ESKIMO PLATE ARMOR

fond of them; as with the southern aborigines, the Eskimo will gamble
away everything they possess. In the descriptions of the various
games the locality where each was observed is given, but it should be
noted that they are not ordinarily limited to any one tribe or district,
but, so far as could be learned, seemed to be generally distributed,
with slight local modifications. Implements used in some of the games
were obtained from widely separated places.

Friendly contests in trials of strength, wrestling, etc, were much
more common before than they have been since the arrival of white
men, their coming having put a stop to the predatory raids of one village upon another and caused a diminution in the rivalry among the

FIG. 120—Boy with toy sled, St Lawrence island.

young men to excel in strength and agility which accompanied the
more warlike spirit of other days.

In addition to the games of the men, others are played by the women
and children. Boys have toy hunting outfits, with models of sleds,
kaiaks, and umiaks, and small bows and arrows for hunting birds; they
also snare birds and set traps for mice and other small game. The girls
play with dolls made of ivory or other material, and also have small
models of dishes and other women's household utensils, with which
they amuse themselves in the house very much after the manner of
children in civilized countries, playing at housekeeping and women's
work of various kinds. Figure 120, from a sketch made by Mr H. W.
Elliott on St Lawrence island, represents the boy Poonook, with his

toy sled. In the background is the shelter over the entrance of the tunnel leading to the interior of the half-underground house, the roof of which appears like a mound on the right.

During one of my sledge journeys I was storm-bound at Cape Darby, near Bering strait, and during the day an old man in the house where I stopped amused me by the ingenuity with which he made intricate patterns of cord, holding the loop between his extended hands after the manner of children making a "cat's cradle." For an hour or more he made a constant succession of patterns with his sinew cord, forming outlines of various birds and other animals of the region. The readiness with which he wove the strings in and out showed that his dexterity must have been gained by long practice. I also heard of this form of amusement among the Eskimo along the coast southward to the mouth of the Kuskokwim.

The following games are in common use throughout this region:

FIRST GAME—(St Michael). A round block about 6 inches long is cut into the form of a large spool, but with the flaring rim of one end replaced by a sharpened point. The top is from $2\frac{1}{2}$ to 3 inches across and has a deep hole in the center. This spool-like object is planted in the floor of the kashim with the large end upward, and an indefinite number of players gather around it seated cross-legged on the floor. Near the spool is a small pile of short sticks, of uniform size, used as counters. These, with a small, pointed wooden dart, in size and shape almost exactly like a sharpened lead pencil, compose the implements of the game. The first player takes the butt of the dart between the thumb and forefinger, with its point upward and his hand nearly on a level with the spool. Then he gives the dart a deft upward toss, trying to cause it to take a curved course, so that it will fall with the point downward and remain fast in the hole at the top of the spool. If he succeeds he takes one of the counting sticks from the pile and tries again; when he misses, the dart is passed to the next player, and so on, until the counters are all gone, when the players count up and the one having the most counters is the winner. Ordinarily this game is played by men, women, or children merely for pastime, but sometimes small articles are staked upon the outcome. It is a source of much sport to the players, who banter and laugh like school children at each other's bad play.

SECOND GAME—(St Michael). A bundle of from fifty to seventy-five small, squared, wooden splints, about 4 inches long and a little larger than a match, are placed in a small pile crosswise on the back of the player's outstretched right hand. The player then removes his hand quickly and tries to grasp the falling sticks between his thumb and fingers, still keeping the palm downward. If one or more of the sticks fall to the ground it is a miss and the next player tries. Every time a player succeeds in catching all of the falling sticks, he lays aside one of them as a counter until all are gone, when each player counts up and the one holding the greatest number is the winner. These squared splints are similar to those used for markers in the first game described. Small stakes are sometimes played for in this game as in the first.

THIRD GAME—(St Michael). The bunch of slender splints already described are also used to play a game exactly like jackstraws. The player grasps the bunch of sticks between the thumb and the forefinger of the right hand, resting one end upon the floor; then he suddenly releases them and they fall in a small heap. The players have a small wooden hook, and each in succession removes as many of the sticks as he can without moving any but the one taken. Each player keeps those he succeeds in removing, and the one holding the largest number at the end is the winner. Both men and women play this game, but usually not together.

FOURTH GAME (*ä-zhŭkh'-ch-tak* of the Unalit)—(St Michael). This is played by men and women during the long twilight nights of June, and is often continued during the whole night. A stake (*nŭ-pŭg'-ŭ-zhŭk*) is driven into the ground so as to project a foot or two. About this, in a circle, some four yards away, sit the men and women players. One of them places some small article of value at the foot of the stake for a prize (*än-khu'-tĭk*). The next player takes a small ring of twisted grass (*ä-zhŭkh'-ch-tak*) about 6 inches in diameter, and tries to toss it so as to encircle the stake. If he misses, the ring is passed to the next player. When one encircles the stake he takes a prize and must substitute for it another of about equal value, but of a different kind. In this way a kind of trading is brought about, since each puts up something of which he has a surplus.

TOP SPINNING (*u-i'-wŭk*)—(Lower Yukon). In winter along the lower Yukon and adjacent region to the south the children of both sexes gather in the kashim, and each child in succession spins its top. The moment the top is spun the owner runs out through the entrance passage and attempts to make a complete circuit of the house and enter again before the top stops spinning. A score is made every time this is done successfully.

DART THROWING (*yokh'-whŭk*)—(St Michael). This is played in the kashim by two or more persons, usually for a prize or stake. The darts are small, short, and made of wood, largest at the point and tapering backward toward the butt, in which is fastened a bird quill for guiding the dart in its flight. In the large end of the dart is fastened a sharp spike of bone, horn, or sometimes of ivory. The target is a small, upright stick of some soft wood planted in the floor. This may be placed in the middle of the room and the players divided into two parties, seated on opposite sides of the target, or it may be placed on one side of the room and the players seated together on the other. In the former case a man is appointed from each side to return the darts to the throwers and to give each player a counter when a point is made. Each player has two darts which he throws one after the other, and a score is made when a dart remains sticking into the target. Ten small wooden counting sticks are placed on the floor by the target, and one of these is given for each score; the side gaining the most of these counters takes the prize, and the game begins again.

At Cape Nome, south of Bering strait, a similar dart game was seen, but there the target was a square, board-like piece of wood with a dark-colored bull's-eye painted in the center. This was set up in the kashim and the men and boys threw their darts at it, scoring when they hit the bull's-eye. The wooden portion of the darts used in this game, both at Cape Nome and St Michael, was from five to six inches in length and from three-fourths of an inch to an inch in diameter at the larger end. Figure 121 represents a dart from Cape Nome, used for throwing at a square board target with a round, black bull's eye painted on its center. The players place the target on one side of the kashim and stand upon the other side to throw, scoring one for each dart that sticks in the bull's-eye. These darts are nearly two feet in length and have a tapering wooden handle, largest at the front, with an ivory point fastened in the lower end by a tapering, wedge-shape point, which is inserted in the split end and lashed firmly. The upper end of the shaft tapers to a small, round point, on which is fastened the end of a feather from a cormorant's tail, which serves to guide the dart in its flight.

NET AND DART-THROWING GAME (*nŭ-g'o'-hlĭ-g'a'-nŭk*)— (St Michael). This is played in the kashim by men only. A small, oval, wooden frame, about three inches long by an inch and a half wide, having the interior finely netted with cord, is hung from the roof and held in place by a cord at each end. It is placed about four feet from the floor in front of the summer entrance or under the smoke-hole in the roof. Each player has a long, slender dart, about three feet in length and a quarter of an inch in diameter, with a barbed point of bone or deerhorn. To the butt end of the dart is fastened a small cord, so that the player can draw it back after throwing. When the point of the dart enters the wooden ring it is held fast by the barbs on the point, and this scores one for the successful player. Under this target each player places some object as a prize. Then all go to one side of the room and throw three darts in succession at the target. Whenever a player pierces the target so that he must remove his dart with his hands, he is entitled to take anything he wishes from the pile of prizes. In this way the game continues until all the articles are disposed of.

(⁵⁄₁₆)

FIG. 121—Dart.

THROWING STICKS (*kĭ-bŭ'-tŭk*)—(St Michael). A rectangular ivory pin, from five to seven inches in length, is planted upright in the floor of the kashim. Each player puts up an object for a prize, and standing at a certain distance from the pin tosses in succession two small, flat, ivory rods toward it. The man whose rod lies closest to the pin when all have thrown is entitled to his choice of the articles staked by the players, and the game proceeds until all of the articles are won. The ivory rods used in this game are from about $2\frac{1}{2}$ to 4 or 5 inches in length, rather flattened, and quadrangular in cross section, the corners rounded, and on one side of each end is a rounded bead, the two beads facing in different directions. The name of these two small rods is the same as that of the game. They are sometimes grooved along one or both faces, and usually are pierced near one end so that they may be strung on a cord with from two to four larger ivory pins like that stuck in the floor. These latter are brought down to a flat, rounded point at one end, while the other is larger and rounded or squared, often with the head of an animal carved upon it.

This collection of rods serves primarily for preparing and twisting the sinew for sinew-backed bows, as has been explained by Mr John Murdoch. These objects, including both classes of rods, were obtained from the Alaskan coast between Kuskokwim river and the vicinity of Point Barrow, as well as from the islands in Bering strait and on St Lawrence island.

A handsome set obtained on Sledge island consists of four of the large pins with the upper ends carved to represent reindeer heads, and two of the ordinary, small, flat rods. These, like most implements of this kind, are made of walrus ivory; occasionally bone is used, but this is uncommon in the region where ivory is found. One set of the flat rods from Hotham inlet, Kotzebue sound, are marked with the raven totem; others have a series of circle-and-dot ornamentation, but many of them are plain. One specimen of the pin from Point Hope has the larger end carved to represent one of the joints in the leg-bone of a mammal, and another set from the same place has carved on them the head of some small animal, probably a fox. Another set of these implements in the National Museum was obtained by Mr Macfarlane at Fort Anderson, in Hudson Bay territory.

FOOTBALL (*i-tĭg'-ŭ-mi-u'-hlu-tĭn*)—(St Michael). The ball (*ŭñ'kak*) used in this game is made of leather, stuffed with deer hair or moss, and varies in size, but rarely exceeds five or six inches in diameter. The game is played by young men and children. The usual season for it is at the end of winter or in spring. I saw it played in various places from Bering strait to the mouth of the Kuskokwim; at Cape Darby it was played by children on the hard, drifted snow; it is also a popular game on the lower Yukon. Two of the participants act as leaders, one on each side choosing a player alternately from among those gathered until they are equally divided. At a given distance apart two conspicuous marks are made on the snow or ground which serve as goals, the players stand each by their goal and the ball is tossed upon the ground midway between them; a rush is then made, each side striving to drive the ball across its adversaries' line.

Another football game is begun by the men standing in two close, parallel lines midway between the goals, their legs and bodies forming two walls. The ball is then thrown between them and driven back and forth by kicks and blows until it passes through one of the lines; as soon as this occurs all rush to drive it to one or the other of the goals.

The northern lights (aurora) of winter are said by these people to be boys playing this game; others say that it is a game being played by shades using walrus skulls as balls.

WOMEN'S FOOTBALL (*ŭñ-käl'-û-g'it*)—(St Michael and neighboring coast region, both north and south). This game is played by women usually during the fall and winter. The ball used is generally considerably larger than the one used in the men's game. The four players stand opposite each other, thus—

Each pair has a ball, which is thrown or driven back and forth across the square. The ball is thrown upon the ground midway between the players, so that it shall bound toward the opposite one. She strikes the ball down and back toward her partner with the palm of her open hand. Sometimes the ball is caught on the toe or hand and tossed up and struck or kicked back toward the other side. The person who misses least or has fewer " dead " balls on her side wins. At times this game is played by only two women.

HAND BALL (*kai-täl'-û-g'ĭt*)—(St Michael). The ball used in this game is a rounded rectangular leather bag about three by six inches, filled with sand or earth. This bag is called *kai'-tuk*. The young men of the village form one side in this game, tossing the ball from one to the other, while the young women are on the opposite side and strive to secure the bag and keep it going among themselves. A player on the same side as another is called *i-li'-ka* (plural, *i-li'-put*) and the opponents are called *i-li-kĭl'-û-g'ĭt*. It is played in May and June, during the long, pleasant twilight nights, sometimes lasting the entire night.

When one of the young men has chanced not to have the ball in his hand for a long time, his comrades cry out that he is "hungry" and try to get the ball to him. The women exert every effort to intercept it and

if they succeed pursue and catch the unlucky player and rub his head
with the ball, telling him that they will "oil his head so that he shall
not starve," while the other players shriek with laughter. This game
goes on night after night during the season on top of a hill near St
Michael, the laughter and cries of the players being heard for hours.

In addition to this game another is played, particularly among the
women, in which the ball is merely tossed from hand to hand.

HOCKEY (*ai'-yu-täl'-û-g'ït* or *püt-k'u-täl'-û-g'ït*)—(St Michael). This
is played with a small ball of ivory, leather, or wood, and a stick
curved at the lower end. The ball and stick are called *pat-k'u'-tûk*.
The ball is placed on the ground or ice and the players divide into two
parties. Each player with his stick attempts to drive the ball across
the opponents' goal, which is established as in the football game.

GRASS-BALL GAME (*mûm'-û-g'u*)—(St Michael). In summer the men
make a stout ball of grass, five or six inches in diameter, from which
the game takes its name. Sides are chosen and each, when having the
ball, pursues the other. The members of each side try to hit their
opponents with the ball while the latter attempt to avoid being struck
or to obtain the ball in order to hit their opponents. The side scoring
the greatest number of hits is the winner.

ROPE JUMPING (*ä-tûkh'-ta-g'ûk*)—(St Michael). This is a summer
game played out of doors. A heavy rope, from 18 to 24 feet in length,
made of braided grass, is held at each end by a man or a woman and
swung in a circle. One player stands in the middle, sidewise to the
rope, and must jump it twice in succession as it is swung around and
then spring away without being touched. He is then replaced by a
companion, who repeats the performance. If either fails he exchanges
place with one of those swinging the rope. This rope is called
pi-hakh'-luk.

BLIND-MAN'S BUFF (*chaf-ta'-g'aun*)—(St Michael). This is played by
young people during spring and summer. One of the players, either a
man or a woman, is blindfolded and the others stand in a circle around
him and set up a shout. After this all try to keep perfectly quiet,
creeping softly about on the ground to avoid being caught, the first
person caught being in turn blindfolded.

HIDE AND SEEK (*i-g'u'-ta-g'a'-tl-hït*)—(St Michael). This game is
played in summer, when the grass is long, by both men and women,
but not together. The players divide into two sides, standing opposite each other and bent over so that the crowns of each opposing pair
rest against each other, their hands being clasped and outstretched on
each side. Then a designated player hides in the grass or behind some
shelter and when well concealed utters a faint cry. The two sides
then separate, the opposing side searching for the one concealed.
When he is found all join as before, with heads and hands together,
while the one successful in discovering the other conceals himself in
the same manner.

TAG (*u-la'-ki-ta'-g'ûk*)—(St Michael). This game is played at any season by men and women divided into equal parties, which are subdivided into pairs. Then a designated player starts off, pursued by the others, the players on the opposite side trying to overtake and touch him before he can touch the mate he was given from his own party. This mate strives to get within reach of his companion, the opposite side meanwhile using every effort to interfere between the two by running after the first and hindering the latter. If the player succeeds in touching his mate before he is touched he wins and another pair of runners come out from his side. If he is touched first by one of his opponents, he loses, and a pair of runners come out from among them and take his place.

TWIN TAG (*ki-hlûkh'-ku-ta'-g'ûk*)—(St Michael). In this game the players are fastened together in pairs, being tied by the ankles. One pair are given a start and are pursued by the others until one of the two is touched by another pair, whereupon the latter take their places. This is a summer game.

RING AROUND (*uhl-tä'*)—(St Michael). The players in this game are either men or women together or separately. The players are divided into two equal parties, each party joining hands and facing toward the center of a circle. When ready they circle about as swiftly as possible, all the time advancing toward a certain point agreed upon, and the circle or ring of players which first reaches the goal is victorious. This game affords much sport, as the members of each ring are eager to reach the goal, but the double motion frequently causes them to stumble and fall promiscuously over one another.

TOSSING ON WALRUS SKIN (*äj-u-täl'-û-g'ĭt*).—I heard of this game from Bering strait to the mouth of the Yukon. A large walrus hide is spread out and hand-holes are cut around its border. One of the players stands upon the center, and a party of men on one side and women on the other, numbering as many as can reach it, take hold of the skin. By united effort the players jerk the skin up, holding it tightly stretched. The person on it is thrown high in the air and if he alights on his feet one of the other side must take his place. Should he fall in any other position he or one of his side must remain on the skin. This is a summer game, but is sometimes practiced by the young men in the kashim during winter.

TUG OF WAR (*tiñ-ukh-tai'-g'aun*)—(St Michael). This is played at any season. A strong rawhide loop is made; the contestants are divided into two parties, and the strongest man of each party grasps the loop with his right hand. The men on each side form a queue with their arms around each other's bodies and pull at a given signal; the side which first looses its hold on the loop is defeated. The loop is called *ki-chĭk'*. This game is played either out of doors or in the kashim, by either men or women; sometimes it is played by a single pair of men or women and is then called *no-kú'-taun*.

ARM PULLING (*käs-o'-g'aun*)—(St Michael). Two men lock their right arms and a string of other men form a queue, pulling on both sides until one gives way. This is a winter contest, engaged in within the kashim.

POLE PULLING (*no-kŭj'-un*)—(St Michael). A round, slender pole, six or eight feet long, is laid on the floor of the kashim and an equal number of men sit upon the floor along each side of it with their knees bent and hands grasping it. At a given signal all pull, the side dragging the other across the central line being victors.

STICK RAISING (*yä-g'u'-tak*)—(St Michael). A round stick a little larger than a broom handle is grasped firmly by two players who are usually standing; one player holds it down at arm's length, grasping it firmly with both hands while the other attempts to raise it above his head.

FINGER PULLING (*a-gu'-li-phun*)—(St Michael). This is played in the kashim by four men; the two strongest players hook their right second fingers and each man is grasped about his right shoulder and under the left arm by his second; then all pull until one is defeated by loosing his hold.

FOOT PULLING (*it-kha'-g'aun*)—(St Michael.) Two men lie upon their faces on the floor of the kashim with their feet together and heads in opposite directions. Their right feet are hooked into a short, rawhide loop, and each tries to crawl away and drag the other backward.

NECK PULLING (*tu-nu-chu'-g'aun*)—(St Michael). Two men kneel on the floor of the kashim, near and facing each other; their heads are bowed and a rawhide loop is placed so as to rest over the backs of their necks. A stick is placed crosswise between each man's teeth, projecting on either side above the cord of the loop so as to keep the latter from slipping over the head. The men then drop forward on their hands and each tries to back away, dragging his adversary; the one who first succeeds is the victor.

HEAD PUSHING (*chuñ-ukh'-tŭ-g'aun*)—(St Michael). Two men go down upon their hands and knees on the kashim floor and, pressing their foreheads together, strive to push each other back from their positions.

BATTERING RAM (*tu'-kŭ-kă-gu'-tă*)—(St Michael). This is played by four men in the kashim. Two of the players each takes his partner upon his shoulder, the latter lying face downward with his body stiffened and feet projecting horizontally in front of the man carrying him. In this position the carriers face each other and run one at the other so that the feet of the two men on their shoulders shall come together, trying in this way to upset each other, the defeated pair falling igno-miniously to the floor.

WRESTLING (*chä'-hluk*)—(St Michael). Wrestling is usually done by each man seizing his opponent by the arms or body, trying to gain

a square fall on the back without the aid of tripping or any other use
of the feet or legs, except as supports.   This is generally done for sport,
but I was told that in ancient times disputed claims for women were
sometimes settled in this manner.   A stranger, upon arrival in a village,
is frequently challenged to wrestle with the local champion.   Powerful
men are very rough in this sport, and one method is to attempt by a
terrific hug to crush the opponent.   One old man told me that he had
seen the blood gush from a wrestler's mouth and nose from the pressure
of his antagonist.   I heard of an instance where a white man visiting
the village of the Malemut at Kotzebue sound during the winter was
repeatedly challenged to wrestle by one of the villagers.   Finally, the
annoyance became so great that the stranger accepted the challenge,
and, being an extremely powerful man, seized the Eskimo and dashed
him to the floor of the kashim so heavily that he was badly hurt.   This
was considered quite legitimate and the stranger was not molested
further.

KNEE WALKING (*chis-ku'mĭ-ûk'*)—(St Michael).   The young men of
a village kneel on the plank flooring of the kashim and holding their
feet up with their hands walk about on bare knees, each trying to
outdo the others in endurance.

HIGH JUMPING (*kût'-khûk*)—(St Michael).   A stick is held or fastened above the floor at a certain distance and the young men try to
excel in leaping over it, the stick gradually being raised to the limit of
the jumpers' powers.

HORIZONTAL JUMPING (*mĭ-chĭkh-tăk*)—(St Michael).   The jumpers
in this game practice it either outside of or within the kashim.   A mark
is made from which the jumping is done and another on the ground or
floor scores the point reached by each.

HURDLE JUMPING (*ya'-lĭ-ku'-juk*)—(St Michael).   Four umiak oars
are placed at an equal distance apart around the sides of the kashim,
about breast high above the floor; the contestants start in pairs, jumping over them one after the other until one of each pair is defeated by
failing to clear one of the oars.

FOOT RACING (*ûk-whaun'*)—(St Michael).   This is a favorite sport
among the Eskimo and is practiced usually in autumn when the new
ice is formed.   The race extends from one to several miles, the course
usually lying to and around some natural object, such as an island or
a point of rocks, then back to the starting point.

KAIAK RACING (*pañ-û-g'aun'*)—(St Michael).   The men, each in his
kaiak, are ranged side by side near the shore, and then at a signal
paddle around a rock or islet, the winner being he who first touches
the shore on returning to the starting point.

Umiak races are also conducted in the same way, and hunters engage
in contests in throwing seal and walrus spears of various kinds.

From Kuskokwim river to Cape Prince of Wales, on both the mainland and the islands, children of both sexes were found using tops.

These are commonly of disk shape, thin at the edge and perforated in the center for a peg. One from Cape Prince of Wales (figure 122) is of walrus ivory; it is 2½ inches in diameter and has a hole an inch wide in the middle, which is closed by a neatly fitted wooden plug of the same thickness as the top, through which passes a spindle-shape peg four inches long. This is the general style of top used in the region mentioned, but another kind is made to be spun with a guiding stick and cord; these are often used by men as well as by boys.

On the lower Yukon the children amuse themselves in winter by spinning tops on the wooden floor of the kashim. The game is played by each child spinning its top and then hurrying out through the long passage to the entrance, making a complete circuit around the outside of the building, then back to the interior, trying to return before the top has ceased spinning. These toys are spun between the two hands, the upper part of the spindle being held upright between the palms.

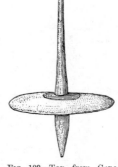

Fig. 122—Top from Cape Prince of Wales (about ½).

Among other games, the children also have a buzz, usually made by stringing a doubly perforated, flattened disk on a cord. The two ends of the cord are tied together and the ends of the loop thus formed are held in their hands, so that by tightening and relaxing their hold the disk is caused to twirl about, exactly as is done with a similar toy by civilized children. These buzzes are usually made of wood, ivory, or bone, although of recent years some are made of metal. I obtained one at St Michael made from the adjoining phalangeal bones of some animal,

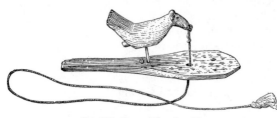

Fig. 123—Toy woodpecker (½).

probably a seal, still united by their cartilage. The string is a single cord of sinew, which is made fast between the two middle bones, and at each end of the string is tied a short cross-stick for grasping.

Another toy obtained at St Michael, represented in figure 123, is the image of a woodpecker made of wood fastened to a small wooden spatula by means of a stout quill in place of legs. The surface of the spatula is dotted over with red paint to represent food. By means of a string fastened to the point of the bird's beak and passing down through a hole in the spatula, the child is enabled to pull the bird's head down. On releasing it, the elasticity of the quill throws it up again, thus giving a pecking motion and imitating the movements of feeding. Various toys of this character are made by the Eskimo to represent familiar animals or birds.

FIG. 124—Toy mouse (about ⅓).

Figure 124 represents a toy obtained at the village of Sabotnisky, on the lower Yukon. It is a slender, flat rod a little over an inch wide and about 16 inches long, perforated with six round holes at equal intervals along its length, through which is passed in and out a sinew cord, having its ends fastened to the extremities of a small, narrow strip of fur, forming an endless loop. Grasping the rod by the handle at one end, the child draws on the free part of the cord, causing the strip of fur to run in and out of the holes along the surface, thus representing a mouse.

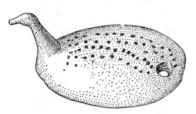

FIG. 125—Toy representing a murre swimming (full size).

The children also have small figures of birds, seals, and other animals, which their fathers carve in ivory, bone, and wood. Along the seacoast ivory is the material ordinarily used for making these objects, but among the Eskimo of the tundras, or along the rivers of the interior, bone or deerhorn is more commonly employed. The bird images usually represent geese, murres, or other waterfowl, and are made flat upon the lower surface, so that they sit upright. On St Lawrence island, and at various other points which were visited, many of these objects were obtained, of which the toy bird shown in figure 125 is an example. They are similar in character to the images with which a sort of game is played among the eastern Eskimo.

In addition to the foregoing objects, dolls made for girls are among the most interesting of the children's toys. On St Lawrence island two were obtained; these are shown in figure 7, plate XCIII, made rudely of wood, and figure 8, plate XCIII, which is of ivory. The makers of these displayed very little skill or

FIG. 126—Clay doll (½).

artistic ability, as might be expected from their general lack of culture in this direction compared with the people of the adjacent American coast. Along the Alaskan shore wherever I went, as well as along

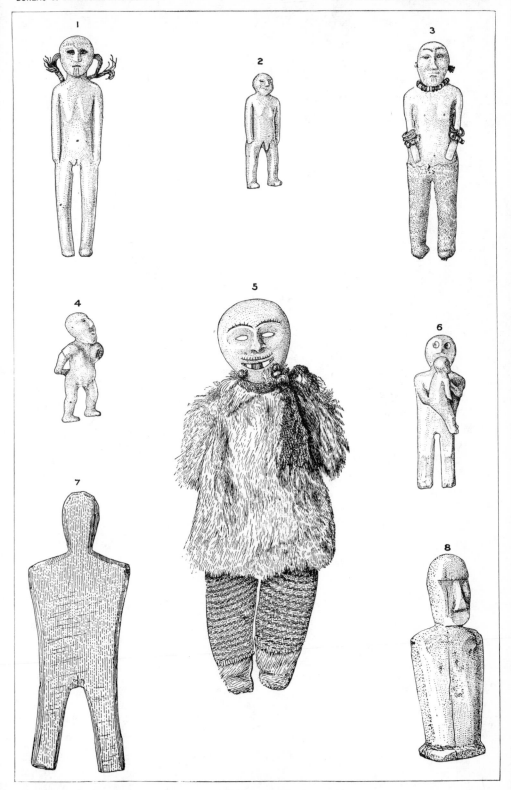

DOLLS (THIRTEEN-SIXTEENTHS)

Yukon and Kuskokwim rivers and on Nunivak island, dolls were found in common use. They are usually small images of wood, ivory, or bone; indeed, the only instance that I saw of the use of clay among the Eskimo for making images of any kind was a pair of rudely modeled dolls representing the head and body, which were obtained at Razbinsky, on the lower Yukon. One of these dolls is shown in figure 126. The inartistic character of these clay figures is in striking contrast to the carvings produced by the same people.

FIG. 127—Wooden doll (¼).

The dolls usually represent the anatomic details of both sexes, and are from an inch to a foot or more in length. Many of them are carved to represent grotesque human figures, but the majority are simply upright ivory images with the arms by the sides (as represented in figure 2, plate XCIII) or held in various positions across the body, sometimes one hand being placed in front and the other behind the back. Many of the natives use hard material merely for the upper half of the body, the legs being made of skin, stuffed with hair or skin to give them a semblance to the natural form.

FIG. 128—Doll (nearly ½).

An ivory figure from Cape Prince of Wales (figure 4, plate XCIII) represents an old man with his hands clasped behind the back. The arms and legs are carved free from the body and the work gives evidence of considerable skill and ingenuity.

Only from Big lake, between the lower Yukon and the mouth of the Kuskokwim, were dolls obtained with heads hollowed out, so that the eyes and the mouth were pierced into the cavity. The back of the heads of these dolls, after the interior had been excavated, were replaced by a thin wooden cover neatly fitted in the opening. Figure 127 represents a hollow-head, wooden doll from Big lake. Figure 5, plate XCIII, from the same locality, is made of bone, with the head fitted on a wooden pin projecting from the body, so that it turns as on a swivel.

Another doll from Big lake (figure 128) is similar to the preceding and is clothed in reindeer skin. The head is made of bone, and the beads attached to a cord passed through holes at the corners of the mouth represent labrets. The interior of the head is excavated.

The faces of dolls made in representation of females are etched to show the eyebrows, and sometimes the tattooing; the faces of dolls made to represent men have labrets of beads or pieces of ivory inserted at the corners of the mouth. The method of dressing the hair of women and their nose- and ear-rings are represented by hair and beads hung in the proper places. Some of the ivory dolls are provided with bracelets and bead necklaces as shown in figure 3, plate XCIII, from Hotham inlet.

FIG. 129—Wooden doll (½).

Large dolls of wood, from the country between Yukon and Kuskokwim rivers, have the eyes and the mouth represented by pieces of ivory inlaid in the wood, as in figure 129, from Kaialigamut. One of the most ingenious of these toys was obtained at Point Hope, on the Arctic coast, and is represented in figure 130. It is made of wood, and the well-carved head has a short string of beads attached to each side of the forehead for earrings, while the labret holes at the corners of the mouth show that it is intended to represent a man. Each eye is indicated by a blue bead, inserted so that the hole in the bead forms the pupil. The neck is in the form of a smooth, round pin, about half an inch in diameter, which sets in a deep socket cut into the shoulders. About the lower end of this pin are fastened two ends of a cord which is passed around in opposite directions and out in front, through two small holes in the body, and are tied together; thence they pass downward through a larger hole to the back. The lower part of the body is grasped from behind by the thumb and last two fingers, leaving the other two fingers resting in the loop of the cord. By slight pressure, either on one side or

FIG. 130—Mechanical doll (½).

the other of the loop, the head of the doll is made to turn to the right or left at will. Another ivory doll (figure 6, plate XCIII), from Unalaklit, represents a woman holding a child in her arms. Similar dolls are sometimes made to represent a small child in the hood of the fur coat, after the fashion in which women are wont to carry their infants throughout this region.

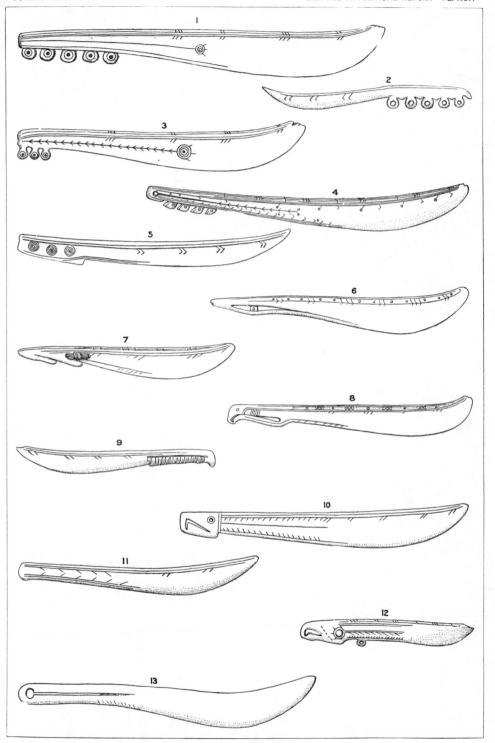

SNOW KNIVES (ABOUT ONE-FOURTH)

The girls frequently have a number of dolls varying in size, the smaller ones being made so that they will stand upright. While making a brief visit to Sledge island, two little girls in the house where we stopped amused us by watching their opportunity, while we were busy about other things, to place their dolls standing in a semicircle before us upon the floor, while they sat quietly behind as though permitting their dolls to take a look at the strangers. In connection with these toys girls have also a complete outfit of toy bedding made from the skins of mice or lemmings, small grass mats, toy boots, mittens, and clothing, all patterned after those used by the people of the locality.

FIG. 131—Toy bear with dog harness (⅓).

Other favorite toys of the children of both sexes are snow knives, which are from four to fifteen inches long and are made of ivory, bone, or wood, the two first-named materials being most commonly used. They are small at the handle and expand toward the end, usually curving upward and sometimes to one side. The makers frequently show great artistic skill in these objects; the handle is often tipped with a carving representing the head of a salmon, gull, seal, or other animal; the grip of the handle is insured by various projections, which sometimes consist of a series of three or more rounded bosses pierced by a small hole in the middle, as in figure 2, plate XCIV, from the lower Yukon. This specimen is well carved from a piece of bone.

Figure 3, plate XCIV, represents a large, handsomely made ivory knife from Koñigunugumut; the raven totem mark is etched on each side; three projecting knobs on the handle are pierced and the holes plugged with wood. Another specimen, from Chalitmut (figure 4, plate XCIV),

FIG. 132—Toy dogs and sled (about ½).

is made of ivory and has four murre heads in relief on the handle; the surface is ornamented with etched lines. An ivory knife from Ikogmut (figure 7, plate XCIV) has two long, rounded projections extending forward from the butt.

A large, handsomely made ivory knife from Koñigunugumut (figure 1, plate XCIV) has on the under side of the handle five rounded projections which are pierced for the insertion of plugs of wood; the raven totem sign is etched on both sides. Figure 5, plate XCIV, illustrates an ivory knife from Cape Vancouver, heavily etched on both sides; on the handle are three sets of concentric circles, pierced in the center and with wooden plugs inserted in the holes. A deerhorn knife from Kushunuk, represented in figure 9, plate XCIV, has a long slit in the handle, in

which is wound a piece of spruce root to afford a firm grip. Another
deerhorn knife, from Big lake (figure 11, plate XCIV), is very plainly
made. A well-made deerhorn knife from the lower Kuskokwim (figure
13, plate XCIV) has the handle pierced with a large hole from which a
slit extends forward.

FIG. 133—Toy bear (½).

Figure 6, plate XCIV, represents a
handsome ivory knife, obtained on
Togiak river by Mr Applegate.
The handle is curiously slit, with a
cross-bar in the opening, and an ordinary conventional design is etched
on the surface. Another knife, obtained also by Mr Applegate at the
same place (figure 8, plate XCIV), is of deerhorn and is elaborately
etched. The end of the handle is carved to represent the head of a
bird, probably a gerfalcon. A well-made ivory knife from Nulukhtulogumut (figure 10, plate XCIV) has the handle carved to represent the

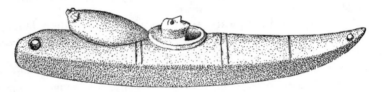

FIG. 134—Toy kaiak from St Lawrence island (¼).

head of a salmon. A small and rather rudely made ivory knife from
Ikogmut (figure 12, plate XCIV) also has the handle carved in the shape
of a salmon-head.

A large number of these knives were collected, most of them being
carved and etched in great variety of pattern. Many of these objects
in the National Museum repre-
sent localities from the extreme
southern limit of the Alaskan
Eskimo nearly to Point Barrow.
These knives are rarely used
for any other purpose than as
toys; the children play with
them in winter, cutting up the
hard, drifted snow, or marking
thereon various fantastic fig-

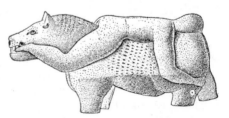

FIG. 135—Ivory image of man and bear (⅓).

ures representing mammals, birds, or other fancies. In a village south
of the Yukon mouth I saw children make figures of animals in the
snow and then run about cutting them up with their knives, evidently
imitating the killing of game by the hunters.

Figure 131 represents a toy figure of a white bear, which was
obtained on the Diomede island. It is made of wood and has a raw-

hide harness on the neck and back, similar to that used for dogs. The body is fashioned from a single piece, but the legs are made separately and are attached to the body by a peg inserted in a hole and fastened by other pegs.

A toy sled from St Lawrence island (figure 132) is carved from a single piece of ivory and has two small ivory figures of dogs attached to it with sinew cord.

Figure 133, from the same locality, represents a toy figure of a white bear carved from a single piece of ivory.

Figure 134 illustrates an ivory model of a kaiak, from St Lawrence island, and is a representation of the boats in use at that place. Looking up from the manhole is a human head carved in relief, and just back of the manhole is represented an inflated sealskin float.

The specimen from Norton bay, shown in figure 135, is an ivory figure of a white bear with a man lying along its back. This toy is intended as an illustration of an occurrence in one of the folktales.

MUSIC AND DANCES

The Eskimo of Bering sea and the lower Yukon are very fond of singing. Songs have a prominent place in their religious observances and festivals, as well as in their sports and dances. They also serve to while away the time when traveling at sea and sometimes on shore. Men are usually the singers, and will often keep up a monotonous chant for hours when traveling a long distance by water, and I often heard my men singing at night during sledge journeys when they were unable to sleep from the severe cold or for other cause. On one occasion I asked one of the men who was singing at night why he did so, and he replied that it made him feel warmer. Frequently songs of this kind, and some of those used while dancing, are a mere series of meaningless syllables, such as at other times serve as a refrain. Songs are composed for various other purposes, sometimes to preserve a recollection of past occurrences, to glorify some event, or for ridiculing one another; these latter are similar to the *nith* songs of Greenland, and are said to have been commonly used before white men came to Alaska. During my residence at St Michael I heard of instances of their having been sung by the Eskimo in some of the villages on the tundra, between the mouths of Kuskokwim and Yukon rivers, before the assembled people in the kashim. The only result was the satisfaction gained by the victor's consciousness that he had enlisted the sympathy of his fellow-townsmen and the chagrin of the one who felt himself worsted.

Songs are employed by shamans in their incantations and during religious festivals. Special songs are sung to the shades of the dead or to the *inuas* of various kinds to which the people are addressing their petitions, either for the purpose of propitiating the superior powers to prevent evil or to secure successful hunting. The songs in memory of the dead are heard at all festivals to departed shades, and at times are of an inexpressibly mournful character.

Almost invariably songs of every description, when sung in the kashim, are accompanied by the beating in regular time of one or more tambourine-like drums in the hands of old men, and the drummers, who are usually the leaders, sometimes sing a song, phrase by phrase, a repetition by the rest of the people following. At other times they are the only singers; this is particularly the case when dances are being performed.

Songs for the great festivals of a religious character and often those in honor of the dead, or for the bladder feast, are practiced for a long period by the villagers so that they may be given correctly at the proper time, the composer of the song usually teaching it to the others a few words at a time. Others of the songs have been handed down from ancient times, being transmitted, like the folktales, from generation to generation.

During one of my sledge journeys I chanced to stop at a village near Cape Vancouver where the people were learning a song for the feast to the dead. In the evening the lights were all extinguished in the kashim and in complete darkness an old man gave out the song, a few words at a time, and about twenty-five men, ranged around the middle of the room, united in singing the words to the time of a single drum beaten by another old man. The burden of the song I did not catch, but the refrain was a repetition of the syllables ûñ'-ai-yă-hai'-yă-yă, which serve for this purpose in many different songs over most of this region.

At another village in the same district a song was rendered in parts, the bass being sung by a number of men who kept excellent time to the beating of several drums, while the women and the boys, who were all arranged together on one side of the room, joined in the chorus every few minutes, producing a very pleasing effect. One song that is sung in a long, wailing chant is very effective, calling on the shades of the dead to enter the offerings that may be given them during the festival in their honor. The part of this song recorded at St Michael is as follows:

Tû-ko'-măl-û-g'ĭ'-ă tai'-kin-ă.   Ä-la'-ai-ya'.   Mŭ-klûg-û-mŭk kän-ûkh'-kûñ-ûm'-kĭn.
Dead ones   come here.   (Chorus.)   Hair sealskin   tent you-will-get (for a)
Ä la'-ai-ya'.
(Chorus.)

Tai'-kin-ă-ka'; tun-tu'-mŭk cho-g'okh'-kûñ-ûm'-kĭn.   Ä-la'-ai-ya'.   Tai'-kin-ă-ka'.
Come here, do;   reindeer skin   bed you will get (for a).   (Chorus.)   Come here, do.

During one festival to the dead that was witnessed the mourners who were making the gift offerings to the namesakes of their deceased relatives, entered and, dancing together in the center of the kashim, sang an invitation to their dead ones to return. The burden of the song was that the absent ones were missed and were begged to return as their friends were lonely. The loud, wailing manner in which this song was rendered to the music of the drums and the steady, monotonous chant of the drummers rendered the whole very effective.

The following two songs give a general idea of the character of those sung at festivals for pastime. The first is a song of a Malemut hunter from the head of Kotzebue sound. He wishes for the time to come when the reindeer shall renew their horns, that the hunting season may begin. It was noted that the same idea was repeated again and again with constant repetition of the same chorus, so that a few phrases did duty for hours:

Ă-ŭñ'-ă-yai'   *ya-ĭ-yae*   *ŭñ-a-ĭ-yă*   *ĭ-yă*   *ai-yae-ig'-ĭ-a*
  (Chorus)   (Chorus)

Co-ai-ă-chŭg'-ŭ-lĭ   *yae-yă-ĭ-a*   *ŭñ'-a-ĭ-yă-ĭ-ya-ai*
  I want   (Chorus)   (Chorus)

ă-to'-ai-găd-ly   *ŭñ-ĭ-yae-yae*   *kin'-gh'-kluñ'-ă*
  very much   (Chorus)   to see

ĭ-yae-ĭ-yă   *nŭg-g'ul-ĭñ.*
  (Chorus)   the deer horns make, etc.

The following song, composed and sung by a man at Cape Prince of Wales in Bering strait, expressed his wish to see the ships come in the spring, because his tobacco was gone:

I-ghĭ-ghŭn-ă   *Ŭñ-ĭ-yă-ae-yă*   *mai'-ŭ-ruk'-ĭ-gă*   *Ĭ-yŭñ-ĭ-yă-yă*
  The mountain   (Chorus)   I wish to climb   (Chorus)

chŭn-mu-i-nak'.   *I-yae-yă*   *Kŭt-kĭt'-kŭ-mă,*
  to get to the water.   (Chorus)   I sit on the top,

kĭ-nĭg'-nai-găk   *I-yŭñ-ă-yă-ya*   *um'-ĭ-ŭk-pŭk-mŭn-ă*
  I wish to see   (Chorus)   the big boats coming

Ă-yŭ-yae-ya   *tĭ-bă'-lae-ka.*
  (Chorus)   tobacco (with).

The following music was written for me by Bishop Seghers, an accomplished Catholic missionary (afterward killed on the upper Yukon), from a song sung by the Eskimo during a dance at Ikogmut on the lower Yukon in the winter of 1879. This gentleman, who was a skilled musician, said that the most remarkable thing he had noted in the songs of the Eskimo, both of the lower Yukon and of the adjacent coast of Bering sea, was the ease and accuracy with which they raised and dropped an exact octave when singing:

Despite the fact that these people are so fond of their own music, they are unable to understand or enjoy that of a more complicated character. At St Michael some of the men were frequently invited into one of the houses where there was a small organ, and the agent of the Fur company would play simple melodies for them. In every instance the visitors kept perfectly quiet, and watched the keyboard of the instrument closely, as if fascinated. Finally, I asked an old man who had attended several of these concerts if he enjoyed the music, and he replied frankly that he did not, because, said he, "I do not understand what the noise says. It sounds confusedly in my ears and is strange to them, so that I do not know what it says. I like better to hear the drum and singing in the kashim, for I understand it." But he added that he liked to watch the movements of the performer's fingers as they sped over the keyboard, the rapid motion pleasing him. I afterward made the same inquiry of other men from various distant localities along the coast, when they heard the music at St Michael, and received an almost identical reply.

The drums used by the Eskimo of western Alaska and on the adjacent coast of Siberia are made in one pattern, having a rounded tambourine-like frame, over one side of which is stretched a thin, parchment like covering, usually made from the bladders of seals and walrus. The cover is held in place by a cord of sinew or rawhide, wound around the outer border of the drum in a sunken groove, enabling the cover to be tightened at will.

The frames, usually made of spruce, are from one to three inches in width and are bent to form a ring, either circular or somewhat pear-shape in outline, measuring from ten to thirty inches in diameter. The largest ones seen in use were in the district between lower Yukon and Kuskokwim rivers. Near the Kuslevak mountains a drum was seen covered with tanned reindeer skin, which was the only exception to the ordinary covering that was noted, and this was due to the fact that the usual material could not be obtained at that point.

Ordinarily the ends of the drum frame overlap and are fastened with sinew or rawhide cords, which pass through holes in the wood; but along the coast from Bering strait northward, drums were seen which had the ends of the frame beveled to wedge-shape points and inserted in a short, intervening piece of ivory of the same width and thickness as the frame. These pieces were beveled with a deep, wedge-shape slot to receive the ends of the wood, and pierced with holes through which were passed wooden pegs to fasten the ends of the frame in place, thus forming a neatly made joint. This splice is carved on its outer border to match the groove on the edge of the frame for the reception of the cover lashings. They are usually fitted with a handle from four to six inches long, with a square notch in its upper surface for the reception of the lower edge of the frame. The latter is ordinarily held in position by sinew lashings passed through holes and thence through corresponding holes in the handle just below the notch, or are passed around the handle. A drum from Sledge island and another from Cape Wankarem, Siberia, are attached to their handles with wooden pegs inserted through holes at the inner end of the handle and through the drum frame in the notch. These handles are commonly plain rods of ivory, deerhorn, or bone, round or oval in section, with the ends rounded, but in many instances they are carved in various patterns.

One of these handles (number 43807), which was obtained at Shakto-lik, is of walrus ivory, and is six inches long by an inch and a half in diameter. It is carved in the form of a walrus, the well-made head being placed at the inner end; on the lower side are four diagonal grooves for finger-rests, and at the rear the animal's flippers are represented. The back is etched with short lines to indicate bristly hairs.

A handle from Point Hope, on the Arctic coast (figure 136) is of ivory, four inches long. At one end is carved a human face, with small blue beads inlaid for eyes and the mouth incised; along the lower side are four finger-grooves, and an ivory strip is fitted in the square slot for the ends of the drum frame. Another specimen from the same place (num-

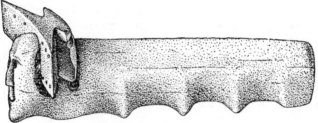

Fig. 136—Drum handle (⅔).

ber 63798) is similar to the preceding, but has the face curiously distorted. The tip of the handle is patched with a block of wood neatly fastened with five wooden pegs.

A handle of reindeer horn from St Michael (figure 137) measures five inches in length and represents the head and neck of a sand-hill crane. The beak is open, and small, round incisions mark the eyes and ears; the slot for the frame of the drum is at the base of the neck, and the wings of the bird are indicated by an incised line on each side, extending diagonally to the rear, where they meet on the back; short, parallel, incised lines represent the quill feathers. A drum obtained at Sledge island (number 45401) has a handle made from a section of deerhorn without ornamentation. The frame, made of spruce, is slightly pear-shape, with the small end next to the

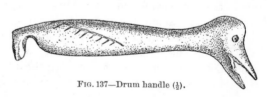

Fig. 137—Drum handle (½).

handle, and is about 20 inches in diameter. The ends overlap and are fastened with sinew cord. It is fastened in the slot of the handle by a wooden pin, and is beveled both ways on the inside from a central ridge. On the outer surface, near the upper edge, is a deep groove to receive the braided sinew cord that fastens the cover, which has the looped end attached to a projecting wooden peg on the frame to the right of the handle.

In a drum (number 38840) obtained at Cape Vancouver, the frame, made of spruce wood, 3 inches broad, is bent in a circle, 28 inches in diameter, the overlapping ends being sewed together with rawhide cord.

Over this frame is stretched a cover of walrus or white-whale intestine, held in place by a cord in a groove around the middle of the frame. It has a large handle, 26 inches long, made of the same material as the frame, and largest on the inner end, which is in the shape of a sea-parrot's head. On the back of the bird's neck is a square notch, an inch deep, into which the frame fits, and outside of which the handle projects about 20 inches. The bill of the sea-parrot is colored red; the rest of the handle is the color of the wood, except a band of red near the middle.

These large drums are frequently held by one man while the other beats them with a long, slender rod. As with the smaller drums, they are frequently struck so that the rod taps against the frame at the same time that it strikes the cover, thus producing a sharp, rapping sound which mingles with the more resonant tone.

The International Polar Expedition obtained at Point Barrow large drums, somewhat similar to that collected by me at Cape Vancouver, with handles also carved on the inner ends to represent the heads of birds, one of which is that of a cormorant and another the head of a murre.

FIG. 138—Ivory baton for beating time on a stick ($\frac{7}{8}$).

In the country between the lower Yukon and the Kuskokwim, as well as on the American shore of Bering strait, I saw large and small drums used at the same time, producing a pleasing combination of sound. The drum is held by the handle in the left hand, the top slightly inclined away from the drummer and about on a level with his chin. When excited by the sound and movement, the drummers sometimes raise the drums almost at arm length, so that the handles are on a level with their brows. They are beaten in measured time, two strokes in quick succession, then a short pause, and two strokes again. Each drummer has a single slender, flat rod about 12 to 16 inches long, which he holds in the right hand.

While witnessing a festival to the dead on the lower Yukon, I saw people dancing near the graves to time beaten with a stick on the end of a log projecting from one of the houses, and another party dancing on the ice on the river to time beaten on a piece of driftwood which had been taken to the river for the purpose. This was the only instance south of Norton sound in which I saw such an accompaniment to dancing. On the American shore of Bering strait, and thence northward

along the Arctic coast, resonant pieces of wood are regularly beaten
to aid the drum accompaniment during dancing. For this purpose a
short, heavy baton of walrus ivory is generally used. Such an instrument (figure 138), was obtained at Port Clarence. It is 10½ inches in
length by an inch in diameter, rounded, beveled at each end, and has
the slight curve of the tusk from which it was made. Fine shavings
are bound around the butt by a braided sinew cord to afford a grip, and
a deerhorn peg close to the projecting end of the handle prevents the
hand from slipping. Extending from near this peg to the other end of
the grip is a loop of twisted sinew cord which aids in holding the instrument firmly. On its outer end the mouth, eyes, and blowholes of a
right whale are represented by incised holes and pits. Between the
blowholes are inserted some small, downy feathers, held in place by
wooden pegs, to represent the spouting of the whale.

In addition to the dances performed during the various festivals and
described in connection with those ceremonies, various others are practiced among the Eskimo with whom I came in contact. These latter
are generally executed for pastime, and are often merely a series of
movements supposed to be graceful or pleasing; at other times they
are distinctly symbolic, frequently carrying out and illustrating a long
narrative by gestures and sometimes accompanied by a song. Dances
are usually accompanied by the beating of one or more drums and by
the singing of the drummers, and sometimes of other males, but at times
the drummers cease, and the dancing continues to the sound of voices.
Some of these performances are extremely grotesque, the dancers being
young men, often quite nude or simply wearing a pair of ornamental
trunks made of fine deerskin, who sing or utter loud cries and leap
about, gesticulating with their arms and legs and contorting their bodies
in every conceivable manner. The object of such dances is apparently
to amuse the spectators, and the successful dancers frequently cause
great laughter among the assembled people by the absurdity of their
attitudes and movements. The young men exert themselves in friendly
rivalry at such times until they are forced to cease from sheer exhaustion.

Both men and women take part in the dances, each having certain
movements peculiar to himself. The women remain with their feet
planted squarely on the floor and, swaying the body and slowly gesticulating with hands and arms, go through the figures permitted to them,
always keeping time to the music. Very commonly the women have a
long, feather wand in each hand which they wave slowly back and forth
as they move. During certain religious festivals they also use finger-
masks—small, round, flat pieces of wood with a projection below, through
which are one or two holes for admitting the first or the first and second
fingers; they are carved to represent a human face or a face supposed to
belong to some animal, an *inua*, or some supernatural being. They
are generally painted and surrounded by a halo-like fringe, formed
by the upstanding hair on a narrow band of skin, usually of the rein-

18 ETH——23

deer or wolf. They are also ornamented with quill feathers of various birds, frequently tipped with down.

The men ordinarily rest the weight of the body first on one foot and then on the other, while the free foot is advanced, the ball resting on the floor and the heel continually raised and brought down with a sounding thump in time to the beating of the drums. At the same time the dancers contort the body and gesticulate with the hands and arms in rythmic motion. Frequently the dancer sings or utters loud cries at regular intervals, springing from one side to the other. The rythmic beating of the drums and the accompanying songs work the dancers to a pitch of great excitement, and they sometimes go on for hours with these violent exertions, the perspiration rolling down their bodies, until they cease from exhaustion.

With rare exceptions the dances are performed in the kashim, taking place during the winter months, that is, from October until the end of April. Both songs and dances are practiced beforehand when preparing for any great festival. In addition to the larger performances accompanying the more important festivals, there are small dances of rather frequent occurrence among the villagers during the early part of winter; but these are informal affairs performed for amusement by a few of the young men.

A ceremonial dance is performed by a stranger who enters for the first time the kashim of a village. On such occasion he is expected to make a small offering or gift of propitiation to the headman, who divides it among the other old men. The stranger then steps out upon the floor and dances for a short time, sometimes singing a song expressing his friendship for the people he is with, or merely a chorus song. In this way he is considered to have introduced himself properly and thus to have gained the freedom of the kashim.

At St Michael we were usually invited to the first dances held in the kashim every autumn. Each year we made a practice of carrying a little tobacco, which we handed to the headman upon entering, and this he would divide into small portions and distribute among the other men. At such times, if one of us would step out upon the floor and execute a short dance after the style of the Eskimo, it was received with great merriment by the assembled villagers.

The dances of the Eskimo, whether on the islands of Bering sea or on the banks of Kuskokwim river, are very similar in general character, but local variations are common. On Sledge Island, in March, 1880, was witnessed a curious and characteristic performance, different from anything seen elsewhere. We found the people on the verge of starvation, and nearly all of their dogs had died from lack of food. Our own dogs were dying from the same cause, so we decided to return at once to the mainland. When the headman of the villagers learned this he came to beg us to remain at least one night with them so that they might show us their appreciation of our visit, promising that the inhabitants would find something with which to feed our dogs and that they would give a dance in the kashim in our honor.

About two hours after dark we were invited into the kashim and given the place of honor at the rear end of the room. Half a dozen men, including the headmen of the village, stepped out in time to singing and drumming, and went through the movements of an ordinary dance such as had been seen at the beginnings of dances at Cape Darby, Unalaklit, and elsewhere southward to the mouth of Kuskokwim river.

One of these dancers wore about his brow a fillet made from the skin of the head and neck of an Adams loon, with the beak left on and projecting over the middle of the forehead; another man wore a fillet made from the white breast of a murre with the wing-feather of a gerfalcon stuck in it so as to stand erect over the forehead.

Then a man and a woman took the floor, performing some figures or movements such as I had seen used by a couple at Unalaklit. Next was a dance of similar character by a half-grown boy and a girl; their motions were greatly varied, but in perfect unison; they postured with the body inclined first to one side and then to the other, alternating with an inclination forward until their heads nearly touched the floor. Many of their movements were characterized by the swaying grace that is notable in many of the dances of these people.

When this was finished nine women and girls seated themselves close together, cross-legged, and stripped to the waist, on a bench extending along one side of the room, facing in one direction along the length of the bench. Drummers and singers struck up a medley different from anything I had ever heard, and the women on the bench responded by executing a long and complicated series of swaying motions with the head, arms, and body, in perfect unison. From where I sat the dancers were in profile, and their light-colored bodies showed in strong contrast against the sooty wall. Their slow, regular motions, with bodies swaying alternately from one side to the other, now inclining forward and then swaying back, the arms constantly waving in a series of graceful movements, presented a remarkably pleasing sight.

The headman asked me if I liked the dance, and I told him that I did and that I thought it a good one, whereupon he seemed greatly pleased and told me that several of the dancers were his wives. Directly afterward he called out something to the singers, and the latter immediately began a different song and the women a different set of motions. In this way the headman changed the dances until over twenty distinct songs and sets of motions had been executed; some of the songs and movements were done in very slow time, while others were rapid. All of the movements were evidently conventional and carefully learned by the performers, as they were executed with great regularity.

On one occasion, at Sabotnisky, on the lower Yukon, a dance was given for my benefit by several villagers. Two women took the most prominent part. One of the performers by her gestures told the story of her father's life and battles during the wars among the villagers preceding the arrival of the white men; the gestures were mainly beyond my comprehension, but the Eskimo about me appeared to understand them all. I could interpret the motions of stealthy approach and retreat, then a struggle with the enemy and the flight, ending by a sudden turn and the killing of a pursuer by a spear thrust. In addition there were a great deal of gesture and posture with hands and bodies which seemed to be full of meaning to the people about me. This woman's companion went through a series of motions describing berry picking and various other occupations of women in the summer and fall. During all their movements both of them were extremely graceful and kept accurate time to the music.

On February 12, 1880, I remained over night in the village of Unalaklit, where a number of dances were given in my honor. Soon after dark I was invited to the kashim, where a dozen young men were stripped to the waist and ranged around the room in a circle. Five or six old men stood near the lamp at the rear end of the room beating a drum and singing one of the common dance songs; the young men postured and leaped with such energy that the perspiration ran down their bodies, as it did also from the faces of the drum men. There seemed to be a rivalry between the musicians and the dancers to outdo one another, and the singers would stop to take breath occasionally, quickly beginning again while the dancers were still panting, causing laughter at the expense of the latter. This continued for some time, until the dancers acknowledged themselves defeated and sat down. Then a young man came out alone, stripped to the waist, and stood before the entrance hole in the middle of the room. On his face was a mask representing a wolf-head. He stood for a few moments appearing to look intently into the hole in the floor while he postured slowly back and forth with his arms and body; while he did this two women came up behind him, stood close by and began gesturing, imitating in perfect time every motion made by him. Then the time of the song suddenly changed, the women stepping out quickly, one upon each side a few paces away, and all three postured, swaying back and forth to the song. The man moved first toward one woman then toward the other with a gliding motion and appeared to try to grasp them with one hand, never losing the time and keeping the motion uniform with the movements of the women. After he had done this he resumed his first position, the women stepped back to their former place, and the dance soon ended. This was said to represent a wolf hunting reindeer.

When this dance ended, the man who wore the wolf mask went out, but came in again very quickly wearing a mask representing a human face; he took the same position as before, beginning with a set of postures of the arms and body different from those seen in the first dance. He was joined by the two women, one on each side of him, and all went through the motion of picking berries, which was done very slowly with a continual graceful swaying of the body. This dance ended the performance.

At Cape Darby, on the same journey, I passed a night with the villagers and was invited into the kashim with my companion to witness a dance given for us. We went in and found the entire population of the village assembled. A small present of tobacco to the headman was our offering as strangers, after which we were given the place of honor by the drummers at the rear end of the room. The song and the drum-beating began at once, with a chorus song of meaningless syllables like those sung in dances of conventional style. A number of men and women kept the floor, going through a series of ordinary postures until they became tired and sat down. These were followed by a man and a woman who came forward and went through a new set of motions, which I was told they had learned from people on the shore of Bering strait. Afterward a woman came out and imitated the gathering of eggs of sea fowl among the rocks. At certain intervals a song accompanied her movements, which was intended to represent the cries of birds startled from their nests.

FEASTS AND FESTIVALS

THE FUNCTION OF THE CELEBRATIONS

Among the Eskimo of lower Kuskokwim and Yukon rivers and thence northward along the coast to Kotzebue sound, as well as on the islands of Bering strait, the festivals form some of the most important features of their social life. The same may undoubtedly be said of the Eskimo elsewhere in Alaska, but these remarks are intended to cover the region over which my personal observations extended.

These festivals serve to enliven the long, depressing evenings of Arctic winter, and at intervals render the cold, stormy season a period of enjoyment and feasting. They serve also to promote friendly intercourse between the people of adjacent villages and districts. Through the festivals comes an interchange of products and manufactures of different localities, and, above all, they are important in expressing and carrying out the religious beliefs and observances of these people.

Nearly or quite all of the formal festivals of the Eskimo in this region are of a more or less religious character. As examples of these may be noted the Bladder feast and the Feast to the Dead.

CALENDAR OF FESTIVALS

Having been more familiar with the Unalit Eskimo of Norton sound than with any others of this region, I subjoin a list of festivals observed among them, although it is probably not complete. A somewhat similar program exists among the other tribes within the limits of the region covered by the present paper. While the same festival may exist in different localities over a considerable area, rites vary locally to a greater or less extent, although the central idea is preserved. Intercourse with the Russians and subsequently with the Americans at St Michael and adjacent parts of Norton sound has modified in many respects the customs of the Eskimo in that region, yet the ancient beliefs and observances are still preserved among the older people.

Certain festivals, however, are no longer celebrated in the district named. Perhaps the most striking change has been in the disuse of masks, which are still used in the complicated ceremonials of the inhabitants of the country lying between the mouths of the Kusko-kwim and the Yukon. Among the Unalit Eskimo about St Michael I noted the following festivals:

1. *Ai-ya'-g'uk*, or Asking festival, which takes place each year about the middle or latter part of November.

2. *Ĭhl'-û-g'ĭ*, the Festival to the Dead. In this there are songs and dances, with food offerings and libations in honor of the dead. It is held the last of November or the first of December.

3. *Chau'-ĭ-yûk*, the Bladder feast. This is held usually during the December moon and sometimes extends into January. It is a festival belonging essentially to the coast people, but is still preserved in modified form among the Eskimo of lower Kuskokwim and Yukon rivers.

4. A repetition of the Festival to the Dead is given at St Michael two days after the close of the Bladder feast, and (5) another just before the opening of the fishing season in spring.

6. *Ĭkh'-tû-ka'-tûkh-tûk*, Great feast to the Dead. This is the most nota-ble of all the festivals, owing to the fact that years are spent in prepar-ing for the display with which it is celebrated. Among the fur traders it is known as the "Ten-year feast," but in reality there is no definite number of years between its recurrence. It is held at the time when the makers consider that they have accumulated sufficient material in the shape of food, skins of fur-bearing animals, and other objects of value to properly honor the shades of their deceased relatives for whose benefit the feast is held.

THE "INVITING-IN" FEAST

I-thû'-ka-gûk, a mask festival, known as the "inviting-in feast," is observed along the lower Yukon and southward to Kuskokwim river. Masks in every variety of shape and form are made by the men for use in it. Some of these are so large that it becomes necessary to hang them from the roof of the kashim by a stout cord, and the owner stands behind with the mask fastened to his head, wagging and swaying it from side to side. The masks are usually carved to represent heads of animals, frequently the totemic animals of the maker, and very often expressing mythological fancies, which will be more fully detailed in treating of masks. The shamans make masks representing the faces of their supernatural or semihuman familiars by whose aid they claim to work their will. The object of these faces is to propitiate and do honor to the animals or beings represented by them, and thus to bring about plenty of game during the coming year and to ward off evil influences. The *inuas* or shades of the various animals are invited and are supposed to be present and enjoy the songs and dances, with the food and drink offerings, given in their honor. The masks are burned at the conclusion of the ceremonies, and should a man sell his mask he must replace it with wood in about equal amount for the sacrificial fire which takes place subsequent to the ceremony. This festival is held usually in January or February of each year. Although I was not able to witness one of these observances, many of the masks used in them were obtained.

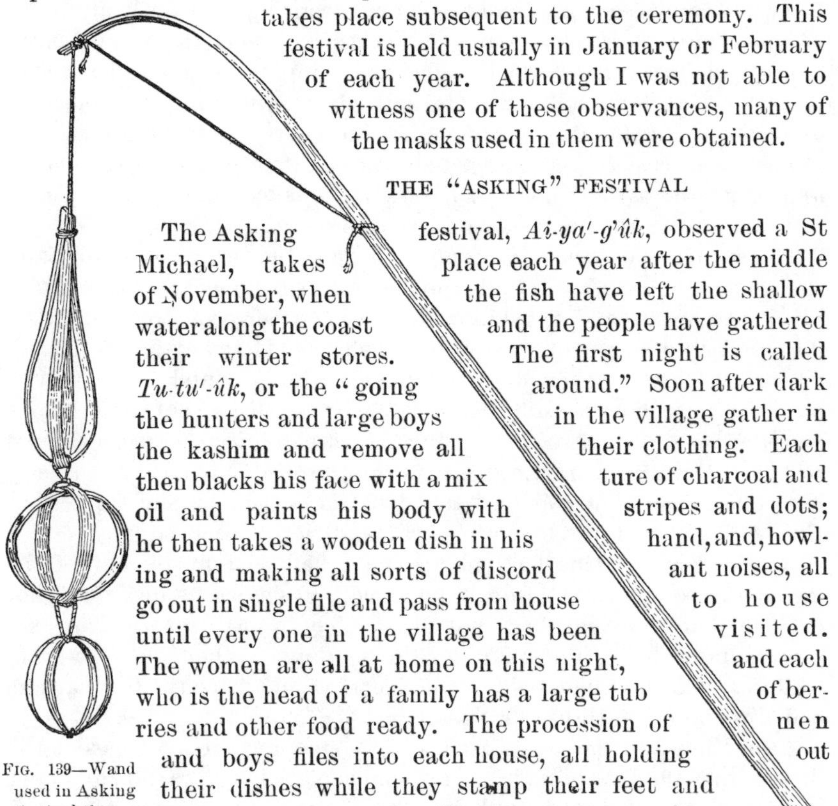

THE "ASKING" FESTIVAL

The Asking festival, *Ai-ya'-g'ûk*, observed a St Michael, takes place each year after the middle of November, when the fish have left the shallow water along the coast and the people have gathered their winter stores. The first night is called *Tu-tu'-ûk*, or the " going around." Soon after dark the hunters and large boys in the village gather in the kashim and remove all their clothing. Each then blacks his face with a mix ture of charcoal and oil and paints his body with stripes and dots; he then takes a wooden dish in his hand, and, howl- ing and making all sorts of discord ant noises, all go out in single file and pass from house to house until every one in the village has been visited. The women are all at home on this night, and each who is the head of a family has a large tub of ber- ries and other food ready. The procession of men

Fig. 139—Wand used in Asking festival (¼).

and boys files into each house, all holding out their dishes while they stamp their feet and utter grunting sounds. The women at every house place food in each of the dishes, and when the round is completed all return to the kashim, shouting and stamping. While in the house their faces are kept turned toward the floor so that they shall not be recognized. Outside the children follow them from house to house, shouting and making a great outcry. When they return to the kashim the soot is washed from their faces and bodies with urine and, giving some of the food to the old men, all sit down to the feast. Next day a wand, called *ai-yă'-g'ûk*, is made by a man chosen for the purpose. This wand has a slender, rod-like handle, with three hanging globes at the outer end. Figure 139 illustrates one of these wands.

In the evening of this day the men are gathered in the kashim and the women in their houses, as on the preceding night. The man who prepared the wand takes it in his hand and stands with it in the middle of the room; any man in the community has the privilege of telling him the name of any article he wishes, sometimes giving him the name of the woman from whom he desires to obtain it. The wand-bearer then goes to the house of the woman named and stands before her, swinging the hanging globes on the wand, at the same time telling her what he has come for, and then stands waiting. The woman thinks of something which she desires in return and tells the wand-bearer, whereupon he returns to the kashim and, swinging the globes before the one who sent him, tells what is desired in return for the object he demanded. In this way every one in the village asks for something. When the messenger has completed his task, the men go to their houses and bring the articles for which they were asked, and when all have returned to the kashim a dance is performed.

The women then come, bringing with them the things asked for, and the exchange is made through the messenger, who must have his face blackened and wear a fishskin coat, or some other poor dress, having a dogskin belt with the tail fastened on behind. If any article is desired which the person asked does not possess, he is bound by custom to obtain it as soon as possible after the festival and present it to the one who wishes it. The two exchanging presents in this way are considered to hold a certain temporary relationship, termed *i-lo'-g'ŭk*. Formerly those once made *i-lo'-g'ŭk* exchanged presents each succeeding year at this festival, but that custom is now less strictly observed.

At the time of this festival any man had a right to request the messenger to inform the woman he named, if she was unmarried, that he wished to share her bed that night. The woman returned answer that he must bring a deerskin for the bedding. When all were gathered in the kashim he gave her the deerskin, and after the festival was ended remained with her for the night.

After the wand has been used while conveying the messages of the different people, it is hung in a conspicuous place in the kashim and kept there until the festival is ended. This instrument is much respected by the community, and it is considered shameful to refuse the requests made with it, and a person doing this would be despised by every one. In some districts this festival is observed by asking presents between persons of the same sex. It exists substantially as described from the vicinity of Bering strait to the mouth of Kuskokwim river, although each locality varies slightly the details and rites performed.

The custom of the men taking women during the night of this festival is observed throughout this district. One variation of the festival is for the messenger to be told secretly the desire of each person, and until all meet in the kashim no one knows with whom he is to exchange. On the lower Yukon and in the adjacent districts to the southward this is accomplished by each person making a small image of the object he desires and hanging it on .the messenger's wand, which is taken into the kashim where all examine the images. Each then takes the image of whatever he wishes to supply, and the messenger tells him from whom it comes and what is desired in return.

THE TRADING FESTIVAL

Another celebration, known as the Trading festival and somewhat allied to the preceding, is held at irregular intervals almost everywhere throughout the region. The following description of its observance at Andreivsky, on the lower Yukon, will serve as an illustration of its character. The fur trader who made the festival was instructed by an old Eskimo and observed all the customary ceremonies.

Early in the winter the trader sent to several villages in the surrounding district a messenger, who was instructed to go to two or three of the best hunters in each place and tell them that the trader thought they had skins of mink, otter, or of other fur-bearing animals, as the case might be. The maker of the feast and the two or three men in each village to whom he sent his special invitation were known during the festival as *näs'kut'* or "heads." Each *näs'kuk'* replied to the messenger that he thought the trader had powder, lead, or whatever else he most desired. Then the messenger went into the kashim and addressed the young men generally, saying that his *näs'kuk'* thought they possessed skins of various kinds. In this way the man went from village to village, learning at the same time the date or time in a certain moon when all could go to the feast. A message of this kind sent to a village is considered as an invitation to the feast to be held at the village of the giver. The messenger having ended his errand, returned, telling the *näs'kuk'* when the guests would arrive; also what each headman among the invited guests wished from him. The chief *näs'kuk'* then prepared for his guests, gathering food in abundance, together with the various articles desired by the people invited. Those who had been invited gathered at a predetermined village and in a body approached the place appointed for the festival.

In the present feast, as soon as the guests came in sight a messenger went to meet them on the ice of the Yukon. He ran out and stopped just before the guests, so that they might send any message they wished to the feast giver. In this instance an old woman sent word to a little girl in the trader's family that she wished a reindeer skin. When the first messenger came back, two others ran out to meet the guests, crying out as they went, "Are we not strong men? Are we not strong men?" Then, as if in reply, "Yes, we are strong; yes, we are strong; we do not steal," and much more of the same kind of self-glorification. Running up close to the guests, they stopped and stared at them without speaking, then turned and ran swiftly back. When they returned, two others ran out in the same way. The last four messengers wore about their heads fillets made of skin from the throats of reindeer, so arranged that the long hairs stood up, looking like crowns.

When the guests were close to the house of the feast giver they stopped and two drums were taken out to them by messengers. Then, while the villagers where the feast was given stood in front of their houses looking at the guests, the latter sang and danced on the ice for a few minutes. After they stopped the people of the trader's village danced and sang a welcome. The dancing and singing of the guests was a propitiatory ceremony, such as is customary with strangers on first entering a kashim, while the dance of the hosts was one of welcome. Then the guests came forward, passing by their hosts without a word, and went into the kashim. As soon as they were seated, the host, or chief *naskuk*, brought in and gave them the articles requested of the messenger when he went out on the ice to meet them. After this, food was distributed to every one. In the evening the "heads" took into the kashim the skins or other articles they had brought. Each *naskuk* must bring at least one of the skins of the kind named by the messengers in the invitation to the feast or he would be shamed. They usually try, in defense of honor, to bring as many skins as possible of each kind requested.

While these skins are being brought in the hosts are seated at one side of the room, beating drums and singing. As the *naskuk* to whom the messenger went first in the village goes in with his furs, the host or chief *naskuk* of the entertainers meets him as the most important guest and puts upon him a new fur coat as a mark of honor. Then as each headman goes in and throws down his skins he executes a short dance in time with the drums, giving a pantomime representing some exploit of his father or of his own, and singing at the same time in praise of the person represented. After this the young men who came on the general invitation bring in their furs, each having at least one skin of the kind desired, but as it is a distinction to bring more, some of them have quite a number; these are thrown in a heap near the lamp at the head of the room. When all of the guests have brought in their skins they sit about the room for a time and sing. The host then takes out the skins brought by the other headmen. He soon returns, bringing to one of the headmen the articles requested of the messenger, these being a fair equivalent for the furs he had brought to the trader. At the same time the host throws down near the lamp some articles of value and dances for a short time. He then goes out and returns with the articles desired by the second headman, and so on until all have received the things they desired. By this time the heap of articles near the lamp has been augmented by the host on each return to the kashim until there is an equivalent for the pile of furs brought by the young men, when it is distributed among them. Then the host entertains the guests by songs and dances and the festival is ended by the distribution of food.

The skins brought by the young men in this instance were taken by the trader, but when the Eskimo give the festival these are distributed among the young men of the village who contribute to the general supply of articles to be distributed among the guests.

In the middle of February, 1880, while at the head of Norton sound, a party of Malemut were met on their way to a trading festival of this kind at Unalaklit. Their sledges were laden with reindeer skins. I afterward learned that they took part in the festival, but being dissatis-fied with the presents given in return for their skins, they took them back and returned home.

In a rude sketch drawn for me by an Eskimo from the Kaviak pen-insula, the figures of a party of men from Cape Prince of Wales are portrayed, showing them on their way to a festival of this kind and being met by the villagers of the place to which they are going.

FEASTS TO THE DEAD

MORTUARY FEASTS IN GENERAL

Every year the *Ĭhl'-û-g'ĭ'* at St Michael is held during the latter part of November or early in December. It is repeated two days after the Bladder feast of autumn and just before the beginning of the salmon fishing in spring. It is given for the sole purpose of making offerings of food, water, and clothing to the shades of those recently deceased, and of offerings to the dead who have not yet been honored by one of the great festivals. The makers of this feast are the nearest rela-tives of those who have died during the preceding year, joined by all others of the village who have not given a great feast to their dead.

The day before the festival, among the Eskimo of St Michael and on the lower Yukon, the nearest male relative goes to the grave of the deceased and plants before it, if it be that of a man, a newly made stake upon which is placed a small model of a seal spear, and if of a woman, a wooden dish. Sometimes the spear model is replaced by the model of a kaiak paddle or an umiak oar. Upon these implements are marked the totems of the dead. At times, however, the totem of the deceased is indicated by a simple wooden image of the totem animal, which is placed on top of the stake. This is the notification which brings the shade from the land of the dead to the grave, where it waits, ready to be called into the kashim by the songs of invitation during the festival.

At the *Ĭhl'-û-g'ĭ'* held the year preceding a great festival to the dead, those making the festival plant other stakes of invitation bearing the same symbols before the graves of those to be honored, and by these graves are sung songs of invitation to the shades, informing them of the approaching festival. It is said that when one of these festivals begins with its opening song of invitation, the shades are in their graves and come thence to the kashim, where they assemble in the fire pit, under the floor. At the proper time they ascend from their place beneath the floor, entering and possessing the bodies of their name-sakes in the kashim, and thus obtaining for themselves the offerings of food, drink, or clothing which are made to these namesakes for the benefit of the deceased. It is by means of such offerings that the shade is believed to obtain the supplies necessary for its wants in the land of the dead.

When the offerings have been made and the songs concluded, the shades are sent back to their abiding place by stamping upon the floor. On the day of the feast no one is permitted to do any work about the village, and all work with sharp-edged or pointed tools is prohibited for fear that some shade may be about, and, being injured, become angry and do harm to the people. All are supposed to take part in this festival whose nearest relatives have died, and in propor-tion to the care and generosity exercised on these occasions the shade is made happy and comfortable.

These Eskimo fear to die unless they have someone to make offer-ings to their memory, and childless persons generally adopt a child so that their shade may not be forgotten at the festivals, as people who have no one to make offerings for them are supposed to suffer great destitution in the other world. For this reason it is regarded as the severest punishment possible for a shade to have these rites neglected by its relatives. When a person has been very much disliked, his shade is sometimes purposely ignored.

At St Michael and the lower Yukon, when this feast is held, each of those who have dead friends to honor takes an oil lamp into the kashim at midday, where the lamps are lighted and arranged around the room a yard or two from the wall on supports about two feet high. If the shade of a man is to be honored a lamp is placed in front of the place he formerly occupied in the room. These lamps are kept burning until the festival is ended, and in this way the shades are supposed to be lighted on their way back to the earth and to receive in the land of the dead the light which they used in their houses. After this an old man takes a drum, and sitting in front of the main lamp in the middle of the room, beats it in slow, regular time, while singing the invitation to the shades, accompanied by all the villagers. This is quite a long song, of which the following few words are given:

Tú-ko'-mäl-û-g'ĭ'-ă,   tai'-kin-ă;   Ä-la'-ai-ya'   mú-klûg'-û-mûk
Dead ones,   come here;   (Chorus)   sealskins (for a)

kän-ûkh'-kûñ-ûm'-kĭn.   Ä-la'-ai-ya'.   Tai'-kin-a'-ka;   tหn-tu'-mûk
tent you will get.   (Chorus.)   Come here, do;   reindeer skins

cho-g'okh'-kûñ-ûm'-kĭn.   Ä-la'-ai-ya'.   Tai'-kin-a'-ka'.
for a bed you will get.   (Chorus.)   Come here, do.

When this is completed the persons who are making the feast rise, and going to the food they have prepared and placed at the doorway, take a small portion from every dish and cast it down on the floor as an offering; then each takes a ladle of water and pours a little on the floor so that it runs through the cracks. In this way they believe that the spiritual essence of the entire quantity of food and water from which the small portions are offered goes to the shade. This essence of the offerings is believed to be transported mysteriously to the abodes of the shades and thus supply their wants until the time of the next festival. After these offerings have been made the festival maker distributes the food that is left among the people present and all eat heartily. Then, with songs and dances, the feast is ended and the shades are dismissed.

GREAT FEAST TO THE DEAD

The great feast to the dead (the ten-year *Egruska* of the fur trader) is the *Ĭkh'-tŭ-ka'-tŭkh-tŭk* of the Unalit at St Michael and the *Ûkh'-tă* or *I'-lĭ-g'ĭ* of the Eskimo at Ikogmut on the lower Yukon. The latter term means "throwing away," from the custom of the feast makers giving away everything during the festival. The nearest relative of a deceased Eskimo in this region must honor the shade of the departed with presents of food, drink, and clothing, through the dead person's namesake at the first festival in honor of the shades following his death; also by small food offerings at each of the following annual observances of this festival until he takes part in the great feast to the dead. The chief mourner is the nearest blood relative, either the father, son, brother, or other near relation. The chief mourner, after the expiration of one or two years, commences to save up valuable articles, such as skins of various kinds, clothing, and other things prized by these people; thus he or she saves for four, six, or even more years until the store of goods has grown to a large amount of property, as these people regard it, often worth hundreds of dollars.

At the same time others in the village are doing the same, until finally a number of persons conclude that they have enough to make one of these great festivals, when they agree on a time for its observance on some day during a certain moon in the ensuing year. Then, at the holding of the next minor feast to the dead, each relative plants his invitation stake before the grave of the one he wishes to honor. The invitation stake consists of a slender wooden rod, four to six feet high, commonly having rings of red paint about its freshly cut surface, and topped by a small, painted, wooden image of the totemic animal of the deceased; this stake is supposed to notify the shade of the dead of the approaching festival. To still further notify the shades, a song of invitation is sung at the minor festival to the dead given the year before the great feast, and as the shades are believed to be present at these festivals, this song is supposed to be heard by them.

With the observance of this great festival a person is supposed to have done his entire duty to the shades of his dead, and thenceforth may abstain from making any further feasts in their honor without being ashamed before his fellow villagers. However, should he lose another very near relation he would be expected to repeat the usual rites, unless there should be someone to take his place. The shade is supposed to be supplied with sufficient food and property at this feast to enable it to exist thenceforth without fear of want.

In January, 1880, I chanced to be at the small village of Razbinsky, on the lower Yukon, when the festival to the dead was held and the villagers were invited to attend the great feast to be given them the next year. This preliminary feast was entirely in the hands of the women, who distributed food and presents among the people and sang the song of invitation to the shades to return again next year. At the same time a slow dance was executed.

I was informed that the great festival to which the shades were invited would be given entirely by men. People from surrounding villages, sometimes in a circuit of nearly 200 miles, are invited by messengers to take part as guests in this feast. The feast makers strive to make as much show as possible and distribute great quantities of food among the guests.

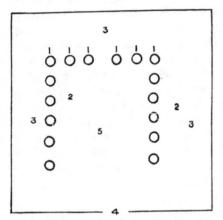

The following is an account of one of these festivals witnessed at Razbinsky in January, 1881, which will give a general idea of their good character. It is from notes made at the time the festival was in progress.

People came to this feast from all the neighboring villages and even from Kuskokwim river, until the village was filled to overflowing. On the evening of the day on which the festival began, the kashim was packed with men, women, and children. A place was given me on a bench in a corner of the room and this was reserved during the entire time of the festival.

FIG. 140—Plan of kashim during mortuary ceremony. (1, six drum men; 2, singers; 3, space occupied by spectators; 4, entrance or doorway; 5, vacant space under which the shades are supposed to gather.)

First evening

At the beginning of the festival the people were arranged in the kashim as shown in the accompanying figure 140.

Six men with drums sat in the rear end of the kashim, facing the door. Along each side, as shown in the diagram, sat a row of men who did the singing. The drummers and singers all sat on long, rude benches. The space from the drummers to the door was unoccupied, but the back and sides of the room were packed with people. Several songs were sung, all expressing welcome to the expected guests. During one of these a man who had come with other guests from Kuskokwim river suddenly appeared in the door, and, raising his voice over the din of the drums and singing, shouted: "Oh, oh, oh, oh, oh! Look at me. What are you saying of us Kuskokwim people? See here what we bring you for presents." He then threw down some skins he had in his hands and went out, but returned immediately, dragging in several large deerskins, which were placed in the same pile, and was followed by four companions, who came from the same place, each of whom added to the pile. My interpreter told me that this was the customary offering of guests who came from a distance.

I then sent him out to my sledge to obtain some articles with which to make our offering in the same manner, so as to observe the custom of propitiatory gifts. He returned with some leaf tobacco, which he brought in while the singing still continued, crying out, as had the others, "Oh, oh, oh, oh, oh! See here. What are you saying about us St Michael people?" Throwing the tobacco on the common heap, he went out and returned with one end of a roll of calico in his hands, drawing the remainder through the entrance hole with great deliberation, to make it appear as long as possible. An old man of the village arose to distribute these offerings, and with this the day's entertainment was closed. This is called the guests' day, or *yu-gûkh'-tut*. The guests from closely neighboring villages are not expected to make propitiatory presents at these festivals, as they reciprocate by giving feasts themselves, but those from afar are looked upon with disfavor unless they make the customary gifts. Should the guest wish to take part in any of the dances, it is almost imperative that he should have made such presents on his arrival. The guests at these festivals are furnished with food both for themselves and their dogs during the time of their attendance.

Second day

The kashim was filled with people in the evening, as it was the day before. The drummers and singers were arranged in the same position, and several songs were sung in time to the drums, one of which, intended to describe the dangers and difficulties of a journey, is translated as follows:

> We will sing a song.
> We will go down the current.
> The waves will rise;
> The waves will fall.
> The dogs will growl at us.

After several songs had been sung, one of the men making the feast came in suddenly with his face bent toward the floor and made a feint as if intending to dance; then wheeled about abruptly and went out. His place was taken at once by five men and five women, also feast givers, dressed in fine new clothing. Some of the women wore men's clothes and some women's garments, thus indicating the sex of the person for whom they were making the feast. After a short dance these five went out and were replaced by others until all the feast givers had danced. This completed the second day's performance. In this dance some of the men wore wolfskin fillets and some of the women fillets made from two ermine skins, the heads of the ermines being joined over the middle of the forehead and the skins drawn back on each side, and hanging over the sides of the face. These were said to be totemic insignia.

Third day

About 4 oclock in the morning all the guests were aroused and called into the kashim, where a fur trader and myself, having come from the most remote country, were given the places of honor on the bench at the back of the room, to the left of the entrance. Next to us were the guests from Kuskokwim river, who came from the next farthest place, the guests being placed in precedence according to the distance from which they had come. The people were all seated in this way under the direction of the old headman of the village, who sits at the left of the drummers during the dances.

When the guests were all seated the villagers came in and filled the vacant places. The seats of the guests thus allotted are reserved throughout the festival, and if a villager happens to be seated in one of them when the guest enters, he at once vacates it in favor of the original occupant; not to do so would be considered gross rudeness and would call forth a reprimand from the old men.

The kashim at this place had two tiers of sleeping benches around its sides, and these were both fully occupied by the guests. The villagers gathered in a compact mass between the vacant space in the middle of the room and the wall, but leaving a passageway along the sides and back of the room, in which were ranged, at regular intervals, twelve clay lamps, supported on wooden posts or wicker-top holders about 30 inches high.

Each of these lamps was filled with seal oil and kept burning day and night during the festival. These lights are said to be made to burn constantly, so that the road back and forth from the land of the dead may be lighted and the shades to be honored may have no difficulty in coming to the feast. If one of the feast makers fails to put up a lamp in the kashim and keep it lighted, the shade he or she wishes to honor would be unable to find its way and would thus miss the feast.

When the people, numbering about two hundred, were seated, an old man took a large drum, about $3\frac{1}{2}$ feet in diameter, and sat on a stool in the middle of the floor just in front of the customary lamp which burns at the back of the room. Then the headman of the village, who had attended to the seating of the guests, sat on a small stool at the right of the drummer, and on the left sat the headman's brother on a similar stool. These acted as directors of the ceremonies and served also the purpose of prompting the drummer during the songs. The arrangement of the kashim was the same as on the first evening.

The feast givers now filed in, each carrying a woven grass bag containing a fine suit of clothing worn during the dance of the preceding evening. At this time each was dressed in his or her poorest and oldest suit of clothing, tied about the waist by a cord of plaited grass.

As they came in, they stooped over and crept softly and humbly to their places in the open space around the sides of the kashim as though trying to avoid being seen. The wearing of old clothing and their coming into the room in this way was to express humility and to show how little they value their offerings. It is said that if one did not enter in this manner, but should hold up his head and afterward not be able to give as much as some of the others, he would be ashamed and become the subject of ridicule; each feast maker is emulous to give more than his fellows, and as no one knows how much the others have to give, they come humbly so as not to assume any credit they may subsequently lose. During all the rites of this festival, even in dancing, they kept their faces cast to the floor to express their humility. From this time forth throughout the festival, the feast makers wore the filthiest and most miserable clothing they had, putting on the fine garments in the grass bags only while performing certain dances. The feast givers are expected to enter the kashim in the humble manner described only when rites are being performed; at other times they come in walking erect and moving briskly.

It is customary for the guests and others aside from the givers of the feast to enter and leave the room slowly and with as little noise as possible, so as not to attract attention, thus showing their respect for the feast givers.

Having ranged themselves around the two sides and back of the room, the feast givers took out the suits of new clothing from the grass bags and exchanged them for their old garments. The wolfskin and ermine fillets, already described, were put on, and the women held in each hand a wand about two feet in length. These were slender sticks, having the quill feathers of the golden eagle bound along their length, and projecting from their tips were three bare vanes of large feathers, each tipped with a tuft of downy plumes.

The drummers began to beat in measured time and sang the song of invitation to the shades as if coming from the mourners. The song, translated, is as follows, each person being supposed to invoke the relation he or she was honoring:

> Come, my brother,
> Return to us again;
> We wait for you;
> Come, brother, come.
>
> (*Chorus*)
> Our mother, come back to us.
> Return once more.
>
> (*Chorus*)
> Return, our father;
> We wait for you;
> Come back to us,
> And we, who are lonely,
> Will give you food—etc.

The singing continued in mournful tones for some time. When it ended a man on one side of the room made a whining cry, which was answered by another feast giver from the opposite side; at this signal all of them arose, the men ranging themselves along the sides of the room while the women filed back and stood behind the drummers, all facing toward the center. The women wore fillets of various kinds and held a feather wand upright in each hand. Then the song of invitation to the shades was repeated by both feast makers and drummers.

Suddenly the time of the drum beats was changed from slow to fast, and two women just behind the drummers stepped forward close to them and began a pantomime dance in imitation of walking; the hands were used for these motions and moved alternately back and forth, the wands being held nearly upright and parallel; at the same time they kept up a slight swaying motion of the body, bending the knees slightly in time to the drums. The other women feast givers stood in their places, and some of them went through the same dance, while others performed various other movements, among which was a pantomime of tying up packages and packing away articles of various kinds by putting them in a pile, then encircling them with a cord and tying it, shown by moving the right hand from right to left over the left arm, all done in perfect time to the music.

Then two men stepped forward, one on each side, one of whom began to imitate the motion of a man's feet walking on snowshoes by the outstretched hands held palm downward and moved alternately back and forth, at the same time stamping heavily with his right foot; the other imitated a bear walking and stopping every now and then, as though raising itself up on its hind feet and staring about. After standing in this way for a few moments with his arms bowed in front of him in an absurdly realistic position, he would again begin stamping heavily on the floor, giving his body a rolling motion, while he moved his hands and arms in imitation of a bear's gait. This was done remarkably well, and great laughter was created, this being the object of the dancer.

Other men among the feast givers then took part in the dance, each pantomiming some occupation of daily life. The most striking of these was an imitation by one of traveling a long distance on snowshoes and winding in and out among the hills. The hands of the performer were in front of him, palms downward, and he moved back and forth with a walking motion, inclining obliquely one way and the other to indicate the slopes of the hills. Then he stopped and appeared to seize and strike something. I could not understand this, but the Eskimo next to me said the man was killing an otter in the snow. Another man imitated making a hole in the ice with his ice chisel, another paddling a kaiak, and so various other pantomimes were executed, every motion being made in time to the drum.

After a time the drummers ceased and rapped sharply on their stools with the drum handles. The dancers stopped and stamped quickly on the floor, first with one foot, then with the other. Each of them raised his hands over his head and drew them down over the body as if wiping something from it. When their hands reached their hips they began slapping their thighs quickly and sat down slowly on the floor. Then the men, with bent bodies, filed slowly back to their original places and sat down by their companions. After sitting quietly for a long time the dancers went home to replace with their old suits the new clothing they had worn during the dance. I was told that the wiping motion, followed by the stamping and the slapping on the thighs, indicated that the feast makers thus cast off all uncleanness that might be offensive to the shades, and thus render their offerings acceptable.

In a short time the namesakes of the dead gathered in the place made for them in the center of the room and sat down. The feast givers then came in, each bearing one or more new wooden buckets containing frozen fish. They went first to the lamps burning for the shades and dropped on the floor by them fragments of the fish as food offerings. Then a bucket of water was given to each of the namesakes, and they dipped their hands twice into it and sprinkled it on the floor, thus making a libation to the shades to accompany the food. After this each feast maker gave the remainder of the fish to the namesake of his dead. After the namesakes had all eaten, the empty dishes were removed. The feast givers then brought in between 3,000 and 4,000 pounds of frozen fish, consisting mainly of loach, whitefish, blackfish, and pickerel, which were placed by the door in individual piles. This fish was in woven-grass bags and frozen solid, having been kept thus since autumn. Each feast giver sat down silently beside his or her pile, and in a few moments a man came in and started to cross the room to his place, when an old man called out some epithet, to which he replied in seeming anger. The first speaker answered, and the two kept up a rapid and apparently angry series of retorts for several minutes.

This byplay, which had been prearranged in order to put the guests in good humor, caused great laughter. When it was finished the feast givers rose and, with wooden mauls and reindeer-horn wedges, separated the masses of frozen fish into fragments, which were distributed among the people, the guests from the greatest distance receiving the most. The fur trader and myself received about 250 pounds each.

Fourth day

Very early in the morning the feast makers came into the kashim and refilled their lamps with seal oil, and then brought in food consisting of whitefish oil, dried salmon, and seal blubber. After they had made their customary offering of small fragments before each of the lamps burning for the dead, the food was distributed among the people, and everyone broke his fast.   After the food was disposed of, songs of invitation were sung to the dead and a dance was performed exactly like that of the previous day.   When this was ended, the feast givers brought in about a ton of fine dried salmon, and each sat down behind his or her pile.   Then a man came in and the same style of word play was engaged in as on the day before, after which the feast givers distributed their salmon, the trader and myself getting about 200 pounds each.   This was followed by an interval of about an hour, when the dance was repeated.   Following this more salmon and a quantity of cranberries were distributed; then another interval ensued, lasting until just before dark, and the dance given in the morning was again repeated, but with a different ending.

As the dance concluded the central drummer, an old man, arose, and, holding the drum and stick overhead, called out, " Turn now as light (of day) goes," and, with a loud, hissing noise, he turned slowly a quarter of a circle with the sun, from left to right, and stopped; after a short pause he turned another quarter of a circle and stopped again, and so on until the circle was completed.   At the same time all the dancers turned, stopped, and started again with the drummer, making the same hissing noise; when the circle was completed the dancers stamped their feet and slapped their thighs to make themselves clean, and all went outside.   About half of the dancers then stood in front of the kashim and began to dance, while most of the others went among the graves, which were just behind the building, and danced before the grave boxes of those in whose honor the feast was given.   At the same time four men who had lost relatives by drowning went to the ice of the Yukon, where they danced.   The old drummer stood on the top of the kashim beating his drum for those dancing before the door; the dancers among the graves had time beaten for them by an old man striking the end of a log projecting from the wall of a house near by, and those who went to the river danced to time beaten on a piece of wood carried by one of the old men.

The reason given for the dance by the graves was that the shades of the dead were believed to have returned from their place of abode in the other world in response to the invitations and to be occupying their grave boxes when not in the kashim, and by the dance the shades were shown that their relatives were taking part in the festival.   At the close of this dance the children of the village, to the number of seventy or eighty, gathered in the kashim, occupying the center of the room in a square body, each child having a small wooden dish and a grass bag in its hands, and shouting in deafening chorus, " Wi-hlu!" (me, too) " Wi-hlu!" " Wi-hlu!"

The women had come in, meanwhile, bringing bags of berries, which they put by handfuls into the dishes of the children, who immediately emptied the dishes into the bags and held them out again, crying for more. This lasted about half an hour, and was greatly enjoyed by the children, each trying to procure more than the next, while the spectators appeared to be much amused.

Meanwhile berries and fish were handed about among the adults, who sat packed around the sides of the room. Then the women feast givers made presents of straw pads for skin boots and finely combed grass for towels, the trader and myself getting our portion. The feast givers then made an offering of water before each of the lamps, by pouring a little on the floor, after which they gave the remainder to the namesakes.

Later the two tiers of benches along the sides of the room were crowded with men, and in the middle of the floor was a compact mass of women and children, leaving a narrow passage around the sides next to the wall, so that the feast givers could move about the lamps.

In a short time they came in and took their usual places by the lamps. The women among them had brought a large number of small articles, such as spruce gum, wooden snow knives for children, wooden ladles, dishes, spruce root used for lashing, willow splints for fish traps, reindeer sinew thread, and various other things. When all were in the room and seated the husband or nearest male relation of each of the women feast givers arose and held up the articles one after another, making depreciative remarks about them, as if they had been obtained so easily that they were of trifling value. One of the men held up some reindeer sinew, saying, "Look at this. What is it? I don't know. I was sitting in the snow last spring and it fell before me from the sky." Another said, holding up another article, "Look at this. It was given me by Charlie" (the fur trader who was with me at the festival). Some of these remarks were quite amusing, causing everyone to laugh heartily, and the whole performance was very much enjoyed.

When the men had finished this preliminary announcement the women arose and each one called out the names of those to whom she wished to make presents, and when the latter answered the articles were handed or tossed to them. As there were a dozen or more persons calling out and replying at the same time, the uproar was very great. Instead of calling the person's real name in every case, some of the women gave them apt nicknames. My presence in the village to obtain ethnological specimens had excited great curiosity, and one woman caused shouts of laughter by crying out, "Where is the buyer of good-for-nothing things?"—and then handed me some presents.

For the first time during any part of the ceremony the feast givers stood erect while distributing these presents. When nearly all of the articles had been distributed, a small stick, attached to the end of a line, was dropped down through the smoke hole in the roof. One of the women feast givers who was sitting below caught hold of it and began to draw in the line. As she did this she sang a slow-measured

song, keeping time to the motions she made in hauling the cord. It
was very mournful, and might have been some old hymn in a minor
key. It ran as follows:

> Oh, my brother, come back to me,
>   *Ai-yă-yă-yai.*
> Come back, my brother, I am lonely,
>   *Ai-yă-yă-yai.*
> My brother come back and we
>   Will give you a small present,
>   *Ai-yă-yă-yai-yae-yai,* etc.

Along the line was fastened a number of articles. Each of the
women had a string, which she drew down in the same manner, singing
a similar song, asking the return of those for whom she mourned, while
the assembled people joined in at intervals wailing a mournful chorus.

The articles fastened to these lines consisted of grass mats, grass
baskets or bags, grass socks, fishskin bags, calico, white drilling, tobacco
bags, wooden dishes, ladles, fishskin boots, workbags, loon-skin bathing
caps, and tool bags. Each line had many of these articles on it, one
kind always predominating, and to the end was fastened one or more
small wooden models of some implement such as small oars, paddles,
or other things symbolical of the occupation of the relative for whom
she was mourning, and from them the sex of the deceased could be
known. As these symbols appeared the women to whom they belonged
would grasp them, and, holding them out at arms' length above their
heads, would cry, "See! I have searched and this is what I have
found," meaning that they had looked for their lost ones and had found
only a toy or implement which they had used.

When the last of the line was drawn in, each song came to a close,
and the articles were untied and placed in a pile before the owner.
When all were ready, they arose and made excuses for the small number of things they had been able to gather for gifts. One woman said,
"I am poor and have no husband, so could get no more." A common
excuse was, "I have been sick a great deal and have been unable to
get more." A woman who had an unusually large number of articles
would announce the number and then make her excuses with mock
humility. One of them had a hundred grass mats and a large number
of grass bags which she had made. Another had sixty grass mats.
One very old woman, on the end of whose line an arrow was tied,
began a song as she drew in the line and was joined by her husband.
Both were very old, and their quavering voices united in a sad wail
for their lost ones, as follows:

> My children, where are you?
>   *Ai-yă-yă-yai.*
> Come back to us, our children,
>   We are lonely and sad.
>   *Ai-yă-yă-yai.*

> For our children are gone,
>   While those of our friends remain.
>   *Ai-yă-yă-yai.*
> Come back, nephew, come back, we miss you;
>   *Ai-yă-yă-yai.*
> Come back to us, our lost ones,
>   We have presents for you.
>   *Ai-yă-yă-yai.*

This song had a wild, mournful harmony, and was sung with an earnestness that made it seem like a requiem for the dead.

When the women had given out all their articles among those present the day's ceremonies were completed.

Fifth day

At midday the men among the feast givers were busy outside the kashim tying together on long rawhide cords various articles, among which were deer- and seal-skins. One man had eighty deerskins, worth in trade one dollar each, and forty large sealskins, each worth two dollars and a half. Others had smaller numbers of the same articles, besides other things, and some men had a mixed assortment, among which I saw over twenty pairs of trousers made of white drilling for summer use, wooden dishes, rabbit-skin coats, and steel fox-traps. The large articles were made into a roll and tied to one end of the cord, and the smaller ones were strung on poles.

The men and the large boys were gathered in the kashim, but no women or children were permitted there at this time. When the male feast makers were ready they went into the kashim and occupied the middle of the room. Their bundles of skins, etc, were then lowered through the smoke hole, four at a time, one at each corner. As the bundles appeared the owners stepped forward and began a song of invitation to the dead, like those sung by the women on the previous day. After the bundles had been raised and lowered from above several times they rested on the floor and were untied. Then the cords were raised and other bundles let down while the singing continued. In this way all the bundles were lowered, the singers received their articles, and the songs were ended. The poles bearing the smaller articles were put down in the same way. When everything was in the kashim the feast givers arose and told how easily they had obtained them, depreciating their value in the same style as had been done with the gifts of the women on the previous day. Then the articles were distributed with excellent judgment. The guests from the interior were given sealskins, the givers saying they did this because seals were scarce with those people. For a similar reason the people from the coast were given reindeer skins.

After this was ended an interval passed during which the women and the children came in. Then the male feast givers brought in a large amount of seal, whale, and fish oil, some back fat of reindeer, several boxes of pilot bread, and other food, which was piled up about the room, each of the owners sitting by his pile. After they had all told how easily they had procured this food, two of them had a mock quarrel similar to the performance on previous days. This depreciation of the articles is to show their humility and lack of pride in their gifts. If this is not done they believe that the shades will become angry and bring sickness or other evil upon the village, and at the same time it serves to assure the people that the givers do not feel proud of their possessions.

When the food was ready for distribution, each person made a small offering, by his or her lamp, of every kind of food and from each bag of oil, dish, or tub, after which the remainder was distributed.

Among the food was a lot of small, bulbous roots, taken by the women from the winter stores of mice on the tundra. After the boxes of pilot bread were emptied of all but the fragments, the small boys, numbering about thirty, were permitted to scramble for them, which they did with great glee and good nature; when the boys had secured all the fragments, they each cast down a few crumbs at the foot of the lamps, as an offering to the shades, and went away. While standing about the room the male feast givers then sang a short, lively song, at the end of which the people carried home the food that had been distributed.

When this had all been taken out of the kashim, a shout was heard at the smoke hole in the roof, and a man cried out: "Your bag is only half full—that is the reason you have been sick," and lowered a large grass bag filled to its utmost capacity. Another man shouted down, "Big sleeper! You slept all the last two years, and are still asleep; that is the reason you have an empty bag." Another cried: "You stole very little last year when the people were away from home; that is the reason your bag is empty."

Accompanied by some such cry, a large bag of things, belonging to each feast maker, male and female, was lowered to the floor. The owners then came forward, opened their bags, and held up the articles contained therein, crying out, often six or eight of them at once, giving an imaginary history of the manner in which they had been obtained, and belittling the efforts required to obtain them. The trader who was with me was named Charlie Peterson, and article after article was held up and its owner would cry out, "I stole this from Charlie;" or, "I took this from Charlie;" or, "I took this from Charlie's man," which seemed to afford considerable amusement. One man held up a rabbit-skin coat, in mock admiration, and said: "This is counted as fine fur upon this side." Each bag contained several suits of fur clothing, intended for the namesakes of the dead. The shouting of the fictitious histories of the articles contained in the bags continued for about two hours. Many of the accounts were extremely ludicrous, causing much merriment.

As each feast giver finished taking the things out of the bag he or she called out, "Come to me, my best beloved relative," at which the namesake of the deceased relative came forward from among the people. The feast giver then removed the clothing from the namesake and replaced it with a complete new suit, the person sitting passively while this was being done. As soon as the new suit had been put upon the namesake, the feast giver gathered up the discarded clothing on the floor with the bags and placed them in the namesake's arms, who returned to his or her place among the villagers. As the namesake turned away the feast giver cried out in a loud voice, bidding the shade of his relative to return to the grave where its bones lay.

This was sometimes accompanied by directions, such as, "Go back to your grave on Clear creek and there circle about it once and then enter your grave box." Others told the shade to circle about its grave three times and enter it. Others told the shade to circle about the village where it was buried and then enter the grave. The dead who were buried beside this village were told to go out and circle about the place or kashim and return to their graves. Shades of persons who had been drowned were bidden to return to the river.

During this festival, from the time the dance of invitation is first performed in front of the graves, the shades of the dead are supposed to congregate in the pit under the floor of the kashim, and there to hear and enjoy everything that goes on. Sometimes they are said to be in the kashim itself, but are invisible. During the last day they are believed to enter the bodies of their namesakes, so that when the clothing is put on the latter the shades are clothed.

When a relative bids a shade to return to its burial place it must obey, and it goes back wearing the essence of the new clothing, as it is believed that when the old clothing is removed from the namesake and the new put on, the spiritual essence of the new garments goes to the shade.

Two men among the namesakes were given complete suits of clothing; also loaded guns, flasks of powder, caps, filled bullet pouches, and similar articles. After receiving their gifts these men danced wildly about, flourishing their guns and shouting in great excitement. One man cried, "You don't believe me; you think I lie, but I will guard and protect the village from danger," at the same time firing his gun toward the roof. The other man who received a gun went through a similar performance. The shouts of twenty or thirty people among the crowd of eager spectators and the firing of guns in the dim light of the feeble oil lamps created a wild scene.

Soon after the new clothing was put on the namesakes, they went to their homes, where they left their extra garments and returned to the kashim. Then the feast givers exchanged their old garments for new ones, taking the old clothing home, where it was left. In an hour everyone had returned to the kashim, the drums were brought out again, and the old men struck up the ordinary chorus song:

Ai-yă-yă-ŭñ-ai-yă, etc.

The boys and the young men occupied the middle of the room, shouting wildly, contorting their bodies, and springing about in great excitement until compelled to stop from lack of breath, but resuming the
dance after a short rest. This was continued without intermission
until the middle of the night.

Until this dance was concluded and the festival thus ended no one
was permitted to leave the village, as it was considered that to do so
would offend the shades and bring misfortune upon the villagers.
After the dance ended a great fire was lighted in the kashim, and the
men took a sweat bath. On the following morning the guests dispersed
to their homes.

On one of my sledge journeys I chanced to arrive at Kushutuk, near
Razbinsky, on the lower Yukon, one night during the great festival to
the dead. At dusk I lighted a candle in the kashim, where none of the
usual seal-oil lamps were burning at the time, and an old man at once
took a pole, seven or eight feet long, and began thumping on the floor
at the head of the room with measured strokes. At the same time two
young men arose and lighted a lamp upon each side of the room.

After about five minutes the old man gave the pole to a boy who continued the thumping for a few minutes longer, until about a dozen of
the feast givers came in, each carrying a grass bag of new clothing.
They crept to their places in the same stooping posture noted at Razbinsky, indicating their humility. After ranging themselves about the
room the feast givers changed their old clothing for the new suits contained in the bag, and several men and women put on wolfskin fillets.
The women all carried feather-ornamented wands. The men formed in
line at the head of the room, standing in front of the drummers and,
when the latter began to beat time and sing, they commenced a dance.
Other men took their places on each side of the room and joined in the
dance, which, including the bear dance, was almost an exact repetition
of the one performed at Razbinsky.

After about five minutes the dancers stamped heavily on the floor, to
cleanse themselves, as they said, and then sat down. Soon after they
went out and brought in food, which they distributed after making the
customary offering to the shades by casting a small portion on the floor.
One of the old men told me that the thumping on the floor was to
arouse the shades and call them to the dance. They were said to be
sitting in the grave boxes, with the body, awaiting the invitation and
to answer the summons at once. They are supposed to enjoy these
dances equally with the living, and as the feasting and dancing please
the invited guests, so are the shades pleased and enlivened. The next
morning I was obliged to resume my journey and so failed to witness
the conclusion of this festival.

At Askinuk, near Cape Vancouver, I was in the kashim about dusk
one evening and found the women learning a song to be given at the

festival to the dead a little later in the season.   Later, during the same evening, I sat with a lighted candle before me in the kashim writing my journal when a number of men came very quietly and seated themselves in a semicircle about me with their backs in my direction so that the light of the candle was shut off from the rest of the room.   I inquired the reason for this and was told they wished to sing but could not while the room was lighted, so they had arranged themselves in this manner to shut off my light from the other part of the room without disturbing me.   I immediately blew out the light, leaving the room in intense darkness, and the song began.   I did not obtain the song, but a chorus of the common syllables, *ûñ'-ai-yă-hai'-yă-yă*, occurred between every few words as they were given out by some of the old men.   About twenty-five men were singing, their heavy bass voices sounding very well.   Each time they came to the end of the portion recited, they closed with a curious kind of howl, and waited until the next words were chanted by the prompters and then went on again. They told me afterward that their reason for practicing this song in utter darkness was that any shade which desired to be present to hear the singing might do so without being driven away by the light.

DOLL FESTIVAL

For notes on the Doll festival (*Yu-gi-yhĭk'* or *I'-tĭ-kă-tah'*), observed at Ikogmut, the reader is referred to the tale of the *Yu-gi-yhĭk'* among the legends, and in this connection attention is also called to the Doll festival, or *Túh-tuhn'*, among the Tinné near Anvik.   The Russian priest at Mission (Ikogmut) regards this festival as idolatrous, and has tried for many years to prevent the people from observing it at that place and in the neighboring villages.   As a consequence, I found it difficult to learn much about it from the Eskimo during my brief stay in that vicinity.

One old man at Ikogmut told me the legend of the *Yu-gi-yhik'*, giving an account of the origin of this festival as kept in their traditions, and added that the day after the images were set up in the kashim the men and the large boys of the place go out to bring firewood to the village, which they leave at the doors of the women and girls with whom they are paired during the festival.

During the continuance of the festival the namesakes of dead men are paired with namesakes of their deceased wives without regard to age, and during this period the men or the boys bring their temporary partners firewood, and the latter prepare food for them, thus symbolizing the former union of the dead.

BLADDER FEASTS

The bladder feast (*Chaú-ĭ-yûk*) occurs annually at St Michael, commencing between the 10th and the 20th of December, the exact date depending on the phase of the moon.

First day

The festival opens by the men giving the kashim, including the fire-pit, a thorough cleaning. After dark all the men, women, and children in the village gather on the roof of the kashim and an old man beats a drum while the people unite in a song addressed to the wild parsnip (*Archangelica*), the stalks of which are standing ungathered on the distant hillsides.

Second day

On the second day four men go out and gather bundles of stalks of the wild parsnip (*i-ki-tŭk*) which they place on top of the entrance way outside the kashim. When evening comes these bundles are taken inside and laid on the floor, while the little boys of the village roll over them and wrestle with one another on top of them; then they are opened, the stalks spread on the floor, and each man takes one in his hand and sits at his place in the kashim uniting with the others in a song asking the stalks to become dry; when the heat of the room dries the stalks they are formed into a large sheaf.

Third day

At daybreak on this morning the sheaf is opened and from its contents a smaller sheaf is made about a foot in diameter, one end of which is thrust down on a stake, four or five feet long, planted in the floor, in front of the oil lamp which ordinarily burns at the rear of the room. When it is daylight each hunter brings into the kashim the inflated bladders of all the seals, whales, walrus, and white bears that he has killed during the year. Each man ties the bladders in a bunch by the necks and these bunches are hung up on seal spears stuck in the wall in a row six or eight feet above the floor, at the back of the room. Food is then brought into the kashim and offerings of small fragments are thrown on the floor before the bladders; a libation of water is also made in the same place; then the food is passed about and everyone partakes of it.

Fourth day

On this morning every hunter takes down his bunch of bladders and marks each with bands and dots of paint made from charcoal and oil; the charcoal used for this purpose is made usually from wild parsnip stalks. In the evening small torches are made from parsnip stalks, which burn with a bright, flaring, resinous flame. Each of the young men takes one of the torches and rushes about the room, leaping and shrieking like a madman, waving the flaming torches about the bladders, so as to bathe them slightly in the fire and smoke, and then into the faces of the men who are sitting about the room. When the place becomes filled with thick smoke this performance ends by the torch bearers jumping wildly about and shouting, while the young men and boys catch one another and in succession each one is forced backward down through the hole in the middle of the floor; everyone resists in a good-natured way until he is overcome and forced through.

Fifth day

On this day the men remain in the kashim and no one is permitted to do any work in the village, while all wait for the full moon. The first night of the waning moon each man ties his bladders into a bundle, which is fastened about the head of a large seal spear, and they are then hung on a line strung across the back of the room. The same day the men go out and make a hole in the sea ice before the village about a quarter of a mile from the shore. When this has been done two men, each with a small seal spear in his hand, run out to the hole in the ice and dip the point of their spears in the water and run back to the kashim as quickly as possible and stir up their bladders with the points of their spears, after which they drop their spears, and, going over to the large bundle of parsnip stalks, strike it with their open hands. Then two or three men start out and repeat this ceremony, and so on until it has been done by every one of the hunters.

When this is finished all the hunters seat themselves around the kashim and join in a song of welcome to the guests, while the other villagers, men, women, and children, file in one after the other and execute a short dance.

Sixth day

Just at sunrise the following morning every man takes his spear, on which the bladders are hung, and, forming a long file, all go out to the hole in the ice as fast as they can run. Reaching this, each kneels down by it, and, tearing the bladders from his spear, thrusts them down one by one through the hole under the ice. When this is finished all return to the village. Meanwhile the old men have brought out the bundle of parsnip stalks from the kashim and, placing them on the sea ice in front of the village, have built a small fire of driftwood. As the men return from the hole, the entire population gathers about the fire and unites in a song of welcome to the guests.

Fire is now applied to the bundle of wild parsnip stalks and they burst into a high, waving flame. As the returning men draw near they start to run for the fire, each leaping through it in succession, uttering a loud whoop in which the villagers join with a chorus of shrieks and cries. On the occasions of my witnessing this rite I was asked by the Eskimo to jump through the flame with the hunters, and as they seemed to think it was required by custom I complied. When the men have all passed through the flame the women and children rush frantically into the fire, stamping and dashing the embers about until it is extinguished, perfectly regardless of burning boots and clothing. Everyone then forms in a line and marches once around the village; sometimes two files are formed which march about the place in opposite directions at the same time.

After this a fire is built in the kashim and the men take a sweat bath. The fire having burned down, the kashim is closed, the floor planks put in place, and the men form a circle around the room, each bent over and having his hands on the nape of the one in front of him; everyone is completely nude. Two nude boys are placed in the middle of the ring while the men circle four times around the room from left to right (with the sun), the boys, except those in the middle of the ring, climbing upon their backs and chasing each other about.

As soon as the four circuits of the room have been completed, the men stop and slap each other heartily upon the back until each has had enough; then they stand back from the hole in the middle of the floor and jump over it until some one nearly falls in. Two lines are now let down from the roof; handles are tied to the ends, which are some distance from the floor, and the men grasp them, attempting to raise themselves up and perform other trials of strength. This ends the festival, but no work must be done in the village during the next four days.

At one of these festivals witnessed at St Michael, the ceremonies of the last morning varied from those described. Just before sunrise a small bunch of dried parsnip stalks was lighted and waved about the bladders and also over and inside the waterproof gut-skin shirts worn by the hunters when in their kaiaks at sea, which were brought in for the purpose. The headman of the village then stood up and each hunter placed beside himself a small bundle of dried grass. The headman took these, one after the other, and passed them about the bladders belonging to their owners, repeating at the same time certain directions to the shades in a low tone of voice. As soon as he had completed this, the hunter to whom the bladders belonged would cry out *"Ai-yai!"* The straws were then lighted and again passed over the bladders, the charred stumps being returned to the side of their owner, after which the hunters made black paint of wild-parsnip charcoal and oil, with which they striped one another's faces and drew a double cross ($\ddagger$) upon the middle of each one's back and chest.

Then each hunter took the spear to which his bladders had been fastened and all marched about the hole in the middle of the floor, each making several feints before putting his bladders through the hole and taking them outside. At the hole in the ice the bladders were burst by means of a seal-claw ice scratcher, and several strands of seal sinew were tied to each before thrusting it under the ice.

On December 15, 1879, I reached Kushunuk, near Cape Vancouver, and found the Bladder festival in progress. Hanging from the roof over the middle of the floor was a fantastic bird-shape image, said to represent a sea gull. It had the primary quill feather of a gull stuck in each side of the body to represent the wings. The body was covered with the skin and feathers of the small Canada goose (*Branta canadensis minima*). It was fastened to a long, slender, rawhide cord which passed through an eye fastened to one of the roof logs, and thence down to the floor on one side of the room. By pulling and

releasing this cord, the image could be made to glide up and down.
Behind this, at the back of the room, was planted a pole about ten feet
long, to the upper end of which a bundle of wild-parsnip stalks was
bound like a great brush or besom. The pole was banded along its
entire length with red and white paint, and fastened on two sides of it,
near the middle, were two pairs of reindeer-skin strips which hung down
two or three feet. On the left side of the room, hung horizontally midway between the floor and ceiling, was a large sheaf of seal and walrus
spears, their heads partly in one direction and partly in another.
Attached to these, a bunch being fastened to each spear, were several hundred seal and walrus bladders, all of which were spotted
and blotched with grayish-white paint; each spear had tied to it the
bladders belonging to its owner. Hanging about the room, singly or
in bunches, were a number of reindeer bladders, but none of these were
hung with those of the seal and the walrus. On the side of the room
opposite the spears and bladders, at an equal height from the floor,
hung a large bundle of wild-parsnip stalks. All about the room and
on the sides were arranged various spears used in hunting seals and
walrus. Under the wild-parsnip stalks and beneath the spears and
bladders was a pile of thirty or forty wooden hunting helmets of various
shapes, some of which were ornamented with carved ivory images,
while others were not thus ornamented; they were painted white or
brown, with white blotches, and on many of them were depicted female
phallic symbols. Back of the entrance hole in the floor stood a large
walrus skull.

When I entered the room one of my dogs followed, and immediately
a man seized a drum and began beating it to exorcise the evil influence
of the dog's presence until it was hastily expelled. I looked about the
room and went over to the bladders and felt one to learn the nature of
the paint with which it was spotted; my movements seemed to startle
the men very much and all raised a loud outcry. I afterward heard
the same cry raised if any loud noise was accidentally made near these
objects. When our camping outfit was brought in from the sledges,
two men took drums, and as the clothing and goods of the traders who
were with me were brought in, the drums were beaten softly and a song
was sung in a low, humming tone, but when our guns and some steel
traps were brought in, with other articles of iron, the drums were beaten
loudly and the songs raised in proportion. This was done that the
shades of the animals present in the bladders might not be frightened.

Early in the evening the boys of the village gathered outside the
kashim and raised a great outcry. An hour later the hunting helmets
were ranged around the kashim, forming a circle on the floor inclosing
the walrus skull and the stake. Very soon after this a bundle of straw,
such as is used for pads in boot soles, was thrown down from the hole
in the roof; a man took this, and holding it at arm's length over his
head while he marched around the ring of helmets, deposited it on the

floor at the base of the stake. The walrus skull was then placed close
to the hole in the floor with a folded straw mat before it; two small
wooden buckets of water were brought in and placed in front of the
hole to symbolize the sea, the hole thus representing a seal hole leading into the sea through the ice. After this no one was permitted to
leave the room until the evening ceremonies were completed, as the exit
hole was the only means of egress and was supposed to be used during
this time by the shades of the animals, and consequently was tabooed.
During this time it became, figuratively, the entrance to the sea.

The men and the boys now put on their helmets, and the one who had
first taken the grass from beside each hunter again took it up and, after
waving it over his head, scattered it in the ring just inside the place
where the circle of helmets had been; this was said to represent the
drift weeds lying on the seashore.

A young man now seated himself under the spears and bladders and
another under the large bundle of wild-parsnip stalks, their feet resting
on the ring of grass. The drums began to beat loudly, and the young
men around the room imitated the notes of the eider duck. In a short
time the men and the boys ranged themselves around the room just
outside the circle made by the grass, the women and the girls being
behind them and next to the wall. The headman chanted a few words
of a song in time to the beating of the drums, which was taken up as
a refrain by every one, including men, women, and boys, each party
repeating it in alternation. During this song one of the young men
imitated in pantomime the motions of a loon and another those of a
murre. These men remained seated upon the floor, swaying their heads
and bodies about in the most singular postures, like those of a bird
diving and swimming under water, or on the surface, pecking with their
beaks, etc, after which they made a flapping motion with their hands as
if rising and flying away, imitating at the same time the cries of the
birds they were representing.

A short interval followed, during which a single drummer and singer
continued the music; then various others of the dancers began similar
bird movements, and all began drumming and singing as before. The
new dancers stood about the ring of grass, and one made the motions
of a beaver at work cutting bushes and building a dam. Another
gestured his encounter with the enemy and his escape from a hostile
force.

Suddenly one of the singers sprang to his feet and, seizing the two
wooden buckets of water, vanished through the hole in the floor. At
the same moment the men and boys ran out to the large bundle of wild-
parsnip stalks and each put his hunting helmet upon it as quickly as
possible. Nearly every one left the kashim at this time, and soon a man
came in who had been stripped to the waist at the outer door. He bore
a wooden dish of food, which he held high over his head, and circled
once around the room as an offering to the shades and *tunghat* in the

sky land; then he stamped on the floor two or three times and the people came in, bringing food, of which he partook.

No further ceremonies were conducted until the middle of the night, when the lights were suddenly extinguished and the shaman uttered, from the roof, a long series of unintelligible words ending with a loud shout, followed by his entry into the kashim. Then the lights were renewed and a bucket of water was placed on the floor under the bladders. A man and three boys then stripped, and one of the boys was placed astride the man's back, where he hung by his arms and legs twined about the man's body; the other two boys stood in a stooping posture in front of the bucket of water, and the man carrying the boy on his back stood beside them.

This man dipped up some water with his hand and tossed it up toward the bladders, so that it fell back in a shower upon the two boys and himself. After doing this for some time he carried the bucket around the room, continually flirting the water up toward the roof with one hand as a libation to the *tunghät* of the air. The boys then knelt in the middle of the room with bowed heads and rounded shoulders while the cold water in the buckets was dashed over them. Shortly after a growling noise was heard under the floor, and a man with the hood of his fur coat over his head and a kaiak paddle in his hand entered and stood in one corner of the room. He was soon followed by another, also carrying a paddle, who went to the corner occupied by the first comer, while the latter went on to the next corner; then a third man came in, and the preceding ones advanced each to the next corner, and the first corner was occupied by the third man; a fourth entered, and the changing of places was continued so that each of the four corners was occupied. These men then marched around the room several times, lifting the bladders with their paddle blades as they passed and knocking down the spears that were stuck up on the walls of the room.

After this they filed out, and the people gathered up the fallen spears, removing their points. The bunch of wild-parsnip stalks was fastened to the stake at the back of the room, and the bundle of spears, to which the bladders were hung, was lowered to a level with the sleeping benches, between three and four feet above the floor. When the four men went outside they planted their paddles, blade downward, in front of the kashim, forming a row across the entrance. To the top of each the owner fastened his wooden hunting helmet, which had been worn under his fur hood when in the kashim. To each helmet was fastened a bunch of straw or grass similar to that used to form the ring on the floor, representing seaweed. To the heads of this grass were fastened a few small, downy gull feathers.

Early on the following morning the old men told us that we must not stamp our feet in the kashim during that day, for fear of alarming the shades of the animals that were expected to be present. The bunch of wild-parsnip stalks was lighted and waved flaming, toward the cardinal points, after which the charred stumps were laid at the foot of the stake. About noon two men took the small bundles of parsnip stalks and lighted them, waving the flame about the bladders, and after carrying them around the room went out through the passageway to the outer door. The charred stalks were then brought back and laid on the floor under the large bundle of stalks on the stake. Nothing more was done until just after noon, when a bag made of sealskin was brought in. The men then took their urine buckets and went outside, carrying the bag, and each poured urine from his bucket upon it, shouting loudly some unintelligible words, after which all came back into the room and stripped themselves to the waist.

Soon afterward the cover was removed from the smoke hole in the roof, and the sealskin bag, having attached to it the four helmets worn by the men who had entered with the paddles on the previous evening, was lowered through the hole by a rawhide line and was hung on the stake at the head of the room; then the owners went to the helmets and removed the grass that was fastened to them, and each tied a few blades to his bunch of bladders. The helmets were then taken down and placed on the floor at the foot of the stake.

Up to this time the seal bag had been empty, but it was now taken down and inflated and hung up by the nose on the middle of the sheaf of spears to which the bladders were fastened; to each hind-flipper was tied a primary wing-feather of the Pacific glaucous gull. There was then an interval without ceremonies lasting until evening.

Early in the evening everyone gathered in the kashim and the walrus skull and the grass mats were placed in the same position as on the previous evening. Suddenly a burning stalk of wild parsnip was waved in the entrance hole from below, a man's head appeared, and a dish of food was placed on the floor and slid across to the corner of the room between the bladders and the stake; the man entered and went over to the bladders, where he stopped. Another man then went through the same performance, waving the burning stalk and sliding in a dish of food, etc, succeeded by two others, until the four men were ranged side by side in front of the bladders. They were the same who had come in with the paddles during a former ceremony.

The first lighted a bunch of parsnip stalks, to which was tied all the points taken from the fallen spears on the preceding night. Waving this about a few times in the corner where his wooden dish had been slid, he raised it over his head and turned once slowly around. After this the blazing mass was waved over the four wooden dishes which had been slid into the corner, over the two empty buckets which had contained the water symbolizing the sea during the last night's ceremonies, and about the bladders and the charred stumps were then laid at the foot of the stake.

He went next to the four wooden dishes and made motions as though scooping up food from them in both hands and casting it toward the bladders; at the same time a man sitting in an obscure corner gave a vigorous pull to the line passing from his hand through a loop in the roof and down to the bladders, which caused them to oscillate violently and was supposed to indicate the acceptance of the offering by the shades of the animals in the bladders.

The other three men repeated these rites in every detail, after which the drums were beaten and the four men executed a curious dance in front of the bladders, which were swung about as before, to indicate their pleasure. The dance was begun by a pecking, jerking motion from side to side and forward, while the dancers moved slowly along in front of the bladders. Then the dance was changed to an oblique galloping movement, after which the arms were tossed up and down, giving the body a jumping motion; then first one leg, then the other, was thrown up and a hop made on the other, followed by quick hops sidewise and long jumps forward, all keeping perfect time to the drums. This dance was said to be an imitation of the movements of seals and walrus.

Throughout the performance a half-grown girl stood beside the four dancers swaying her body back and forth with an undulating motion. The four men repeated their series of motions or dances several times in succession, until they were compelled to stop from exhaustion; when they ceased their places were taken by four others, who repeated the dance, and they in turn by four others, and these again by two other sets, another girl being substituted with each set of dancers.

One of the men told me that each of these sets of dancers comprised only men of the same "kin," by which, so far as I could ascertain, he referred to the gens, since people of the same gens are considered by them as being of the same kin. In this case it evidently implied that four gentes were represented in the festival, as indicated by the totem marks on the four paddles standing before the door.

When the dance ended, the four dishes of food were carried around the hole in the floor, after which their contents were distributed and eaten. In a short time two straw mats were spread on the floor before the entrance hole, and two men stripped to the waist sat upon them, facing the hole. In the pit under the floor were all the hunters who owned the bladders hanging in the kashim, and each had in his hand a small wisp of straw or grass like that already described, which were handed, in succession, to the men on the mats, the one handing them up showing nothing but his hand and arm. As each wisp was passed up, the man who received it called out the name of its owner, who responded by making a short speech, which created great laughter among the people seated around the kashim.

Among other things, the men stated in the speeches that the grass they were handing up served as beds for the *inuas* of the bladders. When each speech was ended, the man who had taken the grass handed it to the man opposite on the other mat, who broke it into halves and bound the two ends together. Then taking up the stump of the parsnip-stalk torch, to which the spearpoints were attached, he lighted it and passed the lighted end over and around the grass, at the same time saying in a loud voice, "When they sit down they are sleepy and fall down;" he then fell, and, rolling over, laid the grass on the floor. This was repeated for every hunter, and symbolized the killing of the seals with the spearpoints which were attached to the torch. In the middle of the night the lamps were again extinguished and the shaman went on the roof, where another speech was made to the bladders through the smoke hole. This speech was ended by a blowing noise, such as is made by seals and walrus when they come to the surface to breathe. Afterward the shaman made a squeaking and grunting noise, such as a pup seal utters when trying to find its mother.

At 4 oclock in the morning everyone arose, and the dances given by sets of four men on the previous night were repeated in all their details, except that fewer motions were made with the arms and the upper part of the body. The woman dancing with each set took the unlighted bunch of parsnip stalks and passed it about the dishes of food before they were offered to the *inuas* of the bladders.

When the dance and the food offerings had been completed, the chief shaman—the one first mentioned as leading the ceremonies and who directed all the observances—lighted a parsnip-stalk torch and passed it about the room, holding it close to the floor. He then circled with it about each of the dancers, who removed their fur coats and the torch was passed about their bodies and inside and about their fur coats. This was said to be done to purify the room and the dancers and to remove any evil influence that might bring sickness or bad luck to the hunters. Four of the men then sat beneath the bladders for a short time, after which they arose and seated themselves close together on the sleeping bench behind the spears and bladders.

A woman then brought in a large wooden bucket of food, and, after passing a lighted parsnip-stalk torch about it, made an offering to the bladders. She then stood in front of the bladders, facing the middle of the room, and so near that the bladders brushed her back when they were swung back and forth a moment later by a man hauling on a cord. The shaman then took a boy about twelve years of age, who was stripped to the waist, and laid him across the entrance hole in the floor, at the same time kneeling over him and making a low noise like the note of the murre. Beneath the floor a man started a song, in which the people in the kashim joined.

Immediately after the song was finished the hunters rushed to the bladders and each took those he owned and fastened them about the heads of two or three of the pointless spearshafts. A song was then sung by the people and the bladders were laid with the spearshafts on the floor by the entrance hole, while all of the other spears, the large stake, and the other things were taken down from the walls, and all the wild-parsnip stalks that remained in the room were tied in a large bundle, which was fastened to the top of the stake like a huge broom or brush. When this was done, the shaman went on the roof and, removing the cover, put in his head repeatedly at each corner of the smoke hole, while he made a grunting noise like a young puppy. Another knelt over the entrance hole in front of the kashim and repeated the noise. It was now 3 oclock, and the spearshafts to which the bladders were fastened were passed up to the shaman through the smoke hole. Their owners immediately went out through the passageway, and each obtaining the shafts bearing his bladders ran rapidly to the foot of the knoll on which the village is located. When the hunters were all outside, the top of the great brush of parsnip stalks on the stake was lighted, making a huge torch, which was passed up through the smoke hole. The chief shaman took it on his shoulder and ran across the snow-covered plain as rapidly as possible, followed by all the men, holding the bladders aloft on the ends of the spearshafts. Behind the hunters ran the women, children, and old men, howling, screaming, and making a great uproar.

The night was cold, calm, and very dark, so that the lurid flame of the torch arose ten or twelve feet, casting a red glare over the snow-covered plain and lighting up the swarm of fantastic, fur-covered figures that went streaming along in wild excitement. Nearly a quarter of a mile from the village the crowd reached the borders of a small pond, where a square hole had been made through the ice, close by which the shaman thrust the lower end of the stake into the snow so that the torch stood erect. The hunters then stood by the hole in the ice and, using a detached spearpoint, ripped open the bladders. Then taking the collapsed bladders in one hand and a kaiak paddle in the other, they marched several times around the hole, each time dipping the point of the paddle blade and the collapsed bladders in the water at the corners of the hole. They then put the bladders one at a time into the water under the ice, where they remained. This ended the ceremony and all returned to the village.

Soon after daybreak four men with their paddles came in and, as before, moved from corner to corner in succession until all were in, when they marched around the room, making no motions with their paddles, and then went out. When the first of these men came in he was greeted by a great shout from everyone in the room, and the other three were greeted successively on their entrance by a loud groaning noise. An hour later the old men told everyone to be quiet, and two men went to the entrance hole in the floor where they sat down side by side. One of them held a bundle of small sticks, each stick representing a hunter, and as he passed these singly from hand to hand the other man rolled over on the floor as he had done with the grass wisps on the previous evening.

During this day all work was prohibited in the village. Even the fur trader and myself were requested to do none, it being explained that to work on this day would cause some of the people to die, since it would offend the shades of the animals. We were also asked to be very careful not to make any noise in the kashim. Every time any sudden noise was accidentally made all of the men present united in a chorus of cries, imitating the notes of the eider duck, so that the shades of seals and other animals whose bladders had been suspended in the room should attribute the noise to those birds rather than to the people. In the afternoon a dance was performed by these men, in time to drums and singing. It consisted of leaping and jumping movements like those already described in the dance to the bladders. That evening the head shaman, stripped to the skin, sat on the straw mat in front of the exit hole in the floor with a fur hood over his head. Some men then bound his hands and feet with rawhide cords and a long cord was fastened to his neck by a slipping noose.

Two assistants then carried him down through the hole and placed him on a grass mat in the fire pit. Another cord was then passed around his hands and knees and bound at the back of his neck, being drawn so tight that his face was brought down between his knees, and in this position he was made fast. One of the assistants went out to guard the outer door of the passageway, while the other came back into the room and, after drawing tight the line fastened to the shaman's neck, spread a grass mat over the hole in the floor. This line held by the assistant now began to run out, then slacken up, then run out again, as though something was traveling away with it below the floor.

This was continued for some time; meanwhile the drumming and singing of the men in the kashim were kept up. Finally a kind of groaning was heard from the shaman and several men ran to the hole with the light, and found him bound as he had been at first, but about five feet from the point where he had been placed.

During the performance the cord fastened to the shaman's neck, one end of which was held by his assistant in the kashim, had been pulled down under the floor for ten or fifteen yards, which must have been done by the assistant outside, as the shaman was bound too securely to do more than hitch a little along the ground, but the people in the kashim believed that the drawing out of the cord had been done by the shaman himself, indicating that he had traveled far away.

When he was unbound he came back into the kashim and sat down before the exit hole. After sitting quietly for a moment he began to tell a long story describing the journey he had just made into the sea, following the shades of the seal bladders. He said that he had talked with all but two of the shades and had seen some shades of the bladders he owned playing together in the water; that some of the shades told him they were very much pleased with the men who had taken them and given them such a fine festival; others complained that the hunters had treated them badly and had not offered them sufficient food. He added that the shades of the bladders swam faster this year than the year before, making it more difficult to overtake them.

During this account the names of the hunters were mentioned and the shaman represented the bladder shades as criticising very harshly the prominent faults of some of them, which seemed to chagrin the victims of this criticism considerably. After this was ended two buckets of water were placed in front of the exit hole in the floor and a man lay down on each side of it. At midnight everyone in the kashim arose and stripped to the skin, the floor was removed, and a great fire made in the pit. When the wood burned down, leaving a bed of glowing coals, the heat became intense, so that the men were in a scorching atmosphere with the perspiration rolling down their bodies. While in this condition all bathed in urine, which had been retained in the wooden buckets. This was said to render them clean from any evil influence that might follow from the recent presence of the shades in their midst, and ended the observances connected with the festival. Until this bath had been taken no one was permitted to leave the kashim, nor during the course of the festival was anyone permitted to hunt or fish.

At this village there were two kashims side by side, half of the village belonging to each. During the time that the feast just described was being observed in one of these houses a similar festival was going on in the other. I was unable to learn anything about the ceremonies conducted there, as my attention was fully occupied in the one where I stopped, but a hasty visit showed that the arrangement of the interior was exactly the same as in the one described, except that in place of a gull's image suspended in the middle of the roof there was a rude wooden image of a man wrapped in the skin of an eider duck.

I was informed here that the bladders were kept in the kashim for seventeen days, with a different set of ceremonies for each day.

Two days after leaving Kushunuk, at the end of the festival, I arrived at the large village of Kaialigamut, situated in the same district, and learned that the bladders had on that morning been put into a small lake near by. In front of the kashim stood a row of four kaiak paddles, their blades planted in the snow, showing that at least some of the observances here were identical with those at Kushunuk.

When I entered the kashim and began to stamp the snow from my feet a chorus of eider-duck sounds was raised by the men, showing that a loud noise was tabooed here also. On noticing this I at once ceased and went to one side of the room to sit down, when one of the old men came over and brushed the snow from my fur clothing, at the same time pointing to an inflated sealskin that hung over my head, and asked me to change to another part of the room.

These people seemed much more strict in their observances than those at Kushunuk, to judge by the excessive caution used to avoid making noise. Any slight noise served to raise a few eider-duck notes, and once when a dog strayed in every one in the kashim grunted vociferously, at which the dog slunk out abashed.

No work was permitted here during this day, and no one was permitted to leave the village until after all had taken a bath on the midnight following. Should this rule be broken they believed that some one would surely die before another feast.

On a December afternoon in 1878 I arrived at Chifukhlugumut, a village near the Yukon, south of Andreivsky, while the people were celebrating the bladder feast. They were gathered in the kashim singing to the beating of three drums, two of which were very large and the other of ordinary size. The large drums were about two and a half feet in diameter and covered with tanned reindeer skin. The songs were sung in very slow time and were descriptive of the wars and exploits of their fathers in ancient times.

The only decorations in the kashim consisted of a bundle of wild-parsnip stalks fastened horizontally to the rear end of the room by means of two wooden pegs, and layers of these stalks about six feet long which were fastened to the wall like screens on the sides of the room.

The drumming and songs were repeated three times during the following afternoon. One of the old men told me that, as they lived far from the seacoast, they had killed no seals nor walrus, so had no bladders to put in the water, consequently they did not burn the stalks of the wild parsnips but put them in the kashim to make offerings to them. At the end of the feast the stalks are laid on the frozen surface of a small river near by, where they remain until carried away by the ice in spring.

Here, as in other villages, no work of any kind was permitted during the festival, and no wood must be cut with an iron ax, but when absolutely necessary bone wedges may be used for splitting firewood. At Kushunuk they used for this purpose a large pick, consisting of a wooden handle with a walrus tusk for the point, the use of iron axes being tabooed there as elsewhere in this region during the continuance of this festival. All loud noises are also forbidden, even out of doors.

At a little village on the Yukon near Andreivsky, on January 17, 1881, I found the people performing their final dance at the close of the bladder feast. This date is a month later than is customary.

The bladders used in this festival are supposed to contain the shades or *inuas* of the slain animals. After an animal is killed the hunter carefully removes and preserves the bladder until the time approaches for the festival. When this time arrives songs are sung and the bladder is inflated and hung in the kashim; the shade of the animal to which the bladder belonged is supposed to remain with it and to exist in the inflated bladder when it is hung in the kashim.

The feast is given for the purpose of pleasing and amusing the shades and thus propitiating them, after which the bladders are taken to a hole in the ice and, after being opened, are thrust into the water under the ice so that the shade may return to its proper element. The shade is supposed to swim far out to sea and there to enter the bodies of unborn animals of their kind, thus becoming reincarnated and rendering game more plentiful than it would be otherwise. If the shades are pleased with the manner in which they have been treated by the hunter who killed the animal they occupied, it is said they will not be afraid when they meet him in their new form and will permit him to approach and kill them again without trouble.

Several of the St Michael Eskimo told me that they knew this reincarnation to be true, as a man living at a village on the outer side of the island killed a seal a few years ago which had the same mark on its bladder that he had put on the bladders at the festival the previous year. It should be noted that each hunter puts his totem mark or other personal sign in red or black paint upon his bladders so that they may be distinguished from those of other hunters. The aromatic smoke and red flames of the resinous stalks of the wild parsnip are thought to be very pleasing to the shades of the animals whose bladders are treated with them, and at the same time the flame drives away any uncleanness and unfavorable influence that may be present.

During the continuance of this festival at St Michael, and at other places where it is observed, no man or large boy sleeps away from the kashim and the men keep rigidly apart from the women. If a man breaks this rule it is said he will have no success as a seal hunter. On this account the men avoid as much as possible going into their own or any other house, for fear of becoming unclean. They bathe twice a day, morning and evening, in the kashim, but their food and water are brought to them as usual by the women.

No females who have reached puberty are permitted near or under the bladders while they hang in the kashim, as they are said to be unclean and might offend the shades. Young, immature girls, however, may go about them as freely as the boys.

During the continuance of this festival it is a necessary observance that the kashim shall never be left entirely vacant. An old man at St Michael told me that during one of these festivals at Pastolik the men forgot this and went to an adjacent kashim for a short time. Suddenly one of them remembered that their kashim had been left vacant and hurried back in time to hear the shades in the bladders talking to one another. One end of the line to which they were hung had become untied and the bladders were said to have moved near the doorway ready to leave, the shades being angry at their neglect.

MASKS AND MASKETTES

Masks were found in use among the Eskimo from Kotzebue sound to the mouth of the Kuskokwim, but their use attains the greatest development in the country along the lower Yukon and thence south-

ward through the intermediate country to the Koskokwim. Formerly
the Eskimo of Norton sound used masks much more than at present,
the influence of white men having considerably modified their ideas and
caused some of the ancient customs to become more or less obsolete.

On the rivers named, and especially on the little-visited marshy plain
lying between the lower courses of these streams, mask festivals were
observed with all their ancient elaboration and strictness of ceremony
during my residence at St Michael. Unfortunately, none of my journeys were made at a time when these festivals were being held, but in
various villages I saw men at work preparing masks for approaching
ceremonies. The significance of the masks described is given from
information obtained directly from the Eskimo, unless otherwise stated.

In connection with the description of these curiously carved and
ornamented objects some prefatory remarks are necessary. Shamans
make masks representing grotesque faces of supernatural beings which
they claim to have seen. These may be *yu-ȧ*, which are the spirits of
the elements, of places, and of inanimate things in general; the *tunghät*, or wandering genii, or the shades of people and animals. The
first-named are seen in lonely places, on the plains and mountains or
at sea, and more rarely about the villages, by the clairvoyant vision of
the shamans. They are usually invisible to common eyes, but sometimes render themselves visible to the people for various purposes.

Many of them, especially among the *tunghät*, are of evil character,
bringing sickness and misfortune upon people from mere wantonness
or for some fancied injury. The Eskimo believe that everything, animate or inanimate, is possessed of a shade, having semihuman form
and features, enjoying more or less freedom of motion; the shamans
give form to their ideas of them in masks, as well as of others which
they claim inhabit the moon and the sky-land. In their daily life, if
the people witness some strange occurrence, are curiously affected, or
have a remarkable adventure, during which they seem to be influenced
or aided in a supernatural manner, the shamans interpret the meaning
and describe the appearance of the being that exerted its power.

Curious mythological beasts are also said to inhabit both land and
sea, but to become visible only on special occasions. These ideas furnish material upon which their fancy works, conjuring up strange forms
that are usually modifications of known creatures. It is also believed
that in early days all animate beings had a dual existence, becoming at
will either like man or the animal forms they now wear. In those early
days there were but few people; if an animal wished to assume its
human form, the forearm, wing, or other limb was raised and pushed up
the muzzle or beak as if it were a mask, and the creature became man-
like in form and features. This idea is still held, and it is believed that
many animals now possess this power. The manlike form thus appearing is called the *inua* and is supposed to represent the thinking part of
the creature, and at death becomes its shade.

Shamans are believed to have the power of seeing through the animal mask to the manlike features behind. The ideas held on this subject are well illustrated in the Raven legends, where the changes are made repeatedly from one form to another.

Masks may also represent totemic animals, and the wearers during the festivals are believed actually to become the creature represented or at least to be endowed with its spiritual essence. Some of the masks of the lower Yukon and the adjacent territory to the Kuskokwim are made with double faces. This is done by having the muzzle of the animal fitted over and concealing the face of the *inua* below, the outer mask being held in place by pegs so arranged that it can be removed quickly at a certain time in the ceremony, thus symbolizing the transformation.

Another style of mask from the lower Kuskokwim has the under face concealed by a small hinged door on each side, which opens out at the proper time in a ceremony, indicating the metamorphosis. When the mask represents a totemic animal, the wearer needs no double face, since he represents in person the shade of the totemic animal.

When worn in any ceremonial, either as a totem mask or as representing the shade, *yu-ǎ* or *tunghâk*, the wearer is believed to become mysteriously and unconsciously imbued with the spirit of the being which his mask represents, just as the namesakes are entered into and possessed by the shades at certain parts of the Festival to the Dead.

In connection with the collection of masks obtained it is interesting that a number of them have wooden models of thumbless hands attached to their sides, the palms of the hands being pierced with large, circular holes; these are usually found on masks representing birds, beasts, and spirits, having some connection with making game more or less plentiful. I am inclined to think that the holes in the palms indicate that the being will not hold the game, but will let it pass through to the earth.

Many of the masks from this region are very complicated, having numerous appendages of feathers and carved wood; these either represent limbs or are symbolic. The masks are also painted to represent features or ideas connected with the mythology of the being.

Mask festivals are usually held as a species of thanksgiving to the shades and powers of earth, air, and water for giving the hunters success. The *inuas* or shades of the powers and creatures of the earth are represented that they may be propitiated, thus insuring further success. Unfortunately, I failed to secure the data by which the entire significance of customs and beliefs connected with masks can be solved satisfactorily. I trust, however, that the present notes, with the explanations and descriptions of the masks, may serve as a foundation for more successful study of these subjects in the future; the field is now open, but in a few years the customs of this people will be so modified that it will be difficult to obtain reliable data. When the Eskimo between Yukon and Kuskokwim rivers become so sophisticated by contact with white men that mask festivals fall into disuse, it will be but a short time until all the wealth of mythological fancy connected with them will become a sealed book.

Among the very large number of these objects obtained some of the more interesting have been chosen for description and illustration, giving with each, so far as possible, its significance. Their wonderful variety and complexity of ornamentation, which is symbolical throughout, evinces a lively fancy in the makers.

Figure 2, plate XCV, shows a long, flat, pear-shape mask from Sabotnisky on the lower Yukon, excavated behind and rather convex in front; it measures 6 by 9 inches, and represents the features of a black bear. On one side, covering the area of the right eye and cheek, is a round, human face overhung by five tufts of human hair, which represents the *inua* of the bear. The main surface of this mask is painted white, bordered by red, the muzzle of the bear and border of the human face being of the same color; the remainder of the face is black. From the left corner of the mouth depends a small, red, wooden appendage representing the lower half of the tongue, which is attached to the interior of the mouth by a small willow splint or peg so that it can move freely. About the sides and upper border of the mask are nine holes where large feathers were inserted upright.

Another mask from the same locality, and very much like the preceding, represents a red bear and has a human face on the right side, painted red; the ears are indicated by small, paddle-shape, flattened sticks lashed to split quills, which are fastened to the sides of the mask by wooden plugs. It is 5½ inches broad by 8 inches long.

The collection contains another mask of the same character representing a red bear, but it is a little larger than either of those described. It is from Starikwikhpak, on the lower Yukon.

The mask shown in figure 4, plate XCV, is from Cape Vancouver. It is an oval representation of a semihuman face, a little over 8 inches high by 5¾ wide, rounded in front and slightly excavated behind. This is a grotesque mask, portraying the features of a *tunghâk*. The right eye is prominent and rounded to the same size and shape as the mouth; the left eye is a crescentic opening about two inches long with the corners turned down and near the upper border of an oval, flattened area on the face. Just above the mouth on the inside is fastened, by means of a peg, a tuft of long reindeer hair, which extends down and out of the mouth and hangs over the chin; there are no nostrils. A large feather tipped with small, downy plumes extends out from each side of the forehead, and another from the top. The border of this mask has a narrow, red band around the top and sides, ending opposite the mouth; the flattened space extending from the crescent-shape eye downward on the cheek is red, coarsely spotted with white; the remainder of the face is white.

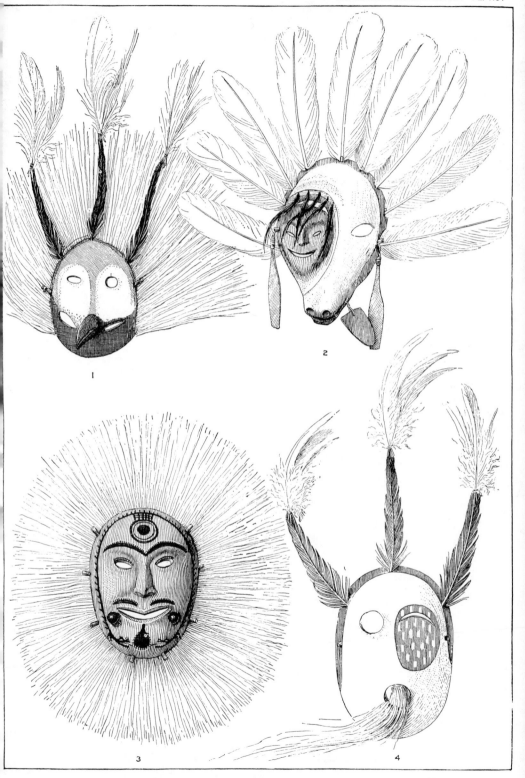

MASKS (ABOUT ONE-FOURTH)

Figure 1, plate xcv, represents a small, flat, rounded mask, 5¾ by 4¼ inches, from Sabotnisky, on the lower Yukon. It is shallowly excavated, and is pierced for the eyes and mouth; the right eye is horizontally oblong, the left is round. The mouth is represented by two flattened, oval openings, inclined toward the center, which is occupied by a rudely carved imitation of an owl's beak, fastened on by means of a square pin fitted into an orifice in the mask. The sides of the face and forehead, with a line descending between the eyes to the beak, are green; an area about each eye and covering the cheeks is white, spotted with red. The beak is not painted, except the red along the grooves marking the gape; the lower sides of the face and the entire chin are black. Three quill feathers tipped with downy plumes are inserted in the forehead. This figure represents the *inua* of the short-ear owl.

Figure 3, plate xcv, from the tundra south of the Yukon mouth, is a well-carved mask representing a human face, 7¼ inches long by 5½ wide, oval in front and deeply concave behind. The features are well carved and smoothly rounded. About the border are set eight wooden pegs, with the ends split for holding a strip of deerskin with outstanding hair to represent the fur hood worn by the Eskimo in winter. It is one of the most carefully modeled of any mask obtained, and is one of the few which represents a human face without distortion of some kind. The eyes and mouth are pierced, and a large globular labret is represented at each corner of the mouth, fastened in place by a wooden pin. The entire face is painted Indian red, with the goatee, mustache, eyebrows, and upper eyelashes black.

Extending over the forehead and down each side of the face is a long, black line with ray-like black markings projecting backward from it; on each side of the chin this black line ends in the head and fore-feet of the alligator-like animal known as *palraiyuk*. A disk-like pendant with two concentric circles and a spot in the center is drawn in black on the forehead, and is connected with the body of the *palraiyuk*, where it crosses the brow, by black cross-lines.

Plate xcvi *a*, from Cape Romanzof, is a very large mask, measuring 12 by 22 inches and 6 inches in depth, carved from a single piece of wood, and is supposed to represent the sea parrot (*Lunda cirrhata*). The open mouth of the bird covers over half the surface, and the points of the mandibles project free from the face. In the open mouth is represented the supposed features of the bird's *inua*. The eyes are narrow and are set obliquely above two widely separated, round nostrils and a broad, semilunar mouth with the corners depressed. Around the border of the mouth of the bird, and thus bordering the inclosed face, are small wooden pegs half an inch in length to represent teeth. On the forehead of the mask, near the base and upper portion of the beak, are carved the eyes of the bird. Surrounding the outer border of the mask, and held out from it half to three-quarters of an inch by wooden pegs, is a hoop of splints. The interior of the mask is roughly excavated, with a projecting lug on each side to prevent it from slipping sidewise on the face, while below another lug serves as a chin rest the wearer. The general surface of the front of the mask is painted a dull blue, coarsely spotted with white; the eyes have white pupils and red irides; the beak of the bird is red, obliquely striped with white, and the sides of its mouth are painted red. The face of the *inua* is white, the interior of the nostrils red, each having four black, ray-like lines drawn from its border about an inch upward on the side of the face.

Plate xcvi *b*, from Cape Romanzof, south of the Yukon mouth, is a very large mask about 30 inches high by 10 inches wide. It is broadly oval below and tapers up into a long projection or neck above, which is formed of a separate piece fitted upon the body of the mask with three pegs, inserted from behind, attaching a projecting shoulder to the main part. On the extreme upper tip is a small figure of a human head. Surrounding the mask on all sides, and held at a short distance from it by lashings of willow root, is a hoop made of two thin, narrow splints. A series of split pegs around the border holds in position a narrow strip of reindeer skin, bearing long, upstanding hairs, which reaches up a little over half way on the neck or handle-like projection, and there its ends are inserted in the wood.

The lower portion or body of the mask represents two faces. The lower, which is much the larger and occupies at least two-thirds of the entire surface, is a grotesque semihuman face, having a huge, crescentic mouth with upturned corners. There are two large, round nostrils in a broad, spreading, rounded nose, and two crescentic eyes with upturned corners, over which hang the broad, heavy eyebrows, which project an inch and a half and sweep down with a crescentic curve over each eye, meeting at an angle on the base of the nose two inches above their lower border. The upper portion of the mask is occupied by the rounded face of some animal, apparently intended to represent a seal, which has a bulging brow and rounded, flat nose with nostrils deeply incised, and a wide, oval mouth, with four square teeth cut in relief on the lower jaw. The eyes are rounded and pierced, with a notch extending downward at the inner corner. The chin of this face rests on the forehead of the huge lower one. The handle-like projection extends upward from the top of the last-described head, and is over 12 inches high; it is flat behind, but rather oval on the sides, and has along its front a deep, rounded groove extending the entire length to the head at the top; along each side is a row of wooden pegs to represent teeth. The head capping this projection is about $2\frac{1}{2}$ inches high and 2 inches broad, representing ordinary human features; it is surrounded on the edges by a groove in which is a band of reindeer skin with the hair projecting like a halo. The large lower face is mainly white, the mouth is red; the line about the upper lip, representing a mustache, is

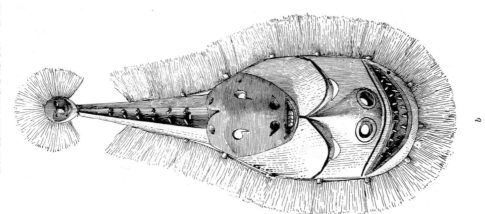

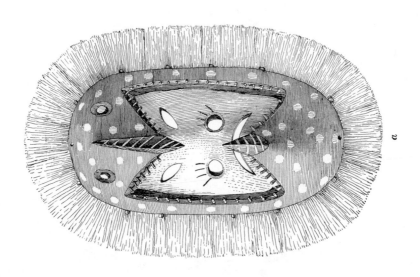

MASKS (ONE-SIXTH)

black, and the circle about each nostril is of the same color; the interior of the nostrils and the line following the outline of the eyebrows are bluish slate color. The animal face resting above this is also colored bluish slate, with the mouth painted red. The front of the projection above is white, the groove being red, as is also the entire face of the small head at the top; the hoop surrounding the border of the mask is also red. The meaning of this mask is unknown, but I would call attention to its general similarity to the composite masks and carvings made among the Tlinket of southern Alaska.

The mask (number 38856) from Sabotnisky is 8½ by 6 inches, and represents a grotesque human countenance. It is oval and deeply excavated behind. Upon the sides are curved ridges in relief to represent ears; the nose is a rounded, triangular piece fastened by two wooden pegs; the eyes and mouth are pierced through the mask, the latter being bordered by a row of reindeer teeth above and below. The face is painted bright red and bordered by a band of reindeer skin with long hair. It is one of the few masks procured that approaches closely to an ordinary human countenance. Its significance was not learned.

Plate XCVIII shows a huge mask, cut from a slab of wood, nearly 2 feet high by 13 inches across, convex on its front and squared in outline, roughly excavated in the back with three projecting lugs for holding the mask in place against the chin and the sides of the face. It represents a gigantic face, with large, rounded blocks of wood for labrets just below the corners of the crescentic mouth. Above these and joining the crescentic mouth on each side projects a flat, paddlelike piece of wood representing a human hand and arm, the former pierced by a large, round hole. Just back of these hands, and fastened up and down along the side of the mask but separated from it by about two inches, are two thin, flat strips of wood about two and a half inches wide, held in place by pegs in the sides of the mask and in the arms. These strips have feathers along their outer edges as ornaments, as has also the squared top of the mask. The mouth is very large, somewhat crescentic in shape, with the corners upturned and extending out along the arms, nearly to the wrists. The nose is large and rounded, with two large, round nostrils, and the eyes, like the nostrils, are pierced through the wood; the brow is very overhanging, and has a row of flat, oval, pointed wooden pegs along its edge to represent eyebrows. In the forehead is cut a square hole a little over two and a half inches in diameter. Below the upper lip there is a row of square, flat wooden pegs along its edge to indicate teeth, matching a similar set in the lower jaw; teeth, both upper and under, are also represented in the portion of the mouth extending along the arms.

On the brow of the mask are the wooden images of five seals and two reindeer. The sides have a row of squared wooden pegs, representing teeth, up and down along its length above the arms, and another set along the bordering flat strip of wood parallel to the side of the mask, thus representing a vertical mouth on each side of the face. The images of the seals, reindeer, labrets, and arms, as well as the teeth and eyebrows, are fastened to the main body of the mask by wooden pegs inserted in holes. The inside of the mouths, on the sides of the head as well as that in the usual place, are painted red, as are also the insides of the hands; the chin is bluish; the labrets are white, with black spots; the arms are blue below and white above, with a black line drawn along the upper border of the mouth, joining the mustache line of the upper lip on the body of the mask. Over each nostril is a curved black line to represent a depression; there is also a broad black band across the region of the eyes from side to side, and a border of red extends along the brow above the pegs, indicating the eyebrows. This image represents the *tunghák* or being that controls the supply of game. It is usually represented as living in the moon. The shamans commonly make a pretense of going to him with offerings in order to bring game into their district when the hunters have been unsuccessful for some time.

Masks of this character are too heavy to be worn upon the face without additional support, so they are ordinarily suspended from the roof of the kashim by strong cords. The wearer stands behind with the mask bound about his head, and wags it from side to side during the dance so as to produce the ordinary motion. I was told that in all the great mask festivals several of these huge objects were usually thus suspended from the roof.

From the lower Kuskokwim there is a circular mask, 15 inches in diameter, in the form of a round board with a human face in relief on its center in front, and excavated in the back. A hoop of splints surrounds the border of this mask, joined to it below and held out from the sides elsewhere to a distance of from one to two inches by lashings. All around the sides and top of the border are set the white, secondary quill-feathers of swans or gulls. Above the forehead on each side is a rudely carved head of a fish, and below on each side of the cheeks is the head of a seal, all of which are set into the mask by pegs in their bases and project forward at right angles to the plane of face. Between these heads and on the border of the board opposite the sides of the face are attached by pegs curious flat representations of thumbless hands with holes in the palms. The mouth is large, wide, rounded at the corners, and set around with the teeth of some mammal. The nostrils are large and rounded; the eyes are oval and set in obliquely with their near cor ners highest. The mouth, nostrils, and eyes are pierced through the wood. The upper portion of this mask is made from a separate piece, which is neatly fitted to the main part and held in place by rawhide lashings. The main color of the front of the mask is white; a band of black encircles the surface an inch or more outside the border of the face. The borders of the face in relief are painted a dull green; the inside of the mouth is red, and a heavy mustache and the depression

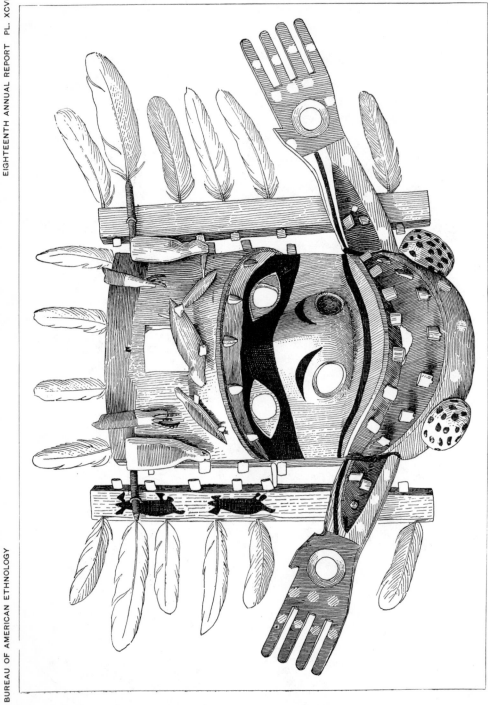

MASK

over each nostril are black. The remainder of the face is white; the hands are red, as are also the two seal-heads; the fish-heads are green. This mask represents the face of a *tunghâk*.

A mask bearing original number 1445, from the country south of the Yukon mouth, represents a human figure with outstretched arms and legs, having a human face in relief on the front of the body. The head, arms, and legs of this figure are attached to the central part of the mask with wooden pins. A hoop fastened to the inside of the arms near the elbows and to the legs at the knees holds the limbs in their outstretched position. On each side of the face on the front of the body is a thumbless hand cut from a flattened piece of wood. These are attached to the mask with flexible pegs of wood. This mask, from the lower part of the body to the top of head, is 14 inches high and nearly 7 inches broad on the body. Its posterior surface is roughly concave, with a projecting ledge of wood near the lower border of excavation, to enable the wearer to seize it with his teeth for the purpose of holding the mask more firmly in position. Around the body of the mask are inserted downy, white swan's feathers; the outstretched hands of the figure are thumbless, as are the hands on nearly all the masks collected in that region. The holes in the palms, which are usually made large and conspicuous, are indicated in this case by small, round punctures about one-tenth of an inch in diameter. The main color of the front of the mask, including the arms, legs, and the hoop, is white. The ears on the head of the figure are represented by small, flat wooden pegs painted red; the mouth is also red. The eyebrows, excavations for the eyes, mustache, and beard are indicated in black paint, the eyebrows and mustache being represented by dots. The arms, between the shoulders and elbows, are surrounded by a black band with a white spot in the middle, and the forearms and the hands to the fingers are red; the ends of the fingers are not painted.

The second pair of hands, mentioned as being on either side of the face in front of the body, are painted like the arms. There is a black band around the thigh with a white spot in the center, and the lower legs and the feet are red, with a white spot on the inside of the calf, which corresponds to a similar spot on the inside of each wrist. The border around the face carved on the front of the body is red, with white dots at regular intervals about the circle. The face itself is white, with eyebrows, snow-goggles, nostrils, a line over each nostril, mustache, and beard represented in black; the lips are painted red. The eyes and the mouth are pierced through. The exact significance of this mask was not learned, but the face on the front of the body undoubtedly represents the supposed features of the *inua* of the being represented by the main figure.

A mask from the lower Kuskokwim (number 64234), 10 by 6½ inches, is oval and deeply excavated, with a convex front imitating a hair seal pierced by four almond-shape openings representing eyes and nostrils.

Just below these the chin is cut away and the carved, wooden head is attached by sinew cords, so that it may be moved up and down, and is controlled by a sinew cord passing through a hole from the rear of the mask to its attachment on the throat. The flippers, both before and behind, are represented by small, paddle-shape wooden attachments fastened to the body with small strips of whalebone. Upon each side of the eyes and nostrils, which are pierced through the face of the mask, are fastened small, wing-like doors, as if to close and cover the face, but they are tied so as to remain permanently open. On each of these doors is painted in black the image of a white whale, and a black line is drawn through the eyes on the face. A stout splint hoop is attached at the shoulders on either side by wooden splints, and surrounds the entire border of the mask, except in front. The face and the interior of the doors are white, with the exception of the black figures mentioned; also all of the seal's head, except the crown and nape, which, with the back of the figure forming the front of the mask, are painted slate color with white spots. This figure is intended to represent a seal, the concealed face on its back being the *inua*.

Figure 1, plate XCVIII, is a long, slender mask representing the head, neck, and beak of a sand-hill crane (*Grus canadensis*). It is 30 inches long, with the head and beak about 24 inches in length, and is rudely carved, having the top of the bird's head excavated for a small lamp, with a hole in front on each side, representing the eyes for the light to shine through. On the beak are a few wooden pegs to indicate teeth, and the slender neck extends down to the breast of the bird where the wood takes a roughly oval form on which is a rudely shaped human face, with the chin narrow and long drawn down. This face is about 5½ inches broad and slightly and roughly excavated behind. The interior of the bird's mouth and the area around the eyes and ears, the sides of the neck, as well as the space about the eyes, nostrils, and interior of the mouth of the human face at the lower portion are painted red. This mask was said to represent the *inua* of the crane. The maker was a shaman, who claimed that once, when he was alone upon the tundra, he saw a sand-hill crane standing at a distance looking at him; as he approached, the feathers on the bird's breast parted, revealing the face of the bird's *inua*, as shown in the carving.

Figure 2, plate XCVIII, from the lower Kuskokwim, is a long, narrow, flattened mask, 11½ by 4½ inches, representing an extremely elongated human countenance with the face divided across the middle, just above the lower point of the nose, and hinged together with rawhide cord so as to move upon itself. The eyes and the mouth are crescentic with down-turned corners; the nose is long and slender with two rounded nostrils pierced through the wood and having a dumbbell-shape pendant on the nose ring. On the middle of the lower lip is a peculiarly shaped labret made of a carved wooden flap, indicating, from the style of wearing this ornament, that the face represented is that of a woman. The upper half of the countenance is painted white and the lower half bluish slate color. Surrounding the upper half, at intervals of about two inches, are inserted white swan feathers. The posterior surface is rudely excavated. The meaning of this mask is not known.

Figure 3, plate XCVIII, from Sabotnisky, on the lower Yukon, is a grotesque human face with the forehead drawn out to the rear as a long, skillet-like handle. This mask is about 20 inches in length, of which the handle or projection back of the forehead represents three-fourths. The inner side is shallowly excavated. The nose is very short and rudely carved, and is placed so far up between the eyes as to leave a very broad, flattened space for the upper lip and cheeks.

Below this is a broad, crescent-shape mouth with corners upturned, and long, widely spaced teeth, represented by wooden pegs. Commencing just at the base of the nose, above the eyes, and extending back along the top of the extension to its extreme posterior end is a deep groove representing a mouth bordered by widely spaced wooden pegs for teeth. Along each side of this are set two feathers. The entire front and upper surface of this mask is painted red, with the face between the mouth and the eyes splashed with blood. This represents some mythical being, but its exact signification was not learned.

Figure 3, plate XCIX, from Paimut, on the lower Yukon, is $8\frac{1}{2}$ by $7\frac{1}{4}$ inches. This is a thin, flattened, rounded mask representing a grotesque semihuman countenance. It has one round eye in the forehead, one in the proper place on the left side, and another in the center of the right cheek. Still another eye, of crescentic shape, is situated just above the round one on the right side. The nose is narrow at the top, curving down to the right and ending in a broad point. The mouth is wide, slit-like, and pierced in two parts, the narrow, slit-like part on the left being separated from the round, eyehole-like opening on the right corner by a narrow, closed space. Surrounding the entire border of the mouth are wooden pegs to represent teeth. The eyebrow above the crescentic eye and a band around the border of the mask, as well as the mouth and the chin, are red. The forehead and the top of the nose are dull green, and the remainder of the face is white. When in use the mask had quill feathers inserted around the edge. This represents the countenance of a *tunghâk* and is from the extreme upper border of the Eskimo territory along the Yukon.

Figure 2, plate XCIX, from Sabotnisky, on the lower Yukon, is a thin, flattened mask, with the posterior side slightly excavated, representing a rude, semihuman face. In the center of the face is a rounded hole for the mouth, with two narrow, slit-like eyeholes above. Surrounding the mouth, between it and the border of the mask, are four broad, concentric grooves. The interior of the mouth and a line around the border of the mask are red, the rest is painted white. This mask also represents the features of a *tunghâk.*

Figure 4, plate XCIX, from Sabotnisky, is 8½ inches long by 6½ inches wide. It is a flattened, rounded mask, slightly excavated behind, with a fantastic human face on the front. The nose is very short, leaving the upper lips and cheek in one broad plane; the mouth is wide and crescentic, with upturned corners. Surrounding the forehead from the ears on either side is a band of deerskin with the hair upstanding. Upon either cheek and from the middle of the forehead extend short pieces of whalebone, having attached to their outer ends slender, wooden, pencil-like appendages about five inches long, which move with the motions of the dancer. Strung along the forehead above the brows are small strips of parchment which are held in place by pegs inserted in the wood and hang down over the eyes. The entire face is painted green and spotted coarsely with dull brown pigment; the sticks on the ends of the whalebone are red. Like preceding masks this represents the face of a *tunghâk*.

Figure 1, plate XCIX, is a thin, flattened mask, measuring 8 by 5½ inches, somewhat quadrate but rounded at the corners. The mouth is crescentic, with the corners turned down, and two round eyeholes pierce the front. Just above the mouth is set a carved attachment representing the top of the head and upper mandible of a bird. A wooden peg inserted below the mouth indicates the lower mandible. Upon each side of the face is attached a long, narrow, flat strip, evidently intended to indicate the doors, which open and close on similar masks made in this district. Two crescentic incisions curving over the eyes represent eyebrows and are colored red. Surrounding the borders of the mask on each side and above are inserted feathers of the horned owl. The main color of the face, as well as the inside of the flaps upon each side is white. The bird's eyes and beak are black, as are also a line across the eyebrows and cheeks, as well as the figures of the seal, walrus, killer whale, reindeer, wolf, and beaver, which are drawn upon the surface of the flaps on each side. This face represents the *inua* of some species of waterfowl, the name of which I did not learn; but from the drawings of the various game animals upon the flaps attached to the sides, I judge that it was used in festivals connected with obtaining success in the hunt, which I learned to be the case with similar masks in that region.

Figure 4, plate C, is a rudely carved figure of the sea parrot (*Mormon arctica*), 7½ inches long by 4½ wide. This represents the upper half of the bird's body as it would appear when swimming on the water. The head and neck are made of a separate piece joined to the body by a round pin. In the upturned beak is the wooden figure of a walrus, the neck of which is made of cloth so as to form a loose joint and permit the head to flap about as the wearer of the mask dances. The mask is surrounded by two successive hoops of splints held in place by being lashed to pegs fastened in holes about the edges. Just in front of these pegs is attached a narrow strip of reindeer skin from which long hairs

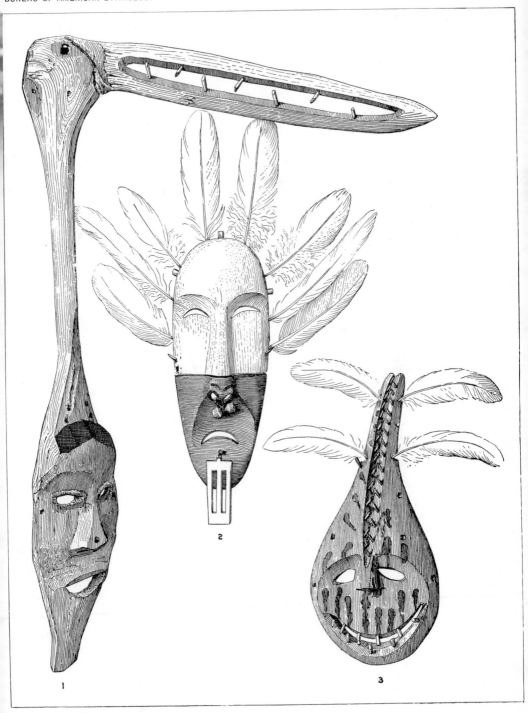

MASKS

project all around like a halo.   This is held in position by being inserted in the split ends of pegs placed around the border of the mask.

To the outer hoop surrounding the mask, one on each side and one on the top, are attached three long quill feathers having the vanes removed on one side and with a tuft of downy feathers tied to their ends.   The bird's wings are represented by small, flat, somewhat paddle-shape pieces, which are fastened to the shoulders of the image with flexible pieces of root inserted in holes, enabling the wings to play as the wearer moved.   Just back of these, one on each side, are rudely cut representations of a pair of thumbless hands with the fingers free and the palms pierced by a large, round hole.   Back of these hands are two paddle-shape attachments of wood, representing the bird's feet, also fastened to the body with flexible pieces of root.   At the posterior end three long, slender, paddle-shape strips are fastened in the same manner to represent the bird's tail.

In the middle of the bird's back, occupying about one-half the space, is a well-carved semihuman face, supposed to represent the *inua* of the bird.   This face has the eyes pierced through the mask; the mouth is represented as open, with the teeth thrown in relief by incised cross lines.   The walrus, bird's beak and feet, the pierced hands on the sides with the exception of the tips of the fingers, the hoops encircling the mask, and the border of the face on the bird's back, are painted red, as well as the outlines of the mouth and the teeth.   The bird's wings, neck, back, and tail-feathers are dull blue.   The bird's face and the pupil of the eye are white and the iris black.   the face on the bird's back is white with black dots to represent the mustache, beard, and eyebrows. The depression just above the nostrils is indicated in black, as is also a representation of snow-goggles drawn across the eyes.

Figure 2, plate C, from Cape Romanzof, south of the mouth of the Yukon, is a mask 9 by 5½ inches, representing a guillemot swimming on the surface of the water.   The head and neck are carved from a separate piece, which is fastened to the body by a peg.   The wings are indicated by thin, flipper-like pieces of wood attached by flexible pieces of root, and at one time the tail was represented by similar appendages which have been broken off and lost.   On the back of this figure is carved in relief a curious, hastate-shape countenance, with the sharp point near the base of the bird's neck.   Near the center of the base of this hastate-shape area on the bird's rump a single round hole pierces the wood and represents an eye.   Below this are placed two obliquely-set, oval nostrils and a crescent-shape mouth with the corners upturned.

The upper part of the head, neck, and body of the bird are painted dull blue, with large white spots.   The lower part of the neck and breast, with the surface of the flippers and the face on the back, are white.   The white face is thinly spotted with black on the sides and lower portion and a single black spot is on the middle of the wing. The interior of the nostrils is dull blue, and a broadly crescentic, white area surrounding the eye is bordered by a narrow black line. The face on the back of the bird represents its *inua*.

Figure 1, plate C, from lower Kuskokwim river, is 11½ inches long by 5 inches wide, and represents a human figure with outspread arms and legs. The head, arms, and legs are set in by squared pegs at their inner portion, which are inserted into holes in the body of the mask. The front of the body of this mask has a grotesque, semihuman face in low relief, shut in by little doors which, hinged upon either side, are made to open outward, and are controlled by sinew cords. This figure is similar in general character, except the doors, to a mask described from the lower Yukon (number 1445). The inside of the head is deeply excavated and the back of the body is shallowly concave. Along the inside of the hands and arms, as well as of the legs to the feet, extend grooves painted red, bordered with black, and set with pegs to represent teeth. This indicates that the being represented was supposed to be provided with mouths all along these portions of its figure. The head has two round eyes and a crescentic mouth with points upturned, but no features in relief. The face on the front of the body has the eyeholes, broadly spaced nostrils, and flattened oval, nearly horizontal mouth pierced through the mask; the mouth is provided with squared, peg-like projections to indicate teeth. The entire mask, when the doors are closed in front, with the exception of the mouth area along the arms and legs, is white.

The inner surfaces of the doors, as well as the concealed face, are white with the exception of the outlined spectacle-like figure covering the eyes, a line indicating the mustache, and the figures of two reindeer upon the inner side of one of the doors and the figures of two seals upon the inner side of the other door, which are black. A narrow strip of deerskin with upstanding hair surrounds the head. Upon each shoulder, as well as along the sides, are inserted white feathers. The exact meaning of this figure is not known, but the doors concealing the face on the front of the body indicate that the concealed features are supposed to represent the inner countenance or *inua* of the being. Other masks of this character were seen in the region between Kuskokwim and Yukon rivers, as well as on the lower Kuskokwim, and in one or more instances I saw masks having an outer or movable portion representing the muzzle of some animal which could be removed at a certain time in the festival by a single motion of the hand. These were used to represent the metamorphosis from the ordinary form of the being indicated to that of its *inua*.

Figure 3, plate C, from Pastolik, at the northern border of the Yukon mouth, is a rather flat, pear-shape mask, 12¾ inches long by 5½ inches broad. It is made with a grotesque, semihuman face on the rounded larger end and tapers back to an obtuse point at the top. On the left side of the face are two rudely carved representations of human legs fastened to the mask by quills. One of these is inserted near the corner of the

MASKS (NEARLY ONE-FOURTH)

mouth and the other just above the top of the face. On the opposite side are two slightly curved pieces of wood of the same size as the legs and fastened to the mask in a similar manner. Each of these pieces has five small, cylindrical sticks an inch and a half long fastened along its lower border by sinew cords. Above these, on the sides of the tapering summit of the mask, are two quills with downy feathers at their tips, and the extreme summit has inserted in it a white swan feather. The face of this mask is very grotesque, one eye being round and nearly in the middle of the upper portion, to the left of which is a crescentic eye over two inches in length, the points of the crescent being toward the center of the face. Between these eyes the ridge of the nose is represented as having a curve similar to the outer border of the crescentic eye, and the nostrils are placed vertically one above the other. The mouth is crescent-shape and twisted around under the large round eye, and in its left corner is a round opening. The teeth are represented by squared, wooden pegs, and the mouth and eyes are pierced through the mask. The face is white, splashed about the mouth with some dark liquid, apparently blood. The two legs, as well as the opposite attachments, are red, as is also a narrow border and the long, pointed extension above the face. The cylindrical pendants are white, and the projection above the face is painted black, with large white spots. This mask represents the features of a *tunghâk*.

Figure 1, plate CI, from south of the lower Yukon, is 12 by 6 inches, and represents a salmon. It is a flat, oval mask, having the head carved from a separate piece and fitted to the front end by a wooden peg. At the other end the tail is represented by two loose pieces on each side, fastened to the mask by pegs. Beneath the throat of the salmon is the wooden effigy of a hair seal, represented as swimming crosswise to the course of the salmon, and fastened in position by a peg. On the back, in front of the tail, is a small model of a kaiak, held upright and crosswise to the length of the fish by a small splint; at one time the kaiak evidently bore the image of a man seated in the manhole.

On each side of the salmon's body are broad, thin, paddle-shape pieces of wood, fastened with pegs, to represent the pectoral fins. Just behind these, and near the tail, on each side, is the flat, wooden image of a small salmon, the mouth, eyes, and gill openings of which are represented by incised lines. Just below the junction of the salmon's neck with the body are incised lines which represent a large mouth with teeth; in the rear of this, on each side, is a large eye cut in relief. The entire back of the fish is occupied by a semihuman face, having a remarkable V-shape mouth, with the corners turned up and the teeth cut in relief; two oval nostrils and the eyes are pierced through the wood. The outline of the mouth and the gill openings of the salmon's head, also of the mouth below the salmon's neck and the outlines of the mouth and teeth in the face on the back, are red; and a band extending from the neck of the salmon around on each side to the end of the tail, as well as the band along the sides of the small fish represented on either side of the salmon, are of the same color. The pupil of the salmon's eye, the outline of the teeth in the large mouth below the neck and outline of the eye just behind this, the spectacle-shape area covering the eyes of the face, the interior of the nostrils, and the line indicating the mustache, as well as a line surrounding the raised border of the face, are black. The remainder of the outer side of the mask, including the seal model and kaiak, are white; the seams on the kaiak, however, are indicated by black lines. About the border of this mask are set white quill-feathers of some gull. The interior is excavated. The face on the back represents the *inua* of the fish.

Figure 2, plate CI, from lower Kuskokwim river, represents the hair seal (*Phoca barbata*). This mask is carved as a flattened image of the common hair seal. It is about 11 inches long by 6 inches in width, and has four large, flipper-shape, wooden attachments to represent the four limbs. These are carved on their borders to represent the toes of the animal, and the eyes, nose, and mouth are well represented on the rounded head. On the seal's back the greater portion of the surface is occupied by a circular face like that of a man, having below the eyes two pear-shape nostrils and a crescentic mouth, with upturned corners, which has a double row of square-cut teeth. The upper surface of this mask is painted white, and the membrane between the toes and the hind-flippers are black. Across the eyes of the human face is marked in black the outline of a pair of snow-goggles. The interior of this mask has a shallow excavation, and the border is surrounded by a groove in which is fastened a strip of skin from the neck of a reindeer, with the long hairs standing out all around like a halo. The face on the back of this mask is supposed to represent the features of the seal's *inua*.

Figure 3, plate CII, from the lower Kuskokwim, measures 7½ by 5 inches. It is an oval, flattened mask of thin material, having carved in slight relief a grotesque human countenance with a Chinese like physiognomy. The almond-shape eyes are set obliquely and the broad, flattened nose with oval nostrils and huge crescentic mouth with upturned corners are curiously like an exaggerated Chinese face. The eyes are indicated by a sunken area on the surface of the wood, in which are pierced the large, round pupils. Teeth are indicated by square-cut, peg-like projections. A band of deerskin with long, projecting hair is set in a groove around the border. A broad, black line is drawn across the eyes, and the upper lip and chin are painted red, the teeth and rest of face being white, including the interior of the eyes. The signification of this mask is unknown.

Figure 2, plate CII, shows a mask, from Sabotnisky, measuring 8½ by 6½ inches. It is a rudely oval representation of a death's-head and is made by using fire to char the wood into the proper shape. The eyes

MASKS (ONE-FIFTH)

are large, irregularly rounded, and pierced through. On each side of the chin are represented two huge labrets, and a roughly fashioned nose and high cheekbones are also indicated. In the rear the mask is slightly excavated, with a ledge to enable the wearer to grasp it with his teeth.

Figure 4, plate CII, from the lower Kuskokwim, measures 6¾ by 7 inches. It is a quadrangular mask, with rounded corners, and is made of a thin, rather flattened piece of wood. It has a broad mouth extending clear across, with the lower jaw carved in a separate piece and hinged near the ends with sinew, so that it can be moved up and down. At the corners of the lower jaw are represented, by squared wooden appendages with small, wooden strips, labret pendants of peculiar style, attached to the chin with whalebone. The mouth above and below is bordered with wooden pegs to represent teeth. Two suboval nostrils, near the middle of the face, and eyes of the same size and shape are pierced through the mask. The pupils are represented by small wooden pegs, carved narrow at the ends and rounded in the middle, set in so that their broad, rounded portion is in the middle of the eye opening. Just above the eye, on each side, and set in by a squared wooden peg, is a somewhat pointed, flattened, or paddle-shape piece of wood representing an ear. Fastened to each side of the face by splints, just above the corners of the mouth, are the ends of two hoops which extend out and around the upper side of the countenance and are held in position by the wrappings of splint; to the outer of these hoops are attached three long feathers with downy plumes at their tips. Fastened immediately about the face of the mask, and held in position by the split ends of pegs set around the border, is a strip of deerskin with long, upstanding hairs, forming a halo-like fringe. This mask represents the *inua* of a Canada lynx. The ear tips are painted black behind, and are white near their bases to represent the markings on the ears of the lynx. The entire face is white, with rounded, bluish spots and a series of brownish blotches along the borders of the mouth, above and below, and a black line is drawn from eye to eye.

Figure 1, plate CII, shows a mask, from south of the Yukon mouth, measuring 6 inches high by 4½ wide. It is thin and rather flat, being only slightly excavated behind, square on top and along the sides, becoming rounded on the lower portion. It represents semihuman features with bird-like mandibles projecting from above and below the mouth, which is broad with the corners upturned, and extends on each side to the extreme borders of the mask. The center of the mouth is pierced through; a round block projects outward between the mandibles and has attached to its outer end by a rag the rudely carved effigy of a walrus head with projecting tusks. The eyes and nostrils are pierced through the mask. Above the eyes, upon each side, are the head and shoulders of a wolf in relief. The remainder of the wolf's body and all its limbs are carved free on a block extending outward horizontally and attached to the side of the mask by wooden pegs so as to be continuous with the part on the mask. These wolves are represented as walking toward the center, their heads close together and tails outstretched in opposite directions. Surrounding the masks at a short distance is a small wooden hoop, in which is inserted three feathers tipped with downy plumes, one on each side and one on top. The forehead, a ring around each eye, a line over the nostrils, the mustache, and the chin, with the entire figure of the wolf on the left side, are black, spotted sparsely with white. The other wolf is white, with the end of its tail and feet black, as are its eyes and nostrils. The inside of the wolves' mouths, the mouth of the mask, including the inside of the mandibles and the figure of the walrus, excepting the tusks, are red. The signification of this mask is unknown, but I believe that the black and white wolves bear a symbolic reference to day and night.

Figure 5, plate CIII, from lower Kuskokwim river, is $7\frac{3}{4}$ by $4\frac{1}{4}$ inches. It is a rudely carved, rather flattened maskette, thin on one side and thicker on the other, with a nearly straight outline along one side and rounded on the other three sides. Facing the straight side of the mask the surface is excavated, leaving a raised edge or rim near the other border, and in the depression thus formed is a rounded, saucer-like excavation about two inches in diameter in which are pierced two holes for eyes and a crescentic mouth. Surrounding the borders of this maskette are two hoops of splint held in position by willow bark lashings. The space occupied by the small face is painted a slaty bluish color, and a band of the same color is drawn along the ridge toward the outer border on the main portion of the maskette; the remainder is white. This maskette represents a half moon and is connected with religious ceremonials held during the winter in that region, but I failed to learn its exact significance.

Figure 4, plate CIII, from lower Kuskokwim river, is $5\frac{3}{4}$ by $3\frac{1}{2}$ inches. It is a small, flattened, rudely shaped maskette, representing a grotesque semihuman countenance with two rounded eyes and an oval mouth piercing the front. The nostrils are indicated by two squared depressions. In the mouth three wooden pegs, two above and one below, indicate teeth. The borders of this object are set with small, white feathers and a rawhide cord is attached to its upper edge for the purpose of sustaining it. It is somewhat pear-shape above, contracting on the sides at a point between the nostrils and the mouth and then expanding to form the rounded chin. Its significance is not known.

Figure 6, plate CIII, is a maskette from the lower Kuskokwim, measuring 5 by $1\frac{3}{4}$ inches. It is a rudely quadrangular, flattened piece of wood, having roughly oval eyes and a crescentic mouth, pierced through. Upon each side of the face are inserted two paddle-shape, slightly curved sticks, expanded toward the ends. From the base of the nose a groove

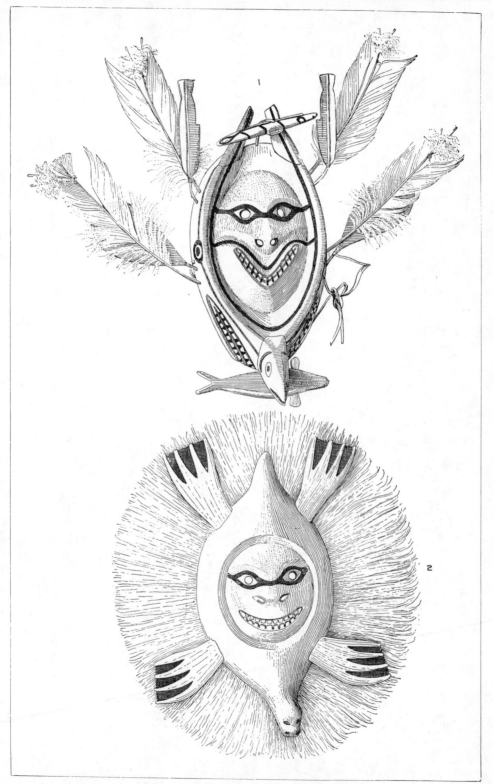

MASKS (ABOUT ONE-FOURTH)

extends along the surface to the upper end. The chin and a space above the eyes are dark slate in color, spotted with white; the remainder is white. The purpose of this maskette is for use in religious observances, but the exact ceremonies in which it figured were not learned.

Figure 2, plate CIII, is a maskette from lower Kuskokwim river. It measures $6\frac{1}{2}$ by $2\frac{3}{4}$ inches, and is a very rudely made specimen, representing semihuman features on a long, thin, quadrangular block of wood. The back portion is very slightly concave; the front has a ridge running down the middle, from which a bevel extends to the outer border on the right side. On the left side the surface of the mask is scooped out parallel to this ridge to a depth of half an inch, so that the ridge rises abruptly from the nearly plane surface on that side. By means of a hinge of bark a long, thin, leaf-like tablet is attached to the left side of the face. This little tablet closes like a door upon the face, covering it completely to the median ridge on that side. The beveled right side of the face has a crescentic eye with the corners pointing downward, and an ovate hole through the little door on the other side of the face serves as an eye for that side when it is closed.

The mouth is rudely and irregularly cut near the lower edge of the maskette, having its left corner drawn up and expanded. A notch in the lower end of the door upon that side serves, when it is closed, as a portion of the mouth. The median ridge described serves as the nose. Upon each side thin, flat strips of wood, somewhat quadrate in shape with a rounded projection at their lower end, are attached by fibrous bark and represent earrings. From the middle of the chin is hung, in the same manner by a peg and a small strip of bark, another similarly shaped, flat strip of wood, with the rounded projection on the lower end but with a squared slit extending up and down its middle. This represents a curious form of labret and, from its position, indicates that the face is intended for that of a woman. The general surface of the maskette, including the fronts of the earrings, the labret, and both sides of the small, leaf-like door are painted white. The nostril on the right side is outlined in black. The earrings and labret have their outer surfaces crossed with black lines, and the rounded lower end is black. The inner side of the little door has painted upon it, in black, the outline of an umiak with the sail up and a solitary human figure in the stern with the arms upraised. The portion of the maskette covered by this leaflet has rudely drawn upon it, in black, four semihuman faces representing mythical beings. Three feathers of the horned owl are stuck along the upper edge. The meaning of this object is unknown.

Figure 3, plate CIII, from the lower Kuskokwim, is a thin disk, $3\frac{1}{4}$ inches in diameter, with the back concavely excavated and the front having a raised ridge slightly within the border, inside of which is a circular face with a distorted semihuman appearance. From the rim mentioned it is beveled both outwardly and inwardly, the inner beveled portion bordering the face. The right eye is indicated by a crescentic hole, with the corners downward; the left eye is marked by an inserted wooden plug projecting about one-fourth of an inch. An almond-shape nostril is the only one represented. The nose, in dim relief, is twisted toward the right; the mouth is large and rounded on the right corner, thence extending across and up on the left side, ending in a sharp angle near the eye peg. In a groove around the border is a strip of reindeer skin with upstanding hair. On each side and at the top are inserted three quills tipped with downy plumes. Distorted countenances of this kind are made to represent the supposed features of a number of supernatural beings known as *tunghät*.

Figure 1, plate CIII, is a maskoid from Razbinsky. It is a roughly rounded block, 2¾ by 3 inches, having at its lower side a projection with a hole for the insertion of one finger. Upon one side is carved a representation of a bird's head; on the other a human countenance is shown. A groove extends around the side of this block at the junction of the two images, in which several feathers are set.

The representation of the entire head of any bird or animal on finger masks is uncommon, this instance being one of the few that came to my notice. The human face is painted red, as are the eyes and mouth of the bird; the bird's face on each side and the line on the top of head are white. The sides of the head and the line extending forward along the ridge of the nose or beak are of slate color. This is used as a finger mask by women in ceremonial dances; the exact meaning is unknown.

From Razbinsky, on the lower Yukon, is a very large and rather roughly made finger mask (number 1620), representing on one side a human face and deeply excavated on the other. It is the largest finger mask that was seen; it measures 4¾ by 7 inches.

Figure 2, plate CIV, is a finger mask from Big lake. It is a square, thin block, with a broad, rounded extension projecting from its lower edge through which are pierced two finger holes. The rear is excavated smoothly. The front has a distorted semihuman face, in slight relief, surrounded by a circular groove; the right eye is almond-shape and is inclined toward the nose. On the left side is a crescentic eye with the corners turned down. The mouth is a flattened oval with the right-hand corner drawn outward and up; the nose is twisted to the left. From the border of the circular countenance to each corner of the block is drawn a black line, and the crescentic eye is surrounded by a black area; the remainder of the face is painted white. Around the border are inserted six long tufts of reindeer hair and six tail-feathers of the old-squaw duck, with tips of plumes. It is used by women in ceremonial dances; otherwise its significance is unknown.

Figures 3 and 4, plate CIV, show two finger masks from Koñigunugumut. Each is made from a discoidal, flattened block 2¾ inches thick, connected by a small neck with a broad wooden attachment, which is

MASKS (NEARLY ONE-FOURTH)

pierced by a doubly rounded hole for the insertion of two fingers. It is surrounded by a groove in which is set a strip of deerskin with the long hair upstanding and with a quill tipped with downy feathers extending out over each side and up from the top. On one side of figure 4 is a grotesque semihuman face, with the mouth commencing as a down-turned corner on the right side, thence extending over and down on the other side, then sweeping up around the left border of the face and forehead. The eye upon the left side is absent; upon the right side is a crescentic eye with corners down-turned, and the nose is curved around toward the right. In the other example (figure 3) the block is surrounded near its border by a ridge from which a narrow bevel extends outward to the edge and another one inward to the border of a face in relief which occupies the middle. This face has no nose, but has the two crescentic eyes inclined downward toward the center and a crescentic mouth with down-turned corners cut into the block. This is used in ceremonial dances, as are other objects of this kind. The distorted countenance of the mask shown in figure 4 represents the supposed features of a *tunghâk*.

Figure 1, plate CIV, from Norton sound, is a rounded, flattened disk, 5 inches long by 2¾ broad, with the center removed, forming a ring and connected below by a short neck to an enlarged ring-like appendage for the insertion of two fingers. The hole through the center is nearly an inch and a half in diameter and is crossed by two small strips of wood. On each face of the disk, or ring, just inside the border, is a shallow groove. Along another groove, around the outer edge of the ring, are inserted five long, downy feathers. This specimen was collected by Mr L. M. Turner, who states that it was intended to represent a star, the feathers indicating the twinkling of the light. This finger mask was used by women in certain ceremonial dances.

Figure 1, plate CV, from Big lake, between Yukon and Kuskokwim rivers, is a ring 4½ inches in diameter inclosing a second ring a little over 2½ inches in diameter, which is attached to the outer one by two projections on opposite sides. On the lower side is a rounded projection about an inch in length and two inches broad, through which are pierced holes for the insertion of two fingers. Each one of the wooden rings is grooved entirely around the middle, and the outer one is beveled on the inner half toward the center, while the inner one is beveled both ways from the middle. The outer ring has its border white, and is black, with white spots, on the beveled inner half. The inner ring has its outer portion white, with black spots, the inner portion being red, with white spots. Surrounding the border is a strip of deerskin with upstanding hair, and five tail-feathers of the old-squaw duck tipped with downy plumes. This mask also is used by women in ceremonial dances, but its signification is unknown.

Figure 3, plate CV, from Pastolik, is 4¾ by 2¾ inches. It is a rudely carved wooden block, roughly pear-shape in outline, with a curiously rounded, semihuman countenance upon the front and deeply but roughly excavated behind. A projection below is pierced with a round hole for the finger. Two round openings for eyes and a larger one representing the mouth pierce the face and are the only indications of a countenance. The face is painted black, with a red border. Upon each side and on the top is inserted a quill with downy plumes at the end. It is a woman's finger mask, used in ceremonial dances, but its meaning is unknown.

Figure 2, plate CV, from Cape Romanof, is a pear-shape ring containing within it a similarly shaped block attached at the sharp point of the ring and having an ob-ovate projection below with a hole in the center

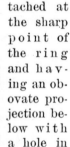
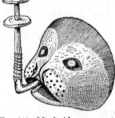

FIG. 141—Maskoid representing a seal-head with rising air bubbles (⅓).

for the insertion of the finger. The outer ring is beveled both outwardly and inwardly, and has a deep groove about its border in which is fastened a strip of reindeer skin having the long hairs upstanding. On each side and above are inserted long feathers from the tail of the oldsquaw duck, tipped with down. The ring and the central block are painted yellowish white on both surfaces, with round red and black dots. This mask was used by the women in ceremonial dances.

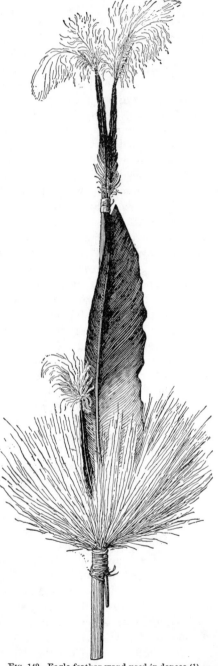

FIG. 142—Eagle-feather wand used in dances (¼).

Figure 141 shows a maskoid, from the lower Yukon, representing the

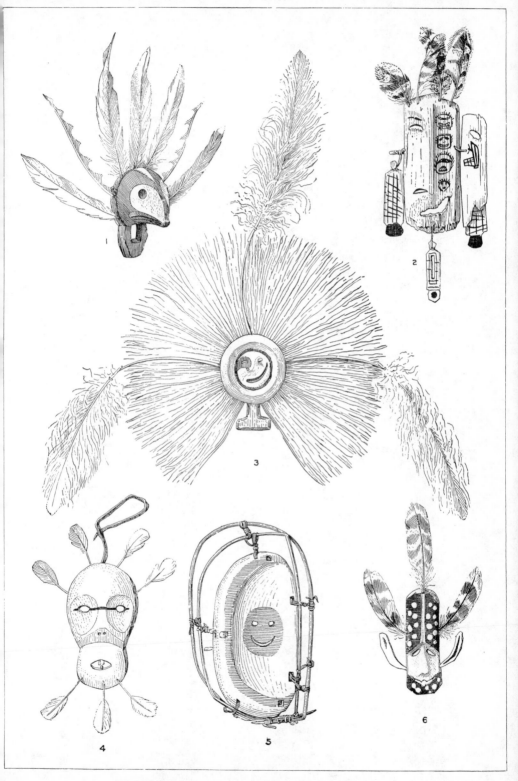

FINGER MASKS AND MASKOIDS (ABOUT ONE-FOURTH)

head of a small hair seal, with a slender rod about 9 inches in length, projecting from the mouth and turning upward, having fastened along its length at regular intervals five flat wooden disks about an inch and a half in diameter, representing bubbles rising on the surface of the water. The seal's face is painted white, with black dots on the muzzle for the whiskers, and the eyes and nostrils are outlined in black. The inside of the mouth is painted red and the top of head light blue. This maskoid is 4½ inches in diameter, and has the posterior side excavated.

Number 33025 is a woman's finger mask, from Chalitmut, south of the Yukon delta. It is a rounded wooden ring, with a wooden disk in the center, held in position by four small, spoke-like attachments from the outer ring. This wooden disk has upon one surface two incised eyes and a down-curved, crescentic mouth. Upon the other surface it has a grotesque mouth twisted far to one side, with a small wooden peg to represent an eye and a small, deep hole for the single nostril. A strip of reindeer skin, with long, upstanding hair, is fastened in a groove extending around the edge of the outer ring. This is used by women during ceremonial dances; its meaning is unknown.

OTHER CEREMONIAL OBJECTS

In addition to the masks various other articles of personal adornment are used during ceremonial dances. Among these may specially be noted the feathered wands used by women and the fillets worn about the head by both men and women. At Cape Nome, on the northern shore of Norton sound, I obtained several specimens of wands made from the quill-feathers of eagles, each of which consists of a single primary feather with a short wooden rod thrust into the truncated quill and held in place by a lashing of sinew. At the tip of the feather are lashed two or three downy plumes from the eagle.

On the coast of Bering sea from Norton bay south to the Kuskokwim somewhat similar wands were in use. On the lower Yukon and thence southward these wands are made by lashing an eagle quill-feather along the length of a slender rod, having fastened at its upper end two or three bare quills several inches in length, with downy plumes attached to the ends, like that shown in figure 142, from Razbinsky. About the

FIG. 143—Eagle-feather wand used in dances (¼).

handle of the wand, surrounding the base of the large quill-feathers, are lashed tufts of wolf hair or reindeer skin with the long hairs projecting.

A wand obtained at Cape Nome (figure 143) measures a little over 30 inches in length; those from the coast of Bering sea, farther to the south, are somewhat longer. These wands are held upright in the hands of the women dancers and are moved back and forth, or from one side to the other, with a slight swaying or beating motion, in time with the movements of the dancers and the beating of the drum.

In addition to the wands mentioned there were obtained at Cape Nome other articles used for personal adornment during the performance of a winter festival at that place. One of these is an armlet (figure 144) consisting of a strap made of tanned sealskin, to which is sewed under an inclosing flap the front part of the lower jaw of a white fox.

At the same place were procured a pair of tanned sealskin gloves with a pair of sea-parrot feet sewed upon their backs.

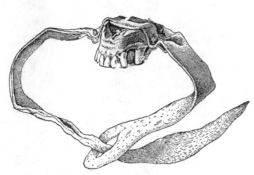

FIG. 144—Armlet worn during dances (⅔).

Used in the same dances at this place is a fillet (original number 6343) made of a small, rounded ring of fine shavings twisted together and having thrust through it a small wooden peg, to the upper end of which, in front, are attached three short eagle feathers about six inches long, and three long eagle quills just behind these. To each side of this ring is attached the end of a narrow rawhide strap for passing over the top of the head. This is worn so that the ring of shavings rests like a pad on the middle of the forehead, with the eagle feathers standing upright.

On Sledge island was seen a fillet, worn by a man during one of the dances, which was made from the skin of the head, neck, and back of the yellow-bill loon.

On Kotzebue sound was obtained one of these headdresses (figure 145). The skin, with feathers in place, had been removed, leaving the beak in position. The skull had also been removed and the skin split along the head and neck both above and below, and a narrow strip from along the middle of the back upon each side formed a continuation of the bands of neck skin. These long strips of skin are tied together at the junction of the neck and the body, thus leaving the skin from the back to hang down twelve or fifteen inches over the wearer's shoulders. The fillet is worn in such a position that the long yellow beak of the bird projects outward over the forehead.

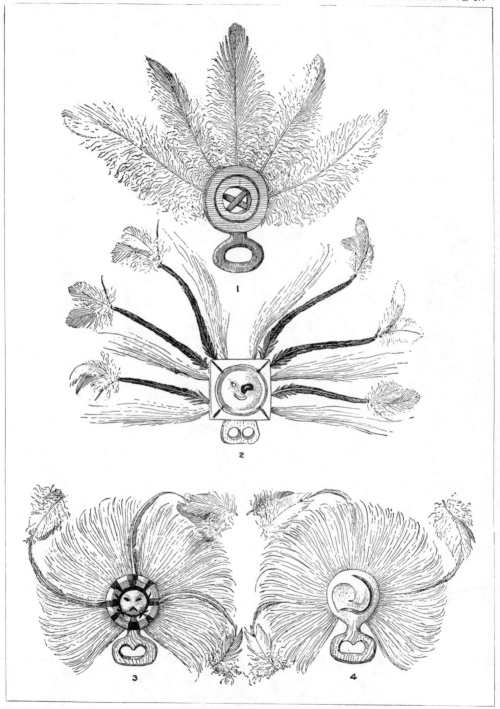

FINGER MASKS (ONE-FIFTH)

On the lower Yukon and thence to Kuskokwim river, the men during certain dances wear broad fillets made of wolfskin or of skin from the neck of the reindeer, with the long hair upstanding. The wolfskin fillets are made from narrow strips of skin taken from the animal's

shoulders or neck, where the fur is longest. These strips are sewed to the edges of a band of tanned sealskin, forming an upstanding ring of fur extending from the edges both upward and downward. On the surface of the intermediate strip of sealskin, which is from two to three inches broad, are sewed narrow, parallel strips of white, parchment-like, tanned sealskin, or reindeer-skin with the hair clipped so as to give it a velvety surface.

Another fillet (figure 146) from the same region is made from a strip of white, parchment-like, tanned sealskin about two inches in breadth, having sewed along its surface two narrow strips of black, tanned sealskin half an inch apart, with two parallel cords sewed to the skin at equal distances between these black bands. The upper border of this fillet has sewed on, in addition, a narrow strip of skin from the neck of the reindeer, with upstanding hair eight inches in length.

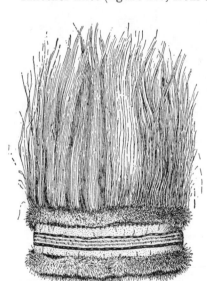

FIG. 145—Loonskin fillet worn in dances.

FIG. 146—Reindeer-skin fillet (¼).

The wolfskin fillet is worn so that one of the bordering lines of wolf hair extends down, concealing the upper half of the face, while the other line of fur stands up about the crown. In the fillet last described the outer standing hairs form a tall, crest-like circle about the crown.

Another kind of fillet is that worn by women during the dances. Two of these were seen at a festival on the lower Yukon, one of which was made from the skin of the white fox with the fur left on, and was formed by a band of skin which extended around the head, with two hanging strips attached over each temple and hanging below the chin on each side. Another was made from skins of the large ermine of that region. First was formed a band with the hair on and about an inch and a half broad, to pass around the head. Attached to this by

Fig. 147—Woman with ermine fillet and eagle-feather wands.

their heads, and hanging down over each side of the face, were two complete ermine skins. The women who wore these also carried eagle-feather wands in their hands during the dances. In the accompanying illustration (figure 147), from a photograph, the ermine-skin fillet described is shown.

Ornamental armlets of various kinds are used by the men in these dances. Figure 1, plate CVI, from Ikogmut, on the lower Yukon, is a good example of these. It is a broad band of reindeer skin with

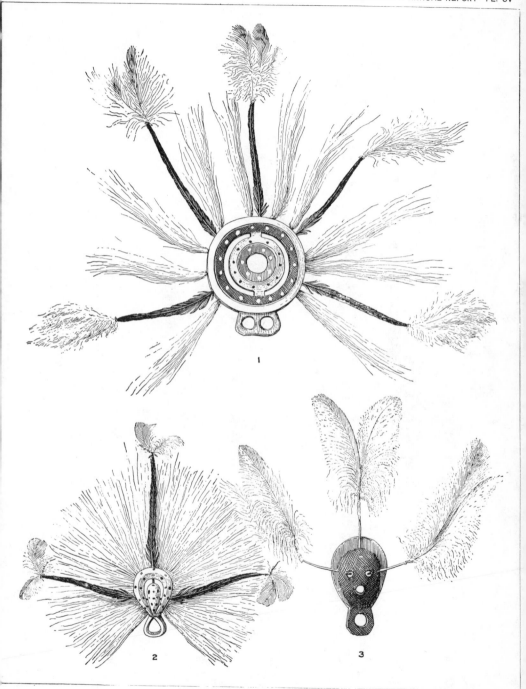

FINGER MASKS (ABOUT ONE-FOURTH)

the hair clipped from it, and used with the hair side outward; the band measures 9 by 3¾ inches. On the outside the border is occupied by three successive narrow bands of skin, the outer one of reindeer, the hair being clipped to about half an inch in length. This is succeeded by a narrow band of skin from the neck of a duck, the feathers forming a narrow border, which is succeeded by a narrow band of skin from the hair seal with the short hairs remaining. Inside of these bordering strips of fur is a surface of tanned skin colored reddish brown. This is surrounded by a narrow strip of white, parchment like sealskin, having set in pairs at regular intervals along the two sides tufts of hair 3½ inches long, dyed reddish brown. The rest of the surface is covered by narrow, alternating strips of white tanned parchment of sealskin divided by equal spaces of the red skin of the background. Each of the white strips is held in place by heavy stitching

Fig. 148—Wristlet from Ikogmut (full size).

of sinew thread sewed over and binding in two or three long, white, reindeer hairs, which are laid along the strips, producing an alternating black and white seam. Along each red strip are four parallel rows of stitches of the same kind, giving the surface of the armlet a longitudinally striped and dotted appearance. This armlet is held in place by leather thongs with the hair left on. A pair of these, fastened at one end of the armlet, is made of alternating pieces of mink, reindeer, and a smooth, dark, tanned skin. They are sewed with sinew and reindeer hair, as described, in seams on the surface of the armlet. To the tips of these thongs are attached several thin strips of sealskin with the hair left on, serving as a sort of tassel. Armlets of this kind have various styles of ornamentation, some of them being fringed with strips of skin still bearing the hair, with their main surfaces of white, parchment-like sealskin, sometimes having little strings of beads as pendants along their borders, or striped with narrow bands of skin or rows of heavy stitching.

Figure 148 shows a wristlet from Ikogmut, on the lower Yukon, used in these dances. It is made of tanned sealskin bordered by a narrow strip with the hair left on. On the rest of the surface there is a series of nine narrow alternating strips of yellowish-white and reddish-brown tanned sealskin, most of which have along their length a row of stripes of the alternating dark and white patterns formed by sewing in white reindeer hairs with sinew thread. At equal intervals in the midst of other bands are two broader strips of the reddish-brown skin, having reindeer hairs crossing their surface and gathered in the middle by the sinew stitching, so that a continuous series of X-shape figures are formed around the entire length of the wristlet.

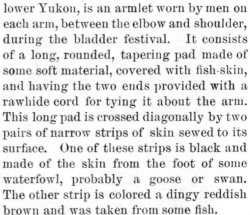

FIG. 149—Armlet worn in dances (¼).

Figure 149, from Sabotnisky, on the lower Yukon, is an armlet worn by men on each arm, between the elbow and shoulder, during the bladder festival. It consists of a long, rounded, tapering pad made of some soft material, covered with fish-skin, and having the two ends provided with a rawhide cord for tying it about the arm. This long pad is crossed diagonally by two pairs of narrow strips of skin sewed to its surface. One of these strips is black and made of the skin from the foot of some waterfowl, probably a goose or swan. The other strip is colored a dingy reddish brown and was taken from some fish.

The pairs of strips mentioned extend from the inside, near the point of the pad, cross over its outer portion, and turn under toward the opposite point again, so that the pairs cross on the outer side near the middle. Inserted in the middle of the pad and projecting back from it, so as to stand out a little from the arm when worn, is a wooden rod having three wooden vanes lashed at each end along its length, to represent the feather vanes used for feathering the butt of an arrow, which this attachment is intended to represent.

The central shaft and one of these wooden vanes are painted red, the other two are dull green. The red vane is crossed by a series of diagonally tapering black lines, broadest along the outer edge, the other two are crossed by a series of black lines extending diagonally from the border of the inner edge.

At Unalakit, on the shore of Norton sound, I obtained a pair of ornamented trunks (number 48799) used in dances by the Malemut. They measure about 15 inches in length and extend from the hip to

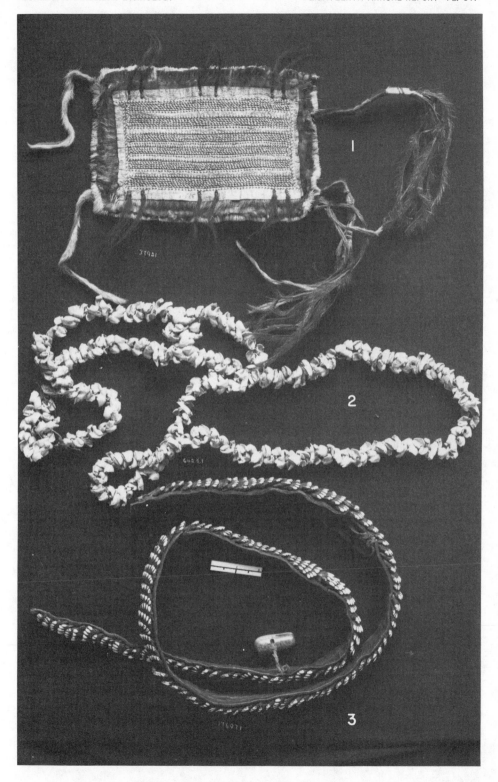

BELTS AND ARMLET (ABOUT ONE-FOURTH)

the upper thigh, and are made of tame reindeer skin mottled white and brown. They have an ornamental strip extending from the lower border on each side and curving upward around the back of the garment, reaching within about 2½ inches of the upper border in the rear. Extending part way down the front of the leg, on each side, is an ornamental band of white deerskin having a seam along the border on one side with a row of small spaced bunches of·red worsted. The ornamental band, which extends from the lower edge of the trousers around to the rear, and the short bands in front, are bordered by a strip of wolverine fur. About the waist is a band containing a drawstring for binding the garment around the hips.

Figure 2, plate CVI, from one of the Diomede islands, is a belt made from the jaws of crabs, worn by women during certain festivals.

RELIGION AND MYTHOLOGY

EFFECT OF CHRISTIAN CONTACT

During the time of my residence in Alaska the Eskimo of the mainland were still firm believers in their ancient religion; but slight modification could be found in their customs, even immediately about St Michael or at Mission (Ikogmut) on the lower Yukon, where the residence of Russian priests during thirty-five or forty years had exerted greater influence against the ancient beliefs than at any other point. Services have been conducted irregularly in the small Greek Catholic churches at the places named, as well as at one or two points farther southward, but the influence on the Eskimo has been very slight. So far as could be observed, the sole effect of the priestly efforts have been to cause the Eskimo to become more secretive than formerly about practicing their religious rites when in the vicinity of white men.

By gifts of small metal crosses, which the people wore as ornaments, and by other means, they were occasionally induced to attend church service. I venture to say that during my residence there not a half dozen full-blood Eskimo could be found in all that region who really understood and believed in the white man's religion, and not one could be found who did not believe implicitly in the power of the shamans and in the religious rites handed down by the elders.

In some districts, notably between lower Kuskokwim and lower Yukon rivers, the ancient rites and beliefs were still practiced in their aboriginal purity. Elsewhere the principal modification was in the gradual but persistent weakening of the old ideas produced by intercourse with the fur traders. This effect was more apparent than real, for the Russians and Americans alike had ridiculed or treated with contempt the old customs, until it had become almost impossible to prevail upon the people to talk of their beliefs and traditions until, by long acquaintance, their confidence had been gained. Curiously enough, the great mask festival (Ă-gaí'-yu-nŭk) of the Eskimo south of the Yukon mouth has supplied terms by which the natives speak of the Greek church and its services among themselves. When they saw the Russian priests in embroidered robes performing the complicated offices of the church it was believed that they were witnessing the white man's method of celebrating a mask festival similar to their own.

WITCHCRAFT

The Eskimo believe that persons dealing in witchcraft have the power of stealing a person's *inua* or shade, so that it will cause him to pine away and die. This I saw illustrated at a village on the lower Yukon, where I had set up my camera to obtain a picture of the people as they were moving about among the houses. When I was focusing the instrument the headman of the village came up and insisted on looking under the cloth. When I permitted him to do this he gazed intently for a minute at the moving figures on the ground glass and then suddenly withdrew his head and shouted at the top of his voice to the surrounding people, "He has all of your shades in this box," whereupon a panic ensued among the group and in an instant they disappeared in their houses.

SHADES OF THE DEAD

A ghost or visible shade is called *ă-lhi-ukh'-tok*, and is a form that an invisible shade may sometimes assume. My inquiries among the people developed the fact that they believe in the existence of two or three distinct forms of the spiritual essence or soul. The *tă-ghûn'-û-g'ăk*, or invisible shade, is formed exactly in the shape of the body, is sentient, and destined for a future life. Another is the *po-klĭhm' tă-ghûn'-û-g'ă*, which has a form exactly like that of the body and is the life-giving warmth. It is without sense and takes flight into the air when a person dies.

From the people with whom I talked I obtained a suggestion of a third kind of shade, which is supposed to remain with the body and to possess evil powers which, however, seem to be limited, but I could not obtain more definite information about it. The shades of the dead are believed to linger for some time in the vicinity of their life scenes, and on the northern shore of Norton sound I learned that for three months after the death of a son the father must not drink from an uncovered vessel, for if he does he may swallow some impurity from the shade that may be present, and die.

During one of my sledge journeys I had an Eskimo with me from the head of Norton sound to Sledge island. During the journey I noticed for some days that whenever he drank he inserted a small dipper beneath his fur coat, and then lowering his face under the collar drank from beneath. On inquiry I was told that this was because his son had died a short time before and he dared not drink from an uncovered vessel, fearing that some emanation from his son's shade might get into the water and, being swallowed, do him harm.

In ancient times the sinews in the arms and legs of a dead person who had been of evil repute during life were cut in order to prevent the shade from returning to the body and causing it to walk at night as a ghoul.

Nearly every attribute possessed by the shades of people is also believed to be possessed equally by the shades of animals, and the *inua* or shade of every animal is believed to possess semihuman form.

There are two places to which the shades of the dead may depart. Some of the Eskimo told me it was believed that the shades of shamans or persons who died by accident, violence, or starvation, go to a land of plenty in the sky, where it has light, food, and water in abundance.

Shades of people who die from natural causes go to the underground land of the dead. There also go the shades of all dead animals, where each kind lives in a village of its own. In this underground world the shades of people depend entirely on the offerings of food, water, and clothing made to them by their relatives in the festivals given to the dead. Even the shades in the land of plenty can be made happier by being remembered with presents in these festivals.

Some few persons are supposed to be uncomfortable after death. These are mainly thieves who steal from their fellow villagers, sorcerers or bad shamans, witches, and the people who practice certain forbidden customs. The shades of evil persons, as well as those of animals, are sometimes believed to return and haunt the vicinity of their burial place. In illustration of this belief I saw a curious custom observed at the village of Kigiktauik. A hunter entered the kashim bringing a red fox which he had just taken from the trap; after skinning it the pelt was stretched and placed in his storehouse. Then he returned to the kashim and, taking the carcass, carefully cut the tendons of the fore and hind legs and a hole at the navel. Carrying the carcass outside he took it to the roof and, opening the smoke hole, held the body over it. The men sitting in the kashim at once united in shouting, "*Än-oḱ'!* (he goes) *Än-oḱ'! Än-oḱ'!*" at the top of their voices. The carcass was then placed on the top of the hunter's storehouse, so that no dogs could reach it. The people told me that by this ceremony the shade of the fox was dismissed either to the land of the dead or back to the tundra, where it would be harmless. If this should not be done it might remain with the body and go about in that shape, doing evil to the hunters or others in the village. The legs must have the tendons cut in order to keep the shade from reentering the body and walking about in that form. No dog must be permitted to touch or defile the body for fear of rendering the shade angry, and thus causing it to bring misfortune to the hunter.

There is considerable difference between the Eskimo of different districts in their manner of regarding the dead. At Razbinsky, on the Yukon, the graves are placed so close to the houses that they form a part of the village, and become excessively offensive during summer. The same custom is observed throughout that section of country.

When the *Corwin* was lying at the head of Kotzebue sound a Malemut begged to be permitted to stay all night on board, because if he went on shore at dusk he would have to paddle by the grave of a man who had died several weeks before.

Among the lower Yukon people it is said that when a person dies he can not see or hear anything at first, but when his body is placed in the grave box his shade becomes clairvoyant and can see all that goes on about him; then other dead people come and point out the road leading to the land of the shades. In this connection reference is made to the tale which gives an account of the return of a girl from the land of the dead and covering the beliefs held on this subject among the lower Yukon Eskimo.

When the shade of a recently deceased person becomes conscious, it rises in form and clothing exactly as in life, and travels along the path that leads away from the grave. The road has many others branching off on one side or the other to villages where the shades of different animals are living, each kind by itself. In these villages the shades of animals occupy houses like those of human beings on earth. Finally the shade arrives at a village, where it is claimed by relatives who have died before, and is taken to a house where it lives an aimless existence, depending on offerings of food, water, and clothing made by relatives during the festivals to the dead.

During this journey from the grave the shade has brought with it the tools placed by its grave with the offerings of food and water. Upon these supplies the shade subsists during its journey to the other world.

On the Yukon a man told me that on the road to the village of the dead the shade is offered water in a bucket, and if it attempts to drink from the large receptacle without using the dipper, the other shades clap the bucket over his head so that he is unable to drink. If a shade disobeys the instructions of the shades in other ways they cause his trousers to slip down so that he can not walk, and they otherwise annoy him.

The first child born in a village after a person dies is given the dead one's name, and must represent that person in subsequent festivals which are given in his honor. This is the case if a child is born in the village between the time of the death and the next festival to the dead. If there be no child born, then one of the persons who helped prepare the grave box for the deceased is given his name and abandons his own for that purpose.

When the festival to the dead is given in which the relatives of the dead person wish to make offerings to the shade, the latter is invited to attend by means of songs of invitation and by putting up sticks with the totem marks of the deceased upon them. The shade becomes notified in this manner and returns to its grave box at the time appointed. Songs of invitation and greeting call the shade from the grave box to the fire pit under the floor of the kashim, where, in company with others, it receives the offerings of food, water, and clothing that are cast on the floor. Then is rendered the song that announces the presence of the namesake, at which the shade enters the form of that person.

The feast giver then removes the new suit of clothing he wears for the purpose and places it upon the namesake, and in doing this the shade becomes newly clothed; the food offerings given to the namesake during this festival are in the same way believed to be really given to the dead. When this ceremony is finished the shade is dismissed back to the land of the dead. During these festivals the shades present, below the floor of the kashim, are supposed to enjoy the songs and dances equally with the living. Songs and dances praising the exploits of the dead are supposed to be especially pleasing to them.

If a person dies without anyone to make a festival for him, or to obtain a namesake, he is forgotten and can never return to these festivals, but must live as the poor and friendless live upon the earth. The shades of all animals are believed to be formed like people, and many kinds are supposed to be able to talk with one another and at times are able to understand the speech of men. The shades of game animals must be propitiated in many ways by offerings and by feasts and dances, as in the Bladder festival.

It is believed that in ancient times all animals had the power to change their forms at will. When they wished to become people they merely pushed up the muzzle or beak in front of the head and changed at once into man-like beings. The muzzle of the animal then remained like a cap on top of the head, or it might be removed altogether, and in order to become an animal again it had only to pull it down. Some animals are still claimed to possess this power, but when they change into people they become invisible except to shamans or others endowed with mystic powers.

GENESIS MYTH—THE RAVEN FATHER

The belief referred to is well illustrated in the raven tales, where the changes are repeatedly made by the characters. In this belief rests the foundation of the mask dances of the Eskimo. The creation of the earth and everything upon it is credited to the Raven Father (*Tu-lu'-kau-gûk*), who is said to have come from the sky and made the earth when everything was covered with water. During a large part of the time he retained the form of a raven and changed to a man at will by pushing up his beak. The raven legends hereafter given render a detailed statement regarding this matter superfluous here.

It should be added, however, that the part played by the raven, as stated in the creation legend, is believed by the Eskimo from Kuskokwim river northward to Bering strait and well around on the Arctic coast. By these legends it will be seen that the Raven came from the sky, where he had a father and where dwarf people were living, and that he made things on earth so much like those in the sky that the shamans still pretend to replace animals on the earth by trips to the sky land.

The first man made on the earth returned to the sky land, where the shades of shamans and people who are recompensed for a violent death also go; the Raven Father is believed still to live there. I was informed that the Eskimo about Norton sound place fragments of dried fish or other food in different places on the tundra as offerings to the Raven Father in the sky; in return for which he gives them fine weather.

The Unalit say that to kill a raven will cause the Raven Father to become very angry and to send bad weather, and the lower Yukon Eskimo dislike and fear ravens as evil birds.

The common mark symbolizing the raven is found upon all kinds of carvings, ornamental work, tools, implements, and utensils among the western Eskimo, as previously described and illustrated. On the ethnological specimens obtained from Point Barrow and through Bering strait to Kuskokwim river, this mark is common. There is an ivory bodkin in the National Museum, brought from the mouth of Mackenzie river, which bears this mark, and I saw the same device tattooed on the forehead of a boy at Plover bay, Siberia (see figure 115).

The Raven Father, who made the land and everything upon it, is the subject of many tales in which he is represented as benefiting mankind. When he returned to the sky he left on earth children like himself, and some of these are the subjects of numerous tales among the Eskimo and adjacent tribes of Tinné, in northern Alaska. These Raven children frequently figure in their tales as boasters or in other discreditable and absurd ways, and while the ravens now living are thought to be descendants of the Raven Father, they have lost their magical powers.

For a long time they were said to have retained their powers of changing back and forth at will from men to birds, but gradually lost these powers until they became ordinary ravens as we see them today.

Many things, such as physical features of the landscape, etc, connected with raven tales are pointed out as evidence of the Raven Father's former presence when the earth was new. Below Paimut on the Yukon is a large block of stone resting near the water's edge which they say was dropped there by the Raven Father after he had made the earth. When he had placed it there he told the people of the Yukon that whenever fish became scarce they must tie an inflated bladder to this stone and throw both into the river, whereupon fish would become plentiful. They say that one year, when fish were very scarce, the shamans did this and when the stone and the bladder struck the water the latter immediately sank out of sight and the stone floated like a piece of dry wood some distance down the river; then it returned upstream of its own volition, went to its former place on the bank and fish immediately became very numerous.

Near St Michael is an island which the Eskimo say was made from the straw pad from a boot which Raven Father once threw into the sea.

In the Raven tales it is made a point to describe the Raven as dressed in dogskin or other miserable garments, and he always occupies a place by the entrance of the kashim where the poor people are seated.

Curious transformations of people into beasts are also believed to have taken place. Among these may be mentioned the one given in the tale of *Ta-ku'-ka*, where a woman became transformed into a red bear, and which also accounts for the manner in which these animals became ferocious.

In another tale the red bears originated from an image made by an old woman near the Yukon. All animals are believed to have changed from the original human-like being, taking throughout life their present form, but the *inua* or shade is still similar to its former appearance.

SUPERNATURAL POWERS

Among the Unalit, who form a typical Eskimo group of this region, the belief exists that there are different ways in which the person may be gifted with supernatural power. Those who are able to foretell are called *ă'-hlu-kai'-lĭñ-ŭk,* " the one who knows everything." There are also people who are clairvoyant, besides wizards or witches who control supernatural beings or *tunghät*, and conjure by means of magic words and in other ways, and know the hidden properties of things.

There are also people who possess the secret of making amulets which serve for various purposes. Occurrences out of the usual order of events are thought to be the work of some supernatural influence. Those possessing power over the invisible world are usually men, but this power is sometimes held by women.

In connection with the belief in supernatural powers is an apparent mystic virtue contained in the number four. In the creation legend the Raven waved his wing four times over the clay images to endow them with life. The first man in the same legend slept four years at the bottom of the sea. The Raven was absent four days in the sky-land when he went to bring berries to the earth. The Whale in which the Raven entered, in another tale, was four days in dying. In the tale of the Strange Boy, from the Yukon, the hero slept in the kashim every fourth night. The woman in the tale of the Land of Darkness, from Sledge island, was told to take four steps, and these transported her to her home from a great distance. In the Bladder festival, witnessed south of the Yukon mouth, four men, representing four gentes, took a prominent part.

In their original beliefs the Eskimo have no conception of a single supreme being or deity, but their spirit world is made up of shades and *tunghät*, which have an existence quite independent of any central authority. At Ikogmut, on the lower Yukon, where the Russians have had a mission for many years, the Eskimo call God *Tun'-rŭñ-ai'-yuk,* or chief *tun-ghâk*, a name which has undoubtedly been introduced with the ideas of the white man's religion. Some of these *tunghät* are more powerful than others, just as some men are more skilful and shrewd than others. Their ideas of the invisible world are based on conditions of the present life with which they are familiar.

They have great faith in the power and wisdom of the shamans, who are the highest authority, to whom all questions of religion and the mysteries of the invisible world are referred.

Among the Unalit and adjacent people of the Bering seacoast the shaman is known as the *tun'-gha-lĭk;* at Point Barrow he is called *añ-alh'-kok.*

A man first becomes aware of possessing shamanic powers by having his attention drawn to some remarkable circumstance or event in his life. Having noticed this, he secures the aid of some old shaman, or practices in secret, to secure control of sufficient power to warrant announcing himself to the people.

A noted shaman of the lower Yukon said that he was first led to become such by having strange dreams and by frequently finding himself when he awoke at a different place from that in which he went to sleep. From this he believed that the invisible powers wished him to become a shaman, so he began to practice and soon succeeded in becoming one.

Every *tun'-gha-lĭk*, as the name implies, is the owner or controller of shades or supernatural beings called *tun'-ghâk*, dual *tun'-ghŭk*, plural *tun'-ghät*. These beings possess supernatural power, and the more of them the shaman subjects to his will the more powerful he becomes. *Tun'-ghät* are believed to be the personifications of various objects and natural forces, or may be wandering shades of men and animals, and are invisible to all except shamans or people possessing clairvoyant powers, unless they become visible to ordinary people in order to accomplish some particular purpose. They have various strange forms, usually manlike, with grotesque or monstrous faces, such as are shown on many of the masks obtained in this region. They have the power of changing their form; in many instances becoming animals or assuming very terrifying shapes. At such times if they render themselves visible to ordinary people the latter may be killed merely by the sight of them.

By their influence over these mysteries the shamans may avert or drive away evil influences of all kinds. If the evil has been produced by some very powerful influence, through the magic of a bad shaman or some wickedly disposed *tun'-ghâk*, the shaman must enlist the aid of others until, by their united power, they finally overcome the possessing *tun'-ghâk* and drive it away.

Among other exercises of their power the shamans claim to make journeys to the land of the dead, and upon their return relate to the people what they have seen in that region, and from this have arisen the ideas commonly diffused among them on this subject. In addition to

the *tunghät* of inanimate things the shamans can see the shades of
dead people or animals which are invisible to persons not specially
endowed.

The shades of people or of animals frequently come at the call of
shamans, doing their bidding, and sometimes the shade of a dead shaman
will appear for this purpose.

The Unalit told me of a shaman who once lived among them and
was aided by his dog, with whom he could talk, the dog being a
tunghâk which had taken that form. A common form of *tunghâk* is
the *yu-ă*, or spirit of the elements, places, and things.

Along the coast of Norton sound and the lower Yukon shamans
sometimes cause the death of new born infants and afterward steal the
body and dry it carefully, in order to keep it and have control of its
shade as a specially strong influence. On the Yukon I heard of an
instance in which one of these men stole the dried body of an infant
from another shaman and by aid of its shade became noted for his
remarkable powers. When he died his relatives were very much afraid
of the small mummy and burned it.

Men who are not shamans, but who understand some of these things,
will sometimes cause the death of a new-born child for the purpose of
having the services of its shade to secure success in hunting. The
child must be killed secretly and its body stolen, so that no one knows
of it; after the body is dried, it is placed in a bag and worn on the
person or carried in a kaiak when at sea. One of the best hunters at
St Michael had such a body, which he carried, wrapped in a little bag,
in his kaiak. By careful inquiry I learned that he had caused its
death and then obtained the body from its grave box near the village
without the knowledge of the mother. It is believed that when the
hunter carries one of these objects the shade of the infant, which is
clairvoyant, assists its possessor in finding game and directs the spear
in its flight so that the animal shall not escape. Owners of these
objects are extremely jealous of them and try to keep their possession
secret. It was by mere accident that I discovered the existence of the
one just mentioned.

At Point Hope, on the Arctic coast, a young man came on board the
Corwin wearing a pair of gloves, on the back of which were sewed a
pair of outspread feet of the sea parrot (*Mormon arctica*). On question-
ing his companions they said that he was a shaman, and once while he
was fishing along the shore one of these birds had alighted on his
hands, leaving its feet to bring him success in salmon fishing.

Shamans are greatly feared, and their advice concerning hunting,
traveling, and other matters of this kind is usually obeyed, but many
failures on their part to give good counsel or to cure sickness may result
in serious consequences. In the fall of 1879 the Malemut of Kotzebue
sound killed a shaman, saying in explanation that he told too many lies.

If a shaman is suspected of using his powers to work evil upon his fellow-villagers he is also in danger of being killed by common consent of the community. I heard of such men being killed in the region lying between the mouths of the Yukon and Kuskokwim for failing to fulfill their predictions and for suspected witchcraft. Observance of various festivals and the attendant rites are usually executed according to instructions of shamans, who learn by the aid of their mysterious power what is acceptable to the shades and the *tunghät*.

The moon is believed to be inhabited by a great man-like being, which controls all the animals that are found on the earth, and when a season of scarcity comes the shamans pretend to go up and make offerings to him. If they succeed in pleasing this being he gives them one of the kind of animals that have become scarce, whereupon the shaman returns with it to the earth and turns it loose, after which the species again becomes plentiful. It is claimed that only in this way can the earth be kept supplied with game, owing to the number killed by hunters and by disease. On one occasion at St Michael, at the beginning of the fall seal hunting, the old head-man of the village was seen to go out secretly and make food offerings to the new moon while he sang a long song of propitiation to the spirit supposed to live in that planet in order to control the supply of game.

The shamans claim that the man who lives in the moon has a very bright face, so that they fear to look at him, and when they come near they must look downward; for this reason two usually go together, since one alone would be abashed. On the Yukon they claim to climb up to the moon, but at the head of Norton sound an old man told me that he used to fly up to the sky like a bird. In all this region the shamans claim to possess the power of visiting the moon. One winter on the lower Yukon, about the middle of February, there was an eclipse of the moon, and soon after throat disease caused the death of about a dozen people. Two shamans, father and son, started to visit the man in the moon to find out why the disease had been sent and to learn how to stop it. The pair were absent from the village several days, and then returned and reported that when they had climbed nearly to the moon the old man became tired and stopped for a while, but the young man went on. When he was near the moon the man came down to meet him and was very angry, asking what he wanted there; the young man was very much frightened, but told the reason for his approach. He was then told that the disease would kill several other people before it would stop; and the moon man was going to keep the young fellow, but his father begged so hard for him from below that he was permitted to return.

On the lower Yukon and southward they say that there are other ways of getting to the moon, one of which is for a man to put a slip noose about his neck and have the people drag him about the interior of the kashim until he is dead. At one time two noted shamans on the Yukon did this, telling the people to watch for them as they would come back during the next berry season. When the season designated had passed, the people of the village said that one of the shamans came back, coming a little out of the ground, looking like a doll, but he was very small and weak and there was no one outside the houses at the time to feed and care for him, except some children, so that he was overlooked and went away again.

Nearly all epidemic diseases are supposed to come from the moon, but occasionally they descend from the sun. An eclipse of the moon is said to foretell an epidemic, and the shamans immediately proceed to learn the cause in order to appease the being living there and, by diverting his anger, save the people. Among the inhabitants along the lower Yukon it is believed that a subtle essence or unclean influence descends to the earth during an eclipse, and if any of it is caught in utensils of any kind it will produce sickness. As a result, immediately on the commencement of an eclipse, every woman turns bottom side up all her pots, wooden buckets, and dishes.

After an eclipse at St Michael the Unalit said that the sun had died and come to life again. The length of duration of an eclipse is said to indicate the severity of the visitation to follow. In the village of Paimut, on the lower Yukon, in December, 1880, I overheard people talking about a recent eclipse of the moon and all agreed that it foreboded either an epidemic or war. Some thought that it meant a raid of the Tinné, living higher up the river, as revenge upon the Eskimo for having killed some moose the year before, the Eskimo evidently thinking that the moose belonged to the people in the region where they are usually found, and their having killed some of the animals would call for reprisals by the Tinné.

South of Cape Vancouver, at the village of Chichiñagamut, we were overtaken by a severe storm and, in order to witness the rites, I paid a shaman to change the weather. After dark he knelt on a straw mat in the middle of the kashim and enveloped himself, with the exception of his face, in a large gut-skin shirt; then, resting his knees and elbows on the floor, he uttered a long speech at the top of his voice. When this was ended he concealed his face in the shirt and made a great variety of grunts, groans, and other noises. During this time two men stood on each side of him and over his back passed a double cord, extending lengthwise of his body, with a stick fastened to each end, which was held fast to the floor on each side of him. When the shaman finished making the noises mentioned a third man made a pantomime with his hands as if lifting some invisible substance from the shaman's back. This motion was repeated a number of times and then the two men raised the sticks to which the cords were tied and circled several times around the shaman, constantly turning their sticks end over end, and finally stopping in their former positions. The shaman then caused his voice to die away in the distance, after which he arose and said that we would have a change of weather in two days.

At the village of Sfugunugumut, in the same district, another shaman attempted to change the weather for my benefit as follows: He put on a gut-skin shirt and was wrapped closely in a large straw mat while squatting in a sitting posture on the floor of the kashim. Four men stood about him, and after he had uttered a long series of curious cries they went through various lifting motions in unison as if raising something from him. Then followed several ventriloquial voices, after which the old man was unwrapped and assured us of good weather in two days.

At a village just north of Cape Vancouver another shaman essayed to conjure the weather for me. He knelt in front of the entrance, inside of the kashim, and held both hands beneath his gut-skin shirt, rattling it about while he uttered various cries and noises. A voice was then made to reply to him from the passageway, after which he assured us of good weather.

At Chalitmut, near the mouth of Kuskokwim river, I arrived late one winter afternoon and found a grass mat hanging over the outer entrance to the kashim. Inside were two shamans at work on the form of a withered old man, who lay with closed eyes on the deerskin in the middle of the floor, evidently too feeble to move. Upon two sides of the room stood a couple of men beating slowly upon drums. The shamans, dressed in gut-skin shirts, were walking about the patient with a strutting gait, each holding one hand before him inside the shirt and the other behind him in the same way, rattling the shirt with both hands. The motions and appearance of the two men were absurdly like those of two game-cocks preparing for battle. During this time they continued uttering cries like those used by the other shamans mentioned when doctoring the weather. Suddenly they dropped upon their knees, one at the old man's head and the other at his feet, both facing him and uttering a series of shrill cries and hisses. Leaping to their feet after this they repeated the cries, and two assistants came forward and went through lifting motions exactly as the men had done to procure good weather. When they had done this the assistants each placed his arms and palms together in front of him and then separated his hands by drawing one back toward the body and pushing the other away from him with a sliding motion. With this the performance ended and the old man was carried out.

In another village, near the one last mentioned, I found a man standing on the roof of a kashim, the door of which was closed by a straw mat and guarded by an old woman who tried to prevent my entrance. Passing her I entered and surprised two shamans performing their incantations over a sick child. The people of the village were seated around the room and the child was lying naked in his mother's lap in the middle of the room. The shamans also were entirely naked and were circling about when I entered, but stopped immediately and the woman hurried out with the child.

One curious method of learning the causes of disease is practiced by the shamans on the plain south of the Yukon mouth. If a man becomes ill they determine the character of his malady by tying a cord attached to the end of a stick to his head or a limb as he lies outstretched, and lifting it by the stick find from the weight of the part the character of the disease. If seriously affected the part is supposed to be very heavy, but becomes lighter or easier to raise as the malady passes away.

In the summer of 1881 my interpreter refused, at the last moment, to go on the *Corwin* with me during our Arctic cruise, saying that the shamans had told him that we would never come back.

One of the greatest feats attributed to the shamans is to visit the land of the dead and come back again; in every district one hears of those who, apparently dead, have been to the land of the shades and returned.

An old shaman from Selawik lake, near Kotzebue sound, told me that a shaman, living there many years ago, died and made such a journey. When he returned he told the people that after his death his shade traveled for two days along the hard, beaten path formed by those who had gone before. During all this time he heard crying and wailing which he knew to be the voices of people on earth mourning for their dead. Then he came to a great village, like those upon the earth, and was met by the shades of two men who led him into a house. In the middle of the room a fire was burning, in front of which were roasting some pieces of meat, stuck on sharp sticks; in this flesh were living eyes which rolled about and watched his movements. His companions told him not to eat any of the meat, as it would be bad for him. After stopping here for a short time he went on and came to the milky way, which he followed for a long distance, finally returning by it to his grave box. When the shade entered the box his body became alive, and rising, he went back to the village and told his friends of his experience.

The old shaman who related the foregoing said that once he himself had died and gone to the land of shades, remaining there until he became tired, when he returned to the earth and entering the body of an unborn child, was born again.

Another method the shamans claim to possess for visiting the land of the dead is practiced in the region south of the lower Yukon as well as about Norton sound. They pretend to be burned to death and afterward to return to life.

At the head of Norton sound my Eskimo guide pointed out the grave of a shaman who had tried to do this, and said that after being burned to death he had failed to return. The man in telling of it seemed to have perfect faith that such a thing was possible, and said that many shamans caused themselves to be burned to ashes and then returned to life, not even their clothing showing a trace of fire. He added that the shaman buried in the grave which we passed had made a mistake in the kind of wood used for the fire, or some other necessary observance had been neglected. This was known from the fact that after he had been burned his body reappeared unharmed except for a small burn on one shoulder, but he failed to become alive. The body was placed over the pyre and a cone of upright drift logs raised over it to mark the spot. My informant added that when people passed this spot they always made small offerings of food and other things to propitiate the shade of the shaman.

The following description of burning a shaman is from a village south of the Yukon mouth, and was obtained from a fur trader who knew the circumstances: The shaman gathered all the villagers into the kashim and, after putting on his fur coat, told them that he wished to be burned and return to them in order that he might be of greater service to the village. He directed that a crib of drift logs should be built waist high, in the form of a square, with an open space in the center, where he could stand. He chose two assistants, whom he paid liberally to attend to the fire and aid him in other ways. His hands and feet were bound and a large mask, covering his face and body to the waist, was put on him. Then the people carried him out and set him inside the crib, after which everyone except the assistants returned to the kashim and the assistants set fire to the pyre in front. Smoke and flames rose from the logs so that the inside of the crib was rendered slightly indistinct; the assistants called out the people, who, when they saw the mask as they had left it, facing them through the smoke, were satisfied. After they had seen it they were ordered to remain within doors until the next morning upon pain of calling down upon them the anger of the *tunghät*.

Immediately after the people went inside the assistants unbound the shaman and substituted a log of wood behind the mask, while the shaman concealed himself near by until the next morning. Meanwhile, the mask and the crib burned to the ground. At daybreak the shaman returned and, taking a couple of firebrands from the smoldering pyre, mounted very quietly on the roof of the kashim and sat by the smoke hole. The gut-skin cover to this outlet was raised and bulging, as usual, from the heat within; over this translucent cover the shaman waved his spark scattering firebrand, at the same time moving his feet about on its surface. The people inside could distinguish the fire and the faint outlines of the feet and said, "He is walking in the air over the window." When he was satisfied that he had created sufficient sensation, he descended, entered the kashim, and was ever afterward considered to be a great shaman. I was told that this ordeal of fire was supposed to endow the person enduring it with the power to cast off or assume the bodily form at will and to greatly increase his power in other ways.

In addition to other supernatural aids that are invoked, amulets and fetiches of wood, stone, bone, or in fact almost anything else will serve.

Frequently the virtue is inherent in the object, but sometimes is secured by means of a shaman's power or the aid of one who knows. In addition to the ordinary *in-g'ukh*, or fetich, an heirloom (*paituk*) may become a fetich by reason of its extreme age and long possession in one family. Such objects are treasured and are handed down from father to son. They are supposed to be endowed with reason and to be gifted with supernatural powers to aid and protect their owners.

With these objects may be classed such things as are used for obtaining success in the hunt—like the dried bodies of newborn infants already described, and others which are supposed to protect their owners from bodily injury.

Women wear belts made from the incisors of reindeer taken out with a small fragment of bone, and attached scale-like to a rawhide strap, overlapping each other in a continuous series. When one of these belts has been in the family a long time, it is believed to acquire a certain virtue for curing disease. In case of rheumatic or other pains the part affected is struck smartly a number of times with the end of the belt and the difficulty is supposed to be relieved.

While at St Michael a shaman sent to me on one occasion to borrow the skin of a pine squirrel, brought from the head of the Yukon, which he used in his conjuring to cure a sick man, and claimed to drive into the squirrel the sickness from the person afflicted, after which the skin was returned to me.

Another method of curing local pain, such as neuralgia, toothache, or similar affections, is for the shaman to suck the skin over the spot vigorously for a time, and then take a small bone or other object out of his mouth, showing it to the patient as the cause of the trouble.

Dogs are never beaten for biting a person, as it is claimed that should this be done the *inua* of the dog would become angry and prevent the wound from healing. During my stay at St Michael a little girl four or five years of age was brought to me to dress her face, which had been badly torn by a savage dog. I told the father that he ought to kill such an animal, to which he replied in alarm, "No, no; that would be very bad for the child; the wound would not heal."

As a rule, married women are very anxious to have a son, and in case of long continued barrenness they consult a shaman, who commonly makes, or has the husband make, a small, doll-like image over which he performs certain secret rites, and the woman is directed to sleep with it under her pillow.

A Kaviagmut from Sledge island, who killed two men on Norton sound during my stay at St Michael, once came to have me cure some sores on his back. When he removed his clothing, I saw that he had on a curious harness-like arrangement of round rawhide cords which went loosely about his neck and, dividing on the chest and back, formed a loop under each arm. On inquiring the meaning of this, he replied that it was to protect him from his enemies. This referred to his fear of blood revenge by relatives of the men he had killed.

Images and masks are used by the people of Point Barrow to bring success in whale hunting. In an umiak at that place I found two masks of human faces mounted on the middle of slightly crescentic boards, to each of which was tied by a sinew cord a small wooden model of a right whale. After considerable effort one of the shields and masks were secured, but the owners absolutely refused to sell the others or any of the little whales, which were well carved and about three inches long. The men said they were used in whale hunting and they did not dare to sell them as, if they did, they would bring them bad luck.

Small carved images of fabulous animals are sometimes carried for the same purpose. In Kotzebue sound a young Malemut white-whale hunter came off to the *Corwin* one day and I found hanging from the framework inside his kaiak, just behind the manhole, a curious wooden image about eight inches long and three inches in diameter. It was

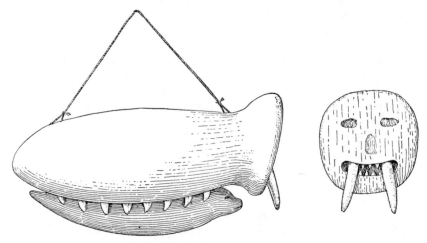

FIG. 150—Fetich from a Malemut kaiak (⅓).

shaped as shown in figure 150. The semihuman face, with holes incised for the eyes and nose, and the deeply cut mouth bordered by teeth, had two large, projecting tusks, which with the teeth were made of walrus ivory. Extending lengthwise along the abdomen was a long, deep slit like a mouth, with a row of peg-like ivory teeth along its edges. Held by the teeth in this mouth was the rudely carved wooden figure of a white whale. I tried to buy the image, but the owner seemed to be alarmed when he found that I had discovered it, and said he would die if he parted with it; thereupon I handed the image back to him and he quickly went ashore and hid it, after which he returned to the vessel.

The images and fetiches used in hunting are supposed to watch for game and, by some clairvoyant power, to see it at a great distance; the hunter is then guided by the influence of the fetich to find it. They are also supposed to guide the spears so that they will be cast straight.

Sometimes the influence of the amulet or fetich is supposed to bring the game to the hunter.

Among the people of Kaviak peninsula and Kotzebue sound a body of the common weasel, which is said to be one of the totem animals of the Eskimo, is very highly prized as a fetich. The body is dried entire and is worn on the belt or carried in a pouch by boys and young men; for this purpose they are valued at the price of a marten skin. The possession of these weasel mummies is supposed to endow their owners with agility and prowess as hunters. In all cases it follows that the owner of a mummy of any animal or of a child carries with it power over its shade, which becomes the servant of the possessor.

The hunter is believed to be able to propitiate and control to a certain extent the shades of sea animals which he kills by keeping them with their bladders and, after the ceremonies and offerings described in the Bladder feast, dismissing them back to the sea to reenter other animals of their kind and so return that he may be able to kill them again. In this way the hunter is believed to be able to procure more game than would be possible were he to allow the shades of the animals killed to go to the land of the dead or to wander freely.

The same belief extends to inanimate objects. When a hunter sells furs it is a common custom for him to cut a small fragment from each skin, usually from the end of the nose, and place it carefully in a pouch. If he sells a seal entire he must cut off the tip of its tongue and swallow it, and sometimes I saw natives swallow fragments from skins they were selling to the traders. Fragments are even cut from garments that they sell, a minute portion being retained in an amulet pouch. In retaining these pieces it is believed that the possessor keeps the essential essence or spirit of the entire article, and is thus certain to become possessed, through its agency, of another of the same kind. Should he neglect to do this in any of the foregoing cases the objects disposed of would be gone forever, and although he might get articles of the same kind, he would obtain fewer than if he had kept the fragment.

In the same manner offerings of small particles of food and a little water from the large quantities distributed at feasts are supposed to convey to the shades the essence or essential parts of the entire amount. In two of the tales it is related that small pieces were taken from skins and afterward these again became full-size skins, to the benefit of their possessor, thus indicating the meaning of this custom.

In the Bladder festivals seen south of the lower Yukon, whenever food and water were brought into the kashim a little of each was cast to the floor and up against the roof as offerings to the shades of the upper and lower worlds.

All places, things, and the elements are supposed each to have a *yu-a* or mystery which is human or semihuman in form, but with grotesque features which are invisible except to shamans and others especially gifted. Hunters at sea and elsewhere in lonely places, when about to eat cast down food and water offerings to the *yu-a* before eating or drinking themselves, and often add propitiatory words. If offended, a *yu-a* has the power of causing a person's death, or making him ill, or taking away his success as a hunter. It is also believed that many animals have supernatural powers of hearing, it being claimed that if they are spoken of, although far away, they will know it. In this respect red and black bears are much feared, and it is said that if a man makes sport of bears or calls them by any disrespectful nickname or epithet, no matter where he is, the bears will hear and will watch for and kill him the next time he enters the mountains. For this reason a hunter who is going out for bears will speak of them with the greatest respect and announce that he is going for some other animal, so that they will be deceived and not expect him. They never like to speak of what they intend to hunt for fear that the animals may hear and give them bad luck. On one occasion I was talking with my guide, who was going reindeer hunting, and spoke of his chances of success in securing deer; he appeared to be offended and reproved me for letting the deer know what he wished to do.

The beaver is another animal that is regarded as especially gifted with power of learning the intentions of people; it is also said to understand what a man says to it, and if a beaver is driven into a hole and the hunter finds that the animal holds down its tail so closely that he can not raise it, all he need do is to say, "Beaver, lift your tail," whereupon the beaver does as told and can be drawn out easily.

The dead bodies of various animals must be treated very carefully by the hunter who obtains them, so that their shades may not be offended and bring bad luck or even death upon him or his people. This is illustrated by the various observances which were seen when a white whale was killed by an Unalit hunter. No one who aids in killing a white whale, or even helps to take one from the net, is permitted to do any work on the four days following, this being the time during which the shade stays with the body. No one in the village must use any sharp or pointed instrument at this time for fear of wounding the whale's shade, which is supposed to be in the vicinity but invisible; nor must any loud noise be made for fear of frightening and offending it. Whoever cuts a white whale's body with an iron ax will die. The use of iron instruments in the village is also forbidden during the four days, and wood must not be cut with an iron ax during the entire season for hunting these animals.

Dogs are regarded as very unclean and offensive to the shades of game animals, and great care is exercised that no dog shall have an opportunity to touch the bones of a white whale. Should a dog touch one of them the hunter might lose his luck—his nets would break or be avoided by the whales and his spears would fail to strike.

One of the best hunters at St Michael once let a dog eat a portion of a white whale's head, and the people attributed to this the fact that he took no more in his net during that season. When the bones of a white whale have been cleaned of the flesh, the hunter takes them to some secluded spot, usually on cliffs fronting the seashore, where dogs do not go, and places them there with several broken spearshafts.

Not far from the village of St Michael is a rocky, shelf-like shelter, facing the sea and very difficult of access. In this I found over twenty white-whale skulls and skeletons, accompanied by numerous broken spearshafts, and near by were other smaller but similar deposits. The lashings and heads of the spears had been removed, only the wooden shafts being left. Usually the spears were thrown down singly, but in one deposit a half dozen were tied together.

FIG. 151—Graphite fetich used in right-whale fishing (about ⅔).

Figure 151, from Aziak or Sledge island, is a beautifully made graphite model of a right whale, eleven inches in length. It is deeply excavated below and has a hole passing through the back to the excavation within. The mouth and blowholes are indicated by grooves in the surface; the hole through the back serves for attaching a stout rawhide cord.

I was told by the people from whom I purchased this object that it was used in right-whale fishing as a kind of charm. The heavy image, hanging to the end of a stout cord, is thrown over the flukes or flippers of the whale, or across its body, and draws the cord down into the water on the other side. Then the men manage to recover the lower end of the cord by reaching below the whale with a long-handle boat hook and draw it in to make it fast.

During the whaling season at Cape Prince of Wales the handles used for water buckets are carved to represent the forms of whales, and small images of these animals, handsomely carved from ivory, are frequently attached to the sides of the buckets. These images also figure in the winter festivals, at which offerings are made to propitiate the shades of those animals. It is with this idea of propitiation that the weights used on cords for making fast to whales after they have been killed are carved to represent these animals.

Figure 152 shows a hollow wooden image of a right whale, from the Diomede islands, used for storing lancepoints, and supposed to have certain occult virtues to aid in giving success to the owner.

Nu-na' hlukh'-tuk is the Unalit name for a spot of ground where certain things are tabooed, or where there is to be feared any evil influence caused by the presence of offended shades of men or animals, or through the influence of other supernatural means. This ground is sometimes considered unclean, and to go upon it would bring misfortune to the offender, producing sickness, death, or lack of success in hunting or fishing. The same term is also applied to ground where certain animals have been killed or have died.

Under the latter circumstance the ground is not considered dangerous unless a person performs there some forbidden act. The ground about the place on the shore where a dead white whale has been beached is so regarded. At such a time to chop wood with an iron ax is supposed to produce death. The same result is said to follow the cutting of wood with an iron ax near where salmon are being dressed.

An old man at St Michael told me that he knew of a case in which an Eskimo began to chop a log near a woman who was splitting salmon, and both of them died soon afterward. The cause of this, he said, was that the *inua* of the salmon and the *yu-a* of the ground did not like it and became angry. When offenses of this kind are committed every one present is supposed to die. If one or more people die suddenly of any strange or unusual disease, the occupants of the dwelling immediately forsake it,

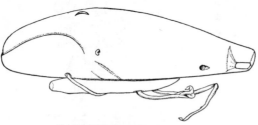

FIG. 152—Whale fetich of wood (⅓).

saying that the place is bad. I saw places of this kind on the Yukon, and a group of four houses were pointed out on the shore of Kotzebue sound that had been deserted by the people because a woman had died there in this manner.

This evil influence in certain spots may be brought about by witchcraft, and while shamans may sometimes succeed in counteracting it, the danger is regarded as great and may even kill the priests as well as other people.

There are other kinds of uncleanness which are less serious, but which produce sickness or bad luck in hunting. These consist of a kind of invisible, impalpable atmosphere like a vapor, which may attach itself to a person from some contamination. If a hunter gets in this condition he becomes much more than ordinarily visible to game, so that his success in the chase is destroyed until he succeeds in becoming clean once more. During menstruation women are considered unclean and hunters must avoid them or become unable to secure game. During the period that the bladders are in the kashim the hunters avoid all intercourse with women, saying that if they fail in this respect the shades will be offended.

Uncleanness of this kind may be removed in some cases by bathing in urine. Sometimes when a man learns that he has become unclean he goes to a grave and scrapes himself from head to foot with a human rib, thus leaving the bad influence at the grave. This condition may be brought about by witchcraft, but usually it is caused by contact with some person or thing already unclean. In the Bladder feast the flames of wild parsnip stalks are supposed to purify the bladders and thereby prevent any influence of this kind. At the same time they are believed to remove from the hunters the influence that may have affected them from their association with so many shades or *inuas*.

In a case that came to my notice one autumn, on Norton sound, a Malemut woman was ill for several months with some uterine trouble, and neither her husband nor other male relative would enter her house during the entire period, saying that if they did so they would become unclean and could kill no more game.

The object illustrated in figure 153 is a grotesque wooden head about three and a half inches long, with the nose of an ermine skin fastened on its forehead and extending thence backward and falling down behind, with the tail and hind feet as pendants. A strip of bear skin on the back of the head furnishes long hair to represent that of a human being. The features are grotesquely carved, with projecting brow, squarely cut nose, deeply incised, triangular eyes, and a crescentic, upturned mouth. A pair of incisors of some rodent project from the upper jaw, curving outward and down over the mouth. The face is painted

FIG. 153—Shaman's doll fetich (½).

dark red, except the area about the mouth, which is blackened with gum, in which are set the teeth. The neck has a round hole in its lower end, apparently for receiving a peg upon which the image was placed. This object was used by a shaman to represent one of his *tunghät*, by whose aid he claimed to accomplish his mysterious works.

MYTHIC ANIMALS

The Unalit and other Eskimo of this region believe in the existence of various fabulous monsters, some of the most important of which are described below. It will be noted that the majority of these beasts are apparently derived from traditional accounts of existing animals or their remains, some of which have already been treated in the chapter relating to masks.

It is said that there are sometimes born, among other beings, monstrous children which begin to devour their mother's breasts as soon as they are made to nurse. One was described to me as having been born at Pikmiktalik many years ago; it devoured its mother's breast, and when the people ran into the house in response to her cries the child escaped through the smoke hole in the roof. When they followed it outside, it was seen sitting between the horns of a reindeer, riding toward the mountains, where it disappeared.

Other curious beings are believed by the people of the lower Yukon to exist in the moon, but are said sometimes to be found on the earth. These are man-like creatures without head or neck, but having a broad mouth, armed with sharp teeth, across the chest. A wooden image of one of these was obtained by me, but it has since been lost.

The ă-mĭ'-kuk is said to be a large, slimy, leathery-skin sea animal with four long arms; it is very fierce and seizes a hunter in his kaiak at sea, dragging both under the water. When it pursues a man it is useless for him to try to escape, for if he gets upon the ice the beast will swim below and burst up under his feet; should he reach the shore the creature will swim through the earth in pursuit as easily as through the water.

Near St Michael the people believe that these creatures swim from the sea up through the land to some land-locked lakes in the craters of extinct volcanoes and to similar inland places. Several dry lake-beds were shown to me in that vicinity as having been drained by these animals when they swam out to the sea, leaving a channel made by their passage through the earth. It is said that if the ă-mĭ'-kuk returns the water follows from the sea and again fills the lake. The idea of this creature may have had its origin in the octopus.

Wĭ'-lŭ-ghó-yŭk is the sea shrew-mouse—a small animal, exactly like the common shrew-mouse in size and appearance, but it possesses certain supernatural powers. It lives on the ice at sea, and the moment it observes a man it darts at him with incredible swiftness, piercing the toe of his boot and crawling all over his body in a moment. If he remains perfectly quiet it disappears by the hole through which it entered without doing him any injury and, after this, he becomes a very successful hunter. If a man stir ever so little, however, while the animal is on him, it instantly burrows into his flesh, going straight to the heart and killing him. Hunters are very much afraid of this animal, and if they chance to come across a shrew-mouse on the ice at sea they stand motionless until the creature goes away. In one case, of which I chanced to hear at St Michael, a hunter who was out on the sea ice in that vicinity during winter stood in one spot for hours, while a shrew-mouse remained near him, and the villagers all agreed that he had a narrow escape.

Az'-ĭ-wû-gûm kĭ-mukh'-tĭ, the walrus dog. This animal is believed to be found in company with large herds of walrus, and is very fierce toward men. It is a long, slender animal, covered with black scales which are tough but may be pierced by a good spear. It has a head, teeth somewhat like those of a dog, and four legs; its tail is long, rounded, and scaly, and a stroke from it will kill a man. The people of the islands in Bering strait told me that sometimes they see these walrus dogs, and that their walrus hunters are very much afraid of them; they also informed me that on one occasion a walrus dog attacked an umiak full of people and killed them all.

The bones of the mammoth which are found on the coast country of Bering sea and in the adjacent interior are said to belong to an animal known as the *kĭ-lúg'-ŭ-wŭk* (*ko-gukh'-pŭk* of the Yukon). The creature is claimed to live under ground, where it burrows from place to place, and when by accident one of them comes to the surface, so that even the tip of its nose appears above ground and breathes the air, it dies at once. This explains the fact that the bones of these animals are nearly always found partly buried in the earth. The Eskimo say that these animals belong to the under world and for that reason the air of the outer world is fatal to them.

Ko'-gat are the *tunghät* of lonely lakes; they are semihuman in form and kill or steal the shade of any person found near their haunts. They have a loud, wailing cry and are much feared.

The *yu-ă* are the shades of inanimate things and the elements and, according to the beliefs of these people, usually have curiously distorted, grotesque faces.

The *nûn'-wûm yú-ă* is the essence or mystery which is believed to be present in or near a lake and when it goes away the lake dries up. These *yu-it* are believed to have the forms of men or women, and when visiting remote lakes people make food offerings to them so that they may be propitiated.

Tĭ'-sĭkh-pŭk, the great worm. This animal, which figures in numerous tales, was shaped like an enormous worm or caterpillar. It lived in the days when animals were supposed to have the power of changing their form at will to that of human beings, and in the tales it is indifferently a worm or a man. Among the carvings in ivory representing this creature were several having the body shaped like a worm with a human face on the head.

I-mŭkh'-pĭ-mĭ ă-klăn'-kun, the sea weasel. The Norton sound people described this as a long, weasel-shape animal found in the sea. They say it has black fur like the shrew-mouse with a white patch between its forelegs. This animal is also known among people living on the islands of Bering strait. There is no question that this myth has its origin in the sea otter, although the latter has been unknown in this region for a long period. Owing to its absence it has been invested with various supernatural traits, among which it is said to bring harm to lonely hunters when it finds them at sea. To this same animal may be ascribed also the *ĭ-mum' tsnĭ'-kak* or *ĭ-mum' pĭkh-tŭkh'-chĭ*, a rare animal said to be like a land otter, but which lives in the sea and is taken by only the best hunters.

Ĭ-mum' ká-bvĭ-ú-gă, sea fox. This is described as being similar in appearance to the red fox, but it is said to live far out at sea and is very fierce, often attacking and killing hunters.

Kăk-whăn'-ú-ghăt kĭg-û-lu'-nĭk. The killer whale (*ăkh'-lut*) is undoubtedly the original of this mythic creature. It is described as being simi-

FIG. 154—Drawing of a composite animal in a wooden tray (⅓).

lar in form to the killer whale and is credited with the power of changing at will to a wolf; after roaming about over the land it may return to the sea and again become a whale. While in the wolf form it is known by the above name, and the Eskimo say they know that this change takes place as they have seen wolf tracks leading to the edge of the sea ice and ending at the water, or beginning at the edge of the water and leading to the shore. This of course results from the breaking away of a portion of the ice on which the wolf tracks had been. These animals are said to be very fierce and to kill men. The same power of changing its form is sometimes credited to the white whale, which interchanges form with the reindeer, as shown in the drawing, reproduced in figure 154, on the bottom of a wooden tray from south of the Yukon mouth. This belief is prevalent among all the Eskimo along the shore of Bering sea.

A strange, crocodile-like animal, known as *păl-raí-yŭk*, is painted on the sides of umiaks and on the inside of wooden dishes (see figures 155, 156) by natives along lower Yukon and Kuskokwim rivers. A mask (plate XCV, 3) from the tundra south of the Yukon mouth has this animal drawn down each side of the face. According to the traditions of the people in this district the climate in ancient times was very much warmer than at present and the winters were shorter. In those days the mythic animals referred to were abundant in the swampy country between the two rivers, being more common near the Kuskokwim, where the climate was more temperate than on the Yukon.

FIG. 155—Drawing of the *păl-raí-yŭk* in a wooden tray (⅓).

In those days the waterfowl and other birds came back from the south in February and the snow melted during that month and the water ran into the passages of houses as it does now in April. At that time the *păl-raí-yŭk* lived in lakes, creeks, and marshes, where it killed men and animals for food. Several of the lower Yukon Eskimo recounted the killing of the last one by a hunter whose wife the beast had caught and devoured while she was getting water from the lake. In the tale of the creation by the Raven, as the latter and the First Man were traveling in the Skyland, the Raven cautioned his companion not to drink from the lakes which were passed, because in them were animals he had made that would seize and destroy any one who ventured near. These were the *păl-raí-yŭk*.

In the drawings of this animal on umiaks, at intervals along the body are open spaces, inside which are represented parts of a human body, showing the belief in its having eaten such food. It was said to live in the water, where it lay hidden among the grass, whence it suddenly rushed to seize a person on the bank or to attack kaiaks when crossing its haunts.

The curious likeness of these animals to the alligator, as shown in the accounts of its habits and in drawings representing it, is very remarkable. Nearly all of the umiaks in the country of the lower Yukon and to the southward have a picture of this animal drawn along the entire length on each side of the boat, with the head near the bow, and the figure is common also on wooden dishes in that region. It appears to be a local myth, and can scarcely have been brought to these people since the advent of the whites. The country where this myth

Fig. 156—Drawing of the *păl-raí-yŭk* on an umiak ($\frac{1}{16}$).

is most prevalent is one of the least visited of any along the coast of Bering sea. The accompanying figure 156 represents a model of an umiak from the lower Yukon, with the animal drawn along the sides.

In one of the Raven tales a large beast is described as having been seen haunting a dry lake bed overgrown with tall grass while Raven and First Man were journeying in the sky land. It is said to have rested by lying down on the tips of the growing grass, without bending the stems. When this animal was killed by the Sky people it was necessary for them first to place logs under it, for when dead it became so heavy that it would sink into the ground as will a lean seal in water. It is described as having a long head and six legs, the hind legs unusually large and the fore ones short, with the small middle pair hanging from the belly. A fine, thick fur, like that on the shrew-mouse, is said to grow all over its body and is thickest about the feet. On the back of the head are a pair of thick, short horns, which extend forward and outward and then curve back at the points. The animal has small eyes and is very dark colored. This undoubtedly refers to the muskox, which has been extinct for ages in the region where these people live.

Tĭñ-mĭ-ûk'-pŭk, the great eagle (Thunderbird). This is described as an enormous eagle which varies in its habits according to locality.

The people of Bering strait said that it preys upon right whales. On a spear-rest used in the bow of an umiak (plate CVI*a*) are etched four of these birds, two upon each side. On one side the birds are represented as having their claws in the backs of the whales, which they are carrying away; on the other side the birds are represented as not yet having seized their prey.

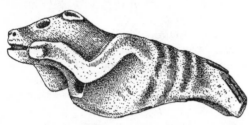

FIG. 157—Ivory carving of a composite animal (⅔).

On the shore of Norton sound the *tǐñ-mǐ-ûk′-pûk* is said to catch either whales or reindeer, and along the lower Yukon it was reported to prey upon people and reindeer. Among the tales herein recorded is one from the lower Yukon describing the last pair of these birds which were believed to have lived there. In that district the top of a mountain below Ikogmut was pointed out as one on which these birds were said to have nested.

Plate CVII *b* shows a handsomely etched ivory pipestem from Norton sound. The side represented in the illustration has several groups of human figures. There is also a kashim with men dancing inside to the music of a drum; others are entering through the summer passageway above ground, and others on the roof. Next is a man with a bow and arrow shooting another who holds a spear upraised. The next is a representation of the Thunderbird seizing a reindeer, followed by the figure of the huge man-worm, or *ti-sǐkh-pûk*, that figures in Eskimo mythology. Other less important figures are also etched on this surface, as is shown in the illustration.

The small sculpin, which is very common along the rocky shore of Norton sound, is called the rainmaker, and the Eskimo say it will cause heavy rain if a person takes one of them in his hand.

Small fragments of quartz crystal are said to be the centers of masses of ice that have frozen harder than usual, so that the cores have turned to stone. These are prized as amulets.

I was told by a fur trader who was familiar with the Nunivak islanders that the latter claim descent from a dog.

FIG. 158—Ivory carving representing the man-worm (full size).

Figure 157, from Cape Darby, on the northern shore of Norton sound, is an ivory carving 3½ inches long, representing the head and shoulders of a white bear and the body of a seal. The bear has in its mouth an object which projects upon either side and is grasped by the paws. This is a well-made carving, and is pierced longitudinally through the under surface for the passage of a cord. It was used as a handle for dragging seals and other heavy bodies over the ice and represents one of the mythic animals of the people on the shore of Bering strait.

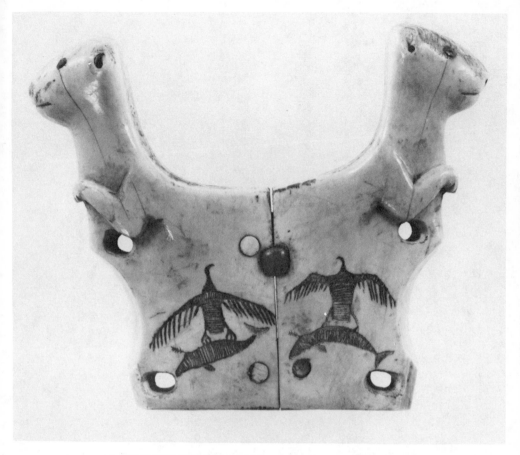

a— SPEAR REST WITH FIGURES OF THUNDERBIRDS CATCHING WHALES

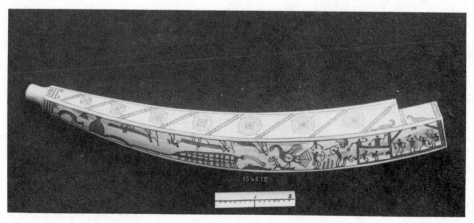

b—IVORY PIPESTEM WITH ETCHED FIGURES OF THE MAN-WORM AND THE THUNDERBIRD

OBJECTS ETCHED WITH MYTHOLOGIC FIGURES

Figure 158, from Cape Vancouver, is a carving of walrus ivory, representing a worm-like body encircled by incised rings to represent the segments, which are colored alternately green and red. On the front end of the body is represented a semihuman face, below which project two paws with four fingers or toes. The carving tapers toward the tail, which is narrow and somewhat flattened, with a hole pierced through for the admission of a cord. This object was used as a pendant on a woman's belt, and represents the man-worm which appears in numerous tales of these people.

Fig. 159—Ivory carving of a mythic animal (full size).

Figure 159, from Cape Vancouver, is a handsome little ivory carving representing the figure of a seal with the mouth of a lamprey; the middle of the body is carved into two joined links. This represents one of the numerous mythic animals supposed to inhabit the sea.

Figure 160, from Sledge island, is an ivory cord handle representing one of the mythic animals believed to inhabit the sea and to be half white bear and half whale.

Fig. 160—Ivory drag handle representing a composite animal (⅔).

Figure 161 shows a cord handle of ivory from Sledge island. It is carved to represent a mythic creature, half seal and half human, that the Eskimo of Norton sound and Bering strait claim exists in the sea. They are said to be caught in nets or killed by hunters at times, and when this happens the one who is responsible for it is presumed to suffer many misfortunes.

Figure 162, from Sledge island, is an ivory handle for a whale float. One end represents a sealhead, and the other the head of one of the mermaid-like beings said to live in the sea and to have the head and shoulders of a human being, the remainder of the animal being like a seal.

Fig. 161—Ivory carving of a mermaid-like creature (₁₀⁶).

Figure 163, from Kushunuk, is a carving of wood three inches in length. It represents the body of a seal with the head and neck of a human being. Upon the shoulders incised lines represent hands and arms; a seal claw is set in the lower part of the breast and curved downward and back. This object represents a mythic animal supposed to live in the sea, and is without definite use. It shows a mermaid-like creature, half human and half seal, described as having the upper part of the body covered with white skin, with long hair on the head, and the legs replaced by a seal's body. It is a mythical conception common among the western Eskimo.

FIG. 162—Ivory float handle with mermaid-like figure (⅔).

Figure 164, from Cape Vancouver, is a carving an inch and three-quarters long, representing a walrus. On the breast is a human face, inclosed within the front flippers and looking forward, intended to represent the features of the walrus *inua*. The body is ornamented with concentric circles

FIG. 162—Ivory float handle with mermaid-like figure (⅔).

FIG. 163—Carving representing a mermaid-like creature (¾).

FIG. 164—Ivory carving showing the face of a walrus *inua* (full size).

with central dots, made by filling round holes in the ivory with wooden plugs. The general execution of this carving is very good, the shape of the walrus, including the tusks, nostrils, and small sunken dots about the muzzle, representing bristles, being well reproduced.

An ivory carving (number 43717), three inches in length, from Nunivak island, represents a seal's body with a man's head and neck. It is pierced crosswise through the shoulders for the passage of a cord, and is used as a fastener for a woman's belt. This represents one of the composite animals which figure in the mythology of this region.

A carving, from Sledge island in Bering strait (number 45236), represents a seal's body with a semihuman face. It is pierced lengthwise along the lower side for the passage of a cord, is used for the same purpose as the specimen last described, and, like it, illustrates a mythic animal.

Another carving (figure 135), from the northern shore of Norton sound, is 4½ inches in length, made from mammoth ivory, and

FIG. 165—Drawing of mythic creature in a wooden tray (⅓).

represents a white bear carrying upon its back the extended figure of a man lying face downward with his head over the animal's hips and grasping it about the haunches. It is a spirited carving, illustrating an incident in one of the Eskimo tales.

Figure 165 is copied from a figure painted on the bottom of a wooden tray (number 38642) obtained at Nulukhtulogumut, and represents a mythical creature described in the tales of that region.

In the Raven tale are described reindeer which came from the sky and which had teeth like dogs. These are said still to exist, but are invisible except to shamans, who see them on the plains and describe them as having a large hole through the body, back of the shoulders. People supposed to be gifted with clairvoyant powers sometimes see and shoot at them, believing them to be like other deer, but no ordinary weapon can kill them. Carvings of these animals were seen among the people south of the Yukon mouth.

In the far north there are said to be men having tails and two faces—one in front and one behind.

CONCEPTION OF NATURAL PHENOMENA

The aurora is believed to be a group of boys playing football, sometimes using a walrus skull as the ball. The swaying movement of the lights back and forth represents the struggles of the players. When the light fades away the Eskimo utter a low whistle, which they say will call the boys back.

The galaxy is said to be the track made by Raven's snowshoes when he walked across the sky during one of his journeys while creating the inhabitants of the earth.

The Pleiades are called the "Little foxes," and are said to be a litter of fox cubs.

The stars of Orion's belt are called the "Great stretchers," being regarded as posts on which rawhide lines are being stretched.

The vertical bar in a parhelion is called the "Sun's walking stick," and shooting stars are termed star dung.

Sirius is the "Moon-dog," which makes high winds when it is near the moon.

TRADITIONAL SHOWERS OF ASHES

The Eskimo have various traditions of occurrences long past. One very old woman on the lower Yukon told me she had heard related by old people when she was a girl that showers of matter like ashes fell there very long ago. The first shower of ashes she heard of was quite deep, killing fish in the rivers and causing the death of many people by starvation.

At St Michael an old man related that before the Russians came to the country he knew of one fall of a strange substance like ashes which covered the ground like a slight fall of snow and adhered to whatever it fell upon so that when rubbed off from wood it left a polished

18 ETH——29

appearance. This man said that such showers were known to have taken place at widely distant intervals and that people were very much frightened by them. After one occurred they saved all the bones and scraps of food, even the skins of animals, after removing the hair, in order to forestall the expected famine. During the cold months of winter following one of these occurrences the people ate every scrap, saving the dried fish and better food for spring, when they feared another fall might take place.

These accounts undoubtedly refer to falls of volcanic ashes from eruptions taking place in the Aleutian islands and other points in this region, and are interesting as showing the manner in which occurrences of this kind are treasured in the memories of these people.

ANIMAL SYMBOLISM

When the first foxes caught in fall are lean the old men predict a hard winter, and if the white geese commence to fly southward early in autumn an early winter is expected to follow.

The names of birds and other forms of animal life used among these people are frequently very expressive, as for instance, the term applied to the emperor goose, which means "the hooded one," and the name for the grass snipe (*Tringa maculata*), called "the walrus talker" from its booming note, which is similar to that of the walrus.

FOLK TALES

SCOPE OF ALASKAN FOLKLORE

The following legends are from various localities. The name of the place whence each was obtained is given at the beginning of each tale. The Alaskan Eskimo possess an almost endless number of tales and legends, which express in many details their religious beliefs and convey in an interesting form an idea of their ancient customs and modes of thought. In a section treating of their mythology are give notes on the supernatural animals and other beings which are mentioned in the legends.

These tales are best known by certain old men who entertain their fellow-villagers by repeating them before the assembled people in the kashim. The Raven legends form a series of culture myths, and are especially popular as accounting for the existence of all things. These have a widely-extended distribution, and I know personally of their existence among the people from Kotzebue sound southward around Bering strait to the mouth of Kuskokwim river. The Raven myth also exists on the Asiatic shore of Bering strait. At Plover bay, Siberia, there was seen a boy 10 or 12 years of age who had the raven totem tattooed on his forehead (figure 115).

Special attention is invited to this series of legends, which are so similar in character to Raven legends existing among the Tlinket of southeastern Alaska. These tales apparently have a common source. The Thunderbird of the Tlinket also appears in the mythology of the Eskimo, at least as far north as Bering strait.

Young men who have an aptitude for learning tales become narrators and repeat them verbatim, even with the accompanying inflections of the voice and gestures. On lower Kuskokwim river and the adjacent district toward the Yukon mouth, some of the important tales are given by two men, who sit cross-legged near together and facing each other; one is the narrator and the other holds a bundle of small sticks in one hand. The tale proceeds and at certain points one of these sticks is placed on the floor between them, forming a sort of chapter mark. If the narrator is at fault he is prompted by his companion. Some of the tales are long, occupying several successive evenings in their recital. The narrators are very careful to repeat them in a certain set phraseology, with repetitions in definitely determined places. When an error is made it is common for the narrator to go back and repeat from some prominent incident. The voice is intoned to imitate the different characters in a more or less dramatic manner, and with the gestures makes a very effective recital. The listeners are quiet and attentive, and at certain incidents express by a word or two their feelings of surprise or satisfaction. These tales are heard with pleasure over and over again, forming the unwritten lore upon which they draw for entertainment during the long winter evenings. During a sledge journey to the mouth of Kuskokwim river in 1879 I was kept awake several nights by young men lying in the kashim repeating for hours the tales they were memorizing, although the other Eskimo slept through it all with perfect indifference.

In addition to the more important tales, which are the property of the men, there are many children's stories, which the women relate, frequently entertaining each other as well as the children; these are short, simple stories and are looked upon as belonging peculiarly to the women. An example of these is the tale of the Raven and the Marmot.

A collection of tales from the shore of Bering strait would undoubtedly give valuable insight into the intercourse formerly held with the Asiatic shore, the tale *Ak'-chĭk-chû'-gŭk* being an example in point. An old man related this tale, at the same time drawing a map showing the course taken by the brothers to Cape Prince of Wales and across the strait to East cape, Siberia, and southward along that coast until they found their sister; the villages were all marked and named, and the map, though rude, gave a good idea of the coastlines and islands.

The tales of these people seem to have originated largely from certain distinct sources; there are tales of hunting and adventure, including voyages and incidents of the ordinary life of the people which may start from someone who recounts an episode in his life in a pleasing manner, so that it is taken up and repeated, with various additions, mainly of a supernatural character, and finally becomes fixed in the tribal folklore.

Another class is made up and recounted by the shamans, or medicine-men, always dealing with supernatural powers and beings, and are intended to increase the public regard for them and their ability to deal with the shades that are believed to exist everywnere, through the propitiation of which the public and private welfare is secured. Many of their festivals have undoubtedly originated from tales told by the shamans regarding visions seen and instructions said to have been obtained from supernatural beings, while asleep or in a trance. One such tale is that of the *Yuguk* festival of the lower Yukon.

FLOOD LEGENDS FROM ST MICHAEL

The Norton sound Eskimo have a legend that in the first days the earth was flooded except a very high mountain in the middle. The water came up from the sea and covered all the land except the top of this mountain; only a few animals were saved, which escaped by going up the mountain side. A few people escaped by going into an umiak and subsisting on the fish they caught until the water subsided. Finally, as the waters lowered, the people who were saved went to live upon the mountains, eventually descending to the coast; the animals also came down and replenished the earth with their kind. During the flood the waves and currents cut the surface of the land into hollows and ridges, and then, as the water receded, it ran back into the sea, leaving the mountains and valleys as they are today. Legends very similar to this are widely spread among other Eskimo on the coast of Bering sea.

TALES OF THE RAVEN (TU-LU-KAU′-GÛK)

THE CREATION

(From Kigiktauik)

The following was related by an old Unalit man living at Kigiktauik, who learned it, when he was a boy, from an old man. Fragments and versions of the same tale were found among the Eskimo from the Arctic coast to the banks of Kuskokwim river. The last portion of this series of legends, describing the recovery of the light by Raven, was repeated by Eskimo from Kotzebue sound, Norton bay, and Kuskokwim and Yukon rivers.

My narrator said that the old man from whom he learned it came from Bering strait, and that always, when he finished the tales on the third evening, he would pour a cup of water on the floor and say: "Drink well, spirits of those of whom I have told."

It was in the time when there were no people on the earth plain. During four days the first man lay coiled up in the pod of a beach-pea (*L. maritimus*). On the fifth day he stretched out his feet and burst the pod, falling to the ground, where he stood up, a full-grown man. He looked about him, and then moved his hands and arms, his neck and legs, and examined himself curiously. Looking back, he saw the pod from which he had fallen, still hanging to the vine, with a hole in the lower end, out of which he had dropped. Then he looked about him again and saw that he was getting farther away from his starting place, and that the ground moved up and down under his feet and seemed very soft. After a while he had an unpleasant feeling in his stomach, and he stooped down to take some water into his mouth from a small pool at his feet. The water ran down into his stomach and he felt better. When he looked up again he saw approaching, with a waving motion, a dark object which came on until just in front of him, when it stopped, and, standing on the ground, looked at him. This was a raven, and, as soon as it stopped, it raised one of its wings, pushed up its beak, like a mask, to the top of its head, and changed at once into a man. Before he raised his mask Raven had stared at the man, and after it was raised he stared more than ever, moving about from side to side to obtain a better view. At last he said: "What are you? Whence did you come? I have never seen anything like you." Then Raven looked at Man, and was still more surprised to find that this strange new being was so much like himself in shape.

Then he told Man to walk away a few steps, and in astonishment exclaimed again: "Whence did you come? I have never seen anything like you before." To this Man replied: "I came from the pea-pod." And he pointed to the plant from which he came. "Ah!" exclaimed Raven, "I made that vine, but did not know that anything like you would ever come from it. Come with me to the high ground over there; this ground I made later, and it is still soft and thin, but it is thicker and harder there."

In a short time they came to the higher land, which was firm under their feet. Then Raven asked Man if he had eaten anything. The latter answered that he had taken some soft stuff into him at one of the pools. "Ah!" said Raven, "you drank some water. Now wait for me here."

Then he drew down the mask over his face, changing again into a bird, and flew far up into the sky where he disappeared. Man waited where he had been left until the fourth day, when Raven returned, bringing four berries in his claws. Pushing up his mask, Raven became a man again and held out two salmonberries and two heathberries, saying, "Here is what I have made for you to eat. I also wish them to be plentiful over the earth. Now eat them." Man took the berries and placed them in his mouth one after the other and they satisfied his hunger, which had made him feel uncomfortable. Raven then led Man to a small creek near by and left him while he went to the water's edge and molded a couple of pieces of clay into the form of a pair of mountain sheep, which he held in his hand, and when they became dry he called Man to show him what he had done. Man thought they were very pretty, and Raven told him to close his eyes. As soon as Man's eyes were closed Raven drew down his mask and waved his wings four times over the images, when they became endowed with life and bounded away as full-grown mountain sheep. Raven then raised his mask and told Man to look. When Man saw the sheep moving away, full of life, he cried out with pleasure. Seeing how pleased Man was, Raven said, "If these animals are numerous, perhaps people will wish very much to get them." And Man said he thought they would. "Well," said Raven, "it will be better for them to have their home among the high cliffs, so that every one can not kill them, and there only shall they be found."

Then Raven made two animals of clay which he endowed with life as before, but as they were dry only in spots when they were given life, they remained brown and white, and so originated the tame reindeer with mottled coat. Man thought these were very handsome, and Raven told him that they would be very scarce. In the same way a pair of wild reindeer were made and permitted to get dry and white only on their bellies, then they were given life; in consequence, to this day the belly of the wild reindeer is the only white part about it. Raven told Man that these animals would be very common, and people would kill many of them.

"You will be very lonely by yourself," said Raven. "I will make you a companion." He then went to a spot some distance from where he had made the animals, and, looking now and then at Man, made an image very much like him. Then he fastened a lot of fine water grass on the back of the head for hair, and after the image had dried in his hands, he waived his wings over it as before and a beautiful young woman arose and stood beside Man. "There," cried Raven, "is a companion for you," and he led them back to a small knoll near by.

In those days there were no mountains far or near, and the sun never ceased shining brightly; no rain ever fell and no winds blew. When they came to the knoll, Raven showed the pair how to make a bed in the dry moss, and they slept there very warmly; Raven drew down his mask and slept near by in the form of a bird. Waking before the others, Raven went back to the creek and made a pair each of stickle-backs, graylings, and blackfish. When these were swimming about in the water, he called Man to see them. When the latter looked at them and saw the sticklebacks swim up the stream with a wriggling motion he was so surprised that he raised his hand suddenly and the fish darted away. Raven then showed him the graylings and told him that they would be found in clear mountain streams, while the sticklebacks would live along the seacoast and that both would be good for food. Next the shrew-mouse was made, Raven saying that it would not be good for food but would enliven the ground and prevent it from seeming barren and cheerless.

In this way Raven continued for several days making birds, fishes, and animals, showing them to Man, and explaining their uses.

After this he flew away to the sky and was gone four days, when he returned, bringing back a salmon for the use of Man. Looking about he saw that the ponds and lakes were silent and lonely, so he created many water insects upon their surfaces, and from the same clay he made the beaver and the muskrat to frequent their borders. Then, also, were made flies, mosquitoes, and various other land and water insects, it being explained to Man that these were made to enliven and make cheerful the earth. At that time the mosquito was like the house-fly in its habits and did not bite as it does now.

Man was shown the muskrat and told to take its skin for clothing. He was also told that the beavers would live along the streams and build strong houses and that he must follow their example, and likewise that the beavers would be very cunning and only good hunters would be able to take them.

At this time the woman gave birth to a child, and Raven directed Man how to feed and care for it, telling him that it would grow into a man like himself. As soon as the child was born, Raven and Man took it to a creek, rubbed it over with clay, and then returned with it to his stopping place on the knoll. The next morning the child was running about pulling up grass and other plants which Raven had caused to grow near by; on the third day the child became a full-grown man.

After this Raven thought that if he did not create something to make men afraid they would destroy everything he had made to inhabit the earth. Then he went to a creek near by, where he formed a bear and gave it life, jumping to one side quickly as the bear stood up and looked fiercely about. Man was then called and told that the bear would be very fierce and would tear him to pieces if he disturbed it. Then were made different kinds of seals, and their names and habits were explained to man. Raven also taught Man to make rawhide lines from sealskin, and snares for deer, but cautioned him to wait until the deer were abundant before he snared any of them.

In time the woman was with child again, and Raven said it would be a girl and they must rub her over with clay as soon as she was born, and that after she was grown she must marry her brother. Then Raven went away to the place of the pea vine, where the first man was found. While he was gone a girl was born and the pair did as they were told, and the next day the girl walked about. On the third day she became a full-grown woman, and was married to the young man as directed by Raven, in order that the earth might be peopled more rapidly.

When Raven reached the pea vine he found three other men had just fallen from the pea pod that gave the first one. These men, like the first, were looking about them in wonder, and Raven led them away in an opposite direction from that in which he had taken the first man, afterward bringing them to firm land close to the sea. Here they

stopped, and Raven remained with them a long time, teaching them
how to live. He taught them how to make a fire drill and bow from a
piece of dry wood and a cord, taking the wood from the bushes and
small trees he had caused to grow in hollows and sheltered places on
the hillside. He made for each of the men a wife, and also made
many plants and birds such as frequent the seacoast, but fewer kinds
than he had made in the land where the first man lived. He taught
the men to make bows and arrows, spears, nets, and all the implements of the chase and how to use them; also how to capture the seals
which had now become plentiful in the sea. After he had taught them
how to make kaiaks, he showed them how to build houses of drift logs
and bushes covered with earth. Now the three wives of the last men
were all pregnant, and Raven went back to the first man, where he
found the children were married; then he told Man about all he had
done for the people on the seacoast. Looking about here he thought the
earth seemed bare; so, while the others slept, he caused birch, spruce,
and cottonwood trees to spring up in low places, and then awoke the
people, who were much pleased at seeing the trees. After this they
were taught how to make fire with the fire drill and to place the spark
of tinder in a bunch of dry grass and wave it about until it blazed,
then to place dry wood upon it. They were shown how to roast fish on
a stick, to make fish traps of splints and willow bark, to dry salmon
for winter use, and to make houses.

Raven then went back to the coast men again. When he had gone
Man and his son went down to the sea and the son caught a seal which
they tried to kill with their hands but could not, until, finally, the son
killed it by a blow with his fist. Then the father took off its skin with
his hands alone and made it into lines which they dried. With these
lines they set snares in the woods for reindeer. When they went to look
at these the next morning, they found the cords bitten in two and the
snares gone, for in those days reindeer had sharp teeth like dogs.
After thinking for a time the young man made a deep hole in the deer
trail and hung in it a heavy stone fastened to the snare so that when
it caught a deer the stone would slip down into the hole, drag the deer's
neck down to the ground, and hold it fast. The next morning when
they returned they found a deer entangled in the snare. Taking it
out they killed and skinned it, carrying the skin home for a bed; some
of the flesh was roasted on the fire and found to be very good to eat.

One day Man went out seal hunting along the seashore. He saw
many seals, but in each case after he had crept carefully up they would
tumble into the water before he could get to them, until only one was
left on the rocks; Man crept up to it more carefully than before, but it
also escaped. Then he stood up and his breast seemed full of a strange
feeling, and the water began to run in drops from his eyes and down
his face. He put up his hand and caught some of the drops to look at
them and found that they were really water; then, without any wish

on his part, loud cries began to break from him and the tears ran down his face as he went home.   When his son saw him coming, he called to his wife and mother to see Man coming along making such a strange noise; when he reached them they were still more surprised to see water running down his face.   After he told them the story of his disappointment they were all stricken with the same strange ailment and began to wail with him, and in this way people first learned how to cry.   After this the son killed another seal and they made more deer snares from its hide.

When the deer caught this time was brought home, Man told his people to take a splint bone from its foreleg and to drill a hole in the large end.   Into this they put some strands of sinew from the deer and sewed skins upon their bodies to keep themselves warm when winter came; for Raven had told them to do this, so that the fresh deerskins dried upon them.   Man then showed his son how to make bows and arrows and to tip the latter with points of horn for killing deer; with them the son killed his first deer.   After he had cut up this deer he placed its fat on a bush and then fell asleep; when he awoke he was very angry to find that mosquitoes had eaten all of it.   Until this time mosquitoes had never bitten people, but Man scolded them for what they had done and said, "Never eat meat again, but eat men," and since that day mosquitoes have always bitten people.

Where the first man lived there had now grown a large village, for the people did everything as Raven directed them, and as soon as a child was born it was rubbed with clay and so caused to grow to its full stature in three days.   One day Raven came back and sat by Man, and they talked of many things.   Man asked Raven about the land he had made in the sky.   Raven said that he had made a fine land there, whereupon Man asked to be taken to see it.   This was agreed to and they started toward the sky where they arrived in a short time.   There Man found himself in a beautiful country with a very much better climate than that on earth; but the people who lived there were very small.   Their heads reached only to his thigh when they stood beside him.   Man looked about as they journeyed and saw many strange animals; also that the country was much finer than the one he had left.   Raven told him that this land, with its people and animals, was the first he had made.

The people living here wore handsomely made fur clothing, worked in ornamental patterns, such as people now wear on earth; for Man, on his return, showed his people how to make clothes in this manner, and the patterns have been retained ever since.   After a time they came to a large kashim, and went in; a very old man, the first made by Raven in the sky land, came out from his place of honor at the head of the room, opposite the door, and welcomed them, telling the people to bring food for the guest from the lower land, who was his friend.   Then boiled flesh of a kind which Man had never eaten before was brought to him.

Raven told him that it was from the mountain sheep and the tame reindeer. After Man had eaten Raven led him on again to show him other
things which he had made, and told him not to try to drink from any of
the lakes they might pass, for in them he had made animals that would
seize and destroy him if he went near.

On the way they came to a dry lake bed in which tall grass was
growing thickly. Lying upon the very tips of this grass, which did not
bend under its weight, was a large, strange-looking animal, with a long
head and six legs. The two hind-legs were unusually large; the fore-
legs were short, and a small pair extended down from the belly. All
over the animal's body grew fine, thick hair, like that on the shrew-
mouse, but it was longer about the feet. From the back of the head
grew a pair of thick, short horns, which extended forward and curved
back at the tips. The animal had small eyes and was of very dark
color or blackish.

Raven told Man that when people wished to kill one of these animals
they first placed logs on the ground under them, for, if they did not, the
animal would sink into the earth when he fell and be lost. In order to
kill one of them many people were needed, and when the animal fell on
the logs other logs must be thrown over it and held down, while two
men took large clubs and beat in its skull between the eyes.

Next they came to a round hole in the sky, around the border of
which grew a ring of short grass, glowing like fire. This, Raven
said, was a star called the Moon-dog (ĭ-ghă-lum kĭ-mukh'-tĭ). The tops
of the grass bordering the hole were gone, and Raven said that his
mother had taken some, and he had taken the rest to make the first fire
on earth. He added that he had tried to make some of this same kind
of grass on the earth but could not.

Man was now told to close his eyes and he would be taken to another
place. Raven took him upon his wings and, dropping through the star
hole, they floated down for a long time, until at last they entered something that seemed to resist their course. Finally they stopped, and
Raven said they were standing at the bottom of the sea. Man breathed
quite easily there, and Raven told him that the foggy appearance was
caused by the water. He said, "I will make some new kinds of animals here; but you must not walk about; you must lie down, and if
you become tired you may turn over upon the other side."

Raven then left Man lying on one side, where he rested for a long
time; finally he awoke, but felt very tired, so he tried to turn over, but
could not. Then Man thought, "I wish I could turn over;" and in a
moment he turned without effort. As he did this he was surprised to
see that his body had become covered with long, white hairs and that
his fingers had become long claws, but he quickly fell asleep again. He
awoke, and turned over and fell asleep three times more. When he
awoke the fourth time Raven stood beside him and said, "I have
changed you into a white bear. How do you like it?" Man tried to

answer, but could not make a sound until the Raven waved his magic wing over him, when he replied that he did not like it, for he would have to live on the sea while his son would be on the shore, and he would feel badly. Then Raven made a stroke with his wings and the bearskin fell from Man and lay empty at one side while he sat up in his original form. Then Raven took one of his tail-feathers, placing it inside the bearskin for a spine, and, after waving his wing over it, a white bear arose. Then they passed on, and ever since white bears have been found on the frozen sea.

Raven asked Man how many times he had turned over, and he answered, " four." " That was four years," said Raven, "for you slept there just four years." They had gone only a short distance beyond this, when they saw a small animal like a shrew-mouse; this was a *wĭ'-lû-gho'-yûk*. It is like the shrew that lives on the land, but this one always lives at sea on the ice. When it sees a man it darts at him, and, entering the toe of his boot, crawls all over his body, after which, if he keeps perfectly quiet, it will leave him unharmed and the man will become a successful hunter. In case the man moves even a finger while this animal is on him, it instantly burrows into his flesh and goes directly to his heart, causing death.

Then Raven made the *ă-mĭ'-kuk*, a large, slimy, leathery-skin animal, with four long, wide-spreading arms. This is a fierce animal, living in the sea, which wraps its arms about a man or a kaiak and drags them under the water; if the man tries to escape from it by leaving his kaiak and getting on the ice it will dart underneath, breaking the ice beneath his feet, and even pursuing him on shore by burrowing through the earth as easily as it swims in the water, so that no one can escape from it when it once pursues him.

Beyond this, they saw two large dark-colored animals, around which swam a smaller one. Raven hurried forward and sat upon the head of the smaller animal, and it became quiet. When Man drew near, Raven showed him two walrus, and said that the animal upon whose head he was borne was a walrus dog (*az-ĭ-wû'-gŭmkĭ-mukh'-tĭ*). This animal, he said, would always go with large herds of walrus and would kill people. It was long and rather slender, covered with black scales which were not too hard to be pierced by a spear. Its head and teeth were somewhat like those of a dog; it had four legs and a long, round tail covered with scales like those on the body; with a stroke of this tail it could kill a man.

Some whales and grampus were seen next. Raven told Man that only good hunters could kill them, and that when one was killed an entire village could feast. Then they saw the *ĭ-mum' ka'-bvĭ-á-gă*, or sea fox, an animal very much like the red fox, except that it lives in the sea and is so fierce that it kills men. Near this were two *ĭ-mum' tsnĭ'-kak* or *ĭ-mum' pĭkh-túkh'-chĭ*, the sea otter, which is like the land otter, but has much finer fur, tipped with white, and is very scarce, only the best hunters being able to capture it. They passed many kinds of fish and then the shore rose before them, and overhead could be seen the ripples on the surface of the water. "Close your eyes, and hold fast to me," said Raven. As soon as he had done this, Man found himself standing on the shore near his home, and was very much astonished to see a large village where he had left only a few huts; his wife had become very old and his son was an old man. The people saw him and welcomed him back, making him their headman; he was given the place of honor in the kashim, and there told the people what he had seen and taught the young men many things. The villagers would have given Raven a seat by the old man in the place of honor, but he refused it and chose a seat with the humble people near the entrance.

After a time the old man began to wish to see the fine sky land again, but his people tried to induce him to stay with them. He told his children that they must not feel badly at his absence, and then, in company with Raven, he returned to the sky land. The dwarf people welcomed them, and they lived there for a long time, until the villagers on the earth had become very numerous and killed a great many animals. This angered Man and Raven so much that one night they took a long line and a grass basket with which they descended to the earth. Raven caught ten reindeer, which he put into the basket with the old man; then one end of the cord was fastened to the basket and Raven returned to the sky, drawing it up after him. The next evening they took the reindeer and went down close to Man's village; the deer were then told to break down the first house they came to and destroy the people, for men were becoming too numerous. The reindeer did as they were told and ate up the people with their sharp, wolf-like teeth, after which they returned to the sky; the next night they came back and destroyed another house with its people in the same manner. The villagers had now become much frightened and covered the third house with a mixture of deer fat and berries. When the reindeer tried to destroy this house they filled their mouths with the fat and sour berries, which caused them to run off, shaking their heads so violently that all their long, sharp teeth fell out. Afterward small teeth, such as reindeer now have, grew in their places, and these animals became harmless.

Man and Raven returned to the sky after the reindeer ran away, Man saying, "If something is not done to stop people from taking so many animals they will continue until they have killed everything you have made. It is better to take away the sun from them so that they will be in the dark and will die."

To this Raven agreed, saying, "You remain here and I will go and take away the sun." So he went away and, taking the sun, put it into his skin bag and carried it far away to a part of the sky land where his parents lived, and it became very dark on earth. In his father's village Raven took to himself a wife from the maidens of the place and lived there, keeping the sun hidden carefully in the bag.

The people on earth were very much frightened when the sun was taken away, and tried to get it back by offering Raven rich presents of food and furs, but without effect. After many trials the people propitiated Raven so that he let them have the light for a short time. Then he would hold up the sun in one hand for two days at a time, so that the people could hunt and get food, after which it would be taken away and all would become dark. After this a long time would pass and it required many offerings before he would let them have light again. This was repeated many times.

Raven had living in this village an older brother who began to feel sorry for the earth people and to think of means by which he could get the sun and return it to its place. After he had thought a long time he pretended to die, and was put away in a grave box, as was customary. As soon as the mourners left his grave he arose and went out a short distance from the village, where he hid his raven mask and coat in a tree; then he went to the spring where the villagers got their water, and waited. In a short time his brother's wife came for water, and after she had filled her bucket she took up a ladle full of water to drink. As she drank, Raven's brother, by a magic spell, changed himself into a small leaf, falling into the ladle, and was swallowed with the water. The woman coughed and then hastened home, where she told her husband that she had swallowed some strange thing while drinking at the spring, to which he paid little attention, saying it was probably a small leaf.

Immediately after this the woman became with child, and in a few days gave birth to a boy, who was very lively and crept about at once and in a few days was running about. He cried continually for the sun, and, as the father was very fond of him, he frequently let the child have it for a plaything, but was always careful to take it back again. As soon as the boy began to play out of doors he cried and begged for the sun more than ever. After refusing for a long time, his father let him take the sun again and the boy played with it in the house, and then, when no one was looking, he carried it outside, ran quickly to the tree, put on his raven mask and coat, and flew far away with it. When he was far up from the sky he heard his father crying out to him, "Do not hide the sun. Let it out of the bag to make some light. Do not keep it always dark." For he feared his son had stolen it to keep it for himself.

Then Raven went home and the Raven boy flew on to the place where the sun belonged. There he tore off the skin covering and put the sun in its place again. From this place he saw a broad path leading far away, which he followed. It led him to the side of a hole surrounded by short grass glowing with light, some of which he plucked. He remembered that his father had called to him not to keep it always dark, but to make it partly dark and partly light. Thinking of this, he caused the sky to revolve, so that it moved around the earth, carrying the sun and stars with it, thus making day and night.

While he was standing close by the edge of the earth, just before sunrise, he stuck into the sky a bunch of the glowing grass that he held in his hand, and it has stayed there ever since, forming the brilliant morning star. Going down to the earth he came at last to the village where the first people lived. There the old people welcomed him, and he told them that Raven had been angry with them and had taken the sun away, but that he had put it back himself so that it would never be moved again.

Among the people who welcomed him was the headman of the sky dwarfs, who had come down with some of his people to live on the earth. Then the people asked him what had become of Man, who had gone up to the sky with Raven. This was the first time the Raven boy had heard of Man, and he tried to fly up to the sky to see him, but found that he could rise only a short distance above the earth. When he found that he could not get back to the sky, he wandered away until he came to a village where lived the children of the other men last born from the pea-vine. There he took a wife and lived a long time, having many children, all of whom became Raven people like himself and were able to fly over the earth, but they gradually lost their magic powers until finally they became ordinary ravens like the birds we see now on the tundras.

RAVEN TAKES A WIFE

(From the Unalit of Norton sound)

For a long time Raven lived alone, but finally became tired of this and decided to take a wife. For this purpose he looked about and noticed that it was late in the fall and that the birds were going southward in large flocks. Then Raven flew away and stopped directly in the path taken by the geese and other wild fowl on their way to the land of summer. As he sat by the way he saw a pretty young Hutchins goose coming near. Then he modestly hid his face by looking at his feet, and as the goose passed he called out, "Who wishes me for a husband? I am a very nice man." Unheeding him, the goose flew on, and Raven looked after her and sighed. Soon after a black brant passed, and Raven cried out as before, with the same result. He looked after her and cried out, "Ah, what kind of people are these? They do not even wait to listen." Again he waited, and a duck passed near, and when Raven cried out she turned a little toward him but passed on. For an instant his heart beat quickly with hope, and as the duck passed, he cried, "Ah, I came very near then; perhaps I shall succeed this time;" and he stood waiting with bowed head.

Very soon a family of white-front Geese came along, consisting of the parents with four brothers and a sister, and the Raven cried out, "Who wishes me for a husband? I am a fine hunter and am young and handsome." As he finished they alighted just beyond him, and he thought, "Now I will get a wife." Then he looked about and saw a pretty white stone with a hole in it lying near; he picked it up and, stringing it on a long grass stem, hung it about his neck. As soon as he had done this he pushed up his bill so that it slid to the top of his head like a mask, and he became a dark-colored young man, who walked up to the Geese. At the same time each of the Geese pushed up its bill in the same manner, and they became nice-looking people. Raven was much pleased with the looks of the girl and, going to her, gave her the stone, choosing her for his wife, and she hung it about her own neck. Then all pushed down their bills, becoming birds again, and flew away toward the south.

The Geese flapped their wings heavily and worked slowly along, but Raven with his outspread wings glided on faster than his party, while the geese looked after him, exclaiming, in admiration, "How light and graceful he is!" At length Raven grew weary, so he said, "We had better stop early and look for a place to sleep." The others agreed to this, so they stopped and were soon asleep.

Early next morning the Geese were astir and wished to be off, but Raven still slept so heavily that they had to arouse him. The father Goose said, "We must make haste, for it will snow here soon; let us not linger."

As soon as Raven was fully awake he pretended to be eager to get away, and, as on the day before, led the others with outspread wings and was greatly admired by his young companions. And so Raven kept on, above or in front of his companions, who made admiring remarks to one another, such as "Ah, see how light and graceful he is." Thus the party traveled on until they stopped one evening upon the seashore, where they feasted upon the berries that were plentiful all about them, and then went to sleep.

Early the next morning the Geese made ready to go without stopping for breakfast. Raven's stomach cried out for some of the fine berries that were so plentiful, but the Geese would not wait, so he dared not object to starting. As they left the seashore the father Goose told them that they would stop to rest once on the way, and the next stretch would bring them to the other shore. Raven began to feel very doubtful about being able to reach the other shore, but he was ashamed to say so and thought he would risk making the attempt; so off they all flew. The Geese flew steadily on and on. After a long time Raven began to fall behind. His wide-spread wings ached, yet the Geese kept on steadily and untiringly. Raven flapped heavily along, and then would glide on outspread pinions for a time, trying to ease his tired wings, but to no purpose, so he fell farther and farther behind. Finally the Geese looked back, and the father Goose exclaimed, "I thought he was light and active, but he must be getting tired; let us wait." Then the Geese settled close together in the water, and Raven came laboring up and sunk upon their backs, gasping for breath. In a short time he partly recovered, and, putting one hand on his breast, said, "I have an arrowhead here from an old war I was in and it pains me greatly; that is the reason I fell behind."

After resting they went on, but the others had to wait for Raven again, and he repeated the story of the arrowhead, which he told them had pierced his heart. Then he had his wife put her hand on his breast to feel it shaking about. She did so, but could feel only his heart beating like a hammerstone and no sign of an arrowpoint, yet she said nothing. Thus they went on, and again they waited for Raven, but now the brothers began to talk about him, saying among themselves, "I do not believe that story about the arrowhead. How could he live with an arrowhead in his heart?"

When they were rested they saw the far-away shore before them. The father Goose now told Raven that they would wait for him no more until they reached the land. Then all arose and flew on, Raven slowly flapping his wings, which felt very heavy. The Geese kept steadily on toward the shore, while Raven sank lower and lower, getting nearer and nearer to the dreaded water. As he came close to the waves he cried and shrieked to his wife, "Leave me the white stone! Throw it back to me!" for it contained magical properties. Thus he kept crying until suddenly his wings lost their power and he floated helplessly in the water as the Geese gained the shore. He tried to rise from the water, but his wings seemed to be weighted down, and he drifted back and forth along the beach. The waves arose, and soon succeeding white caps buried him until he was soaked, and only with the greatest difficulty could he get his beak above the surface to breathe a little between the waves. After a long time a great wave cast him upon the land. Then, as it flowed back, he dug his claws into the pebbles and only by great effort did he save himself from being dragged back again into the sea. As soon as he was able he struggled up the beach, an unhappy-looking object. The water ran in streams from his soaked feathers and his wings dragged on the ground. He fell several times, and at last, with wide-gaping mouth, reached some bushes, where he pushed up his beak and became a small, dark-colored man. Then he took off his raven coat and mask, hanging them on a bush, while he made a fire-drill out of some pieces of wood and soon had a fire burning, before which he dried himself.

THE RAVEN, THE WHALE, AND THE MINK

[This tale is related either separately or in conjunction with the fore-going legend, of which it forms a part.]

After Raven had dried his clothing at the fire he chanced to look toward the sea and saw a large whale passing close along the shore, and he cried out, "When you come up again shut your eyes and open your mouth wide." Quickly putting on his raven coat, he drew down his mask, then, carrying his fire-drill under his wings, flew out over the water. The whale soon came up again and did as it was told, and when Raven saw the open mouth he flew straight down the whale's throat. The whale closed its mouth and went down again, while Raven stood looking about, finding himself at the entrance of a fine room, at one end of which burned a lamp. He went in and was surprised to see a very beautiful young woman sitting there. The place was clean and dry, the roof being supported by the whale's spine, while its ribs formed the walls. From a tube that extended along the whale's backbone, oil was dropping slowly into the lamp. When Raven stepped in the woman started up and cried out, "How came you here? You are the first man who ever came in here." Raven told how he came there, and she asked him to be seated on the other side of the room. This woman was the shade or *inua* of the whale, which was a female. Then she prepared him food, giving him some berries and oil, at the same time telling him that she had gathered the berries the year before. For four days Raven stayed there as the guest of the *inua*, and continually wondered what the tube was that ran along the roof of the house. Each time the woman left the room she told him that he must not touch it. At last, when she left the room again, he went to the lamp, and holding out his claw caught a large drop of the oil and licked it with his tongue. It tasted so sweet that he began to catch and eat other drops as fast as they fell. This soon became too slow for him, so he reached up and tore a piece from the side of the tube and ate it. As soon as this was done a great rush of oil poured into the room, extinguishing the light, while the room itself began to roll wildly about. This continued for four days and Raven was nearly dead from weariness and the bruises which he had received. Then the room became still and the whale was dead, for Raven had torn off a part of one of the heart vessels. The *inua* never came back to the room, and the whale drifted upon the shore.

Raven now found himself a prisoner, and while trying to think of a plan for escaping, heard two men talking on top of the whale, and proposing to bring all of their village mates to the place. This was done very quickly, and the people soon had a hole made through the upper side of the whale's body. This hole was enlarged until, watching his chance while everybody was carrying a load of meat to the shore, Raven flew out and alighted on the top of a hill close by without being noticed. Then he remembered that he had left his fire-drill behind, and exclaimed, "Ah, my good fire-drill; I have forgotten it." He quickly removed his raven mask and coat, becoming a young man again, and started along the shore toward the whale. The people on the carcass soon saw a small, dark-colored man in a strangely made deerskin coat coming toward them, and they looked at him curiously. Raven drew near and said, "Ho, you have found a fine, large whale. Well, I will help you cut him up." He rolled up his sleeves and set to work. Very soon a man working inside the whale's body cried out, "Ah, see what I have found. A fire-drill inside the whale." At once Raven began to roll

18 ETH——30

down his sleeves, saying, "That is bad, for my daughter has told me that if a fire-drill is found in a whale and people try to cut up that whale many of them will die. I shall run away." And away he ran.

When Raven had gone the people looked at one another and said, "Perhaps he is right;" and away they all ran, every one trying to rub the oil off his hands as he went. From his hiding place near by Raven looked on and laughed as the people ran away, and then he went for his mask and coat. After procuring them he returned to the whale and began cutting it up and carrying the flesh back from the shore. As he thought of the feast in store for him he even said, "Thanks" to the shades.

When he had stored away enough meat he wished to save some oil, but had no bag to put it in, so he walked along the shore trying to find a seal. He had gone only a short distance when he saw a mink run swiftly by, and he called out, "What are you running after so fast? Are you going for something to eat?"

Mink stopped, and pushing up his nose like a mask, as Raven had done with his beak, became a small, dark-colored man. Then Raven cried, "Ah, you will be my friend? I have plenty of food, but I am lonely, for I have no one with me." To this Mink agreed, and both walked back to the whale and went to work, but Mink did the most for Raven was very lazy.

They made grass bags and mats for the meat and blubber, storing great quantities of it in holes in the ground. After this was done they built a fine kashim. When it was finished Raven said, "It is lonely; let us make a feast." And he told Mink to go out and invite the sea people to join them.

To this Mink agreed, so next morning he started out, while Raven made a short, round, slender rod, at one end of which he painted two rings with charcoal paint. When he had finished this, he gathered a large ball of sticky spruce gum, which he placed with the rod in the kashim.

Mink soon returned and told Raven that on the morrow plenty of sea people would come to the feast. To this Raven answered, "Thanks." Early the next morning Mink called Raven outside and pointed toward the sea, the surface of which was covered with different kinds of seals coming to the feast. Raven went back into the kashim, while Mink went down to the water to meet the guests and escort them to the house.

As each seal came on shore he pushed up his mask and became a small man, and all entered the house until it was full. Raven looked about at the guests and exclaimed, "What a number of people. How shall I be able to make a feast for all of you? But never mind; let me first rub the eyes of some of you with this stuff, in order that you may be able to see better; it is dark in here."

With his ball of gum Raven then fastened shut the eyes of every seal, except a small one near the door, which he overlooked. The last seal whose eyes were shut was also a small one, and as soon as its eyes were made fast it tried to get them open, and began to cry. The little one by the door cried out to the others, "Raven has stuck your eyes shut, and you can not open them." Then every seal tried to open his eyes, but could not. With the stick he had made the day before Raven now killed all the guests by striking them on the head, each seal man changing back to a seal as it was killed. As soon as the little one by the door saw Raven killing his companions, it ran out and escaped alone into the sea.

When he had finished, Raven turned to Mink and said, "See what a lot of seals I have killed. We will have plenty of oil bags now." Then they made bags of the sealskins and filled them with oil for the winter. Ever since that time Raven and Mink have been friends, and even to this day ravens will not eat the flesh of a mink, be they ever so hungry; and the mink and the raven are often found very close together on the tundras.

THE RED BEAR (TA-KU'-KA)

(From St Michael and Norton sound)

On the seashore, near where the village of Pikmiktalik now stands, there once lived the Eskimo hunter Pi-tĭkh'-cho-lĭk' and his wife Ta ku'-ka. The mountains were filled with great herds of reindeer and the sea was full of seals and fish, so that Pi-tĭkh'-cho-lĭk' brought home an abundance of food and skins.

One fine summer evening Ta-ku'-ka stood on the seashore waiting for her husband's return. She was uneasy and anxious, as he had remained away much longer than usual on his recent hunting excursions, although he had explained to her that the deer were getting farther back into the mountains and the seals were to be found only farther at sea.

After a time Ta-ku'-ka went into the house to attend to her children and when she came out again her husband was putting his kaiak on the framework standing by the house.

She asked him many questions about his long stay, but he replied peevishly that he had gone far out to sea and had remained because he did not wish to come home without game. When they went into the house Ta-ku'-ka placed before him different kinds of food, prepared as he liked it best, but he ate very little, and seemed gloomy and sad. His wife urged him to tell her the cause of his sadness, and at last he said, "If you must know the cause of my sadness, hear it. I feel that I am going to die, and the third day from now will be the time of my death."

At this Ta-ku'-ka began to cry very bitterly, but he stopped her, saying, "Do not cry and make me unhappy while I am with you, but hear my last wishes. When I am dead you must put my kaiak into the water and fasten it to the shore; lay my paddle, spears, and lines upon it in their proper places; dress my body in the waterproof shirt and put me into the kaiak, fastening the shirt to the manhole as you have seen me do when going to sea. Every evening for three days place fish, deer fat, and berries before my body that my *inua* may be satisfied. Do you promise me this?" Ta-ku-'ka promised and wept silently. Pi-tĭkh'-cho-lĭk' did not leave the house again, and he died on the third day. Then Ta-ku'-ka cried very much, but did as she had been told. Every morning she saw that the shade had eaten, for all the food before the body was gone. On the fourth morning, when she went to the shore to lament for her dead as usual, she saw that the kaiak with all its contents had disappeared. Then she threw herself upon the ground and lay there for a long time in her sorrow; finally she remembered her children and went back to the house to care for them. For a long time Ta-ku'-ka worked very hard, gathering berries or catching and drying fish to prepare her store of winter food.

One day while gathering berries she wandered far from home and went to the top of a mountain; there she looked out over the land and far away saw puffs of smoke drifting upward from the ground. This was the first sign she had ever seen of other people, and she decided to go to see what they were like. After some time she drew near the place and crept softly to the edge of the hill, that fell away sharply on one side to the sea, but sloped gradually toward a portion of the inland side. Near the water were three houses, from one of which came the smoke she had seen.

Here Ta-ku'-ka waited quietly to see what kind of people were there, and soon a woman came out, shading her eyes with one hand and looking out to sea; then she hurried back to the house, calling to someone within. At this two other women came out, and all went down to the water's edge, where they began to sing a love song and to dance upon the sand facing the sea. Ta-ku'-ka had been so interested in watching these women and their handsome fur garments that she had not noticed anything else, but now the low, pleasant sound of a man's voice rising in song struck her ear and made her heart beat faster. She looked beyond the women and saw a man urging his kaiak swiftly toward the shore, singing and playfully throwing his seal spear before him, and picking it up as he passed.

When he came near, Ta-ku'-ka recognized the song as one that Pi-tĭkh'-cho-lĭk' used to sing to her in the old days; then the kaiak man came on shore and the women met him with exclamations of pleasure. Ta-ku'-ka could scarcely believe her eyes when she saw that the man was indeed her husband, whom she had believed to be dead. He went into the house with the women, and Ta-ku'-ka felt a strange, fierce anger in her heart, such as she had never known before. She stood on the hillside listening to the songs and laughter coming from the house until far into the night.

Morning came and Pi-tĭkh'-cho-lĭk' came out of the house and arranged his hunting gear upon the kaiak. After saying "good-bye" to the women on the shore he paddled out to sea, singing pleasantly. When he was out of sight Ta-ku'-ka went down from the hillside and followed the women into one of the houses; they seemed surprised to see her, but made her welcome, asking her many questions. They admired her face and its color, which was lighter than theirs, also several tattooed lines on her face, one up and down between her eyes and three that extended down across the chin from her lower lip; they were also pleased with the shape of her garments, which were different from theirs. By and by one of the women said, "You are very handsome with the beautiful lines marked on your face; I would give much if you would teach me how to make my face like yours." Ta-ku'-ka answered, "I will show you how it is done, if I can please you, but it will hurt you and you may not wish to bear the pain." "I shall not mind the pain," said the woman, "for I wish to be handsome, as you are, and am ready to bear it." "Be it as you wish," said Ta-ku'-ka. "Go into the house and make a fire, and put by it a large clay pot, filled with oil; when the oil boils call me. I will make your face beautiful like mine." When the woman had thanked her and had gone to make ready, the other women asked her many questions. "Will it hurt very much?" and "Will she really be as pretty as you are?" and others. To which Ta-ku'-ka replied, "She will not be hurt very much, and she will be prettier even than I."

In a short time the woman came back, saying that the oil was ready. Ta-ku'-ka then went into the house and told her to kneel before the pot of boiling oil and to bend her face over it. As soon as this was done, Ta-ku'-ka grasped her by the hair and thrust her face down into the hot oil and held it there until the woman was dead, saying, "There, you will always be beautiful now." Then she laid the body on the bed platform, and covering the face, went back to the other women. During her absence the other two had been talking together, and when she came back they asked her if she had succeeded in making their companion handsome, and Ta-ku'-ka nodded her head.

Then both women said, "We, too, will make you presents if you will make us beautiful," and she consented. Then all went to the dead woman's house, and Ta-ku'-ka said to her companions, "Do not disturb your friend; she sleeps now and her face is covered so that nothing will break the charm; when she awakes she will be very handsome." After this she killed both the other women as she had the first, saying, as she laid them on the ground, "You, too, will be very pretty." She then made three crosses of sticks and placed them upright in the sand where the women had danced on the shore the evening before, upon which she placed the clothing of the dead women so that a person at a distance would think they were standing there. Thén she took a red bearskin and went back to her hiding place in the rocks. Evening came, and the hunter drew near, singing as on the previous night. No answer reached him, but he thought he saw his wives standing on the shore, and although he raised his song in praise of them, they gave no answer. He became angry and stopped his song; then he began to scold and upbraid them, but still they were silent. Landing, he hurried to the silent figures and then on to the nearest house. There and at the second house he found nothing, but in the last he saw his wives as they lay dead, and Ta-ḱu'-ka heard his cries of sorrow when he saw them.

Pi-tĭkh'-cho-lĭk' rushed raging from the house, wailing with sorrow, shouting in wild anger, "If any bad spirits have done this, I fear them not. Let them come and try to work their evil upon me. I hate and scorn them." All remained quiet. "If any evil shade, man or beast, has done this, let it come out from its hiding place," he shouted, "and dare to face a man who will tear out its heart and eat its blood; oh, miserable good-for-nothing!"

As if in answer, he heard a deep growl coming from the hillside, and there he saw a red bear standing on its hind feet, swaying its body back and forth. This was Ta-ku'-ka, who had placed a flat stone on each side of her body to protect herself from wounds by arrow or spear and had wrapped herself in the bearskin.

Pi-tĭkh'-cho-lĭk' saw her and thought she was really a bear and began calling every opprobrious name he could think of, while he quickly fitted an arrow to his bow and loosed it. The arrow struck one of the stones and fell harmless, and the bear turned its other side toward him. Again he shot a well aimed arrow, and again it fell harmless. Then the bear rushed down the slope straight at him, and Pi-tĭkh'-cho-lĭk''s spear, striking the bear's side, broke in his hands. In a few moments the bear had thrown him down lifeless and torn out and eaten his heart. Then the fury which had urged Ta-ku'-ka on seemed to leave her and her better feelings began to return. She tried to take off the bearskin, but it closed about her so firmly that she could not.

Suddenly Ta-ku'-ka thought of her children at home, so taking her basket of berries from the hilltop, she started for her dwelling. As she went along she began to be frightened at her strange desire for blood, mingled with the thoughts of her children. Hurrying on she came at last to the house and rushed in. The two children were asleep, and as soon as Ta-ku'-ka saw them a fierce, uncontrollable desire for blood again came over her, so that she at once tore them to pieces. After this she went out and wandered over the earth, filled with a desire to destroy every one she came across.

Up to that time red bears had been harmless, but Ta-ku'-ka filled them with her own rage, so that they have been very savage ever since. Finally she reached Kuskokwim river and was killed by a hunter, whose arrow found its way through a crack that had been made in one of the stones on her side.

THE GIANT (KIÑ′-ÄK)

(From Unalaklit, Norton sound)

One dark winter night a woman ran through the village of Nĭkh′-tă and out on to the snow-covered tundra; she was fleeing from her husband whose cruelty had become unbearable. All through the night and for many days afterward she traveled on toward the north, always going around the villages she came near, fearing that she might be pursued. Finally she left all signs of human life behind, and the cold became more and more intense; her small supply of food was exhausted and she began to eat snow to lessen her hunger. One day, as evening drew nigh, she was in such a wind-swept place that she forced herself to go on. At last she saw before her what seemed to be a hill with five elevations on its crest; when she came to it she saw that it looked like an enormous human foot. Removing the snow from between two elevations, that looked like huge toes, she found it warm and comfortable, and slept there until morning, when she started and walked toward a single elevation that showed in the snowy level. This she reached near nightfall and noticed that it appeared to be shaped like a great knee. Finding a sheltered place by it she stayed there until morning, when she went on. That evening a hill like a huge thigh sheltered her for the night. The next night she was sheltered in a round pit-like hollow, around which grew scattered brush; as she left this place in the morning it appeared to her like a great navel.

The next night she slept near two hills shaped like enormous breasts; the night following she found a sheltered, comfortable hollow, where she slept. As she was about to start from there in the morning a great voice seemed to come from beneath her feet, saying: "Who are you? What has driven you to me, to whom human beings never come?" She was very much frightened, but managed to tell her sorrowful tale, and then the voice spoke again: "Well, you may stay here, but you must not sleep again near my mouth nor on my lips, for if I should breathe on you it would blow you away. You must be hungry. I will get you something to eat."

While she waited it suddenly occurred to her that for five days she had been traveling on the body of the giant, Kĭñ′-ă-g′âk′, or Kĭñ′-äk. Then the sky became suddenly obscured, and a great black cloud came swiftly toward her; when it was near she saw that it was the giant's hand, which opened and dropped a freshly killed reindeer, and the voice told her to eat of it. Very quickly she got some of the brushwood that grew all about, made a fire, and ate heartily of the roasted flesh. The giant spoke again: "I know you wish a place in which to rest, and it is best for you to go into my beard where it grows most thickly, for I wish to take breath now and to clear from my lungs the hoarfrost which has gathered there and which bothers me; so go quickly."

She barely had time to get down into the giant's beard when a furious gale of wind rushed over her head, accompanied by a blinding snow-storm, which ended as quickly as it began, after extending far out over the tundra, and the sky became clear once more.

The next day Kiñ-äk told her to find a good place and build herself a hut of hairs from his beard. She looked about and chose a spot on the left side of the giant's nose, not far from his nostril, and built her hut from hairs taken from his mustache. Here she lived for a long time, the giant supplying her wants by reaching out his great hand and capturing deer, seals, and whatever she wished for food. From the skins of wolves, wolverines, and other fur-bearing animals that he caught for her she made herself handsome clothing, and in a little time had on hand a great store of skins and furs.

Kiñ-äk began to find his mustache getting thin, as she used the hairs for firewood, so forbade her using any more of it, but told her to get some of the hair growing down the side of his face whenever she needed any. Thus a long time passed.

One day Kiñ-äk asked her if she would not like to return home. "Yes," she replied, "only I fear my husband will beat me again, and I shall have no one who will protect me."

"I will protect you," said he. "Go and cut the ear tips from all the skins you have and put them in the basket. Then set yourself before my mouth, and whenever you are in danger remember to call, 'Kiñ-äk, Kiñ-äk, come to me,' and I will protect you. Go now and do as I have told you. It is time. I have grown tired of lying so long in one place and wish to turn over, and if you were here you would be crushed." Then the woman did as she had been told, and crouched before his mouth.

At once there burst forth a tempest of wind and fine snow, and the woman felt herself driven before it until she became sleepy and closed her eyes. When she awoke she was on the ground before the houses of Nïkh'-tă, but could not believe it was so until she heard the familiar howling of the dogs. She waited until evening, and after placing the basket of ear tips in her storehouse, entered her husband's home. He had long mourned her as dead, and his pleasure was very great when she returned. Then she told her story and her husband promised never to treat her badly again. When he went to his storehouse the next day he was very much surprised to find it filled with valuable furs, for every ear tip brought by his wife had turned into a complete skin during the night.

These skins made him very rich, so that he became one of the head-men of the village. After a time he began to feel badly because they had no children, and said to his wife, "What will become of us when we are old and weak, with no one to care for us? Ah, if we could but have a son." One day he told his wife to bathe herself carefully; then he dipped a feather in oil and with it drew the form of a boy on her abdomen. In due time she bore a son and they were very happy.

The boy grew rapidly and excelled all of his youthful companions in strength, agility, and marksmanship. He was named Kiñ-äk, in memory of the giant. Then by degrees the husband became unkind and harsh as he had been before, until one day he became so enraged that he caught up a large stick to beat his wife. She ran out of the house in fear, but slipped and fell just outside, and her husband was close upon her when she remembered the giant and called " Kiñ-äk! Kiñ-äk! come to me." Scarcely had she said these words when a terrible blast of wind passed over her, blowing her husband away, and he was never seen again.

The years passed until young Kiñ-äk grew to be a handsome and powerful young man and became a very successful hunter, but he had a fierce and cruel temper. One evening he came home and told his mother that he had quarreled with two of his companions and had killed both of them. His mother remonstrated with him, telling of the danger he would be in from the blood revenge of the relatives of the murdered men. Time went on, and the matter seemed to be forgotten.

Again Kiñ-äk came home with a tale of having killed a companion. After this every few days he would quarrel with someone and end by killing him; at last he had killed so many people that his mother refused to permit him to live with her any longer. He seemed greatly surprised at this, saying, "Are you not my mother? How is it that you can thus treat me?"

"Yes," she replied, " I am your mother, but your evil temper has ended in killing or driving away all our friends. Everyone hates and fears you, and soon no one will be left living in the village except old women and children. Go away; leave this place, for it will be better for all of us."

Kiñ-äk made no reply, but for some time he hunted continually until he had filled his mother's storehouse with food and skins. Then he went to her, saying, "Now that I have provided you with food and skins, as was my duty, I am ready to leave," and he went forth.

By chance he took the same road his mother had traveled during her flight, and came at last to the giant's head. When the giant understood that he was the son of the woman who had been there he permitted the young man to stay on his face, but told him never to come about his lips, for if he ventured there evil would befall him. For some time Kiñ-äk lived there quietly, but at last made up his mind to go upon the giant's lip and see what was there. After a great deal of hard work in getting through the tangled thicket of beard on the giant's chin he reached the mouth. The moment he stepped upon the lips and approached the opening between them a mighty blast of wind swept forth and he was hurled into the air and never seen again.

The giant still lives in the north, although no one has ever been to him since that day; but whenever he breathes the fierce snow-drifting north winds of winter make his existence known.

THE ONE-WHO-FINDS-NOTHING (PI-CHU'-I-LĬÑ-UK)

(From St Michael)

Once there was a small, ugly-face young man who could never find anything that he looked for. Whenever he went out with his sled for wood, he returned without any, because he could never succeed in finding any, not the least piece. Then he entered the kashim and sat down in his place over the entrance way. When he sat down there he would remain quiet for a long time. The one sitting beside him sometimes gave him water, which he would drink and then become quite still again.

If forced to go out, he would put on his boots and go, but would return again very soon and sit as before. Once when thirsty he went out to the water hole for a drink, but when he came to the place he could not find the water hole, as it seemed not to be there. Then he returned to the kashim again without drinking and sat down in his place, the one beside him giving him water.

At night in bed, not being able to sleep and being thirsty, he went out to find his elder brother's house. After much searching he could not find the place, so went back to the kashim and lay down. Awaking in the morning, he took some fishing tackle and went fishing. When he came to the water he could not find it, and after looking for it unsuccessfully he returned without fishing. Thus he came back once more without anything and was hungry also when he sat in his place as usual.

Then he thought, "If I go to pick berries I suppose I will not be able to find any." Taking a wooden bucket he went for berries. After looking, but failing to find any, he returned to his place in the kashim. The next morning, becoming hungry, he took his arrows and went hunting for wild geese. Not finding any, and seeing nothing else, he returned again. Other men brought back hair seals they had killed. The One-who-finds-nothing took his kaiak and putting it into the water went out seal hunting. He hunted long for the seals, but there seemed to be none; and seeing nothing, he came back to his place in the kashim.

Winter came, and he thought, "I do not know what to do with myself." The next day he took his miserable bed and rolled it up with his poor tool bag, put the bundle on his back, and went out to the landward side of the village, beyond the houses, and sat down. Being seated, he took his bundle from his back and, opening it, untied his tool bag. This being done, he scattered the tools about him and threw away the bag. Then he spread down his bed and, sitting upon it, lay back, saying, "Here will I die."

There he lay all night without moving. When the sun came up he heard a Raven croaking, and then its mate. He remained quiet and the Raven came, alighting near him with its mate just beyond. The nearest Raven spoke, saying, "Look! here is something to eat. We have not eaten, and we had better not wait. Let us have his eyes." The farthest Raven answered, "No, he is not dead." "Why does he lie there, then, as if he were dead?" said the first Raven. "No, he is not dead; for look there, there is no smoke[1] by him," replied the second one.

Then the first Raven became enraged and cast himself about, saying, "Why is he thrown out, then? Look at his things scattered about him." "I do not wish any of it," said the mate, "there is no smoke by him. I will leave you." And he flew away. "All right; you can fly off," said the first Raven; "I will have his eyes."

Then the man opened his eyes very slightly and looked sidewise at the Raven. This one, coming toward the small, ugly-face young man, stood there holding up his beak, which became a fine knife. He went nearer, and between his eyelashes the man saw, raised by the hilt, a fine knife. He thought, "I have no knife." Then the point came close to him. He thought again, "I have no knife." He suddenly caught it and snatched it away from the Raven.

Back sprang Raven, and the man sat up. "Give me my knife," said Raven. The man answered, saying, "I have no knife, and this shall be my knife. The Raven replied, "I will pay you for it with all kinds of game."

"No," said the man, "I will not give it back. I always go out hunting and can get nothing." "Then," said the Raven, "if you wish to go back to the village you will not reach there when you try." "I have no knife," replied the man. Here the Raven coughed and fell down, saying, "Thus will you do. Keep my knife, if you prize it," said he, and flew away.

The man sat up, still keeping the knife. Then he started to go back to the village. As he was going his throat contracted, his back bent over in front, and he rested his hands on his knees. Suddenly he became an old man. He could not walk. He lay on his face. He did not stir. He was dead.

Following is the same tale in Eskimo with an English interlinear translation:

Pi-chu'-i-liñ-uk (The One-who-finds-nothing)

Nu-gŭlth'-pĭ-ŭñ'-ĭ-na'-g'ŭk	pi'-chu-i'-tok	ŭ-kukh-tŭkh'-ka-mĭ	ka-mĭgh'-ŭ-
A small, ugly-face young man	(who) can not find (anything)	going out for wood	with a

lu'-nĭ ŭ-kukh'	tai'-g'o-hlŭkh'-tok	ă-ko-ja'-gĭ-jakh'-lu-nĭ	u'-tŭkh-naukh'-tok.
sled the wood	he goes to bring	without finding any	again returned he.

Ú-ku'-gŭ-mŭk	tŭñkh'-pŭ-kĭn'-än-ĭ	u'-tŭkh-naukh'-tok	p'kĭkh'-pŭk-tĭ-kit'-
The wood	having seen none of it	again returned he	without the least

---

[1] Of his burial fire.

naukh-tok chŭñ-i'-năg-ŭ-lu'-nĭ.   Käj'-ĭ-gĭ-naukh'-tok a-mim' ko-l'i'-nun ukh-
came back   having none.   The kashim went into   the   above   sat
he   door

naukh'-tok ukh-chă'-mĭ wi'-tän-aukh'-tok.   Chĭ-kĭ-ĭkh'-kät-nĭ um chûn-ĭk'-
down he   sitting down   there remained he.   When given   (by) along-
                                                              him

hlĭ-mĭ mŭg'-ŭ-naukh'-tok.   Tŭk-hnŭ'-mĭ tau-ătn' wi'-tän-aukh'-tok.   Kum-
side   water drank he.   Finishing   thus   there remained he.   His

gu'-gĭ-nĭ tĭ-gu-a'-mĭ-gĭk ät-nau'-gŭk än-aukh'-tok.   Tslûk-wha'-mĭ än-ûg-ŭ-
boots   taking   putting on went out he.   Outside   defe-

naukh'-tok kho'-hlu-ĭ-ni'-hlu i-tûg'-ŭ-naukh'-tok it-kha'-mĭ ukh-naukh'-tok.
cated he   urinated and   came back he   coming in   sat down he.

Ukh-chŭ'-mĭ wi'-tän-aukh'-tok.   Mŭk'-shu-a'-mĭ än-aukh'-tok la'g'ŭ-mun'
Sitting down   there remained he.   Being thirsty   out went he   to the water-
                                                                   hole

tĭ-bvû-naukh'-tok tĭ-kĭ-chä-mĭu' nau'-gwa la'-gŭkh-tai'-tŭk mŭkh'-pû-kĭn'-
went he   coming to it   again   the water-hole   without drink-
                                                             was not (there)

än-ĭ u-tûkh-naukh'-tok Käj'-ĭ-gĭ'-mun it-kha'-mĭ nu-na'-mi-nun' ukh-cha'-mĭ
ing   returned he again   to the kashim. reaching   to his place   sitting down

wi'-tän-aukh'-tok. Chän-ĭk'-hli-mĭ chi-kĭ-an'-ĭ mûgh'-ŭ-mŭk' mugh'-ŭ-naukh'-
there remained he. The one beside giving   water   drank
                    him

tok tau'-a wi'-tän-aukh'-tok.   U-nug'-ŭ-mĭ kau-âg'-u-jun-ĭ-gĭkh'-ka'-mĭ än-
he thus   there remained he.   At night   not sleeping   out

aukh'-tok än-ĭñ-a'-mĭ nĭ-mun' mŭk'-shu-a'-mĭ ŭ'-gĭ-naukh'-tok nĭ-tai'-g'ŭt-
went he to his elder the house being thirsty   went he   but found it
         brother   of

naukh'-tok nĭ-shog'-ŭ-jakh'-lu-nĭ käj'-ĭ-gĭ-naukh'-tok i'-nûkh-naukh'-tok.
not he   searching much for it   went to the Käj-ga he   laid down he.

Tu-pi'-mĭ män-a'-ko-tŭg'-ĭ-nĭk tĭ-gu'-chä-mĭ män-ûg'-ŭ-jŭg'-ŭ-lu'-nĭ ai-ûg-ŭ-
Awaking   fishing tackle   taking   fishing   went

naukh'-tok.   Mûgh'-ŭ-mun' tĭ-kĭ'-chä-mĭ mûkh-tai'-g'u-tŭk tau'-ă mĭ-shog'-
he.   To the water   coming   water was not   and then searching

ĭ-jakh' lu-nĭ   män-ûkh'-pu-kĭn'-än-ĭ u-tûkh-naukh'-tok tĭ-gĭt-naukh'-tok
unsuccessfully   not fishing   returned again he   brought   he

chûn-i'-năg-ŭ-lu'-nĭ nû'-gû-hu-mĭl'-ĭ-g'ĭ-ă'-whă tĭ-kĭ'-chä-mĭ nu-na'-mi-nun'
nothing   hungry was he also   coming   to his place

ukh-naukh'-tok.   Um'-ju-ûkh'-tĭ-kok ä-chûkh-cho'-ku-ma'-gĭk ä-chûkh'-mĭñ-
sat down he.   Thought he   berries if I go to pick   perhaps I will

ai-tlĭl-û-g'ĭ-añ'-ă.   Käthl-tă'-mŭk tĭ-gu'-cha-mĭ ai-ûkh'-tok ä-chŭs'-ăg-ĭ-
not be able to get   A bucket   taking   goes he   having searched
any.

jăkh'-lu-nĭ u-tûkh'-tok ă-chûkh'-tof-kĭ-na'-nĭ.   Tĭ-kĭ'-cha-mĭ nu-na'-mi-nun'
for them   back went without getting any.   Coming back   to his place
unsuccessfully he

ukh-chă'-mĭ wi'-tauk.   Nŭ'-gû-juñ-a'-mĭ u-nu-â'-ko-ûn-ûkh-chûn' khu'-nĭ-
sitting down   is there. Becoming hungry   morning the next   taking

tĭg'-u-a'-mĭ-gĭ   *ai-ăkh'-tok*   *tĭñ'-û-mĭ-ûkh'-chog-û-lu'-nĭ*   *tĭñ'-û-mĭ-a'-shăg-*
his arrows   goes he   hunting wild geese   for the geese

û-ja'-kok tĭñ'-û-mi-ûkh-tai'-tûk. Tûñ-ĭn'-û-g'i-la'-mĭ u-tûkh'-tok. Yút'-ẃhă
hunted he   wild geese are none.   Seeeing nothing   returned he.   Men other

mûk-hlûg'-ĭn-ĭk   *tĭ'-ki-ok-mĭl-û-g'it*   *ĭhl-mún'*   *pi-ta'-mûkh-nĭk.*   *Ĭm'-ĭ-nă*
hair seals   bringing them   by them-   taken.   That (one)
                         selves

pi'-chu-i'-lĭñ-ok   *kai-a'-nĭ*   *ät-khăkh'-chă-miu*   *ai-akh'-tok*   *mûk'-lûkh-chog'-*
one who finds   his kaiak   putting down   goes he   hair seal
nothing

û-lu'-nĭ.   *Mú-klû'-shăg ĭ-ja'-kok*   *mûk'-lûkh-tai'-tok*   *u-tûkh'-tok*   *tûñkh'-pú-*
hunting.   For hair seals hunts he   hair seals are not   back went he   seeing

kĭn-än'-ĭ   *tĭ-ki'-chă-mĭ*   *ẃi'-tauk.*   *Uk-shog'-û-lu'-nĭ*   *hlu*   *um'-ĭ-a'-gu-tok*
nothing   coming   there.   Winter coming   and   thinks he

ĭhl-mi'-nĭk kai-ukh'-ẃhú-tûk pi-l'hi'.   *U'-nu-ấ'-ko-ûn ă-hli'-kŏ-bvû'-hlu-a'-nĭ*
himself   don't know   what   The next day   his miserable bed
                   to do.

tĭ-gu-o'-mĭu   *hlĭl'-ûg'-û-ẃi'-hlu-a-nĭ*   *ă-hli'-ko-bvúg'-û-mi'-nun*   *i'-mû-gu'-ta*
taking   and his mean tool bag   putting in his bed   rolling it up

ät'-mi-okh'-tok   *ät-mi'-miu*   *ai-ăkh'-tok*   *nu-num*   *ƚun-i'-nun*   *nĭ-tä-lokh'-chă-*
a bundle he   ties it on   goes he   to the   side   the houses
makes   land

mi'-kĭ   *a-ku'-mûk.*   *A-kum'-uñ-am-ĭ*   *ät-mûg'-û-nĭ*   *mä-tûkh'-tai*   *añ-i'-tai*
beyond   sits down.   Being seated   the bundle   taking off   undoing it

añ-i'-chä-mĭ'-kĭ hli'-lûg û-ẃi'-nĭ tĭg-u-a'-miu añ-i'-tăi. Käthl-pûkh-chă'-miu
being undone   the tool bag   taking   undoing it.   Being open

i-man'-ĭ ûkh kă'-kai a-ẃät-mi'-nun hli'-lûg-û-ẃi'-ni-hlu.   *Ă-hli'-û-ku-pa-nĭ*
the con-   throwing   around him   the bag too.   His bedding
tents

tĭ'-gu-a'-miu   *ă-chi'-mi-nun*   *chûkh-tă*   *Kaiñ'-än-un'*   *ă-ko'-mûk*   *nu-ûkh'-tok*
taking   under him   placed   upon it   sitting   lies back he

kän-ûg-û-lu'-nĭ   *"ẃû-nĭ tû-koñ'-û-nok'-hlĭ."*   *U-nukh'-púk tau-atn pú-kĭ'-tĭk-*
saying   "here   will I die."   All night   thus   stirring

shaun'-än-ĭ ẃi'-tauk.   *Úkh'-tok mä-djûkh'-hlu-mûg'-û-lu'-nĭ ni'-tok tu-lu'-*
not   he is thus. Morning it is   and the sun rising   hears he   a

kau-g'úk käl'-û-g'ĭ-û-g'ĭ-ă ẃûn-i'-tän ĭm-ai'-pa-ni'-tok a-hla'-mûk. Pú-kĭ'-tĭk-
raven   croaking   then   its mate hears he   besides.   Remaining

shaun'-än-ĭ ẃi'-tauk.   *Tau-ă' mi-tok' ya-ti'-nun ẃú-ni'-tän im-ai'-pă ya-ti'-*
still he   is there.   And   lights   beyond   and here   its mate beyond
                  then   he   him

nun   *mi-tok'.*   *Tau-atn'*   *pú-kĭ'-tĭk-shaun'-än-ĭ*   *ẃi'-tauk.*   *U-gúk'-hli-ă*
it   lights he.   And yet   he remaining not stirring   is there. The nearest one

kän-ûkh'-tok   *"ta-ẃa'-hlut*   *nû-gĭ'-kak'*   *u-nă*   *nû-g'úk'*   *shai'-tu-guk*
says he   "see here   some food   he   eat   had not better

ẃi'-tûf-kin'-än-uk' i-tog'-û-lau'-úk" ĭñ'-ĭ-nă ai-pan' yak-hli'-än ki-u'-g'ă
wait   eyes let us have"   that   mate   farthest   answers
                      (one)   (the)

"kâñ'-ă tû-ko'-män-u-g'i'-tok." *Iñ-úm yak'-hli-ûn ki-u'-g'ă* *"chä-ku'-nĭ-*
"no   dead is not he."   The one nearest answers "why does he

gĭk ma'-nĭ chä-hlĭkh'-chĭ-kă?" *iñ'-úm yak-hlĭ'-än* *"Kâñ'-ă tû-ko'-män-*
lie here as if thrown out?"   the one farthest "No   dead is

u-g'i'-tok ä-tûm' tûñ'-khu kiñ-un'-û-g'ĭ' po-ĭ-ûkh-tai'-lĭñ-ut." *Ĭm'-ĭ-nă*
not he   for see look here in his place   smoke is none."   That one

u-gúk'-hli-a kän-ûkh'-tok *"chä-lu'-nĭ-gĭk?"* *tau'-ă chu-ûg'-û-jug-û-lu'-nĭ*
nearest   says he   "why is he thrown and then becoming enraged
               (out)?"

chä-hlĭg'-ĭ-nĭ-ûkh'-tă *"ä-tûm' tûñ'-khu chai'-mä-gut' a-wa-ti'-nĭ chä-hlĭl'-*
threw himself about "see here look his things around scat-

û-g'it." *Ĭñ'-ĭ-nă ai'-pă kän-ûkh'-tok "wi'-pĭñ-ai'-tu-ă u-ni-chi'-a-kúm-kĭn*
tered." That one's mate says he   "I do not wish it I will leave you

ä-tûm' tûñ-khu kĭñ-un'-û-g'ĭ pu'-ju-i'-lĭñ-ut." *Tĭñ'-ok* *"tau'-ă tĭñ-ûn"*
for see look in his place there is no smoke." Flies he "All right fly you'

ai-pa kän-ûkh'-tok "wi i-tuñ'-sin-wâg'-û-lĭ." *Ĭm'-ĭ-nă yukh wi-tĭm'-ĭ-*
the mate says he   "I   will have his eyes." That   man opens his

shu-akh'-tok ta-gu'-ya-ga' nu-gúthl-pi-úñ'-ĭ-na'-g'úk. *Tai-ĭñ'-ĭ-nă nûñ'-û-kă-*
eyes a little looks sidewise the small, ugly young man. The one stands
                                                      coming

jĭl'-ĭ-g'ĭ-ă tĭ-gu'-mĭ a'-go-whă chau ikh'-tûk tai'-kä-tûkh'-tok tĭ-ki'-chä-miu'
there   holding a fine knife nearer comes he coming close

tau-atn' kĭ-lúm'-ĭ-lu'-nĭ kû-múg'-û-ja'-mĭ a-gu-lit'-hum ki-ûkh-kog'-û-lu-nĭ
and then watching   eyelashes between looking a little

tĭ-ki'-chä-miu ok-hlĭ-u'-tă chau-ĭg'-ĭ-mi'-nĭk. *Um-ju-ûkh'-tĭ-kok* *"Chau-*
close by raised by the hilt his fine knife.   Thinks he   "I have

bvi'-chu-kwa" *wûn-ĭkh'-whă kä-púk'-ă-ta'-nĭ um-ju-ûkh'-tĭ-kok* *"Chau-*
no knife"   and here the point coming close thinks he   "I have

bvi'-chu-kwa tĭ'-gu-ûkh'-tă ä-hlokh'-hlu-ku akh'-kh-tok. *Ĭm'-ĭ-nă a-ku'-mok.*
no knife" catching it and snatching it back jumps That one sits up he.
               he.

" Chau-i'-kă tai'-sĭ-gu" *kän-ûkh'-tok tu-lu'-kau-g'úk.* *Ĭñ'-ĭ-nă a-ku'-mok*
"My knife give here," says   the raven. That one sits he

"chau-bvi'-tu-a wi-chau-ĭk'-ĭ-chĭ'-ă-kă-kă" ĭm'-ĭ nă ĭñ-ĭ-nă kän-ûkh-tok
"knife I have not my knife it shall be" this one that one says he

"nu-nu'-lĭkh-chĭ-a-kum'-kĭn pĭ-túkh'-kút tä-mai'-tă." *"Kâñ'-ă"* *ĭm'-ĭ-nă*
"I will pay you of game all kinds." "No," this one

u'-nă "tu-niñ-ai'-tă-kă ai-úñ'-g'û-mă pĭ-hlûn'-ĭ-g'ĭ-tu-ă." *Ĭm'-ĭ-nă ĭñ'-ĭ-nă*
to him "I will not I always go out I get nothing." This one that one

tu-lu'-kau-g'uk "pĭkh-shukh-pa'-gún kiñ-u'-nûkh-pĭñ-un' u-túg'-ûs-gu'-ut
the raven "If you wish to return to your place when you go back

tĭ kĭj'-ĭñ-ai'-tutn ki-u'-g'ă "chau-bvi'-tu-ă." Wûn-i'-tän um tu-lu'-kau g'úk
you will not get answered "I have no knife." Here then he the raven
       there   (he)

ko-ĭ-ĭkh'-tok ĭ'-ku-a'-lu-nĭ "wûtn pĭ-chĭ'-ă-kutn chau-i'-kă ĭ-g'ĭlh'-k'-ku'-
coughs he   falling "Thus will you do knife my keep if you

bú-gu" tĭñ'-ok. Núñ-úkh'-cha-mĭ ĭm'-gut úkh'-kokh-kna'-nĭ kä-tokh'-lu-kĭ
prize it" flies he.   Standing up   those   scattered about   gathering up

ĭm'-ĭ-nă chau'-ĭk tĭ-gu'-mĭ-a'-ka u-túkh'-tok u-túkh'-gni-nún'-ĭ-ga'-nĭ ĭg'-ĭ-
that   knife   keeping   goes back he   back when he is going   his

jag'-a ka-hla'-tĭñ-ĭñ'-ok kho'-ka ä-pún'-ĭ-tĭñ-ĭñ'-ok chĭs-kog'-ĭ-nĭ ai-a'-pún'-
throat   contracts it   the back   curves it   on his knees   his hands

ĭñ'-ĭk ki-i'-mă pi-u'-ju-i'-g'u-tok uñ-u'-hlu-úkh'-tok ki-i'-mă pä-lokh'-tok
rest   suddenly   can not walk he   old man becomes he   suddenly   on his face
                                                                                    lies he

pú-kĭ'-tn-u-g''i-tok tau-a'-nĭ tú-ko'-lu-nĭ.
stirs not he   and then   is dead.

THE LONE WOMAN

(From St Michael)

Very long ago there were many men living in the northland, but there was no woman among them. Far away in the southland a single woman was known to live. At last one of the young men in the north started and traveled to the south until he came to the woman's house, where he stopped and in a short time became her husband. One day he sat in the house thinking of his home and said, "Ah, I have a wife, while the son of the headman in the north has none." And he was much pleased in thinking of his good fortune.

Meanwhile the headman's son also had set out to journey toward the south, and while the husband was talking thus to himself the son stood in the entrance passage to the house listening to him. He waited there in the passage until the people inside were asleep, when he crept into the house and, seizing the woman by the shoulders, began dragging her away.

Just as he reached the doorway he was overtaken by the husband, who caught the woman by her feet. Then followed a struggle, which ended by pulling the woman in two, the thief carrying the upper half of the body away to his home in the northland, while the husband was left with the lower portion of his wife. Each man set to work to replace the missing parts from carved wood. After these were fitted on they became endowed with life, and so two women were made from the halves of one.

The woman in the south, however, was a poor needlewoman, owing to the clumsiness of her wooden fingers, but was a fine dancer. The woman in the north was very expert in needlework, but her wooden legs made her a very poor dancer. Each of these women gave to her daughters these characteristics, so that to the present time the same difference is noted between the women of the north and those of the south, thus showing that the tale is true.[1]

---

[1] This tale refers to notable facts in regard to the accomplishments of the women in the districts north and south of St Michael.

THE CIRCLING OF CRANES

(From St Michael and other places on Norton sound)

One autumn day, very long ago, the cranes were preparing to go southward. As they were gathered in a great flock they saw a beautiful young woman standing alone near the village. Admiring her greatly, the cranes gathered about, and lifting her on their widespread wings, bore her far up in the air and away. While the cranes were taking her up they circled below her so closely that she could not fall, and their loud, hoarse cries drowned her calls for help, so she was carried away and never seen again. Ever since that time the cranes always circle about in autumn, uttering their loud cries while preparing to fly southward, as they did at that time.

THE DWARF PEOPLE

(From St Michael and Pikmiktalik)

Very long ago, before we knew of the white men, there was a large village at Pikmiktalik. One winter day the people living there were very much surprised to see a little man and a little woman with a child coming down the river on the ice. The man was so small that he wore a coat made from a single white fox skin. The woman's coat was made from the skins of two white hares, and two muskrat skins clothed the child.

The old people were about two cubits high and the boy not over the length of one's forearm. Though he was so small, the man was dragging a sled much larger than those used by the villagers, and he had on it a heavy load of various articles. When they came to the village he easily drew his sled up the steep bank, and taking it by the rear end raised it on the sled frame, a feat that would have required the united strength of several villagers.

Then the couple entered one of the houses and were made welcome. This small family remained in the village for some time, the man taking his place in the kashim with the other men. He was very fond of his little son, but one day as the latter was playing outside the house he was bitten so badly by a savage dog that he died. The father in his anger caught the dog up by the tail and struck it so hard against a post that the dog fell into halves. Then the father in great sorrow made a handsome grave box for his son, in which he placed the child with his toys, after which he returned into his house and for four days did no work. At the end of that time he took his sled and with his wife returned up the river on their old trail, while the villagers sorrowfully watched them go, for they had come to like the pair very much.

Before this time the villagers had always made a bed for their sleds from long strips of wood running lengthwise, but after they had seen the dwarf's sled with many crosspieces, they adopted this model.

Up to the time when they saw the dwarf people bury their son in a grave box with small articles placed about him, the villagers had always cast their dead out upon the tundra to be the prey of dogs and wild beasts. But thenceforth they buried their dead and observed four days of seclusion for mourning, as had been done by the dwarf.

Since that time the hunters claim that they sometimes see upon the tundra dwarf people who are said usually to carry bows and arrows, and when approached suddenly disappear into the ground, and deer hunters often see their tracks near Pikmiktalik mountains. No one has ever spoken to one of these dwarfs since the time they left the village. They are harmless people, never attempting to do any one an injury.

THE SUN AND THE MOON

(From St Michael)

In a coast village once lived a man and his wife who had two children, a girl and a boy. When these children grew large enough, so that the boy could turn over the gravel stone, he became in love with his sister. Being constantly importuned by the boy his sister finally, to avoid him, floated away into the sky and became the moon. The boy has pursued her ever since, becoming the sun, and sometimes overtakes and embraces her, thus causing an eclipse of the moon.

After his children had gone their father became very gloomy and hated his kind, going about the earth scattering disease and death among mankind, and the victims of disease became his food, until he became so evil that his desire could not be satisfied in this way, so he killed and ate people who were well.

Through fear of this being people threw the bodies of their dead just outside the village that he might be fed without injuring the living. Whenever he came about the bodies would disappear during the night. Finally he became so bad that all the most powerful shamans joined together and, by using their magic powers, were enabled to capture and bind him hand and foot, so that he was no longer able to wander about doing mischief. Although bound and unable to move about, he has still the power to introduce disease and afflict mankind.

To prevent evil spirits from wandering and taking possession of dead bodies and thus giving them a fictitious animation for evil purposes, and in memory of the binding of this evil one, the dead are no longer thrown out, but are tied hand and foot in the position in which the demon was bound and placed in the grave box.[1]

---

[1] There is another Norton sound version of this tale similar to the one from the lower Yukon, which will be given with the tales from that district.

18 ETH——31

THE SUN AND THE MOON

(From the lower Yukon)

In a certain village on the great river once lived four brothers and a
sister. The sister had for a companion a small boy of whom she was
very fond. This boy was lazy and could never be made to work. The
other brothers were great hunters and in the fall hunted at sea, for
they lived near the shore. As soon as the Bladder feast was over
they went to the mountains and hunted reindeer.

The boy never went with them, but stayed at home with the sister,
and they amused each other. One night the sister awoke and found
the boy lying in bed close to her, at which she became very angry and
made him go to sleep in the kashim with the men. The next evening,
when she carried food to her brothers in the kashim she gave none to
the boy; instead, she went home, and after mixing some berries and
deer fat, cut off one of her breasts, placed it in the dish, and carried it
to the boy. Putting the dish before him she said, "You wanted me
last night, so I have given you my breast. If you desire me, eat it."

The boy refused the dish, so she took it up and went outside. As
she went out she saw a ladder leading up into the sky, with a line
hanging down by the side of it. Taking hold of the line, she ascended
the ladder, going up into the sky. As she was going up her younger
brother came out and saw her and at once ran back into the kashim,
telling his brothers. They began at once to scold the boy and ran out
to see for themselves.

The boy caught up his sealskin breeches and, being in such a hurry,
thrust one leg into them and then drew a deerskin sock upon the other
foot as he ran outside. There he saw the girl far away up in the sky and
began at once to go up the ladder toward her, but she floated away, he
following in turn.

The girl then became the sun and the boy became the moon, and ever
since that time he pursues but never overtakes her. At night the sun
sinks in the west and the moon is seen coming up in the east to go
circling after, but always too late. The moon, being without food, wanes
slowly away from starvation until it is quite lost from sight; then the
sun reaches out and feeds it from the dish in which the girl had placed
her breast. After the moon is fed and gradually brought to the full, it
is then permitted to starve again, so producing the waxing and waning
every month.

ORIGIN OF LAND AND PEOPLE

(From the lower Yukon)

In the beginning there was water over all the earth, and it was very
cold; the water was covered with ice, and there were no people. Then
the ice ground together, making long ridges and hummocks. At this
time came a man from the far side of the great water and stopped

on the ice hills near where Pikmiktalik now is, taking for his wife a she-wolf. By and by he had many children, which were always born in pairs—a boy and a girl. Each pair spoke a tongue of their own, differing from that of their parents and different from any spoken by their brothers and sisters.

As soon as they were large enough each pair was sent out in a different direction from the others, and thus the family spread far and near from the ice hills, which now became snow-covered mountains. As the snow melted it ran down the hillsides, scooping out ravines and river beds, and so making the earth with its streams.

The twins peopled the earth with their children, and as each pair with their children spoke a language different from the others, the various tongues found on the earth were established and continue until this day.

THE BRINGING OF THE LIGHT BY RAVEN

(From Paimut, on the lower Yukon)

In the first days there was light from the sun and the moon as we now have it. Then the sun and the moon were taken away, and people were left on the earth for a long time with no light but the shining of the stars. The shamans made their strongest charms to no purpose, for the darkness of night continued.

In a village of the lower Yukon there lived an orphan boy who always sat upon the bench with the humble people over the entrance way in the kashim. The other people thought he was foolish, and he was despised and ill-treated by everyone. After the shamans had tried very hard to bring back the sun and the moon but failed, the boy began to mock them, saying, "What fine shamans you must be, not to be able to bring back the light, when even I can do it."

At this the shamans became very angry and beat him and drove him out of the kashim. This poor orphan was like any other boy until he put on a black coat which he had, when he changed into a raven, preserving this form until he took off the coat again.

When the shamans drove the boy out of the kashim, he went to the house of his aunt in the village and told her what he had said to them and how they had beaten him and driven him out of the kashim. Then he said he wished her to tell him where the sun and the moon had gone, for he wished to go after them.

She denied that she knew where they were hidden, but the boy said, "I am sure you know where they are, for look at what a finely sewed coat you wear, and you could not see to sew it in that way if you did not know where the light is." After a long time he prevailed upon his aunt, and she said to him, "Well, if you wish to find the light you must take your snowshoes and go far to the south, to the place you will know when you get there."

The Raven boy at once took his snowshoes and set off for the south. For many days he traveled, and the darkness was always the same. When he had gone a very long way he saw far in front of him a ray of light, and then he felt encouraged. As he hurried on the light showed again, plainer than before, and then vanished and appeared at intervals. At last he came to a large hill, one side of which was in a bright light while the other appeared in the blackness of night. In front of him and close to the hill the boy saw a hut with a man near by who was shoveling snow from the front of it.

The man was tossing the snow high in the air, and each time that he did this the light became obscured, thus causing the alternations of light and darkness which the boy had seen as he approached. Close beside the house he saw the light he had come in search of, looking like a large ball of fire. Then the boy stopped and began to plan how to secure the light and the shovel from the man.

After a time he walked up to the man and said, "Why are you throwing up the snow and hiding the light from our village?" The man stopped, looked up, and said, "I am only cleaning away the snow from my door; I am not hiding the light. But who are you, and whence did you come?" "It is so dark at our village that I did not like to live there, so I came here to live with you," said the boy. "What, all the time?" asked the man. "Yes," replied the boy. The man then said, "It is well; come into the house with me," and he dropped his shovel on the ground, and, stooping down, led the way through the undergound passage into the house, letting the curtain fall in front of the door as he passed, thinking the boy was close behind him.

The moment the door flap fell behind the man as he entered, the boy caught up the ball of light and put it in the turned up flap of his fur coat in front; then, catching up the shovel in one hand, he fled away to the north, running until his feet became tired; then by means of his magic coat he changed into a raven and flew as fast as his wings would carry him. Behind he heard the frightful shrieks and cries of the old man, following fast in pursuit. When the old man saw that he could not overtake the Raven he cried out, "Never mind; you may keep the light, but give me my shovel."

To this the boy answered, "No; you made our village dark and you can not have your shovel," and Raven flew off, leaving him. As Raven traveled to his home he broke off a piece of the light and threw it away, thus making day. Then he went on for a long time in darkness and then threw out another piece of light, making it day again. This he continued to do at intervals until he reached the outside of the kashim in his own village, when he threw away the last piece. Then he went into the kashim and said, "Now, you good-for-nothing shamans, you see I have brought back the light, and it will be light and then dark so as to make day and night," and the shamans could not answer him.

After this the Raven boy went out upon the ice, for his home was on the seacoast, and a great wind arose, drifting him with the ice across the sea to the land on the other shore. There he found a village of people and took a wife from among them, living with her people until he had three daughters and four sons. In time he became very old and told his children how he had come to their country, and after telling them that they must go to the land whence he came, he died.

Raven's children then went away as he had directed them, and finally they came to their father's land. There they became ravens, and their descendants afterward forgot how to change themselves into people and so have continued to be ravens to this day.

At Raven's village day and night follow each other as he told them it would, and the length of each was unequal, as sometimes Raven traveled a long time without throwing out any light and again he threw out the light at frequent intervals, so that the nights were very short, and thus they have continued.

THE RED BEAR (TA-KÚ-KA)

(From Andreivsky, on the lower Yukon)

On the tundra, south of the Yukon mouth, there once lived an orphan boy with his aunt. They were quite alone, and one summer day the boy took his kaiak and traveled away to see where people lived on the Yukon, of whom he had heard. When he came to the river, he traveled up its course until he reached a large village. There he landed and the people ran down to the shore, seized him, broke his kaiak to pieces, tore his clothing from him, and beat him badly.

The boy was kept there until the end of summer, the subject of continual beating and ill treatment from the villagers. In the fall one of the men took pity on him, made him a kaiak, and started him homeward, where he arrived after a long absence. When he reached home he saw that a large village had grown up by his aunt's house. As soon as he landed, he went to his aunt's house and entered, frightening her very much, for he had been starved and beaten so long that he looked almost like a skeleton.

When his aunt recognized him, she received his story with words of pity, then words of anger at the cruel villagers. When he had finished telling her of his sufferings, she told him to bring her a piece of wood, which he did; this they worked into a small image of an animal with long teeth and long, sharp claws, painting it red upon the sides and white on the throat. Then they took the image to the edge of the creek and placed it in the water, the aunt telling it to go and destroy every one it could find at the village where her boy had been.

The image did not move, and the old woman took it out of the water and cried over it, letting her tears fall upon it, and then put it back in the water, saying, "Now, go and kill the bad people who beat my boy." At this the image floated across the creek and crawled up the other bank, where it began to grow, soon reaching a large size, when it became a red bear. It turned and looked at the old woman until she called out to it to go and spare none.

The bear then went away until he came to the village on the great river. It met a man just going for water and it quickly tore him to pieces; then the bear stayed near this village until he had killed more than half of the people, and the others were preparing to leave it in order to escape destruction. He then swam across the Yukon and went over the tundra to the farther side of Kuskokwim river, killing every one he saw, for the least sign of life seemed to fill him with fury until it was destroyed. From the Kuskokwim the bear turned back, and one day it stood on the creek bank where it had become endowed with life. Seeing the people on the other bank he became filled with fury, tearing the ground with his claws and growling, and began to cross the creek. When the villagers saw this they were much frightened and ran about, saying, "Here is the old woman's dog; we shall all be killed. Tell the old woman to stop her dog." And they sent her to meet the bear. The bear did not try to hurt her, but was passing by to get at the other people when she caught it by the hair on its neck, saying, "Do not hurt these people who have been kind to me and have given me food when I was hungry."

After this she led the bear into her house and, sitting down, told him that he had done her bidding well and had pleased her, but that he must not injure people any more unless they tried to hurt or abuse him. When she had finished telling him this she led him to the door and sent him away over the tundra. Since this time there have always been red bears.

THE LAST OF THE THUNDERBIRDS (MÛ-TÛGH′-O-WĬK)

(From the lower Yukon)

Very long ago there were many giant eagles or thunderbirds living in the mountains, but they all disappeared except a single pair which made their home on the mountain top overlooking the Yukon river near Sabotnisky. The top of this mountain was round, and the eagles had hollowed out a great basin on the summit which they used for their nest, around the edges of which was a rocky rim from which they could look down upon the large village near the water's edge.

From their perch on this rocky wall these great birds would soar away on their broad wings, looking like a cloud in the sky, sometimes to seize a reindeer from some passing herd to bring back to their young; again they would circle out, with a noise like thunder from their shaking wings, and descend upon a fisherman in his canoe on the surface of the river, carrying man and canoe to the top of the mountain. There the man would be eaten by the young thunderbirds and the canoe would lie bleaching among the bones and other refuse scattered along the border of the nest.

Every fall the young birds would fly away into the northland, while the old ones would remain. Then came a time, after many hunters had been carried away by the birds, that only the most daring would go upon the great river. One summer day a brave young hunter started out to look at his fish traps on the river, but before he went he told his wife to be careful and not leave the house for fear of the birds. After her husband had gone the young wife saw that the water tub was empty, so she took a bucket and went to the river for water. As she turned to go back, a roaring noise like thunder filled the air, and one of the birds darted down and seized her in its talons. The villagers cried out in sorrow and despair when they saw her carried to the mountain top.

When the hunter came home the people hastened to tell him of his wife's death, but he said nothing. Going to his empty house he took down his bow and a quiver full of war arrows, and after examining them carefully he started out toward the eagle mountain. Vainly did his friends try to stop him by telling him that the birds would surely destroy him. He would not listen to them, but hurried on. With firm steps at last he gained the rim of the great nest and looked in. The old birds were away, but the fierce young eagles met him with shrill cries and fiery, shining eyes. The hunter's heart was full of anger, and he quickly bent his bow, loosing the war arrows one after another until the last one of the hateful birds lay dead in the nest.

With heart still burning for revenge, the hunter sheltered himself by a great rock near the nest and waited for the parent birds. The old birds came. They saw their young lying dead and bloody in the nest, and uttered such cries of rage that the sound echoed from the farther side of the great river as they soared up into the air looking for the one who had killed their young. Very quickly they saw the brave hunter by the great stone, and the mother bird swooped down upon him, her wings sounding like a gale in the spruce forest. Quickly fitting an arrow to his string, as the eagle came down the hunter sent it deep into her throat. With a hoarse cry she turned and flew away to the north, far beyond the hills.

Then the father bird circled overhead and came roaring down upon the hunter, who, at the right moment, crouched close to the ground behind the stone and the eagle's sharp claws struck only the hard rock. As the bird arose, eager to swoop down again, the hunter sprang from his shelter and, with all his strength, drove two heavy war arrows deep under its great wing. Uttering a cry of rage and spreading abroad his wings, the thunderbird floated away like a cloud in the sky far into the northland and was never seen again.

Having taken blood vengeance, the hunter's heart felt lighter, and he went down into the nest where he found some fragments of his wife, which he carried to the water's edge and, building a fire, made food offerings and libations of water pleasing to the shade.[1]

---

[1] The truth of this tale is implicitly believed by the Eskimo of the lower Yukon. They point out the crater of an old volcano as the nest of the giant eagles, and say that the ribs of old canoes and curiously colored stones carried there by the birds may still be seen about the rim of the nest. This is one of the various legends of the giant eagles or thunderbirds that are familiar to the Eskimo of the Yukon and to those of Bering strait and Kotzebue sound.

THE LAND OF THE DEAD

(From Andreivsky, on the lower Yukon)

[The following tale is known all along the lower Yukon, and was related by an old shaman who said that it occurred several generations ago. It is believed by the Eskimo to have been an actual occurrence, and it gives a fair idea of their belief of the condition of the shade after death.]

A young woman living at a village on the lower Yukon became ill and died. When death came to her she lost consciousness for a time; then she was awakened by some one shaking her, saying, "Get up, do not sleep; you are dead." When she opened her eyes she saw that she was lying in her grave box, and her dead grandfather's shade was standing beside her. He put out his hand to help her rise from the box and told her to look about. She did so, and saw many people whom she knew moving about in the village. The old man then turned her with her back to the village and she saw that the country she knew so well had disappeared and in its place was a strange village, extending as far as the eye could reach. They went to the village, and the old man told her to go into one of the houses. So soon as she entered the house a woman sitting there picked up a piece of wood and raised it to strike her, saying, angrily, "What do you want here?" She ran out crying and told the old man about the woman. He said, "This is the village of the dog shades, and from that you can see how the living dogs feel when beaten by people."

From this they passed on and came to another village, in which stood a large kashim. Close to this village she saw a man lying on the ground with grass growing up through all his joints, and, though he could move, he could not arise. Her grandfather told her that this shade was punished thus for pulling up and chewing grass stems when he was on the earth. Looking curiously at his shade for a time, she turned to speak to her grandfather, but he had disappeared. Extending onward before her was a path leading to a distant village, so she followed it. She soon came to a swift river, which seemed to bar her way. This river was made up of the tears of the people who weep on earth for the dead. When the girl saw that she could not cross, she sat on the bank and began to weep. When she wiped her eyes she saw a mass of straw and other stuff like refuse thrown from houses, floating down the stream, and it stopped in front of her. Upon this she crossed the river as over a bridge. When she reached the farther side the refuse vanished and she went on her way. Before she reached the village the shades had smelled her and cried out, "Someone is coming." When she reached them they crowded about her, saying, "Who is she? Whence does she come?" They examined her clothing, finding the totem marks, which showed where she belonged, for in ancient days people always had their totem marks on their clothing and other articles, so that members of every village and family were thus known.

Just then someone said, "Where is she? Where is she?"—and she saw her grandfather's shade coming toward her. Taking her by the hand, he led her into a house near by. On the farther side of the room she saw an old woman, who gave several grunts and then said, "Come and sit by me." This old woman was her grandmother, and she asked the girl if she wanted a drink, at the same time beginning to weep. When the girl became thirsty she looked about and saw some strange looking tubs of water, among which only one, nearly empty, was made like those in her own village.

Her grandmother told her to drink water from this tub only, as that was their own Yukon water, while the other tubs were all full of water from the village of the shades. When she became hungry her grandmother gave her a piece of deer fat, telling her that it had been given them by her son, the girl's father, at one of the festivals of the dead, and at the same time he had given them the tub of water from which she had just drunk.

The old woman told the girl that the reason her grandfather had become her guide was because when she was dying she had thought of him. When a dying person thinks of his relatives who are dead the thought is heard in the land of shades, and the person thought of by the dying one hurries off to show the new shade the road.

When the season came for the feast of the dead to be given at the dead girl's village, two messengers were sent out, as usual, to invite the neighboring villagers to the festival. The messengers traveled a long time toward one of the villages, and it became dark before they reached it, but at last they heard the drums beat and the sound of the dancers' feet in the kashim. Going in, they delivered to the people their invitation to the feast of the dead.

Sitting invisible on a bench among these people, with the girl between them, were the shades of the grandfather and grandmother, and when the messengers went back to their own village the next day the three shades followed them, but were still invisible. When the festival had nearly been completed, the mother of the dead girl was given water, which she drank. Then the shades went outside of the kashim to wait for their names to be called for the ceremony of the putting of clothing upon namesakes of the dead.

As the shades of the girl and her grandparents went out of the kashim the old man gave the girl a push, which caused her to fall and lose her senses in the passageway. When she recovered she looked about and found herself alone. She arose and stood in the corner of the entrance way under a lamp burning there, and waited for the other shades to come out that she might join her companions. There she waited until all of the living people came out dressed in fine new clothing, but she saw none of her companion shades.

Soon after this an old man with a stick came hobbling into the entrance, and as he looked up he saw the shade standing in the corner with her feet raised more than a span above the floor. He asked her if she was a live person or a shade, but she did not reply, and he went hurriedly into the kashim. There he told the men to hasten out and look at the strange being standing in the passageway, whose feet did not rest on the earth and who did not belong to their village. All the men hurried out, and, seeing her, some of them took down the lamp and by its light she was recognized and hurried into the house of her parents.

When the men first saw her she appeared in form and color exactly as when alive, but the moment she sat down in her father's house her color faded and she shrank away until she became nothing but skin and bone, and was too weak to speak.

Early the next morning her namesake, a woman in the same village, died, and her shade went away to the land of the dead in the girl's place, and the latter gradually became strong again and lived for many years.

THE STRANGE BOY

(From Andreivsky, on the lower Yukon)

At a village far away in the north once lived a man with his wife and one child, a son. This boy was very different from others, and while the village children ran about and shouted and took part in sports with one another, he would sit silent and thoughtful on the roof of the kashim. He would never eat any food or take any drink but that given him by his mother.

The years passed by until he grew to manhood, but his manner was always the same. Then his mother began to make him a pair of skin boots with soles of many thicknesses; also, a waterproof coat of double thickness and a fine coat of yearling reindeer skins. Every day he sat on the roof of the kashim, going home at twilight for food and to sleep until early the next morning; then he would go back to his place on the roof and wait for daybreak.

One morning he went home just after sunrise and found his new clothing ready. He took some food and put on the clothing, after which he told his mother that he was going on a journey to the north. His mother cried bitterly and begged him not to go, for no one ever went to the far northland and returned again. He did not mind this, but taking his bear spear and saying farewell, he started out, leaving his parents weeping and without hope of ever seeing him again, for they loved him very much, and his mother had told him truly that no one ever came back who had gone away from their village to the north.

The young man traveled far away, and as evening came on he reached a hut with the smoke rolling up through the hole in the roof. Taking off his waterproof coat, he laid it down near the door and crept carefully upon the roof and looked through the smoke hole. In the middle of the room burned a fire, and an old woman was sitting on the farther side, while just under him was sitting an old man making arrows. As the young man lay on the roof, the man on the inside cried out, without even raising his head, "Why do you lie there on the outside? Come in." Surprised at being noticed by the old man without the latter even looking up, he arose and went in. When he entered the house the man greeted him and asked why he was going to the north in search of a wife. Continued the old man, "There are many dangers there and you had better turn back. I am your father's brother and mean well by you. Beyond here people are very bad, and if you go on you may never return."

The young man was very much surprised to be told the object of his journey, when he had not revealed it even to his parents. After taking some food he slept until morning, then he prepared to go on his way. The old man gave him a small black object, filled with a yellow substance like the yolk of an egg, saying, as he did so, "Perhaps you will have little to eat on your way, and this will give you strength." The traveler swallowed it at once and found it very strong to the taste, so that it made him draw a deep breath, saying, as he did so, "Ah, I feel strong." Then he took up his spear and went on. Just before night he came to another solitary hut, and, as before, looked in, seeing a fire burning and an old woman sitting on one side and an old man making arrows just below him. Again the old man called out without raising his head, and asked him why he did not come in and not stay outside. He again was surprised by being told the object of his journey, and was warned against going farther. The young man gave no attention to this, but ate and slept as before. When he was ready to set out in the morning the old man saw he could not stay him, so gave him a small, clear, white object, telling the traveler that he would not get much to eat on the road, and it would help him. The young man at once swallowed this, but did not find it as strong as the object he had swallowed the day before. He was then told by the old man that if he heard anything on the way that frightened, him he must do the first thing that came into his mind.

"I will have no one to weep for me if anything should happen," said the traveler, and he journeyed on, spear in hand. Toward the middle of the day he came to a large pond lying near the seashore, so he turned off to go around it on the inland side. When he had passed part of the way around the lake he heard a frightful roar like a clap of thunder, but so loud that it made him dizzy, and for a moment he lost all sense of his surroundings. He hurried forward, but every few moments the terrible noise was repeated, each time making him reel and feel giddy and even on the point of fainting, but he kept on. The noise increased in loudness and seemed to come nearer at every roar, until it sounded on one side close to him. Looking in the direction whence it came, he saw a large basket made of woven willow roots floating toward him in the air, and from it came the fearful noise.

Seeing a hole in the ground close by, the traveler sprang into it just as a terrible crash shook the earth and rendered him unconscious. He lay as if dead for some time, while the basket kept moving about as if searching for him and continuously giving out the fearful sounds. When the young man's senses returned, he listened for a short time, and, everything having become quiet, went outside of his shelter and looked about. Close by was the basket resting on the ground with a man's head and shoulders sticking out of its top. The moment he saw it the young man cried out, "Why are you waiting? Go on; don't stop and give me a good loud noise, you." Then he sprang back into the hole again and was instantly struck senseless by the fearful noise made by the basket. When he had recovered sufficiently he went out again, but could not see the basket. Then he raised both of his hands and called upon the thunder and lightning to come to his aid. Just then the basket came near again, with only the man's head projecting from the top. He at once told the thunder and lightning to roar and flash about the basket, and they obeyed and crashed with such force that the basket shaman began to tremble with fear and fell to the ground.

As soon as the thunder stopped the basket began to retreat, the shaman being almost dead from fear. Then the young man cried out, "Thunder, pursue him; go before and behind him and terrify him." The thunder did so, and the basket floated away slowly, falling to the ground now and then. Then the traveler went on, arriving at a village just at twilight. As he drew near a boy came out from the village to meet him, saying, "How do you come here from that direction? No one ever came here from that side before, for the basket shaman allows no living thing to pass the lake; no, not even a mouse. He always knows when anything comes that way and goes out to meet and destroy it."

"I did not see anything," said the traveler. "Well, you have not escaped yet," said the boy, "for there is the basket man now, and he will kill you unless you go back." When the young man looked he saw a great eagle rise and fly toward him, and the boy ran away. As the eagle came nearer it rose a short distance and then darted down to seize him in its claws. As it came down the young man struck himself on the breast with one hand and a gerfalcon darted forth from his mouth straight toward the eagle, flying directly into its abdomen and passing out of its mouth and away.

This gerfalcon was from the strong substance the young man had been given by the first old man on the road. When the gerfalcon darted from him the eagle closed his eyes, gasping for breath, which gave the young man a chance to spring to one side so that the eagle's claws caught into the ground where he had stood. Again the eagle arose and darted down, and again the young man struck his breast with his hand, and an ermine sprang from his mouth and darted like a flash of light at the eagle and lodged under its wings, and in a moment had eaten its way twice back and forth through the bird's side, and it fell dead, whereupon the ermine vanished. This ermine came from the gift of the second man with whom the traveler had stopped.

When the eagle fell the young man started toward the shaman's house, and the boy cried to him, "Don't go there, for you will be killed." To this the traveler replied, " I don't care; I wish to see the women there. I will go now, for I am angry, and if I wait till morning my anger will be gone and I will not be so strong as I am at present." "You had better wait till morning," said the boy, "for there are two bears guarding the door and they will surely kill you. But if you will go, go then, and be destroyed. I have tried to save you and will have nothing more to do with you." And the boy went angrily back to the kashim. The young man then went on to the house, and looking into the entrance passage, saw a very large white bear lying there asleep. He called out, "Ah, White-bear," at which the bear sprang up and ran at him. The young man leaped upon the top of the passageway and, as the bear ran out at him, drove the point of his spear into its brain, so that it fell dead. Then he drew the body to one side, looked in again, and saw a red bear lying there. Again he called out, "Ah, Red-bear." The red bear ran out at him and he sprang up to his former place. The red bear struck at him with one of its forepaws as it passed, and the young man caught the paw in his hand and, swinging the bear about his head, beat it upon the ground until there was nothing but the paw left, and this he threw away and went into the house without further trouble. Sitting at the side of the room were an old man and woman, and on the other side was a beautiful young woman whose image he had seen in his dreams, which had caused him to make his long journey. She was crying when he went in, and he went and sat beside her, saying, "What are you crying for; what do you love enough to cry for?" To which she replied, "You have killed my husband, but I am not sorry for that, for he was a bad man; but you killed the two bears. They were my brothers, and I feel badly and cry for them." "Do not cry," said he, "for I will be your husband." Here he remained for a time, taking this woman for his wife and living in the house with her parents. He slept in the kashim every fourth night and at home the rest of the time.

After he had lived there for a while, he saw that his wife and her parents became more and more gloomy, and they cried very often. Then he saw things done that made him think they intended to do him evil. Becoming sure of this, he went home one day and, putting his hand on his wife's forehead, turned her face to him, and said: "You are planning to kill me, you unfaithful woman, and as a punishment you shall die." Then taking his knife, he cut his wife's throat, and went gloomily back to his village, where he lived with his parents as

before.   When the memory of his unfaithful wife had become faint, he
took a wife from among the maidens of the village and lived happily
with her the rest of his days.

ORIGIN OF THE YU-GI-YHĬK' OR I'-TĬ-KĂ-TAH' FESTIVAL

(From Ikogmut, on the lower Yukon)

[This festival is observed by the Eskimo of the lower Yukon from
about Ikogmut (Mission) up to the limit of their range on the river.
Beyond that the festival is observed by the Tinné at least as far as
Anvik, they having borrowed it from the Eskimo.   The festival is
characterized by the placing of a wooden doll or image of a human
being in the kashim and making it the center of various ceremonies,
after which it is wrapped in birch-bark and hung in a tree in some
retired spot until the following year.   During the year the shamans
sometimes pretend to consult this image to ascertain what success will
attend the season's hunting or fishing.   If the year is to be a good one
for deer hunting, the shamans pretend to find a deer hair within the
wrappings of the image.   In case they wish to predict success in fishing, they claim to find fish scales in the same place.   At times small
offerings of food in the shape of fragments of deer fat or of dried fish
are placed within the wrappings.   The place where the image is concealed is not generally known by the people of the village, but is a
secret to all except the shamans and, perhaps, some of the oldest men
who take prominent parts in the festival.   An old headman among the
Mission Eskimo informed me that the legend and festival originated
among the people of a place that has long been deserted, near the
present village of Paimut, and that thence it was introduced both up
and down the Yukon and across the tundra to the people living on
lower Koskokwim river.   The names of this festival are derived, first,
Yu-gi-yhĭk from *yu'-gŭk*, a doll or manikin, and *I'-tĭ-kă-tah'* from *i-tŭkh-
tok*, "he comes in," thus meaning the doll festival or the coming-in
festival, the latter referring to the bringing in of the doll from the tree
where it is kept during the year.]

At the foot of the mountains below Paimut, near where a small summer village now stands, there was in ancient days a very large village
of Eskimo, which was so large that the houses extended from the river
bank some distance up the hillside.

In this village lived two young men who were relatives and were also
noted shamans and fast friends.   For a long time they remained unmarried, but at last one of them took a wife, and in the course of time had
a daughter who grew to womanhood, was married, and to her was born
a son.   As soon as this child was born its grandfather killed it and
carried the body out into the spruce forest and hung it to a tree, where
it remained until it was dried or mummified.

Then the old man took it down, placed it in a small bag, which he
hung about his neck by a cord, and wore it secretly under his clothing

as an amulet, thus having the services of its *inua* to assist him in his ceremonies. His wife and daughter, however, knew what he had done with the child.

The unmarried shaman never took a wife, and after his friend began to wear the child about his neck, he frequently saw among the shades that came to do his bidding that of a small, new-born child. What it was or why it came he could not understand, as it did not come at his bidding. This was observed very often, and still he did not know that his friend had the body.

When one of these men was practicing his rites and found it difficult to obtain help from the shades, his friend would assist him to accomplish his object. One fine, warm day the unmarried shaman went up on the hillside back of the village and sat down. As night came on he fell asleep, and as he slept he saw the air filled with falling stars, and then that the sky was sinking toward him until finally it rested upon the hilltop so close that he had barely enough room to move about below it. Looking around, he saw that every star was in reality a round hole in the sky through which the light from above was shining. Raising himself up, he put his head through the nearest star hole and saw another sky with many stars shining above the first one. As he looked, this sky sank slowly down until he could put his head through one of the star holes in it, and above this were shining the stars in still another sky. This, too, sank slowly down, and standing up he found himself breast high above the third sky, and close by was a kashim surrounded by a village like the one in which he lived.

From familiar signs he saw that the men had just taken a sweat bath. A woman was at work covering the air hole in the roof of the kashim with the gut-skin covering, while other women were carrying in food. After looking about for a short time he decided to go into the kashim and see the people. Then raising himself through the star holes he walked to the kashim and entered it through the underground passageway. When he reached the inside he found the room full of people sitting around on the floor and benches. He started to cross the room to take a seat in the place of honor opposite the door, but a man sitting over the main entrance called to him to sit beside him, which he did.

The women were still bringing in food, and the man who had spoken first to the shaman, said, in a low voice, "If you are offered food do not eat it, for you will see that it is not fit to eat." The shaman then looked about the room and saw lying at the side of each man a small wooden image, all of which represented different kinds of mammals, birds, and fishes. Over the lamps beside the entrance door were two slender sticks of wood more than a fathom in length, joined at the lower end and spread apart above like two outspread arms, along the sides of which were fastened swan quills, and the upper end of each stick bore a tuft of wolf hair. These sticks were designed to represent the outspread wings of the Raven father who made the world. Over the entrance to the room hung another pair of these sticks similarly ornamented.

From the roof hung two great hoops extending entirely around the room, one of which was a little below the other, and both were about midway between the roof and the floor. Extending from the roof hole down to the upper hoop were many slender rods, the lower ends of which were fastened to the hoop at regular intervals. Fastened to the hoops and rods in many places were tufts of feathers and down. These hoops and rods represented the heavens arching over the earth, and the tufts of feathers were the stars mingled with snowflakes. The cord suspending the rings passed through a loop fastened to the roof, and the end passed down and was held by a man sitting near the lamp. This man raised and lowered the rings slowly by drawing in and letting out the cord in time to the beating of a drum by another man sitting on the opposite side of the lamp. [This movement of the rings was symbolical of the apparent approach and retreat of the heavens according to the condition of the atmosphere.]

The shaman had just time to notice this much when he saw a woman come in with a dish of food which seemed like freshly-boiled meat. Looking about, she asked, "Where is the guest?"—to which he replied, "Here I am," and she handed him the dish. As soon as the steam cleared away a little the shaman saw lying in the dish a new-born boy who was wriggling about. The shaman was so startled by the sight that he did not know what to do and let the dish turn toward the floor so that the child slipped out and fell. At this moment the shaman felt himself driven head foremost from his seat down through the exit hole in the floor. Starting up, he looked about and found himself reclining upon the mountain top near his village, and day was just breaking in the east. Rising, he hastened down to the village and told his friend, the other shaman, what had occurred to him, and the latter advised that they should unite in working their strongest charms to learn the meaning of this vision. Then they called the shaman's wife and went with her into the kashim where they worked their spells, and it was revealed to them that during the February moon in each year the people of the earth should hold a great festival. They were directed to decorate the kashim just as the shaman had seen it in the sky house, and by the two shamans the people were taught all the necessary observances and ceremonies, during which food and drink offerings were made to the *inuas* of the sky house and songs were sung in their honor. If these instructions were properly followed, game and food would be plentiful on the earth, for the people in the sky house were the shades or *inuas* controlling all kinds of birds and fish and other game animals on the earth, and from the small images of the various kinds which the shaman had seen lying beside the sky people was the supply of each kind replenished on earth. When the sky people or shades were satisfied by the offerings and ceremonies of the earth people, they would cause an image of the kind of animal that was needed to grow to the proper size, endow it with life and send it down to the earth, where it caused its kind to become again very numerous.

ORIGIN OF WINDS

(From the lower Yukon)

In a village on the lower Yukon lived a man and his wife who had no children. After a long time the woman spoke to her husband one day and said, "I can not understand why we have no children; can you?" To which the husband replied that he could not. She then told her husband to go on the tundra to a solitary tree that grew there and bring back a part of its trunk and make a doll from it. The man went out of the house and saw a long track of bright light, like that made by the moon shining on the snow, leading off across the tundra in the direction he must take. Along this path of light he traveled far away until he saw before him a beautiful object shining in the bright light. Going up to it, he found that it was the tree for which he came in search. The tree was small, so he took his hunting knife, cut off a part of its trunk and carried the fragment home.

When he returned he sat down and carved from the wood an image of a small boy, for which his wife made a couple of suits of fur clothing in which she dressed it. Directed by his wife, the man then carved a set of toy dishes from the wood, but said he could see no use for all this trouble, as it would make them no better off than they were before. To this his wife replied that before they had nothing but themselves to talk about, but the doll would give them amusement and a subject of conversation. She then deposited the doll in the place of honor on the bench opposite the entrance, with the toy dishes full of food and water before it.

When the couple had gone to bed that night and the room was very dark they heard several low whistling sounds. The woman shook her husband, saying, "Do you hear that? It was the doll;" to which he agreed. They got up at once, and, making a light, saw that the doll had eaten the food and drank the water, and they could see its eyes move. The woman caught it up with delight and fondled and played with it for a long time. When she became tired it was put back on the bench and they went to bed again.

In the morning, when the couple got up, they found the doll was gone. They looked for it about the house, but could find no trace of it, and, going outside, found its tracks leading away from the door. These tracks passed from the door along the bank of a small creek until a little outside the village, where they ended, as the doll had walked from this place on the path of light upon which the man had gone to find the tree.

18 ETH——32

The man and his wife followed no farther, but went home. Doll had traveled on along the bright path until he came to the edge of day, where the sky comes down to the earth and walls in the light. Close to where he was, in the east, he saw a gut-skin cover fastened over the hole in the sky wall, which was bulging inward apparently owing to some strong force on the other side. The doll stopped and said, "It is very quiet in here. I think a little wind will make it better." So he drew his knife and cut the cover loose about the edge of the hole, and a strong wind blew through, every now and then bringing with it a live reindeer. Looking through the hole, Doll saw beyond the wall another world like the earth. He drew the cover over the hole again and bade the wind not to blow too hard, but he said "Sometimes blow hard, sometimes light, and sometimes do not blow at all."

Then he walked along the sky wall until he came to another opening at the southeast, which was covered, and the covering pressed inward like the first. When he cut this cover loose the force of the gale swept in, bringing reindeer, trees, and bushes. Closing the hole again, he bade it do as he had told the first one, and passed on. In a short time he came to a hole in the south, and when the cover was cut a hot wind came rushing in, accompanied by rain and the spray from the great sea lying beyond the sky hole on that side.

Doll closed this opening and instructed it as before, and passed on to the west. There he saw another opening, and as soon as the cover was cut the wind brought in a heavy rainstorm, with sleet and spray, from the ocean. This opening was also closed, with the same instructions, and he passed on to the northwest, where he found another opening. When the cover to this was cut away a blast of cold wind came rushing in, bringing in snow and ice, so that he was chilled to the bone and half frozen, and he hastened to close it, as he had the others.

Again he went along the sky wall to the north, the cold becoming so great that he was obliged to leave it and make a circuit, going back to it where he saw the opening. There the cold was so intense that he hesitated for some time, but finally cut the cover away. At once a fearful blast rushed in, carrying great masses of snow and ice, strewing it all over the earth plain. He closed the hole very quickly, and having admonished it as usual, traveled on until he came to the middle of the earth plain.

When he reached there he looked up and saw the sky arching overhead, supported by long, slender poles, arranged like those of a conical lodge, but made of some beautiful material unknown to him. Turning again, he traveled far away, until he reached the village whence he had started. There he circled once completely around the place, and then entered one after the other of the houses, going to his own home last of all. This he did that the people should become his friends, and care for him in case his parents should die.

After this Doll lived in the village for a very long time. When his foster parents died he was taken by other people, and so lived for many generations, until finally he died. From him people learned the custom of wearing masks, and since his death parents have been accustomed to make dolls for their children in imitation of the people who made the one of which I have told.[1]

THE STRONG MAN

(From the lower Yukon)

In ancient times a very strong man (Yukhpuk) lived in the Askinuk mountains, near the Yukon river. One day he picked up a part of these mountains and, placing them on his shoulders, carried them out upon the level country, where he threw them down. In this way he made the Kuslevak mountains. When the mountain was thrown from the man's shoulders, the effort caused his feet to sink into the ground so that two deep pits were left, which filled with water, making two small lakes, which now lie at the base of this mountain. From there he traveled up the Yukon, giving names to all the places he passed.

THE OWL GIRL

The lower Yukon Eskimo have a legend that the short-ear owl was once a little girl who lived at a village by the river. She was changed by magic into a bird with a long beak and became so frightened that she sprang up and flew off in an erratic way until she struck the side of a house, flattening her bill and face so that she became just as these owls are seen today.

TALE OF AK′-CHĬK-CHÛ′-GŬK

(From Sledge island)

At the village of Käl-ul′-ĭ-gĭt[2] a terrible wind was blowing, which filled the air with flying snow and kept everyone in the house. One house in the village was occupied by a family of eight people—the parents and five sons and a daughter. The eldest son, named Ak′-chĭk-chû′-gŭk, was noted for the great breadth of his shoulders, and the strength of his hands was greater than that of the most powerful walrus flippers. The daughter was well known for her kindness and beauty.

As the day passed, one of the brothers asked his mother for some food, and she replied that none had been prepared, nor did she have any water with which to cook meat. Turning to the daughter, she told her to take a tub and go down to the water hole in the ice and bring some sea water that she might boil meat. The girl hesitated about going on account of the storm, and the brothers joined with her

---

[1] The path of light mentioned in this tale is the galaxy, which figures in numerous Eskimo myths.
[2] Point Rodney, on the eastern shore of Bering strait.

in trying to persuade the mother to give up the idea of having water brought at that time, but all to no purpose.

Then Ak'-chĭk-chû'-gûk told the youngest brother to go and help his sister, and the pair left the house. After some difficulty in getting to the water hole they rested for a time, and then slowly filled the tub; when it was full they turned back and, with bowed heads, struggled toward the shore in the face of the wind. As they were moving along the path, they suddenly started back in fear, for, in place of the shore, they saw the black, open water in a rapidly widening crack where the ice had broken and was drifting away from the land. Dropping the water tub they ran wildly back and forth along the edge of the ice until they were exhausted. After waiting for some time, the people in the house became alarmed, and one of the brothers ran down to the shore where, by the open water, he saw what had taken place. He hastened back and told his family and, as soon as the storm ceased, the brothers searched the sea as far as they could, but saw nothing of the missing ones. Then one of the brothers traveled along the coast to the north and another went to the south, informing the villagers they met of their loss, but both returned without any tidings.

Spring came, and their mother told the brothers that they must search for their lost ones far along the coast, for it was likely that they had been driven on shore somewhere. The brothers then set to work to build a fine, large umiak; when it was finished they decided to try it before they started on their voyage. Launching the umiak the three younger brothers rowed while Ak'-chĭk-chû'-gûk sat in the stern with the broad-blade steering paddle. They had gone only a short distance when a wild goose came flying by, and the three brothers strained their arms in trying to equal the bird in swiftness, but in vain. Suddenly Ak'-chĭk-chû'-gûk raised the broad paddle and the first stroke caused the umiak to leap forward so suddenly that his brothers were thrown from their seats into the bottom of the boat; after this, he bound them firmly to their seats and had them take in their oars. Then, under his strokes, the umiak darted through the water like an arrow, throwing a streak of foam away on both sides. Very soon they were close alongside the goose, and the bird tried hard to escape from its strange companions, but was quickly passed by the umiak and left far behind.

On another short preparatory trip they made along the coast they landed near a great rock. Ak'-chĭk-chû'-gûk told his brothers to take up some small drift logs on the beach and follow him; then, taking up the rock, he placed it upon his shoulders and carried it up the shore, although his feet sank deep in the earth at every step, so heavy was his burden. At some distance from the water he stopped and had his brothers form a platform of their logs, on which he placed the stone, saying: "Now I will not be forgotten, for the people who come after us will point out this rock and remember my name;" and this is true, for the villagers say that the rock lies there until this day and Ak'-chĭk-chû'-gûk's name is not forgotten.

Then the brothers returned home and completed their preparations for the journey. When everything was ready, Akʹ-chĭk-chûʹ-gûk had his brothers remove all their clothing and, taking his knife, with a single stroke he cut off the head of each. After this he made their mother carry the bodies outside and dismember them, putting the fragments into a great earthen pot, where they were boiled. At first his mother refused, but Akʹ-chĭk-chûʹ-gûk compelled her to obey him. When she had done as she was bid, she came in and told him; then, ordering her to remain in the house and upon no account to come outside until he gave her permission, he went out and, by the aid of a powerful *inua* that did his bidding, restored his brothers to life again.

When all her sons entered the house alive once more, the mother was very glad. At the bidding of Akʹ-chĭk-chûʹ-gûk she put some decayed fish roe and some bird-skin coats into the umiak, and they started on their search, leaving their parents alone. The brothers journeyed on until they reached a large village, where they stopped, and, going into the kashim, asked for tidings of their sister.

The people answered in an unfriendly way, and soon after one of the villagers cried out, " We must kill these men," and everyone seized his weapons and started toward the brothers. Akʹ-chĭk-chûʹ-gûk seemed not to notice the treacherous villagers until they were close to him; then, raising his right arm and placing the elbow against his side, drew the entire arm into his body; as he did this everyone of the villagers was compelled to do the same, and they stood helpless, without the use of their right arms.

" Why do you not kill us ?   Why do you wait ? " and similar mocking taunts were directed to them by Akʹ-chĭk-chûʹ-gûk. When the villagers had promised to let them go in peace, he thrust forth his own arm again, and at once everyone of the villagers was able to do the same; the people then told them that they might hear of their sister in the next village.

After journeying for several days they came to the village and went into the kashim, where again they made inquiries for their sister. As before, the people answered in an unfriendly tone and rushed at the strangers to kill them. Akʹ-chĭk-chûʹ-gûk paid no attention to his enemies until they were close to him, when he suddenly closed both eyes and the villagers were forced to do the same, after which he taunted them as he had taunted the men at the other village, then made them promise not to try to injure himself or his brothers, and restored their sight by opening his own eyes. These people told them that possibly they might get tidings at the next village, so the brothers went on.

When they reached that place they made inquiry, and, as at the other villages, the people wished to kill them, and were quite near the brothers with their weapons raised when Akʹ-chĭk-chûʹ-gûk put his hands on each side of his face and turned his head about on his shoulders so that his face looked backward. Instantly the heads of all the villagers turned around on their shoulders and the backs of their heads rested where their faces should have been, while their bodies were in the position of rushing forward. On getting the usual promise from them, Ak'-chĭk-chû'-gûk replaced the villagers' heads, and the brothers were directed to make inquiries at the next place.

In that village they were attacked again, and the villagers were forced to put their hands behind their backs by the strong magic of the elder brother. Here the people told the brothers that their sister was in the next village, but that she was the wife of a very powerful and wicked shaman, and they tried to keep the brothers from going on, saying that harm would come to them if they did. No heed was given to this, and they went on until they came in sight of the village.

There they stopped while Ak'-chĭk-chû'-gûk smeared his hands and face with the decayed fish roe and changed his fine deerskin clothing for the old bird-skin garments his mother had put in the boat. Then he coiled himself up in the bottom of the boat, bending down his shoulders until he looked like a feeble old man. His brothers were instructed what to do, and, rowing on, they soon landed at the village. Then the brothers started to carry Ak'-chĭk-chû'-gûk into the village, when they were met by several people, among whom was the bad shaman. He asked them why they carried with them such a miserable old man; to which they replied that he did not belong to them, but they had found him on the shore and brought him along with them.

Asking about their sister, they were told that they could see her when they had carried the old man in the kashim. Ak'-chĭk-chû'-gûk was placed in the kashim, where they left him lying apparently helpless. Then they were taken to another house and shown a young woman dressed in fine furs, and were told that she was their sister. The two elder brothers believed this, but the youngest one was suspicious of some wrong, but said nothing and went back to the kashim with the others.

When the brothers were inside the kashim, the shaman went down to the beach, where he untied the lashings of the umiak, rolled the framework up in the cover, and hid it. When night fell and everyone was asleep, the youngest brother crept out and went to the shaman's house. In the passageway he heard a hoarse, choking sound, and at first was frightened, but soon felt stronger and asked, "Who is there?" No reply came, and he went forward carefully until he reached the door beyond which he had heard the strange sound. He listened a moment, and then pushed the door open and went in.

There on the floor lay his sister dressed in coarse, heavy sealskins and bound hand and foot, with a cord drawn tightly about her neck and another fastened her tongue. Very quickly she was released, and then told him that the wicked shaman had kept her in this way and treated her very cruelly; her brother put his hand on her breast and found her so emaciated that the bones were almost through the skin. Leaving her there, he closed the door and soon brought the next elder brother to the girl; after which both went back and, awakening the others, told them what they had seen.

After this all the brothers kept awake and watchful until morning. As dawn appeared the bad shaman came to the window in the roof and cried out, "Now it is time to kill those strangers." Going into the kashim, he sent a man for a large, sharp-edge piece of whalebone, while he had another take away loose planks from the middle of the floor, which left a square open pit several feet deep, and about the edge of this the shaman bound upright the piece of whalebone with the sharp edge. The brothers were then challenged to wrestle with him. Ak'-chĭk-chû'-gûk whispered that they should wrestle with him without fear, as he had killed and restored them to life again before leaving home, so that men could not harm them.

One of the brothers stepped forward, and after a short struggle the shaman stooped quickly, caught the young man by the ankles, and raising him from the floor with a great swing, brought him down so that his neck was cut off across the edge of the whalebone. Casting the body to one side, the shaman repeated the challenge and killed the second brother in the same way. Again the shaman made his scornful challenge, but scarcely had he finished speaking when Ak'-chĭk-chû'-gûk wiped the fish roe from his face and hands, and with a wrench tore the bird-skin coat from his body and sprang up as a powerful young man with anger shining in his eyes.

When the shaman saw this sudden change he started back, with his heart growing weak within him; he could not escape, however, and very soon Ak'-chĭk-chû'-gûk caught him in his arms, pressed in his sides until the blood gushed from his mouth, and, stooping, caught him by the ankles and whirled him over his head and across the whalebone, cutting his neck apart; then he brought the body down again and it fell in two. Throwing aside the fragment in his hand, he turned to the frightened villagers and said, "Is there any relative, brother, father, or son of this miserable shaman who thinks I have done wrong? If there is, let him come forward and take revenge."

The villagers eagerly expressed their joy at the shaman's death, as they had been in constant fear of him, and he had killed every stranger who came to their village. Then Ak'-chĭk-chû'-gûk sent everyone out of the kashim, and soon, by help of his magic, restored his two brothers to life; after this they went out and released their sister, and clothed ing her in fine new garments. She told them of her long drifting on the ice with her brother and of their landing near Uñ-a'-shûk,[1] the village at which they then were; also how the shaman had killed her brother and kept her a prisoner.

The brothers were now treated so kindly by the people in the village

---

[1] Uñ-a'-shûk, a village near St Lawrence bay, on the Siberian shore of Bering strait.

that they lingered there from day to day until a considerable time had elapsed, during which two of them made fine bows and quivers full of arrows, and another made a strong, stone-head spear.

One day nearly all the men were gathered in the kashim when the youngest brother hurried in and said that the sea was covered with umiaks, so that the flashing of their paddles looked like falling rain drops in the sun. The villagers told the brothers that the umiaks were from a neighboring place and that the men in them meant no harm to the people of Uñ-a'-shûk, but were coming to kill the strangers. Hearing this, Ak'-chĭk-chû'-gûk told the villagers to stay within their houses and sent his brothers out to meet the enemy. The umiaks soon came to the shore and a fierce battle ensued. The umiak men tried in vain to kill or wound the brothers, while the latter killed many of them. Finally the youngest brother returned to the kashim, saying that his arrows were exhausted, but that their enemies were nearly all dead. Soon afterward the next younger brother came in and said that all his arrows were gone and only a few of the enemy were left. He had scarcely finished speaking when the third brother came in, his spear all bloody, and told them that only one man had been spared to carry home news of the fate of his comrades. Going out the villagers saw the shore covered with the dead men and were astonished, but they said nothing.

Still the brothers lingered, disliking to begin the long homeward journey, and at last another fleet of umiaks, larger than the first, bearing the friends and relatives of the men slain in the first battle, came in sight; these, the villagers said, were people coming for blood revenge. Again Ak'-chĭk-chû'-gûk sent all of the villagers to their homes, telling them not to leave their houses. When they were gone he sat side by side with his brothers in the kashim and awaited the enemy.

The umiaks came to the shore very quickly, and the warriors, fully armed, hurried to the kashim to seek their victims, coming in such numbers that the last had hard work to get into the house. The brothers sat still in the midst of their enemies, who became quiet when they were all in the house and seemed to be waiting for something. In a few moments two extremely old women came in, each carrying a small grass basket in her hands. One of them sat quietly in a corner while the warriors made room for the other to come up in front of the brothers. She looked at them with an evil eye and drew from the basket a finger bone of one of the men killed in the first battle, setting it up on the floor in front of the youngest brother; then taking out a human rib, she looked fixedly at the young man and struck the bone with the rib, saying at the same time, "He is dead." Instantly the young man fell over from his seat dead. Quickly she placed the second bone in front of another brother and he, too, fell dead from his seat.

At this Ak'-chĭk-chû'-gûk uttered a cry of anger, and springing upon the witch, before anyone could move, caught both her hands and crushed them to a shapeless mass. Then he caught up her basket and scattered about him in a circle all the finger bones it contained. Without a moment's delay he took the rib and striking the bones as quickly as possible, repeated, "He is dead. He is dead. He is dead." And his enemies fell as he moved until not one of them was left alive. Then he exercised his magic power and restored his brothers to life again, after which the villagers were called in. When the latter came and saw the kashim filled with dead men, they were full of fear and told the brothers that so many people had been killed by them that they feared to have them remain there any longer.

The brothers consented to go, and preparing their umiak, they embarked with their sister. Just as they were leaving, the villagers told them to be sure to stop and build a large fire on the beach as soon as they came in sight of their native village. They traveled slowly back as they had come, and finally they were pleased to see their village just ahead of them. At this time the sister was walking along the shore with a dog, towing the boat by means of a long, walrus-hide line. When she saw the houses she remembered the directions of the villagers about building a fire when they came in sight of their home, and reminded her brothers of it, but Ak'-chĭk-chû'-gŭk was eager to complete the journey, and said impatiently, "No, no, we will not trouble ourselves to do that; I wish to hurry home." When the sister turned and started to go on she had scarcely taken a step forward when her feet felt so heavy that she could not raise them. She shrieked in fear, and said, "My feet feel as if they were becoming stone." As she spoke she changed into stone from head to foot. Then the same change occurred with the dog, and out along the line to the boat, changing it and its occupants into stone. There until this day, as a rocky ledge, is the boat where it stopped, the brothers facing their home, and a slender reef running to the land where the towline dropped, while on shore are the stony figures of the girl and the dog.

THE DISCONTENTED GRASS PLANT

(From Sledge island)

Near the village of Pastolik, at the Yukon mouth, grows a tall, slender kind of grass. Every fall just before winter commences the women from the villages go out and gather great stores of it, pulling or cutting it off close to the ground, and making large bundles which they carry home on their backs. This grass is dried and used for braiding mats and baskets and for pads in the soles of skin boots.

One of these Grass-stalks that had been almost pulled out of the ground by a woman, began to think that it had been very unfortunate in not being something else, so it looked about. Almost at first glance it spied a bunch of herbs growing near by, looking so quiet and undisturbed that the Grass began to wish to be like them. As soon as this wish had been formed the Grass-stem became an Herb like those it had envied, and for a short time it remained in peace.

One day it saw the women coming back carrying sharp-pointed picks, with which they began to dig up these herbs and eat some of the roots, while others were put into baskets and carried home. The changeling was left when the women went home in the evening, and having seen the fate of its companions, it wished it had taken another form; so looking about, it saw a small, creeping plant which pleased it, being so tiny and obscure; without delay it wished and became one of them. Again passed a time of quiet, and again came the women tearing up its companions but overlooking the changeling. Once more the latter was filled with fear and by wishing became a small tuber-bearing plant like others growing near. Scarcely had this change been made when a small tundra mouse came softly through the grass and began digging up one of the tubers of a similar plant near by, holding it in its fore-paws and nibbling it, after which the mouse went on again. "To be secure I must become a mouse," thought the changeling, and at once it became a Mouse and ran off, glad of the new change. Now and then it would pause to dig up and eat one of the tubers as the other mouse had done, or it would sit up on its hind feet to look around at the new scenes that came in view. While traveling nimbly along in this manner, the Mouse saw a strange, white object coming toward it, which kept dropping down upon the ground, and after stopping to eat something would fly on again. When it came near the Mouse saw that it was a great white owl. At the same moment the owl saw the Mouse and swooped down upon it. Darting off, the Mouse was fortunate enough to escape by running into a hole made by one of its kind, so the owl flew away.

After a while the Mouse ventured to come out of its shelter, though its heart beat painfully from its recent fright. "I will be an owl," thought the Mouse, "and in this way will be safe." So again it changed with the wish into a beautiful white Owl, and with slow, noiseless wing flaps set off toward the north, pausing every now and then to catch and eat a mouse. After a long flight Sledge island came in view, and the Owl thought it would go there. When far out at sea its untried wings became so tired that only with great difficulty did it manage to reach the shore, where it perched upon a piece of driftwood that stood up in the sand. In a short time it saw two fine-looking men pass along the shore, and the old feeling of discontent arose again. "I will be a man," it thought, and, with a single flap of the wings, it stood upon the ground, where it changed immediately into a fine young Man, but was without clothing. Night came over the earth soon after, and Man sat down with his back against the stick of wood on which, as an Owl, he had perched, and slept there until morning. He was awakened by the warm sun, and upon rising Chûñ-ûh′-lûk, as he called himself, felt stiff and lame from sitting in the cold night air.

Looking about, he found some grass, which he wove into a kind of loose mantle, which helped to keep out the cold, after which he saw some reindeer grazing near by and felt a sudden desire to kill and eat one of them. He crept closely on his hands and knees, and springing forward on the nearest one seized it by the horns and broke its neck with a single effort, threw it over his shoulders, returned, and cast it down near his sleeping place. Then he felt all over the reindeer's body and found that its skin formed a covering which his fingers were unable to penetrate. For a long time he tried to think of a way to remove the skin, and finally noticed a sharp-edge stone, which he picked up and found that he could cut through the skin with it. The deer was quickly skinned, but he felt the lack of a fire with which to cook the flesh. Looking around, he found two round, white stones upon the beach and, striking them together, saw that they gave out numerous sparks. With these and some dry material found along the shore he succeeded in making a fire, upon which he roasted some of the meat. He tried to swallow a very large piece of the meat just as he had eaten mice when he was an Owl, but found that he could not do it; then he cut off some small fragments and ate them. Another night passed, and in the morning he caught another reindeer, and the day following two others; both of these last deer he threw over his shoulders, and at once carried them back to his camping place on the shore. Chûñ-ûh′-lûk found the nights very cold, so he skinned the last two reindeer and wrapped himself from head to foot in their skins, which dried upon him very soon and became like a part of his body. But the nights grew colder and colder, so that Chûñ-ûh′-lûk collected a quantity of driftwood along the shore, with which he made himself a rough hut, which was very comfortable.

After finishing his house he was walking over the hills one day when he saw a strange black animal among some blueberry bushes eating the berries. Chûñ-ûh′-lûk did not at first know whether he should interfere with this unknown animal or not, but finally he caught it by one of its hind legs. With an angry growl it turned about and faced him, showing its white teeth. In a moment Chûñ-ûh′-lûk caught the bear by the coarse hair upon each cheek and swung it over his head, bringing it down to the ground with such force that the bear lay dead; then he threw it across his shoulders and went home.

In skinning the bear Chûñ-ûh′-lûk found that it contained much fat, and that he might have a light in his house if he could find something to hold the grease, for he had found it very dark inside and troublesome to move about. Going along the beach he found a long, flat stone with a hollow in one surface, and in this the oil remained very well, so that when he had put a lighted moss wick into it he saw that his house was lighted as well as he could wish.

In the doorway he hung the bearskin to keep out the cold wind which sometimes had come in and chilled him during the night. In this way he lived for many days, until he began to feel lonely, when he remembered the two young men he had seen when he stood on the shore as an Owl. Then he thought, "I saw two men pass here once, and it can not be far to where others live. I will go and seek them, for it is very lonely here." So he went out in search of people. He wandered along the coast for some distance, and at last came to two fine new kaiaks, lying at the foot of a hill, upon which were spears, lines, floats, and other hunting implements.

After having examined these curiously he saw a path near by, leading up to the top of a hill, which he followed. On the top of the hill was a house with two storehouses in the vicinity, and on the ground in front of him were several recently killed white whales, with the skulls of many others grouped around. Wishing to see the people in the house before showing himself, he crept with noiseless steps into the entrance way and up to the door. Lifting cautiously one corner of the skin that hung in the doorway, he looked in. Opposite the door was a young man sitting at work on some arrows, while a bow lay beside him. Chûñ-ûh′-lûk dropped the curtain and stood quite still for some time, fearing that if he entered the house the young man would shoot him with the arrows before he could make known his good will. He ended by thinking, "If I enter and say, 'I have come, brother,' he will not hurt me," so, raising the curtain quickly, he entered. The householder at once seized the bow and drew an arrow to the head ready to shoot, just as Chûñ-ûh′-lûk said, " I have come, brother." At this the bow and arrow were dropped and the young man cried out with delight, "Are you my brother? Come and sit beside me." And Chûñ-ûh′-lûk did so very gladly. Then the householder showed his pleasure and said, " I am very glad to see you, brother, for I always believed I had one somewhere, but I could never find him. Where have you lived? Have you known any parents? How did you grow up?" and asked many other questions, to which Chûñ-ûh′-lûk replied that he had never known his parents, and described his life by the seashore until he had started on the present search. The householder then said that he also had never known any parents, and his earliest recollection was of finding himself alone in that house, where he had lived ever since, killing game for food.

Telling his brother to follow him, the householder led Chûñ-ûh′-lûk to one of the storehouses, where there was a great pile of rich furs, with an abundance of seal oil and other food. Opening the door of the other storehouse, the newcomer was shown a great many dead people lying there. The householder said he had killed them in revenge for the death of his parents, for he felt certain that they had been killed by these people, so he let no one pass him alive.

When they returned to the house, the brothers fell asleep and slept till morning. At daybreak they arose and, after breakfast, the householder told Chûñ-ûh′-lûk that as he had no bow and arrows, he should stay at home and cook for them both while he went out himself to kill the game. Then he went away and came back at night, bringing some reindeer meat. Chûñ-ûh′-lûk had food ready, and after eating they both went to bed and slept soundly. In this manner they lived for several days, until Chûñ-ûh′-lûk began to tire of cooking and of staying in the house.

One morning he asked permission to go out to hunt with his brother, but the latter refused and started out alone. Soon after, when he began to stalk some reindeer, Chûñ-ûh′-lûk came creeping softly behind and grasped him by the foot, so that without alarming the game his brother should know he was there. Turning, the hunter said angrily, "What do you mean by following me? You can not kill anything without a bow and arrows." "I can kill game with my hands alone," said Chûñ-ûh′-lûk; but his brother spoke scornfully, and said: "Go home, and attend to your cooking." Chûñ-ûh′-lûk turned away, but instead of going home he crept up to a herd of reindeer and killed two of them with his hands, as he had done while living alone. Then he stood up and waved his hands for his brother to come. The latter came, and was very much astonished to see the two reindeer, for he had killed none with his arrows. Chûñ-ûh′-lûk then lifted both of the reindeer upon his shoulders and carried them home.

His brother followed with dark brow and evil thoughts in his heart, until jealousy and anger replaced all the kindly feelings he had for Chûñ-ûh′-lûk, and there was also a feeling of fear after having seen his brother manifest such great strength. During all the evening he sat silent and moody, scarcely tasting the food placed before him, until finally his suspicions and evil thoughts began to produce the same feelings in Chûñ-ûh′-lûk's breast. Thus they sat through the night, each watching the other and fearing some treachery.

The following day was calm and bright, and the householder asked Chûñ-ûh′-lûk if he could paddle a kaiak, to which the latter answered that he thought he could. Then the householder led the way to the kaiaks upon the shore, into one of which he got, and telling Chûñ-ûh′-lûk to follow him in the other. At first Chûñ-ûh′-lûk had some trouble in keeping his kaiak steady, but he soon learned to control it, and they paddled far out to sea. When the shore was very distant they turned back, and the householder said: "Now, let us see who can gain the shore first." Lightly the kaiaks darted away, and first one, then the other, seemed to have the advantage, until at last, with a final effort, they ran ashore, and the rivals sprang up the beach at the same moment. With scowling brow the householder turned to Chûñ-ûh′-lûk and said: "You are no more my brother. You go in that direction and I will go in this," and they turned their backs to each other and separated angrily. As they went Chûñ-ûh′-lûk changed into a Wolverine, his brother becoming a Gray Wolf, and until this day they are found wandering in the same country, but never together.

THE FIRE BALL

(From Sledge island)

In the village of Kiñ-i'-gûn (Cape Prince of Wales), very long ago, there lived a poor orphan boy who had no one to care for him and was treated badly by everyone, being made to run here and there at the bidding of the villagers. One evening he was told to go out of the kashim and see how the weather was. He had no skin boots, and being winter, he did not wish to go, but he was driven out. Very soon he came back and said there was no change in the weather. After this the men kept sending him out on the same errand until at last he came back and told them that he had seen a great ball of fire like the moon coming over the hill not far away. The people laughed at him and made him go out again, when he saw that the fire had come nearer until it was quite close. Then the orphan ran inside telling what he had seen and hid himself because he was frightened.

Soon after this the people in the kashim saw a fiery figure dancing on the gut-skin covering over the roof hole, and directly after a human skeleton came crawling into the room through the passageway, creeping on its knees and elbows. When it came into the room the skeleton made a motion toward the people, causing all of them to fall upon their knees and elbows in the same position taken by the skeleton. Then turning about it crawled out as it had come, followed by the people, who were forced to go after it. Outside the skeleton crept away from the village, followed by all the men, and in a short time everyone of them was dead and the skeleton had vanished. Some of the villagers had been absent when the skeleton, or *tunghâk*, came, and when they returned they found dead people lying on the ground all about. Entering the kashim they found the orphan boy, who told them how the people had been killed. After this they followed the tracks of the *tunghâk* through the snow and were led up the side of the mountain until they came to a very ancient grave, where the tracks ended.

In a few days the brother of one of the men who had been killed went fishing upon the sea ice far from the village. He stayed late, and it became dark while he was still a long way from home. As he was walking along the *tunghâk* suddenly appeared before him and began to cross back and forth in his path. The young man tried to pass it and escape, but could not, as the *tunghâk* kept in front of him, do what he might. As he could think of nothing else, he suddenly caught a fish out of his basket and threw it at the *tunghâk*. When he threw the fish it was frozen hard, but as it was thrown and came near the *tunghâk*, it turned back suddenly, passing over the young man's shoulders, and fell into his basket again, where it began to flap about, having become alive.

Then the fisherman pulled off one of his dogskin mittens and threw it. As it fell near the *tunghâk* the mitten changed into a dog, which ran growling and snarling about the apparition, distracting its attention so that the young man was able to dart by and run as fast as he could toward the village. When he had gone part of the way he was again stopped by the *tunghâk*, and at the same time a voice from overhead said, "Untie his feet; they are bound with cord;" but he was too badly frightened to obey. He then threw his other mitten, and it, too, changed into a dog, delaying the *tunghâk* as the first one had done.

The young man ran off as fast as he could, and fell exhausted near the kashim door as the *tunghâk* came up. The latter passed very near without seeing him and went into the house, but finding no one there, came out and went away. The young man then got up and went home, but did not dare to tell his mother what he had seen. The following day he went fishing again, and on his way came to a man lying in the path whose face and hands were black. When he drew near, the black man told him to get on his back and close his eyes. He obeyed, and in a short time was told to open his eyes. When the young man did this he saw just before him a house and near it a fine young woman. She spoke to him, saying, "Why did you not do as I told you the other night when the *tunghâk* pursued you?" and he replied that he had been afraid to do it. The woman then gave him a magic stone as an amulet to protect him from the *tunghät* in the future, and the black man again took him on his back, and when he opened his eyes he was at home.

After this the young man claimed to be a shaman, but he thought continually of the beautiful young woman he had seen, so that he did not have much power. At last his father said to him, "You are no shaman; you will make me ashamed of you; go somewhere else." The next morning the young man left the village at daybreak, and was never heard of again.

THE LAND OF DARKNESS

(From Sledge island)

Very long ago there lived on Aziak (Sledge) island a man with his wife and little son. The husband loved his wife very much, but was so jealous of her that frequently without cause he treated her very badly. After a time the wife became so unhappy that she preferred to die rather than live with him longer. Going to her mother, who lived near by, she related all her troubles. The old woman listened to the complaints and then told her daughter to take a sealskin and rub it with the excrement of three ptarmigans and three foxes; then to fill a wooden dish with food and with her child upon her back to go and meet her husband, and perhaps all might be well with her.

Doing as she was directed, she went down to the shore to meet her husband. When he came within hearing, however, he began to scold and abuse her as usual, telling her to go home at once and he would give her a beating as soon as he got there. When the poor woman heard this she ran to the edge of a low bluff overhanging the sea, and as her husband drew his kaiak upon the shore she cast her sealskin into the water and leaped after it. Her husband saw this with alarm, and ran quickly to the top of a hill to see what had become of his wife. He saw her sitting upon the extended sealskin, which was supported at each corner by a bladder, floating rapidly away from the shore, for when the woman leaped into the sea, the sealskin she threw in had suddenly opened out and a float appeared at each corner. This caught her upon its surface and held her up safely. Very soon after she began to float away a storm arose and night shut her from her husband's sight, and he went home scolding angrily, blaming every one but himself for his loss.

On and on floated the woman, seated on the magic sealskin, and for several days no land could be seen. She used all her food, but still she floated on until it became unbroken night. After a time she became so exhausted that she fell asleep, and was awakened by several sharp shocks and could hear the waves breaking on a pebbly shore. Realizing this, she began to try to save herself; so she stepped from the sealskin and was greatly pleased to find herself standing on a beach made up of small rounded objects, into which her feet sank ankle deep at every step.

These round objects made her curious, so she stopped and picked up two handfuls of them, putting them in her food dish, after which she went slowly on into the deep blackness. Before she had gone far she came to a house, and, feeling along its side, found the entrance and went in. The passageway was dimly lighted by an oil lamp, showing many deerskins piled on one side, and on the other were pieces of flesh and bags of whale and seal oil. When she entered the house there were two oil lamps burning, one on each side of the room, but no one was at home. Over one of the lamps hung a piece of seal fat, and over the other a piece of reindeer fat, from which the oil dropped and fed the flames, and in one corner of the room was a deerskin bed.

She entered and sat down, waiting for what would come to her. At last there was a noise in the entrance way, and a man said, "I smell strange people." Then the man came into the room, frightening the woman very badly, for his face and hands were coal black. He said nothing, but crossed the room to his bed, where, after stripping the upper part of his body, he took a tub of water and washed himself. The woman was relieved to see that his chest was as white as her own. While sitting here she saw a dish of some cooked flesh suddenly placed inside the door by an unseen person, from which the man helped his guest and then took his own meal. When they had done eating he asked her how she came there, and she told him her story. He told her not to feel badly, and went out and brought in a number of deerskins, telling her to make clothing from them for herself and her child, for she had kept her child safely upon her back all the time. When she told him that she had no needle, he brought her one of copper, which pleased her very much, for until then she had never seen any but bone needles.

For some time they lived thus, until at last the man told her that as they were living alone it would be better for her to become his wife, to which she agreed. The husband then told her not to go outside the house, and they lived quietly together.

While her little boy was playing about one day, he cried out suddenly with delight, and when the woman looked at him she saw that he had spilled the things which she had put in her dish when she stepped on the shore. Examining them, she found they were large, handsome, blue beads.[1]

In time she gave birth to a fine boy, of which her husband was very fond, telling her to be very careful of him. In this way they lived for several years, and in time the boy she had brought with her became a youth. His foster father made him a bow and arrows, and when the boy had killed some birds with them he was allowed to accompany him when hunting. One day the boy killed and brought home two hares, which, like all the animals and birds in this country, were coal black. They were skinned and left outside, and shortly after, freshly cooked and steaming, they were placed just inside the door in a wooden dish, as was always done with their food. The woman noticed for the first time that when the dish was pushed inside the door it was held by two hands.

This remained in her mind until she became suspicious that her husband was not faithful to her. Finally he saw that something troubled her; he asked what it was, and she told him. After sitting and thinking for a short time he asked her if she did not wish to go back to her friends, to which she replied that there was no use in wishing for anything that she could not do. So he said, "Well, listen to my story, I am from Unalaklit, where I had a handsome wife whom I loved, but who had a very bad temper, which troubled me so much that I lost heart and was in despair, and from being a good and successful hunter I could no longer succeed. One day I was paddling in my kaiak far out at sea, filled with heavy thoughts, when a great storm broke upon me and I was unable to return to the shore. The high wind forced my kaiak through the water so fiercely that at last I lost consciousness and remembered no more until I found myself lying bruised and lame upon the shore where you, too, were cast. Beside me was a dish of food, of which I ate, and feeling strengthened, I arose, thinking that the food must have been placed there by some one, and started to search for the people, but could find no one. While my wants were still supplied with food every time I became hungry, the thick darkness hid everything from me; but I could find no people, and when my eyes became accustomed to the unbroken darkness, so that I could see a little, I built this house and since then I have lived here, being cared for by the *inua* who, as you have seen, serves my food. This *inua* usually

---

[1] Beads of this kind are still highly prized by the Eskimo of this coast.

takes the form of a large jelly fish, and although I go hunting it is this being that secures my game for me. I became accustomed to the darkness after a time, but the exposure to the continual blackness has made my face and hands as you see, and that is the reason why I told you not to go outside."

Her husband then told her to follow him, and he led her into the entrance way of the storeroom, which was full of furs, and then he opened a door into another room full of fine furs of the rarest kinds. He then told her to take the ear tips from these skins and put them into her dish with the beads she had found on the shore, and she did so. Then the man said, "You wish to see your old home and I also wish to see my friends, and we will part. Take your boy upon your back, shut your eyes, and take four steps." She did as he told her, and so soon as she had opened her eyes she was obliged to close them, for they were dazzled by the bright sunshine about her. When her eyes became used to the light, she looked about and was greatly surprised to see her old home close by. She went at once to her mother's storehouse and placed in it her wooden dish containing the beads and ear tips she had brought with her. Then she entered the house and was received with great joy, and the news of her return quickly spread through the village. Very soon her former husband came in and she saw with pity that his eyes were red and inflamed from constant weeping for her. He asked her to forgive him for being so harsh, and promised if she would return to him as his wife that he would always treat her kindly. When she had considered this for a long time she finally consented, and for a time she lived happily with him. At length, however, his old habits returned and his wife became unhappy.

Her son became a young man and his mother showed him the beads she had brought from the land of darkness, and also a great pile of rich furs, for every ear tip she had brought back with her had now become a full-size skin. These she gave to her son and then went away and was never seen again by her people. Her son afterward became a headman of the village from his success as a hunter and the wealth of furs and beads given him by his mother.

THE RAVEN AND THE MARMOT

(A woman's tale, from Norton bay)

Once a Raven was flying over a reef near the seashore, when he was seen by some Sea-birds that were perched on the rocks, and they began to revile him, crying, "Oh, you offal eater! Oh, you carrion eater! Oh, you black one!" until the Raven turned and flew away, crying, "*Gnăk, gnăk, gnăk!* why do they revile me?" And he flew far away across the great water until he came to a mountain on the other side, where he stopped.

Looking about he saw just in front of him a marmot hole. The Raven stood by the hole watching, and very soon the Marmot came back bringing home some food. When the Marmot saw the Raven in front of his door he asked him to stand aside, but the Raven refused, saying, "They called me carrion eater, and I will show that I am not, for I will eat you." To this the Marmot answered, "All right; but I have heard that you are a very fine dancer; now, if you will dance, I will sing, and then you can eat me, but I wish to see you dance before I die." This pleased the Raven so much that he agreed to dance, so the Marmot sang, " Oh, Raven, Raven, Raven, how well you dance! Oh, Raven, Raven, Raven, how well you dance!" Then they stopped to rest, and the Marmot said, "I am very much pleased with your dancing, and now I will sing once more, so shut your eyes and dance your best." The Raven closed his eyes and hopped clumsily about while the Marmot sang, " Oh, Raven, Raven, Raven, what a graceful dancer! Oh, Raven, Raven, Raven, what a fool you are!" Then the Marmot, with a quick run, darted between the Raven's legs and was safe in his hole. As soon as the Marmot was safe he put out the tip of his nose and laughed mockingly, saying, *"Chĭ-kĭk-kĭk, chĭ-kĭk-kĭk, chĭ-kĭk-kĭk!* You are the greatest fool I ever saw; what a comical figure you made while dancing; I could hardly keep from laughing; and just look at me; see how fat I am. Don't you wish you could eat me?" And he tormented the Raven until the latter flew far away in a rage.

THE SHAMAN IN THE MOON

(From Kotzebue sound)

A Malemut shaman from Kotzebue sound near Selawik lake told me that a great chief lives in the moon who is visited now and then by shamans, who always go to him two at a time, as one man is ashamed to go alone. In the moon live all kinds of animals that are on the earth, and when any animal becomes scarce here the shamans go up to the chief in the moon and, if he is pleased with the offerings that have been made to him, he gives them one of the animals that they wish for, and they bring it down to the earth and turn it loose, after which its kind becomes numerous again.

The shaman who told me the foregoing said he had never been to the moon himself, but he knew a shaman who had been there. He had been up only as high as the sky, and went up that high by flying like a bird and found that the sky was a land like the earth, only that the grass grew hanging downward and was filled with snow. When the wind blows up there it rustles the grass stems, loosening particles of snow which fall down to the earth as a snowstorm.

When he was up near the sky he saw a great many small, round lakes in the grass, and these shine at night to make the stars. The Malemut of Kotzebue sound also say that the north wind is the breath of a giant, and when the snow falls it is because he is building himself a snow house and the particles are flying from his snow shovel. The south wind is the breath of a woman living in the warm southland.

THE MAN-WORM

(From Kotzebue sound)

[There are various tales among the Eskimo along the east shore of Bering sea and the adjacent Arctic coast in which a Man-worm figures, and among the mythical beings illustrated in the chapter on mythology will be found figures of carvings representing this being.]

In very ancient days there lived a large Worm who was married to a woman, and they had a son who was also a Worm. When the son was fully grown the father told him to go to the middle of the earth plain and there in a small house he would find a wife. The son then used his magic powers and made himself small, so that he could travel faster, and journeyed away. When he came near the small house of which his father had told him, he felt the earth shake and tremble under his feet, and he feared that he would be killed. This happened several times, until finally he reached the house. Here he found that the cause of the shaking of the earth was the talk of an old woman who lived in the house with her daughter. These people received him hospitably, and finding that the girl was very beautiful, he married her. After he had lived there four years he remembered his parents and started to go back to visit them, but on the road he was killed by another Man-worm, who was a shaman. In a short time after this the father felt a strong desire to see his son, so he started to go to him. On the way he found the body of his son, and looking about saw a large village close at hand. He went to the spring where the villagers got their water, and making himself small, hid in it, where, by the use of magic, he killed nearly all the people in revenge for his son's death. When there were only a few people left, an old woman in the village, knowing that some magic was employed against them, worked a strong charm which caused the sea to rise and break the ice upon its surface and carried it over the land until the spring was covered; then the floating ice blocks were dashed together until the Man-worm was ground to pieces and destroyed, so that the people were freed from his magic.

MIGRATION LEGEND

[The following legend was obtained from an old man at Ikogmut, on the lower Yukon. I had no opportunity of verifying any part of it, which was given as a statement of fact.]

Very long ago the Eskimo lived far away from the Yukon, and were continually moving from place to place; traveling from the far east to the west. After long wanderings some of them built a village on the bank of Yukon river, just below where Ikogmut now stands, which increased in size until there were thirty-five kashims. The ruins of this village can be seen at the present time, with large pits where the kashims stood.

Finally the villagers quarreled, formed two parties, and made war against each other. The inhabitants of the surrounding villages had hated these people for a long time on account of their overbearing manner, and when they began to quarrel among themselves the outside people united to make war upon them. These enemies were so powerful that they were able to defeat the divided forces of the villagers in a battle, and those who survived became separated into three parties and dispersed.

One party stopped at the village of Kushunuk, near Cape Vancouver; another party went to Nunivak island, and another traveled on until it reached Bristol bay, and settled near where Nushagak now stands. The people on the great island of Kodiak, having heard of the strangers near Nushagak, sent a war party across from the island to attack them, but the newcomers on Bristol bay succeeded in almost exterminating them. After this the Aleut, on the island of Uminak, heard of the strangers, and of their having defeated the Kodiak men, so they sent out a war party against these people. This time the Yukon men were defeated and lost half their number. Those who were left then joined with some of their friends from Nunivak island and attacked the people living at Goodnews bay, below the mouth of Kuskokwim river, killing them and burning their village.

The victors then built themselves a village in the same locality, where they were living at the time the Russians came to the country. When the Russians came the people on Goodnews bay resisted them for some time, but finally they scattered, some going back to Bristol bay and others settling with their people on Nunivak island. Since then the descendants of these people have gradually returned to Goodnews bay, where they are now living. During the last few years the people on Bristol bay have been gradually working along the coast toward the mouth of the Kuskokwim.

During the time of the migration from the Yukon all of these people spoke one tongue, but having settled at three widely separated places, their languages gradually became different, the people living at Bristol bay and on Nunivak island being nearest alike in speech.

ORIGIN OF THE PEOPLE OF DIOMEDE ISLANDS, AND AT EAST CAPE, SIBERIA

An old man from the Diomede islands told me that it was believed among his people that the first human beings who came to Big Diomede island were a man and a woman who came down from the sky and lived on the island a long time, but had no children. At last the man took some walrus ivory and carved five images of people. Then he took some wood and made five more images from it and put all of them to one side. The next morning the ten dolls had become transformed into ten people. Those coming from the ivory dolls were men, being hardy and brave, and those from the wood were women and were soft and timid. From these ten people came the inhabitants of the islands.

An Eskimo living at East cape, Siberia, told me that the first Eskimo who lived on East cape were a man and a woman who came there in two kaiaks from St Lawrence island. The kaiaks turned to stone when the pair landed, and two peculiarly shaped stones, one on each side of the cape, are pointed out as being these kaiaks. From this pair of people came all of the Siberian Eskimo.

In those days there were two kinds of people on East cape, who could not understand each other, but after a time the other people went away and only the Eskimo were left, as they are today.